Treasures

A Reading/Language Arts Program

McGraw Hill **Macmillan/McGraw-Hill**

Contributors

Time Magazine, The Writers' Express, Accelerated Reader

Students with print disabilities may be eligible to obtain an accessible, audio version of the pupil edition of this textbook. Please call Recording for the Blind & Dyslexic at 1-800-221-4792 for complete information.

B

The McGraw·Hill Companies

 Macmillan/McGraw-Hill

Published by Macmillan/McGraw-Hill, of McGraw-Hill Education, a division of The McGraw-Hill Companies, Inc., Two Penn Plaza, New York, New York 10121.

Printed in the United States of America

3 4 5 6 7 8 9 10 WEB 15 14 13 12 11

Treasures

A Reading/Language Arts Program

Program Authors

Dr. Diane August
Senior Research Scientist, Center for
  Applied Linguistics
Washington, D.C.

Dr. Donald R. Bear
University of Nevada, Reno
Reno, Nevada

Dr. Janice A. Dole
University of Utah
Salt Lake City, Utah

Dr. Jana Echevarria
California State University, Long Beach
Long Beach, California

Dr. Douglas Fisher
San Diego State University
San Diego, California

Dr. David J. Francis
University of Houston
Houston, Texas

Dr. Vicki L. Gibson
Educational Consultant, Gibson Hasbrouck
  and Associates, Massachusetts

Dr. Jan E. Hasbrouck
Educational Consultant – J.H. Consulting
Los Angeles, California

Dr. Scott G. Paris
Center for Research and Practice,
National Institute of Education
Singapore

Dr. Timothy Shanahan
University of Illinois at Chicago
Chicago, Illinois

Dr. Josefina V. Tinajero
University of Texas at El Paso
El Paso, Texas

Macmillan/McGraw-Hill

Program Authors

Dr. Diane August

Center for Applied Linguistics, Washington, D.C.

- Principal Investigator, Developing Literacy in Second-Language Learners: Report of the National Literacy Panel on Language-Minority Children and Youth
- Member of the New Standards Literacy Project, Grades 4–5

Dr. Donald R. Bear

University of Nevada, Reno

- Author of *Words Their Way* and *Words Their Way with English Learners*
- Director, E.L. Cord Foundation Center for Learning and Literacy

Dr. Janice A. Dole

University of Utah

- Investigator, IES Study on Reading Interventions
- National Academy of Sciences, Committee Member: Teacher Preparation Programs, 2005–2007

Dr. Jana Echevarria

California State University, Long Beach

- Author of *Making Content Comprehensible for English Learners: The SIOP Model*
- Principal Researcher, Center for Research on the Educational Achievement and Teaching of English Language Learners

Dr. Douglas Fisher

San Diego State University

- Co-Director, Center for the Advancement of Reading, California State University
- Author of *Language Arts Workshop: Purposeful Reading and Writing Instruction* and *Reading for Information in Elementary School*

Dr. David J. Francis

University of Houston

- Director of the Center for Research on Educational Achievement and Teaching of English Language Learners (CREATE)
- Director, Texas Institute for Measurement, Evaluation, and Statistics

Dr. Vicki Gibson

Educational Consultant Gibson Hasbrouck and Associates, Massachusetts

- Author of *Differentiated Instruction: Grouping for Success*

Dr. Jan E. Hasbrouck

Educational Consultant JH Consulting, Los Angeles

- Developed Oral Reading Fluency Norms for Grades 1–8
- Author of *The Reading Coach: A How-to Manual for Success*

Dr. Scott G. Paris

Center for Research and Practice, National Institute of Education, Singapore

- Principal Investigator, CIERA, 1997–2004

Dr. Timothy Shanahan

University of Illinois at Chicago

- Member, National Reading Panel
- President, International Reading Association, 2006
- Chair, National Literacy Panel and National Early Literacy Panel

Dr. Josefina V. Tinajero

University of Texas at El Paso

- Past President, NABE and TABE
- Co-Editor of *Teaching All the Children: Strategies for Developing Literacy in an Urban Setting* and *Literacy Assessment of Second Language Learners*

Consulting and Contributing Authors

Dr. Adria F. Klein
Professor Emeritus,
California State University,
San Bernardino

- President, California Reading Association, 1995
- Co-Author of *Interactive Writing* and *Interactive Editing*

Dolores B. Malcolm
St. Louis Public Schools
St. Louis, MO

- Past President, International Reading Association
- Member, IRA Urban Diversity Initiatives Commission
- Member, RIF Advisory Board

Dr. Doris Walker-Dalhouse
Minnesota State University,
Moorhead

- Author of articles on multicultural literature and reading instruction in urban schools
- Co-Chair of the Ethnicity, Race, and Multilingualism Committee, NRC

Dinah Zike
Educational Consultant

- Dinah-Might Activities, Inc. San Antonio, TX

Program Consultants

Kathy R. Bumgardner
Language Arts Instructional
Specialist
Gaston County Schools, NC

Elizabeth Jimenez
CEO, GEMAS Consulting
Pomona, CA

Dr. Sharon F. O'Neal
Associate Professor
College of Education
Texas State University
San Marcos, TX

Program Reviewers

Mable Alfred
Reading/Language Arts Administrator
Chicago Public Schools, IL

Suzie Bean
Teacher, Kindergarten
Mary W. French Academy
Decatur, IL

Linda Burch
Teacher, Kindergarten
Public School 184
Brooklyn, NY

Robert J. Dandorph
Principal
John F. Kennedy Elementary School
North Bergen, NJ

Suzanne Delacruz
Principal, Washington Elementary
Evanston, IL

Carol Dockery
Teacher, Grade 3
Mulberry Elementary
Milford, OH

Karryl Ellis
Teacher, Grade 1
Durfee School, Decatur, IL

Christina Fong
Teacher, Grade 3
William Moore Elementary School
Las Vegas, NV

Lenore Furman
Teacher, Kindergarten
Abington Avenue School
Newark, NJ

Sister Miriam Kaeser
Assistant Superintendent
Archdiocese of Cincinnati
Cincinnati, OH

LaVonne Lee
Principal, Rozet Elementary School
Gillette, WY

SuEllen Mackey
Teacher, Grade 5
Washington Elementary School
Decatur, IL

Jan Mayes
Curriculum Coordinator
Kent School District
Kent, WA

Bonnie Nelson
Teacher, Grade 1
Solano School, Phoenix, AZ

Cyndi Nichols
Teacher, Grade K/1
North Ridge Elementary School
Commack, NY

Sharron Norman
Curriculum Director
Lansing School District
Lansing, MI

Renee Ottinger
Literacy Leader, Grades K–5
Coronado Hills Elementary School
Denver, CO

Michael Pragman
Principal, Woodland Elementary School
Lee's Summit, MO

Carol Rose
Teacher, Grade 2
Churchill Elementary School
Muskegon, MI

Laura R. Schmidt-Watson
Director of Academic Services
Parma City School District, OH

Dianne L. Skoy
Literacy Coordinator, Grades K–5
Minneapolis Public Schools
Minneapolis, MN

Charles Staszewski
ESL Teacher, Grades 3–5
John H. William School, No. 5
Rochester, NY

Patricia Synan
New York City Department
of Education

Stephanie Yearian
Teacher, Grade 2
W. J. Zahnow Elementary
Waterloo, IL

Unit 6   The Big Question

How do we solve problems?

Enduring Understanding and Essential Questions

In this unit, students will listen, read, and write about problem solving. As they progress through the unit, they will also develop and apply key comprehension skills that good readers use as they read.

Big Idea	Enduring Understanding	Essential Questions
Theme: Problem Solving	People solve problems in many different ways.	How do we solve problems?

Comprehension	Enduring Understanding	Essential Questions
Problem and Solution Week 1	Good readers pay attention to the problem and how it is solved to help them summarize the plot's main events.	What was the problem in this story, and how was it solved?
Cause and Effect Week 2	Good readers recognize cause and effect relationships to sequence and summarize a plot's main events.	How did recognizing cause and effect relationships help you to sequence and summarize the main events of the plot?
Fact and Opinion Week 3	Good readers verify facts and distinguish them from opinions.	Why is it important to verify facts and distinguish them from opinions?
Draw Conclusions Week 4	Good readers connect information to draw conclusions about how authors present major events in a biography.	How can drawing conclusions help you to identify the major events in this biography?
Author's Perspective Week 5	Good readers use literary language and devices to determine the author's perspective.	What is the author's perspective toward the subject of the selection?

Theme: Problem Solving

Planning the Unit

Using the Student Book

Wrapping Up the Unit

Additional Resources

Unit Opener

Main Selections

Unit Assessment

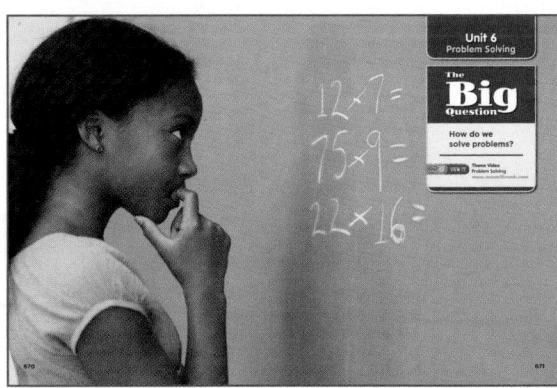

Theme Opener, pp. xvi–672/673

pp. 678–695

pp. 708–721

Unit 6 Planner

ORAL LANGUAGE

- **Listening Comprehension**
- **Speaking/Viewing**

WORD STUDY

- **Vocabulary**
- **Phonics/Word Study**
- **Spelling**

READING

- **Comprehension**
- **Fluency**
- **Leveled Readers**

LANGUAGE ARTS

- **Writing**
- **Grammar**

WEEK 1	WEEK 2
Theme Working Together to Find Solutions	**Theme** Finding Out About the Past
Build Background	**Build Background**
Vocabulary *items, clustered, overflowing, sturdy, glistened, bidding* Dictionary: Unfamiliar Words	**Vocabulary** *reference, disappointment, annoyed, circular, outstretched, conducted* Suffixes
Phonics Words with /ən/	**Phonics** Homophones
Spelling Words with /ən/	**Spelling** Homophones
Comprehension **Strategy:** Analyze Story Structure **Skill:** Problem and Solution	**Comprehension** **Strategy:** Analyze Story Structure **Skill:** Cause and Effect
Fluency Repeated Reading Phrasing	**Fluency** Repeated Reading Intonation/Expression
Approaching *Explorers of the Southwest*	**Approaching** *Buffalo!*
On Level *Explorers of the Southwest*	**On Level** *Camel Ride*
Beyond *Explorers of the Southwest*	**Beyond** *On Board!*
ELL *Explorers of the Southwest*	**ELL** *Camel Ride*
Writing Trait: Ideas	**Writing** Trait: Ideas
Grammar Adverbs	**Grammar** Comparing with Adverbs

Theme: Problem Solving

Unit Opener

Main Selections

Unit Assessment

Unit 6 Contents

Theme: **Problem Solving**

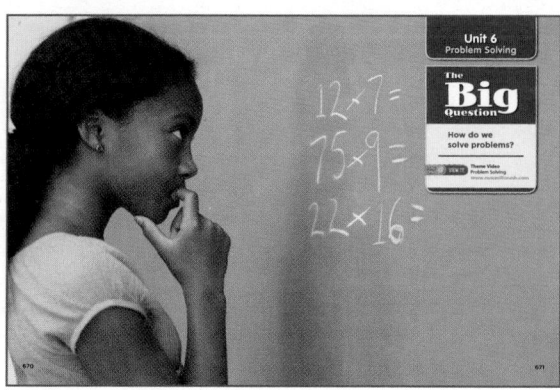

ORAL LANGUAGE

- **Listening Comprehension**

- **Speaking/Viewing**

WORD STUDY

- **Vocabulary**

- **Phonics/Word Study**

- **Spelling**

READING

- **Comprehension**

- **Fluency**

- **Leveled Readers**

LANGUAGE ARTS

- **Writing**

- **Grammar**

WEEK 1	WEEK 2
Theme Working Together to Find Solutions	**Theme** Finding Out About the Past
Build Background	**Build Background**
Vocabulary *items, clustered, overflowing, sturdy, glistened, bidding* Dictionary: Unfamiliar Words	**Vocabulary** *reference, disappointment, annoyed, circular, outstretched, conducted* Suffixes
Phonics Words with /ən/	**Phonics** Homophones
Spelling Words with /ən/	**Spelling** Homophones
Comprehension **Strategy:** Analyze Story Structure **Skill:** Problem and Solution	**Comprehension** **Strategy:** Analyze Story Structure **Skill:** Cause and Effect
Fluency Repeated Reading Phrasing	**Fluency** Repeated Reading Intonation/Expression
Approaching *Explorers of the Southwest*	Approaching *Buffalo!*
On Level *Explorers of the Southwest*	On Level *Camel Ride*
Beyond *Explorers of the Southwest*	Beyond *On Board!*
ELL *Explorers of the Southwest*	ELL *Camel Ride*
Writing Trait: Ideas	**Writing** Trait: Ideas
Grammar Adverbs	**Grammar** Comparing with Adverbs

Unit 6 Planner

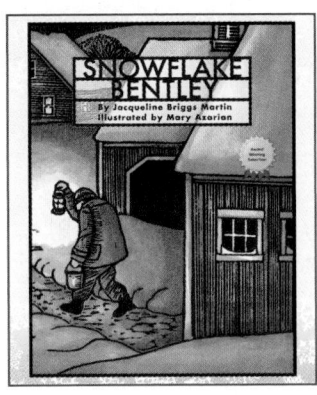

pp. 734–737 pp. 746–767 pp. 778–795

Review and Assess

WEEK 3

Theme
Improving Lives

Build Background

Vocabulary
decades, active, volunteer, transform, violated

Latin, Greek, and Other Linguistic Roots

Phonics
Prefixes

Spelling
Prefixes

Comprehension
Strategy: Generate Questions
Skill: Fact and Opinion

Fluency
Repeated Reading Expression

Approaching
Charles Drew

On Level
Marie Curie

Beyond
Dr. Jonas Salk

ELL
Marie Curie

Writing
Expository: Research Report

Grammar
Negatives

WEEK 4

Theme
Step by Step

Build Background

Vocabulary
technique, foolishness, inspire, evaporate, magnify, annual

Dictionary: Multiple-Meaning Words

Phonics
Suffixes

Spelling
Suffixes

Comprehension
Strategy: Generate Questions
Skill: Draw Conclusions

Fluency
Repeated Reading Accuracy

Approaching
Amazing Stuff

On Level
Amazing Stuff

Beyond
Amazing Stuff

ELL
How Materials Work

Writing
Trait: Sentence Fluency

Grammar
Prepositions

WEEK 5

Theme
Invent It

Build Background

Vocabulary
hilarious, mischief, independence, dizzy, nowadays, came in handy

Dictionary: Idioms

Phonics
Prefixes and Suffixes

Spelling
Prefixes and Suffixes

Comprehension
Strategy: Generate Questions
Skill: Author's Perspective

Fluency
Repeated Reading Rate and Accuracy

Approaching
Who Invented It?

On Level
Thomas Alva Edison

Beyond
Alexander Graham Bell

ELL
A Great Inventor

Writing
Trait: Organization

Grammar
Sentences Using Prepositions

WEEK 6

Show What You Know Spiral Review
Problem and Solution, Cause and Effect, Fact and Opinion, Idioms, Primary Sources

Writing
Expository: Research Report

Unit 6 Assessment, 807M–807N

Comprehension
Problem and Solution, Cause and Effect, Fact and Opinion, Draw Conclusions, Author's Perspective

Vocabulary Strategies
Dictionary: Unfamiliar Words; Idioms; Multiple-Meaning Words; Suffixes; Latin, Greek, and Other Linguistic Roots

Text Features/Literary Elements/Study Skills
Map, Time Lines, Imagery, Metaphor, Figurative Language, Alliteration, Functional Documents

Grammar
Adverbs, Prepositions

Writing
Expository: Research Report

Fluency Assessment

Diagnose and Prescribe
Interpret Assessment Results

Theme: **Problem Solving**

Literature

Student Book

StudentWorks Plus
Online and CD-ROM

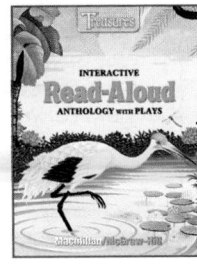

Read-Aloud Anthology
Includes Plays for
Readers Theater

Approaching Level

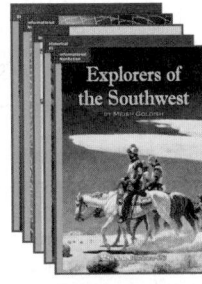

On Level

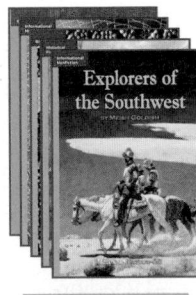

Beyond Level

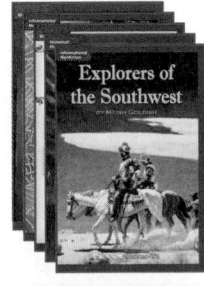

ELL

Leveled Readers

Leveled Classroom Library Books (18)

Teaching Support

Teacher's Edition

Teacher's Resource Book

sturdy   glistened

Vocabulary Cards

Word-Building Cards

those   today

High-Frequency Word Cards

Sound-Spelling Cards

Student Practice

Practice Book

Phonics/Spelling Practice Book

Grammar Practice Book

Home-School Connection

Additional Reproducibles:
Approaching   Beyond

Handwriting
• Cursive

Dinah Zike's Foldables®

Literacy Workstation Flip Charts

Transparencies
Online and CD-ROM

IWB Interactive White Board Ready

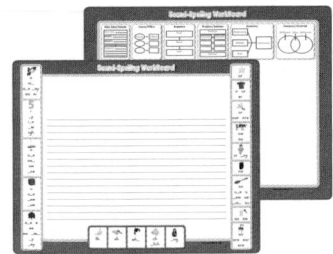
Sound-Spelling WorkBoards

Differentiated Resources

English Language Learners

ELL Resource and Practice Book

Visual Vocabulary Resources

Response to Intervention

Tier 2
• Phonics
• Vocabulary
• Comprehension
• Fluency
• Writing and Grammar

Tier 3

Class Management Tools

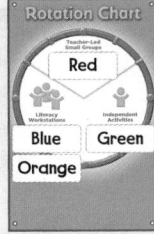
How-to Guide

Rotation Chart

Weekly Contracts

Assessment

Time For Kids
• TFK Teacher's Manual
• Apply Answering Question Strategies

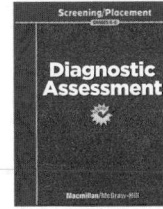
Diagnostic Assessment

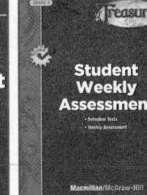
Weekly Assessment

Unit Assessment

Benchmark Assessment

Digital Solutions

Go to **ConnectED** http://connected.mcgraw-hill.com
Online Center

✓ Prepare/Plan

ONLINE www.macmillanmh.com

Teacher's Edition Online

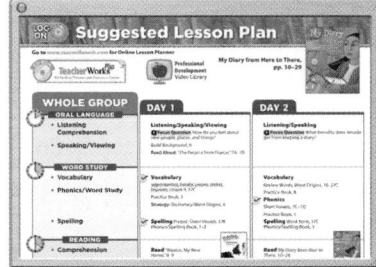

TeacherWorks Plus
All-In-One Planner and Resource Center

Available on CD-ROM
• Interactive Teacher's Edition
• Printable Weekly Resources

Implementation Modules

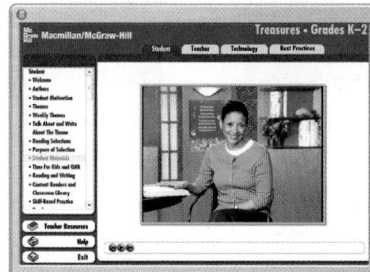

• Support on how to implement the reading program

Balanced Literacy Planner

Balanced Literacy Lesson Plan
▼ **Focus Lesson**
   ▷ Read Aloud
   ▷ Shared Reading
▼ **Word Work**
▼ **Guided Reading**
   ▷ Literacy Centers
▼ **Writing Workshop**

• Create customized weekly balanced literacy planners

ELL Strategies

• Teaching strategies for English Language Learners

Reading Video Library

• Video clips of instructional routines

Leadership Handbook

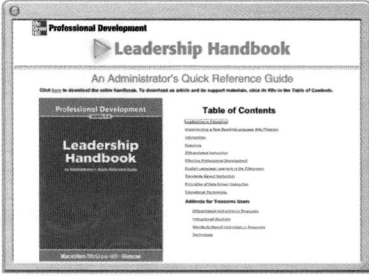

• Professional development for school principals

✓ Teach/Learn

ONLINE www.macmillanmh.com

Interactive Student Book

StudentWorks Plus
Interactive Student Book

• Word-by-Word Reading
• Summaries in Other Languages
• Media Literacy and Research

Animated Activities

• Animated comprehension activities

Theme Videos

• Build background and concept vocabulary

Additional Professional Development

• **Instructional Routine Handbook**
• **Writing Professional Development Guide**
• **Managing Small Groups**
• **Leadership Handbook:**
  An Administrator's Quick Reference Guide

Also available
Reading Yes!
Video Workshops on CD-ROM

LOG ON • VIEW IT • READ IT • LEARN IT • FIND OUT

☑ Assess

Classroom Presentation Toolkit

Weekly transparencies, graphic organizers, and guided instruction and practice

Weekly Activities

- Oral Language
- Research Roadmap
- Research and Inquiry
- Vocabulary and Spelling
- Author and Illustrator

Leveled Reader Database

Search and print Leveled Reader titles

ONLINE www.macmillanmh.com

Formative Assessment

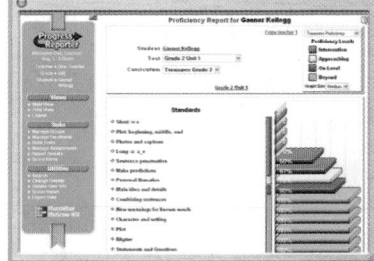

Progress Reporter

- Prescriptions for Reteaching
- Student Profile System

ExamView Test Generator

- Weekly and Unit Tests

Online and CD-ROM materials are **Interactive White Board Ready!**

IWB

Available on CD

AUDIO CD
- **Listening Library**
- **Fluency Solutions**
- **Sound Pronunciation**

CD-ROM

StudentWorks *Plus*
Interactive Student Book
- **Skill Level Up!**
- **Vocabulary PuzzleMaker**

Accelerated Reader
- Accelerated Reader Quizzes

Theme: Problem Solving

Diagnostic Assessments

Screening, Diagnosis, and Placement

Use your state or district screener to identify students at risk. In addition, see tests in our **Diagnostic Assessment** book for information on determining the proficiency of students according to a specific standard or prerequisite skill. The results of the tests will help you place students in the program.

Diagnostics should be given at the beginning of the school year after you have had time to observe students and they have become familiar with classroom routines. Use the diagnostics to determine students in need of intervention or to identify specific prerequisite skill deficiencies that you need to teach during Small Group differentiated instruction time.

Progress Monitoring Assessments

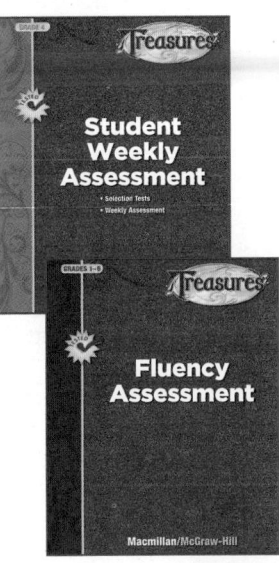

Meeting Grade-Level Expectations

Use the weekly and unit tests (every 6–8 weeks). Multiple questions and next-steps information are provided.

Ongoing Informal Assessments

- Daily Quick Check Observations
- Weekly Tests/Selection Tests; Comprehension Check Questions (Student Book)
- Weekly Fluency Practice Book Passages

Formal Assessments

- Unit Assessments
- Fluency Assessments
- Running Records

Summative Assessments

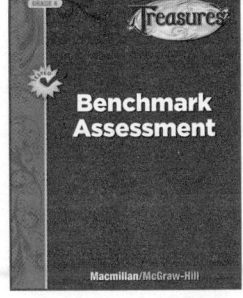

Links to the State Test

Use the State Assessment and the tests provided in the **Benchmark Assessment**. Give every trimester, midyear, or at the end of the year to determine whether students have mastered the grade-level content standards and to document long-term academic growth.

Digital Assessment

 **Assessment Online**
- Administer the **Weekly** and **Unit Assessment** electronically
- Score all tests electronically
- Prescriptions for Reteaching
- Student Profile System

 **Test Generator**
- Available on CD-ROM
- **Weekly** and **Unit Assessments**

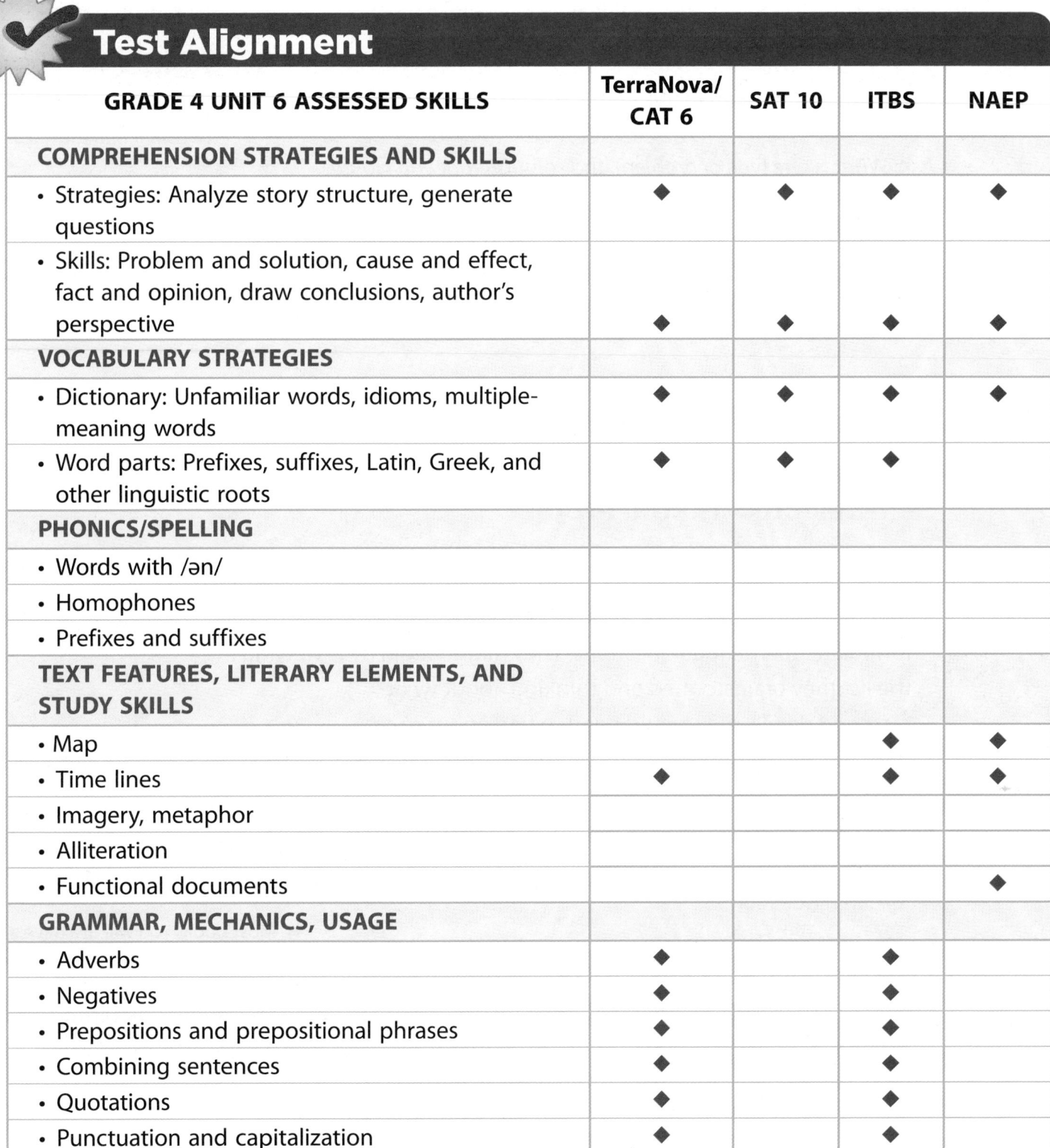

Test Alignment

GRADE 4 UNIT 6 ASSESSED SKILLS	TerraNova/ CAT 6	SAT 10	ITBS	NAEP
COMPREHENSION STRATEGIES AND SKILLS				
• Strategies: Analyze story structure, generate questions	◆	◆	◆	◆
• Skills: Problem and solution, cause and effect, fact and opinion, draw conclusions, author's perspective	◆	◆	◆	◆
VOCABULARY STRATEGIES				
• Dictionary: Unfamiliar words, idioms, multiple-meaning words	◆	◆	◆	◆
• Word parts: Prefixes, suffixes, Latin, Greek, and other linguistic roots	◆	◆	◆	
PHONICS/SPELLING				
• Words with /ən/				
• Homophones				
• Prefixes and suffixes				
TEXT FEATURES, LITERARY ELEMENTS, AND STUDY SKILLS				
• Map			◆	◆
• Time lines	◆		◆	◆
• Imagery, metaphor				
• Alliteration				
• Functional documents				◆
GRAMMAR, MECHANICS, USAGE				
• Adverbs	◆		◆	
• Negatives	◆		◆	
• Prepositions and prepositional phrases	◆		◆	
• Combining sentences	◆		◆	
• Quotations	◆		◆	
• Punctuation and capitalization	◆		◆	

KEY

TerraNova/CAT 6	TerraNova, The Second Edition
SAT 10	Stanford Early Achievement Test
ITBS	Iowa Tests of Basic Skills
NAEP	National Assessment of Educational Progress

Theme Project

Introduce the Theme Write this theme statement on the board: *People solve problems in many different ways.*

Ask: *What is one type of problem and solution that you would like to research and explore?*

Encourage students to brainstorm various types of problems and solutions, from math problems to scientific or medical problems to political problems. They will use their research to create a booklet detailing one problem and solution.

Theme Launcher Video
www.macmillanmh.com

Research and Inquiry
Self-Selected Theme Project

Step 1 **State the Problem and Identify Needed Information** Tell students that they will gather information about problems and solutions and formulate open-ended questions. They might begin by reviewing the list they brainstormed and thinking about what facts and details they would need to find about each problem and solution.

Step 2 **Research Plan** Have students generate a research plan for gathering relevant information about the major research question.

Step 3 **Gathering Sources** Have students follow the research plan to locate information about their problem and solution. For example, some students might examine biographies, textbooks, periodicals, videos, and encyclopedias. Others might use almanacs, atlases, and Web sites. Review how to use different materials.

Step 4 **Synthesizing** After students collect their research information, have them take simple notes and sort evidence by topic and subtopic.

See the Unit Closer on pages 807K–807L for **Step 5: Create the Presentation** and **Step 6: Review and Evaluate**.

Research Strategies

Use Text Features

- Skimming and scanning will help you to quickly identify important information.

- Most books you will use have a table of contents, preface, index, and footnotes.

- Most articles you will use for research have headings and subheadings. Many contain sidebars.

- Look for bold or colored type.

Minilesson

Conducting Interviews

Explain Interviewing an expert on a subject and even taking a field trip to gather information can be useful research strategies. Once you locate an expert to interview, write a letter to introduce yourself and your project. Make an appointment and keep it. Plan your questions ahead of time, and ask permission to record the interview using a tape recorder or by taking notes. Be careful to quote him or her accurately. On your works cited page, include the person's name, how you conducted the interview (in person or over the phone, for example), and the date and time the interview took place.

Discuss Ask: *Why might you choose to interview a person instead of using a printed source of information?* (A person would have personal experiences with the topic.)

Apply Arrange students in small groups and have them brainstorm a list of people they could interview for their theme projects. Have students arrange, plan, and conduct interviews as appropriate to their theme project topics.

Minilesson

Identifying Source Information

Explain Identifying your research sources is important for several reasons. First, it helps you to organize your information and make it easier to return to a source again later, if needed. Second, it shows your audience what kinds of sources you used and the quality of the information your research presentation is based on. Finally, you must include all source information, including the author's name and the source's title, publisher, and publication date, on your works cited page.

Discuss Ask: *Where should you record information about the research sources you use?* (Once you have decided to use a source, take a moment to record the source information at the top of page on which you are recording notes.)

Apply Arrange students in pairs. Have students take turns using each other's notes and source information to locate the source in the library or media center. Students should use the author, title, publisher, publication year, and page numbers to locate the information referenced in the notes.

LISTENING AND SPEAKING

WORKING IN GROUPS

Remind students to

- respectfully ask questions to obtain or clarify information;

- stay focused on the topic and ask relevant questions;

- use formal and informal language to respond to others' ideas and share information with others in an appropriate way.

See Listening and Speaking Checklists in **StudentWorks Plus**.

$$12 \times 7 =$$

$$75 \times 9 =$$

$$22 \times 16 =$$

Unit 6
Problem Solving

The Big Question

How do we solve problems?

LOG ON ▶ VIEW IT

Theme Video
Problem Solving
www.macmillanmh.com

670

671

Introduce Theme Project

PROBLEM SOLVING

Review with students what they have learned so far about identifying problems and solutions.

- Help students apply their knowledge of problem and solution to research. What is the question they want to answer? How can different sources help solve their research questions?

- Read and discuss the Research Activity on page 672. Help students begin thinking about the problem and solution they would like to focus on for their theme project.

Gifted Talented

Connect to Content

Scientific Problem Solving

Explain that scientists are in the business of solving problems and coming up with solutions for scientific mysteries. Scientists use tools and methods to collect and analyze information, conduct scientific inquiry, and propose possible solutions. Often, it takes repeated investigations to find the solution to a scientific problem.

How do we solve problems?

People solve problems in many different ways. The solution depends on the type of problem. To solve a math problem, you may have to apply what you know about numbers or measurement. To solve a health problem, you may have to visit a doctor. To solve a problem with a friend, you may need to sit down with him or her, or know about people and their emotions.

Problem solving can be as complex and varied as the problems themselves.

Learning about problem solving can help you better understand the problems you face and their possible solutions.

Research Activities

Throughout the unit, you will be gathering information about various types of problems and their solutions. Choose one problem and solution to focus your research on. Use graphic aids to create a booklet explaining the problem and solution.

Keep Track of Ideas

As you read, keep track of all you are learning about problem solving. Use the **Layered Book Foldable**. On the front sheet, write the Unit Theme: *Problem Solving*. On each next sheet, write the facts you learn each week that will help you in your research and in your understanding of the Unit Theme.

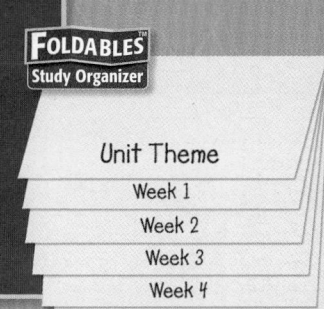

FOLDABLES
Study Organizer

Unit Theme
Week 1
Week 2
Week 3
Week 4
Week 5

Digital Learning

LOG ON ▶ FIND OUT www.macmillanmh.com

StudentWorks Plus
Interactive Student Book

- **Research Roadmap**
  Follow a step-by-step guide to complete your research project.

Online Resources
- Topic Finder and Other Research Tools
- Videos and Virtual Field Trips
- Photos and Drawings for Presentations
- Related Articles and Web Resources
- Web Site Links

People and Places

Lillian Gilbreth 1878–1972
Known as "The First Lady of Engineering," Lillian Gilbreth studied how people could use their time more efficiently. She was also the mother of 12 children. Her children wrote a book, *Cheaper by the Dozen*, about their large, famous family.

KEEP TRACK OF IDEAS

Go to page 22 of the **Foldables Book®** book for instructions on how to create the Layered Book study organizers for this unit. Give students time to create the organizers.

Reread "Keep Track of Ideas" on page 673 of the **Student Book**. Model how students will be using their study organizers to keep track of ideas as they read through the selections in the unit. Explain that keeping track of ideas they read about will help them with ideas for their own theme project.

RESEARCH TOOLS

Tell students that as they read the stories in the unit, they will learn about how people work together to solve problems. Students will be able to use the Research Tools to help them learn more about the importance of problem-solving and methods that have worked for other people.

LOG ON ▶

StudentWorks Plus
Interactive Student Book

Plan, Organize, and Synthesize Activities that will assist students in research planning, organization, and presentation.

Listening and Speaking Resources that will help students apply listening and speaking techniques.

Week 1 ★ At a Glance

Priority Skills and Concepts

 Comprehension
- **Strategy:** Analyze Story Structure
- **Skill:** Problem and Solution
- Sequence
- **Genre:** Expository, Fiction

 Robust Vocabulary
- **Selection Vocabulary:** *items, clustered, overflowing, sturdy, glistened, bidding*
- **Strategy:** Dictionary/Unfamiliar Words

 **Fluency**
- Phrasing

 Phonics/Spelling
- **Word Study:** Words with /ən/, Multisyllabic Words
- **Spelling Words:** *robin, button, bacon, reason, cotton, sunken, eleven, cousin, woven, raisin, wagon, muffin, widen, wooden, ridden, common, proven, often, penguin, skeleton*
- *medal, pupil, paddle*

 Grammar/Mechanics
- Adverbs
- *Good* vs. *Well*

 Writing
- **Trait: Ideas**
- Supporting Details

Key

 Tested in program    Review Skill

Digital Learning

Digital solutions to help plan and implement instruction

☑ Teacher Resources

LOG ON ▶

ONLINE
www.macmillanmh.com

▶ **Teacher's Edition**
* Lesson Planner and Resources also on CD-ROM

TeacherWorks Plus

▶ **Formative Assessment**
* ExamView® on CD-ROM also available

Progress Reporter

▶ **Instructional Resources**
* Unit Videos
* Classroom Presentation Toolkit

 VIDEO

▶ **Professional Development**
* Video Library

Professional Development

☑ Student Resources

LOG ON ▶

ONLINE
www.macmillanmh.com

▶ **Interactive Student Book**

 *StudentWorks Plus*

▶ **Leveled Reader Database**

▶ **Activities**
* Research Toolkit
* Oral Language Activities
* Vocabulary/Spelling Activities

 Listening Library
* Recordings of Student Books and Leveled Readers

 Fluency Solutions
* Fluency Modeling and Practice

Weekly Literature

Theme: Working Together to Find Solutions

Student Book

StudentWorks Plus
Interactive Student Book

- Word-by-Word Reading
- Summaries in Multiple Languages
- Comprehension Questions

Leah's Pony
Written by Elizabeth Friedrich
Illustrated by Michael Garland

Main Selection
Genre Historical Fiction

Grandma's Story
by Marcus Kharana

Preteach Vocabulary and Comprehension
Genre Fiction

SOIL TURNED TO DUST

Social Studies

Paired Selection
Genre Expository

Support Literature

INTERACTIVE Read-Aloud ANTHOLOGY with PLAYS

Interactive Read-Aloud Anthology
- Listening Comprehension
- Robust Vocabulary
- Readers Theater Plays for Fluency

Resources for Differentiated Instruction

Leveled Readers: Social Studies

GR Levels P–U

| Genre | Expository |

- Same Theme
- Same Vocabulary
- Same Comprehension Skills

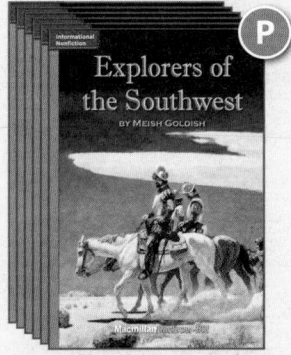

Approaching Level (P)

On Level (R)

Beyond Level (U)

ELL (P)

Leveled Reader Database
Go to www.macmillanmh.com.

Leveled Practice

| Approaching | On Level | Beyond | ELL |

Leveled Classroom Library

| Approaching | On Level | Beyond |

Response to Intervention

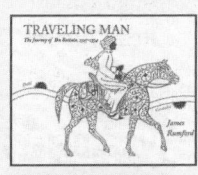

Tier 2

- Phonics
- Vocabulary
- Comprehension
- Fluency
- Writing and Grammar

Tier 3

Assessment

Time For Kids

- TFK Teacher's Manual
- Apply Answering Question Strategies

Weekly Assessment

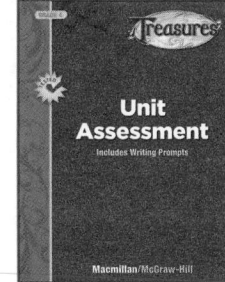
Unit Assessment

Benchmark Assessment

HOME-SCHOOL CONNECTION

- Family letters in English and Spanish
- Take-Home Stories and activities

Online Homework
www.macmillanmh.com

Leah's Pony
Written by Elizabeth Friedrich
Illustrated by Michael Garland

Go to **www.macmillanmh.com** for Online Lesson Planner

CD-ROM
TeacherWorks *Plus*
All-In-One Planner and Resource Center

Professional Development
Video Library

Leah's Pony,
pp. 678–695

WHOLE GROUP

ORAL LANGUAGE

- **Listening Comprehension**
- **Speaking/Viewing**

WORD STUDY

- **Vocabulary**
- **Phonics/Word Study**
- **Spelling**

READING

- **Comprehension**
- **Fluency**

LANGUAGE ARTS

- **Writing**
- **Grammar**

ASSESSMENT

- **Informal/Formal**

DAY 1

Listening/Speaking/Viewing
❓ **Focus Question** What problem do the people in the photo on pages 674–675 face? How are they being helped?

Build Background, 674
Read Aloud: "On Our Own," 675A–675B

✔ **Vocabulary**
items, clustered, overflowing, sturdy, glistened, bidding, 677, 703C
Practice Book, 227
Strategy: Dictionary/Unfamiliar Words, 676

✔ **Spelling** Pretest Words with /ən/, 703E
Phonics/Spelling Book, 151–152

Read "Grandma's Story," 676–677

✔ **Comprehension,** 677A–677B
Strategy: Analyze Story Structure

Skill: Problem and Solution
Practice Book, 228

✔ **Fluency** Model Fluency, 675B

Writing
Daily Writing Write a list of things that you might see on a farm that you would not see in the city.

✔ **Trait: Ideas**
Supporting Details, 701A–701B

✔ **Grammar** Daily Language Activities, 703G
Adverbs, 703G
Grammar Practice Book, 126

Quick Check Vocabulary, 676
Comprehension, 677B

Student Book

DAY 2

Listening/Speaking
❓ **Focus Question** What will happen to Leah's pony?

Vocabulary
Review Words, Dictionary, 678, 703C
Practice Book, 233

✔ **Phonics**
Words with /ən/, 675C–675D
Practice Book, 226

Spelling Word Sorts, 703E
Phonics/Spelling Book, 153

Read *Leah's Pony,* 678–695

✔ **Comprehension,** 678–695
Strategy: Analyze Story Structure

Skill: Problem and Solution
Practice Book, 229

✔ **Fluency** Repeated Reading: Phrasing, 697A

Student Book

Writing
Daily Writing Write a list of questions you would have for someone who lived through the Great Depression.

✔ **Reading/Writing Connection,** 702–703

Grammar Daily Language Activities, 703G
Adverbs, 703G
Grammar Practice Book, 127

Quick Check Phonics, 675D
Comprehension, 695

SMALL GROUP Lesson Plan   Differentiated Instruction 674G–674H

Priority Skills

Vocabulary	Comprehension	Writing	Social Studies
Dictionary/Unfamiliar Words	**Strategy:** Analyze Story Structure **Skill:** Problem and Solution	Trait: Ideas Supporting Details	Summarize reasons for exploration and settlement, and identify explorers

DAY 3

Listening/Speaking

❷ **Focus Question** How are Leah's experiences similar to those of Grandma in "Grandma's Story"?

Summarize, 697

Vocabulary

Review Words, Related Words, 703D

Spelling Word Meanings, 703F
Phonics/Spelling Book, 154

Read *Leah's Pony*, 678–695

Student Book

✔ **Comprehension**
Comprehension Check, 697

Review Skill: Sequence, 697B
Practice Book, 231

✔ **Fluency** Repeated Reading: Phrasing, 697A
Practice Book, 230

Writing

Daily Writing Write a paragraph comparing and contrasting the lives of a girl during the Great Depression and today.

Trait: Ideas
Supporting Details, 703A

✔ **Grammar** Daily Language Activities, 703G
Mechanics and Usage, 703H
Grammar Practice Book, 128

Quick Check Fluency, 697A

DAY 4

Listening/Speaking/Viewing

❷ **Focus Question** How does "Soil Turned to Dust" give you a better understanding of the events in *Leah's Pony*? Use details from both texts to explain your answer.

✔ **Vocabulary**

Review Words, Morphology, 703D

Spelling Proofread, 703F
Phonics/Spelling Book, 155

Read "Soil Turned to Dust," 698–701

Student Book

✔ **Comprehension**
Genre: Expository

Text Feature: Map, 698
Practice Book, 232

Fluency Repeated Reading: Phrasing, 697A

Writing

Daily Writing Think about having to sell a favorite possession. Write a paragraph telling how you would feel.

Trait: Organization
Narrowing a Topic, 703A

Grammar Daily Language Activities, 703G
Adverbs, 703H
Grammar Practice Book, 129

Quick Check Vocabulary, 703D

DAY 5
Review and Assess

Listening/Speaking/Viewing

❷ **Focus Question** Imagine you were alive during the Dust Bowl. Brainstorm different things you could do to help your family and community.

✔ **Vocabulary**

Assess Words, Connect to Writing, 703D

✔ **Spelling** Posttest, 703F
Phonics/Spelling Book, 156

Read Self-Selected Reading, 674K
Practice Book, 234

Student Book

✔ **Comprehension**
Connect and Compare, 701

✔ **Fluency** Practice, 674K

✔ **Writing**

Daily Writing Write a review of a book or movie about a girl and her horse. Include a brief description and explain why you would or would not recommend it.

Conferencing, 703B

✔ **Grammar** Daily Language Activities, 703G
Adverbs, 703H
Grammar Practice Book, 130

Weekly Assessment, 703II–703JJ

Differentiated Instruction

What do I do in small groups?

Teacher-Led Small Groups

Independent Activities

 LOG ON

Focus on Skills

IF... students need additional instruction, practice, or extension based on your **Quick Check** observations for the following priority skills

 **Phonics/Word Study**
Words with /ən/

 Vocabulary Words
items, clustered, overflowing, sturdy, glistened, bidding
Strategy: Dictionary/Unfamiliar Words

 Comprehension
Strategy: Analyze Story Structure
Skill: Problem and Solution

 Fluency

THEN...

Approaching / **ELL**	Preteach and Reteach Skills
On Level	Practice
Beyond	Enrich and Accelerate Learning

Suggested Small Group Lesson Plan

 CD-ROM **TeacherWorks** *Plus* All-In-One Planner and Resource Center

	DAY 1	**DAY 2**
Approaching Level **Tier 2** • **Preteach/Reteach** **Tier 2 Instruction**	• Prepare to Read, 703I • Academic Language, 703I • Preteach Vocabulary, 703K	• Comprehension, 703M Analyze Story Structure/Problem and Solution **ELL** • Leveled Reader Lesson 1, 703N
On Level • **Practice**	• Vocabulary, 703S • Phonics, 703S Words with /ən/ **ELL**	• Leveled Reader Lesson 1, 703U
Beyond Level • **Extend/Accelerate** **Gifted and Talented**	• Leveled Reader Lesson 1, 703Y • Analyze Information, 703Y	• Leveled Reader Lesson 2, 703Z • Synthesize Information, 703Z
ELL • **Build English Language Proficiency** • See **ELL** in other levels.	• Prepare to Read, 703AA • Academic Language, 703AA • Preteach Vocabulary, 703BB	• Vocabulary, 703BB • Preteach Main Selection, 703CC

Small Group

Focus on Leveled Readers

Leveled Reader Library

Levels P–U

   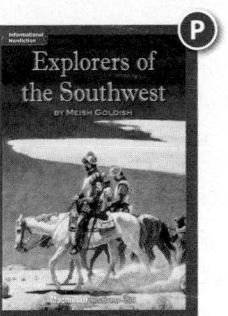

Approaching   **On Level**   **Beyond**   **ELL**

Science

Social Studies

Teacher's Annotated Edition

Summarize reasons for exploration and settlement, and identify explorers.

Additional Leveled Readers

LOG ON ▶ **Leveled Reader Database**
www.macmillanmh.com

Search by

- Comprehension Skill
- Content Area
- Genre
- Text Feature
- Guided Reading Level
- Reading Recovery Level
- Lexile Score
- Benchmark Level

Subscription also available.

Manipulatives

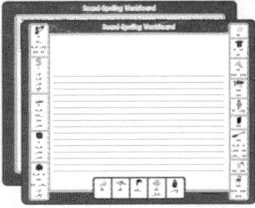

Sound-Spelling WorkBoards

Sound-Spelling Cards

High-Frequency Word Cards

Visual Vocabulary Resources

DAY 3	DAY 4	DAY 5
• Phonics Maintenance, 703J Words with /ən/ **ELL**	• Reteach Phonics Skill, 703J Words with /ən/ **ELL** • Review Vocabulary, 703L • Leveled Reader Lesson 3, 703P	• High-Frequency Words, 703L • Fluency, 703Q • Self-Selected Independent Reading, 703R • Book Talk, 703P
• Leveled Reader Lesson 2, 703O • Leveled Reader Lesson 2, 703V	• Fluency, 703T	• Self-Selected Independent Reading, 703T • Book Talk, 703V
• Phonics, 703W Words with /ən/ **ELL**	• Vocabulary, 703W • Compare Primary Sources, 703W • Fluency, 703X	• Self-Selected Independent Reading, 703X • Evaluate Information, 703X • Book Talk, 703Z
• Vocabulary, 703BB • Grammar, 703EE	• Vocabulary, 703BB • Writing/Spelling, 703FF • Preteach Paired Selection, 703CC • Fluency, 703DD • Leveled Reader, 703GG	• Vocabulary, 703BB • Leveled Reader, 703GG • Self-Selected Independent Reading, 703DD • Book Talk, 703HH

Managing the Class

What do I do with the rest of my class?

- Practice Book and Reproducibles
- ELL Practice Book
- Leveled Reader Activities
- Literacy Workstations
- Online Activities

Classroom Management Tools

Weekly Contract

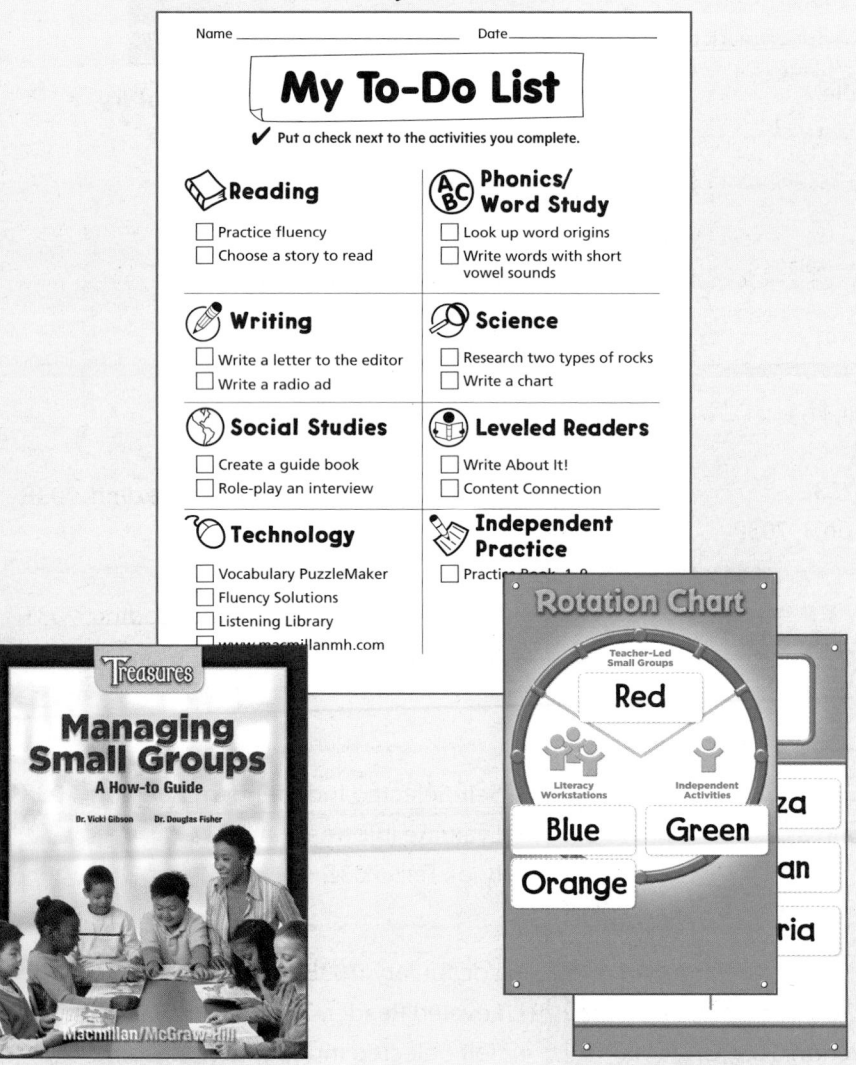

Name _____ Date _____

My To-Do List

✔ Put a check next to the activities you complete.

📖 Reading
- ☐ Practice fluency
- ☐ Choose a story to read

🔤 Phonics/Word Study
- ☐ Look up word origins
- ☐ Write words with short vowel sounds

✏️ Writing
- ☐ Write a letter to the editor
- ☐ Write a radio ad

🔬 Science
- ☐ Research two types of rocks
- ☐ Write a chart

🌎 Social Studies
- ☐ Create a guide book
- ☐ Role-play an interview

⚓ Leveled Readers
- ☐ Write About It!
- ☐ Content Connection

🖱 Technology
- ☐ Vocabulary PuzzleMaker
- ☐ Fluency Solutions
- ☐ Listening Library
- ☐ www.macmillanmh.com

🖌 Independent Practice
- ☐ Practice Book, 1-8

Rotation Chart

Teacher-Led Small Groups

Red

Literacy Workstations | Independent Activities

Blue | Green

Orange

How-to Guide

Managing Small Groups — A How-to Guide

Dr. Vicki Gibson · Dr. Douglas Fisher

Rotation Chart

Digital Learning

LOG ON ▶

StudentWorks Plus™

Interactive Student Book

StudentWorks Plus Online
- Summaries in Multiple Languages
- Word-by-Word Reading
- Comprehension Questions

Meet the Author/Illustrator

Rosalyn Schanzer

- As a child, Rosalyn loved reading stories about horses.
- She lives with her husband, her two children, and her dog named Jones.
- Rosalyn worked for years illustrating other people's books before finally deciding to write her own.

Other books by Rosalyn Schanzer
- Schanzer, Rosalyn. *Escaping to America: A True Story.* New York: HarperCollins, 2000.
- Schanzer, Rosalyn. *Gold Fever.* Washington, D.C.: National Geographic Society, 1999.

- Other Books by the Author or Illustrator

Leveled Practice

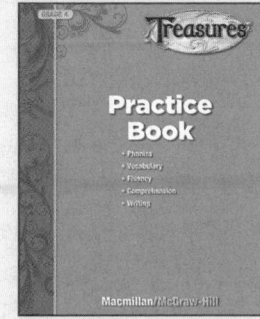

Treasures

Practice Book
- Phonics
- Vocabulary
- Fluency
- Comprehension
- Writing

Macmillan/McGraw-Hill

On Level

Treasures

English Language Learner Practice Book

Macmillan/McGraw-Hill

ELL

Also Available:

Approaching Reproducible

Beyond Reproducible

Independent Activities

ONLINE INSTRUCTION www.macmillanmh.com

Oral Language Activities

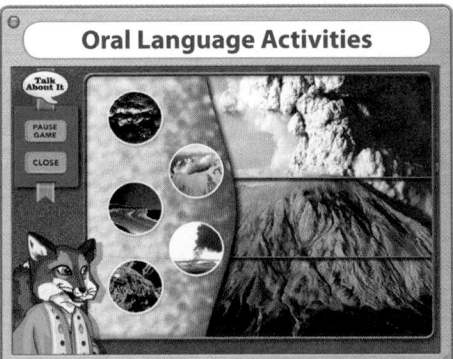

- Focus on Vocabulary and Concepts
- English Language Learner Support

Vocabulary/Spelling Activities

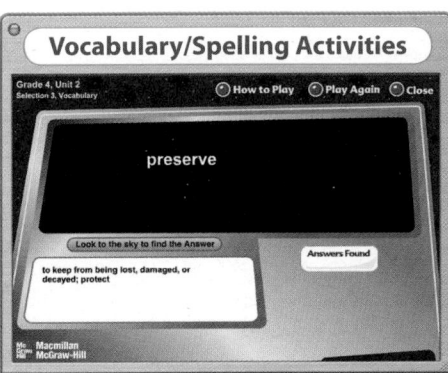

- Differentiated Lists and Activities

Leveled Reader Database

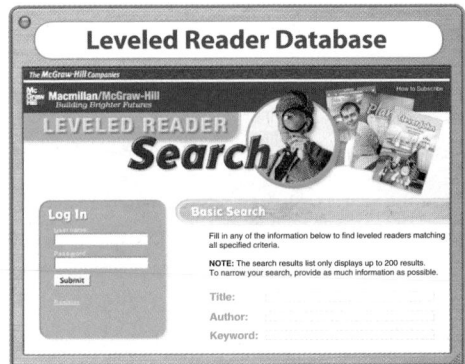

- Leveled Reader Database
- Search titles by level, skill, content area, and more

Research Toolkit

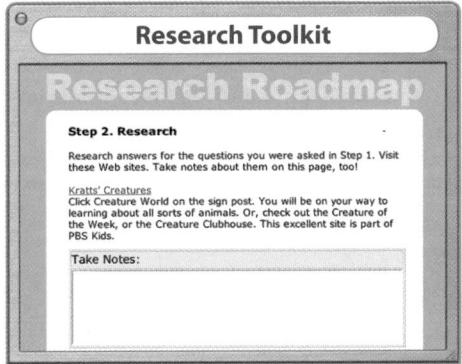

- Research Roadmap
- Research and Presentation Tools
- Theme Launcher Video
- Links to Science and Social Studies

Available on CD

LISTENING LIBRARY
Recordings of selections
- Main Selections
- Paired Selections
- Leveled Readers

VOCABULARY PUZZLEMAKER

FLUENCY SOLUTIONS
Recorded passages at two speeds for modeling and practicing fluency

Leveled Reader Activities

Approaching

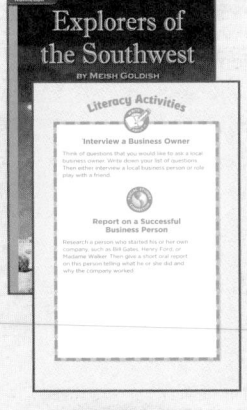

On Level

Beyond

ELL

See inside cover of all Leveled Readers.

Literacy Workstations

See lessons on pages 674K–674L.

Managing the Class

What do I do with the rest of my class?

 **Reading**

Objectives

- Develop fluency through partner-reading
- Read independently for a sustained period of time; use **Practice Book** page 234 for Reading Strategies and Reading Log

---

 **Reading** **FLUENCY** — 20 Minutes

- Select a paragraph from the Fluency passage on page 230 of your Practice Book.
- With a partner, take turns reading the sentences aloud. Pause briefly at commas and stop at end punctuation.

Extension

- Read the paragraph three times. Emphasize a different word in a sentence each time.
- Discuss how the meanings change when you emphasize different words.
- Listen to the Audio CD.

> **Things you need:**
> - Practice Book

Fluency Solutions Listening Library · 51

Reading **Independent Reading** — 20 Minutes

- Read a mystery story.
- Take notes about the problem the main character is trying to solve.
- Remember to make sure you know what is happening in the story.
- Use what you have learned about asking questions to help you understand.

Extension

- Use your notes to fill in a Problem and Solution chart. What was the problem? How was it solved?
- Share your answers with a partner.

> **Things you need:**
> - book
> - pen and paper

For more books about Creative Solutions, go to the Author/Illustrator section of www.macmillanmh.com · 52

Phonics/Word Study

Objectives

- Write definitions for unfamiliar words
- Identify words with /ən/
- Sort words with /ən/ sounds

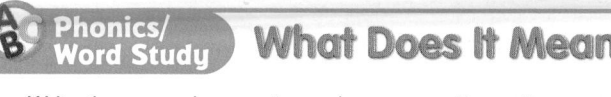 **Phonics/ Word Study** **What Does It Mean?** — 20 Minutes

- Write these words on note cards: *glistened, bidding, overflowing,* and *clustered.* On a separate piece of paper, write one definition for each word.

overflowing

Extension

- Draw a picture that represents the meaning of each word.
- Ask a partner which word matches each picture.

> **Things you need:**
> - dictionary
> - note cards
> - pen and paper
> - colored pencils or markers

For additional spelling and vocabulary games, go to www.macmillanmh.com · Vocabulary PuzzleMaker · 51

Phonics/ Word Study **Words with /ən/** — 20 Minutes

- Create a Three-Pocket Foldable®.
- On each pocket, write *-in, -on, -en.*
- On note cards, write these words: *woven, button, skeleton, vitamin,* and *proven.*
- Underline the letters in each word that make the /ən/ sound.
- Sort the cards in the correct pockets.

Extension

- Use your note cards to write funny sentences for each word. Write your sentence on the back of the correct card.

FOLDABLES

- Three-Pocket Foldable®

woven · -in · -on · -en

For additional vocabulary and spelling games, go to www.macmillanmh.com · **FOLDABLES®** · 52

Literacy Workstations

Reading | **Phonics/ Word Study** | **Writing** | **Science/ Social Studies**

Literacy Workstation Flip Charts

Writing

Objectives

- Write a character sketch
- Write questions for an interview with a weather forecaster

Content Literacy

Objectives

- Research information about droughts in the United States
- Research information about the Great Depression
- Select and use reference sources

Writing — A Character Sketch
20 Minutes

- Choose one of your favorite characters from a story.
- Write a character sketch that describes him or her.
- Begin your sentences in different ways to add interest to your writing.

Extension

- Draw a picture of your character.
- Write labels around your drawing that describe various character traits. For example, a label near the heart might say "kind person."

Things you need:
- pen and paper
- colored pencils

Internet Research and Inquiry Activity
Students can find more facts at www.macmillanmh.com

51

Science — Drought
20 Minutes

- Use an almanac, encyclopedia, or the Internet to locate places in the United States where there is drought.
- Make a list of states that regularly suffer from drought.

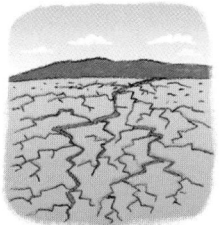

Extension

- How are plants, animals, and people affected by a drought? Write a paragraph.

Things you need:
- almanac, encyclopedia, or online resources
- pen and paper

Internet Research and Inquiry Activity
Students can find more facts at www.macmillanmh.com

51

Writing — A Weather Forecast
20 Minutes

- Imagine that you are going to interview your local TV weather forecaster.
- Write five questions you might ask this person in an interview.

Why I Would Not Want to Be a Weather Forecaster

Extension

- Would you like to be a weather forecaster? Write a paragraph telling why or why not.

Things you need:
- pen and paper

52

Social Studies — The Great Depression
20 Minutes

- Work with a partner. Use the encyclopedia, history book, or the Internet to learn how the Great Depression affected people where you live.
- Take notes, and share them with a partner.

FIRST NATIONAL BANK

Extension

- What questions would you ask people who lived during the Great Depression? Write five questions.

Things you need:
- encyclopedia, history book, or online resources
- pen and paper

52

WHOLE GROUP

ORAL LANGUAGE
- Build Background
- Connect to Theme
- Read Aloud

✓ **PHONICS/WORD STUDY**
- Words with /ən/

✓ **VOCABULARY**
- Dictionary: Unfamiliar Words
- Teach Words

✓ **COMPREHENSION**
- Strategy: Analyze Story Structure
- Skill: Problem and Solution

SMALL GROUP

- Differentiated Instruction, pp. 703I–703HH

WORKING TOGETHER To Find Solutions

674

Oral Language

Build Background

ACCESS PRIOR KNOWLEDGE

Share the following information: The people in this photo lived long ago. They are all standing together because they have a problem—they do not have jobs and they are hungry. They lived during a very difficult time when jobs were hard to find. However, others are cooperating to help these people by offering free food. (Notice the sign on the window.) This is one solution to, or way to fix, their problem.

Write the following words on the board, and briefly define each using the **Define/Example/Ask** routine: **solution** (the answer to a problem), **accomplish** (achieve a goal), **cooperating** (working together to achieve a goal).

FOCUS QUESTION Ask students to read "Talk About It" on **Student Book** page 675. Then have students turn to a partner and describe the photo. Ask:

- How does cooperating with others makes it easier to accomplish a solution? Explain.

- How would you help solve the problem of people needing jobs and not having money for food?

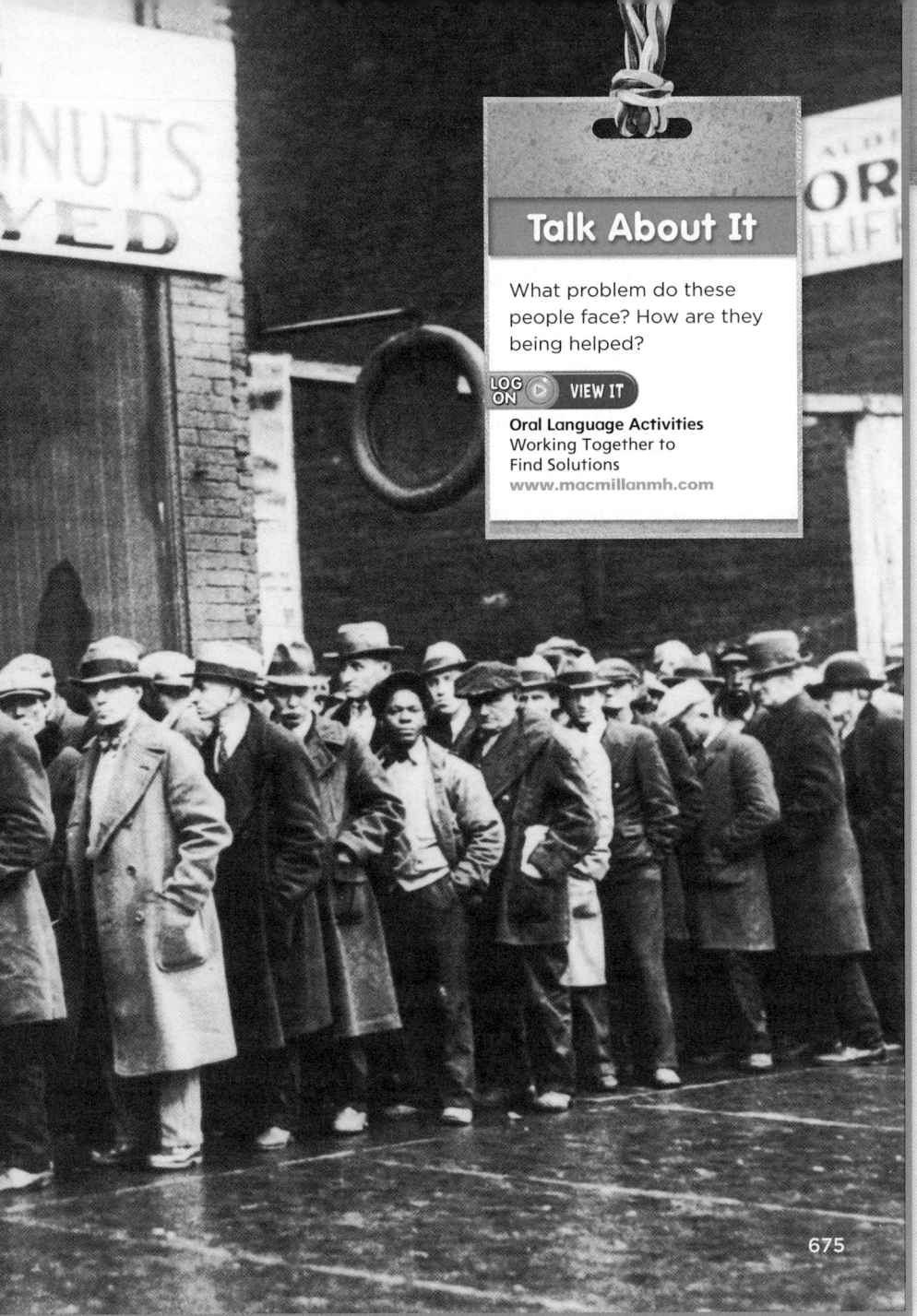

Talk About It

What problem do these people face? How are they being helped?

LOG ON ▶ **VIEW IT**

Oral Language Activities
Working Together to
Find Solutions
www.macmillanmh.com

675

Use the Picture Prompt

BUILD WRITING FLUENCY

Ask students to write in their Writer's Notebooks about what they do to solve a problem. They should write as much and as well as they can for 15 minutes without stopping. Meet with individuals during Writing Conference time to provide feedback and revision assignments. Students should self-correct any errors they find.

Connect to the Unit Theme

DISCUSS THE BIG IDEA

When people work together, often they find solutions to problems more easily.

Tell students that in this unit they will read about people who solved problems in creative ways. Ask:

- How might you improve something in your community?

- How can imagination and teamwork make you a good problem-solver?

USE THEME FOLDABLES

Write the **Big Idea** statement on the board. Ask students to copy it on their Unit Theme Foldables. Remind them to add details as they complete this week's readings.

Dinah Zike's
FOLDABLES®
Study Organizer

Unit Theme
Week 1
Week 2
Week 3
Week 4
Week 5

Layered Book

ELL ENGLISH LANGUAGE LEARNERS

Beginning	Intermediate	Advanced
Use Visuals Tell students about the photograph. *The people are standing together. They are waiting in line to get some help.* Then ask students to tell you about the photograph. If the answer is correct, repeat it in a louder and slower voice so the rest of the class may hear.	**Describe** Ask students to tell what is happening in the photograph. *Why are the people standing together? Is it important to cooperate?* Correct grammar and pronunciation in students' responses as needed.	**Discuss** Ask students to elaborate on cooperation and how it helps people find solutions. *Is it better to cooperate than act alone? Why or why not?* Clarify students' responses.

Objectives

- Identify the characteristics of narrative nonfiction
- Develop vocabulary
- Read sentences fluently, focusing on phrasing

Materials

- Read-Aloud Anthology, pp. 93–96

Read Aloud

Read "On Our Own"

Read Aloud

GENRE: Literary Text/Literary Nonfiction

Present the key characteristics of **narrative nonfiction**, a form of literary nonfiction:

- **Narrative nonfiction** is factual information presented in the form of a story.
- The information usually is presented in **sequence**, or the order in which events really occurred.

FOCUS ON VOCABULARY

Introduce the following words, using the **Define/Example/Ask** routine. Tell students that knowing these words will help them understand what it was like aboard the *Kon-Tiki*. Explain that the story is an excerpt from *Kon-Tiki: A True Adventure of Survival at Sea.*

Vocabulary Routine

Use the routines below to discuss the meaning of each word.

Define: A **current** is a strong flow of water.
Example: The current pulled the boat out to sea.
Ask: Why do some sea creatures use currents to travel in the ocean?

Define: **Sheets** are large, flat surfaces.
Example: It was raining so hard that the rain was coming down in sheets. It looked like a wall of water!
Ask: Which would you describe as a sheet of ice—an ice cube or a frozen lake?

Define: A **cabin** is a small room aboard a ship.
Example: The cabin had a bed, a sink, and a small window to look out onto the ocean.
Ask: How is a cabin like a bedroom? How is it different?

LISTENING FOR A PURPOSE

Ask students to listen carefully as you read "On Our Own" on **Read-Aloud Anthology** pages 93–96. Use the Think Alouds and genre study provided.

ELL Interactive Reading Build students' oral language by discussing the basic meaning of the narrative.

- Point to the picture of the raft. Name the basic parts, such as the sail and the mast, and have students repeat. Point to the oar and tell students that the sailors use it to steer the raft.

- After reading the first page, say: *The weather is stormy. Let's list details that help us picture the sea during this weather.* (Details include *waves were stronger, wind blew harder,* and *hissing sound.*) Ask: *Can the sailors control the raft?* (no)

- After the final paragraph, say: *Think about how the author uses figurative language to create imagery. What does an angry ocean look like? What might a friendly ocean look like?* Help students recognize that a friendly ocean is calm without big waves or strong winds.

Think/Pair/Share Use **Copying Master 5**, "I noticed the author used …," to help students share details about the story. Then have them turn to a partner and orally summarize the story, using their analysis of the author's words and style to guide them. Finally, have a few students share their summaries with the class.

RESPOND TO THE NARRATIVE NONFICTION

Ask students the Think and Respond questions on page 96. Then have them tell how they might have felt if they had been sailors aboard the *Kon-Tiki.*

Model Fluency

Reread the narrative. Tell students that this time you want them to focus on one aspect of how you read—your **phrasing**.

Explain that good readers read with emotion. They pause after each line that ends with punctuation, and pay attention to the type of punctuation to read with the right intonation and expression. Model an example.

Think Aloud Listen as I read the part where night falls. "When night came, the wind blew harder than ever. We could see the white tops of waves in the moonlight. They were as high as the top of our cabin! We waited for one to crash down over our heads." Did you notice how I started reading this part slowly, but then added stress to my voice when I saw the exclamation mark? Reading it this way made the scene sound dramatic. Now you try. Repeat each sentence after me, using the same phrasing that I do.

Establish Fluency Focus Remind students that you will be listening for these same qualities in their reading throughout the week. You will help them improve their reading by adjusting their phrasing for clarity and drama.

Point out that good readers show their understanding of a story by reading it with appropriate phrasing. It shows that the reader is analyzing the story while reading.

Readers Theater

BUILDING LISTENING AND SPEAKING SKILLS
Distribute copies of "The Camera in the Attic," **Read-Aloud Anthology** pages 203–219. Assign parts. Have students practice throughout the unit. Have students present the play or perform a dramatic reading at the end of the unit.

ELL

Discuss Genre Review the characteristics of a nonfiction narrative with students. Ask: *What can you learn from a nonfiction narrative? How is the information told? What is* On Our Own *about? How did the people survive the storm?* Have students describe the main ideas of the story in phrases or sentences. Correct the meaning of students' responses as needed.

Objective
- Decode multisyllabic words with /ən/

Materials
- Practice Book, p. 226
- Word-Building Cards
- Transparency 26
- Teacher's Resource Book, p. 145

ELL

Practice Activities
Distinguishing the final vowel in the spelling of words ending with /ən/ will be difficult for some students. Repeated use of words in modeled-writing activities will help students learn the correct spelling over time. Use the Approaching Level lesson on page 703J for additional practice. See language transfers on pages T16–T31.

HOMEWORK | **Practice Book,** page 226

Listen for the final /ən/ sounds at the end of the following words:

wood**en**   oft**en**   rais**in**   reas**on**   bac**on**

The /ən/ sounds can be spelled -**en**, -**in**, or -**on**.

| bacon | proven | button | eleven | cousin | dozen |
| women | reason | shaken | listen | common | cotton |

Write a word from the box to complete each sentence. Underline the letters that represent the /ən/ sounds.

1. Were there any _____women_____ at the mining camps?
2. Nine plus two is one less than a _____dozen_____.
3. Do you know the _____reason_____ why the computer turned into a time machine?
4. Miners fried up lots of _____bacon_____ for their breakfasts.
5. General stores in San Francisco sold yards of _____cotton_____ for all the clothes the miners would need.
6. My great-grandfather had a _____cousin_____ who was a gold miner.
7. The earthquake left them feeling very _____shaken_____ up.
8. I love to _____listen_____ to stories about the Gold Rush.
9. Most of the miners could sew a patch or a _____button_____ on their clothes.
10. The pigeon is a _____common_____ bird in many cities.

Approaching Reproducible, page 226

Beyond Reproducible, page 226

Word Study

✔ Words with /ən/

EXPLAIN/MODEL

Display the **Word-Building Cards** -in, -on, -en. Tell students that words that end with a vowel + n (and have an unaccented last syllable) have final syllables that are pronounced alike. The final syllables all sound like the on in person. The /ən/ sound can be spelled -in, -on, or -en, but the pronunciation does not change. Use the words below as examples:

- cab**in**   • lem**on**   • ov**en**

Write the sample words on the board, underline the final syllable, and model blending each one.

Think Aloud Let's look at the first word I wrote: cabin. I see that this word begins with cab. This is a closed syllable because it ends with a consonant, so I will pronounce the vowel with the short sound of a: /kab/. The second syllable is unaccented, so I pronounce it with the /ən/ sound. When I blend the sounds together, I get /kab ən/. I know that word—it's a small room on a ship.

PRACTICE/APPLY

Read the Word List Display **Phonics Transparency 26**. Ask students to underline the vowel + n at the end of the words. Then have them read the words aloud. Emphasize that the pronunciation is always the same in an unaccented syllable with a vowel + n. Finally, have students sort the words in their Writer's Notebooks.

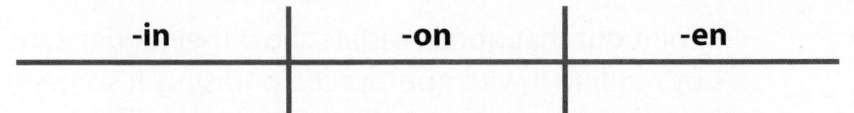

tighten	satin	kitchen	wagon
eleven	cousin	glisten	common
cotton	rotten	raisin	happen
pumpkin	dolphin	muffin	melon
dragon	reason	goblin	chicken

Phonics Transparency 26

-in	-on	-en

Read Multisyllabic Words

TRANSITION TO LONGER WORDS Help students use their knowledge of phonics patterns, compound words, and word parts to decode longer words. Have students read the word in the first column, then model how to read the longer word in the second column. Point out the added syllable(s), such as a prefix or base word, to help students gain awareness of these common word parts.

melon	watermelon	muffin	ragamuffin
common	uncommon	open	reopen
season	preseason	lighten	enlighten
woven	handwoven	son	poison
band	abandon	button	unbutton
proven	unproven	fasten	unfasten

Phonics Transparency 26

BUILD WORDS Use **Word-Building Cards** *en, in, on, less, light, hard, wov, rais, wag, drag, sat, treas, seas.* Display the cards. Have students use the cards to build as many multisyllabic /ən/ words as possible. These and other words can be formed: *lessen, lighten, harden, woven, raisin, wagon, dragon, satin, treason, season.*

APPLY DECODING STRATEGY Guide students to use the Decoding Strategy to decode the following words: *lemonade, unseasoned, unreasonable, dragonfly, personable, vitamin.* Write each word on the board. Tell students to use step 4 of the Decoding Strategy procedure to identify word parts and blend them together to read longer words.

Build Fluency

SPEED DRILL Distribute copies of the **/ən/ Speed Drill, Teacher's Resource Book** page 145. Use the Speed Drill routine to help students become fluent reading words with the final /ən/ sound.

Quick Check

Can students read words with /ən/?

During **Small Group Instruction**

Tier 2

If No → **Approaching Level** Reteach the skill using the lesson on p. 703J.

If Yes → **On Level** Consolidate the learning using p. 703S.

Beyond Level Extend the learning using p. 703W.

DAILY **Syllable Fluency**

Use Word-Building Cards 251–260. Display one card at a time. Have students chorally read each common syllable. Repeat at varying speeds and in random order. Have students work with partners during independent time to write as many words as they can containing each syllable.

cen   bi   act

Decoding Strategy

Decoding Strategy Chart

Step 1	Look for word parts (prefixes) at the beginning of the word.
Step 2	Look for word parts (suffixes) at the end of the word.
Step 3	In the base word, look for familiar spelling patterns. Think about the six syllable-spelling patterns you have learned.
Step 4	Sound out and blend together the word parts.
Step 5	Say the word parts fast. Adjust your pronunciation as needed. Ask yourself: "Is this a word I have heard before?" Then read the word in the sentence and ask: "Does it make sense in this sentence?"

© Macmillan/McGraw-Hill

Vocabulary

STRATEGY
DICTIONARY

Unfamiliar Words Remind students to use a dictionary to determine the meanings of unfamiliar words—words they do not know—and to check the meanings of words they have tried to figure out through context clues. Point out that a dictionary contains definitions, pronunciations, spellings, and word histories. Students should use a dictionary when they read and when they write.

Ask students to read "Unfamiliar Words" in the bookmark on **Student Book** page 676. Then model for them how to use a dictionary to find the meaning of the word *clustered*.

Think Aloud When I read the word *clustered,* I'm not sure what it means. The word *together* makes me think it means "grouped," but I'm going to use a dictionary to check. Words in a dictionary are arranged alphabetically, so first I find the *C* section. Then I scan the guide words at the top of each page to help me find the page with *clustered*. The simplest form of a word is defined, so I find the word *cluster. Cluster* means "group together," so *clustered* means "grouped together." This meaning makes sense in the sentence.

Read "Grandma's Story"

As you read "Grandma's Story" with students, ask them to identify clues that reveal the meanings of the highlighted words. Tell students that they will read these words again in *Leah's Pony*.

Vocabulary

sturdy	bidding
items	overflowing
clustered	glistened

Dictionary

Unfamiliar Words are words you do not know. You can find the meaning, syllabication, and pronunciation of unfamiliar words in a dictionary. Look up the meaning of the word *clustered*.

Grandma's Story

by Marcus Kharana

My grandmother had been in a wheelchair for a long time. "Why is that, Grandma?" I asked her one day.

"When I was 12," she said, "I had polio." Grandma told me that polio harmed the lungs and muscles. Some people died of it. Many people who lived lost the use of their legs or arms. "President Roosevelt even had it," Grandma said. "Now, thank goodness, there is a vaccine for it." Grandma lived, but she would not be able to walk. Her family felt lucky.

To get around, Grandma told me, she needed a **sturdy**, strong wheelchair. Her family was poor, and this was a hard time for everyone. But the neighborhood decided to help them raise money for a wheelchair by having a sale. Everyone looked around their homes and found **items** that they would be glad to part with.

These things were **clustered** together in the community center basement and given price tags. The nicer pieces, such as furniture and paintings, were placed in an auction. All the money that came from the auction **bidding** and the sale would help pay for the wheelchair.

676

Quick Check

Can students identify word meanings?

During **Small Group Instruction**

Tier 2

If No → | Approaching Level | Reteach the words using the Vocabulary lesson, pp. 703K–703L.

If Yes → | On Level | Consolidate the learning using p. 703S.

| Beyond Level | Extend the learning using p. 703W.

Gifted & Talented

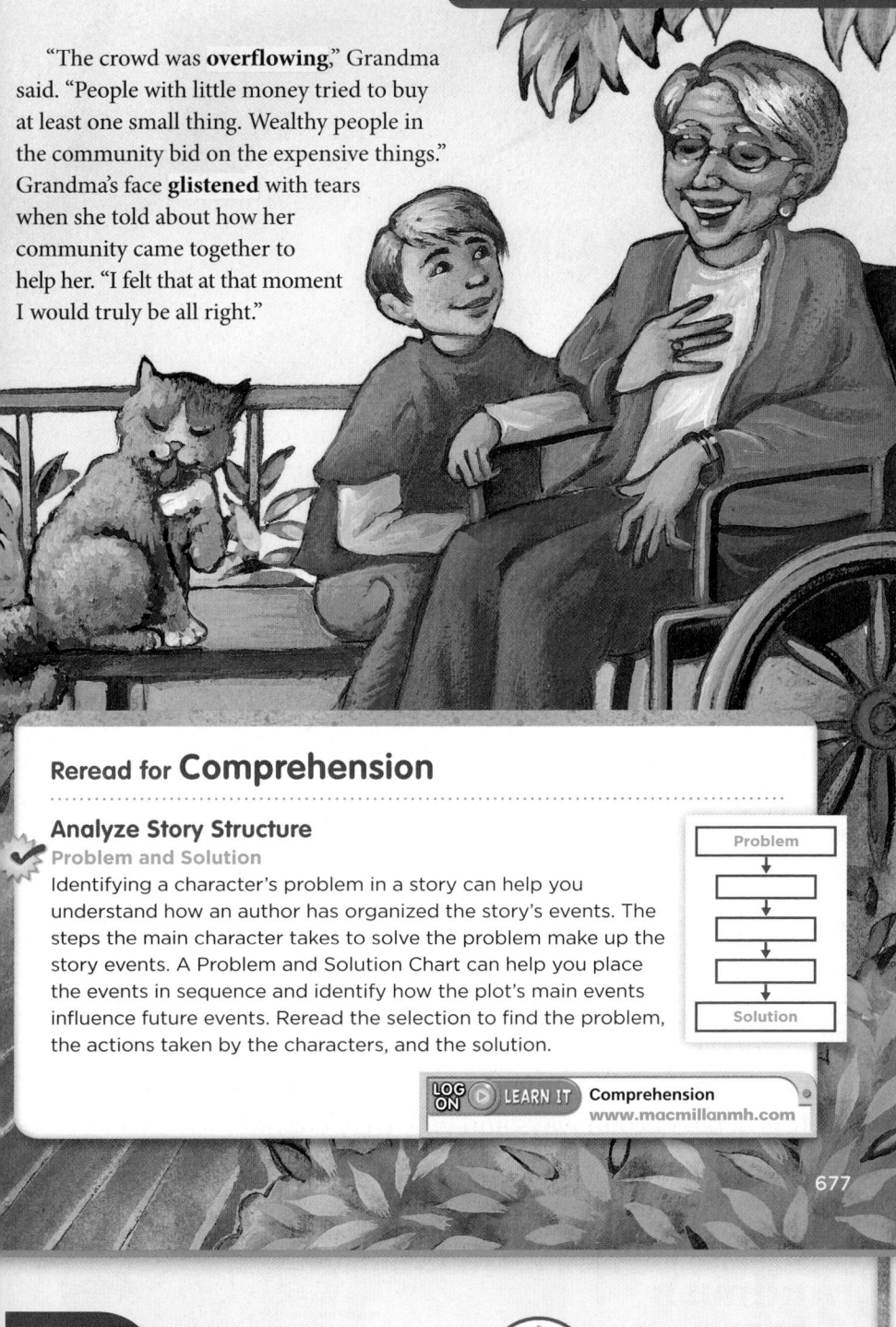

"The crowd was **overflowing**," Grandma said. "People with little money tried to buy at least one small thing. Wealthy people in the community bid on the expensive things." Grandma's face **glistened** with tears when she told about how her community came together to help her. "I felt that at that moment I would truly be all right."

Reread for **Comprehension**

Analyze Story Structure
Problem and Solution

Identifying a character's problem in a story can help you understand how an author has organized the story's events. The steps the main character takes to solve the problem make up the story events. A Problem and Solution Chart can help you place the events in sequence and identify how the plot's main events influence future events. Reread the selection to find the problem, the actions taken by the characters, and the solution.

Problem
↓
↓
↓
↓
Solution

LOG ON ▶ **LEARN IT** **Comprehension**
www.macmillanmh.com

677

Vocabulary

✓ **TEACH WORDS**

Introduce each word using the **Define/Example/Ask** routine. Model reading each word using the syllable-scoop technique.

Vocabulary Routine

Define: **Items** are single objects that are part of a larger group or collection.
Example: The items in my backpack include a notebook, a pencil, and my jacket.
Ask: What are some items you might find in a kitchen? EXAMPLE

- When things are **clustered**, they are grouped together. *The children were clustered together around the campfire.* What is an antonym for *clustered*? ANTONYM

- When something is **overflowing**, it is spilling out of its container because there is too much of it. *After the heavy rain, the river was overflowing.* Should you put another piece of trash in a trash can that is overflowing? Why or why not? EXPLANATION

- Something that is **sturdy** is strong and well built. *The sturdy tree had a thick trunk and heavy branches.* What is an antonym for *sturdy*? ANTONYM

- When something **glistened**, it sparkled and shined. *The diamond glistened in the sun.* What are some things you have seen that glistened? EXAMPLE

- **Bidding** is making an offer of money for something. *The bidding for the antique vase started at 100 dollars.* Which would you rather be bidding on—an old radio or a new bicycle? Why? EXPLANATION

ELL

Preteach Vocabulary See pages 703BB and 703K to preteach the vocabulary words to **ELL** and **Approaching Level** students. Use the **Visual Vocabulary Resources** to demonstrate and discuss each word. To further reinforce concepts, have students complete page 300 in the **ELL Resource Book**.

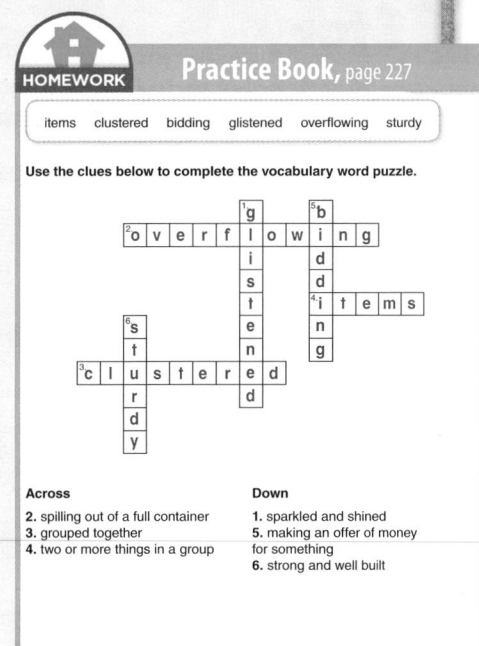

HOMEWORK **Practice Book,** page 227

items   clustered   bidding   glistened   overflowing   sturdy

Use the clues below to complete the vocabulary word puzzle.

Across
2. spilling out of a full container
3. grouped together
4. two or more things in a group

Down
1. sparkled and shined
5. making an offer of money for something
6. strong and well built

Approaching Reproducible, page 227
Beyond Reproducible, page 227

Objectives

- Analyze story structure
- Identify problem and solution
- Use academic language: *analyze, story structure, problem, solution, plot*

Materials

- Transparencies 11, 26a, 26b
- Practice Book, p. 228

Skills Trace

Problem and Solution

Introduce	573A–573B
Practice/ Apply	574–591; Practice Book, 192–193
Reteach/ Review	597M–597Z, 677A–677B, 678–697, 703M–703Z; Practice Book, 228–229
Assess	Weekly Tests; Units 5, 6 Tests
Maintain	723B

ELL

Academic Language
Preteach the following academic language words to **ELL** and **Approaching Level** students during Small Group time: *analyze, story structure, problem, solution.* See pages 703AA and 703I.

Reread for
Comprehension

STRATEGY
ANALYZE STORY STRUCTURE

What Is It? **Story structure** is the way an author organizes the events of the plot using story elements such as character and setting. These events give the story a beginning, middle, and an end.

Why Is It Important? Analyzing story structure helps readers sequence, summarize, and remember the plot's main events.

SKILL
PROBLEM AND SOLUTION

What Is It? Most plots focus on a **problem** and **solution**. The **problem** is something that the characters want to do, change, or need to find out. The steps the characters take to try and solve the problem make up the events of the plot. The **solution** is the way the problem is solved.

Why Is It Important? The problem, the steps taken to solve it, and the solution are an essential part of story structure. Identifying them helps the reader recognize the impact of the plot's main events on future events. Readers who understand how a problem is solved are better able to determine the theme of the story as well as why the characters act in certain ways and why they change.

Student Book pages 676–677 available on Comprehension Transparencies 26a and 26b

- The **problem** usually is introduced at or near the beginning of a story. Good readers identify the problem. Then they examine the actions or steps the main characters take to try to solve the problem. Sometimes an action fails to solve the problem.

- The point where the characters begin to find a solution is called the *turning point*. To recognize the turning point, students should pay close attention to the interaction of characters, including their relationships, their decisions, and the changes they undergo.

- The **solution** to the problem usually is revealed at the end of the story. It tells the outcome, or how the problem is solved.

MODEL

How Do I Use It? Read aloud the first three paragraphs of "Grandma's Story" on **Student Book** page 676. Use **Transparency 11** to record the problem on the Problem and Solution Chart.

Think Aloud When I read the second paragraph, I understand that Grandma is going to describe a problem in her past. She begins by explaining that she had polio as a child. Although she could no longer walk, her family felt lucky because she survived. Then, in the third paragraph, Grandma says that she needed a wheelchair, but that her family was poor. This is the problem: although Grandma needed a wheelchair, her family could not afford to buy one. I will keep reading to find out how the problem is solved.

GUIDED PRACTICE

Continue by helping students identify the steps that the characters take to help Grandma solve her problem. Remind students to consider what the neighbors do first, next, and last.

APPLY

Have students identify the solution to the problem. Then have them complete the Problem and Solution Chart. Ask students to use the chart to retell the story, maintaining meaning and logical order.

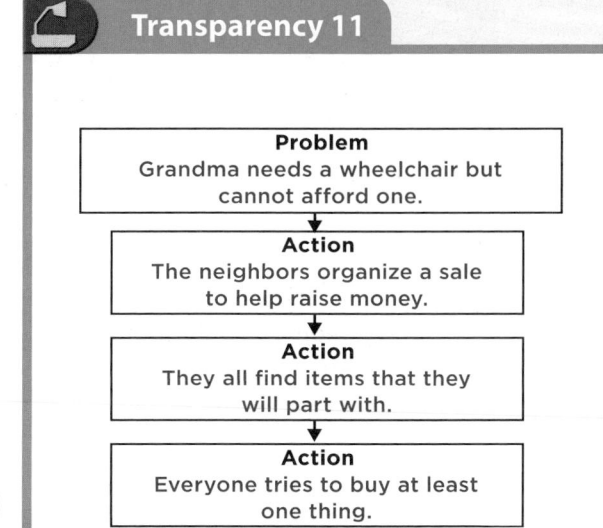

Transparency 11

Problem
Grandma needs a wheelchair but cannot afford one.

Action
The neighbors organize a sale to help raise money.

Action
They all find items that they will part with.

Action
Everyone tries to buy at least one thing.

Solution
The sale raises enough money for Grandma to have a wheelchair.

Graphic Organizer Transparency

Quick Check

Can students identify the problem and solution in a story?

Tier 2

During **Small Group Instruction**

If No → **Approaching Level** Reteach the skill using the Comprehension lesson, p. 703M–703P.

If Yes → **On Level** Consolidate the learning using pp. 703U–703V.

Beyond Level Extend the learning using pp. 703Y–703Z.

HOMEWORK

Practice Book, page 228

When you read a story, look for the **problem** that the main character has. It may influence all the events that follow. Notice the steps the character takes to find the **solution** to the problem.

Read the passage and each question. Underline the answer in the passage. Then write the answers below. Possible responses p

Ding! Ding! Ding! Marta heard the bell of the ice-cream truck. It was the hottest week of the year, and she felt like she was going to melt. Marta wanted an orange ice pop—she could almost taste it. She counted the money in her pocket: 26 cents. Ice pops cost $1.50. She did not have enough money. Marta remembered that her brother owed her $2.00. She knocked on his bedroom door, but he wasn't home.

Then Marta got an idea. She went to the kitchen and found an ice-cube tray. Carefully, she poured some orange juice into the tray. She covered the tray with plastic wrap and stuck a toothpick into each square. Then she put the tray in the freezer and waited. In a couple of hours, she checked the freezer. She had twelve orange ice pops—enough to last all week.

1. Who is the main character? _____ Marta

2. What is the problem? Marta wants an orange ice pop, but she doesn't have enough money.

3. What is the first thing Marta does to solve her problem? She tries to find her brother.

4. How does Marta solve her problem? She makes her own ice pops.

5. What might happen next? She might sell homemade ice pops.

Approaching Reproducible, page 228

Beyond Reproducible, page 228

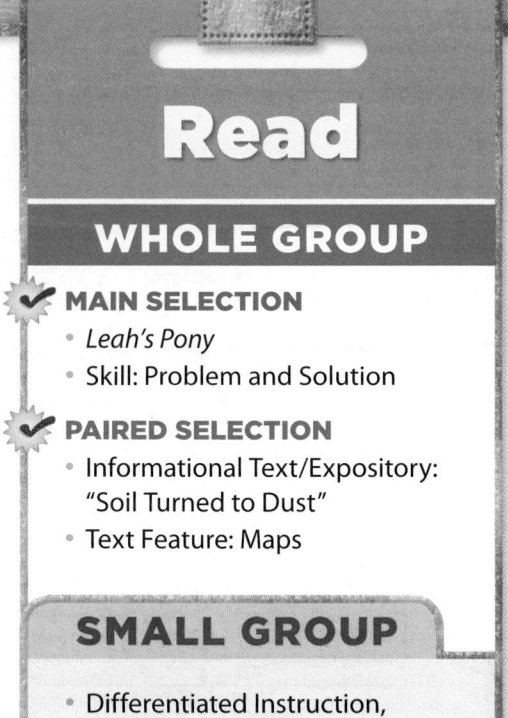

Read

WHOLE GROUP

✔ **MAIN SELECTION**
- *Leah's Pony*
- Skill: Problem and Solution

✔ **PAIRED SELECTION**
- Informational Text/Expository: "Soil Turned to Dust"
- Text Feature: Maps

SMALL GROUP

- Differentiated Instruction, pp. 703I–703HH

Main Selection

GENRE: Historical Fiction

Have a student read the definition of Historical Fiction on **Student Book** page 678. Tell students to look for events and details that reflect the time and place in which the story is set.

 **STRATEGY**
ANALYZE STORY STRUCTURE

Review with students that story structure refers to the way an author organizes the events of the plot using story elements such as character and setting.

 **SKILL**
PROBLEM AND SOLUTION

Remind students that identifying the problem and the steps taken to find a solution helps readers sequence and summarize the plot's main events and recognize their influence on future events.

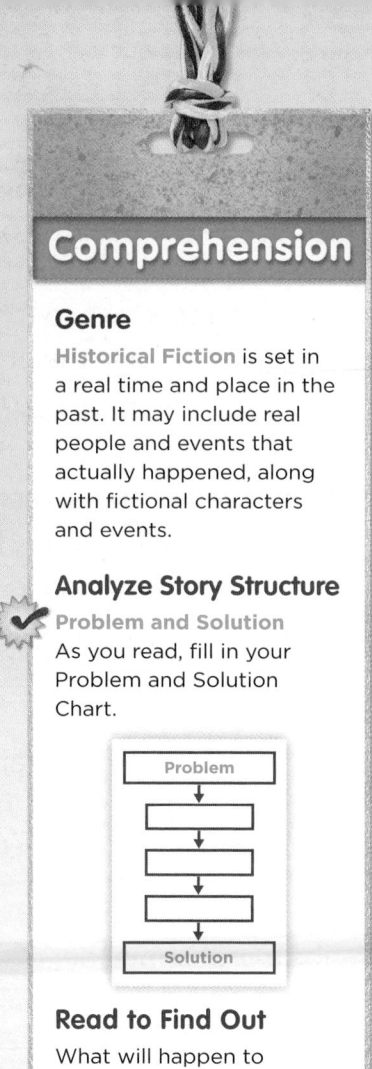

Comprehension

Genre

Historical Fiction is set in a real time and place in the past. It may include real people and events that actually happened, along with fictional characters and events.

Analyze Story Structure

✔ **Problem and Solution** As you read, fill in your Problem and Solution Chart.

Problem
↓
↓
↓
↓
Solution

Read to Find Out

What will happen to Leah's pony?

678

Vocabulary

Vocabulary Words Review the tested words while reading: **items, clustered, overflowing, sturdy, glistened,** and **bidding.**

Additional Selection Words Students may be unfamiliar with these words. Pronounce the words, give student-friendly explanations as needed, and help students use the previously taught vocabulary strategies: context clues, dictionary, word parts.

pasture (p. 681): a field of grass and plants used for feeding horses, cattle, and other livestock

auction (p. 685): a public sale at which goods and property are sold to the highest bidder

gullies (p. 687): ditches or valleys originally created by running water

cultivate (p. 690): to get land ready for growing crops

Leah's Pony

Written by Elizabeth Friedrich
Illustrated by Michael Garland

679

Preview and Predict

QUICK WRITE Ask students to read the title, preview the illustrations, and make predictions about the story.

Set Purposes

FOCUS QUESTION Discuss the "Read to Find Out" question on **Student Book** page 678. Remind students to look for the answer as they read.

Collect questions about the selection from the class. Have students use the questions to establish purposes for reading. Each student should choose one question and look for the answer as he or she reads.

Read *Leah's Pony*

Use the questions and Think Alouds to support comprehension instruction.

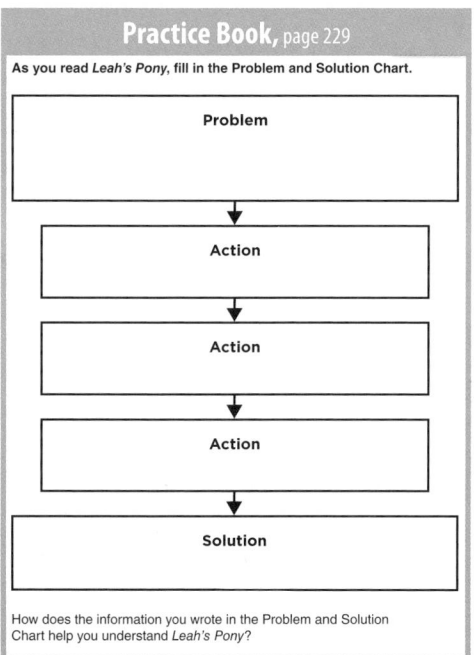

Practice Book, page 229

As you read *Leah's Pony*, fill in the Problem and Solution Chart.

Problem

↓

Action

↓

Action

↓

Action

↓

Solution

How does the information you wrote in the Problem and Solution Chart help you understand *Leah's Pony*?

Approaching Reproducible, page 229
Beyond Reproducible, page 229

Read the Main Selection

Preteach	Read Together	Read Independently
Have Approaching Level students and English Language Learners listen to the selection on **StudentWorks Plus**, the interactive e-Book, before reading with the class.	Use the prompts to guide comprehension and model how to complete the graphic organizer. Have students use **Think/Pair/Share** to discuss the selection.	If students can read the selection independently, have them read and complete the graphic organizer. Suggest that they use their purposes to choose their reading strategies.

Interactive Student Book

Develop Comprehension

1 STRATEGY

ANALYZE STORY STRUCTURE

 **Teacher Think Aloud** When I read on page 681 that Leah's father buys her a pony the year that the corn grows tall, I know that corn is an important crop to this family. It helps them afford to buy special things. As I read the rest of page 681, I learn what happens in the months afterward. Leah is taught how to saddle her pony, and she spends all summer riding and grooming him. She rides him into town to hear Mr. B. say that her pony is the finest around. So far I don't see a problem that any of the characters have. As I read, I will **analyze** the **story structure**, and pay close attention to how the characters' actions and plot events influence what happens later in the story.

680

Monitor Comprehension

Monitor and Clarify: *Reread*

Explain Tell students that when something they read does not make sense, they can read that part again, either silently to themselves or aloud to a partner. Rereading can help students to clarify and adjust their understanding. It can also remind them of story details they might have missed on their first reading.

Discuss Ask students to describe Leah's pony using details from the story. If they cannot remember the details, prompt them to reread the first paragraph on page 681. (The details are *strong and swift and sturdy* and *a snip of white at the end of his soft black nose.*)

Apply As students read the selection, remind them to go back and reread as necessary to find details or to clarify any phrases or parts of the story that may be confusing.

The year the corn grew tall and straight, Leah's papa bought her a pony. The pony was strong and swift and **sturdy**, with just a snip of white at the end of his soft black nose. Papa taught Leah to place her new saddle right in the middle of his back and tighten the girth around his belly, just so.

That whole summer, Leah and her pony crossed through cloud-capped cornfields and chased cattle through the pasture.

Leah scratched that special spot under her pony's mane and brushed him till his coat **glistened** like satin.

1

Each day Leah loved to ride her pony into town just to hear Mr. B. shout from the door of his grocery store, "That's the finest pony in the whole county."

2

681

Develop Comprehension

2 CHARACTER

In the last paragraph on page 681, what do we learn about the **character** of Mr. B. and about his interaction with Leah? (Mr. B., the owner of the town's grocery store, seems to be very observant as well as very kind and friendly. He notices how fine Leah's pony is, and he goes out of his way to say nice things to Leah about him. She seems to like Mr. B.'s enthusiastic words, since she rides into town especially to hear them.)

Phonics/Word Study

APPLY DECODING SKILLS While reading, point out words with the sound/spelling patterns, syllable types, and word parts students have recently learned. Help students blend these words. You may wish to focus on selection words with the /ən/ ending: *tighten, satin, kitchen,* and *wagon.*

Beginning	Intermediate	Advanced
Access Content Preteach story content, build language, and develop meaning using the Interactive Question-Response Guide in the **ELL Resource Book**, pages 288–297. Give ample time for students to respond. They may point or use words or short phrases to respond.	**Describe** Preteach story content, build language, and develop meaning using the Interactive Question-Response Guide in the ELL Resource Book, pages 288–297. Have students respond in complete sentences. Repeat their responses, correcting pronunciation or grammar as needed.	**Explain** Complete the Intermediate task with students. Elicit details from students for their responses.

Develop Comprehension

3 MONITOR AND CLARIFY: REREAD

Why did the corn fail to grow tall? **Reread** page 682 to find the answer. (The first sentence states that the corn grew *no taller than a man's thumb,* but it doesn't tell why the corn did not grow tall. Rereading the rest of the page reveals that the nights were *hot* and *dry* and the sky was *black with dust.* These words reveal drought conditions that are not good for growing corn.)

4 SKILL
PROBLEM AND SOLUTION

What **problem** is Leah's family facing? What are two actions the family takes to try to **solve** the problem? (The dry, dusty weather has kept the corn from growing, so Leah's family is facing hard times. Papa tries to solve the problem by selling pigs and some cattle; Mama makes underwear from flour sacks.) Add the problem and actions to your Problem and Solution Chart.

Problem
The dry, dusty weather has kept the corn from growing, so Leah's family is facing hard times.

↓

Action
Papa sells pigs and some cattle.

↓

Action
Mama makes underwear from flour sacks.

3 The year the corn grew no taller than a man's thumb, Leah's house became very quiet. Sometimes on those hot, dry nights, Leah heard Papa and Mama's hushed voices whispering in the kitchen. She couldn't understand the words but knew their sad sound.

Some days the wind blew so hard it turned the sky black with dust. It was hard for Leah to keep her pony's coat shining. It was hard for Mama to keep the house clean. It was hard for Papa to carry buckets of water for the sow and her piglets.

682

Comprehension

Literary Devices: *Sensory Words*

Explain Authors use special literary devices such as sensory words to help readers understand exactly what the characters are experiencing. For example, the simile *glistened like satin* on page 681 helps readers see and feel the pony's coat. Sensory words such as *hushed* and *whispering* appeal to our sense of hearing.

Discuss Have students list some of the sensory words and phrases on pages 682–683 and the sense to which each one appeals. (hot, dry nights—touch; black with dust—sight; fresh, hot coffee cake baking—smell)

Apply As they read, have students notice other sensory words and images that describe the setting of *Leah's Pony*. Have them list the words and images and share their lists with a partner.

Soon Papa sold the pigs and even some of the cattle. "These are hard times," he told Leah with a puzzled look. "That's what these days are, all right, hard times."

Mama used flour sacks to make underwear for Leah. Mama threw dishwater on her drooping petunias to keep them growing. And, no matter what else happened, Mama always woke Leah on Saturday with the smell of fresh, hot coffee cake baking.

4

5

683

Develop Comprehension

5 **STRATEGY**
ANALYZE STORY STRUCTURE

Teacher Think Aloud I realize that to **analyze story structure**, I need to identify each of the main story elements. I notice that setting is an especially important element in the way this story is structured. I understand from the text that the setting is a farm community where people grow corn and own animals such as cattle, pigs, and ponies. There is a town with a grocery store nearby. When the corn is tall, Leah's father buys her a pony. However, when events happen that affect this farming community, other changes follow. What events help create the hard times Papa talks about on page 683?

PARTNERS Prompt students to apply the strategy in a Think Aloud by describing the events that led up to the hard times.

Student Think Aloud I know that the weather changed and became very hot and dry and windy. Then the corn didn't grow tall. Farmers probably had a hard time earning a living. Also, everything became covered with dust. The wind seemed to turn the sky black with dust. These are some of the events that made life hard for everybody in the story.

Develop Comprehension

6 SEQUENCE

Sequence is the order of events in a story. Signal words such as *first*, *next, then*, and *finally* often indicate a sequence of events. What happens on the day after the grasshoppers eat the trees bare? What signal words help you recognize the sequence of events? (The neighbors fill their truck and stop by to say they are moving to Oregon. The words *The next day* signal the sequence.) Why is their departure an important event? (Their departure shows that things are growing worse and worse. Some people feel they can no longer live on their farms.)

7 GENRE: Historical Fiction

How does the illustration on page 684 indicate that *Leah's Pony* is **historical fiction**? Explain. (Historical fiction tells about a real time in the past. The text says that Leah's neighbors left for Oregon in an old truck. This illustration, however, shows a truck that is not only old but also really old-fashioned. Trucks like this one can mostly be seen in old movies or photographs, or in museums. This illustration is a clue that the story is set in the past.)

One hot, dry, dusty day grasshoppers turned the day to night. They ate the trees bare and left only twigs behind.

6 The next day the neighbors filled their truck with all they owned and stopped to say good-bye. "We're off to Oregon," they said. "It must be better there." Papa, Mama, and Leah waved as their neighbors wobbled down the road in an old truck **7 overflowing** with chairs and bedsprings and wire.

684

Connect to Content

DROUGHT

Tell students that in the 1930s, during the period known in the United States as the Great Depression, a terrible drought devastated many farming communities. In one area of the country, a region that included parts of Texas and other states, the soil became so dry that it blew away in dust storms. This area, known as the Dust Bowl, is the setting for *Leah's Pony*. Tell students they will read more about the Dust Bowl in the selection "Soil Turned to Dust" on page 698.

Point out that drought continues at times to be a serious problem in the United States and around the world. Have students choose and research an area that has been affected by drought in the last fifty years. Ask, *How have residents responded to drought conditions? What steps have been taken to reduce suffering caused by drought?* Ask students to share and discuss their findings with the class.

The hot, dry, dusty days kept coming. On a day you could almost taste the earth in the air, Papa said, "I have something to tell you, Leah, and I want you to be brave. I borrowed money from the bank. I bought seeds, but the seeds dried up and blew away. Nothing grew. I don't have any corn to sell. Now I can't pay back the bank," Papa paused. "They're going to have an auction, Leah. They're going to sell the cattle and the chickens and the pickup truck." **8**

Leah stared at Papa. His voice grew husky and soft. "Worst of all, they're going to sell my tractor. I'll never be able to plant corn when she's gone. Without my tractor, we might even have to leave the farm. I told you, Leah, these are hard times." **9**

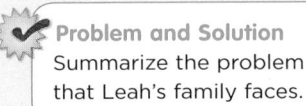

✓ **Problem and Solution**
Summarize the problem that Leah's family faces.

685

Develop Comprehension

8 STRATEGY
DICTIONARY

 What reference source could you use to find the meaning of the **unfamiliar word** *auction*? (a dictionary) What is an auction? (It's a sale at which people bid on items, and the items are sold to the highest bidder.)

9 SKILL
PROBLEM AND SOLUTION

 Summarize the **problem** that Leah's family faces. (The hot, dry, dusty weather has kept the corn from growing and has led to hard times. Now Papa cannot pay back the money he borrowed from the bank, so the bank is going to sell many of the family's things, including Papa's tractor. Without the tractor, Papa won't ever be able to plant corn. The family may have to leave the farm.) **Add** this information in the problem section of your Problem and Solution Chart.

Problem
The dry, dusty weather has kept the corn from growing, so Leah's family is facing hard times. Since Papa cannot pay the bank back, the bank is auctioning off some of the family's belongings, including the tractor. The family may have to leave the farm.

↓

Action
Papa sells pigs and some cattle.

↓

Action
Mama makes underwear from flour sacks.

Develop Comprehension

10 **MAKE INFERENCES**

Do you think there have been auctions in this community before? What clues does the author provide to help you make this **inference**? (An auction is not just a sale to Leah. The author states that "Leah knew what an auction meant." This means that she has experienced them before. Her friends or neighbors may have resorted to an auction when they faced hard times.)

Leah knew what an auction meant. She knew eager faces with strange voices would come to their farm. They would stand outside and offer money for her Papa's best bull and Mama's prize rooster and **10** Leah's favorite calf.

686

Vocabulary

Word Parts: *Compound Words*

Explain/Model Tell students that a compound word is a word made of two smaller words. Point to the word *outside* on page 686.

Think Aloud I see the smaller words *out* and *side* in the word *outside*. I know that *out* means *in the open* or *not enclosed*, and *side* is a place that is neither *front* nor *back*. When I put the meanings together, I can determine that *outside* is someplace not enclosed by walls. When I reread the paragraph, this meaning makes sense.

Practice/Apply As students read, have them note compound words such as *windowpane* on page 687 and *sunburned* on page 689. Have students tell what smaller words form the compound words and what the compound words mean. Have students check the meanings using context clues and a dictionary.

All week Leah worried and waited and wondered what to do. One morning she watched as a man in a big hat hammered a sign into the ground in front of her house.

Leah wanted to run away. She raced her pony past **11** empty fields lined with dry gullies. She galloped past a house with rags stuffed in broken windowpanes. She sped right past Mr. B. sweeping the steps outside his store. **12** **13**

687

Develop Comprehension

11 MONITOR AND CLARIFY: REREAD

Why is Leah riding her pony so quickly? **Reread** to determine the answer. (The last three sentences of the second paragraph describe Leah riding, but they do not explain why she is riding so quickly. The first sentence states the reason: Leah wanted to run away.)

12 SUMMARIZE

A *summary* tells the most important events in a story. How would you **summarize** the story up to this point? Describe the events in sequence and use your Problem and Solution Chart to help you. (Leah's family lives on a farm. When times are good, Leah's father gives her a horse. When the weather turns hot and dry, the crops do not grow and Papa cannot repay the money he borrowed from the bank. The bank is getting ready to auction many of their belongings.)

13 SELF-SELECTED STRATEGY USE

What strategies have you used so far to help you understand this selection? Where did you use them? Why? How did they help?

 **RETURN TO PREDICTIONS AND PURPOSES**

Have students respond to the selection by confirming or revising their predictions and purposes for reading. Direct them to revise or write additional questions to help focus their attention.

Stop here if you wish to read this selection over two days.  STOP

Extra Support

Problem and Solution

Guide students who need help identifying the problem and understanding why Leah is worried and wants to run away. Have them go back and reread the first paragraph on page 685. Ask: *Can Papa pay the bank?* (no) *What is going to happen because he can't pay the bank?* (The bank is going to have an auction of farm property.) Then have them read the second paragraph. Ask: *What are they going to sell that makes Papa worry?* (his tractor) *What will happen if the tractor is sold?* (Papa will not be able to plant corn, so the family might have to leave the farm.) Guide students to combine these ideas to state the problem. (Papa can't pay the bank, so the bank may sell his tractor and he won't be able to plant corn. As a result, the family may have to leave the farm.)

Develop Comprehension

14 | **STRATEGY**
ANALYZE STORY STRUCTURE

How has Leah's past relationship with Mr. B. helped to influence what she decides to do now?

Student Think Aloud The text says that Leah offers to sell her pony to him. Leah knows that Mr. B. admires her pony, and in the past she also has had a friendly relationship with the store owner. If she needs someone to buy her pony, she probably feels that Mr. B. is the best choice . He certainly would take good care of her pony.

15 | **SKILL**
PROBLEM AND SOLUTION

What important step does Leah take to solve her family's **problem**? (She tells Mr. B that he can buy her pony.) Add this information to your Problem and Solution Chart.

Problem
The dry, dusty weather has kept the corn from growing, so Leah's family is facing hard times. Since Papa cannot pay the bank back, the bank is auctioning off some of the family's belongings, including the tractor. The family may have to leave the farm.

↓

Action
Papa sells pigs and some cattle.

↓

Action
Mama makes underwear from flour sacks.

↓

Action
Leah tells Mr. B. that he can buy her pony.

688

At last Leah knew what she had to do. She turned her pony around and rode back into town. She stopped in front of Mr. B.'s store. "You can buy my pony," she said. **14**

Mr. B. stopped sweeping and stared at her. "Why would you want to sell him?" he asked. "That's the finest pony in the county." **15**

Leah swallowed hard. "I've grown a lot this summer," she said. "I'm getting too big for him." **16**

Sunburned soil crunched under Leah's feet as she walked home alone. The auction had begun. Neighbors, friends, strangers—everyone **clustered** around the man in the big hat. "How much for this wagon?" boomed the man. "Five dollars. Ten dollars. Sold for fifteen dollars to the man in the green shirt." **17**

Papa's best bull.

Sold.

Mama's prize rooster.

Sold.

Leah's favorite calf.

Sold.

689

Develop Comprehension

16 **MAKE INFERENCES**

Is Leah telling Mr. B. the truth when she says that she has outgrown the pony? Use details from the text to explain your **inference**. (Leah is not telling Mr. B. the truth. She has to swallow hard before she explains why he can buy her pony. Swallowing before speaking shows that she either needs to think about her answer or that she is trying hard not to cry. Also, she just rode her pony to Mr. B's store, which she wouldn't have been able to do if she were telling the truth.)

17 **SKILL**
PROBLEM AND SOLUTION

 When Leah walks home alone, it is clear that she has sold her pony. How might this step be a turning point in solving the family's **problem**? (The step will give Leah some money to help her family. It is a turning point not only because it might solve her family's problem, but also because Leah has decided to make the huge personal sacrifice of giving up her pony.)

Text Evidence

Problem and Solution

Reread Question 17 aloud. Then ask, *What questions can you raise to figure out why Leah has sold her pony, and why this is a turning point?* (What happened to make her decide to sell him? Why did she think selling him would solve her family's problem?) *After her neighbors leave for Oregon, what specific events lead up to Leah's decision?* (First, she learns that her family might have to sell the tractor and move. Then, she sees the auction sign. After she gallops off, she sees Mr. B. sweeping the steps.) *Where in the text can you find this information?* (on pages 685–687) *How does this information help you understand Leah's decision?* (Leah needs money to buy the tractor and save the farm. Seeing Mr. B. reminds her that he might want the pony and would be a good owner.)

Develop Comprehension

18 **CHARACTER, SETTING, PLOT**

Who is the man in the big hat, and why does Leah's bid make him laugh? (He is the man in charge of the auction. He laughs because the bid is so low. He thinks that she is making a joke.) How is bidding a dollar a plot event that creates surprise, interest, and tension? (It creates them in the reader and the onlookers as well as in the auctioneer because the tractor is worth much more than one dollar. Also, readers realize that Leah has taken the huge step of selling her pony, but that she received very little money in return. It is possible that she still won't have enough money to buy the tractor. The reader wonders what will happen next.) How does everyone at the auction behave after Leah's bid? (No one moves or breathes.)

Leah clutched her money in her hand. "It has to be enough," she whispered to herself. "It just has to be."

"Here's one of the best **items** in this entire auction," yelled the man in the big hat. "Who'll start the **bidding** at five hundred dollars for this practically new, all-purpose Farmall tractor? It'll plow, plant, fertilize, and even cultivate for you."

It was time. Leah's voice shook. "One dollar."

The man in the big hat laughed. "That's a low starting bid if I ever heard one," he said. "Now let's hear some serious bids."

18 No one moved. No one said a word. No one even seemed to breathe.

690

"Ladies and gentlemen, this tractor is a beauty! I have a bid of only one dollar for it. One dollar for this practically new Farmall tractor! Do I hear any other bids?"

Again no one moved. No one said a word. No one even seemed to breathe.

"This is ridiculous!" the man's voice boomed out from under his hat into the silence. "Sold to the young lady for one dollar." **19**

The crowd cheered. Papa's mouth hung open. Mama cried. Leah proudly walked up and handed one dollar to the auctioneer in the big hat.

691

Develop Comprehension

19 SKILL
PROBLEM AND SOLUTION

 How has selling her pony allowed Leah to help her family? (Because Leah has sold her pony, she has a small amount of money to bid on the tractor. When no one bids against her, she is able to buy the tractor for her family.) Add this information to your Problem and Solution Chart.

Problem
The dry, dusty weather has kept the corn from growing, so Leah's family is facing hard times. Since Papa cannot pay the bank back, the bank is auctioning off some of the family's belongings, including the tractor. The family may have to leave the farm.

↓

Action
Papa sells pigs and some cattle.

↓

Action
Mama makes underwear from flour sacks.

↓

Action
Leah tells Mr. B. that he can buy her pony.

↓

Action
Leah bids on her family's tractor and buys it for one dollar.

ELL ENGLISH LANGUAGE LEARNERS

STRATEGIES FOR EXTRA SUPPORT

Question 19 PROBLEM AND SOLUTION

Help students recognize the connection between selling the pony and saving the family's farm. Ask: *What does Leah do with her pony?* (She sells it to Mr. B.) *What do you think Mr. B. gives Leah for her pony?* (money—at least one dollar) *What does Leah do with the money that she gets for her pony?* (She bids on the tractor.) *Is Leah able to buy the tractor?* (Yes.) *How will the tractor help her family?* (They will be able to continue to plant crops.) You may want to show this sequence of events with simple illustrations or a flow chart.

Develop Comprehension

20 SEQUENCE

Think about the **sequence of events**. What happens after Leah buys her family's tractor? (Other people offer low bids on the remaining items; after buying the items, they return them to Leah's parents.)

21 STRATEGY
DICTIONARY

Pages 692–693 contain words related to farming that may be **unfamiliar**. If the words *plow* and *coop* are unfamiliar to you, where can you find the definitions? (a dictionary) What is a plow? (a tool for preparing soil) What is a coop? (a cage or pen, usually for chickens)

22 THEME

How might the actions of Leah and the neighbors be a clue to the story's message or theme? (Leah and the neighbors both behave in unselfish ways that help solve her family's problem. These actions may be a clue that part of the story's message is the importance of being unselfish.)

"That young lady bought one fine tractor for one very low price," the man continued. "Now how much am I bid for this flock of healthy young chickens?"

20 "I'll give you ten cents," offered a farmer who lived down the road.

"Ten cents! Ten cents is mighty cheap for a whole flock of chickens," the man said. His face looked angry.

Again no one moved. No one said a word. No one even seemed to breathe.

"Sold for ten cents!"

The farmer picked up the cage filled with chickens and walked over to Mama. "These chickens are yours," he said.

The man pushed his big hat back on his head. "How much for this good Ford pickup truck?" he asked.

"Twenty-five cents," yelled a neighbor from town.

Again no one moved. No one said a word. No one even seemed to breathe.

"Sold for twenty-five cents!" The man in the big hat shook his head. "This isn't supposed to be a penny auction!" he shouted.

The neighbor paid his twenty-five cents and took the keys to the pickup truck. "I think these will start your truck," he whispered as he dropped the keys into Papa's shirt pocket.

Leah watched as friends and neighbors bid a penny for a chicken or a nickel for a cow or a quarter for **21** a plow. One by one, they gave everything back to **22** Mama and Papa.

Listening/Speaking

Discuss the opinions the author of *Leah's Pony* has regarding farmers. Ask: *Do you think the author has a positive or a negative view of the farmers in the story?* Remind students they may need to make inferences or draw conclusions based on evidence in the story.

Gather several recent articles from magazines, newspapers and the Internet dealing with the status of American farmers today. Read or have students read these articles aloud to find out how the media views farms and farmers. Ask: *Does the author of this article state his or her opinions about farmers? If so, what opinions are included?*

Have students compare the opinions in the story with those in the articles. Ask: *Did your opinions on farmers change after hearing the articles?* Have each student share his or her opinions with the class. Remind students to emphasize their most important points.

The crowds left. The sign disappeared. Chickens scratched in their coop, and cattle called for their corn. The farm was quiet. Too quiet. No familiar whinny greeted Leah when she entered the barn. Leah swallowed hard and straightened her back.

That night in Leah's hushed house, no sad voices whispered in the kitchen. Only Leah lay awake, listening to the clock chime nine and even ten times. **23** Leah's heart seemed to copy its slow, sad beat.

693

Comprehension

Literary Device: *Theme*

Explain Point out that there are recurring themes throughout literature from different cultures and time periods. Some themes are implied and some are directly stated. Have students think of television shows, movies, and books that have similar themes.

Discuss Ask students whether or not the theme is implied or directly stated in *Leah's Pony*. Discuss the theme. Ask students if they can think of a movie that has a similar theme.

Apply Encourage students to think of examples of recurring themes from other cultures and times. Ask, *How are these themes treated in works from different cultures? Why do you think these themes are universal?*

Develop Comprehension

23 SEQUENCE

What happens after the auction ends? (The farm quiets down. First the crowds leave. Next the sign is taken down. However, the farm feels too quiet to Leah. When she enters the barn, she hears no familiar whinny. That night, she lays awake. First the clock strikes nine and then ten o'clock. The night seems to pass slowly.)

24 STRATEGY
ANALYZE STORY STRUCTURE

The story begins when Leah gets her pony. What does the illustration on page 694 show? Based on the illustration, what do you predict may happen at the end of this story? (The illustration shows Leah opening the barn door and looking surprised to see a pony. Based on what I see, I predict that Leah will either get her pony back or get a new pony.)

Develop Comprehension

25 SKILL

PROBLEM AND SOLUTION

What did Leah do to help solve her family's troubles? (Through the unselfish act of selling her pony, Leah raises money to buy her family's tractor and save her family's farm. Her unselfishness is rewarded when Mr. B. returns her pony to her.) **Add** this information to your Problem and Solution Chart.

24

694

Problem
The dry, dusty weather has kept the corn from growing, so Leah's family is facing hard times. Since Papa cannot pay the bank back, the bank is auctioning off some of the family's belongings, including the tractor. The family may have to leave the farm.

↓

Action
Papa sells pigs and some cattle.

↓

Action
Mama makes underwear from flour sacks.

↓

Action
Leah tells Mr. B. that he can buy her pony.

↓

Action
Leah bids on her family's tractor and buys it for one dollar.

↓

Solution
Leah saves her family's farm, and Mr. B. returns her pony to her.

The next morning Leah forced open the heavy barn doors to start her chores. A loud whinny greeted her. Leah ran and hugged the familiar furry neck and kissed the white snip of a nose. "You're back!" she cried. "How did you get here?"

Then Leah saw the note with her name written in big letters:

> Dear Leah,
>
> This is the finest pony in the county. But he's a little bit small for me and a little bit big for my grandson.
>
> He fits you much better.
>
> Your friend,
> Mr. B.
>
> P.S. I heard how you saved your family's farm. These hard times won't last forever.

And they didn't.   **25**

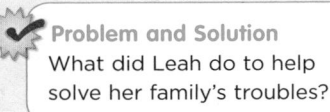
Problem and Solution
What did Leah do to help solve her family's troubles?

695

Quick Check

Can students identify the problem and the steps taken to solve it?

During **Small Group Instruction**

If No → **Approaching Level** Reteach the skill and have students apply it to a simpler text. Use Leveled Reader lessons, pp. 703N–703P.

If Yes → **On Level** Have students apply the skill to a new text to consolidate learning. Use Leveled Reader lessons, pp. 703U–703V.

Beyond Level Have students apply the skill to a more complex text to extend learning. Use Leveled Reader lessons, pp. 703Y–703Z.

Develop Comprehension

RETURN TO PREDICTIONS AND PURPOSES

Review students' predictions and purposes for reading. Did students find out what happened to Leah's pony? (Yes, they learned that Leah sold her pony to help her family buy a tractor and save the farm. But then they find out that the pony's new owner kindly returned him to Leah.)

REVIEW READING STRATEGIES

- **Analyze Story Structure** In what ways did analyzing the story structure help you better understand the selection?

- **Monitor and Clarify: Reread** Do you understand the strategy of rereading when something is unclear or you need to find details? When might you use it again?

- **Decoding** What difficult words did you encounter? How did the Reading Multisyllabic Words strategy help you sound out these words?

- **Self-Selected Strategy Use** What strategies did you use to make sense of what you read? Where? How were these strategies helpful?

 ### RESPONSE TO LITERATURE

Have students tell how they would feel about giving up something they loved to help their family or a friend. Prompt them to use sensory words such as those in the selection to help the reader understand the feelings and actions that they describe.

Author

TRAVEL BACK IN TIME WITH ELIZABETH FRIEDRICH AND MICHAEL GARLAND

Have students read the biographies of the author and illustrator. Ask:

■ How might Elizabeth Friedrich's childhood experiences on a farm have inspired *Leah's Pony*?

■ How do Michael Garland's illustrations help you understand what Elizabeth Friedrich is describing?

WRITE ABOUT IT

Author's Craft: Sensory Words
Lead students in a discussion about the sensory words used in the selection to describe the weather and its impact. Then have students write about a time when weather or some other aspect of nature created a problem for them or someone they know. Direct them to describe the problem the weather caused and how they solved it. Remind them to use sensory words to help readers understand both the problem and the solution.

Author's Purpose

Remind students that a story's theme is the message that the writer wants to communicate. Suggest that students use their Problem and Solution Charts to help them summarize and explain the theme of *Leah's Pony*. Students should identify the importance of unselfish actions.

TRAVEL BACK IN TIME WITH

ELIZABETH FRIEDRICH AND MICHAEL GARLAND

Elizabeth Friedrich was born in San Francisco, California. As a child, she loved to visit her aunt and uncle's farm in Missouri. *Leah's Pony* is based in part on what she learned there.

Today, Friedrich and her family live on a 150-year-old farm in New Hampshire, where she has a horse and six sheep. When she is not writing or working on her farm, she enjoys collecting antiques, reading, and traveling.

Michael Garland was born and raised in New York City. No stranger to children's books, Garland has both written and illustrated many books for young people. His books include *Dinner at Magritte's*, *Circus Girl*, and *My Cousin Katie*. He lives with his wife and three children in Patterson, New York.

LOG ON ▶ **FIND OUT**

Author Elizabeth Friedrich
Illustrator Michael Garland
www.macmillanmh.com

Another book by Michael Garland

✔ **Author's Purpose**

Explain the message or theme of *Leah's Pony*. Use details from the story.

696

Author's Craft

Sensory Words

As we read, we create mental images based on words in the text that appeal to our five senses. These are called **sensory words**.

■ Sensory words often are vivid adjectives, adverbs, and verbs. Example: "Sunburned soil crunched under Leah's feet as she walked home alone," (p. 689). The adjective *sunburned* and the verb *crunched* help readers see, hear, and perhaps even feel the soil as Leah walks on it.

■ Ask students how sensory words help readers create a mental image of the problem faced by Leah and her family.

■ Have students find other examples of sensory words and phrases. Discuss their effectiveness.

 LOG ON ▶ LEARN IT **Comprehension**
www.macmillanmh.com

Comprehension Check

Summarize

To summarize *Leah's Pony* use the most important details in the selection. Your Problem and Solution Chart may help you.

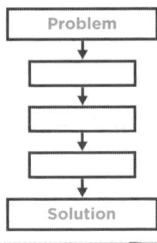

Problem
↓
↓
↓
↓
Solution

Think and Compare

1. Why do Leah's neighbors go to Oregon? Details

2. What happened right before the man in the big hat started the **bidding** for the flock of young chickens? Sequence

3. Summarize the problem that Leah's family faced and the events that led to the solution of the problem. Analyze Story Structure: Problem and Solution

4. Identify if the narrator of the story is first or third person. How would the story be different if the author had made Leah the narrator? Author's Purpose

5. Read "Grandma's Story" on pages 676–677. How are Leah's and Grandma's experiences similar? Use details from both selections in your answer. Reading/Writing Across Texts

697

Make Connections

Text-to-Self Have students respond to the following question to make connections to their own lives. Use the Think Aloud to model a response. *How might you help a friend who had to sell a beloved possession at a tag sale?*

Think Aloud: I could follow the example set by characters in the story. Like Leah's neighbors, I might offer to buy the item at a price I could afford. Then I could return the item to my friend. That way my friend could still enjoy the item.

Text-to-World Have students respond to the following question to make connections to the world. Use the Think Aloud to model a response. *Why are neighbors important?*

Think Aloud: Neighbors help Leah's family, and neighbors have helped my family. So one reason neighbors are important is because they help one another.

 **Comprehension Check**

SUMMARIZE

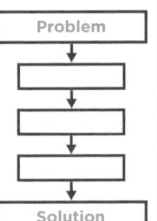 Have partners summarize the selection. Remind students to use their Problem and Solution Chart to organize their ideas.

THINK AND COMPARE

Text Evidence

1. **Details** <u>Answer stated in text</u> They think it must be better there. LOCATE

2. **Sequence** <u>Answer stated in text</u> Before the bidding for the chickens started, Leah handed the auctioneer a dollar for the tractor. COMBINE

3. **Analyze Story Structure: Problem and Solution** <u>Answer</u> The problem was how to survive and keep the farm in hard times. They tried to solve the problem by selling things, borrowing money, and saving money. <u>Evidence</u> Papa sold livestock and borrowed from the bank. Mama made underwear from flour sacks. Leah sold her pony. CONNECT

4. **Author's Purpose** <u>Answer</u> The narrator is third person. As narrator, Leah might have confided more of her feelings. <u>Evidence</u> The narrator is the author not a story character. She uses the pronoun *she* to refer to Leah rather than *I*. She doesn't reveal too much about Leah's feelings. ANALYZE

5.  **Text-to-Text** Leah's experience is similar to Grandma's because they both need something that they cannot afford: Leah wants to buy her family's tractor, and Grandma needs to buy a wheelchair. The community helps them get what they need. COMPARE TEXT

Objectives

- Read fluently with appropriate phrasing
- Rate: 113–133 WCPM

Materials

- Transparency 26
- Practice Book, p. 230
- Fluency Solutions Audio CD

ELL

Develop Comprehension
Write on the board the amount asked for Leah's family's tractor (five hundred dollars) and the amount that Leah offers (one dollar) to show students the difference between the two amounts. Then, point out the sentences *No one moved. No one said a word. No one even seemed to breathe.* Explain that authors use repetition to show importance.

Practice Book, page 230

As I read, I will pause at commas and end punctuation.

	A coral reef is a shelf that runs along the coastlines of
12	countries throughout the world. Coral reefs are found in
21	shallow, warm waters all over the world.
28	Among all these reefs, there is one that stands out. It is
40	the Great Barrier Reef along the coast of Australia. It is
51	remarkable for many reasons. One is its length—over 1,250
60	miles. It is the largest coral reef ecosystem in the world,
71	and the largest organic structure on the planet. It is also
82	home to numerous kinds of sea life.
89	About 40,000 years ago, the Aboriginal peoples were
96	the only humans living on the Australian continent. They
105	fished and hunted along parts of the Great Barrier Reef.
115	For a long period of time they were the only people who
127	knew the reef existed.
131	When sailors began to explore the world, their boats
140	sometimes hit the sharp coral that was under the water,
150	sinking their vessels. The reef remained a mystery. 158

Comprehension Check

1. What details support the idea that the Great Barrier Reef is remarkable? **Main Idea and Details** The Great Barrier Reef is very long, is the largest coral reef ecosystem in the world, and is the largest organic structure on the planet.
2. Why were the sailors unaware of the coral reef? **Cause and Effect** The sailors were new to that part of the world. They didn't discover the reef until their boats had hit it.

	Words Read	–	Number of Errors	=	Words Correct Score
First Read		–		=	
Second Read		–		=	

Approaching Reproducible, page 230

Beyond Reproducible, page 230

Fluency

Repeated Reading: Phrasing

EXPLAIN/MODEL Model reading **Transparency 26** for students fluently and with appropriate phrasing. Remind students to pay attention to commas and end punctuation as they read to help them read with appropriate phrasing. They should pause briefly at commas and longer at periods, question marks, or exclamation marks.

 Transparency 26

> "Here's one of the best items in this entire auction," yelled the man in the big hat. "Who'll start the bidding at five hundred dollars for this practically new, all-purpose Farmall tractor? It'll plow, plant, fertilize, and even cultivate for you."
>
> It was time. Leah's voice shook. "One dollar."
>
> The man in the big hat laughed. "That's a low starting bid if I ever heard one," he said. "Now let's hear some serious bids."
>
> No one moved. No one said a word. No one even seemed to breathe.
>
> "Ladies and gentlemen, this tractor is a beauty! I have a bid of only one dollar for it. One dollar for this practically new Farmall tractor! Do I hear any other bids?"
>
> Again no one moved. No one said a word. No one even seemed to breathe.
>
> "This is ridiculous!" the man's voice boomed out from under his hat into the silence. "Sold to the young lady for one dollar."

Fluency (from *Leah's Pony,* pp. 690–691)

PRACTICE Model reading the entire passage aloud. Next, read one sentence at a time, having students echo-read each sentence back. Then have them echo-read with a partner. Remind students to use punctuation as a guide to appropriate phrasing and to read in a way that shows their comprehension of the passage.

 DAILY FLUENCY Students will practice fluency using **Practice Book** page 230 or the **Fluency Solutions Audio CD**. The passage is recorded at a slow practice speed and a faster fluent speed.

Quick Check

Can students read fluently with appropriate phrasing?

During **Small Group Instruction**

If No → **Approaching Level** Use the Fluency lesson and model, p. 703Q.

If Yes → **On Level** See Fluency, p. 703T.

Beyond Level See Fluency, p. 703X.

Comprehension

REVIEW SKILL
SEQUENCE

EXPLAIN/MODEL

- Review with students that authors usually present plot events in **sequence**, or time order. Understanding sequence in a story can help the reader summarize the plot's main events and explain their influence on future events.

- When events are told in time order, authors often use signal words such as *first*, *next*, *then*, and *finally* to show the sequence.

- Sometimes the order of events described in the story is different from the order in which the events happened. For example, a second or third event may be described before a first event. Readers must **make inferences** to determine the sequence.

Model how to identify the sequence of events in "Grandma's Story." Point out that the story opens when Grandma has been in a wheelchair for a long time. *When I was 12* signals to the reader that Grandma is going to tell about a sequence of events that happened in the past. Explain that readers must ask themselves what happens first, next, and last. Model this for students by asking what happens first. In this case, the first event is that Grandma gets polio.

PRACTICE/APPLY

Have partners or small groups sequence and summarize the plot's main events in *Leah's Pony*. Use these questions to assist the students.

- What happens after the corn grows no taller than a man's thumb? (People talk in hushed voices. The wind turns the sky black. It becomes hard to keep the pony's coat shiny or to clean the house.)

- What does Leah do after her father tells her that the tractor will be sold? (First she starts to run away. Then she changes her mind and sells her pony to Mr. B.)

- What is the last event that takes place? (The last event is that Mr. B. returns Leah's pony to her.)

Have students summarize the story by retelling events in sequence. Remind students to focus on the main events. Then have a few students share their groups' summaries with the class. Point out that an event that comes before another does not necessarily cause it. Discuss which events in the story directly lead to future events.

PRACTICE BOOK See **Practice Book** page 231 for First and Third Person Narrators.

Objective

- Identify and summarize the sequence of events in a selection

Skills Trace

Sequence	
Introduce	107A–107B
Practice/ Apply	108–121; Practice Book, 39–40
Reteach/ Review	125M–125Z, 229A–229B, 230–251, 257M–257Z; Practice Book, 84–85
Assess	Weekly Tests; Units 1, 2, 5 Tests
Maintain	153B, 285B, 641A–641B, 642–659, 663M–663Z, 697B

Paired Selection

GENRE: Informational Text/Expository

Have students read the bookmark on **Student Book** page 698. Explain that expository writing gives information about a topic or topics. Point out that a textbook is one form of expository writing.

Remind students that a textbook

- gives information about subjects that are taught in school;
- often includes features such as maps, photographs, captions, and charts that give additional information;
- may use headings and different typefaces to emphasize important information.

Text Feature: Maps

Point out the **map** on page 701.

Explain that this map shows the states that were affected by the extreme drought in the 1930s.

- A map is a flat drawing of a place that combines text and illustrations to show how things are connected or related.
- A map's title tells what the map shows.
- A map might have a key. The key tells you what the symbols or colors on the map stand for.

Have students look at the map on page 701. Ask them to read the title of the map and explain what the map shows. (The title is The Dust Bowl States, 1930s. The map shows the states that were affected by the dust storms.)

Social Studies

Genre

Expository selections, such as **textbook excerpts**, present facts and ideas about a topic. They often include text features, such as photographs, primary sources, and maps.

✔ **Text Feature**

Maps are drawings that show the surface features of an area such as a state or country.

Content Vocabulary

drought

Dust Bowl

Great Depression

698

SOIL TURNED TO DUST

by Miriam Ramirez

DURING THE 1930s, many states were affected by a **drought**. A drought occurs when little or no rain falls. This drought lasted for so many years that the soil turned to dust.

The map on page 701 shows which states were affected by the drought. This area of the United States became known as the **Dust Bowl**.

Farmers in this area once had plentiful crops. Many had planted larger fields in order to meet the demand for wheat around the world.

Then, during the late 1920s, the rains came less and less often. The soil began to dry up and the wheat died. Strong winds blew the soil away in huge dust storms.

Some farmers borrowed money from banks to help them survive. They had hoped to pay back the banks with money from selling wheat. When there was no wheat to sell, the banks forced the farmers to sell their homes and land. Soon, some of the banks began to have problems and had to close as well.

Content Vocabulary

Explain the words using the **Define/Example/Ask** routine. Definitions are provided for this activity.

- A **drought** is a situation in which the land gets little or no rainfall. How might people have to change their lifestyles because of a drought?

- The **Dust Bowl** was an area devastated by a series of dust storms in the Great Plains during the 1930s, caused by droughts and poor farming practices. Why do you think that many people in the Dust Bowl moved away?

- The **Great Depression** was a period of American history, from 1929 to 1939, when the economy collapsed. Many people could not find jobs, and farms and businesses had to close. Would 1932 have been a good time to open a clothing store? Why or why not?

Many families left the Dust Bowl to find work to support their families and faced great hardships. People all over the country had a hard time finding jobs. This is one reason why those years became known as the **Great Depression**.

The government hired a photographer, Dorothea Lange, to take pictures during this period. One of her photographs is called "Migrant Mother." Lange said that this photo showed a "hungry and desperate mother . . . who had just sold the tires from her car to buy food."

Eventually the rains came back and crops began to grow again. Even so, it took many years for life to return to normal. Most people who lived during those hard times would never forget them.

Dorothea Lange took this photo of a migrant mother in the Dust Bowl.

699

Paired Selection

Read "Soil Turned to Dust"

As students read, remind them to apply what they have learned about expository writing and reading maps. Also have them identify clues to the meanings of highlighted words. Students may set their own purposes for reading.

1 CAUSE AND EFFECT

What **effects** did the drought and dust storms have on farmers? (The droughts dried up the soil, so the wheat died. Without wheat to sell, farmers did not earn money. They borrowed money from banks but could not repay it, so many farmers lost their farms and land. Eventually, banks closed as well.)

2 USE PRIMARY SOURCES

How does the photograph help you picture how people felt during the Great Depression? (The mother in the photograph looks sad, tired, and hopeless. Her expression helps me understand how difficult life was during that time.)

Use the Interactive Question-Response Guide in the **ELL Resource Book**, pages 298–299, to help students gain access to the paired selection content.

Comprehension

Primary Sources

Explain Point out the photograph on page 699. Explain that a primary source is a first-hand account or record of an event or time period by a person who experienced that event or time.

Discuss Have students brainstorm different kinds of primary sources. They should recognize that photographs, letters, songs, interviews, and journals are all primary sources.

Apply Have students each locate a primary source about the Dust Bowl in a reference book or on the Internet and share it with the class. Have students tell how their understanding of the Dust Bowl has changed based on these primary sources.

Paired Selection

3 USE PRIMARY SOURCES

How does Woody Guthrie describe the dust storm? (There is so much dust, it blocked out the sun.) According to the song, what does Guthrie plan to do because of the dust? (move away)

4 TEXT FEATURE: MAPS

Which part of the United States was affected by the dust storms of the 1930s? (The middle of the country from North Dakota to Texas) How does the map key help you understand what happened in the 1930s? (The key helps me understand that five states were part of the Dust Bowl, but that many other states were damaged by the dust storms.)

In April 1935, when he was living in Pampa, Texas, Woody Guthrie wrote this song about a dust storm he saw.

Woody Guthrie

SO LONG, It's Been Good to Know Yuh (Dusty Old Dust)

So long, it's been good to know ye,
So long, it's been good to know ye,
So long, it's been good to know ye,
This dusty old dust is a-getting my home,
And I've got to be drifting along.

A dust storm hit, and it hit like thunder;
It dustedus over and it covered us under;
Blocked out the traffic and blocked out the sun,
Straight for home all the people did run.

Families in the Dust Bowl were often displaced and forced to live in their cars.

700

Practice Book, page 232

A **compass rose** shows north, south, east, and west. The **map key**, or **legend**, explains the symbols on the map.

Use the map to answer each question.

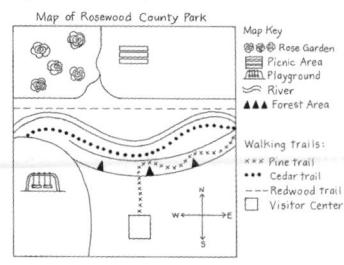

Map of Rosewood County Park

1. The picnic area is to the east of **the Rose Garden**
2. Which trail would you take to walk through the forest area? **the Pine trail**
3. Can you take the Cedar trail to get to the Redwood trail? Explain. **No, the river separates them.**
4. It is possible to get from the Visitor Center to the Rose Garden. What is missing from the map? **the bridge**

Approaching Reproducible, page 232
Beyond Reproducible, page 232

ELL

Content Words Clarify the meaning of the content vocabulary using context clues. To describe the definition of *draught*, have students reread the first paragraph on page 698 and identify words that describe draught *(little or no rain falls)*. Then have students restate the definition of draught. Correct students' responses for meaning as needed. Repeat the process for *Dust Bowl* and *Great Depression*.

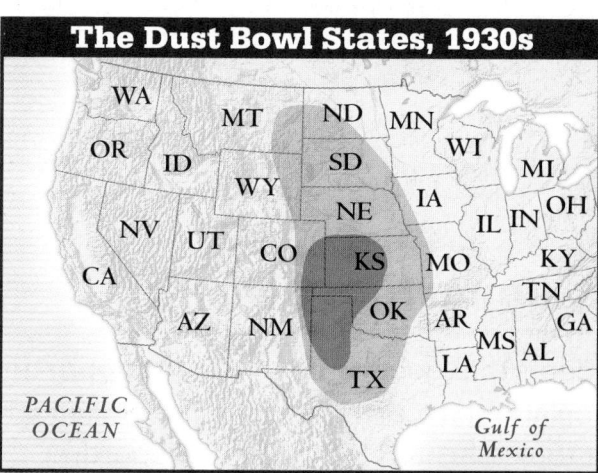

The Dust Bowl States, 1930s 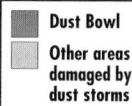 **4**

A Map Key explains the symbols and color coding used on the map.

Dust Bowl

Other areas damaged by dust storms

 Connect and Compare

1. Look at the map on page 701. What states are part of the Dust Bowl? **Reading a Map**

2. How do the photographs, song, and map add to the information presented in the textbook excerpt? **Apply**

3. How does "Soil Turned to Dust" give you a better understanding of the events in *Leah's Pony*? Use details from both texts to explain your answer. **Reading/Writing Across Texts**

 **Social Studies Activity**

Use maps and online references to research the effects of the Dust Bowl in Texas or Kansas. Write a summary of your research and present it to the class.

 **Social Studies** Dust Bowl
www.macmillanmh.com

701

Paired Selection

Connect and Compare

1. Colorado, Kansas, Oklahoma, Texas, and New Mexico were the five states in the Dust Bowl. READING A MAP

2. The photograph, song, and map give more information about what it was like during the 1930s. The photograph and song are primary sources that help show how people felt during that time. APPLY

3. **FOCUS QUESTION** "Soil Turned to Dust" helps me understand that the events that occurred in *Leah's Pony* occurred during the 1930s. Leah and her family lived in the Dust Bowl.

READING/WRITING ACROSS TEXTS

Social Studies Activity

Students might want to use a cause and effect graphic organizer to help them understand and summarize their research findings.

Connect to Content

RESEARCH AND INQUIRY

Give a Dramatic Reading Remind students that the dust storms devastated many people's lives. Farmers had to make difficult decisions. Some migrated to other parts of the country. Others stayed and endured the extreme conditions.

Have students locate primary sources, such as letters or interviews, that help convey the difficult choices farmers had to make. How did farmers feel about leaving their farms? Where did farmers go? How did the farmers who stayed survive? Students should look for primary sources that shed light on the impact on your state or region.

Students should present a dramatic reading of the primary source.

Professional Development
GRADES 3–6

Writing Guide

Macmillan/McGraw-Hill

UNIT 6
Developing Expository Writing

WEEK 1	**Strong Sentences/Trait: Ideas** Supporting Details, 701A
	• Reading/Writing Connection, 702
	• Minilessons, 703A Ideas: Supporting Details Organization: Narrow the Topic
	• Conferencing Routine, 703B
WEEK 2	**Strong Paragraphs/Trait: Ideas** Main Idea and Details
WEEK 3	**Research Report**
WEEK 4	**Strong Sentences/Trait: Sentence Fluency** Transition Words and Phrases
WEEK 5	**Strong Paragraphs/Trait: Organization** Writing a Conclusion
WEEK 6	**Research Report**

Trait: Ideas
Strong Sentences: Supporting Details

TEACH/MODEL Tell students that good writers include **supporting details** to give information about a topic. These details help readers visualize and learn about topics. In narrative writing, supporting details can show actions and describe characters, setting, and plot. In expository writing, supporting details can be facts, explanations, or examples.

Point out that using supporting details in their writing can help students build **strong sentences** that make information clear to their readers. Then write the following sentences and read them aloud:

> Topic: rainbows
> Details:
> The colors in a rainbow are red, orange, yellow, green, blue, indigo, and violet.
> Flowers can be red, orange, yellow, or violet, too.
> Sometimes people see rainbows after a rainstorm.
> Rainbows appear in the sky when sunlight shines on water drops in the sky.
> Clouds are in the sky on rainy days, too.

First, ask students to name the topic (rainbows). Explain that three of the details are supporting details because they give information about the topic. Then reread each detail and ask whether it is a supporting detail and why. Finally, write the following paragraph:

> A rainbow is an arc of color in the sky. The colors in the rainbow are red, orange, yellow, green, blue, indigo, and violet. Sometimes people see rainbows after a rainstorm. Why? Rainbows appear when sunlight shines on water drops in the sky.

Read aloud the paragraph. Note that you did not include the sentences about flowers and clouds. Ask how the supporting details you did include help students understand and visualize rainbows.

Teacher Write Aloud

PRACTICE/APPLY Further explore with students the use of supporting details. Remind them that supporting details support, or tell about, the topic. Good writers do not include details that do not support the topic. Write the sentences below on the board. Then complete the Teacher Think Aloud.

> Topic: dolphins
> Details:
> Dolphins are intelligent and friendly animals.
> Dolphins live in the ocean, but they are not fish.
> Sharks live in the ocean, too. They are fish.
> Dolphins are mammals.
> People are mammals, too.
> Dolphins do not breathe underwater but come to the surface to breathe air.

Teacher Think Aloud What is the topic? (dolphins) There is a list of details, but only some of the details give information about dolphins. Let me read the first detail: *Dolphins are intelligent and friendly animals.* Is that a good supporting detail for the topic? Yes, it is a supporting detail because it gives information about dolphins. I will use that detail to support the topic.

Complete the Think Aloud by asking which other details are supporting details. Then write a paragraph, with student input, that combines the details on the board. For example:

> Dolphins are intelligent and friendly animals. Even though dolphins live in the ocean, they are not fish. Dolphins are mammals. Dolphins do not breathe underwater but come to the surface to breathe air.

 **Draft** Display the writing prompt on **Writing Transparency 86**. Remind students to use supporting details to support the topic. Circulate and provide Over-the-Shoulder Conferences as students work.

Objective
- Write supporting details

Materials
- Writer's Notebooks
- Writing Transparency 86

Daily Journal Prompts

Focus on Supporting Details

Use these and other prompts for independent daily journal writing.

- Write about a moment when you got a special gift. What was the gift, and why was it special?

- Write about a moment when you learned something interesting.

- Write about a moment when you looked up at the sky.

- Write about a moment when you visited a special place.

 Transparency 86

Write about an animal that you think is special. You can tell what the animal looks like, or you can tell why you think the animal is special.

Writing Transparency

Reading and Writing Connection

Trait: Ideas

SUPPORTING DETAILS

Remind students that supporting details give information about the topic. Supporting details can be facts, examples, or explanations. Good writers use supporting details to help readers better understand what they are reading.

Read the Passage

Use the example from *Leah's Pony* to show how the author uses supporting details to give readers more information about how Leah makes a decision.

- Have students read the bookmark. Remind them that a topic is the subject that the writer is writing about.

  Ask: *When have you had to make a difficult decision?*

- Then have students chorally read the excerpt from *Leah's Pony*. Direct their attention to the callout. Have students identify and discuss the supporting details that tell about what Leah does and the decision she makes.

  Ask: *What supporting details best help you picture Leah wanting to run away? What supporting details help you understand Leah's decision?*

Reading and Writing Connection

Writing

✓ **Trait: Ideas**
Good writers use **supporting details** to give more information about a topic.

Read the passage below. Notice how the author Elizabeth Friedrich uses supporting details to give information about a topic.

An excerpt from
Leah's Pony

The author uses supporting details to show what Leah does when she wants to run away. She also uses supporting details to show what Leah decides to do.

All week Leah worried and waited and wondered what to do. One morning she watched as a man in a big hat hammered a sign into the ground in front of her house.

Leah wanted to run away. She raced her pony past empty fields lined with dry gullies. She galloped past a house with rags stuffed in broken windowpanes. She sped right past Mr. B. sweeping the steps outside his store.

At last Leah knew what she had to do. She turned her pony around and rode back into town. She stopped in front of Mr. B.'s store. "You can buy my pony," she said.

Leah's Pony
Written by *Elizabeth Friedrich*
Illustrated by *Michael Garland*

702

Respond to the Selection

Have students write a response to the selection.

✓ **Engagement** Help students deepen their connection to the text and discover their own perspective.

- *Focus on a moment when you had to do something that you really did not want to do.*

✓ **Response** Help students explore more deeply their reactions to particular passages in the reading.

- *Focus on a moment in the story when Leah makes a decision. Use text evidence in your writing.*

✓ **Literary Analysis** Help students deepen their connection to the text and discover their own perspective.

- *Focus on a place in which you thought the author did a good job using supporting details. Use text evidence in your writing.*

Read and Find

Read Kyle's writing below. How does he use supporting details to show the difference between a pony and a horse? Use the checklist below to help you.

My Pony

by Kyle Y.

Some people think my pony is a horse, but ponies are different from horses. First of all, my pony is smaller than a horse. It has a thicker mane and a thicker tail. My pony has shorter legs than a horse does, too. It also has a smaller head.

If you already know a lot about ponies, you would know right away that my pony is not a horse. If you did not know a lot about ponies, now you do and will be able to tell the difference between a pony and a horse!

Read about Kyle's pony.

Writer's Checklist

✓ Does the writing have a topic?

✓ Does the author write **supporting details** that tell about the topic?

☑ Do all the details support the topic?

703

Read the Student Model

Have students chorally read the student model at the top of **Student Book** page 703. Discuss how this student writer used supporting details to give information about a topic. Use the Writer's Checklist.

Journal Prompt

Draft Write the following prompt on the board. Have students write a response to the prompt.

Think about a moment when you did something to help someone in your family. Then write about it. Be sure to include details that support your topic.

Tell students that you will be reading and commenting on their writing during Writing Conference time.

Model how to use the Writer's Checklist so students can write and revise their work. Then ask:

- *What is the moment you chose?*
- *What supporting details did you include? Will readers be able to use the details to clearly picture that moment? If not, what details could you add?*

ELL ENGLISH LANGUAGE LEARNERS

Beginning	Intermediate	Advanced
Write Sentences Provide model sentences based on the Journal Prompt: *My brother needed help when ___. I wanted to help, so I ___. First I ___. Then I ___. My brother was ___ for my help.* Help students add supporting details.	**Describe** Ask students to write three sentences based on the Journal Prompt. Have them make sure that the sentences give supporting details. Provide a model if necessary. Read their sentences, correcting grammar and spelling as needed.	**Narrate** Ask students to respond to the Journal Prompt. Have them include supporting details to give information about the topic.

Objectives

- Write supporting details
- Write strong sentences

Materials

- Writer's Notebooks
- Teacher's Resource Book, p. 203

ELL

Expand Vocabulary Write these words on the board: *sky, moon, planet, stars, constellation.* Say each word and have students repeat it. Then use the word in a sentence to demonstrate its meaning. Have students illustrate the word.

HOMEWORK Teacher's Resource Book, page 203

1. Read the topic and the three details.
   Topic: Marta likes to study the night sky.
   a. Tonight Marta sees a crescent moon that looks like a white banana.
   b. Marta loves bananas and eats one every day for her after-school snack.
   c. On clear nights, Marta points out the Big Dipper constellation.

2. Circle the two details that support the topic.

3. Write one more supporting detail about the night sky.

Example: Last month, Marta watched a planet shining brightly in the night sky.

4. Now write a paragraph using the topic and the three supporting details.

Minilessons

Minilesson 1 Ideas/Supporting Details

TEACH/MODEL

Remind students that they have been working on identifying supporting details, which include facts, examples, and explanations. Today they will practice that again. Have students use **Teacher's Resource Book** page 203. Ask students to read the first direction, the topic, and the details.

PRACTICE/APPLY

Have students work independently to circle the supporting details (**a** and **c**), to add a supporting detail, and to use the sentences in a paragraph. When they are finished, ask students to share their work during Sharing Circle.

Minilesson 2 Organization/Narrow a Topic

TEACH/MODEL

Explain that one kind of expository writing is a research report. When a writer chooses a topic for a research report, it's important that the topic is not too broad. One way to narrow a topic is to ask questions about it. Then a writer can use the answers to include supporting details that give information about the topic. Write the following topic and questions:

> Topic: my favorite sport
> Questions:
> Why is that your favorite sport?
> How do you play your favorite sport?
> What professional teams play your favorite sport?
> What is the history of your favorite sport?

Discuss the questions. Explain that answering all the questions in a report would be too much; the topic would be too broad. Point out that writing a response to any one of the last three questions would help narrow the topic of a research report.

PRACTICE/APPLY

In their Writer's Notebooks, have students write a topic that they are interested in. Then ask them to write questions to narrow the topic.

Conferencing Routine

Dynamic Feedback System

 Step 1 Read and appreciate the writing.

 Step 2 Notice how the student uses the targeted skill. (e.g., supporting details: Ask: *Does the writer include supporting details? Do all the details tell about the topic?*)

 Step 3 Write comments that show how the writing has an impact on you. Direct your comments to those places in the piece where the student has used the targeted skill.

 Step 4 Meet with and give the student a revision assignment.

Write Effective Comments

Ideas At least one of your comments should highlight the way the student uses **supporting details**. Here are some sample comments.

- These details give me a lot of information about the topic.

- This is a great supporting detail. It really helps me understand what I am reading about.

- I'm curious. How does this detail relate to the topic?

Revision Assignments

Ideas Here are some examples of effective revision assignments for supporting details.

 - ***Reread your entry.*** *Find a place in your writing where you think additional supporting details would give more information about the topic. Write two supporting details to help the reader imagine the moment.*

 - **[Underline a section.]** Mark a specific section of a student's writing and ask the student to revise it in a specific way.

 - **[Underline a section.]** *Read the part that I underlined. How would adding details here support the topic? Write two sentences with supporting details.*

5-Day Vocabulary

Connect Language Arts

WHOLE GROUP

✓ **VOCABULARY**
- Tested Words

✓ **SPELLING**
- Words with /ən/

✓ **GRAMMAR**
- Adverbs

SMALL GROUP

- Differentiated Instruction, pp. 703I–703HH

ON YOUR OWN

Practice Book, page 233

A **dictionary** can help you find the meanings, pronunciations, and syllabication of **unfamiliar words.**

Look at this dictionary entry for an unfamiliar word. Use the definition and sample sentence to help answer the questions that follow. **Possible responses provided.**

av•id (av´id) *adjective.* **1.** very eager. *She is an avid reader.*

1. What does *avid* mean, in your own words?
   enthusiastic

2. Use *avid* in another sentence.
   I am an avid baseball fan.

3. How would you find the meaning of the word *incognito*?
   I would use a dictionary.

4. Use a dictionary. Write the meaning of *incognito* below.
   in disguise

5. Use a dictionary. Write the number of syllables in *incognito* below.
   four

Approaching Reproducible, page 233
Beyond Reproducible, page 233

Build Robust Vocabulary

Day 1 Teach/Practice

CONNECT TO WORDS

- Practice this week's vocabulary words using the following prompts:

1. Would you be able to have a collection without *items*? Why or why not?

2. Would you describe a single flower as being *clustered* in a vase? Why or why not?

3. If a party were *overflowing* with people, would you describe it as a success? Why or why not?

4. If a chair is not *sturdy*, what might happen when you sit on it?

5. What is a synonym for *glistened*?

6. If you are *bidding* on something, is it guaranteed that you will be able to buy it? Explain.

ACADEMIC VOCABULARY

- Review the important academic vocabulary words for the week. These words include: *narrative nonfiction, sequence, analyze story structure, problem, solution, plot, historical fiction, textbooks,* and *maps.*

- Write each word on the board. Define each using student-friendly language, and ask students to select the word you are defining. Then point to words in random order for students to define.

Day 2 Review

CONNECT TO WORDS

- Review the definitions of this week's vocabulary words using **Student Book** pages 676–677. Then discuss each word using the following prompts:

1. What *items* would you take with you on a visit to the beach?

2. Would you want to live in a neighborhood where the homes are *clustered* together? Why or why not?

3. If your glass of milk is *overflowing,* have you poured too much liquid or not enough?

4. Why would you want your backpack to be *sturdy*?

5. If an ice-covered road *glistened,* what would it look like?

6. How is *bidding* like a competition?

DICTIONARY: UNFAMILIAR WORDS

- Remind students that they can use a dictionary to find the meaning of an unfamiliar word as well as to find pronunciations and syllabications.

- Display **Transparency 51**. Read the first sentence, and model using a dictionary to find the meaning of the underlined word.

- Have students use a dictionary to define the underlined words in the remaining sentences.

- Have students write their own dictionary entries for this week's vocabulary words in their Writer's Notebooks. Instruct them to include an example sentence.

Day 3 — Reinforce

CONNECT TO WORDS

- Ask students to create Word Squares for each word in their Writer's Notebooks.

- In the first square, students should write the word. (Example: *glistened*)

- In the second square, students should write their own definition of the word and any related words, such as synonyms. (Example: *shimmered, shined, sparkled, gleamed*)

- In the third square, students should draw a simple illustration that will help them remember the word. (Example: a drawing of a diamond ring)

- In the fourth square, students write nonexamples, including antonyms for the word. (Examples: *dull, dim, faded*)

RELATED WORDS

- Classifying synonyms can increase their vocabulary awareness. Help students generate words related to the word *clustered*.

- Draw a word web on the board. Write *clustered* in the center.

- Have students record synonyms for *clustered* on the outer spokes. Tell students to use a thesaurus to help them generate words. Add words such as *gathered, bunched, collected,* and *grouped* if they are not mentioned.

- Afterward have partners create and complete analogies using the words.

Day 4 — Extend

CONNECT TO WORDS

- Review this week's vocabulary using the following sentence stems. Have students orally complete each one.

  1. The items in my closet include ____.

  2. The ____ clustered together so that they could ____.

  3. The bathtub was overflowing because ____.

  4. If you didn't carry ____ in a sturdy box, they would ____.

  5. The ____ glistened in the sunshine.

  6. In order to buy something that you are bidding on, you must ____.

MORPHOLOGY

- Identifying prefixes can raise students' word consciousness. Use the vocabulary word *overflowing* as a springboard for students to learn other words.

- Write *overflowing* on the board. Underline the prefix *over*. Explain that *over-* means "too much" and comes from the Old English word *ofer*. Something that is *overflowing* spills because there is too much of it to be contained.

- Write the words *overcook* and *overuse* on the board. Have students underline *over-* in each word.

- Use the word parts to define each word. Tell students that to *overcook* something is to cook it too much. Have them define *overuse*.

Day 5 — Assess and Reteach

POSTTEST

- Display **Transparency 52**. Have students complete the cloze sentences using one of this week's vocabulary words.

- Note how quickly and accurately students can complete this task. Work with students who make errors or require too much time to complete this task during Small Group time.

CONNECT TO WRITING

- Have students write sentences in their Writer's Notebooks using this week's vocabulary. Tell students to write sentences that provide information they learned from this week's readings.

- **ELL** Provide the Day 4 sentence stems for students needing extra support.

5-Day Spelling

Go to pages T14–T15 for **Differentiated Spelling Lists**.

Words with /ən/

Spelling Words

robin	cousin	ridden
button	woven	common
bacon	raisin	proven
reason	wagon	often
cotton	muffin	penguin
sunken	widen	skeleton
eleven	wooden	

Review medal, pupil, paddle
Challenge violin, vitamin

Dictation Sentences

1. A <u>robin</u> made a nest in our tree.
2. Please push the elevator <u>button</u>.
3. We cooked <u>bacon</u> and spinach omelets.
4. I gave a <u>reason</u> for being late.
5. I am wearing green <u>cotton</u> socks.
6. We came across a <u>sunken</u> ship.
7. There are <u>eleven</u> kids on my team.
8. My <u>cousin</u> is visiting from Mexico.
9. The scarf was <u>woven</u> out of wool.
10. There is a <u>raisin</u> in this cookie.
11. I pulled my brother in a **wagon**.
12. I ate a warm blueberry <u>muffin</u>.
13. They plan to <u>widen</u> our street.
14. The old <u>wooden</u> steps are rotting.
15. I have never <u>ridden</u> a horse.
16. Paul and I have a lot in <u>common</u>.
17. It cannot be <u>proven</u> that the money was stolen.
18. Do you go to the beach <u>often</u>?
19. I spotted a <u>penguin</u> at the zoo.
20. We saw a dinosaur <u>skeleton</u>.

Review/Challenge Words

1. She won a <u>medal</u> for her bravery.
2. Tim is a <u>pupil</u> at the school.
3. One <u>paddle</u> fell into the lake.
4. He played his <u>violin</u> in the concert.
5. Take a <u>vitamin</u> for good health.

The word in **bold** is from this week's selections.

Day 1 Pretest

ASSESS PRIOR KNOWLEDGE

- Model for students how to spell the word *person*. Segment the word syllable by syllable, then attach a spelling to each syllable. Point out that -*on* is the /ən/ spelling in this word.

- Use the Dictation Sentences. Say the underlined word, read the sentence, and repeat the word. Have students write the words.

- Have students self-correct their tests. Point out that the /ən/ sounds have three possible spellings: -*in*, -*on*, or -*en*.

- Have students cut apart the **Spelling Word Cards BLM** on **Teacher's Resource Book** page 69 and figure out a way to sort them. Have them save the cards for use throughout the week.

Day 2 Word Sorts and Review

SPIRAL REVIEW

Review the final /əl/ spellings. Write *medal*, *pupil*, and *paddle* on the board. Have students identify other words with the final /əl/ sound that are spelled these three different ways.

WORD SORTS

- Have students take turns sorting the word cards and explaining how they sorted them. When students have finished the sort, discuss any words that have unexpected vowel spellings (*bacon*).

- Review the spelling words, pointing out the /ən/ spellings. Use the cards from the Spelling Word Cards BLM. Write the key words *robin*, *button*, and *sunken* on the board. Model how to sort the words by the *schwa* spelling. Place one or two cards beneath the correct key words.

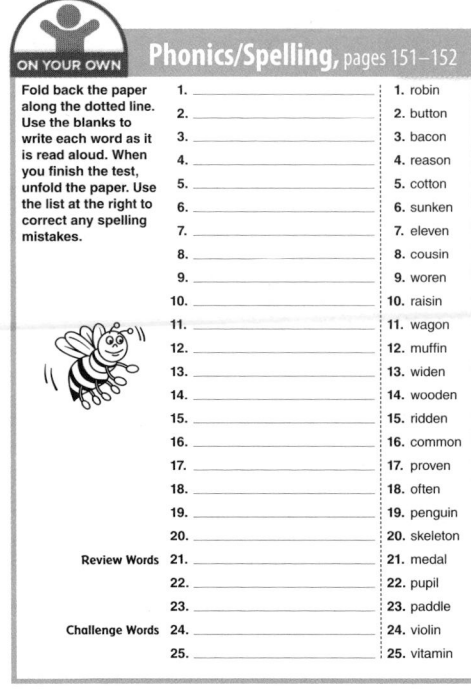

ON YOUR OWN Phonics/Spelling, pages 151–152

Fold back the paper along the dotted line. Use the blanks to write each word as it is read aloud. When you finish the test, unfold the paper. Use the list at the right to correct any spelling mistakes.

1.	1. robin
2.	2. button
3.	3. bacon
4.	4. reason
5.	5. cotton
6.	6. sunken
7.	7. eleven
8.	8. cousin
9.	9. woren
10.	10. raisin
11.	11. wagon
12.	12. muffin
13.	13. widen
14.	14. wooden
15.	15. ridden
16.	16. common
17.	17. proven
18.	18. often
19.	19. penguin
20.	20. skeleton
Review Words 21.	21. medal
22.	22. pupil
23.	23. paddle
Challenge Words 24.	24. violin
25.	25. vitamin

HOMEWORK Phonics/Spelling, page 153

bacon	cotton	muffin	button
woven	cousin	proven	often
ridden	robin	raisin	widen
wagon	eleven	reason	sunken
common	penguin	skeleton	wooden

End Game!

This week's spelling words contain /_n/. Write each spelling word under the correct spelling pattern ending.

-in
1. cousin
2. penguin
3. raisin
4. robin
5. muffin

-en
6. eleven
7. proven
8. often
9. wooden
10. sunken
11. woven
12. widen
13. ridden

-on
14. cotton
15. reason
16. cannon
17. bacon
18. button
19. wagon
20. skeleton

Day 3 — Word Meanings

CATEGORIES

Read each group of words below. Ask students to copy the words into their Writer's Notebooks, completing each group by adding a spelling word that fits in the same category.

1. ham, sausage, ____ (*bacon*)
2. sparrow, pigeon, ____ (*robin*)
3. wool, silk, ____ (*cotton*)
4. three, seven, ____ (*eleven*)

Challenge students to come up with other similar word groups to which they can add Spelling Words, Review Words, or Challenge Words.

Have partners write a sentence for each spelling word, leaving a blank space where the word should go. They can exchange papers and fill in the blanks.

Day 4 — Proofread

PROOFREAD AND WRITE

Write these sentences on the board. Have students circle and correct each misspelled word.

1. I offin hit the wrong butten. (*often, button*)
2. I ate bakin, eggs, and a muffen. (*bacon, muffin*)
3. Sometimes my couson makes raisen toast. (*cousin, raisin*)
4. A pengin jumped onto the woodin ship. (*penguin, wooden*)

Remind students to use print and electronic resources as well as spelling patterns and rules to check spellings.

Error Correction Students who struggle choosing the correct ending spelling for these words will need additional reading and writing practice. Continue to have students sort the words and use the word sorts for reading and writing activities.

Day 5 — Assess and Reteach

POSTTEST

Use the Dictation Sentences on page 703E for the Posttest.

If students have difficulty with any words in the lesson, have them place the words on a list called *Spelling Words I Want to Remember* in their Writer's Notebooks. Look for students' use of these words in their writings.

Challenge students to find words for each /ən/ spelling and add them to their Writer's Notebooks.

Discuss print and electronic resources that students can use to determine or check the correct spellings of words that they find troublesome. For example, have a student demonstrate how to check spellings using a dictionary and using a spelling check tool on the computer. Remind students that a computer will not find when they misspell a word as another word.

HOMEWORK — Phonics/Spelling, page 154

bacon	cotton	muffin	button
woven	cousin	proven	often
ridden	robin	raisin	widen
wagon	eleven	reason	sunken
common	penguin	skeleton	wooden

A. What's the Word?

Complete each sentence with a word from the spelling list.

1. The __reason__ they went west was to find gold.
2. Some men left their __cotton__ fields in search of gold.
3. There were three __common__ paths to California in 1849.
4. The family traveled in a __wooden__ wagon.
5. Some miners used a small __wagon__ to haul their gold.
6. They found a __sunken__ ship filled with gold.
7. Miners __often__ risked their health searching for gold.
8. They had __ridden__ for miles with no sign of water.
9. Earlier promises of gold in California had __proven__ to be untrue.
10. He wore a fancy jacket with each __button__ made of pure gold.

B. Analogies

An analogy is a statement that compares sets of words that are alike in some way: *Night* is to *day* as *black* is to *white*. This analogy points out that *night* and *day* are opposite in the same way that *black* and *white* are opposite.

Use the spelling words to complete the analogies below.

11. *Bear* is to *polar bear* as *bird* is to __penguin__
12. *Plum* is to *prune* as *grape* is to __raisin__
13. *Wood* is to *frame* as *bones* are to __skeleton__
14. *Mom* is to *child* as *aunt* is to __cousin__

ON YOUR OWN — Phonics/Spelling, page 155

A. Proofreading Activity

There are six spelling mistakes in this poem. Circle the misspelled words. Write the words correctly on the lines below.

The Gold Rush Ghosts

Have you heard the tale of the lady
Who wears the (cottin) dress?
They (offen) say she's waiting,
And won't accept she's dead.
All day she sits on her (woodun) chair
Staring out to see
If her lover has (riden) by outside.
For someday his bride she'll be.

But her true love hasn't (provin)
That he's a rightful man.
He's still searching for a gold mine
Like every (commen) man.
So she still sits and he still rides,
These two unhappy souls.
She never will see her love
And he never will find gold.

1. __cotton__
2. __often__
3. __wooden__
4. __ridden__
5. __proven__
6. __common__

B. Writing Activity

Write a poem of your own. Use at least three spelling words in your poem. Answers will vary.

HOMEWORK — Phonics/Spelling, page 156

Look at the words in each set below. One word in each set is spelled correctly. Use a pencil to fill in the circle next to the correct word. Before you begin, look at the sample set of words. Sample A has been done for you. Do Sample B by yourself. When you are sure you know what to do, you may go on with the rest of the page.

Sample A:
- Ⓐ frosen
- Ⓑ frozen
- Ⓒ frozon
- Ⓓ froson

Sample B:
- Ⓔ poisen
- Ⓕ poyzon
- Ⓖ poysen
- Ⓗ poison

1.
- Ⓐ baken
- Ⓑ backen
- Ⓒ bacin
- Ⓓ bacon

2.
- Ⓔ woven
- Ⓕ wovin
- Ⓖ wovon
- Ⓗ wovenn

3.
- Ⓐ riden
- Ⓑ riddin
- Ⓒ ridden
- Ⓓ riddin

4.
- Ⓔ wagon
- Ⓕ wagen
- Ⓖ wagin
- Ⓗ waggon

5.
- Ⓐ comon
- Ⓑ common
- Ⓒ commen
- Ⓓ commun

6.
- Ⓔ coton
- Ⓕ cottin
- Ⓖ kotten
- Ⓗ cotton

7.
- Ⓐ kuzzin
- Ⓑ cusin
- Ⓒ couson
- Ⓓ cousin

8.
- Ⓔ robbin
- Ⓕ robin
- Ⓖ roben
- Ⓗ robben

9.
- Ⓐ ealeven
- Ⓑ eleven
- Ⓒ eelevin
- Ⓓ elevin

10.
- Ⓔ pennguin
- Ⓕ penguin
- Ⓖ pengwin
- Ⓗ pingwin

11.
- Ⓐ mufin
- Ⓑ muffen
- Ⓒ muffin
- Ⓓ mufein

12.
- Ⓔ proven
- Ⓕ proveen
- Ⓖ provon
- Ⓗ prooven

13.
- Ⓐ rasen
- Ⓑ razin
- Ⓒ raisin
- Ⓓ raisen

14.
- Ⓔ reason
- Ⓕ reesin
- Ⓖ reeson
- Ⓗ reasin

15.
- Ⓐ skelletin
- Ⓑ skeletin
- Ⓒ scheleton
- Ⓓ skeleton

16.
- Ⓔ buttin
- Ⓕ button
- Ⓖ butten
- Ⓗ buton

17.
- Ⓐ often
- Ⓑ offen
- Ⓒ offin
- Ⓓ oftin

18.
- Ⓔ widin
- Ⓕ widon
- Ⓖ widen
- Ⓗ wyden

19.
- Ⓐ sunkin
- Ⓑ sunkan
- Ⓒ sunken
- Ⓓ suncken

20.
- Ⓔ woulden
- Ⓕ widen
- Ⓖ wooden
- Ⓗ woodden

5-Day Grammar

Daily Language Activities

Write the sentences on the board.

DAY 1
A Dust Bowl is one of the topics in my book about america. Of the last two periods we studied, its the most interesting. (1: The Dust Bowl; 2: America; 3: it's; 4: more)

DAY 2
Lance do you see the bugs. Do you think they were smallest than the others you saw? (1: Lance,; 2: bugs?; 3: smaller)

DAY 3
Yes Rebecca. I look close at them, and they are smaller then the others. (1: Yes, Rebecca.; 2: looked; 3: closely; 4: than)

DAY 4
Paul was a well inventor. He pushed a butten for no reasen and sudden went back in time. (1: good; 2: button; 3: reason; 4: suddenly)

DAY 5
The japanese man tryed to speak clear. His english teacher helped him. (1: Japanese; 2: tried; 3: clearly; 4: English)

 ## Adverbs

 Day 1 **Introduce the Concept**

INTRODUCE ADVERBS

Present the following:

- An **adverb** is a word that tells more about a verb.

- Adverbs are different from adjectives, which are words that describe nouns or pronouns. An adjective may tell what kind, which, or how many of something, but an adverb tells when, where, or how the action of a sentence takes place.

- Adverbs can be written before or after the verbs they describe: *Happily,* we walked up the aisle to receive our awards. We walked *happily* up the aisle to receive our awards.

- Many adverbs end in *-ly.* These usually tell how: We jogged *quickly.*

 See Grammar Transparency 126 for modeling and guided practice.

HOMEWORK **Grammar,** page 126

- **Adjectives** and **adverbs** should not be confused.
- An **adjective** describes nouns. It gives information about a *person, place,* or *thing.*
- An **adverb** tells more about the verb, such as *how, when,* or *where* an action takes place.

Read each sentence and look at the underlined word. Then tell if the word is an adjective or an adverb.

1. In 1848, many people quickly moved to California in search of gold. **adverb**
2. The forty-niners hoped to become rich men. **adjective**
3. I like to read interesting stories about the California Gold Rush. **adjective**
4. Show your father the treasure map that you found recently. **adverb**
5. The miner dug deeply into the hole to see if there was gold inside. **adverb**
6. I do not think that what you found in the river is real gold. **adjective**
7. On our field trip to the gold mine, our guide led us through a dark tunnel. **adjective**
8. Matt and Eric were standing by a muddy road. **adjective**
9. Raven always wanted to travel back in time to see how her neighborhood used to look. **adverb**
10. They eagerly waited to join the wagon train to California. **adverb**

Day 2 **Teach the Concept**

REVIEW ADVERBS

Review how students can recognize adverbs using yesterday's **Grammar Practice Book** page 126.

INTRODUCE ADVERBS THAT TELL WHEN, WHERE, AND HOW

- Adverbs that tell **when** or indicate frequency include *soon, often, late, usually,* and *never:* Myra arrived *late* to the show. Fred is *never* early to practice.

- Adverbs such as *up, down, here,* and *there* can tell **where**: She sat *there.*

- Adverbs that end in *-ly,* like *happily,* and *extremely* can tell **how** or indicate intensity: Margaret *happily* helped her mother cook dinner. My kitten is *extremely* frisky.

 See Grammar Transparency 127 for modeling and guided practice.

ON YOUR OWN **Grammar,** page 127

- An **adverb** is a word that tells more about a verb.
- Some adverbs tell *how* an action takes place. These adverbs may describe how completely an action is performed.
- Some adverbs tell *when* an action takes place. These adverbs may describe how often an action takes place.
- Some adverbs tell *where* an action takes place.

Underline the adverb in each sentence. Then write if the adverb tells *how, when,* or *where* the action takes place.

1. My mother and I went to the library together for information about our ancestors. **how**
2. Tomorrow we will visit our local museum of natural history. **when**
3. Were they traveling far in search of gold? **where**
4. Did James Marshall first find gold at Sutter's Mill? **when**
5. John Sutter, Jr., built a new city nearby along the Sacramento River. **where**
6. We patiently sifted the sand for gold. **how**
7. Our uncle examined the rock thoroughly. **how**
8. He carelessly threw the stone back in the water. **how**
9. That greedy miner looked at them suspiciously. **how**
10. We then found the gold. **when**

Day 3 — Review and Practice

REVIEW TYPES OF ADVERBS

Review how to identify adverbs and the three questions they answer. Also review how adverbs can show frequency (*usually, sometimes*) and intensity (*almost, a lot, extremely*).

MECHANICS AND USAGE: GOOD VS. WELL

- *Good* is an adjective and should be used only to modify nouns: Charlotte is a *good* swimmer.

- *Well* is an adverb when it is used to modify verbs: Roxanne drives *well*. *Well* is an adjective when it refers to health: Kelvin doesn't feel *well* today.

- In general, an adjective is not used to describe a verb, nor an adverb to describe a noun.

Day 4 — Review and Proofread

REVIEW ADVERBS

Ask students to explain what adverbs do. Have them explain how they differ from adjectives. Remind students that adverbs can show frequency (*always, often*) and intensity (*almost, barely*).

PROOFREAD

Have students correct the errors in the following sentences.

1. I did good on the test about the Gold Rush. (well)

2. I got a good score because I studied good. (studied well)

3. That's a very happily dog. (happy)

4. Working in his room, he wrote his report very quick. (quickly)

Day 5 — Assess and Reteach

ASSESS

Use the Daily Language Activity and **Grammar Practice Book** page 130 for assessment.

RETEACH

Use Grammar Practice Book page 130 and selected pages from the **Grammar and Writing Handbook** for additional reteaching. Remind students that it is important to use adverbs correctly as they speak and write.

Check students' writing for use of the skill and listen for it in their speaking. Assign Grammar Revision Assignments in their Writer's Notebooks as needed.

See Grammar Transparency 128 for modeling and guided practice.

See Grammar Transparency 129 for modeling and guided practice.

See Grammar Transparency 130 for modeling and guided practice.

HOMEWORK — **Grammar,** page 128

- *Good* is an adjective and is used to describe nouns.
- *Well* is an adverb that tells *how* about a verb.
- Do not confuse the adjective *good* with the adverb *well*.
- Use *well* as an adjective when you refer to someone's health.

Complete each sentence by writing the word *good* or *well* on the line.

1. Today our team did _____ **well** _____ in the class treasure-hunt game.

2. Our teacher hid the treasure pieces so _____ **well** _____ that they were very hard to find.

3. It was a _____ **good** _____ experience to win the game for a second year.

4. The other team also did _____ **well** _____, but we found the pieces faster than they did.

5. Though I didn't feel _____ **well** _____, I helped find the last, hidden treasure piece.

6. This river is a _____ **good** _____ place to look for gold pieces.

7. Grandfather, would it be a _____ **good** _____ idea to look for gold in the river?

8. If we pan for gold all day and night, we should do _____ **well** _____.

9. We can have a _____ **good** _____ time swimming in the water if we do not find anything.

10. Is your father feeling _____ **well** _____ enough to come with us?

ON YOUR OWN — **Grammar,** page 129

- An **adverb** is a word that tells more about a verb.
- Some adverbs tell *how* an action takes place.
- Most adverbs that tell *how* end in **-ly**. They are formed by adding **-ly** to an adjective. The adverb *well* also tells *how*.

A. Read the magazine article below, and circle the six incorrect adverbs. Then write the words correctly on the lines below.

When the gold miners of 1849 were looking for gold, they (frequent) found shiny stones in their pans. However, not all were true gold. Fool's gold, also called pyrite, is a stone that some miners (mistaken) confused with the real thing. What if you ever find a rock that looks like gold? These three ways can (quick) help you find out if it is real gold or fool's gold.

First, look carefully and (good) at the color. Both are shiny and yellow-colored, but real gold also has a silver tone. The color of fool's gold is more like brass. Next, look at the shape. Fool's gold forms cubes and larger shapes. Real gold comes in chunks, flakes, or sheets. Last, (brisk) rub it against another hard object and smell it. Gold has no smell, but fool's gold will smell like rotten eggs. Maybe that's why they call it *fool's gold!*

1. **frequently**   3. **quickly**   5. **usually**
2. **mistakenly**   4. **well**   6. **briskly**

B. Rewrite the above article with the correct adverbs on the lines.

HOMEWORK — **Grammar,** page 130

Read each sentence. Then using the clue in the parentheses, circle the letter of the correct adverb that completes each sentence.

1. After gold was discovered at Sutter's Mill, many people moved _____. (where?)
   - a. there
   - b. well
   - c. briefly
   - d. quietly

2. Her grandfather traveled _____ to California to search for gold. (how?)
   - a. today
   - b. outside
   - c. bravely
   - d. ahead

3. Her grandfather shouted _____ when he saw a piece of gold in the river. (how?)
   - a. well
   - b. next
   - c. around
   - d. gleefully

4. His shouting was so loud, it could be heard way out _____. (where?)
   - a. there
   - b. first
   - c. often
   - d. silent

5. _____ people came from everywhere to see why her grandfather was shouting. (when?)
   - a. Forcefully
   - b. Wisely
   - c. Eagerly
   - d. Soon

6. _____ he realized that it was just a piece of fool's gold. (when?)
   - a. Unhappily
   - b. Excitedly
   - c. Immediately
   - d. Nearly

Daily Planner

DAY 1	• Prepare to Read • Academic Language • Vocabulary (Preteach)
DAY 2	• Comprehension • Leveled Reader Lesson 1
DAY 3	• Phonics/Decoding • Leveled Reader Lesson 2
DAY 4	• Phonics/Decoding • Vocabulary (Review) • Leveled Reader Lesson 3
DAY 5	• High-Frequency Words • Fluency • Self-Selected Reading

Interactive Student Book

If you wish to preteach the main selection, use StudentWorks Plus for:

• Vocabulary Preteaching
• Word-by-Word Highlighting
• Think Aloud Prompts

Academic Language

Academic words include those harder Tier 2 words that appear in much of students' reading materials as well as the language of instruction. The words chosen for instruction were selected from the **Living Word Vocabulary** list and Avril Coxhead's list of **High-Incidence Academic Words**.

Approaching Level

Prepare to Read

Objective	Preview *Leah's Pony*
Materials	• **StudentWorks Plus** • self-stick notes

PREVIEW TEXT

- Have students preview *Leah's Pony* using **StudentWorks Plus**. This version of the Student Book contains oral summaries in multiple languages, story recording, word-by-word highlighting, Think Aloud prompts, and comprehension-monitoring questions.

- Remind students that listening carefully to and following along with the word-by-word reading will help them prepare for the reading of the selection with the class. Ask students to place self-stick notes on any challenging words or places that confuse them. Discuss these with students prior to the reading of the selection with the rest of the class.

- Tell students to write three or four sentences in their Writer's Notebooks telling what they learned about Leah's problem and how she tried to solve it.

Academic Language

Objective	Teach academic language
Materials	• none

PRETEACH LANGUAGE OF INSTRUCTION

Tell students that there are many important lesson words you will be using this week. You want them to become familiar with these words *before* the lessons. These words also appear in the directions of the tests they will be taking this year.

Preteach the following academic words: *sequence, analyze, problem, solution, historical,* and *primary sources.*

- Define each word using student-friendly language. Tell students that *sequence* is the order in which events happen or steps are taken in real life or in a story. Sometimes an author will tell events out of order.

- In addition, relate each word to known words. For example, connect *problem* to *a situation that presents a challenge* and *solution* to *the time when the challenge is overcome.*

- Highlight these words when used throughout the week and reinforce their meanings.

Approaching Level

Phonics/Decoding

Objective Decode words with /ən/

Materials
- **Approaching Reproducible,** p. 226
- **Sound-Spelling Workboards**

✓ PHONICS MAINTENANCE

Tier 2

- Distribute a **Workboard** to each student. Say a syllable type that was previously taught, such as a consonant + -le syllable. Have students find the **Sound-Spelling Card** on the board for the syllable type.

- Review the spelling(s) for different types of syllables and for the /ən/ ending by providing a sample word. Guide students to write the word on the board. Model how to segment the word and write the spelling for each sound or syllable, as needed. In addition, point out spelling hints, such as keeping the consonant + -le together in the same syllable in longer words.

- Dictate the following words for students to spell: *reason, simple, pumpkin, table, eagle, fatten*. Write each word on the board, and have students self-correct their work.

RETEACH SKILL

Words with /ən/ Display the Sound-Spelling Cards -in, -on, and -en. Review that, in an unaccented syllable, these spellings stand for the /ən/ sound. Provide a sample word for each spelling.

- Write the words below on the board. Model how to decode the first word in each row, then guide students as they decode the remaining words. For the multisyllabic words, divide the words into syllables using the syllable-scoop technique to help students read one syllable at a time.

- When completed, point to the words in random order for students to chorally read. Repeat several times.

rot	rotten	hid	hidden	sad	sadden
ribbon	robin	risen	frozen	reason	treason
token	taken	mitten	muffin	lemon	linen
poison	basin	season	fasten	napkin	pumpkin
oven	woven	even	event	open	raisin
silken	satin	quicken	ridden	written	whiten

Corrective Feedback

Throughout the lessons, provide feedback based on students' responses. If the answer is correct, ask another question. If the answer is tentative, restate key information to assist the student. If the answer is wrong, provide corrective feedback such as hints or clues, refer to a visual such as a Sound-Spelling Card or story illustration, or probe with questions to help the student clarify any misunderstanding.

Approaching Reproducible, page 226

The ending sounds in the words **cannon, muffin,** and **golden** are the same—/ən/. These sounds can be spelled **-on, -in,** or **-en.**

A. Find and circle each word from the box. Then write the word on the line.

eaten   sunken   season   open   bacon   cousin   reason   often

1. a v l (often) h o t — often
2. f e g w a (cousin) — cousin
3. t y (reason) p o n — reason
4. n m q (eaten) u n e — eaten
5. s p (open) j e o n k — open
6. a (sunken) c i x y — sunken
7. (bacon) w u n v o n — bacon
8. l d f (season) o — season

B. Circle the words that end with the /ən/ sounds.

9. green   (eleven)   sailor
10. (raisin)   raising   rain
11. between   using   (button)
12. along   (muffin)   train

Approaching Level

Vocabulary

Objective   Preteach selection vocabulary
Materials
- **Visual Vocabulary Resources**
- **Approaching Reproducible,** p. 227
- **Vocabulary Cards**

PRETEACH KEY VOCABULARY

Tier 2

Introduce the Words Use the **Visual Vocabulary Resources** to preteach the key selection words *items, clustered, overflowing, sturdy, glistened,* and *bidding.* Use the following routine, which appears in detail on the cards.

- Define the word in English, and provide the example given.

- Define the word in Spanish, if appropriate, and indicate if the word is a cognate.

- Display the picture, and explain how it illustrates or demonstrates the word.

- Then engage students in structured partner-talk about the image, using the key word.

- Ask students to chorally say the word three times.

- Point out any known sound-spellings or focus on a key aspect of phonemic awareness related to the word.

- You may wish to also distribute copies of the Vocabulary Glossary in the **ELL Resource Book**.

REVIEW PREVIOUSLY TAUGHT VOCABULARY

Display the **Vocabulary Cards** from the previous four weeks. Say the meanings of the words, one by one, and have students identify them. Then point to words in random order for students to provide definitions and related words they know.

Dictionary: Unfamiliar Words Have students use a dictionary to find the following words: *glisten, shimmer, silken,* and *satin.* Have students discuss the origins, pronunciations, syllabication, and meanings of these four words Then have students reread the third paragraph on page 681 of *Leah's Pony.* Have students write a sentence describing the pony's coat using the words *shimmered* and *silken* instead of the words *glistened* and *satin.*

Approaching Reproducible, page 227

> items   clustered   bidding   glistened   overflowing   sturdy
>
> **A. Read the vocabulary words. Write the correct word in each sentence below.**
>
> **1.** At the farm sale, three people were ___**bidding**___ on the old truck.
>
> **2.** The fruit on the trees ___**glistened**___ like jewels.
>
> **3.** I stood on a ___**sturdy**___ box to pick the apples.
>
> **4.** Berries were ___**clustered**___ on the low plants.
>
> **5.** Soon my pail was ___**overflowing**___ with sweet berries.
>
> **6.** There were so many different ___**items**___ to choose from at the farm stand.
>
> **B. Write your own sentences using four of the vocabulary words.**
> **Answers will vary.**
>
> **7.** _____
>
> **8.** _____
>
> **9.** _____
>
> **10.** _____

Approaching Level

Vocabulary

Objective   Review vocabulary and high-frequency words
Materials   • **Vocabulary Cards**   • **High-Frequency Word Cards**

✔ REVIEW VOCABULARY

Review the Words Display the **Vocabulary Cards** *items, clustered, overflowing, sturdy, glistened*, and *bidding*. Point to each word, read it aloud, and have students chorally repeat.

Then have students answer the following questions and explain their answers:

■ Which are *items*—books or libraries?

■ Which is *clustered*—a display of apples in a supermarket or a single apple in a bowl?

■ Which is *overflowing*—a cup filled past the top or a cup filled halfway?

■ Which is *sturdy*—a house made of brick or a house made of straw?

■ Which *glistened* in the sunshine—the polished crystal vase or the faded curtains?

■ Which is more like *bidding*—buying or selling?

HIGH-FREQUENCY WORDS

Tier 2

Top 250 Words The ability to read accurately and effortlessly the most frequently used words in written English will help students develop reading fluency. Display **High-Frequency Word Cards** 201–210. Then do the following:

■ Display one card at a time, and ask students to chorally state each word.

■ Have students spell each word aloud.

■ Ask students to write each word in their Writer's Notebooks as they state aloud each letter. Then have them read the word again.

■ When completed, quickly flip through the Word Card set as students chorally read the words.

■ Provide opportunities for students to use the words in speaking and writing. For example, provide sentence starters, such as *Look at the clock and tell me the _____*, for oral and written practice. Or point to a Word Card and ask a question, such as *What word is an antonym for* together? (*apart*)

■ Continue the routine throughout the week.

ELL

Practice Vocabulary Pair students of different proficiency. Orally model the vocabulary in sentences. For example: *I made a list of items I need for the camping trip.* On the board, provide sentence frames for pairs to copy and complete using the vocabulary. For example: *The glass building _____ in the sunlight.* (glistened)

Word Webs

Have students create word webs in their Writer's Notebooks for each vocabulary word. Write the related words provided, and ask students to add other words, phrases, and illustrations.

Student Book

Corrective Feedback

Provide additional instruction for students who struggle with the concept of problem and solution. Read the first three paragraphs with students. Ask: *What does Grandma need that she doesn't have?* Help students recognize that Grandma's need for a wheelchair is her problem. Then read the rest of the selection with students. Ask: *How does Grandma get what she needs? Be specific.* Explain that the events that they list all lead to the solution, which is that Grandma gets her wheelchair because her neighbors hold a fundraising auction.

Approaching Level

Comprehension

Objective Reteach analyze story structure and problem and solution
Materials • **Student Book:** "Grandma's Story"

 **RETEACH THE STRATEGY: ANALYZE STORY STRUCTURE**

Tier 2

- **Define** Remind students that story structure is the way that an author organizes the events of the plot using story elements such as character and setting. Point out that analyzing story structure helps readers sequence and summarize the plot's main events. Review with students that most stories have a beginning, a middle, and an end.

- **Relate to Real Life** Ask students to imagine that they see a friend reading a list of players chosen for the soccer team and hear her shout, "All right! I made the team!" What might students expect to happen next? Perhaps their friend would become busy with soccer training. Then she might take part in a big game. Would her team win? Would it lose? Would an injury keep her from playing? How would she react to any of these events? If an author was writing her story, these events would be part of the story structure.

- **Set Purposes** Remind students that good readers analyze story structure as they read to help them better understand the story's characters, events, and theme.

RETEACH THE SKILL: PROBLEM AND SOLUTION

- **Define** Tell students that the problem is something that the main characters want to do or need to change. The steps that the characters take to solve the problem are an important part of the story structure. These steps or actions influence what happens later in the story. The solution is the way that the problem is solved.

- **Relate to Real Life** Tell students that rain on a day when they were supposed to go to the beach is a problem. Going to the movies, playing inside with a friend, or choosing another day to go are a few possible solutions.

- **Set Purposes** Remind students that good readers identify the problem and then look for the steps that the main characters take to solve it. Recognizing the problem and solution helps the reader better understand the story.

- **Apply** Have students identify the problem in "Grandma's Story." Then have them list the steps that lead to the solution. Students will apply this skill to a simpler text as they read *Explorers of the Southwest*.

Approaching Level

Leveled Reader Lesson 1

Objective Read to apply skills and strategies
Materials • **Leveled Reader:** *Explorers of the Southwest*

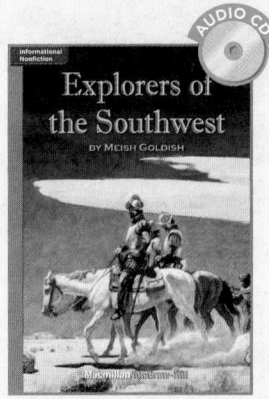

Leveled Reader

BEFORE READING

Preview and Predict Have students read the title and preview the first chapter. Ask them to make predictions about the problems and challenges that the explorers confronted. Students should note any questions they have before they read.

 **Review Vocabulary Words** Have students read the vocabulary words on the inside front cover. Briefly define each and ask students to state related words they have learned.

Set a Purpose for Reading *Let's read to find out what main problem each explorer faced and how the problem was solved.*

DURING READING

STRATEGY
ANALYZE TEXT STRUCTURE

Remind students that text structure is the way that an author organizes the information in a text.

SKILL
PROBLEM AND SOLUTION

Tell students that as they read, they should identify the problem and look for the actions or steps that an explorer took to find a solution. Read Chapter 1 with students. Help them fill in the Problem and Solution Chart.

As you read, help students decode unknown words. In addition, ask open-ended questions to facilitate rich discussion, such as *What is this explorer trying to find out or do? Does the author state the problem clearly?* Build on students' responses to help them develop a deeper understanding of the text.

To check students' understanding, stop after every two pages and have students restate the problem faced by the explorer before reading on. Also have students restate the actions or steps taken to solve the problem in sequence. Help struggling students reread difficult passages.

AFTER READING

Ask students to consider the solutions to the problems. Ask, *Are these the solutions that you were expecting? Explain.*

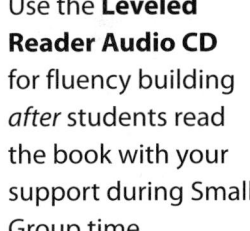

Digital Learning

Use the **Leveled Reader Audio CD** for fluency building *after* students read the book with your support during Small Group time.

Leveled Reader

Approaching Level

Leveled Reader Lesson 2

Objective Reread to apply skills and strategies and develop fluency

Materials
- **Leveled Reader:** *Explorers of the Southwest*
- **Approaching Reproducible,** p. 230

BEFORE READING

Review the Strategy and Skill Review students' completed Problem and Solution Charts from the first read. Point out that authors may structure the information in a text in sequence to show how a problem is solved.

Review Vocabulary Words Have students search the book for each vocabulary word. Ask them to read aloud the sentence containing the word and state the word's definition or provide related words. Direct students to use a dictionary to help them with any words, as needed.

Set a Purpose for Reading *Let's reread to check our understanding of the problems and solutions described in the text and to work on our reading fluency.*

DURING READING

Reread *Explorers of the Southwest* with students. Have them read silently, two pages at a time, or read aloud to a partner. Stop and have students restate the steps taken to solve a problem before they read the next two pages. Model presenting the steps, as needed.

AFTER READING

Check Comprehension Have partners complete the Comprehension Check on page 24. Review students' answers. Help them find evidence for their answers in the text.

MODEL FLUENCY

Model reading the fluency passage on **Approaching Reproducible** page 230. Tell students to pay close attention to your phrasing as you read. Then read one sentence at a time, and have students echo-read the sentences, copying your phrasing.

During independent reading time, have students work with a partner using the fluency passage. One student reads aloud, and the other repeats each sentence. If students need additional support, have them listen to the "practice speed" version of the passage on the **Fluency Solutions Audio CD**.

Approaching Reproducible, page 230

As I read, I will pause at commas and end punctuation.

	Fish swim in almost every body of water in the
10	world. Some are freshwater fish, and others are saltwater
19	fish. Herbivorous (hur-BIV-uh-ruhs) fish eat only grasses
26	and other plants. Carnivorous (kahr-NIV-uh-ruhs) fish eat
33	other fish and animals.
37	Some fish are small and docile, such as minnows. Other
47	fish are large predators, such as sharks. Some fish give
57	birth to live baby fish, and others lay eggs. Scientists
67	estimate that there are over 20,000 species of fish in all,
77	and those are just the ones we know about.
86	What is a fish, anyway? Fish are vertebrate animals.
95	That means that they have backbones. Fish are
103	cold-blooded creatures, and most breathe using gills.
110	They have swum on our planet for about 500 million
119	years.
120	There are three main kinds of fish: jawless,
128	cartilaginous, and bony. 131

Comprehension Check

1. Why did the author write this passage? **Author's Purpose** The author wrote this passage to inform the reader about fish.

2. How are herbivorous and carnivorous fish alike and different? **Compare and Contrast** They are both kinds of fish, but herbivorous fish eat plants, while carnivorous fish eat other animals.

	Words Read	−	Number of Errors	=	Words Correct Score
First Read		−		=	
Second Read		−		=	

Approaching Level

Leveled Reader Lesson 3

Objectives Build fluency

Materials • **Leveled Reader:** *Explorers of the Southwest*
• **Approaching Reproducible,** p. 230

✔ FOCUS ON FLUENCY

Timed Reading Tell students that they will be doing a final timed reading of the fluency passage on **Approaching Reproducible** page 230 that they have been practicing. With each student, follow these directions:

- Place the passage facedown.

- When you say "Go," the student begins reading the passage aloud.

- When you say "Stop," the student stops reading the passage.

As they read, note words students mispronounce and their overall phrasing. Stop after one minute. Help students record and graph the number of words they read correctly.

REREAD PREVIOUSLY READ BOOKS

- Distribute copies of the past six **Leveled Readers**. Have students select two to reread. Tell students that rereading these books will help them develop their skills. The more times they read the same words, the quicker they will learn these words. This will make the reading of other books easier.

- Circulate and listen in as students read. Stop them periodically and ask how they are figuring out difficult words and how they are monitoring their comprehension. Note students who need additional work with specific decoding or comprehension skills.

- Encourage students to read other previously read Leveled Readers during independent reading time or for homework.

Meet Grade-Level Expectations

As an alternative to this day's lesson, guide students through a reading of the On Level Leveled Reader. See page 703U. Since both books contain the same vocabulary, phonics, and comprehension skills, the scaffolding you provided will help most students gain access to this more challenging text.

Book Talk

Bringing Groups Together Students will work with peers of various language and reading abilities to discuss this week's Leveled Readers. Refer to page 162 in the **Teacher's Resource Book** for more about how to conduct a Book Talk.

Leah's Pony

Written by Elizabeth Friedrich
Illustrated by Michael Garland

Student Book

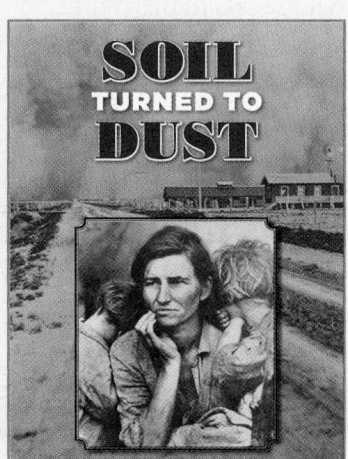

SOIL TURNED TO DUST

Student Book

Decodable Text

Use the decodable stories in the **Teacher's Resource Book** to help students build fluency with basic decoding patterns.

Approaching Level

Fluency

Objectives Reread selections to develop fluency; develop speaking skills
Materials • **Student Book:** *Leah's Pony,* "Soil Turned to Dust"

REREAD FOR FLUENCY

- Have students reread a portion of *Leah's Pony*. Suggest that they focus on two to four of their favorite pages from the selection. Work with students to read the pages with appropriate phrasing.

- Provide time for students to read their sections of text to you. Comment on their phrasing, and provide corrective feedback by modeling proper fluency.

DEVELOP SPEAKING/LISTENING SKILLS

- Have students practice reading the song at the end of "Soil Turned to Dust."

- Work with students to read the song with appropriate phrasing. Remind them that song lyrics are similar to poetry. Model reading two lines at a time. Emphasize the way in which reading with appropriate phrasing makes the meaning of a text clear. Have students repeat.

- Provide time for students to read the song to partners. Ask students to comment on their partner's phrasing and overall fluency.

- Challenge students to memorize and recite part of the song for the class.

Approaching Level

Self-Selected Reading

Objective   Read independently to analyze story structure and identify problem and solution

Materials   • **Leveled Classroom Library**   • other fiction books

APPLY SKILLS AND STRATEGIES TO INDEPENDENT READING

- **Independent Reading** Have students choose a fiction book such as a **Leveled Classroom Library** book for sustained silent reading. (See the **Theme Bibliography** on pages T8–T9 for book suggestions.) Remind them that the problem is what the main character or characters are trying to change or do, and the solution is how the problem is fixed or solved. Have students read their books and record notes about the problem and solution on a Problem and Solution Chart.

- **Show Evidence of Reading** While reading, students may generate a reading log or journal. After reading, ask students to use their Problem and Solution Chart and logs to paraphrase the content of the book, maintaining meaning and logical order. They may write or orally state a summary of the book. Provide time for students to share their summaries and comment on their reactions to the book while participating in Book Talks. Ask: *Did you enjoy this story? Why or why not? Why might a friend of yours enjoy reading this book?*

Daily Planner

DAY 1	• Vocabulary • Phonics
DAY 2	• Leveled Reader Lesson 1
DAY 3	• Leveled Reader Lesson 2
DAY 4	• Fluency
DAY 5	• Self-Selected Reading

ELL

Practice Vocabulary Pair ELL students with native speakers. On the board, provide sentence frames for pairs to copy and complete using the vocabulary and additional words when necessary. For example: *The _____ house survived the _____ without any damage.* (sturdy; storm)

Sound-Spelling WorkBoard

On Level

Vocabulary

Objective Review vocabulary
Materials • **Vocabulary Cards**

 **REVIEW PREVIOUSLY TAUGHT WORDS**

Review the Words Display the **Vocabulary Cards** *items, clustered, overflowing, sturdy, glistened,* and *bidding*. Point to each word, read it aloud, and have students chorally repeat.

Then provide the following Yes/No questions. Ask students to answer each question, justifying their answer. Allow other students to respond. Use the discussions to determine each student's depth of word knowledge.

- Would it be surprising if a store had no *items* for sale?
- In big cities, are buildings often *clustered* together?
- If your piggy bank is *overflowing,* have you saved much money?
- If you are standing on a *sturdy* ladder, do you probably feel safe?
- Would you say that a rusty old car *glistened* in the sunlight?
- If you are *bidding* on something, do you want to buy it?

Phonics/Word Study

Objective Decode multisyllabic words with /ən/
Materials • **Word-Building Cards** • **Sound-Spelling WorkBoards**

RETEACH SKILL

- **Words with /ən/** Display the **Word-Building Cards** *-in, -on,* and *-en.* Review that in an unaccented syllable, these spellings all stand for the /ən/ sound. Provide a sample word for each spelling.

- Write the words below on the board. If necessary, divide the words into syllables using the syllable-scoop technique to help students read one syllable at a time. When completed, point to the words in random order for students to chorally read.

sadden	person	cousin	reason	ragamuffin
listen	glisten	whiten	women	watermelon
abandon	eleven	oxygen	open	reopen

- **Spelling** Dictate the following words for students to spell on their **WorkBoards**: *reopen, mistaken, raisin, uncommon, abandon.* Model how to segment words, such as spelling a word syllable by syllable.

On Level

Fluency

Objectives Reread selections to develop fluency; develop speaking skills

Materials • **Student Book:** *Leah's Pony*, "Soil Turned to Dust"

✔ REREAD FOR FLUENCY

- Have students reread *Leah's Pony*. Work with students to read with appropriate phrasing. Model as needed.

- Provide time for students to read a section of text to you. Comment on their phrasing and provide corrective feedback.

DEVELOP SPEAKING/LISTENING SKILLS

- Have students practice reading page 698 of "Soil Turned to Dust" aloud. Work with them to read the page with appropriate phrasing, keep words together in meaningful chunks. Model reading the passage a few lines at a time.

- Have students prepare summaries of the information on page 698 and deliver their summaries orally to the class. Remind them to use appropriate phrasing when they deliver their summaries.

- Have students practice reading the Woody Guthrie song on page 700 of the Student Book. Model reading it a few lines at a time. Have students use the punctuation in the song as a guide to appropriate phrasing of the lyrics.

Self-Selected Reading

Objective Read independently to identify problem and solution

Materials • **Leveled Classroom Library** • other fiction books

APPLY SKILLS AND STRATEGIES TO INDEPENDENT READING

- **Read Independently** Have students choose a fiction book such as a **Leveled Classroom Library** book for sustained silent reading. (See the **Theme Bibliography** on pages T8–T9 for book suggestions.) Have students read their books and record notes about the problem and solution on their Problem and Solution Chart.

- **Show Evidence of Reading** While reading, students may generate a reading log or journal. After reading, ask students to use their Problem and Solution Chart to write or orally state a summary of the book. Provide time for students to share their summaries and their reactions to the book through Book Talks. Ask: *Was the problem faced by the main character or characters interesting? Was the solution satisfying? Why or why not?*

Student Book

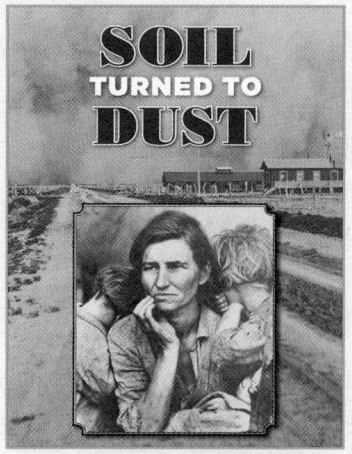

Student Book

On Level

Leveled Classroom Library
See Leveled Classroom Library lessons on pages T2–T7.

Leveled Reader

On Level

Leveled Reader Lesson 1

Objective Read to apply strategies and skills

Materials • **Leveled Reader:** *Explorers of the Southwest*

BEFORE READING

Preview and Predict Have students read the title and preview the book by reading the chapter titles and looking at the illustrations. Ask students to make predictions about what problems and solutions will be described in the text.

Review Vocabulary Words Have students read the vocabulary words on the inside front cover. Ask students to state related words they have learned. Review definitions, as needed.

Set a Purpose for Reading *Let's read to find out what main problems the explorers faced and how they tried to solve them.*

DURING READING

STRATEGY
ANALYZE TEXT STRUCTURE

Remind students that analyzing text structure helps readers identify, understand, and remember key information about a topic.

SKILL
PROBLEM AND SOLUTION

Review with students that a problem is the challenge faced by the individuals portrayed in a text. The solution is how the problem is solved. The steps that individuals take to solve a problem often are presented in sequence.

Read Chapter 1 with students. Ask open-ended questions to facilitate rich discussion, such as *What are these explorers trying to find out or do? What actions are they taking to solve problems?* Build on students' responses. Then have them fill in the first section of the Problem and Solution Chart and continue reading.

Dictionary: Unfamiliar Words As they read, have students point out this week's new vocabulary words and any context clues that the author provides, such as nearby words with similar meanings. Have students use a dictionary to find definitions, as needed.

AFTER READING

Ask students to choose one explorer and identify how that individual solved a problem. Ask: *Is this the solution that you were expecting? Was the solution a successful one?* Have them explain their answers.

On Level

Leveled Reader Lesson 2

Leveled Reader

Objective Reread to apply skills and strategies and develop fluency

Materials
• **Leveled Reader:** *Explorers of the Southwest*
• **Practice Book,** p. 230

BEFORE READING

Review the Strategy and Skill Review students' completed Problem and Solution Charts from the first read. Point out that the problem is the challenge faced by the individual or individuals portrayed in the text, and the solution is how the problem is fixed or solved. When students analyze text structure, they notice how the steps or actions taken to solve a problem lead to the solution.

If students' Problem and Solution Charts are incomplete, provide a model chart or use a student chart and revise it as a group. Have students copy the revised chart in their Writer's Notebooks.

Set a Purpose for Reading *Let's reread to check our understanding of the explorers' problems and solutions and to work on our reading fluency.*

DURING READING

Reread *Explorers of the Southwest* with students. Have them read silently, two pages at a time, or read aloud to a partner. Stop and have students identify any problems or solutions presented in the text before they read the next two pages. Also have students restate in sequence actions or steps taken to solve the problems. Model presenting events in sequence, as needed.

AFTER READING

Check Comprehension Have partners complete the Comprehension Check on page 24. Review students' answers. Help students find evidence for their answers in the text.

MODEL FLUENCY

Model reading the fluency passage on **Practice Book** page 230. Tell students to pay close attention to your phrasing as you read. Then read one sentence at a time, and have students echo-read the sentences, copying your phrasing.

During independent reading time, have students work with a partner using the fluency passage. One student reads aloud, and the other repeats each sentence. If students need additional support, have them listen to the "practice speed" version of the passage on the **Fluency Solutions Audio CD**.

Book Talk

Bringing Groups Together
Students will work with peers of various language and reading abilities to discuss this week's **Leveled Readers**. Refer to page 162 in the **Teacher's Resource Book** for more about how to conduct a Book Talk.

Practice Book, page 230

As I read, I will pause at commas and end punctuation.

	A coral reef is a shelf that runs along the coastlines of
12	countries throughout the world. Coral reefs are found in
21	shallow, warm waters all over the world.
28	Among all these reefs, there is one that stands out. It is
40	the Great Barrier Reef along the coast of Australia. It is
51	remarkable for many reasons. One is its length—over 1,250
60	miles. It is the largest coral reef ecosystem in the world,
71	and the largest organic structure on the planet. It is also
82	home to numerous kinds of sea life.
89	About 40,000 years ago, the Aboriginal peoples were
96	the only humans living on the Australian continent. They
105	fished and hunted along parts of the Great Barrier Reef.
115	For a long period of time they were the only people who
127	knew the reef existed.
131	When sailors began to explore the world, their boats
140	sometimes hit the sharp coral that was under the water,
150	sinking their vessels. The reef remained a mystery. 158

Comprehension Check

1. What details support the idea that the Great Barrier Reef is remarkable? **Main Idea and Details** The Great Barrier Reef is very long, is the largest coral reef ecosystem in the world, and is the largest organic structure on the planet.

2. Why were the sailors unaware of the coral reef? **Cause and Effect** The sailors were new to that part of the world. They didn't discover the reef until their boats had hit it.

	Words Read	–	Number of Errors	=	Words Correct Score
First Read		–		=	
Second Read		–		=	

Daily Planner

DAY 1	• Leveled Reader Lesson 1
DAY 2	• Leveled Reader Lesson 2
DAY 3	• Phonics
DAY 4	• Vocabulary • Fluency
DAY 5	• Self-Selected Reading

ELL

Self-Monitor Vocabulary
Have student pairs of different proficiency identify and define unfamiliar words from the main selection using a dictionary. Challenge students to use the new words in sentences. Monitor students as they complete the activity.

Beyond Level

Phonics/Word Study

Objectives   Decode multisyllabic words with /ən/
Materials   • none

EXTEND/ACCELERATE

- **Read Multisyllabic Words with /ən/** Write the words below on the board. Challenge students to read the words, using known word parts. When completed, point to the words in random order for students to chorally read.

mistaken	ragamuffin	uncommon	forsaken
reopen	refasten	reasonable	preseason
unfrozen	unwoven	eleven	glistening
personal	impersonate	handmaiden	accordion

- **Define the Words** Ask students to use their knowledge of word parts to figure out the meanings of the above words. Then have partners find the words in a dictionary and confirm or revise the meanings. Challenge students to use these words in this week's writing assignments.

- **Spell Words with /ən/** Dictate the following words for students to spell: *unspoken, aspirin, hobgoblin, beholden, unbutton.* Write the words for students to self-correct.

Vocabulary

Objectives   Review primary sources; compare primary sources
Materials   • primary sources from books or the Internet about the Great Depression

ENRICH VOCABULARY

- **Review Primary Sources** Remind students that a **primary source** is an account of actual events spoken or written by someone who witnessed or took part in those events. Maps and photographs can also be primary sources. Remind students of the primary sources found in "Soil Turned to Dust."

- **Compare Primary Sources** Gather a number of primary sources about the Great Depression. Have partners select two or more primary sources from among those collected. Tell students to compare their sources. Ask: *What information did the sources have in common? Do you think the sources you examined were reliable? Why or why not?* Have students use a dictionary to look up any unfamiliar words they find during their reading.

Beyond Level

Fluency

Objectives Reread selections to develop fluency; develop speaking skills
Materials • **Student Book:** *Leah's Pony*, "Soil Turned to Dust"

REREAD FOR FLUENCY

- Have students reread *Leah's Pony*. Work with students to read the selection with appropriate phrasing.

- Provide time for students to read a section of text to you. Comment on their phrasing and provide corrective feedback.

DEVELOP SPEAKING/LISTENING SKILLS

- Have students practice reading page 698 of "Soil Turned to Dust." Model reading a few sentences at a time. Work with students to use punctuation as a guide to meaning and phrasing.

- Have students orally state a summary of the information on page 698 of "Soil Turned to Dust." Remind them to use their own words in their summaries. Have them speak their summaries with appropriate phrasing. Ask students to discuss whether the summaries included the main facts.

Self-Selected Reading

Objective Read independently to identify problems and solutions
Materials • **Leveled Classroom Library** • other fiction books

APPLY SKILLS AND STRATEGIES TO INDEPENDENT READING

- **Read Independently** Have students choose a fiction book such as a **Leveled Classroom Library** book for sustained silent reading. (See the **Theme Bibliography** on pages T8–T9 for book suggestions.) Have students fill in their Problem and Solution Charts as they read.

- **Show Evidence of Reading** While reading, students may generate a reading log or journal. After reading, ask students to use their Problem and Solution Chart to write or orally state a summary of the book, maintaining meaning and logical order. Provide time for students to share their summaries and other comments through Book Talks. Ask: *Would you recommend this book? Why or why not?*

- **Evaluate** Have students compare the problem and solution in the book they chose to those in *Leah's Pony*. Ask students to write a paragraph suggesting a different solution to the problem either in *Leah's Pony* or in the other fiction book they read.

Leah's Pony
Written by Elizabeth Friedrich
Illustrated by Michael Garland

Student Book

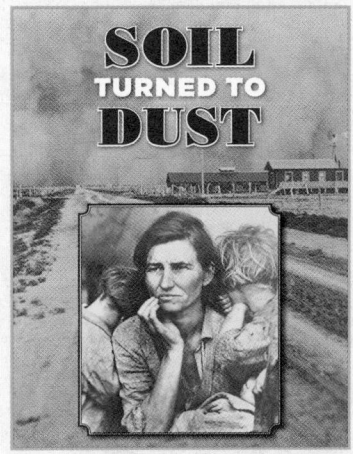

SOIL TURNED TO DUST

Student Book

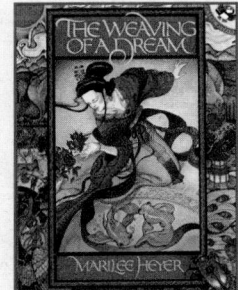

Beyond

Leveled Classroom Library
See Leveled Classroom
Library lessons on pages T2–T7.

Leveled Reader

Beyond Level

Leveled Reader Lesson 1

Objective	Read to apply strategies and skills
Materials	• **Leveled Reader:** *Explorers of the Southwest*

BEFORE READING

Preview and Predict Have students preview the book by reading the title and chapter titles and looking at the illustrations. Ask students to make predictions about the problems that will be described in the text and how they will be solved.

 **Review Vocabulary Words** Have students read the vocabulary words on the inside front cover. Ask students to state each definition and any related words they have learned.

Set a Purpose for Reading *Let's read to find out what main problems the explorers faced and how they tried to solve them.*

DURING READING

 **STRATEGY**
ANALYZE TEXT STRUCTURE

Remind students that analyzing text structure helps readers understand the pattern an author has used to organize information.

 **SKILL**
PROBLEM AND SOLUTION

Ask students to define the terms *problem* and *solution*. Point out that the steps or actions taken to solve a problem often are organized in sequence.

Read the book with students. Ask open-ended questions to facilitate rich discussion, such as *What were the explorers trying to find out or do? What challenges and difficulties did they face?* Build on students' responses to help them develop a deeper understanding of the text. Have students fill in the Problem and Solution Chart independently as they read.

AFTER READING

Compare Information Have students compare and contrast the problems faced by the explorers. Ask: *Who took the most effective action to solve a problem? Were the solutions temporary or enduring?* Have students share their ideas with the class.

Analyze Have students think about a problem they faced in their own lives. Have them write a short essay telling about the problem and the steps they took to solve it.

Gifted Talented

Beyond Level

Leveled Reader Lesson 2

Objectives Reread to apply skills and strategies and develop fluency
Materials • **Leveled Reader:** *Explorers of the Southwest*
          • **Beyond Reproducible,** p. 230

Leveled Reader

BEFORE READING

Review the Strategy and Skill Review students' completed Problem and Solution Charts from the first read. Remind them that the problem is what the individuals in the text are trying to change or do, and the solution is the way the problem is resolved. Analyzing text structure helps readers understand the pattern the author has used to organize information and to remember key points.

If students' Problem and Solution Charts are incomplete, provide a model chart or use a student chart and revise it as a group. Have students copy the revised chart in their Writer's Notebooks.

Set a Purpose for Reading *Let's reread to check our understanding of the problems and solutions described in the text and to work on our reading fluency.*

DURING READING

Have students reread *Explorers of the Southwest* silently or with a partner. If reading in pairs, prompt students to stop every two pages and summarize events or ask their partner probing questions.

AFTER READING

Check Comprehension Have students independently complete the Comprehension Check on page 24. Review students' answers. Help students find evidence for their answers in the text.

Synthesize Challenge students to brainstorm ways that individuals can help others solve problems or survive hard times. Students might mention possibilities ranging from personal efforts to help a friend to volunteer activities to benefit a charity.

MODEL FLUENCY

Model reading the fluency passage on **Beyond Reproducible** page 230. Tell students to pay close attention to your phrasing. Then read one sentence at a time, and have students echo-read the sentences, copying your phrasing.

During independent reading time, have students work with a partner using the fluency passage. One student reads aloud, and the other repeats each sentence. Students can check their fluency by reading along with the "expert speed" version of the passage on the **Fluency Solutions Audio CD.**

Book Talk

Bringing Groups Together Students will work with peers of various language and reading abilities to discuss this week's **Leveled Readers.** Refer to page 162 in the **Teacher's Resource Book** for more about how to conduct a Book Talk.

Beyond Reproducible, page 230

As I read, I will pause at commas and end punctuation

     Marco Polo was born around 1254 in Venice, Italy. His father and
11 uncles were successful merchants. When Marco was born, his father,
21 Niccolo, and his uncle, Maffeo, were in Constantinople. The Polos left
32 Constantinople in about 1260. They set out eastward, along the Black
42 Sea. Marco did not meet his father until years later.
52   In this period, the Mongol Empire ruled much of Asia. Local
63 Mongol leaders, or khans, ruled different regions. The greatest was
73 Kublai Khan, the ruler of Cathay. That was what medieval Europeans
84 called China. After four years of travel, the Polos reached the Great
96 Khan's court. He was probably at his summer palace. It was called
108 Shang-du, or Xanadu (ZAN-ah-doo).
112   The Polos won Kublai Khan's favor. After a while, he sent them back
125 home to Europe. Their trip paved the way for Marco's own adventures.
137   The Polos could not stay home for long, since Kublai Khan was
149 expecting them back. Marco's father and uncle left again after being
160 home for only two years. This time, the teenaged Marco went with
172 them. They traveled by camel across what is now Turkey and
183 northern Iran. 185

Comprehension Check

1. Why do you think trading trips took years? **Cause and Effect**
   Trading trips took years because there were no paved roads, and ships depended on the wind.
2. What kinds of characteristics did the Polos have? **Plot They were very brave and adventurous.**

	Words Read	−	Number of Errors	=	Words Correct Score
First Read		−		=	
Second Read		−		=	

ELL ENGLISH LANGUAGE LEARNERS

Prepare to Read

Content Objective Explore farm life during the time of the Dust Bowl
Language Objective Use key words to describe farm life during the Dust Bowl
Materials • StudentWorks Plus

BUILD BACKGROUND KNOWLEDGE

All Language Levels

- Have students preview *Leah's Pony* using **StudentWorks Plus**, which contains oral summaries in multiple languages, online multilingual glossaries, word-by-word highlighting, and questions that assess and build comprehension.

- Students can build their word-reading fluency by reading along as the text is read or by listening during the first reading and, at the end of each paragraph, returning to the beginning of the paragraph and reading along.

- Students can build their comprehension by reviewing the definitions of key words in the online glossary and by answering the comprehension questions. When appropriate, the text required to answer the question is highlighted to provide students with additional support and scaffolding.

- After reading, ask students to respond to these questions: *Have you ever had to give up something important to you? How did you feel?*

Academic Language

Language Objective Use academic language in classroom conversations

All Language Levels

- This week's academic words are **boldfaced** throughout the lesson. Define the word in context, and provide a clear example from the selection. Then ask students to generate an example or a word with a similar meaning.

Academic Language Used in Whole Group Instruction

Theme Words	Key Selection Words	Strategy and Skill Words
solution	**items**	**analyze**
accomplish	**clustered**	**story structure**
cooperating	**overflowing**	**problem**
	sturdy	**solution**
	glistened	**adverbs**
	bidding	**unfamiliar words**

Daily Planner

DAY 1	• Build Background Knowledge • Vocabulary
DAY 2	• Vocabulary • Access to Core Content *Leah's Pony*
DAY 3	• Vocabulary • Grammar • Access to Core Content *Leah's Pony*
DAY 4	• Vocabulary • Writing/Spelling • Access to Core Content "Soil Turned to Dust" • Leveled Reader *Explorers of the Southwest*
DAY 5	• Vocabulary • Leveled Reader *Explorers of the Southwest* • Self-Selected Reading

StudentWorks Plus
Interactive Student Book

Use StudentWorks Plus for:
- Vocabulary Preteaching
- Word-by-Word Highlighting
- Think Aloud Prompts

Cognates

Help students identify similarities and differences in pronunciation and spelling between English and Spanish cognates.

solution	*solución*
cooperating	*cooperar*
item	*ítem*
analyze	*analizar*
structure	*estructura*
problem	*problema*
adverb	*adverbio*

Vocabulary

Language Objective Demonstrate understanding and use of key words by describing farm life at the time of the Dust Bowl

Materials • **Visual Vocabulary Resources**
• **ELL Resource Book**

PRETEACH KEY VOCABULARY

Use the **Visual Vocabulary Resources** to preteach the key selection words *items, clustered, overflowing, sturdy, glistened,* and *bidding.* Focus on two words per day. Use the following routine, which appears in detail on the cards.

Beginning/Intermediate

■ Point out any known sound-spellings, or focus on a key aspect of phonemic awareness related to the word.

All Language Levels

■ Define the word in English, and provide the example given.

■ Define the word in Spanish, if appropriate, and indicate if the word is a cognate.

■ Display the picture, and explain how it illustrates the word. Engage students in a structured activity, using the key word.

■ Ask students to chorally say the word three times.

■ Distribute copies of the Vocabulary Glossary in the **ELL Resource Book** on page 300.

PRETEACH FUNCTION WORDS AND PHRASES

All Language Levels

Use the Visual Vocabulary Resources to preteach the function words and phrases *swallow hard, hard times, cluster around,* and *wobble down* [*the road*]. Focus on one word or phrase per day. Use the detailed routine on the cards.

■ Define the word in English and, if appropriate, in Spanish. Point out if the word is a cognate.

■ Refer to the picture and engage students in talk about the word. For example, students will partner-talk using sentence frames.

■ Ask students to chorally repeat the word three times.

TEACH BASIC WORDS

Beginning/Intermediate

Use the Visual Vocabulary Resources to teach the basic words *tractor, pickup truck, auction, gully/gullies, petunias,* and *cornfield.* Teach these "farm" words using the routine provided on the card.

Visual Vocabulary Resources

ELL Resource Book, page 300

Use the word chart to study this week's vocabulary words.
Write a sentence using each word in your writer's notebook.

Word	Context Sentence	Illustration
sturdy	The chair was small but sturdy, strong enough for an adult.	
items	She carried as many items to the check out table as she could.	What items might you find at a grocery store?
clustered	The group clustered together to surprise the birthday girl.	
bidding	The woman started the bidding at fifty dollars.	
overflowing	The sink is overflowing with dirty dishes.	
glistened	The stars glistened in the sky.	

ELL Resource Book

ELL ENGLISH LANGUAGE LEARNERS

Access to Core Content

Content Objective Read grade-level text

Language Objective Discuss text, using key words and sentence frames

Materials • **ELL Resource Book,** pp. 288–299

✔ PRETEACH MAIN SELECTION (PAGES 678–695)

All Language Levels

Use the Interactive Question-Response Guide on **ELL Resource Book** pages 288–297 to introduce students to *Leah's Pony.* Preteach half of the selection on Day 2 and half on Day 3.

- Use the prompts provided in the guide to develop meaning and vocabulary. Use the partner-talk and whole-class responses to engage students and increase student-talk.

- When completed, have partners reread the story.

PRETEACH PAIRED SELECTION (PAGES 698–701)

All Language Levels

Use the Interactive Question-Response Guide on ELL Resource Book pages 298–299 to preview the paired selection, "Soil Turned to Dust." Preteach the selection on Day 4.

Beginning	**Intermediate**	**Advanced**
Use Visuals During the Interactive Reading, select several illustrations that show a problem. Describe them and have students summarize what you said.	**Describe** During the Interactive Reading, select a few lines of text that describe a problem or a solution. After you have read and explained it, have students retell, based on the text.	**Discuss** During the Interactive Reading, select a passage of text that describe a problem or a solution. After you have read and explained it, have students discuss the problem or solution, based on the text.

ELL ENGLISH LANGUAGE LEARNERS

Fluency

Content Objectives Reread selections to develop fluency; develop speaking skills
Language Objective Tell a partner what a selection is about
Materials **Student Book:** *Leah's Pony,* "Soil Turned to Dust"
  • **Teacher's Resource Book**

REREAD FOR FLUENCY

Beginning

- Have students read the decodable passages in the **Teacher's Resource Book**, pages 30–31.

Intermediate/Advanced

- Have students reread two to four of their favorite pages from *Leah's Pony.* Help them read the pages with accurate phrasing. For example, read the first paragraph and have students echo. Then have them chorally reread additional paragraphs.

- Provide time for students to read their sections of text to you. Comment on their phrasing, and provide corrective feedback by modeling proper fluency.

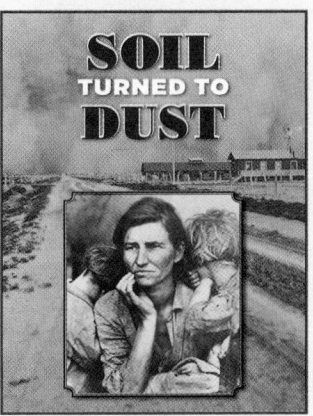

Student Book

DEVELOP SPEAKING/LISTENING SKILLS

All Language Levels

- Have students practice reading the song at the end of "Soil Turned to Dust." Work with them to read with accurate phrasing.

- Model reading a few lines of the song at a time. Emphasize the way in which reading with accuracy makes details clear. Have students tell their partner about the song. Provide the sentence frame *This song is about ____.*

Self-Selected Reading

Content Objective Read independently
Language Objective Orally retell information learned
Materials • **Leveled Classroom Library** • other fiction books

APPLY SKILLS AND STRATEGIES TO INDEPENDENT READING

All Language Levels

- Have students choose a fiction book for independent reading. (See the **Theme Bibliography** on pages T8–T9 for book suggestions.)

- After reading, ask students to orally summarize and share their reactions to the book with classmates. Ask: *Would you recommend this book to a classmate? Why or why not?*

Leveled Classroom Library
See Leveled Classroom
Library lessons on pages T2–T7.

ELL ENGLISH LANGUAGE LEARNERS

Transfer Skills

Adverbs Adverbs are not used in Hmong. Instead, two repeated verbs commonly take the place of a verb and adverb. For example, *I run run to school* for *I run quickly to school.* Write several sentence pairs using verbs and adverbs on the board, simulating each action as you say sentences, such as *I walk quickly; I walk slowly.* Have students repeat. See language transfers on pages T16–T31.

Corrective Feedback

During Whole Group grammar lessons, follow the routine on the **Grammar Transparencies** to provide students with extra support. This routine includes completing the items with English Language Learners while other students work independently, having students reread the sentences with partners to build fluency, and providing a generative task, such as writing a new sentence using the skill.

Grammar

Content Objective Identify adverbs
Language Objective Speak in complete sentences, using sentence frames

✓ ADVERBS

Beginning/Intermediate

- Remind students that an adverb is a word that tells more about a verb. An adverb tells how, when, or where the action of a verb takes place. Many adverbs end in *-ly*. Write the following sentences on the board and underline the adverbs: *The family sadly left the farm. They loaded the truck yesterday.* Ask: *How did the family leave? When did they load the truck?* Point out that adverbs can come before or after the verbs they describe.

All Language Levels

- Review adverbs. Write sentences on the board, such as those provided below. Have students underline the adverb in each sentence and say whether it tells how, when, or where. Have them say: *The adverb is ___. It tells ___.*

  Leah wished she could run <u>away</u>.

  Mr. B. <u>gladly</u> bought the pony.

  The auction would start <u>soon</u>.

  The farm animals sold <u>quickly</u>.

PEER DISCUSSION STARTERS

All Language Levels

- Write the following sentences on the board:

  Living on a farm is ___.   I learned that the drought caused ___.

- Pair students and have them complete each sentence frame. Have them expand on their sentences by providing as many details as they can from this week's readings. Circulate, listen in, and take note of each student's language use and proficiency.

Beginning	**Intermediate**	**Advanced**
Use Visuals Describe the illustrations in *Leah's Pony* to students. Ask: *What do you see?* Help them point and name adverbs.	**Describe** Ask students to describe the illustrations in *Leah's Pony* using adverbs. Have them use complete sentences. Model sentences as needed.	**Describe** Ask students to describe the illustrations in *Leah's Pony* using adverbs. The have them add adjectives in their descriptions.

ELL ENGLISH LANGUAGE LEARNERS

Writing/Spelling

Content Objective Spell words correctly
Language Objective Write in complete sentences, using sentence frames

All Language Levels

- Write the key vocabulary words on the board: *items, clustered, overflowing, sturdy, glistened, bidding.* Have students copy each word on their **WorkBoards**. Help them say each word and then write a sentence for it. Provide sentence starters such as:

  Some items that belong on a desk are ___.

  All the kids clustered together when ___.

  When the bathtub is overflowing, you have to ___.

  You need a sturdy chair because ___.

  The diamond glistened ___.

  I joined in the bidding by ___.

Beginning/Intermediate

- Help students spell words using their growing knowledge of English sound-spelling relationships. Model how to segment the word students are trying to spell, and attach a spelling to each sound (or spellings to each syllable if a multisyllabic word). Use the **Sound-Spelling Cards** to reinforce the spellings for each English sound.

Advanced

- Dictate the following words for students to spell: *hidden, robin, ribbon, muffin, rotten, poison.* Use the Sound-Spelling Cards to guide students as they spell each word.

- When completed, review the meanings of words that can be easily demonstrated or explained. Use actions, gestures, and available pictures.

Sound-Spelling WorkBoard

Phonics/Word Study

For English Language Learners who need more practice with this week's phonics/spelling skill, see the Approaching Level lesson on page 703J. Focus on minimal contrasts, articulation, and those sounds that do not transfer from the student's first language to English. See language transfers on pages T16–T31.

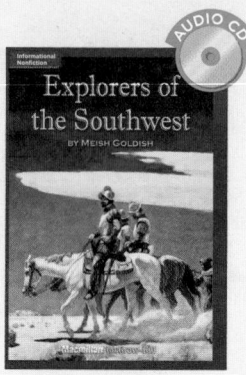

Leveled Reader

ELL ENGLISH LANGUAGE LEARNERS

Leveled Reader

Content Objective Read to apply skills and strategies

Language Objective Retell information, using complete sentences

Materials • **Leveled Reader:** *Explorers of the Southwest*
  • **ELL Resource Book,** p. 301
  • **Visual Vocabulary Resources,** pp. 499–504

✔ BEFORE READING

All Language Levels

■ **Preview** Read the title *Explorers of the Southwest*. Ask: *What's the title? Say it again.* Repeat with the author's name. Then look at the illustrations in the book. Use simple language to tell about each page. Immediately follow up with questions, such as *What kind of things do explorers do? What did the explorers find in the New World?*

■ **Review Skills** Use the inside front cover to review the comprehension skill and vocabulary words.

■ **Set a Purpose** Say: *Let's read to find out about the explorers who built new communities in the Southwest.*

DURING READING

All Language Levels

■ Have students read each page aloud using the differentiated suggestions. Provide corrective feedback, such as modeling how to blend a decodable word or clarifying meaning by using techniques from the Interactive Question-Response Guide.

■ **Retell** After every two pages, ask students to state the main ideas they have learned so far. Help them to complete the Problem and Solution Chart. Restate students' comments when they have difficulty using story-specific words. Provide differentiated sentence frames to support students' responses and engage students in partner-talk where appropriate.

Vocabulary

Preteach Vocabulary Use the routine in the **Visual Vocabulary Resources**, pages 499–504, to preteach the ELL Vocabulary listed in the inside front cover of the **Leveled Reader**.

Beginning	Intermediate	Advanced
Echo-Read Have students echo-read after you.	**Choral-Read** Have students chorally read with you.	**Choral-Read** Have students chorally read.
Check Comprehension Point to pictures and ask questions, such as *This is a map. What does the map show?*	**Check Comprehension** Ask questions/prompts, such as *What did De Vaca looking for in the New World? Did he find it? Who is Estevan?*	**Check Comprehension** Ask: *What did Estevan do? What did Coronado find at Cibola? Why was he angry when he arrived at Cibola?*

ELL ENGLISH LANGUAGE LEARNERS

AFTER READING

Use the chart below and Think and Compare questions in the Leveled Reader to determine students' progress.

Think and Compare	Beginning	Intermediate	Advanced
1 Look back at page 5. What is one problem that de Vaca faced? What solution does he find? **(Problem and Solution)**	Possible responses: Nonverbal response. Got lost. Became hungry and sick. Sailed west.	Possible responses: De Vaca and his men got lost and they were hungry and sick. They sailed west.	Possible responses: De Vaca and his men got lost and they were hungry and sick. They built rafts and sailed west.
2 Think of things you do to get along with new people. Then read page 15 again. What do you think Coronado could have done to get along better with the Zunis? **(Analyze)**	Possible responses: Nonverbal response. Be friendly. Don't order people.	Possible responses: Coronado could have been friendlier. He shouldn't have ordered the Zunis to accept the King of Spain as their ruler.	Possible responses: Coronado shouldn't have ordered the Zunis to accept the King of Spain as their ruler. He should have tried to be more understanding of the Zunis.
3 The Southwest explorers became heroes in their home countries. What famous people today are considered heroes? Why are they admired? **(Apply)**	Possible responses: Nonverbal response. Lance Armstrong. Win races. Help people.	Possible responses: Lance Armstrong is a hero. He won lots of races and he helps people.	Possible responses: Lance Armstrong is a hero because he won lots of championships which inspire others and he helps people.

BOOK TALK

Develop Listening and Speaking Skills Distribute copies of **ELL Resource Book**, page 301, and form small groups. Help students determine the leader to discuss Book Talk questions. Tell students to remember the following while engaged in the activity:

- Share information in cooperative learning interactions. Remind students to work with their partners to retell the story and complete any activities. Ask: *What happened next in the story?*

- Express opinions, ideas, and feelings on a variety of social and academic topics. Ask: *What do you think about the characters in the story?*

ELL Resource Book

Book Talk

Bringing Groups Together Students will work with peers of varying language abilities to discuss the questions for the Book Talk activity. Form groups so that students who read Beyond Level, On Level, Approaching Level, and ELL Leveled Readers are in the same group for the activity.

Progress Monitoring

Weekly Assessment

ASSESSED SKILLS

Vocabulary: Vocabulary Words, Dictionary: Unfamiliar Words

- Comprehension: Problem and Solution
- Grammar: Adverbs
- Phonics/Spelling: Words with /ən/

Selection Test for Leah's Pony Also Available

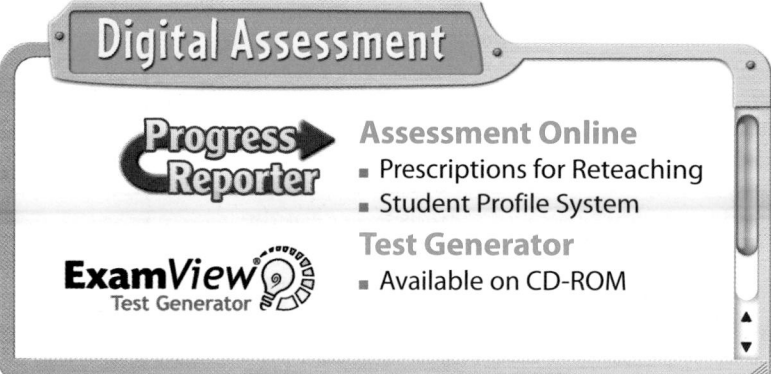

Digital Assessment

Progress Reporter

Assessment Online
- Prescriptions for Reteaching
- Student Profile System

Test Generator

ExamView® Test Generator
- Available on CD-ROM

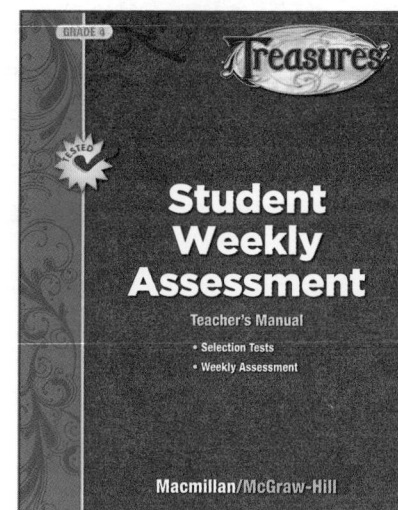

**Weekly Assessment
Unit 6 Week 1**

Fluency Assessment

Assess fluency for one group of students per week.
Use the Oral Fluency Record Sheet to track the number of
words read correctly. Fluency goal for all students:
113–133 words correct per minute (WCPM).

Approaching Level	Weeks 1, 3, 5
On Level	Weeks 2, 4
Beyond Level	Week 6

Fluency Assessment

Diagnose	IF...	Prescribe THEN...

Review the assessment answers with students. Have them correct their errors. Then provide additional instruction as needed.

	IF...	**THEN...**
VOCABULARY WORDS **VOCABULARY STRATEGY** Dictionary: Unfamiliar Words	0–2 items correct ...	See **Vocabulary Intervention Teacher's Edition.** **LOG ON** ▶ Online Practice: Go to www.macmillanmh.com. **CD-ROM** Vocabulary PuzzleMaker
COMPREHENSION Skill: Problem and Solution	0–3 items correct ...	See **Comprehension Intervention Teacher's Edition.** **SPIRAL REVIEW** See Problem and Solution lesson in Unit 6 Week 2, page 723B.
GRAMMAR Adverbs	0–1 items correct ...	See **Writing and Grammar Intervention Teacher's Edition.**
PHONICS AND SPELLING Words with /ən/	0–1 items correct ...	**LOG ON** ▶ Online Practice: Go to www.macmillanmh.com. See **Phonics Intervention Teacher's Edition.**
FLUENCY	109–112 WCPM	**AUDIO CD** Fluency Solutions Audio CD
	0–108 WCPM	See **Fluency Intervention Teacher's Edition.**

Response to Intervention

To place students in Tier 2 or Tier 3 Intervention use the *Diagnostic Assessment*.

- Phonics
- Vocabulary
- Comprehension
- Fluency
- Writing and Grammar

Week 2 ★ At a Glance

Priority Skills and Concepts

 ### Comprehension
- **Strategy:** Analyze Story Structure
- **Skill:** Cause and Effect
- Problem and Solution
- **Genre:** Myth, Science Fiction, Expository

 ### Robust Vocabulary
- **Selection Vocabulary:** *reference, disappointment, annoyed, circular, outstretched, conducted*
- **Strategy:** Word Parts/Suffixes

 ### Fluency
- **Intonation/Expression**

 ### Phonics/Spelling
- **Word Study:** Homophones, Multisyllabic Words
- **Spelling Words:** *root, tale, wade, tail, prince, dough, moose, prints, we've, weave, whose, who's, route, boulder, bolder, weighed, patience, patients, doe, mousse*
- *cotton, muffin, eleven*

 ### Grammar/Mechanics
- **Comparing with Adverbs**
- **Review Punctuation and Capitalization**

 ### Writing
- **Trait: Ideas**
- Main Idea and Details

Key

 Tested in program   Review Skill

Digital Learning

Digital solutions to help plan and implement instruction

☑ Teacher Resources

LOG ON ▶

ONLINE www.macmillanmh.com

▶ **Teacher's Edition**
  - Lesson Planner and Resources also on CD-ROM

TeacherWorks*Plus*

▶ **Formative Assessment**
  - ExamView® on CD-ROM also available

 Progress Reporter

▶ **Instructional Resources**
  - Unit Videos
  - Classroom Presentation Toolkit

 VIDEO

▶ **Professional Development**
  - Video Library

Professional Development

☑ Student Resources

LOG ON ▶

ONLINE www.macmillanmh.com

▶ **Interactive Student Book**

StudentWorks*Plus*

▶ **Leveled Reader Database**

▶ **Activities**
  - Research Toolkit
  - Oral Language Activities
  - Vocabulary/Spelling Activities

 Listening Library
  - Recordings of Student Books and Leveled Readers

 Fluency Solutions
  - Fluency Modeling and Practice

Weekly Literature

Theme: Finding Out About the Past

Student Book

Interactive Student Book

- Word-by-Word Reading
- Summaries in Multiple Languages
- Comprehension Questions

The Gold Rush Game
by William F. Wu

illustrated by Cornelius Van Wright and Ying-Hwa Wright

Main Selection

Genre | Science Fiction

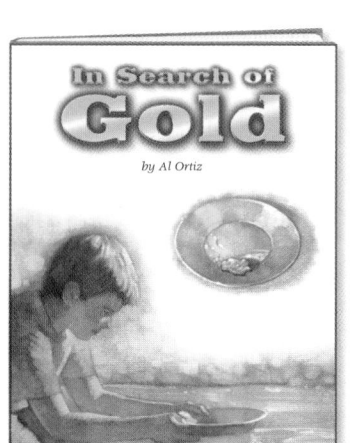

In Search of **Gold**
by Al Ortiz

Preteach Vocabulary and Comprehension

Genre | Fiction

GOLD
by Jan Jensen

Paired Selection

Genre | Expository

Support Literature

INTERACTIVE **Read-Aloud** ANTHOLOGY with PLAYS

Interactive Read-Aloud Anthology
- Listening Comprehension
- Robust Vocabulary
- Readers Theater Plays for Fluency

Resources for Differentiated Instruction

Leveled Readers

GR Levels Q–T

Genre	Expository

- Same Theme
- Same Vocabulary
- Same Comprehension Skills

Q

Approaching Level

R

On Level

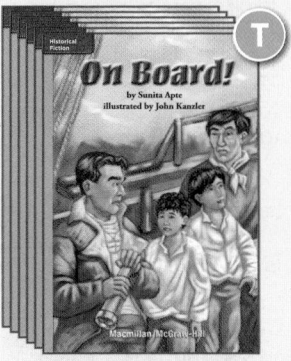

T

Beyond Level

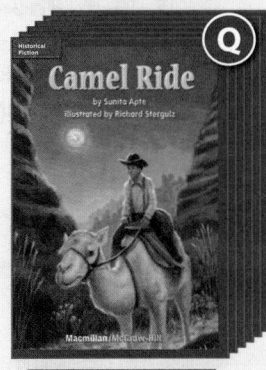

Q

ELL

Leveled Reader Database
Go to www.macmillanmh.com.

Leveled Practice

Approaching	On Level	Beyond	ELL

Leveled Classroom Library

Approaching	On Level	Beyond

Response to Intervention

 **Tier 2**

- Phonics
- Vocabulary
- Comprehension
- Fluency
- Writing and Grammar

 **Tier 3**

Assessment

Time For Kids

- TFK Teacher's Manual
- Apply Answering Question Strategies

Student Weekly Assessment

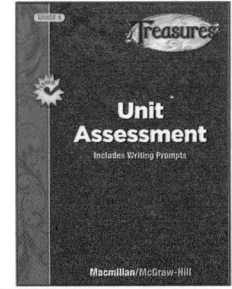
Unit Assessment
Includes Writing Prompts

Benchmark Assessment

Weekly Assessment   Unit Assessment   Benchmark Assessment

HOME-SCHOOL CONNECTION

- Family letters in English and Spanish
- Take-Home Stories and activities

Home-School Connection

Online Homework
www.macmillanmh.com

Go to **www.macmillanmh.com** for Online Lesson Planner

TeacherWorks Plus
All-In-One Planner and Resource Center

Professional Development Video Library

The Gold Rush Game, pp. 708–721

WHOLE GROUP

ORAL LANGUAGE

- **Listening Comprehension**
- **Speaking/Viewing**

WORD STUDY

- **Vocabulary**
- **Phonics/Word Study**
- **Spelling**

READING

- **Comprehension**

- **Fluency**

LANGUAGE ARTS

- **Writing**

- **Grammar**

ASSESSMENT

- **Informal/Formal**

DAY 1

Listening/Speaking/Viewing

? Focus Question What do you think it would have been like to take part in a gold rush?

Build Background, 704

Read Aloud: "The Golden Wish," 705A–705B

Vocabulary
reference, disappointment, annoyed, circular, outstretched, conducted, 707, 729C
Practice Book, 236

Strategy: Suffixes, 706

Spelling Pretest: Homophones, 729E
Phonics/Spelling Book, 157–158

Read "In Search of Gold," 706–707

Comprehension, 707A–707B
Strategy: Analyze Story Structure

Skill: Cause and Effect
Practice Book, 237

Fluency Model Fluency, 705B

Writing

Daily Writing What would be difficult about being a miner in the days of the Gold Rush? What struggles might they have faced?

Trait: Ideas
Main Idea and Details, 727A–727B

Grammar Daily Language Activities, 729G
Comparing with Adverbs, 729G
Grammar Practice Book, 131

Quick Check Vocabulary, 706
Comprehension, 707B

DAY 2

Listening/Speaking

? Focus Question How did Eric and Matt affect the future by going back into the past?

Vocabulary
Review Words, Suffixes, 708, 729C
Practice Book, 242

Phonics
Read Homophones, 705C–705D
Practice Book, 235

Spelling Word Sorts, 729E
Phonics/Spelling Book, 159

Read *The Gold Rush Game,* 708–721

Comprehension, 708–721
Strategy: Analyze Story Structure

Skill: Cause and Effect
Practice Book, 238

Fluency Repeated Reading: Intonation/Expression, 723A

Writing

Daily Writing Why was gold so important to people in the days of the Gold Rush? Write a few sentences to explain your answer.

Reading/Writing Connection, 728–729

Grammar Daily Language Activities, 729G
Comparing with Adverbs, 729G
Grammar Practice Book, 132

Quick Check Phonics, 705D
Comprehension, 721

SMALL GROUP Lesson Plan **Differentiated Instruction 704G–704H**

Priority Skills

Vocabulary	Comprehension	Writing	Science
Vocabulary Words Suffixes	**Strategy:** Analyze Story Structure **Skill:** Cause and Effect	Trait: Ideas Main Idea and Details	Knows that matter has physical properties

DAY 3

Listening/Speaking

❷ Focus Question How is Larry's experience similar to that of the prospectors in *The Gold Rush Game*? How is it different?

Summarize, 723

Vocabulary

Review Words, Related Words, 729D

Spelling Word Meanings, 729F
Phonics/Spelling Book, 160

Read *The Gold Rush Game*, 708–721

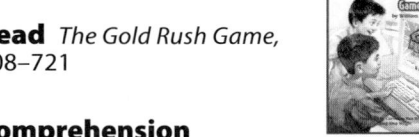
Student Book

Comprehension
Comprehension Check, 723

Review Skill: Problem and Solution, 723B
Practice Book, 240

Fluency Repeated Reading: Intonation/Expression, 723A
Practice Book, 239

Writing

Daily Writing Write a journal entry about a time that you looked hard for something that was like "gold" to you.

Trait: Ideas
Main Idea and Details, 729A

Grammar Daily Language Activities, 729G
Mechanics and Usage, 729H
Grammar Practice Book, 133

Quick Check Fluency, 723A

DAY 4

Listening/Speaking/Viewing

❷ Focus Question Think about the setting of *The Gold Rush Game*. From what you have read in this article, why did the boys find Wong Daido near a river?

Vocabulary

Content Vocabulary: *precious, historians, environment,* 724

Review Words, Morphology, 729D

Spelling Proofread, 729F
Phonics/Spelling Book, 161

Read "Gold!" 724–727

Student Book

Comprehension
Science: Expository

Text Feature: Time Line, 724
Practice Book, 241

Fluency Repeated Reading: Intonation/Expression, 723A

Writing

Daily Writing Suppose you are a miner who has traveled far to look for gold. Write a letter to your family about your new life in California.

Trait: Organization
Create Paragraphs, 729A

Grammar Daily Language Activities, 729G
Comparing with Adverbs, 729H
Grammar Practice Book, 134

Quick Check Vocabulary, 729D

DAY 5
Review and Assess

Listening/Speaking/Viewing

❷ Focus Question Why has gold been highly prized throughout the centuries?

Vocabulary

Assess Words, Connect to Writing, 729D

Spelling Posttest, 729F
Phonics/Spelling Book, 162

Read Self-Selected Reading, 704K
Practice Book, 243

Student Book

Comprehension
Connect and Compare, 727

Fluency Practice, 704K

Writing

Daily Writing Most miners were part of the Gold Rush because they wished they could have lots of money. What is one of your wishes? Write a poem about your wish.

Conferencing, 729B

Grammar Daily Language Activities, 729G
Comparing with Adverbs, 729H
Grammar Practice Book, 135

Weekly Assessment, 729II–729JJ

Differentiated Instruction

What do I do in small groups?

Teacher-Led Small Groups

Independent Activities

IF... students need additional instruction, practice, or extension based on your  **Quick Check** observations for the following priority skills

Phonics/Word Study
Homophones

Vocabulary Words
reference, disappointment, annoyed, circular, outstretched, conducted
Strategy: Word Parts/Suffixes

Comprehension
Strategy: Analyze Story Structure
Skill: Cause and Effect

Fluency

THEN...

Approaching / **ELL**	Preteach and Reteach Skills
On Level	Practice
Beyond	Enrich and Accelerate Learning

 **LOG ON**  **Suggested Small Group Lesson Plan**

 CD-ROM **TeacherWorks** *Plus* All-In-One Planner and Resource Center

	DAY 1	**DAY 2**
Approaching Level **Tier 2** • **Preteach/Reteach** **Tier 2 Instruction**	• Prepare to Read, 729I • Academic Language, 729I • Preteach Vocabulary, 729K	• Comprehension, 729M Analyze Story Structure/Cause and Effect **ELL** • Leveled Reader Lesson 1, 729N
On Level • **Practice**	• Vocabulary, 729S • Phonics, 729S Homophones **ELL**	• Leveled Reader Lesson 1, 729U
Beyond Level • **Extend/Accelerate** **Gifted and Talented**	• Leveled Reader Lesson 1, 729Y • Analyze Information, 729Y	• Leveled Reader Lesson 2, 729Z • Synthesize Information, 729Z
ELL • **Build English Language Proficiency** • **See ELL in other levels.**	• Prepare to Read, 729AA • Academic Language, 729AA • Preteach Vocabulary, 729BB	• Vocabulary, 729BB • Preteach Main Selection, 729CC

Small Group

Focus on Leveled Readers

Leveled Reader Library

Levels Q–T

Ⓠ
Buffalo!
by Sunita Apte
Illustrated by Courtney A. Martin
Macmillan/McGraw-Hill

Approaching

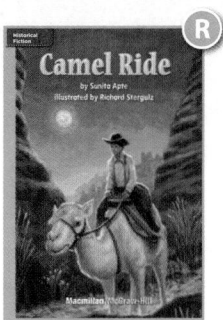
Ⓡ
Camel Ride
by Sunita Apte
Illustrated by Richard Stergulz
Macmillan/McGraw-Hill

On Level

Ⓣ
On Board!
by Sunita Apte
illustrated by John Kanzler
Macmillan/McGraw-Hill

Beyond

Ⓠ
Camel Ride
by Sunita Apte
Illustrated by Richard Stergulz
Macmillan/McGraw-Hill

ELL

Additional Leveled Readers

LOG ON ▶ **Leveled Reader Database**
www.macmillanmh.com

Search by
- Comprehension Skill
- Content Area
- Genre
- Text Feature
- Guided Reading Level
- Reading Recovery Level
- Lexile Score
- Benchmark Level

Subscription also available.

Manipulatives

Sound-Spelling WorkBoards

Sound-Spelling Cards

High-Frequency Word Cards

Visual Vocabulary Resources

DAY 3

- Phonics Maintenance, 729J
  Homophones **ELL**
- Leveled Reader Lesson 2, 729O

- Leveled Reader Lesson 2, 729V

- Phonics, 729W
  Homophones **ELL**

- Vocabulary, 729BB
- Grammar, 729EE

DAY 4

- Reteach Phonics Skill, 729J
  Homophones **ELL**
- Review Vocabulary, 729L
- Leveled Reader Lesson 3, 729P

- Fluency, 729T

- Vocabulary, 729W
- Write an Autobiography, 729W
- Fluency, 729X

- Vocabulary, 729BB
- Writing/Spelling, 729FF
- Preteach Paired Selection, 729CC
- Fluency, 729DD
- Leveled Reader, 729GG

DAY 5

- High-Frequency Words, 729L
- Fluency, 729Q
- Self-Selected Independent Reading, 729R
- Book Talk, 729P

- Self-Selected Independent Reading, 729T
- Book Talk, 729V

- Self-Selected Independent Reading, 729X
- Evaluate Information, 729X
- Book Talk, 729Z

- Vocabulary, 729BB
- Leveled Reader, 729GG
- Self-Selected Independent Reading, 729DD
- Book Talk, 729HH

Managing the Class

What do I do with the rest of my class?

- Practice Book and Reproducibles
- ELL Practice Book
- Leveled Reader Activities
- Literacy Workstations
- Online Activities

Classroom Management Tools

Weekly Contract

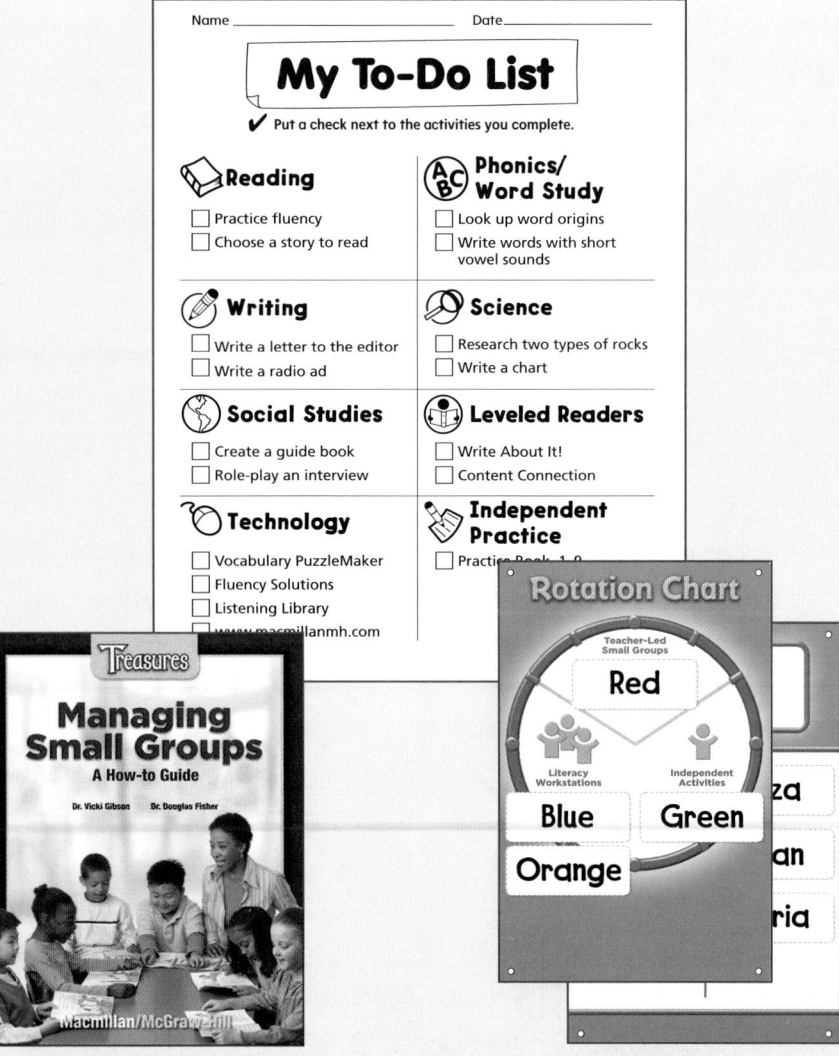

Name _____ Date _____

My To-Do List

✔ Put a check next to the activities you complete.

📖 **Reading**
- ☐ Practice fluency
- ☐ Choose a story to read

🔤 **Phonics/Word Study**
- ☐ Look up word origins
- ☐ Write words with short vowel sounds

✏️ **Writing**
- ☐ Write a letter to the editor
- ☐ Write a radio ad

🔬 **Science**
- ☐ Research two types of rocks
- ☐ Write a chart

🌍 **Social Studies**
- ☐ Create a guide book
- ☐ Role-play an interview

⚓ **Leveled Readers**
- ☐ Write About It!
- ☐ Content Connection

🖱 **Technology**
- ☐ Vocabulary PuzzleMaker
- ☐ Fluency Solutions
- ☐ Listening Library
- ☐ www.macmillanmh.com

✍ **Independent Practice**
- ☐ Practice Book, 1–9

Rotation Chart

Teacher-Led Small Groups

Red

Literacy Workstations   Independent Activities

Blue   Green

Orange

How-to Guide

Treasures

Managing Small Groups
A How-to Guide

Dr. Vicki Gibson   Dr. Douglas Fisher

Macmillan/McGraw-Hill

Rotation Chart

Digital Learning

LOG ON ▶

StudentWorks Plus

Interactive Student Book

StudentWorks Plus Online
- Summaries in Multiple Languages
- Word-by-Word Reading
- Comprehension Questions

Meet the Author/Illustrator

Rosalyn Schanzer

- As a child, Rosalyn loved reading stories about horses.
- She lives with her husband, her two children, and her dog named Jones.
- Rosalyn worked for years illustrating other people's books before finally deciding to write her own.

Other books by Rosalyn Schanzer
- Schanzer, Rosalyn. *Escaping to America: A True Story*. New York: HarperCollins, 2000.
- Schanzer, Rosalyn. *Gold Fever*. Washington, D.C.: National Geographic Society, 1999.

- Other Books by the Author or Illustrator

Leveled Practice

Treasures

Practice Book
- Phonics
- Vocabulary
- Fluency
- Comprehension
- Writing

Macmillan/McGraw-Hill

On Level

Treasures

English Language Learner Practice Book

Macmillan/McGraw-Hill

ELL

Also Available:

Approaching Reproducible

Beyond Reproducible

Independent Activities

Oral Language Activities

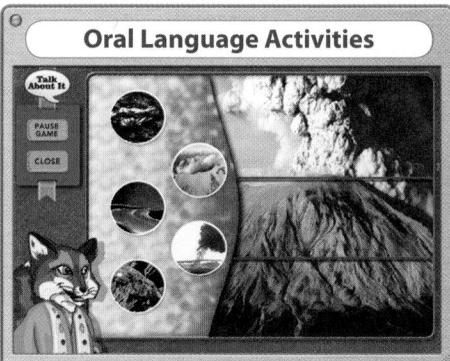

- Focus on Vocabulary and Concepts
- English Language Learner Support

Vocabulary/Spelling Activities

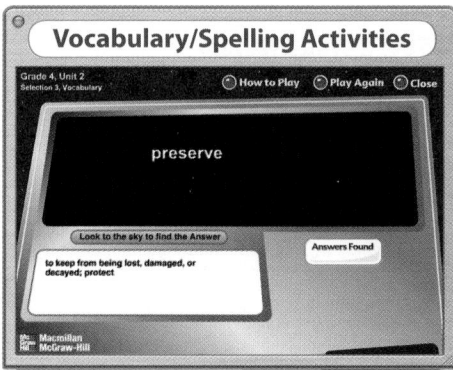

- Differentiated Lists and Activities

Leveled Reader Database

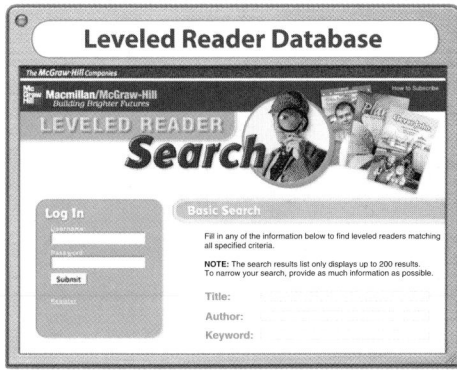

- Leveled Reader Database
- Search titles by level, skill, content area, and more

Research Toolkit

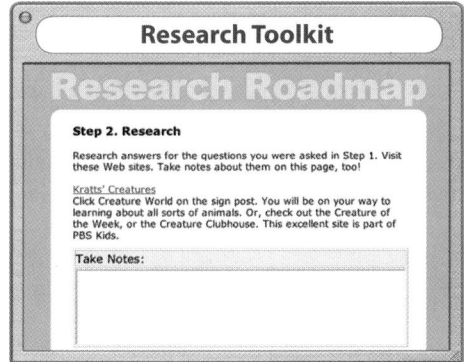

- Research Roadmap
- Research and Presentation Tools
- Theme Launcher Video
- Links to Science and Social Studies

Available on CD

LISTENING LIBRARY
Recordings of selections
- Main Selections
- Paired Selections
- Leveled Readers

VOCABULARY PUZZLEMAKER

FLUENCY SOLUTIONS
Recorded passages at two speeds for modeling and practicing fluency

Leveled Reader Activities

Approaching   **On Level**   **Beyond**   **ELL**

See inside cover of all Leveled Readers.

Literacy Workstations

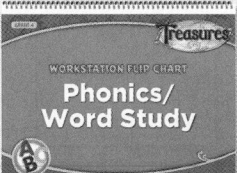

See lessons on pages 704K–704L.

Managing the Class

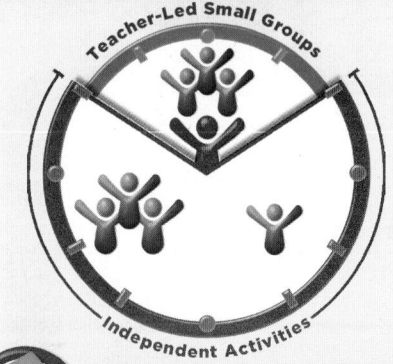

What do I do with the rest of my class?

Reading

Objectives
- Develop fluency through partner-reading
- Read independently for a sustained period of time; use **Practice Book** page 243 for Reading Strategies and Reading Log

 **Reading** FLUENCY — 20 Minutes

- Select a paragraph from the Fluency passage on page 239 of your Practice Book.
- With a partner, take turns reading the sentences with expression. Slow down if you come to unfamiliar words and break them into syllables. Pause briefly between phrases.

Extension
- Read each sentence again, paying attention to difficult words. Repeat until you can say those words without pausing.
- Listen to the Audio CD.

Things you need:
- Practice Book

Fluency Solutions Listening Library — 53

Reading Independent Reading — 20 Minutes

- Read a science fiction story. Identify details that describe cause-and-effect relationships and write them in your response journal.
- Remember to check your understanding as you read.

Extension
- Compare the science fiction story with a realistic fiction story.
- How would the story be different if it were realistic?

Things you need:
- science fiction books
- pen and paper

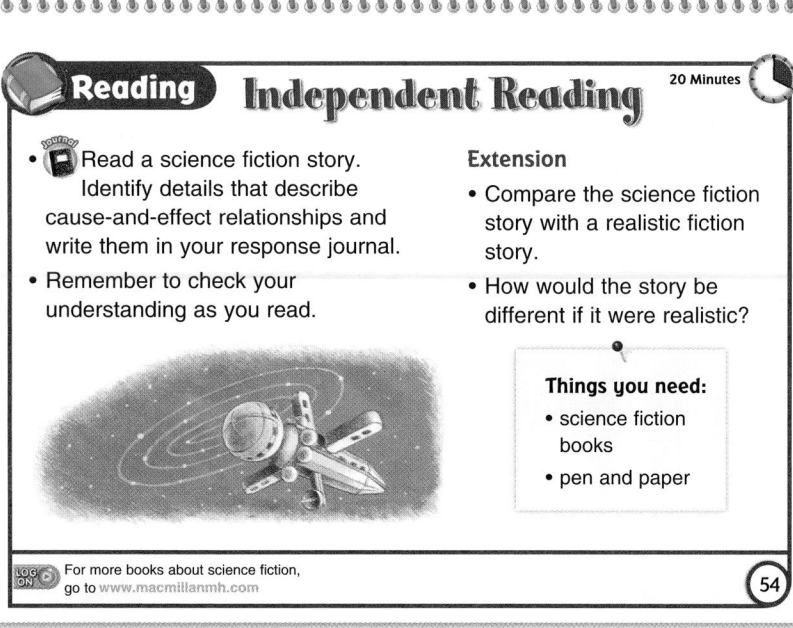

For more books about science fiction, go to www.macmillanmh.com — 54

Phonics/Word Study

Objectives
- List homophones
- Add endings to base words

Phonics/Word Study Homophones — 20 Minutes

- Create a Table or Chart Foldable®.
- Write *Homophones* at the top. Fold paper into two columns.
- List as many homophones in the two columns as you can.
- See if your partner can add more homophones to your list.

Extension
- With a partner, draw a picture for each new set of homophones.

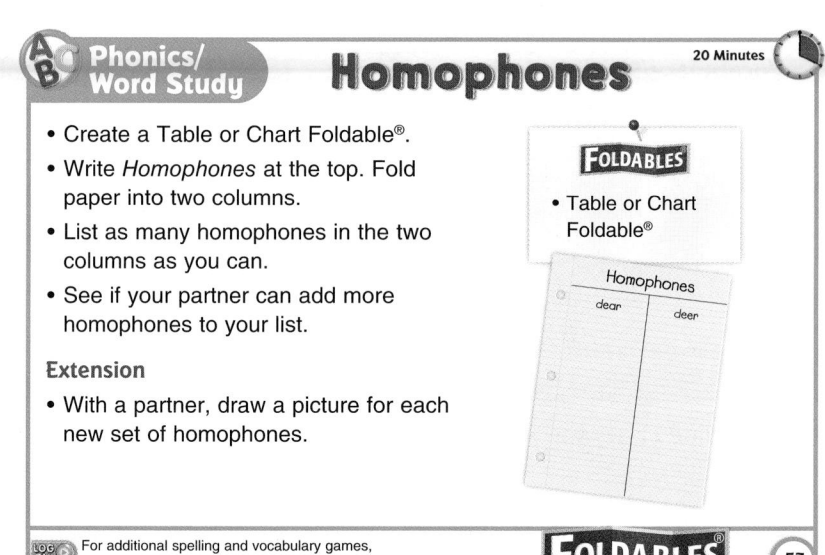
FOLDABLES
- Table or Chart Foldable®

Homophones
| dear | deer |

For additional spelling and vocabulary games, go to www.macmillanmh.com — **FOLDABLES**® — 53

Phonics/Word Study Words with -ed — 20 Minutes

- Rewrite the following sentences by adding the -ed ending to the correct words. Add or delete words if necessary.
  1. I will conduct a search for the missing ring.
  2. I will watch the ball bounce across the field.

Extension
- Write three new sentences that include only base words.
- Exchange sentences with a partner and have him or her rewrite the sentences adding -ed to the base words.

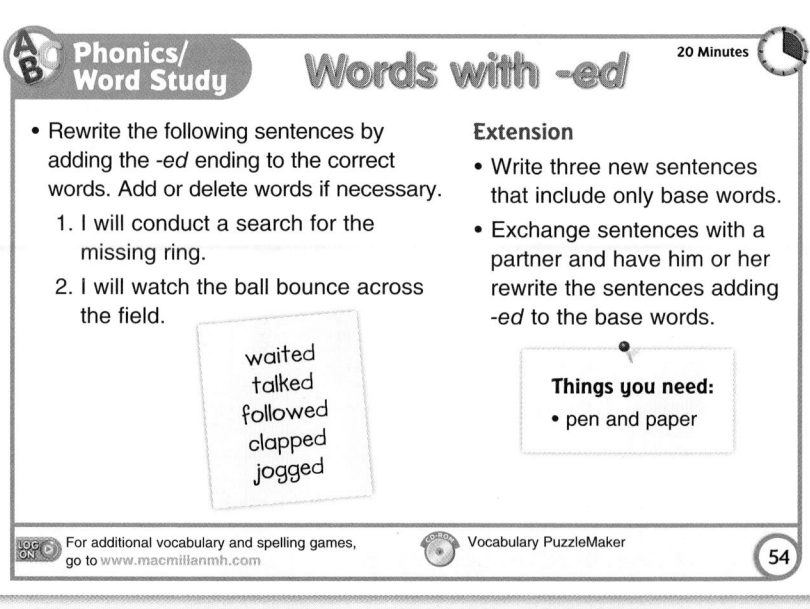
waited
talked
followed
clapped
jogged

Things you need:
- pen and paper

For additional vocabulary and spelling games, go to www.macmillanmh.com — Vocabulary PuzzleMaker — 54

Literacy Workstations

 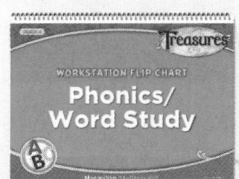  

Literacy Workstation Flip Charts

Writing

Objectives

- Write a paragraph about a real-life event
- Create illustrations and captions to support text
- Write a headline for a newspaper or magazine article

Content Literacy

Objectives

- Use an encyclopedia to research gold and its properties
- Research events during the Gold Rush

Writing — Something's Missing!   20 Minutes

- Write a paragraph telling about a time when you lost something.
- Include what you lost and the steps you took to try to find it.

Extension

- Draw small illustrations to support each step you took to find the lost item.
- Include a brief caption for each one.
- Read your paragraph with a partner.

Things you need:
- pen and paper
- colored pencils or markers

53

Science — Go for the Gold!   20 Minutes

- How does gold get from the ground to the ring on your finger? How does matter change in the process? Use an encyclopedia or the Internet to find out.
- Make a list of five things that you learned about gold.

Extension

- Make up five True/False questions based on the facts you learned. Then ask a partner to answer them.

Things you need:
- encyclopedia or online resources
- pen and paper

53

Writing — Write a Headline   20 Minutes

- Read a magazine or newspaper article about a mystery.
- Write a new headline for the article that will make readers want to learn more.

MYSTERY SOLVED

NEW CLUES HELP SOLVE MYSTERY

FAMOUS DETECTIVE JOINS THE CASE

CASE CONTINUES

Extension

- Write a continuation of the story you read. Was the mystery ever solved? Include further details in the last paragraph.

Things you need:
- magazine and newspaper articles
- pen and paper

54

Social Studies — When Did It Happen?   20 Minutes

- Use an encyclopedia to find out the key events of the California Gold Rush. Make a time line of these events.
- Tell how the state's population grew.

Extension

- Use history books or the Internet to find out what events led people to move to your state. Write a paragraph about the events.

Things you need:
- encyclopedia or history book
- pen and paper

Internet Research and Inquiry Activity
Students can find more facts at www.macmillanmh.com

54

ORAL LANGUAGE
- Build Background
- Connect to Theme
- Read Aloud

✔ **PHONICS/WORD STUDY**
- Homophones

✔ **VOCABULARY**
- Suffixes
- Teach Words

✔ **COMPREHENSION**
- Strategy: Analyze Story Structure
- Skill: Cause and Effect

SMALL GROUP

- Differentiated Instruction, pp. 729I–729HH

FINDING OUT ABOUT THE PAST

704

Oral Language

Build Background

ACCESS PRIOR KNOWLEDGE

Share the following information: The men in this photo from the past are panning for gold, or using a pan to look for gold from the bottom of a river. In 1848 gold was discovered in California. Once the news spread, many people moved out west hoping to become rich. Though we did not live then, we can use research and our imaginations to discover what it might have been like.

Write the following words on the board, and briefly define each using the **Define/Example/Ask** routine: **discover** (see or find for the first time), **research** (study to find and learn facts), **imagination** (the ability to form pictures or ideas in your mind).

FOCUS QUESTION Ask students to read "Talk About It" on **Student Book** page 705. Then have students turn to a partner and describe the photo. Ask:

- Would you like to have lived during the Gold Rush? How do you imagine your life would have been different?

- What would you do if you wanted to discover more about this time?

Talk About It

What do you think it would have been like to take part in a gold rush?

LOG ON ▶ VIEW IT

Oral Language Activities
Finding Out About the Past
www.macmillanmh.com

705

Use the Picture Prompt

BUILD WRITING FLUENCY

Ask students to write in their Writer's Notebooks about researching the past. Students should write as much as they can as well as they can for 15 minutes without stopping. Meet with individuals during Writing Conference time to provide feedback and revision assignments. Students should self-correct any errors they notice prior to the conference.

Connect to the Unit Theme

DISCUSS THE BIG IDEA

We can discover the past through research, but it takes imagination to make the past come to life. Ask students what they have read about working as a team.

- What problems did people who lived in the past have to face?

- How might working together have helped them?

USE THEME FOLDABLES

Write the **Big Idea** statement on the board. Ask students to copy it on their Unit Theme Foldables. Remind them to add details as they complete this week's readings.

Dinah Zike's
FOLDABLES®
Study Organizer

Unit Theme
Week 1
Week 2
Week 3
Week 4
Week 5

Layered Book

ELL ENGLISH LANGUAGE LEARNERS

Beginning	Intermediate	Advanced
Use Visuals Tell students about the photograph. *In 1848 people discovered gold in California. These men are looking for gold. They want to get rich.* Then ask students to tell you about the men in the photograph. Repeat correct responses in a louder and slower voice so the rest of the class may hear.	**Describe** Ask students to tell what the men in the photograph are doing. *What are they looking for? Why do they want to find gold?* Correct grammar and pronunciation in students' responses as needed.	**Discuss** Ask students to imagine what it might be like to look for gold. *What kinds of things would you do to find gold?* Elaborate on or restate students' responses.

Objectives

- Identify the characteristics of a myth
- Develop vocabulary
- Read sentences fluently, focusing on intonation/expression

Materials

- Read Aloud Anthology, pp. 105–110

Read Aloud

Read "The Golden Wish"

Read Aloud

GENRE: Literary Text/Folktale (Myth)

Discuss how **myths** are like and unlike other types of folktales, such as legends and fables. Share these key characteristics of a myth:

- Myths are stories that teach lessons or explain something in nature.

- Many myths use gods and goddesses as characters, as well as humans. Some myths also involve monsters or other imaginary creatures.

- A number of well-known myths originated in ancient Greece. These and other myths are often retold and exist in many versions.

FOCUS ON VOCABULARY

Introduce the following words, using the **Define/Example/Ask** routine. Tell students that knowing these words will help them analyze the Greek myth and the lesson that it teaches.

Vocabulary Routine

Use the routines below to discuss the meaning of each word.

Define: An **unconquerable** person is someone who cannot be defeated.
Example: The football team was unconquerable and won every game.
Ask: What animals in nature seem to be unconquerable?

Define: **Blighted** means "harmed or destroyed."
Example: The farmer's crops were blighted by the drought.
Ask: What might be blighted by a tornado?

Define: **Alchemy** is the magical ability to turn something common into something valuable.
Example: The woman tried to use alchemy to turn the rock into gold.
Ask: Why would people want to practice alchemy?

LISTENING FOR A PURPOSE

Ask students to listen carefully as you read "The Golden Wish" on **Read-Aloud Anthology** pages 105–110. Use the Think Aloud and Genre Study prompts provided.

ELL Interactive Reading Build students' oral language by engaging them in talk about the myth's basic meaning.

- Point to the picture of the man on page 105. Tell students the man is a king. Have students describe how he is feeling. (sad, upset)

- After the first paragraph, say: *The king is also a fool. What does the author mean by this? What is always on the king's mind?*

- After the second page, ask: *Why is King Midas becoming so angry?*

- At the end of the story, ask: *What are some of the effects of King Midas's golden touch on him and the other characters?*

Think/Pair/Share Use **Copying Master 3**, "I was able to picture in my mind . . . ," to prompt students to share a part of the myth they were able to visualize. Then have them turn to a partner and orally summarize the myth. Finally, have a few students share their summaries with the class.

RESPOND TO THE MYTH

Ask students the Think and Respond questions on page 110. Have students compare and contrast the characters and events in this myth with the characters and events in other myths or traditional tales they know. Then tell them to turn to a partner and summarize and explain the theme and discuss some other lessons that might be taught through mythology. Have students share their ideas.

Model Fluency

Reread the myth. Tell students that this time you want them to focus on one aspect of how you read—your **expression** and **intonation**.

Point out that, as you read, your tone of voice changes at times. This is known as intonation. For example, you stress important words or phrases, and your voice rises in tone for questions and exclamations. Model reading with good intonation and expression for students.

Think Aloud Listen as I read the last part of "The Golden Wish." Pay particular attention to how I stress certain words to give them more emphasis as I read:
Never again did he dream of gold—except in nightmares. Never again did he yearn to own gilded ornaments and mounds of yellow riches. No, no! For Midas had learned his lesson, hadn't he? Now he thought about jewels, instead.
Did you notice how I emphasized certain words using a different tone of voice? Which words were they? Now you try. Repeat each line after me, using the same expression that I use.

Establish Fluency Focus Remind students that you will be listening for this same quality in their reading throughout the week. You will help them improve their reading by adjusting their intonation to add emphasis to important words and phrases and to reflect punctuation.

Readers Theater

BUILDING LISTENING AND SPEAKING SKILLS
Distribute copies of "The Camera in the Attic," **Read-Aloud Anthology** pages 203–219. Assign parts. Have students practice throughout the unit. Have students present the play or perform a dramatic reading at the end of the unit.

ELL

Discuss Genre Review the characteristics of a myth with students. Ask: *How are myths similar to folktales? How are they different? What is "the Golden Wish" about? Who is Midas? What happened when Midas got his wish?* Repeat students' responses, correcting grammar and pronunciation as needed. Elicit details to support students' responses.

Objective
- Decode homophones

Materials
- Practice Book, p. 235
- Word-Building Cards
- Transparency 27
- Teacher's Resource Book, p. 146

ELL

Homophones Read aloud each pair of homophones slowly and point out the spelling of each word. Then identify the meaning of each word with students. Remind them that homophones sound alike but have different spellings and meanings. Use the Approaching Level lesson on page 729J for additional practice. See language transfers on pages T16–T31.

HOMEWORK — Practice Book, page 235

Homophones are words that sound the same but are spelled differently and have different meanings. The words **right** and **write** are homophones.
    right = correct   write = make marks on paper

Fill in each blank with the correct homophone.

1. **tale / tail**   He told a ___tale___ about a lion that lost its ___tail___.

2. **patience / patients**   The doctor encouraged his ___patients___ to have more ___patience___ while they waited to see him.

3. **dough / doe**   The ___doe___ and her fawns ate the ___dough___ that the baker left on the window sill.

4. **wade / weighed**   She tried to ___wade___ across the river wearing a backpack that ___weighed___ 90 pounds.

5. **bolder / boulder**   The skier grew ___bolder___ after he jumped over the ___boulder___.

6. **plain / plane**   We flew in a ___plane___ over the ___plain___ where the buffalo roamed.

7. **week / weak**   I felt ___weak___ for a ___week___.

8. **aloud / allowed**   "There are no photos ___allowed___," the guide said ___aloud___.

Approaching Reproducible, page 235
Beyond Reproducible, page 235

Word Study

Homophones

EXPLAIN/MODEL

Explain to students that certain words, such as *heir* and *air*, sound alike but have different meanings and spellings. These sets of words are called **homophones**. The way a homophone is used in a sentence can help readers figure out its meaning.

Write the homophone sets below on the board. Explain that some homophone sets have more than two words with the same pronunciations, such as *do, due,* and *dew*.

- *ate/eight*
- *tail/tale*
- *sweet/suite*
- *lessen/lesson*
- *rain/reign/rein*

Think Aloud Look at the first set of homophones I wrote. The first word is the past tense of *eat*. The second word is a number. The two words sound exactly the same, but, as you can see, they are spelled very differently. When I read these words, I can see that they are spelled differently. When I have to write these words, if I am unsure of which one to write and I know how to spell both words, I can use a dictionary to find their meanings and determine which word best fits in the context of the sentence.

PRACTICE/APPLY

Read the Word List Display **Transparency 27**. The first two lines include homophones that students will encounter in the upcoming selections. The first word in each pair appears in one of the selections. Have students underline the letters that are changed when spelling each word in the pair and then chorally read the words.

root	route	doe	dough
who's	whose	queues	cues
new	knew	rode	road
piece	peace	wait	weight
need	knead	pride	pried
thrown	throne	hour	our

Phonics Transparency 27

Read Multisyllabic Words

TRANSITION TO LONGER WORDS Write the homophone sets below on the board, or use **Transparency 27**. Have students use their knowledge of phonics patterns and word parts to decode the words.

Model how to determine the meaning of each word by pointing to it and using it in a clear context sentence. Then have students say the words and use them in their own sentences.

ceiling	sealing	weather	whether
cymbal	symbol	principle	principal
mustard	mustered	colonel	kernel
presence	presents	patients	patience
cereal	serial	aisle	I'll
isle	cents	sense	scents

Phonics Transparency 27

APPLY DECODING STRATEGY Guide students to use the Decoding Strategy to decode the following words: *berry, bury, minor, miner, capital, capitol, residence, residents*. Write each word on the board. Remind students to look for common spelling patterns in step 3 of the Decoding Strategy procedure.

Build Fluency

SPEED DRILL Distribute copies of the **Homophones Speed Drill** on **Teacher's Resource Book** page 146. Use the Speed Drill routine to help students become fluent in reading homophones.

Quick Check

Can students recognize and use homophones?

During **Small Group Instruction**

Tier **2**

If No → | Approaching Level | Reteach the skill using the lesson on p. 729J.

If Yes → | On Level | Consolidate the learning using p. 729S.

| Beyond Level | Extend the learning using p. 729W.

DAILY **Syllable Fluency**

Use **Word-Building Cards** 266–280. Display one card at a time. Have students chorally read each common syllable. Repeat at varying speeds and in random order. Have students work with partners during independent time to write as many words as they can containing each syllable.

Decoding Strategy

Decoding Strategy Chart

Step 1	Look for word parts (prefixes) at the beginning of the word.
Step 2	Look for word parts (suffixes) at the end of the word.
Step 3	In the base word, look for familiar spelling patterns. Think about the six syllable-spelling patterns you have learned.
Step 4	Sound out and blend together the word parts.
Step 5	Say the word parts fast. Adjust your pronunciation as needed. Ask yourself: "Is this a word I have heard before?" Then read the word in the sentence and ask: "Does it make sense in this sentence?"

© Macmillan/McGraw-Hill

Vocabulary

STRATEGY
WORD PARTS

Suffixes Explain that a suffix comes at the end of a word and attaches to a base word or root. Suffixes change the meanings of the words to which they are added. Knowing the meanings of suffixes can help a reader predict a word's meaning and part of speech.

Some suffixes, such as -*ar* and -*ment*, as in *circular* and *disappointment*, come from Latin. Others, such as -*ist* as in *scientist*, come from Greek. Still other suffixes have roots in other languages. For example, the suffix -*ward*, meaning "moving in a particular direction," as in *backward*, comes from German.

Explain that adding -*ar* to a noun changes it into an adjective. Model using knowledge of word parts to predict the meaning of *circular*.

Think Aloud One of the vocabulary words for this passage is *circular*. The word looks similar to *circle*, but it has an ending added to it. The spelling of the base word *circle* has been changed due to the ending being added. This ending is the suffix -*ar* which means "resembling." I can put the base word and suffix together to determine that *circular* is an adjective that means "resembling a circle."

Read "In Search of Gold"

As you read "In Search of Gold" with students, ask them to identify clues that reveal the meanings of the highlighted words. Tell students they will read these words again in *The Gold Rush Game*.

Vocabulary

reference	conducted
disappointment	annoyed
circular	outstretched

✔ Suffixes

Suffixes are word parts added to the ends of words to change their meaning. The Latin suffix
-*ar* = resembling
circular = resembling a circle

In Search of Gold

by Al Ortiz

Mr. Rodriguez's fourth-grade class was on a field trip at the Sutter Gold Mine. Larry couldn't wait to load up on gold. He even brought along some photos of gold nuggets to use as a **reference**. He didn't want to pick up "fool's gold" by mistake.

Larry's class boarded the Boss Buggy Shuttle that would take them down into the mine. Everyone had to wear a hard hat for safety. On the ride down, their guide, Ron, gave them some information about the Gold Rush.

"Many prospectors came to this area beginning in 1848," explained Ron. "A prospector is someone who searches for valuable metals like gold."

Margaret commented, "Everyone must have gotten rich!"

"Actually," said Ron, "not everyone was successful. Many left the mines filled with regret and **disappointment**. People often turned to farming or ranching to make a living instead."

706

Quick Check

Can students identify word meanings?

Tier 2

During **Small Group Instruction**

If No → **Approaching Level** Reteach the words using the Vocabulary lesson, pp. 729K–729L.

If Yes → **On Level** Consolidate the learning using p. 729S.

Gifted Talented

Beyond Level Extend the learning using p. 729W.

The underground tour lasted about an hour. Then it was time to go to the mining flumes and pan for gold. Ron handed out pans and demonstrated how to swirl them around in a **circular** motion.

"It's okay to let some of the water splash out," said Ron. "If there's any gold in your pan, it will sink to the bottom."

Larry found an open place at one of the flumes. With his arm **outstretched**, he dipped his pan below the surface of the water. Then he swished around the water. "Nothing," he said with a sigh.

Larry **conducted** the same search several times. He was beginning to get **annoyed**. Then, he noticed something at the bottom of his pan. Larry angled the pan so he could get a better look. Whatever it was, it glinted in the sunlight. Larry pulled out the photos and compared them with what was in his pan. Then he went to show Ron.

"You've found gold!" Ron exclaimed in surprise.

Everyone gathered around to see. It was just a small piece, but Larry felt like he had hit the jackpot.

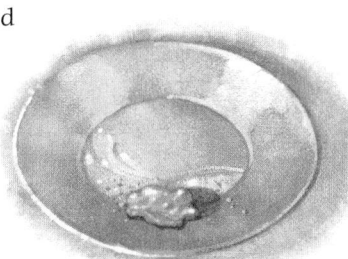

Reread for **Comprehension**

Analyze Story Structure

Cause and Effect A cause is an event or action that causes or makes something happen. An effect is what happens because of an event or action. Identifying them can help you understand how an author has organized these events. A Cause and Effect Chart can help you to sequence cause and effect relationships, and identify how these events influence future events in the plot. Reread the selection and fill in your Cause and Effect Chart to figure out what happens and why.

Cause → Effect
→
→
→
→

LOG ON ▶ **LEARN IT** Comprehension
www.macmillanmh.com

707

Preteach Vocabulary See pages 729BB and 729K to preteach the vocabulary words to **ELL** and **Approaching Level** students. Use the **Visual Vocabulary Resources** to demonstrate and discuss each word. To further reinforce concepts, have students complete page 312 in the **ELL Resource Book**.

HOMEWORK **Practice Book,** page 236

| annoyed | circular | outstretched |
| conducted | reference | disappointment |

A. Draw a line to match the vocabulary word to its meaning.

1. reference   a. reaching out
2. disappointment   b. led
3. annoyed   c. round, like a circle
4. circular   d. upset
5. outstretched   e. the feeling when something doesn't happen the way you hoped it would
6. conducted   f. a source of reliable information

B. Write a paragraph or two using as many of the vocabulary words as possible. Possible response provided.

   By the stream stood some prospectors. Looking hopeful, the man in the center held a *circular* pan in his *outstretched* hands. The others leaned over to look at something that glinted in the sun.

   "That's fool's gold again, Mike!" said one of the men, with an *annoyed* face.

   With *disappointment*, Mike emptied the pan.

Approaching Reproducible, page 236
Beyond Reproducible, page 236

Vocabulary

✔ TEACH WORDS

■ Introduce each word using the **Define/Example/Ask** routine. Model reading each word using the syllable-scoop technique.

Vocabulary Routine

Define: A **reference** is a source, or a mention of a source, of information.
Example: The reference at the end of the chapter guided him to read more books by the author.
Ask: When might you use a reference?
EXAMPLE

■ When things do not happen the way a person wants or expects, he or she faces **disappointment**. *Her disappointment at not getting an A caused Jean to work harder.* What is an antonym for *disappointment?* ANTONYM

■ If the movement or shape of something is **circular**, it is round like a circle. *The circular patterns of the fireworks were beautiful.* What else moves in or has a circular pattern? PRIOR KNOWLEDGE

■ Something that is **outstretched** is extended outward. *The horse's outstretched neck crossed the finish line first.* When might you see a person with a hand outstretched? EXAMPLE

■ A person who **conducted** an activity managed or led it. *The scientist conducted an experiment on plant growth.* Describe a task that you conducted. DESCRIPTION

■ A person who is **annoyed** is bothered to the point of being upset or angry. *We were annoyed that people had left litter on the beach.* Describe a situation when you felt annoyed. DESCRIPTION

Objectives

- Analyze story structure
- Identify cause and effect
- Use academic language: *analyze, story structure, cause, effect*

Materials

- Transparencies 5, 27a, 27b
- Practice Book, p. 237

Skills Trace

Cause and Effect

Introduce	203A–203B
Practice/ Apply	204–219; Practice Book, 75–76
Reteach/ Review	225M–225Z, 707A–707B, 708–723, 729M–729Z; Practice Book, 237–238
Assess	Weekly Tests; Units 2, 6 Tests
Maintain	251B, 333B, 737B

ELL

Academic Language
Preteach the following academic language words to ELL and Approaching Level students during Small Group time: *analyze, story structure, cause, effect*. See pages 729AA and 729I.

Reread for
Comprehension

STRATEGY
ANALYZE STORY STRUCTURE

What Is It? **Story structure** refers to the way an author organizes the events of the plot, using story elements such as character and setting, and literary devices such as flashback and foreshadowing.

Why Is It Important? Recognizing how story events are organized can help readers comprehend and summarize the story and determine the influence of the plot's main events on future events.

SKILL
CAUSE AND EFFECT

What Is It? A **cause** is an event or action that makes something happen. An **effect** is what happens as a result of an event or action. To identify cause-and-effect relationships between events, ask "What happened?" to find the effect, and "Why?" to find the cause.

Why Is It Important? Cause-and-effect relationships help make up the events in a story, and they make more sense when readers understand why things happen and what makes them happen. Recognizing cause-and-effect relationships can also help readers explain the influence of the plot's main events on future events.

Transparency 27a

Vocabulary

reference   conducted
disappointment   annoyed
circular   outstretched

Suffixes

Suffixes are word parts added to the ends of words to change their meaning. The Latin suffix *-ar* = resembling
circular = resembling a circle

In Search of Gold
by Al Ortiz

Mr. Rodriguez's fourth-grade class was on a field trip at the Sutter Gold Mine. Larry couldn't wait to load up on gold. He even brought along some photos of gold nuggets to use as a **reference**. He didn't want to pick up "fool's gold" by mistake.

Larry's class boarded the Boss Buggy Shuttle that would take them down into the mine. Everyone had to wear a hard hat for safety. On the ride down, their guide, Ron, gave them some information about the Gold Rush.

"Many prospectors came to this area beginning in 1848," explained Ron. "A prospector is someone who searches for valuable metals like gold."

Margaret commented, "Everyone must have gotten rich!"

"Actually," said Ron, "not everyone was successful. Many left the mines filled with regret and **disappointment**. People often turned to farming or ranching to make a living instead."

706

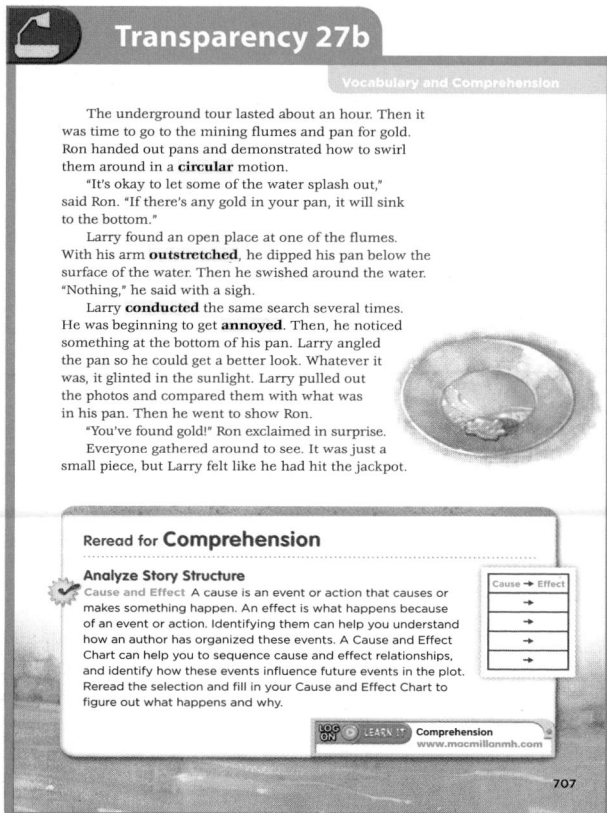

Transparency 27b

Vocabulary and Comprehension

The underground tour lasted about an hour. Then it was time to go to the mining flumes and pan for gold. Ron handed out pans and demonstrated how to swirl them around in a **circular** motion.

"It's okay to let some of the water splash out," said Ron. "If there's any gold in your pan, it will sink to the bottom."

Larry found an open place at one of the flumes. With his arm **outstretched**, he dipped his pan below the surface of the water. Then he swished around the water. "Nothing," he said with a sigh.

Larry **conducted** the same search several times. He was beginning to get **annoyed**. Then, he noticed something at the bottom of his pan. Larry angled the pan so he could get a better look. Whatever it was, it glinted in the sunlight. Larry pulled out the photos and compared them with what was in his pan. Then he went to show Ron.

"You've found gold!" Ron exclaimed in surprise.

Everyone gathered around to see. It was just a small piece, but Larry felt like he had hit the jackpot.

Reread for Comprehension

Analyze Story Structure

Cause and Effect A cause is an event or action that causes or makes something happen. An effect is what happens because of an event or action. Identifying them can help you understand how an author has organized these events. A Cause and Effect Chart can help you to sequence cause and effect relationships, and identify how these events influence future events in the plot. Reread the selection and fill in your Cause and Effect Chart to figure out what happens and why.

Cause	→	Effect
	→	
	→	
	→	
	→	

Comprehension
www.macmillanmh.com

707

Student Book pages 706–707 available on Comprehension Transparencies 27a and 27b

- **Explicit** cause-and-effect relationships in a text are signaled by clue words and phrases such as *because, so, in order to,* or *as a result.* **Implicit** cause-and-effect situations do not have signal words and must be inferred from the logical sequence of events.

- One cause can sometimes have multiple effects, and an effect can sometimes have more than one cause. In addition, in a chain cause and effect, an event causes something to happen, and this effect in turn is the cause of another effect. Recognizing these relationships can help students determine how the plot's main events can often influence future events.

MODEL

How Do I Use It? Read the first two paragraphs of "In Search of Gold" on **Student Book** page 706. Use **Transparency 5** to create a Cause and Effect Chart for the events in the story.

Think Aloud I know that authors don't always directly state what caused certain things to happen. The cause-and-effect relationship may be implicit, so I will have to use clues from the story to help me. For example, what caused Larry to want to "load up on gold"? In the story, I read that they are going to a gold mine and that gold is valuable, so Larry probably wants to strike it rich like the prospectors wanted to do in 1848. I will add this information to my Cause and Effect Chart.

GUIDED PRACTICE

Tell students to read the next two paragraphs and tell what caused people to come to the Sutter Mine in 1848. (Someone must have discovered a lot of gold there, and many people thought they could get rich, too.) Ask what the author says happened when people did not find any gold. (They looked for other ways to make a living.) Have students use their answers to add to the Cause and Effect Chart.

APPLY

Have students reread the rest of "In Search of Gold" and complete the chart. Have them explain why Larry felt like he had "hit the jackpot."

Quick Check

Can students identify cause-and-effect relationships in a story?

During **Small Group Instruction**

Tier 2

If No → | Approaching Level | Reteach the skill using the Comprehension lesson, pp. 729M–729P.

If Yes → | On Level | Consolidate the learning using pp. 729U–729V.

| Beyond Level | Extend the learning using pp. 729Y–729Z.

Transparency 5

Cause and Effect Chart

Cause	→	Effect
Larry wanted to strike it rich.	→	He could not wait to load up on gold.
Someone found a lot of gold at Sutter Mine.	→	Many people went there to try their luck.
Many people did not find gold.	→	They had to make a living in other ways.
Larry found a small piece of gold.	→	He felt like he had hit the jackpot.

Graphic Organizer Transparency

HOMEWORK   **Practice Book,** page 237

A **cause** is what makes something happen. If you can answer the question "Why did that happen?", then you know the cause. What happens as a result of the cause is the **effect**. If you can answer the question "What happened?", then you know the effect.

Read the passage below. As you read, think about causes and effects. Then answer the questions.

Sam Brannan was a merchant in San Francisco. When he heard that gold had been found near the American River, he knew just what to do. He bought up every pickax, shovel, and pan in the entire city. Then he ran through the streets of San Francisco spreading the news about the discovery of gold.

Because Brannan was the only merchant who had tools to sell, he could charge as much as he wanted. Prospectors were willing to spend $15.00 for a pan that was worth only 60 cents. It wasn't long before Brannan became one of the richest men in California—without ever panning for gold!

1. What caused Sam Brannan to buy up all the mining tools?
   He wanted to be the only merchant with tools.

2. What was the effect of Brannan's spreading the news about gold?
   Many people came to him to buy pans and shovels.

3. What caused miners to pay $15.00 for a 60-cent pan? They had no other choice. They couldn't buy pans elsewhere.

4. What was the effect of so many prospectors buying Brannan's tools?
   Brannan became very rich.

Approaching Reproducible, page 237

Beyond Reproducible, page 237

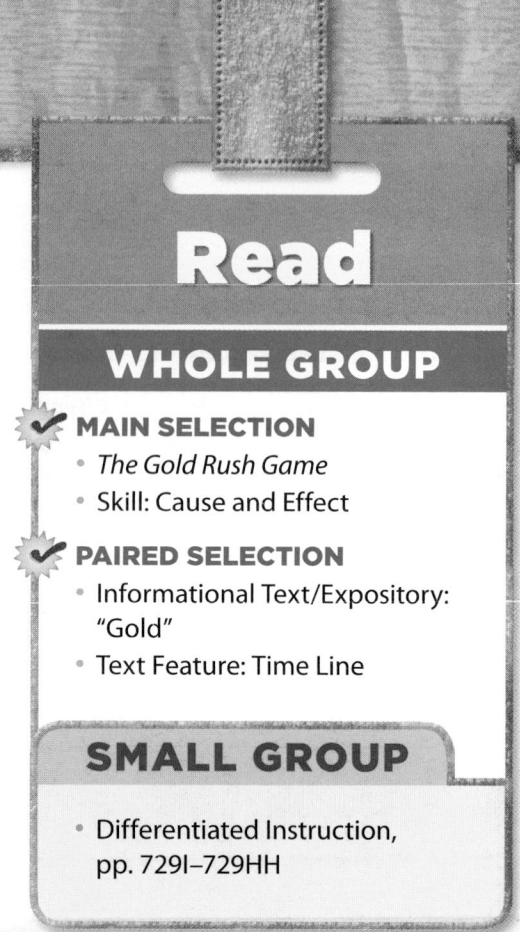

Read

WHOLE GROUP

✔ **MAIN SELECTION**
- *The Gold Rush Game*
- Skill: Cause and Effect

✔ **PAIRED SELECTION**
- Informational Text/Expository: "Gold"
- Text Feature: Time Line

SMALL GROUP

- Differentiated Instruction, pp. 729I–729HH

Main Selection

GENRE: Literary Text/Fiction

Read the definition of Science Fiction on **Student Book** page 708. As they read, students should look for elements of fantasy and the use of technology that may not exist yet. Point out time travel is common in science fiction.

 **STRATEGY**
ANALYZE STORY STRUCTURE

Remind students that story structure refers to the way an author organizes the events of the plot using literary elements such as character and setting.

 **SKILL**
CAUSE AND EFFECT

Cause-and-effect relationships make up the events of a story. Often one event or action in the plot will lead directly to another event or action. Recognizing these relationships can help readers explain the influence of the plot's main events on future events.

Comprehension

Genre

Science Fiction is a story that includes fictional events based on actual or invented scientific or technological discoveries.

Analyze Story Structure
Cause and Effect
As you read, fill in your Cause and Effect Chart.

Cause → Effect
→
→
→
→

Read to Find Out

How did Eric and Matt affect the future by going back into the past?

708

Vocabulary

Vocabulary Words Review the tested words while reading: **reference, disappointment, annoyed, circular, outstretched,** and **conducted**.

Additional Selection Words Students may be unfamiliar with these words. Pronounce the words, give student-friendly explanations as needed, and help students use previously taught vocabulary strategies: context clues, dictionary, word parts.

queues (p. 710): long braids of hair that hang down the back

ivory (p. 719): a hard, white substance that makes up the tusks of some animals, such as elephants

Internet (p. 721): a network that links computers all over the world

The Gold Rush Game

by William F. Wu

illustrated by Cornelius Van Wright and Ying-Hwa Hu

709

Preview and Predict

QUICK WRITE Tell students to read the title, preview the illustrations, think about the genre, and make predictions about the story. Students may include what they know about the Gold Rush.

Set Purposes

FOCUS QUESTION Discuss the "Read to Find Out" question on **Student Book** page 708. Remind students to look for the answer as they read and have them also set their own reading purposes.

Point out the Cause and Effect Chart in the Student Book and on **Practice Book** page 238. Explain that students will fill it in as they read.

Read *The Gold Rush Game*

Use the questions and Think Alouds to support instruction about the comprehension strategy and skill.

Practice Book, page 238

As you read *The Gold Rush Game*, fill in the Cause and Effect Chart.

Cause	→	Effect
	→	
	→	
	→	
	→	

How does the information you wrote in the Cause and Effect Chart help you to analyze the story structure of *The Gold Rush Game*?

Approaching Reproducible, page 238
Beyond Reproducible, page 238

Read the Main Selection

Preteach	Read Together	Read Independently
Have Approaching Level students and English Language Learners listen to the selection on **StudentWorks Plus**, the interactive e-Book, before reading with the class.	Use the prompts to guide comprehension and model how to complete the graphic organizer. Have students use **Think/Pair/Share** to discuss the selection.	If students can read the selection independently, have them read and complete the graphic organizer. Suggest that they use their purposes to choose their reading strategies.

LOG ON StudentWorks Plus
Interactive Student Book

Develop Comprehension

1 STRATEGY
ANALYZE STORY STRUCTURE

Teacher Think Aloud The author begins the story by introducing some characters. I can tell that Eric and Matt will be important characters because they are about to play a game that is also the title of the selection. It seems as if the author will use what happens to these characters to help **structure** the **story**. The author also states that Eric's parents are tracing their family tree, and that they bought the Gold Rush game for Eric. I think that these events might be important parts of the story structure as well. As I read, I will pay close attention to ways in which playing the game may help inform Eric about his family tree.

2 SKILL
CAUSE AND EFFECT

Why do Eric's parents buy him the Gold Rush game? (They want him to learn about his great-great-great grandfather.) Add this information to your Cause and Effect Chart.

Cause	→	Effect
Eric's parents want him to learn about their family history.	→	They buy him the Gold Rush game.

Eric Wong looked at his new game on the computer screen. "Let's play." He clicked the button to start.

1 "The Gold Rush," his friend Matt O'Brien read out loud, as he rolled his chair closer. "What's that mean? I want to see it! Come on, I'm going first."

"I'm older," said Eric. "Besides, it's my game."

2 "Be nice." Eric's mom came up behind them. "We bought the game so Eric could learn more about the Gold Rush," she said to Matt. "His dad and I are tracing our family tree. Eric's great-great-great grandfather on his dad's side came to California from China during the Gold Rush, but we don't know much about him."

"Hey, look at the game," said Eric. On the screen, he saw steep, mountain slopes covered with tall, green trees. Some men wearing broad-brimmed hats rode horses along a muddy path, leading mules with bundles on their backs. Picks and shovels were tied to the bundles. Chinese men, with long, braided queues down their backs, squatted by a rushing river.

"Who are those guys?" Matt asked. "Are they looking for gold?"

"They might be," said Eric's dad as he came into the room. He held out a small piece of paper with two Chinese characters written on it. "This is the name of our ancestor who first came to California. I don't know Chinese, but my grandfather wrote it down for me when I was growing up."

710

Monitor Comprehension

Monitor and Clarify: *Paraphrase*

Explain Tell students that they can check their understanding of what they have read by restating the main points in their own words. They should make sure they can restate important details and that they do not include their own opinions.

Discuss Ask: *Why is paraphrasing a passage a good way to make sure you understand it?* (You can properly restate a passage in your own words only if you know what it means.)

Apply Have students paraphrase the paragraph in which the author describes the Gold Rush game. (In the game, some Chinese men are riding horses in an area with mountains, trees, and a running river. These men are leading mules carrying bundles that have picks and shovels tied to them. Other men are by the river.)

Eric turned and looked. "What was his name?"

"Daido," his dad said. "I'll say it slower, 'Dye-doe.' It means 'Great Path.' That's a good name for a man who took a great adventure traveling across the Pacific Ocean to a new land. In Chinese, his family name would be given first. And so, he was called Wong Daido."

"Wong Daido," Eric repeated. "Yeah."

"Do you know how to write that?" Matt asked, looking at the name.

"No." Eric shrugged.

"We'll let you play your game," said Eric's mom. "Come on, dear." She and Eric's dad walked away.

"Look." Eric pointed to the screen. A miner wearing a broad-brimmed gray hat lifted a rock showing a button that said, "Press if you dare."

"I dare you," Matt said loudly.

"I'm doing it." **Annoyed**, Eric pressed the button.

711

Develop Comprehension

3 MONITOR AND CLARIFY: PARAPHRASE

Paraphrase what happens when Eric and Matt start playing the game. (They see a button on the screen, and Eric presses it after Matt dares him to.)

Phonics/Word Study

APPLY DECODING SKILLS While reading, point out words with the sound/spelling patterns, syllable types, and word parts students have recently learned. Help students blend these words. You may wish to focus on selection words that are homophones: *queues, miner, you're,* and *past.*

ELL ENGLISH LANGUAGE LEARNERS

Beginning	Intermediate	Advanced
Access Content Preteach story content, build language, and develop meaning using the Interactive Question-Response Guide in the **ELL Resource Book**, pages 302–309. Give ample time for students to respond. They may point or use words or short phrases to respond.	**Describe** Preteach story content, build language, and develop meaning using the Interactive Question-Response Guide in the ELL Resource Book, pages 302–309. Have students respond in complete sentences. Repeat their responses, correcting pronunciation or grammar as needed.	**Explain** Complete the Intermediate task with students. Elicit details from students for their responses.

Develop Comprehension

4 STRATEGY
WORD PARTS

What is the base word of *miner*? (*mine*) What does the verb *mine* mean? (to take minerals out of the earth) How does adding the **suffix** *-er* to the end of *mine* change the meaning? (Adding the suffix changes the word from a verb to a noun naming someone who performs that verb's action. A miner is a person who takes minerals from the earth.)

5 PROBLEM AND SOLUTION

What do Eric and Matt do on page 712 that helps them find out about Eric's family history? (They travel back in time to 1849 and start asking about Wong Daido, Eric's great-great-great grandfather.)

---

4 Suddenly Eric and Matt found themselves standing in a narrow space between two large, tall rocks by the muddy road in the mountains, with trees towering over their heads. Miners and prospectors walked and rode past. Eric's heart beat faster with excitement, but he was also a little scared.

"What happened?" Matt asked. "This is creepy. Where are we?"

Eric smelled the scent of pine trees and kicked at the mud. "I think we're really in the Gold Rush. We went back in time!"

"Did you say, back in time?" Matt stared around them in shock.

5 "Come on." Eric walked up to the mysterious miner who had lifted the rock. "Do you know a man named Wong Daido?" Eric carefully pronounced his ancestor's name, remembering to put his family name first.

The miner laughed. Then he looked closely at Eric and Matt. "You're not from around here are you?"

"No, we're not," said Eric hoping the man wouldn't ask any more questions.

"Do you know how many people are in this area? We're on the Feather River upstream from Marysville, in the western foothills of the Sierra Nevada in California. Men came to find gold. We're called the Forty-niners because so many of us have come this year."

"What year?" Matt asked, his eyes wide.

6 "1849, of course," said the miner. He frowned. "Don't you boys know what year it is? Gold was discovered in this area last year. Now, Forty-niners are coming from all over America and **7** lots of other places."

> Cause and Effect
> Why did Eric and Matt find themselves back in 1849?

712

713

Develop Comprehension

6 SKILL
CAUSE AND EFFECT

Why did Eric and Matt find themselves back in 1849? Add the answer to your Cause and Effect Chart. (Somehow, pressing the button on the computer game sent them to another time and place.) How might this main event in the plot of the story influence future events? (Now that Eric and Matt have gone back in time to the days of the Gold Rush, they may meet Eric's relative, Wong Daido.)

Cause	➡	Effect
Eric's parents want him to learn about their family history.	➡	They buy him the Gold Rush game.
Eric pushes a button on the screen.	➡	Eric and Matt end up in 1849 during the California Gold Rush.

7 GENRE: Literary Text/Fiction

What details in the story so far show that it is science fiction? (The boys travel back in time by pressing a button on a computer game. Time travel is not possible, so this use of technology is fictional.) What aspects of the plot, characters, and setting are realistic? (Though the characters from the present and the past would never meet in real life, they speak and behave like real people. The settings are also realistic because the Gold Rush actually happened.)

The Gold Rush Game **713**

Develop Comprehension

8 SUMMARIZE

Summarize the information that the prospector tells Eric and Matt on pages 712 and 714. (In 1849 men traveled long distances to come to California to prospect for gold that had been discovered there the year before. The men were called Forty-niners because they came in 1849. Marysville was a new town started by the Forty-niners that some of the men lived in while they looked for gold. Others lived in camps.)

"How do they get here?" Eric asked.

"I came overland from the eastern United States by wagon train. A good friend of mine took a ship from the east coast south around Cape Horn at the tip of South America. From China, other men come on ships across the Pacific Ocean."

"But where do they live?" Eric asked. "I don't see any houses here."

"Marysville is a new town," said the miner. "It was started by miners and prospectors. But men also live in camps, sometimes together and sometimes on their own, while they look for gold." He pointed to the river. "But the best way to **8** find a Chinese miner is to ask other Chinese miners."

714

Vocabulary

Dictionary: Multiple-Meaning Words

Explain/Model Explain that some words in this story, such as *queue, pan, current*, and *chop*, are multiple-meaning words. These are words that are spelled and pronounced the same but have different meanings that can be determined using context clues or a dictionary. Two meanings of *queue* are "a braid of hair" and "a line of waiting people." In this story, the first meaning fits best.

Think Aloud: I see the word *pan* on page 715. I know that one type of pan is used in the kitchen. Used in that sense, the word is a noun. That meaning does not fit here since *pan* is used as a verb. From context, I know it must mean a way to find and separate gold.

Practice/Apply Write *current*. List possible meanings, such as *flowing water* and *happening now*. Have students use context clues to find its meaning in the last paragraph on page 715. ("flowing water")

Matt ran down to the edge of the river, where a Chinese miner squatted by the rushing water, swirling sand in a metal pan.

Eric hurried after him. "Hey, mister, is your name Wong Daido?"

"No." The man shook his head. Then he gave Eric a little smile and pointed downstream. "You see that man? His name is Wong."

Matt ran down the bank, but this time Eric ran, too. They stopped next to Mr. Wong together, near a big tree growing right beside the river.

"Are you named Wong Daido?" Eric asked.

Mr. Wong was a little younger than the other Chinese miner. His long, braided queue swung behind him as he looked up. "I am," he said, giving both boys a big smile. "Why do you ask?"

Eric was afraid to explain he and Matt had traveled through time from the future. He was sure Mr. Wong wouldn't believe him and might chase them away, so he changed the subject. "My name's Eric, and this is my friend Matt. Have you found any gold?"

"Not today. Some days I find enough gold to buy food that will last until the next time I find gold. I filed this claim so I have the right to pan gold here. The river washes gold dust downstream, so I catch river water, mud, and sand in this pan and try to find it." He moved the pan in a **circular** motion, so that water sloshed out with some of the sand. "Gold is heavy, so it stays in the pan."

"Wow," said Matt. "And the river's so fast."

"Don't you have to get sand from the bottom of the river?" Eric asked. "It looks really deep right here!"

"It's very deep here," said Mr. Wong. "The riverbank drops steeply from the edge of the water and the current's very fast. But I can take the sand and mud right here at the edge and pan it. And the water itself carries sand, even when it looks clear. On a good day, the water brings gold to me." **9**

Develop Comprehension

9 STRATEGY
ANALYZE STORY STRUCTURE

Teacher Think Aloud The author seems to be using Eric's and Matt's trip back in time to provide information about Eric's ancestor and about the Gold Rush. I have learned that people came from many faraway places to look for gold in California. The author also reveals how the prospectors lived and how they panned for gold. We are also introduced to Wong Daido at this point in the story. What kind of character is he, based on what we read on page 715?

PARTNERS

Prompt students to apply the strategy in a Think Aloud.

Student Think Aloud Wong Daido seems friendly, because he greets Eric and Matt with a big smile. When the boys ask him if he found any gold, he patiently responds and tells them information about how gold is collected. He seems genuinely interested in answering their questions.

Develop Comprehension

10 | **SKILL**
CAUSE AND EFFECT

 What **effects** does the sudden earthquake have on the characters? Add this information to your Cause and Effect Chart. (Mr. Wong falls into the river. The boys act quickly to save him. They bend a tree branch down into the river so that Mr. Wong can be pulled out of the water.) How might this cause-and-effect situation affect future events in the story? (Because Matt and Eric saved Wong's life, he may try to repay them in some way.)

Cause	→	Effect
Eric's parents want him to learn about their family history.	→	They buy him the Gold Rush game.
Eric pushes a button on the screen.	→	Eric and Matt end up in 1849 during the California Gold Rush.
An earthquake happens suddenly.	→	Mr. Wong is knocked into the river. Eric and Matt save him.

Suddenly the ground shook. Eric and Matt thumped backward into a sitting position in the mud. Mr. Wong fell into the river with a splash.

10 "It's an earthquake!" Eric jumped up again. He had felt small earthquakes before, and this one was so quick it had ended already. When he looked up, he saw Mr. Wong in the river, desperately holding onto a tree root with both hands. The power of the river current pulled his legs downstream and he struggled to hold his head above the water. "Help me!"

Eric and Matt grabbed his arms and pulled, but the river current was too strong and Mr. Wong was too heavy for them to help.

"We have to save him," Eric called desperately to Matt. "If we don't, my family won't ever be born. And I won't be here!"

Eric saw a tree branch hanging low. "Come on! Help me pull the branch down!" He took the branch in both hands and bent his knees so his weight pulled it down. When Matt grabbed it, too, the branch lowered to Mr. Wong.

With an **outstretched** hand Mr. Wong grasped the branch.

11 "Matt, let go!" Eric and Matt released the branch and the branch slowly moved upward again, pulling Mr. Wong out of the water. He got his feet back on the river bank and let go of the branch. Mr. Wong took several moments to catch his breath. His clothes were so wet they stuck to him. "Aiee! You two saved my life. Thank you."

12

716

Text Evidence

Cause and Effect

Remind students that when they answer a question about a selection, they will often need to find evidence in the text to support their answer. Reread question 11 aloud. Ask: *What questions could you ask to help you find the information that would answer this question?* (Who is Wong Daido? Why is rescuing him from the river so important to Eric and Matt?) *Where would you look to find the information to help you answer these questions? Point to the information when you find it.* (On page 710 the author introduces Wong Daido as Eric's great-great-great grandfather.) *How does this information help you to answer the question?* (If Wong Daido had drowned in the river, none of Eric's ancestors and relatives would have been born, and he would cease to exist in the future.)

Develop Comprehension

11 | **SKILL**
CAUSE AND EFFECT

 What **effect** did saving Mr. Wong's life have on the future? (If Mr. Wong were to drown in the river, none of his descendants, including Eric, would ever have been born.)

12 **SELF-SELECTED STRATEGY USE**

What strategies have you used so far to help you understand the selection? Where did you use them? Why? How did they help?

 **RETURN TO PREDICTIONS AND PURPOSES**

Have students respond to the selection by confirming or revising their predictions and purposes for reading. Direct them to revise or write additional questions to help focus their attention as they continue to read the selection.

Cause and Effect
What effect did saving Mr. Wong's life have on the future?

717

Extra Support

Cause and Effect

If students are having difficulty, guide them through the process of identifying causes and effects. Have them reread the last three paragraphs on page 716. Ask: *What is the effect of Eric and Matt pulling the branch down?* (The branch lowers to Mr. Wong.) *What is the effect of the boys letting the branch go?* (The branch moves upward, pulling Mr. Wong out of the water.) Remind students that the effect is what happens after the cause. A cause always leads to an effect. Say: *In the sentence "His clothes were so wet they stuck to him," what is the cause and what is the effect?* (The cause is that his clothes were wet; the effect is that his clothes stuck to him.) Explain that in some cause-and-effect relationships the effect is listed first even though it happens after the cause.

Stop here if you wish to read this selection over two days.

Develop Comprehension

13 MAKE INFERENCES

Why does Eric jab Matt in the ribs? Explain using details from the story. (Before Eric jabs Matt, Mr. Wong says his dream is to find some gold and raise a family in America. After Eric jabs Matt, Eric smiles when he thinks about how Mr. Wong's dream has come true. Eric probably jabs Matt to stop him from saying anything. Eric does not want Mr. Wong to know that he is his great-great-great grandson. There would be no way to explain how they came from the future.)

"Mine too," said Eric. "You're welcome."

"I thought I was going to drown. Everything I have dreamed about would have come to an end." He paused and looked down at the ground. "I came from a poor peasant village in southern China," Mr. Wong went on. "I hope to find some gold and send for a woman I love. We'll marry here and raise a family in America—at least, I hope so."

"Hey, that's good," said Matt. "Because—"

Eric jabbed Matt with his elbow and interrupted, ". . . because it's a good idea." He smiled, knowing that Mr. Wong's dream was going to come true.

13

718

"I don't have much to offer in return for my life," said Mr. Wong. He reached into his pocket and pulled something out. "This is my chop."

Eric and Matt looked. It was a small piece of ivory, with unfamiliar shapes carved on the bottom. "What's it for?" Eric asked.

"I'll show you." Mr. Wong pushed the bottom into a smooth spot of mud next to the river. When he lifted it, three marks were in the mud. "That's my name, Wong Daido. I don't have any gold today. But I would like you to accept this as my gift. I will always remember you."

Eric took the chop. "That's very nice of you. Thanks."

"I should return to my camp and dry off," said Mr. Wong.

"I think we better go home, too," said Eric. "We enjoyed meeting you!" He carefully put the chop in his pants pocket.

"Thank you again for your help," said Mr. Wong. "Goodbye." He picked up his pan and walked away from the river toward the muddy road.

719

Develop Comprehension

14 PROBLEM AND SOLUTION

SPIRAL REVIEW

Mr. Wong wants to repay the boys for saving his life, but he did not find any gold that day. How does he solve this problem? (Mr. Wong does not have any gold and he does not have much else to offer, so he gives the boys a small piece of ivory. He calls it a chop, and the chop has his name carved on it.)

Develop Comprehension

15 **STRATEGY**

ANALYZE STORY STRUCTURE

What problem do Eric and Matt have after they travel back in time? How does the author use dialogue to resolve the problem?

Student Think Aloud The boys realize that pressing the computer button caused them to travel back in time, but there is no computer in the past. They discuss the problem and decide to try and find the two large, tall rocks where they first appeared back in time. When they find the rocks they return to the present. They conclude that passing between the rocks causes time travel.

16 **SKILL**

CAUSE AND EFFECT

What **effect** does Wong Daido's gift to Eric have on him and his family? (Eric shows his parents the chop to prove that he went back in time. The chop also has Wong Daido's name on it.) Add this information to your Cause and Effect Chart.

Cause	→	Effect
Eric's parents want him to learn about their family history.	→	They buy him the Gold Rush game.
Eric pushes a button on the screen.	→	Eric and Matt end up in 1849 during the California Gold Rush.
An earthquake happens suddenly.	→	Mr. Wong is knocked into the river. Eric and Matt save him.
Mr. Wong gives Eric his chop.	→	Eric can prove he went back in time and met Mr. Wong.

15

"How do we get back to our time?" asked Matt. "Maybe we should try to find those big rocks. But where are they?"

"Come on," Eric said to Matt. "I remember where they are. Maybe we'll find some kind of clue there that will help us get back." He led Matt back into the space between the two big rocks where they had walked out. Suddenly they were back in Eric's living room in front of the computer.

"Wow! It worked. Those rocks must be some kind of doorway into the past." Matt looked at the computer screen. "That's a great game!"

"Who's winning?" Eric's mom asked, as she and his dad came in.

"Mom! Dad!" Eric called out. "We went into the game and back in time!"

"Yeah," said Matt. "We met Eric's great-great-great grandfather!"

Eric's mom and dad laughed.

"I love the way these games build imagination while they teach history," said Eric's mom. "Isn't that nice?"

720

Listening/Speaking

Have students reread the last paragraph on page 720. Discuss how Eric's mom seems to feel about computer games. Ask: *What do you think is the author's opinion of computer games? Did Eric and Matt use the Gold Rush game for entertainment, information, or both?* Have students share their own opinions.

Gather several articles from magazines, newspapers, and the Internet that discuss the purpose for and effectiveness of computer games. Read or have students read these articles aloud to find out how the media views these games. Ask: *Does the author of this article include his or her opinions of computer games? What opinion(s) does the author share?*

Have students compare the opinions in the story and articles. Ask: *Did your opinion of computer games change after reading the story? The articles?* Have each student share his or her revised opinions, using examples, experiences, and anecdotes to clarify their points.

"Dad! He told us he filed a claim for his mine along the Feather River!"

"Well, I know from what I read in my grandfather's journal that Daido did file a claim. Let's see if we can find out if it was along the Feather River." Eric's dad moved to the computer and **conducted** an Internet search. After a while he looked up in surprise. "Wong Daido did file a claim in that area in 1849. I found a **reference** to it."

"Do you believe me now?" Eric asked.

"C'mon, Eric. Do you expect me to believe you actually went back in time?"

"No, I guess not." Eric felt a wave of **disappointment**, then suddenly reached into his pocket. "Maybe this will convince you!" He pulled out the chop. "Dad! Look at the name: Wong Daido." Smiling, Eric held it up. **16**

On the chop, a little bit of gold dust from the river glinted in the light.

721

Develop Comprehension

RETURN TO PREDICTIONS AND PURPOSES

Review students' predictions and purposes. Were they able to find which parts of the story are science and which are fiction? (Using a computer to learn about the Gold Rush is science; actually traveling back in time is fiction.)

REVIEW READING STRATEGIES

- **Analyze Story Structure** In what ways did analyzing how the author structured the story help you to understand the selection?

- **Monitor and Clarify: Paraphrase** Do you understand the strategy of paraphrasing to show your understanding of story events?

- **Decoding** What difficult words did you encounter? How did the Reading Multisyllabic Words strategy help you sound out these words?

- **Self-Selected Strategy Use** What strategies did you use to make sense of what you read? Where? How were these strategies helpful?

RESPONSE TO LITERATURE

Provide the following writing prompt: *Write about what you would do if you traveled back in time to the Gold Rush. Use details from the story to support your answer.*

As students write, remind them to

- show their understanding of the story;

- give examples from the story;

- use correct grammar and spelling.

Author and Illustrator

FILE A CLAIM WITH WILLIAM, CORNELIUS, AND YING-HWA

Have students read the biographies of the author and the illustrators. Ask:

- How does William F. Wu combine his love of history and love of writing in this selection?

- How do the different backgrounds and cultures of Cornelius Van Wright and Ying-Hwa Hu make the illustrations true to life?

- Have students research the biography of William F. Wu. Ask them to look for similarities and differences between events and characters in his life and in *The Gold Rush Game*.

WRITE ABOUT IT

Author's Craft: Dialogue Have students reread the dialogue on page 712. Discuss how the author includes dialogue to inform and to entertain. Have students write a dialogue between themselves and a friend, using both facts and opinions to inform and entertain.

Author's Purpose

Suggest that students look for clues in the story that help reveal William F. Wu's message in *The Gold Rush Game*. They should recognize that one message might be that learning about family history can be important and exciting and should use relevant supporting details from the story.

File a Claim with William, Cornelius, and Ying-Hwa

William F. Wu has liked history since he was a boy. During recess at school, he and his friend acted out famous historical events. William also enjoyed writing stories and poems. He first thought about becoming a writer when he was eight years old.

Cornelius Van Wright and Ying-Hwa Hu are a husband and wife team who have been illustrating books for over 15 years. Cornelius studied art in New York City, while Ying developed her art skills in Taiwan and Minnesota. With such different backgrounds, the two try to combine their different cultures into each illustration for this story.

LOG ON ▶ FIND OUT
Author William F. Wu
Illustrators Cornelius Van Wright and Ying-Hwa Hu
www.macmillanmh.com

✔ **Author's Purpose**
What message or lesson was the author trying to communicate to readers in this story? Use evidence and details from the story to support your answer.

722

Author's Craft

Dialogue

Authors use dialogue in a variety of ways. One effective use is to give key information informally. Example: *"What year?" Matt asked, his eyes wide. "1849, of course," said the miner.* (page 712) The author conveys important information through dialogue, rather than just stating the date in prose.

- Have students scan the selection for historical and other facts that are presented in dialogue, such as *"From China, other men come on ships across the Pacific Ocean."* (page 714)

- Readers can also analyze characters' thoughts, traits, and motivations through dialogue. Example: *"C'mon, Eric. Do you expect me to believe you actually went back in time?"* (page 721) Here the author reveals that Eric's dad is doubtful.

Comprehension Check

Summarize

To summarize *The Gold Rush Game* use the most important details from the story. Information from your Cause and Effect Chart may help you.

Cause → Effect
→
→
→
→

Think and Compare

1. What gift did Mr. Wong give to Eric and Matt? Details

2. Why did Eric press the button in the computer game? Analyze Story Structure: Cause and Effect

3. Summarize the main events in the plot that happen after Mr. Wong fell into the river. Summarize

4. Why did the author have Mr. Wong give Eric and Matt his chop? How did this action influence the events at the end of the story? Author's Purpose

5. Read "In Search of Gold" on pages 706–707. How is Larry's experience similar to that of the prospectors in *The Gold Rush Game*? How is it different? Use details from both selections to explain. Reading/Writing Across Texts

723

Make Connections

Text-to-Self Have students respond to the following question to make connections to their own lives. Use the Think Aloud to model a response. *How would you change the plot to include one of Matt's ancestors?*

Think Aloud: I might include an Irish ancestor who was also a prospector. I would have him be friends with Mr. Wong, and he would talk to Eric and Matt as well.

Text-to-World Have students respond to the following question to make connections to the world. Use the Think Aloud to model a response. *Why is it important for people to use a reference to learn about their family's history?*

Think Aloud: Using a reference is important because a reference contains facts that would allow me to find true information about my family.

Comprehension Check

SUMMARIZE

Have partners summarize *The Gold Rush Game* in their own words. Remind students to use their Cause and Effect Charts to help them.

THINK AND COMPARE
Text Evidence

1. **Details** <u>Answer stated in text</u> He gave them his chop, which was a piece of ivory with his name carved into it. LOCATE

2. **Cause and Effect** <u>Answer stated in text</u> Eric pressed the button because Matt dared him to. COMBINE

3. **Summarize** <u>Answer</u> Eric and Matt decide to save him. <u>Evidence</u> First the boys try to pull Mr. Wong out of the river, but the current is too strong. Next, they pull a tree branch down near Mr. Wong. He grabs onto the branch. When the boys let go, the branch bends up, pulling him out of the water. CONNECT

4. **Author's Purpose** <u>Answer</u> Mr. Wong gave them his chop as a thank-you gift. It proved to Eric's parents that they had traveled back in time. <u>Evidence</u> Mr. Wong told the boys that he wanted them to have his chop in return for saving his life. Later, Eric showed it to his parents to show that he met Mr. Wong. ANALYZE

5. **Text-to-Text** Larry went looking for gold using the same technique that the prospectors used in *The Gold Rush Game*. While those prospectors looked for gold every day, Larry and his class were only on a one-day tour. COMPARE TEXT

Objectives
- Read fluently with good intonation and expression
- 113–133 WCPM

Materials
- Transparency 27
- Practice Book, p. 239
- Fluency Solutions Audio CD

ELL

Develop Fluency Help students understand the overall meaning of the passage before focusing on fluency work. Read through the passage slowly first, using gestures to convey meaning. The second time through, echo-read with students. The third time through, read at a quicker pace.

Practice Book, page 239

As I read, I will pay attention to my intonation and expression.

	In the early 1800s, the United States needed room to grow.
10	Most people lived in the East. The cities were crowded. New land
22	was expensive. Young families couldn't afford to buy farms.
31	Then the United States government purchased land from
39	France. The government also acquired land from Mexico. Soon the
49	country stretched all the way to the Pacific Ocean. People looked
60	to the setting sun with outstretched arms and said, "Go west!"
71	Settlers rode in wagons or on horses. They followed long, dusty
82	trails across hot plains for thousands of miles. There was no shelter.
94	People slept in tents on the ground. They had to watch out for wild
108	animals like wolves and snakes. The trip west could take months.
119	Then a railroad was built that stretched from the East Coast
130	almost to the West Coast. The railroad made travel faster. More
141	people poured into the new lands. The settlers quickly built small
152	towns where the farming, fishing, and mining were good. 161

Comprehension Check Possible responses provided.
1. What was life like in the East in the 1800s? **Main Idea and Details**
   The cities were crowded and land was expensive.

2. What enabled people to move west? **Cause and Effect** They bought land from France and acquired more land from Mexico.

	Words Read	−	Number of Errors	=	Words Correct Score
First Read		−		=	
Second Read		−		=	

Approaching Reproducible, page 239

Beyond Reproducible, page 239

Fluency

Repeated Reading: Intonation/Expression

EXPLAIN/MODEL Explain that part of reading with expression is intonation, including stressing important words. Model reading **Transparency 27** with good expression. Be sure to group words in phrases and to pause for punctuation. Explain that the text has been marked with slashes that indicate pauses and stops. A single slash indicates a pause, usually between phrases. A double slash indicates a stop, usually between sentences. Point out that you will vary your expression to express the characters' feelings shown by the dialogue.

 Transparency 27

> Suddenly Eric and Matt found themselves standing in a narrow space between two large,/ tall rocks by the muddy road in the mountains,/ with trees towering over their heads.// Miners and prospectors walked and rode past.// Eric's heart beat faster with excitement,/ but he was also a little scared.//
>
> "What happened?"/ Matt asked./ "This is creepy.// Where are we?"//
>
> Eric smelled the scent of pine trees and kicked at the mud.// "I think we're really in the Gold Rush.// We went back in time!"//

Fluency (from *The Gold Rush Game*, p. 712)

PRACTICE/APPLY Reread the first two sentences with students. Then divide them into two groups, and have groups alternate reading sentences with good expression. Remind students to pay attention to the meaning of the text as they read.

 DAILY FLUENCY Students will practice fluency using **Practice Book** page 239 or the **Fluency Solutions Audio CD**. The passage is recorded at a slow practice speed and a faster fluent speed.

Quick Check

Can students read fluently with good expression?

During **Small Group Instruction**

If No → **Approaching Level** Use the Fluency lesson and model, p. 729Q.
If Yes → **On Level** See Fluency, p. 729T.
          Beyond Level See Fluency, p. 729X.

Comprehension

REVIEW SKILL
PROBLEM AND SOLUTION

EXPLAIN/MODEL

Point out that the plot of most stories includes one or more problems that the characters need to solve.

- The **problem** is what the main characters want to do or change, or need to find out. The events in the story result from the characters' attempts to solve that problem.

- The **solution** is the way in which the main characters fix, or solve, the problem. The main solution often comes near the end of a story; however, characters do not always solve their problems.

- Recognizing the problems and solutions in a story can help readers identify and keep track of story events. Readers can also see how certain events can influence characters' actions and future events.

Discuss the main problem of "In Search of Gold." Model by reading the first paragraph and pointing out that Larry is the main character and the problem is that he wants to find gold. Assist students in finding the solution by asking them if Larry found gold by the end of the story. Have them reread the last two paragraphs if necessary.

PRACTICE/APPLY

Have students work with partners to find problems and solutions in *The Gold Rush Game*. Remind partners to discuss how each problem influences later events in the story.

- On page 710, what problem do Eric's parents face? (They are making a family tree but do not know much about Eric's great-great-great grandfather.) Does the author provide a solution right away? Explain. (No, the problem is not solved until the end of the story, when the characters work together to find out more about Eric's great-great-great grandfather.)

- On page 716, what problem does Mr. Wong face? (He has fallen into the river because of an earthquake.) What problem does Eric face? (If he and Matt do not save Mr. Wong, Eric's family will never exist.) How do they solve their problems? (Eric and Matt save Mr. Wong's life by using a branch to pull him out of the river.)

- Which is the main problem of the story? Explain. (Eric's family doesn't know about his great-great-great grandfather. It affects later events.)

PRACTICE BOOK See **Practice Book** page 240 for Paraphrasing Independent Reading.

Objective

- Identify problem and solution

Skills Trace

Problem and Solution

Introduce	573A–573B
Practice/ Apply	574–591; Practice Book, 192–193
Reteach/ Review	597M–597Z, 677A–677B, 678–697, 703M–703Z; Practice Book, 228–229
Assess	Weekly Tests; Units 5, 6 Tests
Maintain	723B

Paired Selection

GENRE: Informational Text/Expository

Have students read the bookmark on **Student Book** page 724. Explain that expository writing gives information about something.

Remind students that an expository article

- provides facts and details about a specific event, place, person, or thing;

- sometimes contains photographs or illustrates information in other ways, such as through charts or time lines;

- may have headings to help organize the information.

Text Feature: Time Line

EXPLAIN Point out the **time line** on page 726.

Tell students that a time line is a record of historical events in the order in which they occurred. This time line shows important events in the history of gold.

- A time line highlights key events that happen over a certain time.

- A time line may cover either a short or long period of time.

- A time line may be presented horizontally or vertically. It may also be illustrated.

Have students explain how the time line on page 726 is organized. (horizontally, from left to right) Discuss why there are not events listed for every year. (The time line only shows the most important events.)

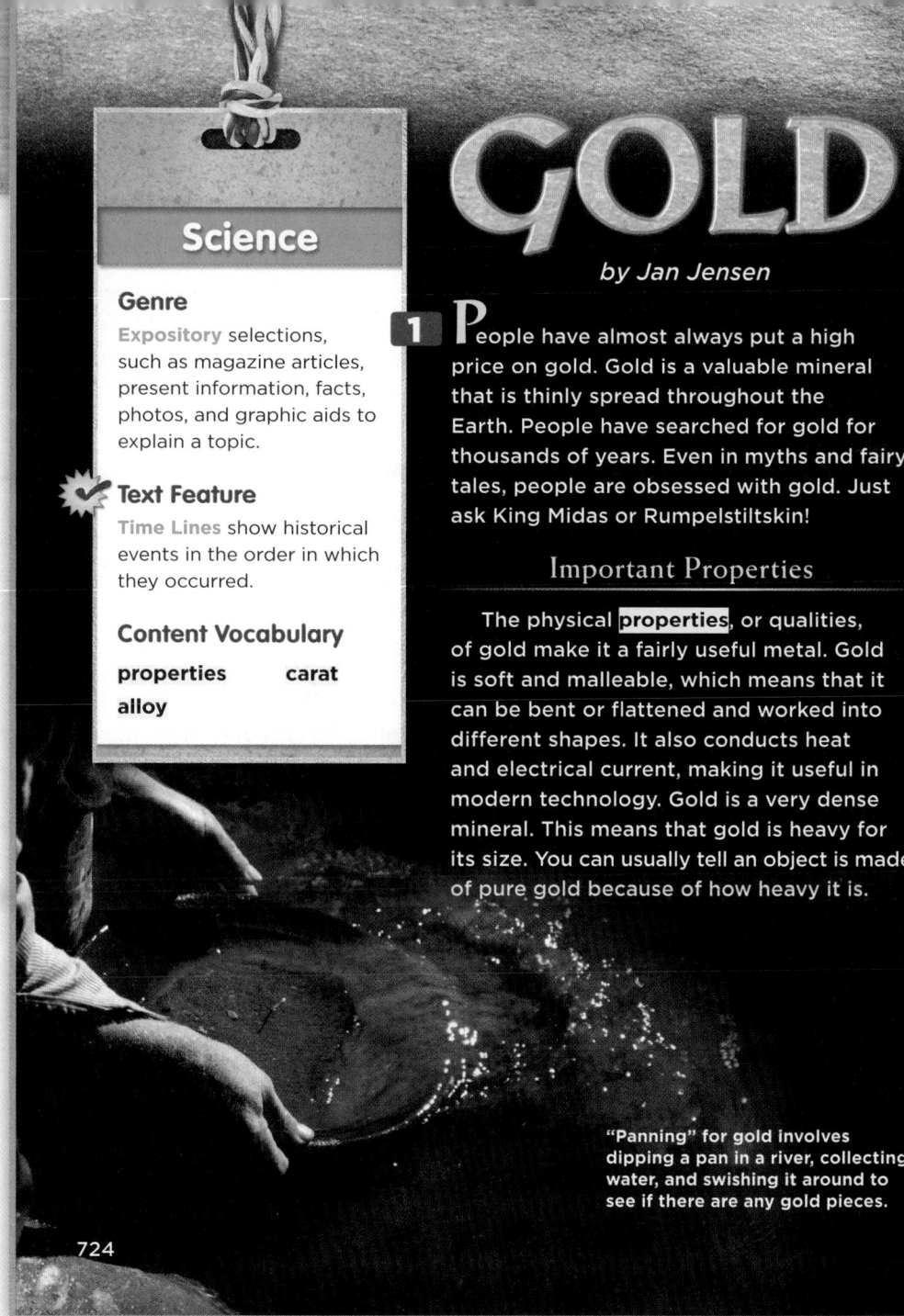

Science

Genre

Expository selections, such as magazine articles, present information, facts, photos, and graphic aids to explain a topic.

Text Feature

Time Lines show historical events in the order in which they occurred.

Content Vocabulary

properties   carat

alloy

GOLD
by Jan Jensen

1 People have almost always put a high price on gold. Gold is a valuable mineral that is thinly spread throughout the Earth. People have searched for gold for thousands of years. Even in myths and fairy tales, people are obsessed with gold. Just ask King Midas or Rumpelstiltskin!

Important Properties

The physical **properties**, or qualities, of gold make it a fairly useful metal. Gold is soft and malleable, which means that it can be bent or flattened and worked into different shapes. It also conducts heat and electrical current, making it useful in modern technology. Gold is a very dense mineral. This means that gold is heavy for its size. You can usually tell an object is made of pure gold because of how heavy it is.

"Panning" for gold involves dipping a pan in a river, collecting water, and swishing it around to see if there are any gold pieces.

724

Content Vocabulary

Explain the words using the **Define/Example/Ask** routine. Definitions are provided for this activity.

- **Properties** are distinctive features of something. What are the properties of water?

- An **alloy** is a mixture of two or more metals. Why might someone mix an expensive metal with a less expensive metal?

- A **carat** is a unit of measurement for gold. If pure gold is 24 carats, would a ring made of 12 carats be worth more or less than one made of 24 carats?

Gold can be measured using different types of instruments. This gold is being measured using a scale.

A Rare Metal

Perhaps gold's most important property is its rarity. There just isn't much of it around, which is why it is so valuable. Kings and other leaders would often keep most of the gold for themselves. Some of them also believed that gold had magical properties. When they wore crowns and necklaces made of gold, they certainly drew attention wherever they went!

Using Gold

Today, gold is most commonly used as part of an alloy. This means that it is mixed with other metals to make a little bit go a long way. This process can also change the properties of the gold. When mixed with silver or copper, the gold becomes harder. This makes it less likely to get scratched or dented.

GOLDEN FACTS

- If you filled a two-liter bottle with gold, it would weigh over 85 pounds!

- One ounce of gold can be stretched into a thin wire that from end to end would cover 50 miles.

The word *gold* comes from an Old English word, *gelo*, which means *yellow*.

725

Connect to Content

Remind students that gold is often found in hard nuggets. Have students research how gold is transformed from nuggets into jewelry, including how gold is heated and cooled to change from a solid to a liquid and back to a solid. They may compile their research in a flowchart or a report.

Paired Selection

Read "Gold"

As students read, remind them to apply what they have learned about reading time lines. Also have them identify clues to the meanings of highlighted words and set their own purposes for reading.

1 **GENRE:** Informational Text/Expository

Look at the images on the first two pages and then read the first two paragraphs of the selection. How can you tell the selection is **expository**? (It includes photographs and headings; the first two paragraphs contain facts about gold.)

2 **CAUSE AND EFFECT**

Why did kings and other leaders keep gold for themselves? (Gold is rare, which makes it valuable. People also thought that gold had magical powers. Kings and other important people kept the gold for themselves and used it to make crowns and necklaces that others would admire.)

Use the Interactive Question-Response Guide in the **ELL Resource Book**, pages 310–311, to help students gain access to the paired selection content.

Paired Selection

 **3 MAKE INFERENCES**

Why might someone buy something that is gold-plated? (Gold-plated items are more affordable than solid gold. Gold is very valuable, so sometimes another metal is used and then coated with gold.)

 **4 TEXT FEATURE: TIME LINE**

Look at the time line on page 726. What is the purpose of this time line? (The purpose is to show in sequential order the important events in the history of gold.)

 **5 TEXT FEATURE: TIME LINE**

The time line shows events from 4,000 B.C. to when? (1900) What happened in 1492? (Christopher Columbus came to the Americas looking for gold.)

3 This gold bracelet is 24 carats. It was made in the 1800s in India.

How Many Carats

A **carat** is a unit of measurement that tells how much actual gold is in an alloy. Pure gold is 24 carats. If you buy a ring that is 12 carat gold, half of it might be another metal, such as nickel or platinum. If something is described as gold-plated, there is only a thin layer of gold on the outside. The rest of the item might be made of a heavy metal such as lead to give it the weight and heft of gold.

Golden Moments in History

4
5 **Reading a Time Line**
This time line shows some important events in the history of gold.

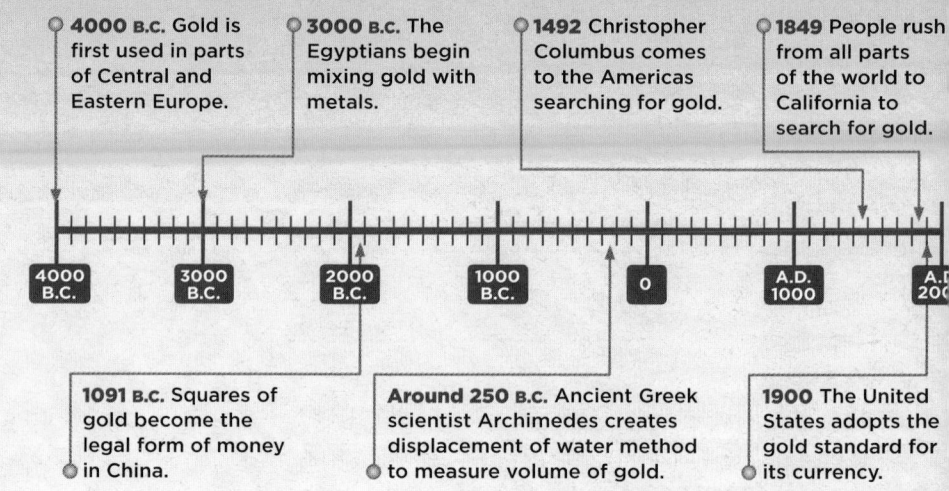

4000 B.C. Gold is first used in parts of Central and Eastern Europe.

3000 B.C. The Egyptians begin mixing gold with metals.

1492 Christopher Columbus comes to the Americas searching for gold.

1849 People rush from all parts of the world to California to search for gold.

1091 B.C. Squares of gold become the legal form of money in China.

Around 250 B.C. Ancient Greek scientist Archimedes creates displacement of water method to measure volume of gold.

1900 The United States adopts the gold standard for its currency.

726

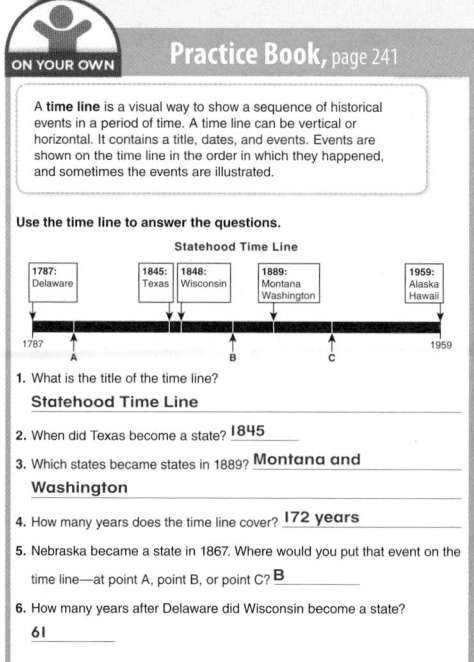

ON YOUR OWN

Practice Book, page 241

A **time line** is a visual way to show a sequence of historical events in a period of time. A time line can be vertical or horizontal. It contains a title, dates, and events. Events are shown on the time line in the order in which they happened, and sometimes the events are illustrated.

Use the time line to answer the questions.

Statehood Time Line

| 1787: Delaware | 1845: Texas | 1848: Wisconsin | 1889: Montana Washington | 1959: Alaska Hawaii |

1787   A   B   C   1959

1. What is the title of the time line?
   Statehood Time Line
2. When did Texas become a state? **1845**
3. Which states became states in 1889? **Montana and Washington**
4. How many years does the time line cover? **172 years**
5. Nebraska became a state in 1867. Where would you put that event on the time line—at point A, point B, or point C? **B**
6. How many years after Delaware did Wisconsin become a state?
   61

ELL

Content Words Clarify the meaning of the content vocabulary using synonyms or context clues. To describe the definition of *properties*, have students read the second paragraph on page 724 and identify words that describe properties, such as *qualities, soft, can be bent.* Then have students restate the definition of *properties.* Correct students' responses for meaning as needed. Repeat the process for *carat* and *alloy.*

Approaching Reproducible, page 241
Beyond Reproducible, page 241

Rich Prospects

Even today, some people hope to "strike it rich" by finding gold. Though it exists as a hot fluid deep inside the Earth, it most often appears on the surface as flakes or small nuggets in streams and rivers. Because of its weight, gold can be separated from other rocks and minerals using a simple pan. Water washes away the lighter elements, leaving gold behind.

It may take a long time to find a little bit of gold, but with the price of gold still high around the world, it can be well worth the effort!

Gold bars back up the world's currency.

Connect and Compare

1. Look at the time line. What is the next event after the Egyptians began mixing gold with metals? **Using a Time Line**

2. What properties does gold have that makes it useful? **Apply**

3. Think about the setting of *The Gold Rush Game*. From what you have read in this article, why did the boys find Wong Daido near a river? **Reading/Writing Across Texts**

Science Activity

Choose another metal, such as silver or copper, and use reference sources to research its history. Write a brief report about the metal and include a time line.

LOG ON ▶ FIND OUT **Science** Gold
www.macmillanmh.com

Paired Selection

Connect and Compare

1. Squares of gold are used as money in China. **USING A TIME LINE**

2. Gold is malleable, so it can be formed into many different shapes. It conducts heat and electricity. It can be mixed with other metals to make it harder. **APPLY**

3. **FOCUS QUESTION** The boys found Wong Daido near a river because he was looking for gold. Gold often appears as small nuggets in rivers.

   READING/WRITING ACROSS TEXTS

Science Activity

As needed, help students to research the information. Remind students that they can add illustrations to their time lines. Have them present their findings to the class.

RESEARCH AND INQUIRY

Write a Research Report

Remind students that gold melts when heated.

Have students research what happens to the physical properties of gold when it is heated. Why do people melt gold? At what temperature does gold melt? Which physical properties change when gold moves from a solid to a liquid form?

When students have completed their research, have them write a research report and share it with the class.

WRITING WORKSHOP

- Developing Expository Writing
- Trait: Ideas
- Main Idea and Details

Professional Development
GRADES 3–6

Writing Guide

Macmillan/McGraw-Hill

UNIT 6
Developing Expository Writing

Trait: Ideas
Strong Paragraphs: Main Idea and Details

TEACH/MODEL Remind students that supporting details give information about a topic. Explain that a research report is about one topic but it has a lot of information about that topic. The writer organizes the information into paragraphs. Each paragraph has one **main idea** that is often stated in a **topic sentence**. The other sentences in the paragraph are supporting details that give information about the main idea of that paragraph.

Tell students that writers of research reports use reliable sources to find information about, or supporting details for, their main ideas. Explain that good writers create **strong paragraphs** by paraphrasing, or using their own words, to tell about what they've learned from different sources. Write this paragraph, and read it aloud:

> Cheetahs are fast runners. In fact, they are the fastest land animals. Cheetahs live on the savannahs in Africa. Cheetahs can run up to 70 miles per hour. They can speed up from 0 mph to 60 mph in 3 seconds! Cheetahs have smaller heads and smaller ears than other big cats do.

Explain that this paragraph is from a research report about cheetahs. Point out the main idea of this paragraph: *Cheetahs are fast runners.* Tell students that even though all the details give information about the topic of cheetahs, only three details support the main idea that cheetahs are fast runners. As you reread each detail, ask if it supports the main idea. Cross out the two sentences that do not support the main idea (sentences 3 and 6). Then reread the paragraph. Ask how each supporting detail supports the main idea.

Teacher Write Aloud

PRACTICE/APPLY Further explore with students the use of main ideas and details. Remind them that details tell about the main idea of a paragraph and that good writers do not include details that do not support the main idea. Write the sentences below on the board. Then complete the Teacher Think Aloud.

> Topic: cheetahs
>
> Main idea: Cheetahs have a unique appearance.
>
> Details:
>
> A cheetah has short, tan fur with black spots.
>
> A cheetah does not roar but does purr.
>
> There are no spots on a cheetah's stomach fur.
>
> A cheetah hunts in the early morning or evening.
>
> A cheetah has black marks that go from the corners of its eyes down the sides of its nose.

Teacher Think Aloud The previous paragraph about cheetahs told how fast they are. That was its main idea. Now I will write another paragraph about cheetahs. The main idea of this paragraph is *Cheetahs have a unique appearance.* Let me read the first detail: *A cheetah has short, tan fur with black spots.* Does that tell what a cheetah looks like? Yes, it does. It is a supporting detail, so I will include it in the paragraph.

Complete the Think Aloud by asking if each detail is a supporting detail. Then write the following paragraph. Stop to discuss how each detail supports the main idea.

> Cheetahs have a unique appearance. A cheetah has short, tan fur with black spots. There are no spots on a cheetah's stomach fur. A cheetah has black marks that go from the corners of its eyes down the sides of its nose. If you see a picture of a big cat with those spots and marks, you know it is a cheetah.

 **Draft** Display the writing prompt on **Writing Transparency 87**. Remind students to use supporting details to give information about the main idea of their paragraph. Circulate and provide Over-the-Shoulder Conferences as students work.

Daily Journal Prompts

Focus on Main Ideas and Details

Use these and other prompts for independent daily journal writing.

- Write about a moment when you explored something new.

- Write about your favorite animal.

- Write about something you learned at school last week.

- Write about an activity that you love to do.

 Transparency 87

What is something that you know a lot about? Write a paragraph to tell what you know about that thing.

Write

Reading and Writing Connection

Trait: Ideas

MAIN IDEA AND DETAILS

Remind students that supporting details give information about the main idea of a paragraph. Good writers use supporting details that help readers understand the main idea, which is often stated in a topic sentence. Supporting details can be examples, facts, or explanations.

Read the Passage

Use the example from *Gold* to show how the author uses supporting details to help readers better understand the main idea.

- Have students read the bookmark. Explain that a paragraph's main idea is what the paragraph is about and that supporting details give more information about the main idea.

  Ask: *When have you seen or touched something gold?*

- Then have students chorally read the excerpt from *Gold*. Direct their attention to the callout. Have students identify and discuss the main idea and its supporting details.

  Ask: *Which supporting detail did you find most interesting? Why?*

Reading and Writing Connection

Writing

✓ **Trait: Ideas**
Good writers choose details that support their **main idea**.

Read the passage below. Notice how the author Jan Jensen uses details that support a main idea.

An excerpt from Gold

The author writes a paragraph about the qualities of gold. The supporting details give information about the main idea.

The physical properties, or qualities, of gold make it a fairly useful metal. Gold is soft and malleable, which means that it can be bent or flattened and worked into different shapes. It also conducts heat and electrical current, making it useful in modern technology. Gold is a very dense mineral. This means that gold is heavy for its size. You can usually tell an object is made of pure gold because of how heavy it is.

728

Respond to the Selection

Have students write a response to the selection.

✓ **Engagement** Help students deepen their connection to the text and discover their own perspective.
- *Focus on something that you put a high price on.*

✓ **Response** Help students explore more deeply their reactions to particular passages in the reading.
- *Focus on the paragraph that interested you most. Use text evidence in your writing.*

✓ **Literary Analysis** Help students deepen their connection to the text and discover their own perspective.
- *Focus on a place where the supporting details helped you understand a main idea. Use text evidence in your writing.*

Read and Find

Read Eva's writing below. How does she use a main idea and supporting details? Use the checklist below to help you.

Rivers
by Eva C.

Throughout history, people have used rivers in many ways. People get water and food from rivers. They use rivers to travel from one place to another. Loggers float logs down rivers. Many people use rivers for recreation. They kayak, canoe, and fish in rivers. In the 1800s, people looked for gold in rivers like the Feather River in California.

Read about how people use rivers.

Writer's Checklist

✓ Does the writing have a main idea?

✓ Does the author include details that give information about the main idea?

☑ Do all the details support the **main idea**?

729

Read the Student Model

Have students chorally read the student model at the top of **Student Book** page 729. Discuss how this student writer used supporting details to give information about a main idea. Use the Writer's Checklist.

Journal Prompt

Draft Write the following prompt on the board. Have students write a response to the prompt.

What is your favorite way to travel—by foot, by bike, by horseback, or by some other way? Write a paragraph about how you like to travel.

Tell students that you will be reading and commenting on their writing during Writing Conference time.

Model how to use the Writer's Checklist so students can write and revise their work. Then ask:

■ *What method of traveling did you choose?*

■ *What is the main idea of your paragraph? What facts, details, and explanations did you include? Will readers be able to use these supporting details to understand your main idea? If not, what could you add?*

Write

Objectives

- Write supporting details for a main idea
- Create paragraphs

Materials

- Writer's Notebooks
- Teacher's Resource Book, p. 204

ELL

Expand Vocabulary Write these words on the board: *roots, trunk, bark, leaves, branches, twigs.* Say each word, and have students repeat it. Then draw a tree on the board. Have students label the parts of the tree. Ask: *Which part anchors the tree, or keeps it from falling over? What else do roots do for the tree?*

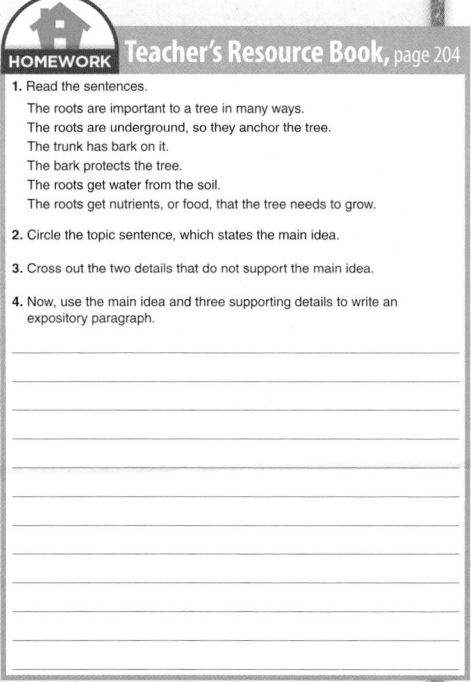

HOMEWORK Teacher's Resource Book, page 204

1. Read the sentences.
   The roots are important to a tree in many ways.
   The roots are underground, so they anchor the tree.
   The trunk has bark on it.
   The bark protects the tree.
   The roots get water from the soil.
   The roots get nutrients, or food, that the tree needs to grow.

2. Circle the topic sentence, which states the main idea.

3. Cross out the two details that do not support the main idea.

4. Now, use the main idea and three supporting details to write an expository paragraph.

Minilessons

Minilesson 1 Ideas/Main Idea and Details

TEACH/MODEL

Remind students that they have been working on main idea and details. Today they will practice that again. Have students use **Teacher's Resource Book** page 204. Ask students to read the first item.

PRACTICE/APPLY

Have students work independently to follow the rest of the directions. When they are finished, ask students to share their work during Sharing Circle. Have students tell how each supporting detail supports the main idea in the topic sentence.

Minilesson 2 Organization/Create Paragraphs

TEACH/MODEL

Remind students that a paragraph has a main idea and supporting details. Explain that when writers organize their writing, they begin a new paragraph each time they write about a new main idea. Write the following paragraph on the board:

> Trees are important to squirrels. Squirrels get food from trees. They store their food in trees for the winter. Trees protect squirrels from larger predators. Tree squirrels, like the gray squirrel, make their homes in trees. Many animals make their homes in trees. Birds build nests in the branches of trees. Monkeys and chimpanzees live in trees. Some snakes also live in trees. The snakes find food in their tree homes.

Read the paragraph. Point out that it has two main ideas, each of which is stated in a topic sentence: *Trees are important to squirrels* and *Many animals make their homes in trees.* This paragraph should be broken into two separate paragraphs, one for each main idea.

PRACTICE/APPLY

In their Writer's Notebooks, have students rewrite the paragraph as two paragraphs. Remind them to include one main idea and its supporting details in each paragraph.

Conferencing Routine

Dynamic Feedback System

 Step 1 Read and appreciate the writing.

 Step 2 Notice how the student uses the targeted skill. (e.g., main idea and details: Ask: *Does each paragraph have a main idea stated in a topic sentence and supporting details?*)

 Step 3 Write comments that show how the writing has an impact on you. Direct your comments to those places in the piece where the student has used the targeted skill.

 Step 4 Meet with and give the student a revision assignment.

Write Effective Comments

Ideas At least one of your comments should highlight the way the student uses **main idea and details**. Here are sample comments.

- Each of your paragraphs has a main idea. That helps me understand your writing.

- I'm confused here. How does this detail support the main idea?

- These are great supporting details! They give facts and examples to help me understand the main idea.

Revision Assignments

Ideas Here are some examples of effective revision assignments for main idea and details.

 - **Reread your entry.** *Find a place where you think additional supporting details would give more information about the main idea. Write two details to help the reader imagine the moment.*

 - **[Underline a section.]** Mark a specific section of a student's writing and ask the student to revise it in a specific way.

 - **[Underline a section.]** *Read the part that I underlined. How many main ideas are in this paragraph? Which details support each idea? Create a paragraph for each main idea.*

Teacher-to-Teacher

Over-the-Shoulder Conferences

Use these quick, focused opportunities to comment while students are writing.

- **Step 1** Quietly move close enough to a student that you can read the journal entry he or she is writing.

- **Step 2** Read part of what you see. You don't need to start from the beginning or read the entire piece.

- **Step 3** Show the student a spot in the writing where he or she is using a particular skill or describing something that piques your interest.

- **Step 4** Whisper a sentence or two about why you noticed that spot in the writing, and ask a question that will nudge the student to add main ideas and/or supporting details.

- **Step 5** Move on to the next student. Select students strategically. You should see 12–15 students in a 15-minute period.

Research Proven Writing Approach

The Writers' Express
Immediate Impact. Lasting Transformation.   wex.org

Connect
Language Arts

✔ **VOCABULARY**
- Tested Words

✔ **SPELLING**
- Homophones

✔ **GRAMMAR**
- Comparing with Adverbs

SMALL GROUP

- Differentiated Instruction, pp. 729I–729HH

ON YOUR OWN — **Practice Book,** page 242

A **suffix** is a word part that can be added to the end of a base word. Adding a suffix to a base word changes its meaning. When added to the end of a verb, the suffix -er or -or means "a person who."

teach + er = teacher (a person who teaches)
act + or = actor (a person who acts)

Many suffixes come from Greek and Latin. For example, -logue or -log is a Greek suffix that means "to speak" and -able or -ible is a Latin suffix that means "capable or worthy of."

A. Look for the verb. Then add the correct suffix to make a word that means the same as the entire phrase in bold.

1. **A person who travels** across time is a time ___ traveler
2. **A person who mines** for gold is a ___ miner
3. In the 1800s, many people traveled by sea. And **a person who worked on the sailing ships** was called a ___ sailor
4. Wong Daido was **a person who survived** the river current. He was a ___ survivor

B. Underline the suffix in each word below. Then write the meaning of each word on the lines provided.

5. dialogue ___ a conversation between two or more persons
6. monologue ___ a part of drama in which an actor speaks alone
7. likable ___ easily liked
8. flexible ___ capable of being bent

Approaching Reproducible, page 242
Beyond Reproducible, page 242

Build Robust Vocabulary

Day 1 — Teach/Practice

CONNECT TO WORDS

- Practice this week's vocabulary words using the following prompts:

  1. What could you use as a *reference* when giving a speech about your favorite sport?

  2. Why might you consider a movie to be a *disappointment*?

  3. What objects on cars are *circular*?

  4. When might you need to have your arms *outstretched*?

  5. If someone *conducted* an experiment, how would they want it to turn out?

  6. What might children do to make adults feel *annoyed*?

ACADEMIC VOCABULARY

- Review the important academic vocabulary words for the week. These words include *analyze, story structure, cause, effect, problem, solution, science fiction, intonation,* and *expression*.

- Write each word on the board. Define each using student-friendly language, and ask students to select the word you are defining. Then point to words in random order for students to define.

Day 2 — Review

CONNECT TO WORDS

- Review the definitions of this week's vocabulary words using **Student Book** pages 706–707. Then discuss each word using these prompts:

  1. What in this classroom could you use as a *reference* for a report?

  2. Would getting an A on a test be a *disappointment*?

  3. What in this classroom has a *circular* shape?

  4. Is a bird with *outstretched* wings more likely to be flying or walking?

  5. Would someone who *conducted* a survey fill out a form or collect it?

  6. Would an *annoyed* person be happy or upset?

SUFFIXES

- Remind students that adding a suffix changes a word's meaning and often its part of speech. The suffixes -er and -or mean "one who" and originally derive from Latin. The suffix -ar means "resembling."

- Display **Transparency 53**. Model adding the suffix -or to *prospect*. Read the sample sentence.

- Have students add -er, -or, or -ar to the remaining words and then use each new word in a sentence.

- Point out that when a base word ends in e, students may need to drop the e before adding a suffix that begins with a vowel. Also use *angle* and *angular* to review how the spelling of a base word can change when -ar is added.

Day 3 — Reinforce

CONNECT TO WORDS

- Have students create Word Squares for each word in their Writer's Notebooks.

- In the first square, students write the word. (Example: *annoyed*)

- In the second square, students write their own definition of the word and any related words, such as synonyms. (Examples: *upset, perturbed, irritated*)

- In the third square, students draw a simple illustration that will help them remember the word. (Example: a drawing of a person waiting impatiently in line)

- In the fourth square, students write nonexamples, including antonyms for the word. (Example: *happy, calm*)

RELATED WORDS

- The classification of related words can help improve students' vocabularies. Help students generate words related to *circular*.

- Draw a word web on the board. Write *circular* in the center of the web.

- Have students list words related to *circular* in the other spaces of the web. Suggest that students organize the words on the web by category. Tell them to include words for things that are circular, such as *wheel*, or that move in a circular pattern, such as *merry-go-round*.

- Students can use a print or online thesaurus as a resource.

Day 4 — Extend

CONNECT TO WORDS

- Review this week's vocabulary using the following sentence stems. Have students orally complete each one.

  1. I used the ____ as a reference.
  2. I felt such disappointment when ____.
  3. The ____ was circular in shape.
  4. I outstretched my fingers to ____.
  5. The ____ conducted the ____.
  6. The ____ annoyed me when I was ____.

MORPHOLOGY

- Use the selection word *historians* as a springboard for learning other words. Tell students that learning about Latin and Greek roots can help raise their word consciousness.

- Write the word *historians* on the board. Explain that the word comes from the Latin and Greek root *historia* meaning "learning or knowing by inquiry." *Historians* are people who know about past events by finding out information or inquiring about them.

- Write the words *history* and *prehistoric* on the board. Have students underline the root in each word, taking note of the prefixes and suffixes added to the root.

- Use the word parts to define each word. Explain that *history* means "the record of past events" and *prehistoric* means "before history."

Day 5 — Assess and Reteach

POSTTEST

- Display **Transparency 54**. Have students complete the cloze sentences using one of this week's vocabulary words.

- Note how quickly and accurately students can complete this task. Work with students who make errors or require too much time to complete this task during Small Group time.

CONNECT TO WRITING

- Have students write sentences in their Writer's Notebooks using this week's vocabulary. Tell students to write sentences that provide information they learned from this week's readings.

- **ELL** Provide the Day 4 sentence stems for students needing extra support.

5-Day Spelling

Go to pages T14–T15 for **Differentiated Spelling Lists**.

 # Homophones

Spelling Words

root	prints	bolder
tale	we've	weighed
wade	weave	patience
tail	whose	patients
prince	who's	doe
dough	route	mousse
moose	boulder	

Review cotton, muffin, eleven
Challenge straight, strait

Dictation Sentences

1. A tree **root** grew out of the ground.
2. Have you heard the <u>tale</u> of Paul Bunyan?
3. Do you like to <u>wade</u> in the ocean?
4. My dog wagged his <u>tail</u> excitedly.
5. The <u>prince</u> lives in the castle.
6. It's fun to roll out cookie <u>dough</u>.
7. The <u>moose</u> has large antlers.
8. She <u>prints</u> her letters carefully.
9. <u>We've</u> been here all day.
10. Can you <u>weave</u> on a loom?
11. <u>Whose</u> jacket is on the floor?
12. **Who's** coming to the party?
13. We took the quickest <u>route</u> home.
14. We climbed over a <u>boulder</u>.
15. He acts <u>bolder</u> outside of school.
16. The baby <u>weighed</u> seven pounds.
17. Have <u>patience</u> with your brother.
18. My doctor is kind to her <u>patients</u>.
19. We saw a **doe** run in the woods.
20. I tasted the chocolate <u>mousse</u>.

Review/Challenge Words

1. My shirt is made of pure <u>cotton</u>.
2. I ate a toasted corn <u>muffin</u>.
3. He turned <u>eleven</u> years old.
4. Draw a <u>straight</u> line.
5. The <u>strait</u> was too narrow for the boat to pass through.

Words in **bold** are from this week's selections.

Day 1 Pretest

ASSESS PRIOR KNOWLEDGE

- Model for students how to spell the word *root*. Segment the word sound by sound, then attach a spelling to each sound. Point out that the spelling *oo* is used for the /ü/ sound.

- Use the Dictation Sentences. Say the underlined word, read the sentence, and repeat the word. Have students write the words.

- Have students self-correct their tests. Point out that hearing a homophone in context can help determine which spelling to use.

- Have students cut apart the **Spelling Word Cards BLM** on **Teacher's Resource Book** page 70 and figure out a way to sort them. Have them save the cards for use throughout the week.

Day 2 Word Sorts and Review

SPIRAL REVIEW

Review final /ən/ spellings. Write *cotton, muffin*, and *eleven* on the board. Have students identify other words with the schwa + n sound that are spelled these three different ways.

WORD SORTS

- Have students take turns sorting Spelling Word Cards and explaining how they sorted them. When they finish, discuss any words that have silent letters. (*dough, whose, weighed*)

- Review the spelling words, pointing out the homophone spellings. Use the cards on the Spelling Word Cards BLM. Write the key words *root, tale, prince, dough*, and *weave* on the board. Model how to sort the words by vowel sound. Note how the same vowel sound can be spelled in different ways. Place one card beneath the correct key words.

ON YOUR OWN Phonics/Spelling, pages 157–158

Fold back the paper along the dotted line. Use the blanks to write each word as it is read aloud. When you finish the test, unfold the paper. Use the list at the right to correct any spelling mistakes.

1.		1. root
2.		2. tale
3.		3. wade
4.		4. tail
5.		5. prince
6.		6. dough
7.		7. moose
8.		8. prints
9.		9. we've
10.		10. weave
11.		11. whose
12.		12. who's
13.		13. route
14.		14. boulder
15.		15. bolder
16.		16. weighed
17.		17. patience
18.		18. patients
19.		19. doe
20.		20. mousse
Review Words 21.		21. cotton
22.		22. muffin
23.		23. eleven
Challenge Words 24.		24. straight
25.		25. strait

HOMEWORK Phonics/Spelling, page 159

doe	boulder	patience	mousse
who's	weighed	tail	dough
route	patients	prince	whose
weave	tale	bolder	root
moose	prints	wade	we've

There are ten pairs of spelling words that are homophones. They sound the same but are spelled differently. Sort the homophones into pairs. Write each pair on the lines below.

1.	doe	dough
2.	bolder	boulder
3.	route	root
4.	patience	patients
5.	moose	mousse
6.	prince	prints
7.	who's	whose
8.	wade	weighed
9.	weave	we've
10.	tail	tale

Order Please!

Write the following words in alphabetical order: patience, weighed, tail, dough, whose, weave, bolder, root, moose, and prints.

11.	bolder	16.	root
12.	dough	17.	tail
13.	moose	18.	weave
14.	patience	19.	weighed
15.	prints	20.	whose

Day 3 — Word Meanings

DEFINITIONS

Read each definition below. Ask students to copy the definitions into their Writer's Notebooks, and then write the correct spelling word for each.

1. a female deer (*doe*)
2. a story (*tale*)
3. walk in shallow water (*wade*)
4. a large rock (*boulder*)
5. people who visit a doctor (*patients*)

Challenge students to write definitions for other spelling, review, or challenge words. Have them create a list and exchange it with a classmate who can try supplying the correct spelling word for each definition.

Have students create crossword puzzles, using clues for homophone pairs. They can exchange papers and solve each other's puzzles.

Day 4 — Proofread

PROOFREAD AND WRITE

Write these sentences on the board. Have students circle and correct each misspelled word.

1. You need patients when you make bread doe. (*patience, dough*)
2. The prints enjoys eating lemon moose. (*prince, mousse*)
3. Who's tale is longer, the mouse's or the lion's? (*Whose, tail*)
4. To get to Root 4, we make a right at the big bolder. (*Route, boulder*)
5. Weave never wade ourselves on this kind of scale. (*We've, weighed*)

Error Correction Point out that homophones are often misspelled because they sound the same. Remind students of the importance of knowing the meaning of the word in order to decide which homophone to use. Students should use context clues and/or a dictionary if necessary.

Day 5 — Assess and Reteach

POSTTEST

Use the Dictation Sentences on page 729E for the Posttest.

If students have difficulty with any words in the lesson, have them place the words on a list called *Spelling Words I Want to Remember* in their Writer's Notebooks. Look for students' use of these words in their writings.

Point out that students may need to check a dictionary or electronic resource often as they learn how to spell homophones. They may find the same spelling rules and patterns that help them spell other words less helpful with homophones.

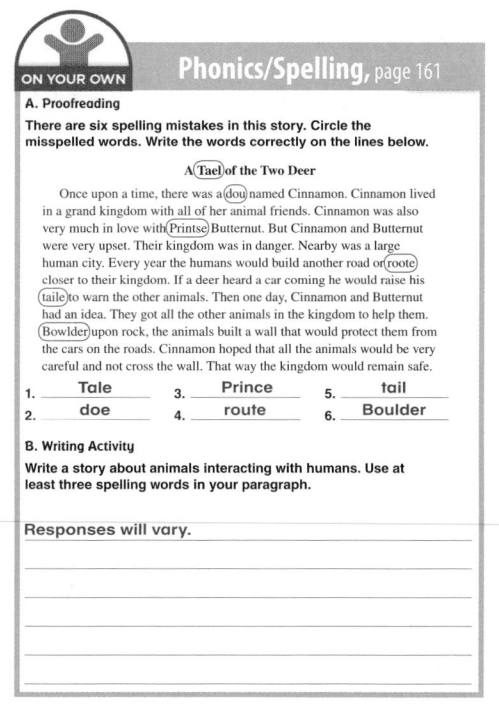

5-Day Grammar

 ## Comparing with Adverbs

Daily Language Activities

Write the sentences on the board.

DAY 1

Natasha's cat was nice, but mine was nicest. Peters pet was hungryest than Molly's pet. The mouse seemed to listen polite. (1: nicer; 2: Peter's; 3: hungrier; 4: politely.)

DAY 2

Sarah is a well listener. She listens more hard than I do. She asked curiouslier than Al about our trip to the city. (1: good; 2: harder; 3: more curiously)

DAY 3

Sarah and me enjoy vacations, but Gerard enjoy them more of all. He gets ready fastest than we do in the mornings. (1: and I; 2: Gerard enjoys; 3: most of all; 4: faster)

DAY 4

The bus ride seemed more slower than last time. "Weave got to go to the second floor." my teacher said. (1: seemed slower; 2: We've; 3: floor,)

DAY 5

I saw well sights on our field trip. When it was time to go, it was most sad than before? (1: good; 2: was sadder; 3: before.)

ELL

Use Concrete Examples

Demonstrate the difference between *more* and *most*. For example, have a student count *quickly*, another *more quickly* than the first, and a third *most quickly* of all. Create a sentence about each. Emphasize that adverbs compare actions instead of things.

Day 1 Introduce the Concept

INTRODUCE COMPARING WITH ADVERBS

Present the following:

- Adverbs can be used to compare two or more actions.

- To compare using most one-syllable adverbs, add -er or -est: Amelia tried *harder* than her teammate. Ken tried the *hardest* of all.

- The words *more* and *most* are usually used with adverbs with two or more syllables to make comparisons: Tom read *more carefully* than Monica. I read the *most carefully* of all.

- When adverbs are used with *more* or *most*, they do not change their endings to make comparisons.

 See Grammar Transparency 131 for modeling and guided practice.

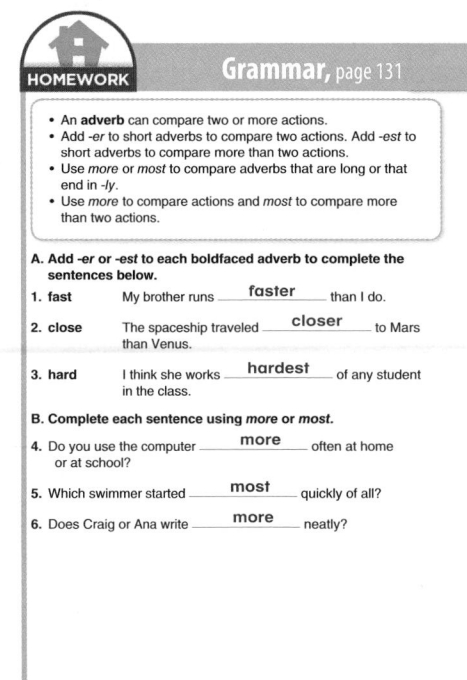

HOMEWORK **Grammar,** page 131

- An **adverb** can compare two or more actions.
- Add -er to short adverbs to compare two actions. Add -est to short adverbs to compare more than two actions.
- Use *more* or *most* to compare adverbs that are long or that end in -ly.
- Use *more* to compare actions and *most* to compare more than two actions.

A. Add -er or -est to each boldfaced adverb to complete the sentences below.

1. **fast**   My brother runs ___faster___ than I do.

2. **close**   The spaceship traveled ___closer___ to Mars than Venus.

3. **hard**   I think she works ___hardest___ of any student in the class.

B. Complete each sentence using *more* or *most*.

4. Do you use the computer ___more___ often at home or at school?

5. Which swimmer started ___most___ quickly of all?

6. Does Craig or Ana write ___more___ neatly?

Day 2 Teach the Concept

REVIEW COMPARING WITH ADVERBS

Discuss with students how to compare with adverbs. Have them share some basic rules for deciding whether to add -er or -est or to use *more* and *most*.

INTRODUCE COMPARING WITH IRREGULAR ADVERBS

Present the following:

- To make comparisons using the adverb *well*, use *better* and *best*: Shania works *well* in math. Bob works *better*. Mike works *best* of all.

- To make comparisons using the adverb *badly*, use *worse* and *worst*: I swam the 100-meter *badly*. I swam *worse* last week. I swam *worst* of all when I first started.

 See Grammar Transparency 132 for modeling and guided practice.

ON YOUR OWN **Grammar,** page 132

- Use *more* or *most* to form comparisons with adverbs that end in -ly or with longer adverbs. Use *more* to compare two actions. Use *most* to compare more than two actions.
- To make comparisons using the adverb *well*, use *better* and *best*.
- To make comparisons using the adverb *badly*, use *worse* and *worst*.

A. Use *more* or *most* with the underlined adverb in each first sentence to complete the two sentences that follow.

1. The train that Chester was on shook harshly as it moved on the track.
   The second train shook ___more harshly___ every now and then.
   But the subway car shook ___most harshly___ of all.

2. Harry Cat speedily jumped toward Chester and Tucker Mouse.
   Chester jumped the ___most speedily___ of all into the matchbox.
   Chester jumped ___more speedily___ than Harry Cat.

B. Use *better* or *best* or *worse* or *worst* to replace the underlined adverb in the two sentences that follow.

3. Chester chirps well when he is excited.
   Chester chirps ___better___ when he is scared than when he is tried.
   But Chester chirps ___best___ of all when he is happy.

4. He sings badly when it is very hot.
   He sings ___worse___ when he is sick than when he is healthy.
   He sings ___worst___ of all when he has a cold.

Day 3 · Review and Practice

REVIEW COMPARING WITH IRREGULAR ADVERBS

Review how to make comparisons using *well* and *badly*.

MECHANICS AND USAGE: REVIEW PUNCTUATION AND CAPITALIZATION

- Use a comma before coordinating conjunctions, after a beginning dependent clause, and to separate three or more items in a series.

- Capitalize sentence beginnings, proper adjectives, and proper nouns such as names of books, historical events, and nationalities. Also capitalize the first word in a quotation that is a full sentence.

- A comma or period always goes inside closing quotation marks. A question or exclamation mark goes inside when part of the quotation.

See Grammar Transparency 133 for modeling and guided practice.

HOMEWORK — **Grammar,** page 133

- Every sentence begins with a capital letter.
- Use the correct end mark for each sentence.
- Capitalize proper nouns and proper adjectives, such as South African. Also capitalize the first word in the title of a book or the name of a historical event, as well as each important word after that.
- Capitalize the first word in a quotation that is a full sentence.
- Use a comma to separate three items in a series, as well as before coordinating conjunctions that join compound sentences.

Rewrite each sentence correctly by adding commas and quotation marks where they belong.

Luis: sara, are carpenter ants a type of american ant?
Sara, are carpenter ants a type of American ant?

Sara: a book I read, the world of ants, says that carpenter ants dig wood!
A book I read, The World of Ants, says that carpenter ants dig wood!

Luis: yes, after they dig the wood, they live in the caverns they made.
Yes, after they dig the wood, they live in the caverns they made.

Sara: Three kinds of ants are the queen the males and the workers.
Three kinds of ants are the queen, the males, and the workers.

Luis: the other ants take special care of the queen.
The other ants take special care of the queen.

Sara: what are those little white things, luis?
What are those little white things, Luis?

Day 4 · Review and Proofread

REVIEW MORE COMPARING WITH IRREGULAR ADVERBS

Have students explain when to use -er, -est, more, and most. Review the comparative and superlative forms of adverbs.

PROOFREAD

Have students correct errors in the following sentences.

1. My cousin ate well, but I ate weller. (better)

2. Charlie tried hard, but Gretchen tried hardest than Charlie. (harder)

3. Thomas liked waffles and pancakes for breakfast, but he liked eggs more of all. (most)

4. My grandma decided she would live happier in the country than in the city. (more happily)

See Grammar Transparency 134 for modeling and guided practice.

ON YOUR OWN — **Grammar,** page 134

A. Read the magazine article below and circle six incorrect uses of adverbs.

Last week, a baby bird was lucky found in a nest near school. The winds blew coldly than the bird could stand, so it chirped loud and hid inside the nest. Then a boy and his uncle heard it chirping frantically than it had earlier. It was the tiniest bird they had ever seen.

They kind took the bird to the zoo. Because the workers there are taking good care of it, the bird is doing much more well than before.

B. Rewrite the above article with the correct adverbs on the lines below.

Last week, a baby bird was luckily found in a nest near school. The winds blew more coldly than the bird could stand, so it chirped loudly and hid inside the nest. Then a boy and his uncle heard it chirping more frantically than it had earlier. It was the tiniest bird they had ever seen.

They kindly took the bird to the zoo. Because the workers there are taking good care of it, the bird is doing much better than before.

Day 5 · Assess and Reteach

ASSESS

Use the Daily Language Activity and **Grammar Practice Book** page 135 for assessment.

RETEACH

Use Grammar Practice Book page 135 and selected pages from the **Grammar and Writing Handbook** for additional reteaching. Remind students that it is important they use adverbs correctly as they speak and write.

Check students' writing for use of the skill, and listen for it in their speaking. Assign Grammar Revision Assignments in their Writer's Notebooks.

See Grammar Transparency 135 for modeling and guided practice.

HOMEWORK — **Grammar,** page 135

A. For each of the adverbs below, write the form you would use to compare two things. Then choose one of the adverbs you formed and use it in a sentence.

1. cute — cuter
2. curiously — more curiously
3. careful — more carefully
4. soon — sooner
5. gloomily — more gloomily
6. tall — taller
7. young — younger
8. Sentences will vary.

B. For each of the following adverbs, write the form you would use to compare more than two things. Then choose one of the adverbs you formed and use it in a sentence.

9. graciously — most graciously
10. playfully — most playfully
11. poor — poorest
12. heavily — most heavily
13. hard — hardest
14. sweetly — most sweetly
15. sad — saddest
16. Sentences will vary.

Daily Planner

DAY 1	• Prepare to Read • Academic Language • Vocabulary (Preteach)
DAY 2	• Comprehension • Leveled Reader Lesson 1
DAY 3	• Phonics/Decoding • Leveled Reader Lesson 2
DAY 4	• Phonics/Decoding • Vocabulary (Review) • Leveled Reader Lesson 3
DAY 5	• High-Frequency Words • Fluency • Self-Selected Reading

LOG ON **StudentWorks** Plus

Interactive Student Book

If you wish to preteach the main selection, use StudentWorks Plus for:

• Vocabulary Preteaching
• Word-by-Word Highlighting
• Think Aloud Prompts

Academic Language

Academic words include those harder Tier 2 words that appear in much of students' reading materials as well as the language of instruction. The words chosen for instruction were selected from the **Living Word Vocabulary** list and Avril Coxhead's list of **High-Incidence Academic Words**.

Approaching Level

Prepare to Read

Objective   Preview *The Gold Rush Game*
Materials   • **StudentWorks Plus**   • self-stick notes

PREVIEW THE MAIN SELECTION

■ Have students preview *The Gold Rush Game* using **StudentWorks Plus**, the interactive eBook. This version of the selection contains oral summaries in multiple languages, story recording, word-by-word highlighting, Think Aloud prompts, and comprehension-monitoring questions.

■ Remind students that listening carefully to and following along with the word-by-word reading will help them prepare for the reading of the selection with the class. Ask students to place self-stick notes on any challenging words or places that confuse them. Discuss these with students prior to the reading of the selection with the rest of the class.

■ Tell students to write three or four sentences in their Writer's Notebooks telling what they learned about Chinese prospectors during the Gold Rush in California.

Academic Language

Objective   Teach academic language
Materials   • none

PRETEACH LANGUAGE OF INSTRUCTION

Tell students that there are many important lesson words you will be using this week. You want them to become familiar with these words *before* the lessons. These words also appear in the directions of the tests they will be taking this year.

Preteach the following academic words: *science fiction, cause, effect, analyze story structure, problem, solution, suffixes,* and *homophones.*

■ Define each word using student-friendly language. Tell students that *science fiction* is a type of made-up story that involves fantasy and science or technology that often does not yet exist in real life.

■ In addition, relate each word to known words. Connect, for example, *cause* and *effect* to what happens and what made it happen, *analyze story structure* to understanding how a story is organized, and *homophones* to words that sound the same but are spelled differently and have different meanings.

■ Highlight these words when used throughout the week, and reinforce their meanings.

Approaching Level

Phonics/Decoding

Objective   Decode homophones

Materials   • **Approaching Reproducible,** p. 235   • **Word-Building Cards**
                  • **Sound-Spelling WorkBoards**

Sound-Spelling WorkBoard

✔ PHONICS MAINTENANCE

Tier 2

- Distribute a **WorkBoard** to each student. Say a syllable type that was previously taught, such as a closed syllable, an open syllable, a consonant + *le* syllable, or an *r*-controlled vowel syllable. Have students find the **Word-Building Cards** for these syllables.

- Review the spelling for each syllable and for homophones by providing sample words and, in the case of homophones, word pairs. Guide students to write the word. Model how to segment the word and write the spelling for each sound or syllable, as needed. In addition, point out spelling hints, such as that a final unaccented syllable ending with a vowel plus *n* can be spelled *-en, -in,* or *-on,* as in *shaken, basin,* and *button.*

- Dictate the following words for students to spell, and provide a sentence for each homophone: *carton, mitten, stable, purple, bear/ bare, blew/blue.* Write each word on the board, and have students self-correct their work.

RETEACH SKILL

Homophones Point to the homophones on the board. State each spelling, and have students provide sample sentences.

- Write the words below on the board. Model how to decode the first word in each row, then guide students as they decode the remaining words. For the multisyllabic words, divide the words into syllables using the syllable-scoop technique to help students read one syllable at a time. Provide sentences for context.

- When completed, point to the words in random order for students to chorally read. Repeat several times.

ad	add	affect	effect	ate	eight
I'll	aisle	isle	cent	sent	scent
based	baste	berry	bury	chews	choose
he'll	heal	heel	main	Maine	mane
tacks	tax	thyme	time	forth	fourth
plain	plane	way	weigh	which	witch

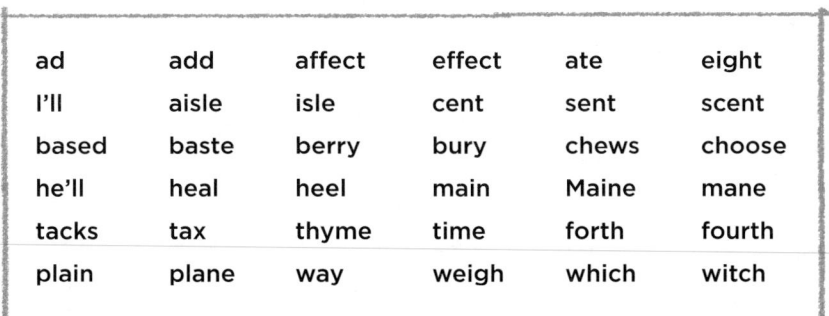

Approaching Reproducible, page 235

Say these words: *tail, tale.*
Some words sound the same, but have different spellings and meanings. These words are called **homophones**.
The words *hour* and *our* are homophones.
     hour = 60 minutes   our = belonging to us

For each set of words, cross out the word that is not a homophone.

1. prince	~~pinch~~	prints
2. ~~meant~~	meet	meat
3. too	two	~~toy~~
4. ~~seed~~	sea	see
5. pear	~~par~~	pair
6. not	knot	~~note~~
7. ~~war~~	wear	where
8. made	maid	~~mad~~
9. wade	~~wait~~	weighed
10. ~~pot~~	root	route
11. ~~done~~	doe	dough
12. patients	patience	~~pencils~~

Approaching Level

Vocabulary

Objective Preteach selection vocabulary

Materials
- **Visual Vocabulary Resources** • **Vocabulary Cards**
- **Approaching Reproducible,** p. 236

PRETEACH KEY VOCABULARY

Tier 2

Introduce Words Use the **Visual Vocabulary Resources** to preteach the key selection words *reference, disappointment, annoyed, circular, outstretched, conducted*. Use the following routine, which appears in detail on the cards.

- Define the word in English, and provide the example given.

- Define the word in Spanish, if appropriate, and indicate if the word is a cognate.

- Display the picture, and explain how it illustrates or demonstrates the word.

- Then engage students in structured partner-talk about the image, using the key word.

- Ask students to chorally say the word three times.

- Point out any known sound-spellings or focus on a key aspect of phonemic awareness related to the word.

- You may wish to also distribute copies of the Vocabulary Glossary in the **ELL Resource Book**.

REVIEW PREVIOUSLY TAUGHT VOCABULARY

Display the **Vocabulary Cards** from the previous six weeks. Say the meanings of each word, one by one, and have students identify them. Then point to words in random order for students to provide definitions and related words they know.

Context Clues Remind students that context clues are clues within the text that help a reader figure out what a word means. Have students write a context sentence for each vocabulary word. For example, *With her arms* outstretched, *Jane was able to reach from one end of the table to the other*.

Approaching Reproducible, page 236

| annoyed | circular | outstretched |
| conducted | reference | disappointment |

A. Write a word from the vocabulary list to complete each sentence.

1. Many gold seekers felt __disappointment__ because they found very little of it.

2. To pan for gold, you have to swirl a pan of river water in a __circular__ motion.

3. The old miner shook my __outstretched__ hand when we met.

4. John __conducted__ a search for the lost dog.

5. When I wrote my report on the Gold Rush, I used encyclopedias for __reference__.

6. I felt __annoyed__ that I didn't live back then. I would have loved to pan for gold.

B. Write a sentence that includes two of the vocabulary words.
Possible response provided.

7. I was really annoyed when nothing glinted in my circular pan.

Approaching Level

Vocabulary

Objective Review vocabulary and high-frequency words
Materials • **Vocabulary Cards** • **High-Frequency Word Cards**

✔ REVIEW VOCABULARY

Review Words Display the **Vocabulary Cards** for *reference, disappointment, annoyed, circular, outstretched*, and *conducted*. Point to each word, read it aloud, and have students chorally repeat.

Then ask the following questions. Allow other students to respond and discuss answers.

■ When have you used a *reference*?

■ Explain a time in which you experienced *disappointment*.

■ What is something that can make you feel *annoyed*?

■ Do you own anything with a *circular* shape or pattern?

■ Describe a situation when your arms would be *outstretched*.

■ Tell about a time when you *conducted* yourself politely.

HIGH-FREQUENCY WORDS

Tier 2

Top 250 Words The ability to read accurately and effortlessly the most frequently used words in written English will help students develop reading fluency. Display **High-Frequency Word Cards** 211–220. Then do the following:

■ Display one card at a time, and ask students to chorally state each word.

■ Have students spell each word aloud.

■ Ask students to write each word in their Writer's Notebooks as they state aloud each letter. Then have them read the word again.

■ When completed, quickly flip through the Word Card set as students chorally read the words.

■ Provide opportunities for students to use the words in speaking and writing. For example, provide sentence starters such as *I used the _____,* for oral and written practice. Or ask a question, such as *To what places can you walk?* (when pointing to the *walk* word card)

■ Continue the routine throughout the week.

ELL

Practice Vocabulary Pair students of different proficiency. Orally model the vocabulary in sentences. For example: *I used three references to write my history report.* On the board, provide sentence frames for pairs to copy and complete using the vocabulary. For example: *I felt _____ when I did not make the baseball team.* (*disappointment*)

Word Webs

Have students create word webs in their Writer's Notebooks for each vocabulary word. Write the related words provided, and ask students to add other words, phrases, and illustrations.

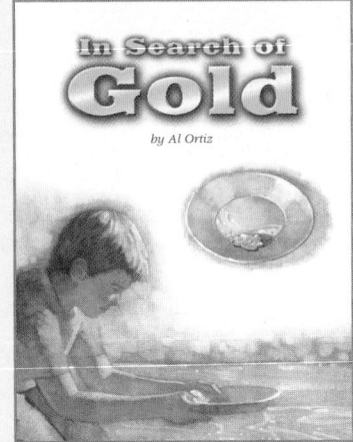

Student Book

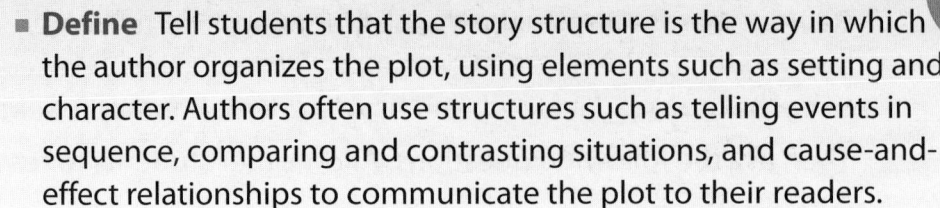

Approaching Level

Comprehension

Objective Reteach analyze story structure and cause and effect

Materials • **Student Book:** "In Search of Gold"

RETEACH STRATEGY: ANALYZE STORY STRUCTURE

Tier 2

- **Define** Tell students that the story structure is the way in which the author organizes the plot, using elements such as setting and character. Authors often use structures such as telling events in sequence, comparing and contrasting situations, and cause-and-effect relationships to communicate the plot to their readers.

- **Relate to Real Life** Have students imagine that they are writing a short story. Before they can begin, they need to determine who will be in the story and where it will take place. They also need to decide how they are going to structure their story. Will they tell the events in sequence? Will the setting have an effect on the actions of the characters? Explain that before authors write a story, they need to decide what structure they want to use to tell their story.

- **Set Purposes** Remind students that good readers analyze the story's structure while they read. If the reader can explain how the story is organized, he or she reads on. If not, he or she must go back and reread.

Corrective Feedback

Reread the story with students. Have them identify causes and effects in the story. Ask questions, such as *What was the cause for the students wearing hard hats? What was the effect of Larry angling his pan in the sunlight?*

RETEACH SKILL: CAUSE AND EFFECT

- **Define** Tell students that cause-and-effect relationships provide structure for a story. Each event or action often leads directly to or influences another event or action in the future. A cause tells why something happens, and the effect tells what happened.

- **Relate to Real Life** Have students think about the weather. Remind them that the weather outside can be the cause for how they dress, what activities they do, and how they feel. For example, if it is cold outside, they need to dress warmly, they may want to play a game inside, and they may feel disappointed that they cannot do something outside. Those are the effects of the cold weather.

- **Set Purposes** Remind students that good readers search for causes and effects as they read. This helps readers better understand why certain events happen and why the characters act the way they do.

- **Apply** Work with students to identify examples of causes and effects in "In Search of Gold." Then use those examples to analyze the structure of the story. Have students restate your analysis in their own words. Students will apply this strategy and skill to a simpler text as they read *Buffalo!*

Approaching Level

Leveled Reader Lesson 1

Objective Read to apply skills and strategies
Materials • **Leveled Reader:** *Buffalo!*

BEFORE READING

Preview and Predict Have students read the title and preview the first chapter. Tell students to make predictions about this chapter. Students should note any questions they have before they read.

 **Review Vocabulary Words** Have students read the vocabulary words on the inside front cover. Briefly define each and have students state related words they have learned.

Set a Purpose for Reading *Let's read to find out about buffalo.*

DURING READING

 **STRATEGY**
ANALYZE STORY STRUCTURE

Remind students that determining a story's structure will involve recognizing how its characters, settings, and events are organized and related to each other.

SKILL
CAUSE AND EFFECT

As they read, remind students to think about cause-and-effect relationships and how one event in the story influences another. Read Chapter 1 with students. Help them complete a Cause and Effect Chart.

As you read, help students decode unknown words. In addition, ask open-ended questions to facilitate rich discussion, such as *Why did the author structure this story through journal entries? How does this help us to learn about the main characters?* Build on students' responses to help them develop a deeper understanding of the text.

Stop after every two pages, and have students summarize to check their understanding before reading on. If they struggle, help students reread the difficult pages or passages. Then model summarizing orally.

AFTER READING

Tell students to compare *The Gold Rush Game* to *Buffalo!* Ask: *How are these stories similar? How are they different?* Have students comment on what they found most interesting in both.

Leveled Reader

Digital Learning

Use the **Leveled Reader Audio CD** for fluency building *after* students read the book with your support during Small Group time.

Leveled Reader

Approaching Level

 **Leveled Reader Lesson 2**

Objective	Reread to apply skills and strategies and develop fluency
Materials	• **Leveled Reader:** *Buffalo!*
	• **Approaching Reproducible,** p. 239

BEFORE READING

 **Review the Strategy and Skill** Review students' completed Cause and Effect Charts from the first read. Remind students that the effect is what happened, and the cause is the reason for what happened.

Review Vocabulary Words Have students search the book for each vocabulary word. Tell students to read aloud the sentence containing the word and state the word's definition or provide related words. Point out words with suffixes that appear in the text.

Set a Purpose for Reading *Let's reread to check our understanding of the information in the book and to work on our reading fluency.*

DURING READING

Reread *Buffalo!* with students. Have them read silently two pages at a time or read aloud to a partner. Stop and have students summarize before they read the next two pages. Model summarizing orally, as needed.

AFTER READING

Check Comprehension Have partners complete the Comprehension Check on page 20. Review students' answers. Help students find evidence for their answers in the text.

MODEL FLUENCY

Model reading the fluency passage on **Approaching Reproducible** page 239. Tell students to pay close attention to your intonation and expression as you read. Then read one sentence at a time and have students echo-read the sentences, copying your expression.

During independent reading time, have students work with a partner using the fluency passage. One student reads aloud while the other repeats each sentence back. If students need additional support, have them listen to the "practice speed" version of the passage on the **Fluency Solutions Audio CD**.

Approaching Reproducible, page 239

As I read, I will pay attention to my intonation and expression.

	Gold is a shiny metal. It is rare and hard to find. It has
14	been a valuable metal since ancient times. People pay
23	a lot of money for it. A few ounces of gold are worth
36	hundreds of dollars. People will travel a long way and
46	risk danger in search of it. When someone does find
56	gold, the news spreads quickly.
61	As the United States grew, people went west, where
70	they discovered new things. Some found good farmland.
78	Others found a place for raising cattle. A few found gold.
89	This was always the most exciting news.
96	The years from 1848 to 1900 were a time of great
105	gold rushes in the United States. Thousands of people
114	hoped to strike it rich. California's Gold Rush is the most
125	famous. But there were others. Gold was discovered
133	in Georgia. There was a rush for gold in Colorado. 143

Comprehension Check Possible responses provided.

1. What happened when gold was discovered? **Cause and Effect People rushed to find it.**

2. In history, how has the discovery of gold affected people? **Main Idea and Details The discovery of gold caused so much excitement in people that they were willing to travel a long way and risk their lives in the hopes of finding some gold.**

	Words Read	−	Number of Errors	=	Words Correct Score
First Read		−		=	
Second Read		−		=	

Approaching Level

Leveled Reader Lesson 3

Objective   Build fluency

Materials
- **Leveled Reader:** *Buffalo!*
- **Approaching Reproducible,** p. 239

✓ FOCUS ON FLUENCY

Timed Reading Tell students that they will be doing a final timed reading of the fluency passage on **Approaching Reproducible** page 239 that they have been practicing. With each student, follow these directions:

- Place the passage facedown.

- When you say "Go," the student begins reading the passage aloud.

- When you say "Stop," the student stops reading the passage.

As they read, note words students mispronounce and their overall expression. Stop after one minute. Help students record and graph the number of words they read correctly.

REREAD PREVIOUSLY READ BOOKS

- Distribute copies of the past six **Leveled Readers**. Have students select two to reread. Tell students that rereading these books will help them develop their skills. The more times they read the same words, the quicker they will learn these words. This will make the reading of other books easier.

- Circulate and listen in as students read. Stop students periodically and ask them how they are figuring out difficult words and how they are monitoring their comprehension. Note students who need additional work with specific decoding or comprehension skills.

- Encourage students to read other previously read Leveled Readers during independent reading time or for homework.

Meet Grade-Level Expectations

As an alternative to this day's lesson, guide students through a reading of the On Level Leveled Reader. See page 729U. Since both books contain the same vocabulary, phonics, and comprehension skills, the scaffolding you provided will help most students gain access to this more challenging text.

Book Talk

Bringing Groups Together Students will work with peers of various language and reading abilities to discuss this week's Leveled Readers. Refer to page 158 in the **Teacher's Resource Book** for more about how to conduct a Book Talk.

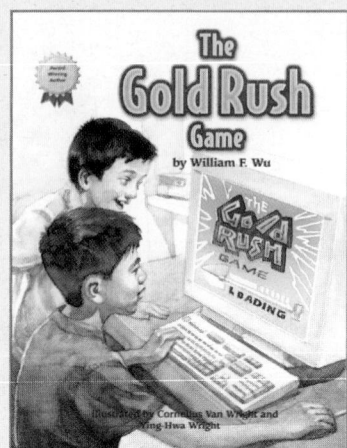

Student Book

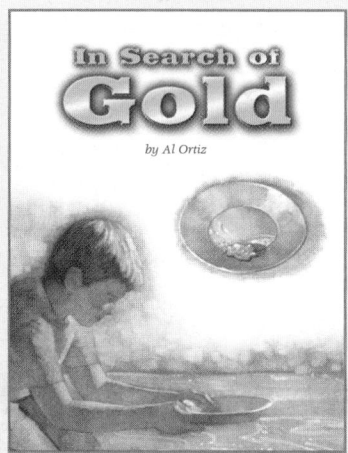

Student Book

Approaching Level
Fluency

Objectives Reread selections to develop fluency; develop speaking skills

Materials • **Student Book:** *The Gold Rush Game*, "In Search of Gold"

✔ REREAD FOR FLUENCY

- Have students reread a portion of *The Gold Rush Game*. Suggest that they focus on one to two of their favorite pages from the selection. Work with students to read the pages with the appropriate expression.

- Provide time for students to read their sections of text to you. Comment on their expression, and provide corrective feedback by modeling proper fluency.

DEVELOP SPEAKING/LISTENING SKILLS

- Have students practice reading the second page of "In Search of Gold."

- Work with students to read with appropriate expression. Model reading a few sentences at a time. Use intonation, or tone of voice, for emphasis and to convey feeling. Have students repeat.

- Provide time for students to read half of the page aloud to partners. Have students name the ways their partner expressed emotion or emphasized words with expression.

- Have students use what they learned in the story to give step-by-step instructions for panning for gold. Remind them to use intonation when they speak, in order to gain the interest of their listeners. Have partners give each other feedback on their directions.

Approaching Level

Self-Selected Reading

Objective   Read independently to identify cause-and-effect relationships and analyze story structure

Materials   • **Leveled Classroom Library**   • other fiction books

APPLY SKILLS AND STRATEGIES TO INDEPENDENT READING

- **Read Independently** Have students choose a fiction book for sustained silent reading such as a **Leveled Classroom Library** book. (See the **Theme Bibliography** on pages T8–T9 for suggestions.) Remind them to look for causes and effects as they read in order to better analyze the story structure. Have students read their books and record causes and effects on a Cause and Effect Chart.

- **Show Evidence of Reading** While reading, students may generate a reading log or journal. After reading, have students use their Cause and Effect Charts to write or orally state a summary of the book, maintaining meaning and logical order. Provide time for students to share their summaries and other comments through Book Talks. *Would you recommend this book to a classmate? Why or why not?*

Approaching

Leveled Classroom Library
See Leveled Classroom
Library lessons on pages T2–T7.

On Level

Vocabulary

Objectives Review vocabulary
Materials • **Vocabulary Cards**

REVIEW PREVIOUSLY TAUGHT WORDS

Review the Words Display the **Vocabulary Cards** for *reference, disappointment, annoyed, circular, outstretched,* and *conducted.* Point to each word, read it aloud, and have students chorally repeat.

Then provide the following discussion questions. Allow several students to respond to each question. Use the discussions to determine each student's depth of word knowledge.

- In what situations would you need to have or use a *reference*?
- When might students feel *disappointment*?
- If someone *annoyed* you, how would you react?
- What *circular* objects can you find in a classroom?
- When might you reach for *outstretched* arms?
- If a boss *conducted* a meeting, who might be there?

Phonics/Word Study

Objectives Decode multisyllabic homophones
Materials • **Sound-Spelling WorkBoards**

RETEACH SKILL

- **Homophones** Write homophones, such as *beach/beech, altar/alter,* and *bolder/boulder.* Have students read them. Point out the words in each pair sound the same but have different meanings and spellings. Provide sample sentences for each homophone.

- Write the words below on the board. If necessary, divide the words into syllables using the syllable-scoop technique to help students read one syllable at a time. When completed, point to the words in random order for students to chorally read.

capital	capitol	ceiling	sealing	choral	coral
carrot	caret	carat	petal	pedal	peddle
patience	patients	weather	whether	Sunday	sundae

- **Spelling** Dictate these words for students to spell on their **WorkBoards**: *lesson, lessen, aloud, allowed, naval, navel.* Give example sentences as needed. Model how to segment words, such as spelling a word syllable by syllable.

Daily Planner

DAY 1	• Vocabulary • Phonics
DAY 2	• Leveled Reader Lesson 1
DAY 3	• Leveled Reader Lesson 2
DAY 4	• Fluency
DAY 5	• Self-Selected Reading

ELL

Practice Vocabulary Pair ELL students with native speakers. On the board, provide sentence frames for pairs to copy and complete using the vocabulary and additional words when necessary. For example: *I felt _____ when I did not make the _____ team.* (*disappointment; softball*)

Sound-Spelling WorkBoard

On Level

Fluency

Objectives Reread selections to develop fluency; develop speaking skills
Materials • **Student Book:** *The Gold Rush Game*, "In Search of Gold"

REREAD FOR FLUENCY

- Have students reread *The Gold Rush Game*. Work with them to read with appropriate intonation and expression. Model as needed.

- Provide time for students to read a section of text to you. Comment on their expression and provide corrective feedback.

DEVELOP SPEAKING/LISTENING SKILLS

- Have students practice reading "In Search of Gold."

- Work with students to read with appropriate expression. Model reading a few sentences at a time. Use intonation, or tone of voice, for emphasis or to convey feeling. Have students repeat.

- Provide time for students to read the second page aloud to partners. Tell students to name the ways their partner expressed emotion or emphasized words using expression.

- Have students think of a time that they found something important they were looking for. Tell them to create a brief oral narrative to share with a partner.

Self-Selected Reading

Objective Read independently to identify cause-and-effect relationships and analyze story structure
Materials • **Leveled Classroom Library** • other fiction books

APPLY SKILLS AND STRATEGIES TO INDEPENDENT READING

- **Read Independently** Have students choose a fiction book for sustained silent reading. (See the **Theme Bibliography** on pages T8–T9 for book suggestions.) Remind them to look for causes and effects as they read, in order to better analyze the story structure. Have students read their books and record causes and effects on a Cause and Effect Chart.

- **Show Evidence of Reading** While reading, students may generate a reading log or journal. After reading, have students use their Cause and Effect Charts and logs to paraphrase the book, maintaining meaning and logical order. Provide time for students to share their summaries and comments while participating in Book Talks. Ask: *How did the author structure the plot in your book? Would you have changed anything about the structure?*

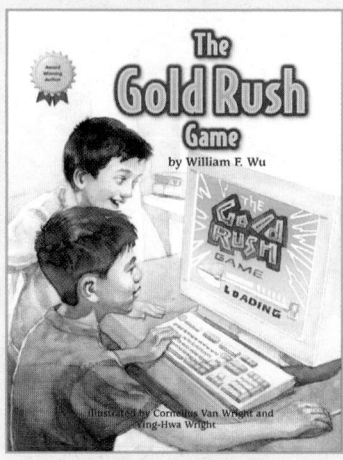

Student Book

Student Book

On Level
Leveled Classroom Library
See Leveled Classroom Library lessons on pages T2–T7.

Leveled Reader

On Level

Leveled Reader Lesson 1

| **Objective** | Read to apply strategies and skills |
| **Materials** | • **Leveled Reader:** *Camel Ride* |

BEFORE READING

Preview and Predict Have students read the title and preview the book by reading the chapter titles and looking at the illustrations. Have students predict what this book is about and how the author structured the story.

 **Review Vocabulary Words** Have students read the vocabulary words on the inside front cover. Have students state related words they have learned. Review definitions, as needed.

Set a Purpose for Reading *Let's read to find out who is taking a camel ride.*

DURING READING

 **STRATEGY**
ANALYZE STORY STRUCTURE

Remind students that the structure of the story will involve the setting and characters, or people and places, and how the author chooses to organize the events. Discuss why setting may be particularly important in this book.

 **SKILL**
CAUSE AND EFFECT

Remind students that causes and effects play a part in the story structure, as one event causes others to take place. Prompt them to think about the causes of various events or happenings in the book.

Read Chapter 1 with students. Ask open-ended questions to facilitate rich discussion, such as *Does the author structure the story clearly? How could the author tell us more about the character of Cole?* Build on students' responses to help them develop a deeper understanding of the text. Have students fill in the Cause and Effect Chart as they continue reading.

Suffixes As they read, have students point out this week's new vocabulary words and identify any words with suffixes they notice.

AFTER READING

Have students discuss responsibility. *When is doing the right thing difficult? When is it easy?* Students may discuss their own family responsibilities or their responsibilities at school.

On Level

Leveled Reader Lesson 2

Objective Reread to apply skills and strategies and develop fluency

Materials • **Leveled Reader:** *Camel Ride*
• **Practice Book,** p. 239

BEFORE READING

Review the Strategy and Skill Review students' completed Cause and Effect Charts from the first read. Remind students that analyzing story structure involves understanding how the author chooses to organize the events of the story.

An analysis of story structure will include an understanding of how the author uses causes and effects and how the events in a story interconnect. If students' Cause and Effect Charts are incomplete, provide a model chart or use a student chart and revise it as a group. Have students copy the revised chart in their Writer's Notebooks.

Set a Purpose for Reading *Let's reread to check our understanding of the information in the book and to work on our reading fluency.*

DURING READING

Reread *Camel Ride* with students. Have them read silently two pages at a time, or read aloud to a partner. Stop and have students summarize before they read the next two pages. Model summarizing orally, as needed.

AFTER READING

Check Comprehension Have partners complete the Comprehension Check on page 20. Review students' answers. Help students find evidence for their answers in the text.

MODEL FLUENCY

Model reading the fluency passage on **Practice Book** page 239. Tell students to pay close attention to your expression, particularly your intonation—the way you change your tone of voice and emphasize important words. Then read one sentence at a time, and have students echo-read the sentences, copying your expression.

During independent reading time, have students work with a partner using the fluency passage. One student reads aloud while the other repeats each sentence back. If students need additional support, have them listen to the "practice speed" version of the passage on the **Fluency Solutions Audio CD**.

Leveled Reader

Book Talk

Bringing Groups Together Students will work with peers of various language and reading abilities to discuss this week's **Leveled Readers**. Refer to page 158 in the **Teacher's Resource Book** for more about how to conduct a Book Talk.

Practice Book, page 239

As I read, I will pay attention to my intonation and expression.

	In the early 1800s, the United States needed room to grow.
10	Most people lived in the East. The cities were crowded. New land
22	was expensive. Young families couldn't afford to buy farms.
31	Then the United States government purchased land from
39	France. The government also acquired land from Mexico. Soon the
49	country stretched all the way to the Pacific Ocean. People looked
60	to the setting sun with outstretched arms and said, "Go west!"
71	Settlers rode in wagons or on horses. They followed long, dusty
82	trails across hot plains for thousands of miles. There was no shelter.
94	People slept in tents on the ground. They had to watch out for wild
108	animals like wolves and snakes. The trip west could take months.
119	Then a railroad was built that stretched from the East Coast
130	almost to the West Coast. The railroad made travel faster. More
141	people poured into the new lands. The settlers quickly built small
152	towns where the farming, fishing, and mining were good. 161

Comprehension Check Possible responses provided.

1. What was life like in the East in the 1800s? **Main Idea and Details**
   The cities were crowded and land was expensive.

2. What enabled people to move west? **Cause and Effect** They bought
   land from France and acquired more land from Mexico.

	Words Read	–	Number of Errors	=	Words Correct Score
First Read		–		=	
Second Read		–		=	

Daily Planner

DAY 1	• Leveled Reader Lesson 1
DAY 2	• Leveled Reader Lesson 2
DAY 3	• Phonics
DAY 4	• Vocabulary • Fluency
DAY 5	• Self-Selected Reading

ELL

Self-Monitor Vocabulary
Have student pairs of different proficiency identify and define unfamiliar words from the main selection using a dictionary. Challenge students to use the new words in sentences. Monitor students as they complete the activity.

Beyond Level

Phonics/Word Study

Objective Decode multisyllabic homophones
Materials • none

EXTEND/ACCELERATE

- **Read Multisyllabic Homophones** Write the words below on the board. Challenge students to read the words, using known word parts. When completed, point to the words in random order for students to chorally read.

cereal	serial	cymbal	symbol
dessert	desert	overdo	overdue
manner	manor	presence	presents
principal	principle	stationary	stationery

- **Define Words** Have students use their knowledge of word parts to figure out the meanings of the above words. Then have partners find the words in a dictionary and confirm or revise the meanings. Challenge students to use these words in this week's writing assignments.

- **Spell Homophones** Giving example sentences, dictate these words for students to spell: *reseed, recede, independents, independence*. Write the words for students to self-correct.

Vocabulary

Objectives Review time lines; write an autobiography
Materials • none

ENRICH VOCABULARY

- **Review Time Lines** Remind students that the author uses a time line in "Gold!" to organize important information about gold. The time line lists the information in chronological order. Have students brainstorm some important events in their lives, then create a time line listing those events in chronological order.

- **Write an Autobiography** Explain that an autobiography is the story of a person's life written by that person. Gather several autobiographies for students to peruse. Have students use the time lines they created to write short autobiographies. Remind students to write the events of their lives in chronological order, incorporating this week's vocabulary when appropriate. Have students compare their autobiographies with those they reviewed.

Gifted & Talented

Beyond Level

Fluency

Objectives Reread selections to develop fluency; develop speaking skills
Materials • **Student Book:** *The Gold Rush Game*, "In Search of Gold"

REREAD FOR FLUENCY

- Have students reread *The Gold Rush Game*. Work with students to read with the appropriate expression.

- Provide time for students to read a section of text to you. Comment on their expression and provide corrective feedback by modeling proper fluency.

DEVELOP SPEAKING/LISTENING SKILLS

- Have students practice reading "In Search of Gold."

- Work with students to read with appropriate expression. Model reading a few sentences at a time. Use intonation, or tone of voice, for emphasis or to convey feeling. Have students repeat.

- Provide time for students to read the selection aloud to partners. Have students name ways their partner expressed emotion or emphasized words using expression and intonation.

Self-Selected Reading

Objective Read independently to identify cause and effect and analyze story structure
Materials • **Leveled Classroom Library** • other fiction books

APPLY SKILLS AND STRATEGIES TO INDEPENDENT READING

- **Read Independently** Have students choose a fiction book such as a **Leveled Classroom Library** book for sustained silent reading. (See the **Theme Bibliography** on pages T8–T9 for book suggestions.) Remind them to look for causes and effects as they read, in order to better analyze the story structure. Have students read and record causes and effects on a Cause and Effect Chart.

- **Show Evidence of Reading** While reading, students may generate a reading log or journal. After reading, tell students to use their Cause and Effect Charts to write or orally state a summary of the book, maintaining meaning and logical order. Provide time for students to share their summaries and comments through Book Talks. Ask: *Did the author effectively structure the plot of the story?*

- **Evaluate** Ask students to think of how the book they read relates to the unit theme, Problem Solving. Have students discuss times when they have worked to solve problems.

Student Book

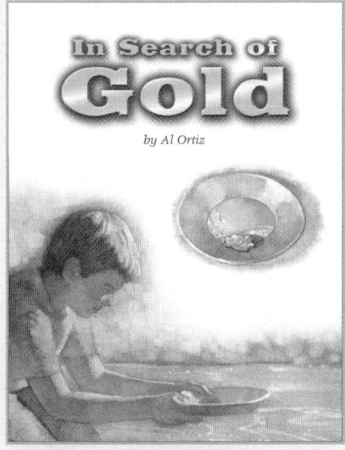

Student Book

Beyond
Leveled Classroom Library
See Leveled Classroom Library lessons on pages T2–T7.

Leveled Reader

Beyond Level

Leveled Reader Lesson 1

Objective	Read to apply strategies and skills
Materials	• **Leveled Reader:** *On Board!*

BEFORE READING

Preview and Predict Have students preview the book by reading the title and chapter titles and looking at the illustrations. Have students predict what this book is about and the types of information they might learn.

 **Review Vocabulary Words** Have students read the vocabulary words on the inside front cover. Tell students to state each definition and any related words they have learned.

Set a Purpose for Reading *Let's read to find out what happens on board this ship.*

DURING READING

 **STRATEGY**
ANALYZE STORY STRUCTURE

Tell students to define the word *structure*. Remind students that story structure involves the story's characters, setting, and plot, and how the author uses these and other elements to organize the story.

SKILL
CAUSE AND EFFECT

Tell students to define the terms *cause* and *effect*. Remind students that every event is an effect of some cause and that the cause usually influences story events in the future.

Read the book with students. Ask open-ended questions to facilitate rich discussion, such as *Why does the author focus on the effect of the hurricane on the two boys? How could the author have explained the causes and effects more clearly?* Build on students' responses to help them develop a deeper understanding of the text. Have students fill in a Cause and Effect Chart independently as they read.

AFTER READING

Compare Tell students to compare the structures of *The Gold Rush Game* and *On Board!* Have students comment on the elements of each that were the most different.

Analyze Have students imagine that they were on the ship with the main characters in *On Board!* Ask them to write a scene with a cause-and-effect set of events. When they are finished, they can trade scenes with a partner and discuss the causes and effects they find.

Gifted & Talented

Beyond Level

Leveled Reader Lesson 2

Objective Reread to apply skills and strategies and develop fluency
Materials • **Leveled Reader:** *On Board!*
• **Beyond Reproducible,** p. 239

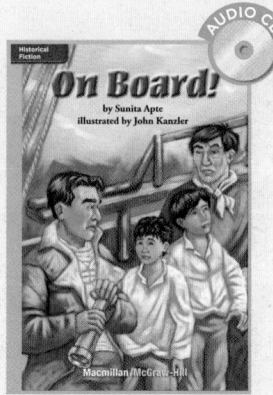

Leveled Reader

BEFORE READING

Review the Strategy and Skill Review students' completed Cause and Effect Charts from the first read. Remind students that an analysis of story structure will include an understanding of how the author uses the different elements to organize the events of the story.

Cause-and-effect relationships are important to most stories. These relationships help the author communicate the events of the plot, including how one event influences a future event. If students' Cause and Effect Charts are incomplete, provide a model chart or use a student chart and revise it as a group. Have students copy the revised chart in their Writer's Notebooks.

Set a Purpose for Reading *Let's reread to check our understanding of the information in the book and to work on our reading fluency.*

DURING READING

Have students reread *On Board!* silently or with a partner. If reading in pairs, prompt students to stop every two pages and ask their partner questions about causes and effects and story structure.

AFTER READING

Check Comprehension Have students independently complete the Comprehension Check on page 20. Review students' answers. Help students find evidence for their answers in the text.

Synthesize Have students imagine that they are interviewing someone on the boat. Tell them to write both the questions and answers, and share with a partner when they are finished.

MODEL FLUENCY

Model reading the fluency passage on **Beyond Reproducible** page 239. Tell students to pay close attention to your intonation and expression as you read. Then read one sentence at a time and have students echo-read the sentences, copying your expression.

During independent reading time, have students work with a partner using the fluency passage. One student reads aloud while the other repeats each sentence back. Students can check their fluency by reading along with the "expert speed" version of the passage on the **Fluency Solutions Audio CD**.

Book Talk

Bringing Groups Together
Students will work with peers of various language and reading abilities to discuss this week's **Leveled Readers**. Refer to page 158 in the **Teacher's Resource Book** for more about how to conduct a Book Talk.

Beyond Reproducible, page 239

As I read, I will pay attention to my intonation and expression.

	If you want to know how a city is made, San Francisco is a good
15	place to learn.
18	The first residents of the area that became San Francisco were
29	Native Americans. For more than 10,000 years, the Ohlone nation lived
39	there. The land wasn't called San Francisco back then and there were
51	no buildings. The land was filled with trees, fields, and wild animals.
63	The Ohlone was not a single nation. It was actually a group of more
77	than 40 different bands. They lived in the same area, but had different
89	languages and customs. The name *Ohlone* actually means "western people."
99	The Ohlone did not live in a single place. They wandered the forests
112	and hills looking for food. If the land seemed good, they set up camp.
126	If not, they moved on.
131	There were usually many plants to eat and animals to hunt. The
143	Ohlone built small boats from wood and reeds. They had access to
154	many rivers, a giant bay, and the Pacific Ocean. There was not much
167	competition between the bands because there was so much food. They
178	shared the land and traded food and supplies. These natural riches
189	would eventually bring other wanderers and explorers. 196

Comprehension Check Possible responses provided.
1. Why was there little competition between the Ohlone bands? **Cause and Effect** There was so much food in their area that they did not have to compete.

2. Was the San Francisco area a good place to live? Why or Why not? **Main Idea and Details** Yes. The Ohlone could gather food on land or from the waters. They traded peacefully among themselves.

	Words Read	−	Number of Errors	=	Words Correct Score
First Read		−		=	
Second Read		−		=	

Daily Planner

DAY 1	• Build Background Knowledge • Vocabulary
DAY 2	• Vocabulary • Access to Core Content *The Gold Rush Game*
DAY 3	• Vocabulary • Grammar • Access to Core Content *The Gold Rush Game*
DAY 4	• Vocabulary • Writing/Spelling • Access to Core Content "Gold!" • Leveled Reader *Camel Ride*
DAY 5	• Vocabulary • Leveled Reader *Camel Ride* • Self-Selected Reading

Interactive Student Book

Use StudentWorks Plus for:
- Vocabulary Preteaching
- Word-by-Word Highlighting
- Think Aloud Prompts

Cognates

Help students identify similarities and differences in pronunciation and spelling between English and Spanish cognates.

imagination	*imaginación*
reference	*referencia*
circular	*circular*
analyze	*analizar*
cause	*causa*
effect	*efecto*
suffixes	*sufijos*
adverbs	*adverbios*

ELL ENGLISH LANGUAGE LEARNERS

Prepare to Read

Content Objective Describe life during the time of the Gold Rush

Language Objective Use key words to describe how research and our imaginations can help us learn about the Gold Rush

Materials • **StudentWorks Plus**

BUILD BACKGROUND KNOWLEDGE

All Language Levels

- Have students preview *The Gold Rush Game* using **StudentWorks Plus**, which contains oral summaries in multiple languages, online multilingual glossaries, word-by-word highlighting, and questions that assess and build comprehension.

- Students can build their word-reading fluency by reading along as the text is read or by listening during the first reading and, at the end of each paragraph, returning to the beginning of the paragraph and reading along.

- Students can build their comprehension by reviewing the definitions of key words in the online glossary and by answering the comprehension questions. When appropriate, the text required to answer the question is highlighted to provide students with additional support and scaffolding.

- After reading, ask students to respond to these questions: *Would you like to visit the past? What time period would you visit? Why?*

Academic Language

Language Objective Use academic language in classroom conversations

All Language Levels

- This week's academic words are **boldfaced** throughout the lesson. Define the word in context and provide a clear example from the selection. Then ask students to generate an example or a word with a similar meaning.

 Academic Language Used in Whole Group Instruction

Theme Words	Key Selection Words	Strategy and Skill Words
discover research imagination	reference disappointment annoyed circular outstretched conducted	analyze story structure cause effect suffixes adverbs

ELL ENGLISH LANGUAGE LEARNERS

Vocabulary

Language Objective Demonstrate understanding and use of key words by describing how imagination can make the past come to life

Materials • Visual Vocabulary Resources
• ELL Resource Book

PRETEACH KEY VOCABULARY

Use the **Visual Vocabulary Resources** to preteach the key selection words *reference, disappointment, annoyed, circular, outstretched*, and *conducted*. Focus on two words per day. Use the following routine, which appears in detail on the cards.

Beginning/Intermediate

■ Point out any known sound-spellings, or focus on a key aspect of phonemic awareness related to the word.

All Language Levels

■ Define the word in English, and provide the example given.

■ Define the word in Spanish, if appropriate, and indicate if the word is a cognate.

■ Display the picture, and explain how it illustrates the word. Engage students in a structured activity, using the key word.

■ Ask students to chorally say the word three times.

■ Distribute copies of the Vocabulary Glossary, **ELL Resource Book** page 312.

PRETEACH FUNCTION WORDS AND PHRASES

All Language Levels

Use the Visual Vocabulary Resources to preteach the function words and phrases *Internet search, squat by, travel overland*, and *broad-brimmed*. Focus on one word or phrase per day. Use the detailed routine on the cards.

■ Define the word in English and, if appropriate, in Spanish. Point out if the word is a cognate.

■ Refer to the picture and engage students in talk about the word. For example, students will partner-talk using sentence frames.

■ Ask students to chorally repeat the word three times.

TEACH BASIC WORDS

Use the Visual Vocabulary Resources to teach the basic words *miner, wagon train, foothills, gold dust, shovel*, and *pick*. Teach these "gold rush" words using the routine provided on the card.

Visual Vocabulary Resources

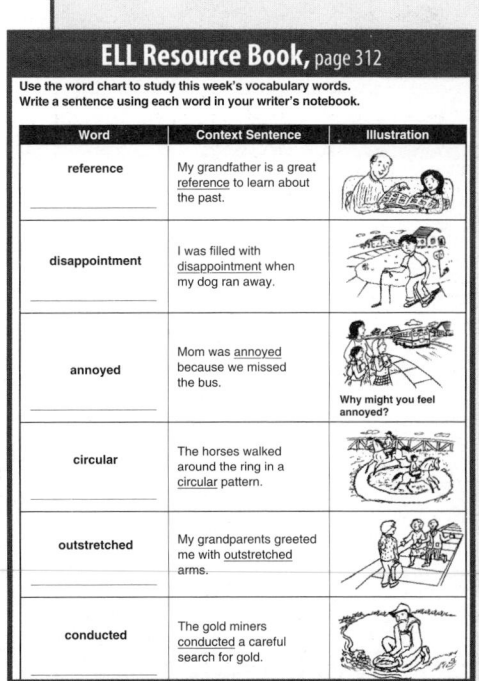

ELL Resource Book, page 312

Use the word chart to study this week's vocabulary words.
Write a sentence using each word in your writer's notebook.

Word	Context Sentence	Illustration
reference	My grandfather is a great <u>reference</u> to learn about the past.	
disappointment	I was filled with <u>disappointment</u> when my dog ran away.	
annoyed	Mom was <u>annoyed</u> because we missed the bus.	Why might you feel annoyed?
circular	The horses walked around the ring in a <u>circular</u> pattern.	
outstretched	My grandparents greeted me with <u>outstretched</u> arms.	
conducted	The gold miners <u>conducted</u> a careful search for gold.	

ELL Resource Book

ELL ENGLISH LANGUAGE LEARNERS

Access to Core Content

Content Objective Read grade-level text
Language Objective Discuss text, using key words and sentence frames
Materials • **ELL Resource Book,** pp. 302–311

PRETEACH MAIN SELECTION (PAGES 708–721)

All Language Levels

Use the Interactive Question-Response Guide on **ELL Resource Book** pages 302–309 to introduce students to *The Gold Rush Game*. Preteach half of the selection on Day 2 and half on Day 3.

- Use the prompts provided in the guide to develop meaning and vocabulary. Use the partner-talk and whole-class responses to engage students and increase student talk.
- When completed, have partners reread the story.

PRETEACH PAIRED SELECTION (PAGES 724–727)

All Language Levels

Use the Interactive Question-Response Guide on ELL Resource Book pages 310–311 to preview the paired selection "Gold!" Preteach the selection on Day 4.

Beginning	Intermediate	Advanced
Use Visuals During the Interactive Reading, select several illustrations that show a cause or an effect in the plot. Describe them and have students retell what you said.	**Identify** During the Interactive Reading, select a few lines of text that describe a cause and an effect. After you have read and explained it, have students identify the cause, based on the text.	**Describe** During the Interactive Reading, select a passage of text. After you have read and explained it, have students describe the cause and effect, based on the passage.

ELL ENGLISH LANGUAGE LEARNERS

Fluency

Content Objectives Reread selections to develop fluency; develop speaking skills

Language Objective Tell a partner what a selection is about

Materials • **Student Book:** *The Gold Rush Game,* "Gold"
• **Teacher's Resource Book**

✓ REREAD FOR FLUENCY

Beginning

- Have students read the decodable passages on pages 32–33 in the **Teacher's Resource Book**.

Intermediate/Advanced

- Have students reread two to four of their favorite pages from *The Gold Rush Game.* Work with students to read the pages with the appropriate intonation. For example, read a few lines of the dialogue with another student. Point out how you change your intonation to express how the characters are feeling. Then have students chorally read additional lines of dialogue for the class.

- Provide time for students to read their sections of text to you. Comment on their intonation and expression, and provide corrective feedback by modeling proper fluency.

DEVELOP SPEAKING/LISTENING SKILLS

All Language Levels

- Have students practice reading "Gold." Work with them to read with the appropriate intonation and expression.

- Provide time for students to read several paragraphs aloud to a partner. Have students tell their partner about the article. Provide the sentence frame: *I learned that ___ .*

Self-Selected Reading

Content Objective Read independently

Language Objective Orally retell information learned

Materials • **Leveled Classroom Library** • other fiction books

APPLY SKILLS AND STRATEGIES TO INDEPENDENT READING

All Language Levels

- Have students choose a fiction book for independent reading. (See the **Theme Bibliography** on pages T8–T9.)

- After reading, tell students to orally summarize and share their reactions to the book with classmates. Ask: *Would you recommend this book to a classmate? Why or why not?*

Student Book

Leveled Classroom Library
See Leveled Classroom
Library lessons on pages T2–T7.

Transfer Skills

Adverbs Adverbs are not used in Hmong. Instead, two repeated verbs commonly take the place of a verb and adverb. For example, *I searched searched for gold* for *I searched longer for gold*. Model how to use adverb comparisons in sentences. Write on the board: *Minh jumps higher than Sam.* Then act out the example. Have students repeat the sentence and help them form their own sentences using adverb comparisons. See language transfers on pages T16–T31.

Corrective Feedback

During Whole Group grammar lessons, follow the routine on the **Grammar Transparencies** to provide students with extra support. This routine includes completing the items with English Language Learners while other students work independently, having students reread the sentences with partners to build fluency, and providing a generative task, such as writing a new sentence using the skill.

ELL ENGLISH LANGUAGE LEARNERS

Grammar

Content Objective Identify adverb comparisons
Language Objective Speak in complete sentences, using sentence frames

COMPARING WITH ADVERBS

Beginning/Intermediate

- Review adverbs. Remind students that adverbs can be used to compare two or more actions. Write on the board: *Lou dug faster than most miners. Larry dug the fastest of all.* Underline *faster* and *fastest*. Point out that to compare, ending *-er* or *-est* is added to most one-syllable adverbs. Then write on the board: *Tom searched more carefully than Will. Rob searched the most carefully of all the miners.* Underline *more carefully* and *most carefully*. Review that for adverbs with two or more syllables, *more* or *most* is added before the adverb. Finally, review the irregular comparative adverbs *good, better, best* and *bad, worse, worst*.

All Language Levels

- Review how to compare with adverbs. Have students underline and correct comparative adverbs in the sentences below. *The correct adverb is ____.*

  Luke mined for gold <u>fastest</u> than Edward.
  Covered wagons moved <u>more slower</u> than trains.
  Sam's piece of gold shined <u>brightliest</u> of all the pieces.

PEER DISCUSSION STARTERS

All Language Levels

- Write the following sentences on the board:

  The Gold Rush ____.   *I learned that miners ____.*

- Pair students and have them complete each sentence frame. Have them expand on their sentences by providing as many details as they can from this week's readings. Circulate, listen in, and take note of each student's language use and proficiency.

Beginning	Intermediate	Advanced
Use Visuals Describe the illustrations in *The Gold Rush Game* to students. Help students point and name adverbs and form comparative adverbs. Use them in sentences for students to repeat.	**Compare** Ask students to describe the illustrations in *The Gold Rush Game* using comparative adverbs. Have them use complete sentences. Model sentences as needed.	**Compare** Ask students to describe the illustrations in *The Gold Rush Game* using comparative adverbs. Have them use adverbs with one syllable and more than two syllables in their comparisons.

ELL ENGLISH LANGUAGE LEARNERS

Writing/Spelling

Content Objective Spell words correctly
Language Objective Write in complete sentences, using sentence frames

All Language Levels

■ Write the key vocabulary words on the board: *reference, disappointment, annoyed, circular, outstretched, conducted*. Have students copy each word on their **WorkBoards**. Help them say each word and then write a sentence for it. Provide sentence starters such as:

> *A dictionary is a good reference for ___.*
>
> *People might feel disappointment when ___.*
>
> *We were annoyed that ___.*
>
> *Something that moves in a circular motion is ___.*
>
> *He outstretched his arms to catch the ___.*
>
> *The group conducted a search to find ___.*

Beginning/Intermediate

■ Help students spell words using their growing knowledge of English sound-spelling relationships. Model how to segment the word students are trying to spell and attach a spelling to each sound (or spellings to each syllable if a multisyllabic word). Use the **Sound-Spelling Cards** to reinforce the spellings for each English sound.

Advanced

■ Dictate the following words for students to spell: *tail/tale, knead/ need, blue/blew, scent/cent*. Guide students using the Sound-Spelling Cards as they spell each word.

■ When completed, review the meanings of words that can be easily demonstrated or explained. Use actions, gestures, and available pictures.

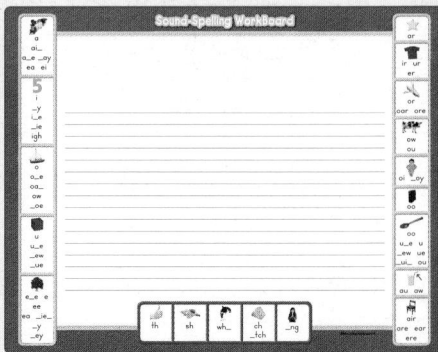

Sound-Spelling WorkBoard

Phonics/Word Study

For English Language Learners who need more practice with this week's phonics/spelling skill, see the Approaching Level lesson on page 729J. Focus on minimal contrasts, articulation, and those sounds that do not transfer from the student's first language to English. See language transfers on pages T16–T31.

Leveled Reader

Vocabulary

Preteach Vocabulary Use the routine in the **Visual Vocabulary Resources**, pages 505–510, to preteach the ELL Vocabulary listed in the inside front cover of the **Leveled Reader**.

ELL ENGLISH LANGUAGE LEARNERS

Leveled Reader

Content Objective Read to apply skills and strategies

Language Objective Retell information using complete sentences

Materials • **Leveled Reader:** *Camel Ride*
• **ELL Resource Book,** p. 313
• **Visual Vocabulary Resources,** pp. 505–510

BEFORE READING

All Language Levels

■ **Preview** Read the title *Camel Ride*. Ask: *What's the title? Say it again*. Repeat with the author's name. Then look at the illustrations in the book. Use simple language to tell about each page. Ask questions, such as *What kinds of things do people do on a ranch? Do camels usually live on a ranch? Where do camels live? What kind of climate do they like?*

■ **Review Skills** Use the inside front cover to review the comprehension skill and vocabulary words.

■ **Set a Purpose** Say: *Let's read to find out what happens at the ranch after the camels arrive.*

DURING READING

All Language Levels

■ Have students read each page aloud using the differentiated suggestions. Provide corrective feedback, such as modeling how to blend a decodable word or clarifying meaning by using techniques from the Interactive Question-Response Guide.

■ **Retell** After every two pages, ask students to state the main ideas they have learned so far. Help them to complete the Cause and Effect Chart. Restate students' comments when they have difficulty using story-specific words. Provide differentiated sentence frames to support students' responses and engage students in partner-talk where appropriate.

Beginning	Intermediate	Advanced
Echo-Read Have students echo-read after you.	**Choral-Read** Have students chorally read with you.	**Choral-Read** Have students chorally read.
Check Comprehension Point to pictures and ask questions, such as *Do you see an animal? What kind of animal is it? Point to a ranch.*	**Check Comprehension** Ask questions/prompts, such as *What does Cole think about the new ranch hands? Why is Cole suspicious?*	**Check Comprehension** Ask: *What are the two new ranch hands planning to do? How did Cole find out about their plan?*

ELL ENGLISH LANGUAGE LEARNERS

AFTER READING

Use the chart below and Think and Compare questions in the **Leveled Reader** to determine students' progress.

Think and Compare	Beginning	Intermediate	Advanced
1 Why does Cole need to find the sheriff? (*Cause and Effect*)	Possible responses: Nonverbal response. Father is in danger.	Possible responses: Cole's father is in danger.	Possible responses: Cole needs the sheriff's help because his father is in danger from the two new ranch hands. They want to take over the mine.
2 What would you have done if you were in Cole's place? (*Synthesize*)	Possible responses: Nonverbal response. Find sheriff.	Possible responses: I would do the same things that Cole did and go to the sheriff.	Possible responses: I would have done the same things as Cole and asked the sheriff for help.
3 Would camels be useful in the Southwest today? Why or why not? (*Apply*)	Possible responses: Nonverbal response. Yes. Travel through Southwest in deserts.	Possible responses: Yes, we could use camels to travel through deserts.	Possible responses: Yes, its would be useful to have camels in the Southwest because people could use them to travel through deserts.

BOOK TALK

Develop Listening and Speaking Skills Distribute copies of **ELL Resource Book** page 313 and form small groups. Help students determine the leader to discuss the Book Talk questions. Tell students to remember the following while engaged in the activity:

- Narrate, describe, and explain with specificity and detail. Ask: *Where did the story take place? Can you describe the setting? What else did you notice?*

- Express opinions, ideas, and feelings on a variety of social and academic topics. Ask: *What do you think about the characters in the story?*

- Employ self-corrective techniques and monitor their own and other students' language production. Students should ask themselves: *What parts of this passage were confusing to me? Can my classmates help me clarify a word or sentence that I don't understand?*

ELL Resource Book

Book Talk

Bringing Groups Together Students will work with peers of varying language abilities to discuss the Book Talk questions. Form groups so that students who read the Beyond Level, On Level, Approaching Level, and ELL Leveled Readers are in the same group for the activity.

Progress Monitoring
Weekly Assessment

ASSESSED SKILLS

- Vocabulary: Vocabulary Words, Suffixes
- Comprehension: Cause and Effect
- Grammar: Comparing with Adverbs
- Phonics/Spelling: Homophones

Selection Test for **The Gold Rush Game** *Also Available*

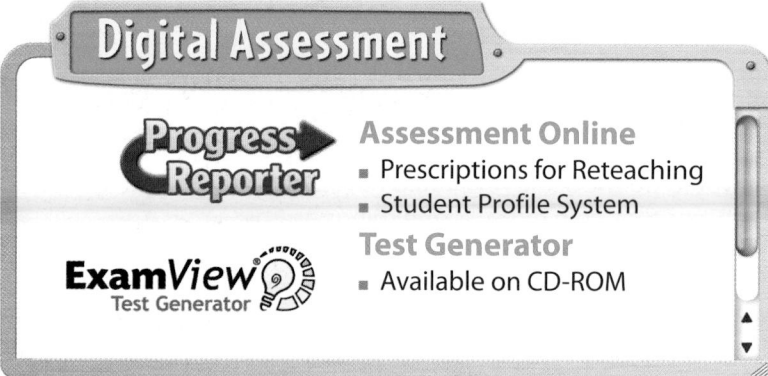

Digital Assessment

Progress Reporter

Assessment Online
- Prescriptions for Reteaching
- Student Profile System

ExamView Test Generator

Test Generator
- Available on CD-ROM

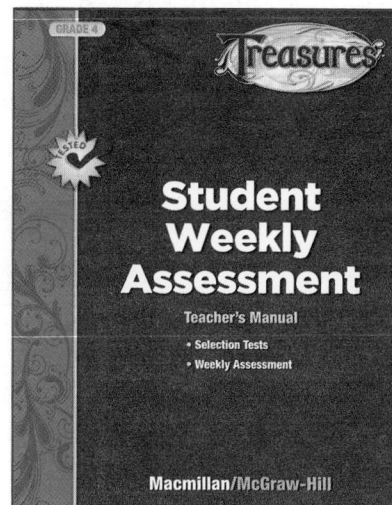

**Weekly Assessment
Unit 6 Week 2**

Fluency Assessment

Assess fluency for one group of students per week. Use the Oral Fluency Record Sheet to track the number of words read correctly. Fluency goal for all students: **113–133 words correct per minute (WCPM)**.

Approaching Level	Weeks 1, 3, 5
On Level	Weeks 2, 4
Beyond Level	Week 6

Fluency Assessment

Diagnose		Prescribe
Review the assessment answers with students. Have them correct their errors. Then provide additional instruction as needed.		
	IF...	**THEN...**
VOCABULARY WORDS VOCABULARY STRATEGY Suffixes	0–2 items correct …	See **Vocabulary Intervention Teacher's Edition.** LOG ON ▶ Online Practice: Go to www.macmillanmh.com. CD-ROM Vocabulary PuzzleMaker
COMPREHENSION Skill: Cause and Effect	0–3 items correct …	See **Comprehension Intervention Teacher's Edition.** SPIRAL REVIEW See Cause and Effect lesson in Unit 6 Week 3, page 737B.
GRAMMAR Comparing with Adverbs	0–1 items correct …	See **Writing and Grammar Intervention Teacher's Edition.**
PHONICS AND SPELLING Homophones	0–1 items correct …	LOG ON ▶ Online Practice: Go to www.macmillanmh.com. See **Phonics Intervention Teacher's Edition.**
FLUENCY	109–112 WCPM	AUDIO CD Fluency Solutions Audio CD
	0–108 WCPM	See **Fluency Intervention Teacher's Edition.**

Response to Intervention

To place students in Tier 2 or Tier 3 Intervention use the *Diagnostic Assessment*.

- Phonics
- Vocabulary
- Comprehension
- Fluency
- Writing and Grammar

Week 3 ★ At a Glance

Priority Skills and Concepts

 Comprehension
- **Strategy:** Generate Questions
- **Skill:** Fact and Opinion
- Cause and Effect
- **Genre:** Biography, Expository

 Robust Vocabulary
- **Selection Vocabulary:** *decades, active, transform, volunteer, violated*
- **Strategy:** Latin, Greek, and Other Linguistic Roots

 Fluency
- **Expression**

 Phonics/Spelling
- **Word Study:** Prefixes, Multisyllabic Words
- **Spelling Words:** *discourage, disappoint, disbelief, distrust, disloyal, misplace, mislabel, mislead, misstep, misnumber, nonfat, nonfiction, nonsense, nonstop, unable, unplug, uncertain, uncomfortable, uncover, unclean*
- *prince, weighed, bolder*

 Grammar/Mechanics
- **Negatives**
- **Correcting Double Negatives**

 Writing
- **Research Report**

Key

 Tested in program  Review Skill

Digital Learning

Digital solutions to help plan and implement instruction

☑ Teacher Resources

LOG ON ▶

ONLINE www.macmillanmh.com

▶ **Teacher's Edition**
- Lesson Planner and Resources also on CD-ROM

TeacherWorks Plus

▶ **Formative Assessment**
- ExamView® on CD-ROM also available

Progress Reporter

▶ **Instructional Resources**
- Unit Videos
- Classroom Presentation Toolkit

VIDEO

▶ **Professional Development**
- Video Library

 **Professional Development**

☑ Student Resources

LOG ON ▶

ONLINE www.macmillanmh.com

▶ **Interactive Student Book**

StudentWorks Plus

▶ **Leveled Reader Database**

▶ **Activities**
- Research Toolkit
- Oral Language Activities
- Vocabulary/Spelling Activities

 Listening Library
- Recordings of Student Books and Leveled Readers

 Fluency Solutions
- Fluency Modeling and Practice

Weekly Literature

Theme: Improving Lives

Student Book

LOG ON StudentWorks *Plus*
Interactive Student Book

- Word-by-Word Reading
- Summaries in Multiple Languages
- Comprehension Questions

Comprehension

Genre
Expository text, such as a magazine article, presents facts and information.

Generate Questions
Fact and Opinion
A fact is something that can be proven true using reference sources. An opinion is a belief that does not have to be supported by facts.

▼ Dolores Huerta and supporters celebrate the birthday of César Chávez in Los Angeles in 2006.

Real World Reading

Taking the Lead

How did Dolores Huerta help solve the problems faced by farmworkers?

Dolores Huerta is an important leader in the Latino community. She has spent the last few **decades** helping farmworkers. After college, Huerta became a teacher. Many of her students' parents worked on farms. Their children often came to school hungry. Huerta realized that these families needed help.

"I couldn't stand seeing farmworker children come to class hungry and in need of shoes," Huerta has said. "I thought I could do more by organizing their parents than by trying to teach their hungry children."

Main Selection
Genre Expository

A Fight Against Injustice

Preteach Vocabulary and Comprehension
Genre Expository

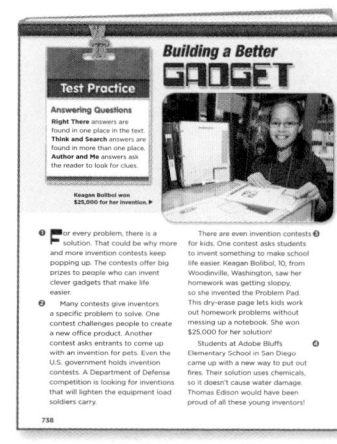

Building a Better GADGET

Test Practice
Genre Expository

Support Literature

Treasures
INTERACTIVE Read-Aloud ANTHOLOGY with PLAYS

Interactive Read-Aloud Anthology
- Listening Comprehension
- Robust Vocabulary
- Readers Theater Plays for Fluency

Resources for Differentiated Instruction

Leveled Readers

GR Levels P–U

| Genre | Biography |

- Same Theme
- Same Vocabulary
- Same Comprehension Skills

P — Charles Drew by Steven Otfinoski
Approaching Level

R — Marie Curie by Meish Goldish
On Level

U — Dr. Jonas Salk by Cliff Clark
Beyond Level

Q — Marie Curie by Meish Goldish
ELL

 **LOG ON** ▶ **Leveled Reader Database**
Go to www.macmillanmh.com.

Leveled Practice

Approaching — Approaching Reproducibles
On Level — Practice Book
Beyond — Beyond Reproducibles
ELL — English Language Learner Practice Book

Leveled Classroom Library

Approaching — TRAVELING MAN

On Level — CLEVER TORTOISE

Beyond — The Weaving of a Dream

Response to Intervention

 **Tier 2**

- Phonics
- Vocabulary
- Comprehension
- Fluency
- Writing and Grammar

 **Tier 3**

Assessment

Time For Kids
- TFK Teacher's Manual
- Apply Answering Question Strategies

Student Weekly Assessment
Weekly Assessment

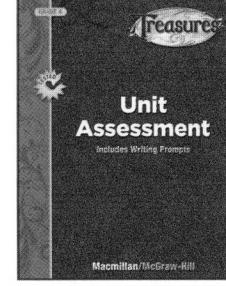
Unit Assessment
Unit Assessment

Benchmark Assessment
Benchmark Assessment

 🏠 **HOME-SCHOOL CONNECTION**

- Family letters in English and Spanish
- Take-Home Stories and activities

Home-School Connection

LOG ON ▶ **Online Homework**
www.macmillanmh.com

Go to **www.macmillanmh.com** for Online Lesson Planner

Teacher Works *Plus*
All-in-One Planner and Resource Center

Professional Development Video Library

Taking the Lead, pp. 734–737

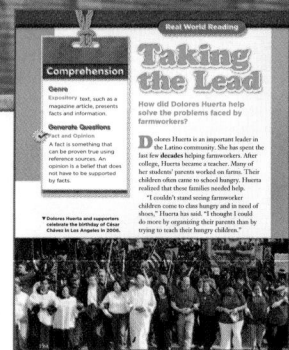

WHOLE GROUP

ORAL LANGUAGE
- **Listening Comprehension**
- **Speaking/Viewing**

WORD STUDY
- **Vocabulary**
- **Phonics/Word Study**
- **Spelling**

READING
- **Comprehension**
- **Fluency**

LANGUAGE ARTS
- **Writing**
- **Grammar**

ASSESSMENT
- **Informal/Formal**

DAY 1

Listening/Speaking/Viewing

? Focus Question How can solving problems in your community improve the lives of others?

Build Background, 730

Read Aloud: "Mary Anning and the Sea Dragon," 731A–731B

Vocabulary
decades, active, volunteer, transform, violated, 733, 741G
Practice Book, 245

Strategy: Word Parts/Latin, Greek, and Other Linguistic Roots, 732

Spelling Pretest: Prefixes, 741I
Phonics/Spelling Book, 163–164

Read "A Fight Against Injustice," "A Place to Heal," and "Summer Camp," 732–733

Student Book

Comprehension, 733A–733B
Strategy: Generate Questions

Skill: Fact and Opinion
Practice Book, 246

Fluency Model Fluency, 731B

Writing

Daily Writing Describe a time when nothing could stop you from finishing a project.

Research Report, Plan/Prewrite, 741A

Grammar Daily Language Activities, 741K
Negatives, 741K
Grammar Practice Book, 136

Quick Check Vocabulary, 733
Comprehension, 733B

DAY 2

Listening/Speaking

? Focus Question How did Dolores Huerta help solve the problems faced by farmworkers?

Vocabulary
Review Words, Latin, Greek, and Other Linguistic Roots, 734, 741G
Practice Book, 251

Morphology
Prefixes, 731C–731D
Practice Book, 244

Spelling Word Sorts, 741I
Phonics/Spelling Book, 165

Read *Taking the Lead,* 734–737

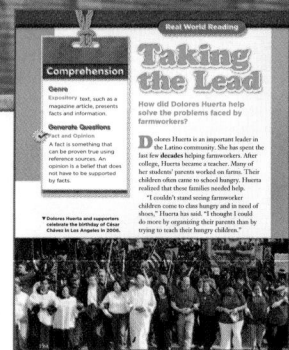
Student Book

Comprehension, 734–737
Strategy: Generate Questions

Skill: Fact and Opinion
Practice Book, 247

Fluency Repeated Reading: Expression, 737A

Writing

Daily Writing Write about one community of people you would like to help.

Research Report, Draft, 741B

Grammar Daily Language Activities, 741K
Negatives, 741K
Grammar Practice Book, 137

Quick Check Phonics, 731D
Comprehension, 737

SMALL GROUP Lesson Plan

Differentiated Instruction 730G–730H

Priority Skills

Vocabulary	Comprehension	Writing	
Vocabulary Words **Word Parts:** Latin, Greek, and Other Linguistic Roots	**Strategy:** Generate Questions **Skill:** Fact and Opinion	Research Report	

DAY 3

Listening/Speaking

? Focus Question How is the organization LULAC in "A Fight Against Injustice" similar to the Community Service Organization?

Vocabulary

Review Words, Related Words, 741H

Spelling Word Meanings, 741J
Phonics/Spelling Book, 166

Read *Taking the Lead,* 734–737

Student Book

Comprehension
Comprehension Check, 737

Review Skill: Cause and Effect, 737B
Practice Book, 249

Fluency Repeated Reading: Expression, 737A
Practice Book, 248

Writing

Daily Writing Why do you think Dolores Huerta had the laws changed to allow people to vote in Spanish instead of English?

Research Report, Revise and Conferencing, 741C–741E

Grammar Daily Language Activities, 741K
Mechanics and Usage, 741L
Grammar Practice Book, 138

Quick Check Fluency, 737A

DAY 4

Listening/Speaking/Viewing

? Focus Question What do you think of the Problem Pad? Review this invention and tell whether or not you would buy one. Use details from the article in your review.

Vocabulary

Review Words, Morphology, 741H

Spelling Proofread, 741J
Phonics/Spelling Book, 167

Read "Building a Better Gadget," 738–739

Test Practice: Answering Questions

Student Book

Research and Study Skills
Functional Documents, 737C–737D
Practice Book, 250

Fluency Repeated Reading: Expression, 737A

Writing

Daily Writing Design an invention contest. What problems in your school need a solution?

Writing Prompt, 740–741

Research Report, Conferencing, Proofread/Edit, 741E–741F

Grammar Daily Language Activities, 741K
Negatives, 741L
Grammar Practice Book, 139

Quick Check Vocabulary, 741H

DAY 5
Review and Assess

Listening/Speaking/Viewing

? Focus Question What generalizations can you make about the personalities of people who help their communities? What makes them different from everyone else?

Vocabulary

Assess Words, Connect to Writing, 741H

Spelling Posttest, 741J
Phonics/Spelling Book, 168

Read Self-Selected Reading, 730K
Practice Book, 252

Comprehension
Strategy: Generate Questions

Skill: Fact and Opinion

Fluency Practice, 730K

Writing

Daily Writing Write steps one can take to organize a group of people, the way Dolores Huerta did.

Research Report, Publish and Share, 741F

Grammar Daily Language Activities, 741K
Negatives, 741L
Grammar Practice Book, 140

Weekly Assessment, 741MM–741NN

Differentiated Instruction

What do I do in small groups?

Teacher-Led Small Groups

Independent Activities

Focus on Skills

IF... students need additional instruction, practice, or extension based on your  **Quick Check** observations for the following priority skills

✔ **Phonics/Word Study**
Prefixes

✔ **Vocabulary Words**
decades, active, volunteer, transform, violated
Strategy: Latin, Greek, and Other Linguistic Roots

✔ **Comprehension**
Strategy: Generate Questions
Skill: Fact and Opinion

✔ **Fluency**

THEN... | **Approaching** **ELL** | Preteach and Reteach Skills |
| **On Level** | Practice |
| **Beyond** | Enrich and Accelerate Learning |

 LOG ON ▶ ## Suggested Small Group Lesson Plan

 CD-ROM TeacherWorks *Plus* All-In-One Planner and Resource Center

	DAY 1	**DAY 2**
Approaching Level **Tier 2** • **Preteach/Reteach** **Tier 2 Instruction**	• Prepare to Read, 741M • Academic Language, 741M • Preteach Vocabulary, 741O	• Comprehension, 741Q Generate Questions/Fact and Opinion **ELL** • Leveled Reader Lesson 1, 741R
On Level • **Practice**	• Vocabulary, 741W • Phonics, 741W Prefixes **ELL**	• Leveled Reader Lesson 1, 741Y
Beyond Level • **Extend/Accelerate** **Gifted and Talented**	• Leveled Reader Lesson 1, 741CC • Analyze Information, 741CC	• Leveled Reader Lesson 2, 741DD • Synthesize Information, 741DD
ELL • **Build English Language Proficiency** • See **ELL** in other levels.	• Prepare to Read, 741EE • Academic Language, 741EE • Preteach Vocabulary, 741FF	• Vocabulary, 741FF • Preteach Main Selection, 741GG

Focus on Leveled Readers

Leveled Reader Library

Levels P–U

Approaching

On Level

Beyond

ELL

Manipulatives

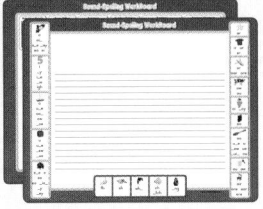
Sound-Spelling WorkBoards

Sound-Spelling Cards

about
today

High-Frequency Word Cards

Visual Vocabulary Resources

Additional Leveled Readers

LOG ON **Leveled Reader Database**
www.macmillanmh.com

Search by

- Comprehension Skill
- Content Area
- Genre
- Text Feature
- Guided Reading Level
- Reading Recovery Level
- Lexile Score
- Benchmark Level

Subscription also available.

DAY 3

- Phonics Maintenance, 741N
  Prefixes **ELL**
- Leveled Reader Lesson 2, 741S

- Leveled Reader Lesson 2, 741Z

- Phonics, 741AA
  Prefixes **ELL**

- Vocabulary, 741FF
- Grammar, 741II

DAY 4

- Reteach Phonics Skill, 741N
  Prefixes **ELL**
- Review Vocabulary, 741P
- Leveled Reader Lesson 3, 741T

- Fluency, 741X

- Vocabulary, 741AA
- Compare Biographies, 741AA
- Fluency, 741BB

- Vocabulary, 741FF
- Writing/Spelling, 741JJ
- Fluency, 741HH
- Leveled Reader, 741KK

DAY 5

- High-Frequency Words, 741P
- Fluency, 741U
- Self-Selected Independent Reading, 741V
- Book Talk, 741T

- Self-Selected Independent Reading, 741X
- Book Talk, 741Z

- Self-Selected Independent Reading, 741BB
- Evaluate Information, 741BB
- Book Talk, 741DD

- Vocabulary, 741FF
- Leveled Reader, 741KK
- Self-Selected Independent Reading, 741HH
- Book Talk, 741LL

Managing the Class

What do I do with the rest of my class?

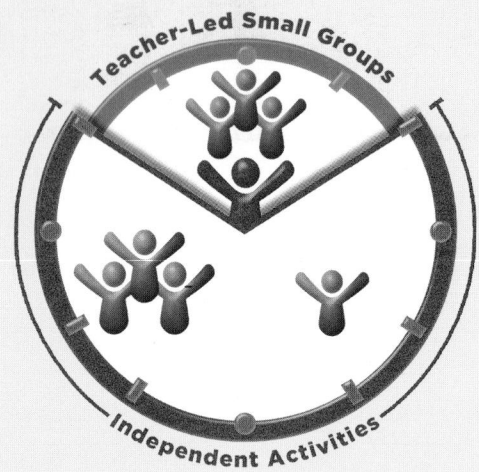

- Practice Book and Reproducibles
- ELL Practice Book
- Leveled Reader Activities
- Literacy Workstations
- Online Activities

Classroom Management Tools

Weekly Contract

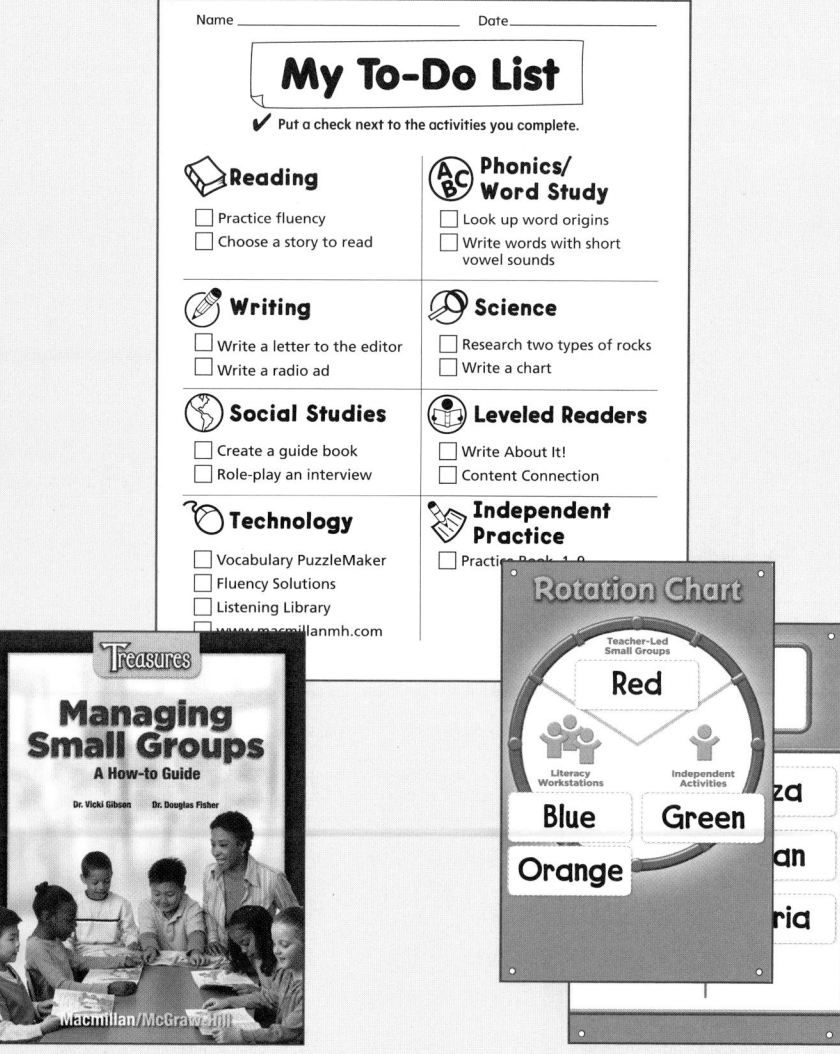

My To-Do List

✔ Put a check next to the activities you complete.

Reading
- [ ] Practice fluency
- [ ] Choose a story to read

Phonics/Word Study
- [ ] Look up word origins
- [ ] Write words with short vowel sounds

Writing
- [ ] Write a letter to the editor
- [ ] Write a radio ad

Science
- [ ] Research two types of rocks
- [ ] Write a chart

Social Studies
- [ ] Create a guide book
- [ ] Role-play an interview

Leveled Readers
- [ ] Write About It!
- [ ] Content Connection

Technology
- [ ] Vocabulary PuzzleMaker
- [ ] Fluency Solutions
- [ ] Listening Library
- [ ] www.macmillanmh.com

Independent Practice
- [ ] Practice Book 1–9

Managing Small Groups: A How-to Guide
Dr. Vicki Gibson Dr. Douglas Fisher
Macmillan/McGraw-Hill

How-to Guide

Rotation Chart

Teacher-Led Small Groups
Red
Literacy Workstations Independent Activities
Blue Green
Orange

Rotation Chart

Digital Learning

StudentWorks Plus
Interactive Student Book

StudentWorks Plus Online
- Summaries in Multiple Languages
- Word-by-Word Reading
- Comprehension Questions

Meet the Author/Illustrator

Rosalyn Schanzer
- As a child, Rosalyn loved reading stories about horses.
- She lives with her husband, her two children, and her dog named Jones.
- Rosalyn worked for years illustrating other people's books before finally deciding to write her own.

Other books by Rosalyn Schanzer
- Schanzer, Rosalyn. *Escaping to America: A True Story.* New York: HarperCollins, 2000.
- Schanzer, Rosalyn. *Gold Fever.* Washington, D.C.: National Geographic Society, 1999.

- Other Books by the Author or Illustrator

Leveled Practice

Practice Book
- Phonics
- Vocabulary
- Fluency
- Comprehension
- Writing

Macmillan/McGraw-Hill

On Level

English Language Learner Practice Book

Macmillan/McGraw-Hill

ELL

Also Available:
Approaching Reproducible
Beyond Reproducible

Independent Activities

Oral Language Activities

- Focus on Vocabulary and Concepts
- English Language Learner Support

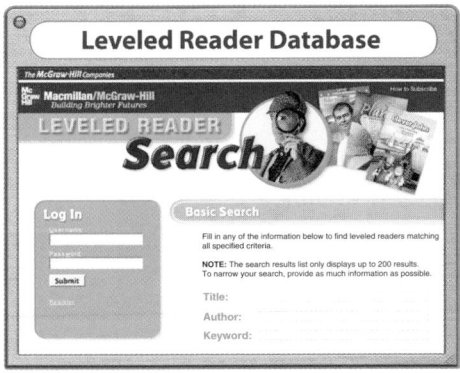

Leveled Reader Database

- Leveled Reader Database
- Search titles by level, skill, content area, and more

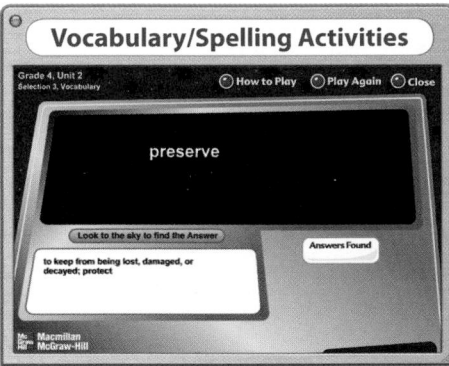

Vocabulary/Spelling Activities

- Differentiated Lists and Activities

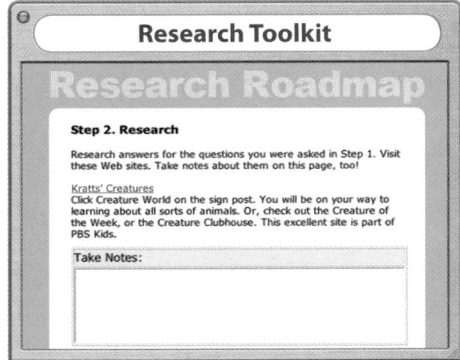

Research Toolkit

- Research Roadmap
- Research and Presentation Tools
- Theme Launcher Video
- Links to Science and Social Studies

Available on CD

LISTENING LIBRARY
Recordings of selections
- Main Selections
- Paired Selections
- Leveled Readers

VOCABULARY PUZZLEMAKER

FLUENCY SOLUTIONS
Recorded passages at two speeds for modeling and practicing fluency

Leveled Reader Activities

Approaching

On Level

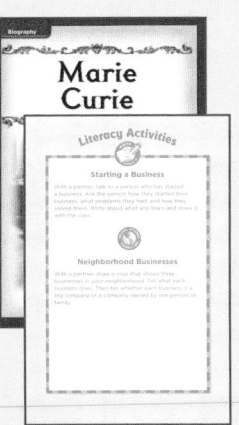

Beyond

ELL

See inside cover of all Leveled Readers.

Literacy Workstations

Reading

Writing

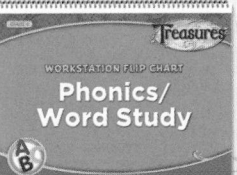
Phonics/Word Study

Science/Social Studies

See lessons on pages 730K–730L.

Managing the Class

What do I do with the rest of my class?

 **Reading**

Objectives

- Develop fluency through partner reading
- Read independently for a sustained period of time; use **Practice Book** page 252 for Reading Strategies and Reading Log

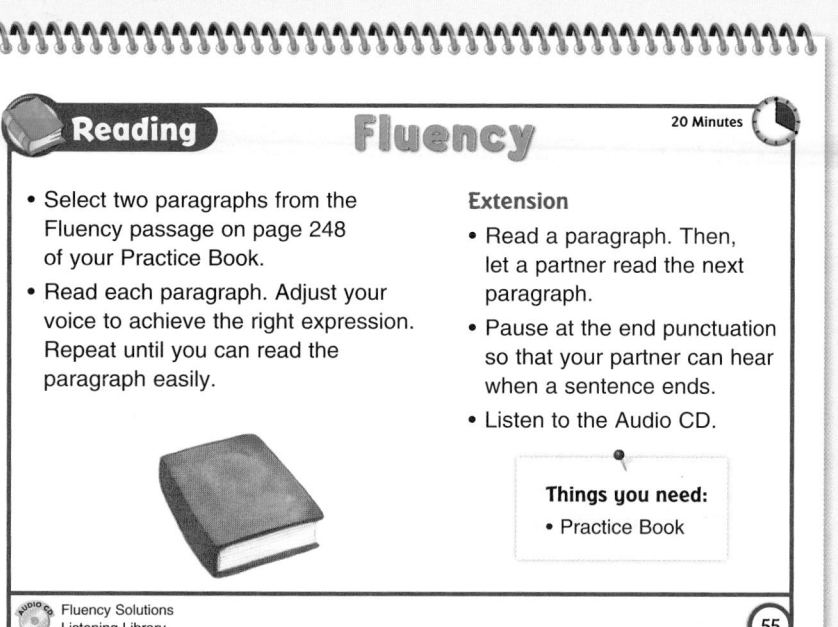

Reading — *Fluency* — 20 Minutes

- Select two paragraphs from the Fluency passage on page 248 of your Practice Book.
- Read each paragraph. Adjust your voice to achieve the right expression. Repeat until you can read the paragraph easily.

Extension

- Read a paragraph. Then, let a partner read the next paragraph.
- Pause at the end punctuation so that your partner can hear when a sentence ends.
- Listen to the Audio CD.

Things you need:
- Practice Book

Fluency Solutions
Listening Library — 55

Reading — *Biography* — 20 Minutes

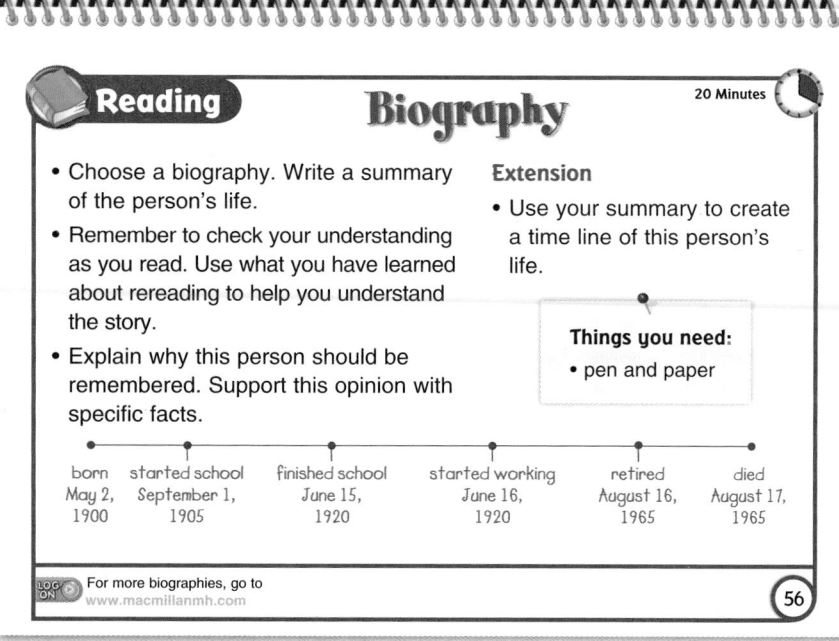

- Choose a biography. Write a summary of the person's life.
- Remember to check your understanding as you read. Use what you have learned about rereading to help you understand the story.
- Explain why this person should be remembered. Support this opinion with specific facts.

Extension

- Use your summary to create a time line of this person's life.

Things you need:
- pen and paper

| born May 2, 1900 | started school September 1, 1905 | finished school June 15, 1920 | started working June 16, 1920 | retired August 16, 1965 | died August 17, 1965 |

For more biographies, go to www.macmillanmh.com — 56

 **Phonics/Word Study**

Objectives

- Identify Greek roots
- Identify prefixes in words
- List words with prefixes

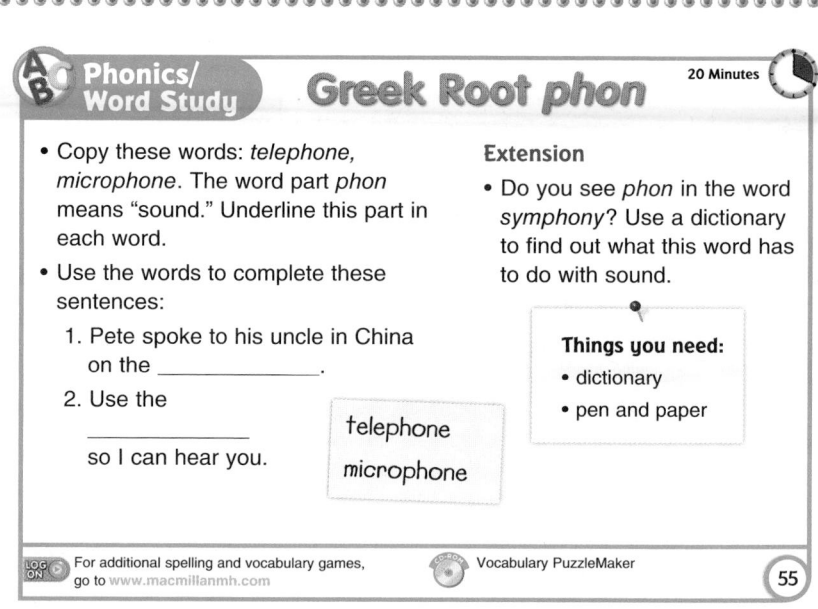

Phonics/Word Study — *Greek Root phon* — 20 Minutes

- Copy these words: *telephone*, *microphone*. The word part *phon* means "sound." Underline this part in each word.
- Use the words to complete these sentences:
  1. Pete spoke to his uncle in China on the _____.
  2. Use the _____ so I can hear you.

telephone
microphone

Extension

- Do you see *phon* in the word *symphony*? Use a dictionary to find out what this word has to do with sound.

Things you need:
- dictionary
- pen and paper

For additional spelling and vocabulary games, go to www.macmillanmh.com — Vocabulary PuzzleMaker — 55

Phonics/Word Study — *Prefixes* — 20 Minutes

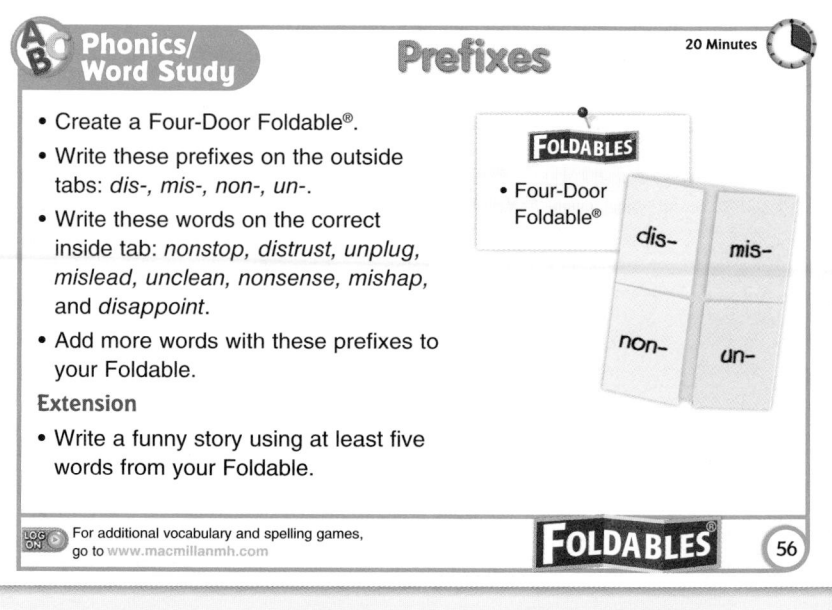

- Create a Four-Door Foldable®.
- Write these prefixes on the outside tabs: *dis-*, *mis-*, *non-*, *un-*.
- Write these words on the correct inside tab: *nonstop, distrust, unplug, mislead, unclean, nonsense, mishap,* and *disappoint*.
- Add more words with these prefixes to your Foldable.

FOLDABLES
- Four-Door Foldable®

dis- *mis-* *non-* *un-*

Extension

- Write a funny story using at least five words from your Foldable.

For additional vocabulary and spelling games, go to www.macmillanmh.com — **FOLDABLES®** — 56

Literacy Workstations

 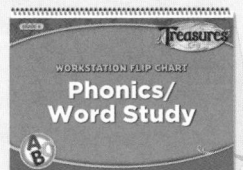  

Reading | Phonics/Word Study | Writing | Science/Social Studies

Literacy Workstation Flip Charts

Writing

Objectives

- Write a paragraph about a place in the community
- Write questions to ask someone who has been in the community a long time

Writing — The World Around You
20 Minutes

- Pick a place in your community. It could be a farm or a park.
- Make a list of details about this place. Use questions like these to help you think of details: What does it look like? How does it smell? What is it used for? When was it built? What is its name? Who usually goes there?

Extension

- Write a paragraph about the place you chose. Be sure to write a good topic sentence and support it with details from your list.
- Draw a picture of the place to support your paragraph.

Things you need:
- pen and paper
- colored pencils or markers

55

Writing — A Time Long Ago
20 Minutes

- Imagine you lived in your community twenty or thirty years ago. What do you think your community looked like back then?
- Choose an elderly person who has lived in your community for many years.
- Write five questions you would ask this person about what the community was like twenty or thirty years ago.

Extension

- Share your list of questions with a partner. Can your partner help you think of any additional questions to ask? Revise your list as needed.

Things you need:
- pen and paper

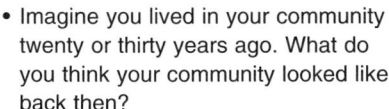

56

Content Literacy

Objectives

- Research the accuracy of voter polls
- Conduct a survey to gather information
- Research social movements of farm workers

Science — Take a Survey
20 Minutes

- When people leave a voting place, different groups or organizations may sometimes ask them how they voted or how they feel about an issue. This is called a poll.
- Use the Internet to research how often polls of citizens are useful or correct. Is the method scientific?
- Record your findings.

Extension

- Take a survey of a small group of classmates on how they feel about a subject, such as nutritious food, getting exercise, or recycling.
- Record your results using percentages.

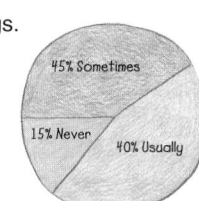

How many students eat a nutritious breakfast?
45% Sometimes, 15% Never, 40% Usually

Things you need:
- online resources
- pen and paper

55

Social Studies — Social Movements
20 Minutes

- Many social movements involve gaining rights for all people in the United States. Use the Internet to research the social movements that farm workers have been involved in.
- On fact cards, write three social concerns of farm workers.

Extension

- Make a chart that compares the goals of the civil rights movement to the goals of social movements involving farm workers.

CIVIL RIGHTS NOW
AND JUSTICE FOR ALL

Things you need:
- encyclopedia or online resources
- index cards
- pen and paper

Internet Research and Inquiry Activity
Students can find more facts at www.macmillanmh.com

56

WHOLE GROUP

ORAL LANGUAGE
- Build Background
- Connect to Theme
- Read Aloud

✓ **PHONICS/WORD STUDY**
- Prefixes

✓ **VOCABULARY**
- Latin, Greek, and Other Linguistic Roots
- Teach Words

✓ **COMPREHENSION**
- Strategy: Generate Questions
- Skill: Fact and Opinion

SMALL GROUP

- Differentiated Instruction, pp. 741M–741LL

Oral Language

Build Background

ACCESS PRIOR KNOWLEDGE

Share this information: The people in the photo are participating in a protest. They are trying to save a hospital from closing. The people came up with a strategy and are coordinating their efforts. Working together to make a plan happen is one way to improve people's lives in your community.

Write these words on the board, and briefly define each using the **Define/Example/Ask** routine: **coordinate** (put ideas and people together for a common effort), **strategy** (a plan), **improvements** (changes done to make something better).

Talk About It

How can solving problems in your community improve the lives of others?

LOG ON ▶ **VIEW IT**

Oral Language Activities
Improving Lives
www.macmillanmh.com

730

FOCUS QUESTION Ask students to read "Talk About It" on **Student Book** page 730. Then have students turn to a partner and describe the photo. Ask:

- Did you ever come up with a strategy to get something done? Explain.

- Why is it important for people to coordinate their efforts when working to improve the community?

SAVE OUR HOSPITAL

MARTIN LUTHER KING JR./DREW MEDICAL CENTER

Improving Lives

731

Use the Picture Prompt

BUILD WRITING FLUENCY

Ask students to write in their Writer's Notebooks about how to improve in their community. Tell students to write as much as they can as well as they can for 15 minutes without stopping. Meet with individuals during Writing Conference time to provide feedback and revision assignments. Students should self-correct any errors they notice prior to the conference.

Connect to the Unit Theme

DISCUSS THE BIG IDEA

Local citizens solve difficult problems to improve the lives of those in their communities. Ask students what they have learned so far in this unit about problem solving.

- What are some strategies that people have used to solve problems?
- Why is it important to help your own community to solve problems?

USE THEME FOLDABLES

Write the **Big Idea** statement on the board. Ask students to copy it on their Unit Theme Foldables. Remind them to add details as they complete this week's readings.

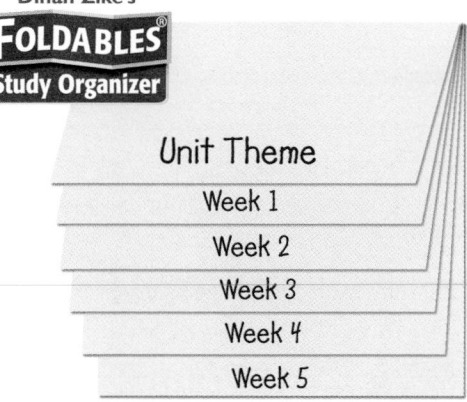

Dinah Zike's
FOLDABLES
Study Organizer

Unit Theme
Week 1
Week 2
Week 3
Week 4
Week 5

Layered Book

ELL   ENGLISH LANGUAGE LEARNERS

Beginning	Intermediate	Advanced
Use Visuals Tell students about the photograph. *The people are protesting. They want to save the hospital. They want to improve people's lives.* Then ask students to tell you what the photograph is about. Repeat correct responses in a louder and slower voice so the rest of the class may hear.	**Describe** Ask students to tell what the people in the photograph are doing. *Why are they protesting? What can you do to make improvements in your community?* Correct grammar and pronunciation in students' responses as needed.	**Discuss** Ask students to discuss how people or groups create a strategy. Ask students to elaborate on or clarify another students' response.

Objectives

- Identify the characteristics of a biography
- Develop vocabulary
- Read sentences fluently, focusing on expression

Materials

- Read Aloud Anthology, pp. 114-119

Read Aloud

Read "Mary Anning and the Sea Dragon"

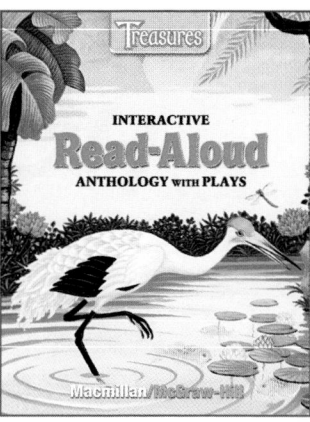

Read Aloud

GENRE: Literary Nonfiction/Biography

Share with students the following key characteristics of a **biography**:

- A **biography** tells a true story about a real person. Shorter biographies are called biographical sketches and may just focus on one or two key events.

- In some biographies, the author makes up dialogue and some details to flesh out the story and add interest. The story, however, describes real people and events, and its main facts are true.

FOCUS ON VOCABULARY

Introduce the following words, using the **Define/Example/Ask** routine. Tell students that knowing these words will help them understand what Mary Anning did and why it was important.

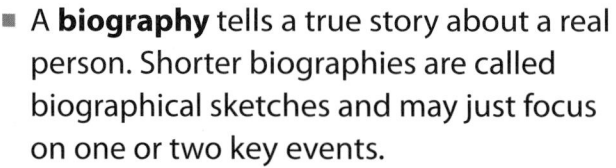

Vocabulary Routine

Use the routines below to discuss the meaning of each word.

Define: **Curiosities** are unusual things found in nature.
Example: These brightly colored feathers are beautiful curiosities.
Ask: Which would be curiosities—seashells or gum wrappers?

Define: **Pounds** are a type of money used in England.
Example: The traveler had to exchange his American dollars for English pounds.
Ask: Would you be able to use pounds to buy food at your local market?

Define: To **pry** is to remove something that is hard to get out.
Example: The rock was stuck in the ground, so I had to pry it out.
Ask: What might you have to pry out of someone's hands?

LISTENING FOR A PURPOSE

Tell students to listen carefully as you read "Mary Anning and the Sea Dragon" on **Read-Aloud Anthology** pages 114–119. Use the Think Alouds and Genre Study provided.

ELL Interactive Reading Build students' oral language by discussing the basic meaning of the passage.

- Point to the picture of Mary Anning. Ask: *What unusual thing is she doing? What tools is she using?*

- After the first page, say: *Turn to your partner. Explain why Mary looks for rocks and other curiosities.*

- After the third page, ask: *Why did Mary do most of this work by herself? What does your answer tell you about her?*

- At the end of the biography, ask: *What did Mary discover? Why was her discovery important?*

Think/Pair/Share Use **Copying Master 7**, "This was mostly about. . .," to help students evaluate and discuss the selection. When completed, have students turn to a partner and orally summarize the biography and discuss what it reveals about Mary Anning.

RESPOND TO THE BIOGRAPHY

Ask students the Think and Respond questions on page 119. Then have students discuss what qualities Mary had that made her an important historical figure. Have students determine the ways in which the author made these qualities clear to the reader.

Model Fluency

Reread the biography. Tell students that this time you want them to focus on your **expression** as you read. Remind students that when you read with expression you demonstrate your comprehension.

Point out that you can show feeling and interest by the way you read aloud. You read the dialogue to express each character's feelings. You read the narration in a lively way, too.

Think Aloud Listen as I read the part where Mary shows the creature to her family. Listen to the expression in my voice as I try to sound like the people who are talking:

"Ugh, a crocodile!" her cousin Sarah said.

"What would a crocodile be doing in England?" asked Mary's older brother, Joseph. "It's a sea dragon!"

"Even if there's more to this sea dragon and she can get it out, who on earth would want it in their parlor?" Aunt Ruth frowned.

Did you notice how I said the word *ugh* as if I were disgusted? Did you notice how I sounded excited when I read Joseph's words and displeased when I read Aunt Ruth's words? Now you try. Repeat each sentence after me. Use the same expression that I do.

Establish Fluency Focus Remind students that you will be listening for these same qualities in their reading throughout the week. You will help them improve their reading by using expression to keep the text lively and interesting and to show their comprehension.

Objective
- Decode multisyllabic words with prefixes

Materials
- Practice Book, p. 244
- Word-Building Cards
- Transparency 28
- Teacher's Resource Book, p. 147

ELL

Write Sentences Write the following pairs of words on the board: *courage/discourage, understand/misunderstand, sense/nonsense, interested/uninterested*. Construct sentences with students for each pair of words, and discuss how the prefix changes the meaning of the word. Use the Approaching Level lesson on page 741N for additional practice.

HOMEWORK | **Practice Book,** page 244

When added to the beginning of a word, a **prefix** changes the meaning of the word. Prefixes may come from Latin or Greek or have other linguistic roots.
The prefixes **un-**, **non-**, and **dis-** mean "not" or "the opposite of."

- **dis** + trust = distrust   to not trust
- **non** + sense = nonsense   something that doesn't make sense
- **un** + covered = uncovered   the opposite of covered

The prefix **mis-** means "badly" or "incorrectly."

- **mis** + spell = misspell   to spell incorrectly

Underline the prefix in the following words. Then write the meaning of the word. Possible responses provided.

1. <u>dis</u>obey not obey
2. <u>un</u>sure not sure
3. <u>mis</u>behave behave badly
4. <u>non</u>sense the opposite of sense
5. <u>un</u>happy not happy
6. <u>dis</u>like not like
7. <u>mis</u>understand understand incorrectly
8. <u>dis</u>connect not connect
9. <u>un</u>believable not believable
10. <u>mis</u>calculate calculate incorrectly

> **Approaching Reproducible,** page 244
> **Beyond Reproducible,** page 244

Word Study

 ## Prefixes

EXPLAIN/MODEL

Explain that a prefix is a group of letters added to the beginning of a base word to make a new word with a different meaning. Recognizing common prefixes can help students decode words and understand their meanings.

Introduce these common prefixes. Write each sample sentence on the board, underlining the word with the prefix. Read and define the prefix. Then use the prefix's meaning to model how to determine the meaning of the underlined words.

- **dis-, non-, un-** "not" or "the opposite of"
  I looked at the scoreboard in <u>disbelief</u>.
  <u>Nonsense</u> poems can be very funny.
  She was <u>uninterested</u> in watching the movie.
- **mis-** "bad" or "wrong"
  You can easily <u>misunderstand</u> someone if you don't listen.

Think Aloud Look at the word *disbelief*. The beginning, or prefix, of the word is *dis-*. The prefix *dis-* means "not" or "the opposite of," so *dis + belief* means "lack of belief." Someone who expresses disbelief might say, "It didn't happen" or "I don't believe it."

Point out that, like other word parts, prefixes often are derived from Latin, Greek, or other languages. For example, *dis-* and *non-* come from Latin and *mis-* comes from German.

PRACTICE/APPLY

Read the Word List Display **Transparency 28**. Help students draw a line to separate the prefix from the word to which it was added. Have students define the prefix. Then help students decode each word and tell what it means.

dislike	disown	distrust	displace
nonfat	nonstop	nonstick	nonfiction
uncut	unfit	unseen	unsure
misdo	misfile	mistreat	mischoose

Phonics Transparency 28

Read Multisyllabic Words

TRANSITION TO LONGER WORDS Display the prefixes and words below using **Transparency 28**. Have students chorally read the prefix in the first column. Then tell students to underline the prefix in the longer word in the second column. Model how to read the word and determine its meaning. When they are finished, have students chorally read the words. Point out each word in random order and at varying speeds.

dis	disorder	disagree	discomfort
non	nondairy	nonviolent	nonpayment
un	unbroken	unfriendly	uncontrollable
mis	misrepresent	misjudging	misunderstood

Phonics Transparency 28

BUILD WORDS Use **Word-Building Cards** *dis, non, mis, un, speak, trust, stop, lead, treat, plug, clear, fat, loyal*. Display the cards. Have students use the word parts to build as many multisyllabic words with the prefixes *dis-, non-, un-,* and *mis-* as possible. These and other words can be formed: *distrust, disloyal, nonstop, nonfat, misspeak, mistrust, mislead, unplug, unclear.*

APPLY THE DECODING STRATEGY Guide students to use the Decoding Strategy to decode the following words: *disconnected, nonbreakable, mispronounced, unidentified.* Write each word on the board. Remind students to look for common word parts, such as prefixes, in step 1 of the Decoding Strategy procedure. Conclude by discussing the meaning of each word.

Build Fluency

SPEED DRILL Distribute copies of the **Prefixes Speed Drill, Teacher Resource Book** page 147. Use the Speed Drill routine to help students become fluent reading words with these prefixes.

Quick Check

Can students read words with prefixes?

During **Small Group Instruction**

Tier 2

If No → **Approaching Level** Reteach the skill using the lesson on p. 741N.

If Yes → **On Level** Consolidate the learning using p. 741W.

Beyond Level Extend the learning using p. 741AA.

Decoding Strategy

Decoding Strategy Chart

Step 1	Look for word parts (prefixes) at the beginning of the word.
Step 2	Look for word parts (suffixes) at the end of the word.
Step 3	In the base word, look for familiar spelling patterns. Think about the six syllable-spelling patterns you have learned.
Step 4	Sound out and blend together the word parts.
Step 5	Say the word parts fast. Adjust your pronunciation as needed. Ask yourself: "Is this a word I have heard before?" Then read the word in the sentence and ask: "Does it make sense in this sentence?"

© Macmillan/McGraw-Hill

Vocabulary

STRATEGY
WORD PARTS

Latin, Greek, and Other Linguistic Roots Remind students that a **root** is the basic part of a word that gives the word its main meaning. Explain that many English words have Greek, Latin, or other linguistic roots.

Model how recognizing common roots can help clarify the meaning of unfamiliar words. Discuss words such as *local* (from the Latin *loc* ["place"]) and *phonograph* (from the Greek *phon* ["sound"] + *graph* ["write"]). Point to the word *children* on page 732. Tell students that words such as *children* and *childish* come from the Old English word *cild*, meaning "young person."

Think Aloud One of the vocabulary words for this week is *decades*. The first part of the word is *deca-* which is both a Latin and Greek root meaning "ten." I can use that root to help me figure out that *decades* means "groups of ten years." Now, when I read, I can look for words that might have the same root.

Discuss the word *injustice* (from the Latin *jus* ["right, law"]). Have students brainstorm other words with the same root.

Read "A Fight Against Injustice"

As you read "A Fight Against Injustice" and "A Place to Heal" with students, ask them to identify clues that reveal the meanings of the highlighted words. Tell students that they will read these words again in *Taking the Lead*.

✓ Vocabulary

decades	transform
active	violated
volunteer	

A Fight Against Injustice

Like other immigrant groups, Mexican Americans have faced difficulties in the United States. They have fought hard to overcome prejudice.

From the 1800s through the middle of the 1900s, Mexican Americans were not allowed to vote if they did not understand English. Latinos who knew English had to pay to vote. Finding work was tough because few people would hire Latinos. Like African Americans, they also faced segregation. Latinos weren't allowed in "white-only" public places. Latino children had to go to "Mexican schools."

732

In 1929, Latino leaders and workers joined together to solve these problems. They formed a group called League of United Latin American Citizens (LULAC). In its first year, LULAC helped desegregate public places in Texas. In 1947, LULAC ended school segregation in California. The organization also worked to make schools better. In the **decades** that followed, LULAC fought for equal rights for Latinos.

Today, the group continues its work. The creation of a LULAC National Youth Group shows that young Latinos are also **active** in this fight for equality.

ELL

Preteach Vocabulary See pages 741FF and 741O to preteach the vocabulary words to **ELL** and **Approaching Level** students. Use the **Visual Vocabulary Resources** to demonstrate and discuss each word. To further reinforce concepts, have students complete page 316 in the **ELL Resource Book**.

HOMEWORK | Practice Book, page 245

A. Complete the story by filling in the blanks with vocabulary words.

decades	active	transform	volunteer	violated

Shawn is a ___volunteer___ at his community's recreation center. He noticed that some of the playground equipment hadn't been replaced in ___decades___. He suggested a fundraiser to raise money for new equipment. Then he took an ___active___ role in planning a talent show. When the new equipment arrived, Shawn was excited because he knew it would ___transform___ the recreation center. Now he supervises younger children on the equipment to make sure safety rules aren't ___violated___.

B. Write two sentences about a way you would like to help in your community. Use a vocabulary word in each sentence. Underline the words that you use. **Responses will vary.**

_____

_____

_____

_____

_____

Approaching Reproducible, page 245
Beyond Reproducible, page 245

A Place to Heal

TIME FOR KIDS

How do you help kids who have lived through wars? One solution is to send them to camp!

The camp is run by the Global Children's Organization (GCO). GCO was started by Judith Jenya in 1993. She wanted to give hope to young war victims. She created camps in Northern Ireland and the Balkans. Jenya says that kids need "air, water, and hope."

"It's impossible to comprehend the horrors these children have lived through," says **volunteer** Carol Tanenbaum. "But it's so amazing to see how quickly some of them **transform**. They're kids again."

Volunteers Carol and Fred Tanenbaum are surrounded by happy campers. ▼

Summer Camp Solution

Camp counselors at Global Children's Organization (GCO) have a tough job. They help child victims of war do typical camp activities, such as swimming, dancing, and singing. Teaching kids to swim is easy. Trying to fix their personal problems is hard.

Jesse Bernstein is a volunteer. She saw that war had **violated** the kids' feelings of trust and security. A few campers even had trouble sleeping. "We'd have to stay with them until they had fallen asleep," she says.

Volunteers like Jesse help campers with their fears. They also show kids that problems can be solved peacefully, as a team.

Kids enjoy swimming at a Global Children's Organization camp. It is located on an island in Croatia.

733

Quick Check

Can students identify word meanings?

During **Small Group Instruction**

Tier 2

If No → Approaching Level Reteach the words using the Vocabulary lesson, pp. 741O–741P.

If Yes → On Level Consolidate the learning using p. 741W.

Beyond Level Extend the learning using p. 741AA.

Gifted Talented

Vocabulary

✓ **TEACH WORDS**

Introduce each word using the **Define/Example/Ask** routine. Model reading each word using the syllable-scoop technique.

> ## Vocabulary Routine
>
> **Define:** Counting by **decades** means counting ten years at a time.
> **Example:** *My grandmother has been alive for six decades, or sixty years.*
> **Ask:** How many years are in two decades? Explain. EXPLANATION

- If you are **active**, you do a lot of things and stay busy. *I am active in the school band, the newspaper, and the track team.* Tell about things that people your age can do to stay active. EXAMPLE

- To **transform** something means to change its appearance in a big way. *We helped transform the empty lot into a beautiful park.* What is a synonym for *transform*? SYNONYM

- A **volunteer** is someone who helps but is not paid money to do so. *Mrs. Lee works two days a week as a volunteer in the school library.* What is one way that you can be a volunteer? EXAMPLE

- Someone or something that has been **violated** has been ignored or disturbed in a cruel or harmful way. *The woman's rights were violated when she was not allowed to vote.* What word means the opposite of *violated*? ANTONYM

Objectives

- Generate questions
- Distinguish facts from opinions
- Explain how to verify facts
- Use academic language: *generate, fact, opinion, verify*

Materials

- Transparency 28
- Practice Book, p. 246

Skills Trace

Fact and Opinion	
Introduce	329A–329B
Practice/ Apply	330–333; Practice Book, 111–112
Reteach/ Review	337Q–337DD, 733A–733B, 734–737, 741Q–741DD, Practice Book, 246–247
Assess	Weekly Tests; Units 3, 6 Tests
Maintain	455B, 527B, 769B

ELL

Academic Language
Preteach the following academic language words to **ELL** and **Approaching Level** students during Small Group time: *generate questions, fact, opinion.* See pages 741EE and 741M.

733A Unit 6 Week 3

Reread for
Comprehension

STRATEGY
GENERATE QUESTIONS

What Is It? Remind students that they can generate different types of questions as they read. They can ask literal questions about specific details in the text or interpretive and evaluative questions about the meaning and importance of information.

Why Is It Important? Asking questions helps readers understand information about a topic and recognize relationships among ideas in a text. If an answer to a question does not make sense, readers can use a self-correction technique to clarify their understanding.

SKILL
FACT AND OPINION

What Is It? Review with students that a **fact** is a statement that can be verified or proven true by using a reference source. An **opinion** is an expression of what someone thinks or believes.

Why Is It Important? Recognizing facts and distinguishing them from opinions can help readers judge the validity of information in a text. Readers can **verify**, or confirm, facts as necessary. They can also decide whether their own opinions agree with the author's opinions.

Student Book page 733 available on Comprehension Transparency 28

- As they read, students should ask themselves whether statements in a text are facts backed up by historical or scientific data or whether they are opinions or beliefs. Signal words such as *I think, I feel, I believe,* and *perhaps* are clues that a statement is an opinion. Students also should watch for signs of bias, persuasive language, and opinions presented as facts.

- Not everyone has the same opinions on a topic. If a statement is an opinion, students can decide whether or not they agree with it. They can form their own opinions based on facts in the text, their own prior knowledge and experience, or additional research.

MODEL

How Do I Use It? Read aloud the first two paragraphs of "A Place to Heal" on **Student Book** page 733.

Think Aloud When I read the second paragraph, I notice that the author says Jenya started GCO in 1993. I can verify this fact by looking it up in a newspaper, an encyclopedia, or on a reliable Web site. However, I also notice Jenya's statement that kids need "air, water, and hope." There is no way to verify that kids need hope. This is Jenya's opinion. Now I am going to ask, *Do I agree with her opinion?* Based on my own knowledge and experience, I think her opinion makes sense. I agree that most kids probably need hope.

GUIDED PRACTICE

Reread the third paragraph of "A Place to Heal." Help students recognize that most of the statements by Carol Tanenbaum are her opinions. Guide students in identifying the persuasive words that she uses to express her opinions such as *impossible* and *amazing*.

APPLY

Have students reread the "Summer Camp" section. Ask: *What fact can you find in the first paragraph? How do you know this information is factual?* (Counselors teaching activities such as swimming, dancing, and singing can be verified.) Have students distinguish facts from opinions in the rest of the article and explain how to verify the facts.

Quick Check

Can students distinguish facts from opinions in a text?

During **Small Group Instruction**

Tier 2

If No → **Approaching Level** Reteach the skill using the Comprehension lesson, pp. 741Q–741T.

If Yes → **On Level** Consolidate the learning using pp. 741Y–741Z.

Beyond Level Extend the learning using pp. 741CC–741DD.

HOMEWORK **Practice Book,** page 246

A **fact** is a statement that can be proven. You can use reference sources to verify facts. An **opinion** is a statement that tells what a person thinks or believes. It cannot be proven. Facts and opinions can appear together.

A. Read the passage. Then write three facts and three opinions presented in the passage on the lines provided.

Oceanography is the most interesting branch of science. Oceanographers go whale watching and even swim with sharks. Doing that must be really scary. They study all the animals in the ocean. Oceanographers also scuba dive. They learn to use computers that tell them about water. They even study weather. I think that being an oceanographer would be the best job in the world!

Possible responses provided.

Facts:
- Oceanographers whale watch.
- They study all the animals in the ocean.
- They learn to use computers.

Opinions:
- Oceanography is the most interesting branch of science.
- Swimming with sharks must be really scary.
- Being an oceanographer would be the best job in the world.

B. In your opinion, what is the best job in the world? Write a paragraph that contains facts and opinions to answer this question.
Answers will vary. Check that students' paragraphs contain both facts and opinions.

Approaching Reproducible, page 246
Beyond Reproducible, page 246

Read

WHOLE GROUP

✓ **MAIN SELECTION**
- *Taking the Lead*
- Skill: Fact and Opinion

✓ **TEST PRACTICE**
- "Building a Better Gadget"
- Answering Questions

SMALL GROUP

- Differentiated Instruction, pp. 741M–741LL

Main Selection

GENRE: Informational Text/Expository

Read the definition of Expository text on **Student Book** page 734. Remind students to look for information in the photographs as well as in the text.

STRATEGY
GENERATE QUESTIONS

Review with students that they should generate literal, interpretive, and evaluative questions as they read. Asking and answering questions about the text can help readers better understand the selection.

SKILL
FACT AND OPINION

To fully understand a topic, readers need to be able to distinguish facts from opinions in a text. A fact is a true statement that can be verified using reference sources. An opinion expresses what someone thinks or believes.

Comprehension

Genre

Expository text, such as a magazine article, presents facts and information.

Generate Questions

✓ **Fact and Opinion**
A fact is something that can be proven true using reference sources. An opinion is a belief that does not have to be supported by facts.

▼ Dolores Huerta and supporters celebrate the birthday of César Chávez in Los Angeles in 2006.

Taking the Lead

How did Dolores Huerta help solve the problems faced by farmworkers?

Dolores Huerta is an important leader in the Latino community. She has spent the last few **decades** helping farmworkers. After college, Huerta became a teacher. Many of her students' parents worked on farms. Their children often came to school hungry. Huerta realized that these families needed help.

"I couldn't stand seeing farmworker children come to class hungry and in need of shoes," Huerta has said. "I thought I could do more by organizing their parents than by trying to teach their hungry children." **1**

734

Vocabulary

Vocabulary Words Review the tested vocabulary words: **decades, active, transform, volunteer,** and **violated.**

Additional Selection Words Students may be unfamiliar with these words. Pronounce the words, give student-friendly explanations as needed, and help students use the previously taught vocabulary strategies: dictionary, word parts, context clues.

organizer (p. 735): someone who helps people form a group to make plans and work on problems

labor (p. 735): having to do with workers or working

dwellings (p. 736): places in which to live

foundation (p. 736): an organization that is supported by donations

▲ Dolores Huerta during a grape pickers' strike

Law and Order

Huerta believed she could be of great service to her community. She became **active** in 1955, when she helped to form the Community Service Organization (CSO). The CSO helped Latinos and farmworkers in California. Huerta listened to the problems farmworkers faced and fought hard to fix them.

While working with the CSO, Huerta tried to make laws fair for farm laborers. One problem she faced was that many farmworkers couldn't read or understand English. Huerta pushed for a law to allow people to vote in Spanish. She also supported a law to let Californians take their driver's license exam in their native language. Without these laws, Huerta argued, people's rights would be **violated**.

Doing More

At the CSO, Huerta worked with another powerful organizer, César Chávez. He also fought for the rights of farmworkers. In 1962, the two began another labor group called the National Farm Workers Association. The group's goal was to organize farmworkers.

Over the years, Huerta and Chávez have helped **transform** the lives of farmworkers. Together, they worked to get higher wages for farm laborers. Huerta organized meetings between large farming companies and workers. She helped save the farmworkers' jobs when they were about to lose them. She stood up for their rights and quickly became a leader and hero to many.

Dolores Huerta and César Chávez meet during a strike by grape pickers. ▼

735

Read the Main Selection

Preteach	Read Together	Read Independently
Have Approaching Level students and English Language Learners listen to the selection on **StudentWorks Plus**, and use the **ELL Resource Book**, pages 314–315 before reading with the class.	Use the prompts to guide comprehension and model how to complete the graphic organizer. Have students use **Think/Pair/Share** to discuss the selection.	If students can read the selection independently, have them read and complete the graphic organizer. Suggest that they use their purposes to choose their reading strategies.

Interactive Student Book

Preview and Predict

QUICK WRITE Ask students to read the title, preview the photographs and captions, think about the genre, and write predictions about what they expect to learn about Dolores Huerta.

Set Purposes

FOCUS QUESTION Discuss with students the question under the title of the article on page 734. Point out the Fact and Opinion Chart on **Practice Book** page 247. Explain that students will use it to distinguish between facts and opinions as they read.

Read *Taking the Lead*

1 **STRATEGY**
GENERATE QUESTIONS

Teacher Think Aloud As I read the first paragraph on page 734, I ask the question, *Who is the subject of this article?* The answer is Dolores Huerta, a leader in the Latino community. I also notice that the author says Huerta is *important.* This is a word that gives an opinion. As I read, I am going to ask, *Why is Huerta important?* What other questions can you ask to help you understand this article?

PARTNERS

Prompt students to apply the strategy in a Think Aloud.

Student Think Aloud I read in the second paragraph that Huerta thought she could do more for farm families by organizing parents than by teaching children. This was her opinion. As I read, I am going to ask, *What did she do to organize farm workers?* I also want to know, *How did her efforts help farm families?*

Develop Comprehension

2 SKILL
CAUSE AND EFFECT

Remind students that a **cause** is an action or event that makes something happen. An **effect** is what happens as the result of a cause. What caused Huerta and Chávez to form the National Farm Workers Service Center? (They saw a need to do more for others, especially regarding housing.) What was one effect of their forming the Center? (Affordable housing was built for farmworkers and Latino families.)

3 SKILL
FACT AND OPINION

What facts can you identify in the first paragraph of the section subtitled "Family First"? (Huerta has 11 children, 20 grandchildren, and 5 great-grandchildren; she has won many awards.) How do you know they are facts? (They can be verified in a reference book or on a reliable online site.) What opinions do you recognize? (Huerta's work isn't easy; she shows no signs of slowing down.) Add the facts and opinions to your Fact and Opinion Chart.

Fact	Opinion
Huerta has won many awards.	Huerta's work isn't easy.
Huerta is the mother of 11 children, 20 grandchildren, and 5 great-grandchildren.	Huerta shows no signs of slowing down.

Huerta and Chávez saw a need to do more for others, so they formed the National Farm Workers Service Center. They found that many workers did not have houses. To help solve this problem, the Center built 4,200 homes and apartments for working families. The dwellings are priced so that farmworkers and Latino families can afford to live there. People in Texas, Arizona, New Mexico, and **2** California are helped by these lower-cost homes.

Family First

Families are important to Dolores Huerta. She is the mother of 11 children, and she has 20 grandchildren and five great-grandchildren. She has won many awards for her **volunteer** efforts. Her work isn't easy, but even in her 70s, she continues to fight for equal rights for poor **3** and working families. She shows no signs of slowing down.

Today, she is the president of the Dolores Huerta Foundation. She often travels around the country to give speeches and to teach future leaders. Crowds of people gather to hear Huerta talk about issues that affect immigrants, families, and workers.

"No matter how poor you are," Huerta has said, "no matter if you lack a formal education, we can do things, we can change things. The secret is taking responsibility."

▲ Dolores Huerta still draws crowds. Here she speaks at a rally in Los Angeles.

736

Quick Check

Can students distinguish facts from opinions in a text and explain how to verify what is a fact?

During **Small Group Instruction**

If No → Approaching Level Reteach the skill using a simpler text. Use Leveled Reader lessons, pp. 741R–741T.

If Yes → On Level Have students apply the skill to a new text to consolidate learning. Use Leveled Reader lessons, pp. 741Y–741Z.

Beyond Level Have students apply the skill to a more complex text to extend learning. Use Leveled Reader lessons, pp. 741CC–741DD.

Famous Women

Dolores Huerta joined the National Women's Hall of Fame in 1993. Read about some of the other women who have also made a big difference in the world.

Hermine Dalkowitz Tobolowski worked hard for equal rights. She was given the nickname "Mother of the Texas Equal Rights Amendment" after she helped pass an equal rights amendment to the Texas constitution.

Virginia Apgar developed a test called the Apgar Score in 1952. This test lets doctors know whether a newborn baby needs special help to stay alive. The Apgar Score has saved the lives of countless infants.

Patricia Locke worked to preserve the languages and spiritual traditions of Native Americans. She helped start Native American-run colleges and helped guarantee Native Americans the right to practice their traditions.

Think and Compare

1. Who formed the National Farm Workers Service Center?

2. Identify a fact from the article. How would you verify, or check the fact?

3. Summarize the main idea and supporting details in this article.

4. How is the organization LULAC in "A Fight Against Injustice" similar to the Community Service Organization?

737

TIME FOR KIDS

Develop Comprehension

Comprehension Check

SUMMARIZE/WRITING FRAME

Have students summarize the selection using the Nonfiction Text Structure Writing Frame Reproducible on **Teacher's Resource Book** page 177. Remind them to use their Fact and Opinion Charts as they complete their summaries.

THINK AND COMPARE
Text Evidence

1. **Details** <u>Answer stated in text</u> Dolores Huerta and César Chávez formed the National Farm Workers Service Center. **LOCATE**

2. **Fact and Opinion** <u>Answer stated in text</u> Students should choose a fact and explain that it can be verified using reference sources such as encyclopedias or reliable online sites. **COMBINE**

3. **Main Idea and Details** <u>Answer</u> It is mainly about how Dolores Huerta fought for the rights of poor and working families, especially families of Latinos and farmworkers. <u>Evidence</u> She helped form organizations that fought to make laws fair to farmworkers, to secure higher wages for them, and to save their jobs. **CONNECT**

4. **Text-to-Text** Both organizations help Latino families. Both organizations were founded by Latino leaders and workers. **COMPARE TEXT**

ELL

Transitions The nonfiction writing frames are especially useful for English Language Learners when speaking and writing because they focus on key transition words. Suggest that all students use these frames when presenting information to the class.

HOMEWORK
Reproducible, page 177

Sequence Writing Frame

A. Summarize *Taking the Lead.*
Use the Sequence Writing Frame below.

Dolores Huerta is an important leader in the Latin community.

After college, Dolores Huerta _____

In 1955, she _____

In 1962, she teamed up with _____ to _____

Over the years, she _____

Today, Dolores Huerta _____

Dolores Huerta has changed the lives of many people throughout California and beyond.

B. Rewrite the completed summary on another sheet of paper. Keep it as a model for writing a summary of an article or selection using this text structure.

Objectives
- Read fluently with expression
- 113–133 WCPM

Materials
- Transparency 28
- Practice Book, p. 248
- Fluency Solutions Audio CD

ELL

Quotations Explain that nonfiction articles sometimes include the exact words spoken by the people being written about. These words are enclosed in quotation marks. Remind students that readers should read these words aloud in the way they think the speaker actually said them. Have students read the quotation that concludes *Taking the Lead*. Ask: *How would Huerta sound when she is saying these words?*

Practice Book, page 248

As I read, I will pay attention to expression.

	Thousands of years ago, pharaohs ruled the great kingdom
9	of Egypt. When pharaohs died, they were buried in tombs
19	with their treasures. One of these pharaohs was very young.
29	His name was King Tutankhamen (TOOT-ahngk-ah-muhn).
34	The entrance to Tutankhamen's tomb was well hidden.
42	The Egyptians built tombs that were hard to find and even
53	harder to enter. They made secret entrances and false passages.
63	Soon after the king was buried, robbers broke into the
73	tomb and took some of the treasures. The tomb was then
84	resealed. It stayed buried in the sand for thousands of years.
95	In the early 1900s, an Englishman named Lord Carnarvon
103	began the search for this pharoah's tomb. Carnarvon believed
112	that the king was buried in the Valley of the Kings.
123	In 1907, Carnarvon began working with a man named
131	Howard Carter. Carter was an artist for paleontologists.
139	He made drawings of the fossils and other findings. Carter
149	and Carnarvon began a search for King Tutankhamen's
157	tomb. It was a search that would last for many years. 168

Comprehension Check Possible responses provided.

1. How do you know that King Tutankhamen's tomb was hard to find? **Main Idea and Details** You know the tomb was hard to find because Carnarvon and Carter's search took many years.

2. Why did the Egyptians build tombs that were hard to find? **Cause and Effect** The Egyptians built tombs that were hard to find to make it more difficult for robbers to steal from the tombs.

	Words Read	−	Number of Errors	=	Words Correct Score
First Read		−		=	
Second Read		−		=	

Approaching Reproducible, page 248

Beyond Reproducible, page 248

Fluency
Repeated Reading: Expression

EXPLAIN/MODEL Model reading **Transparency 28** with appropriate expression. Remind students that an important part of fluent reading is expression—showing the feelings of the characters (real or fictional) and even the narrator by the lively, involved way you read. Tell students that they will be doing an echo-reading.

Transparency 28

Families are important to Dolores Huerta. She is the mother of 11 children, and she has 20 grandchildren and five great-grandchildren. She has won many awards for her volunteer efforts. Her work isn't easy, but even in her 70s, she continues to fight for equal rights for poor and working families. She shows no signs of slowing down.

Today, she is the president of the Dolores Huerta Foundation. She often travels around the country to give speeches and to teach future leaders. Crowds of people gather to hear Huerta talk about issues that affect immigrants, families, and workers.

"No matter how poor you are," Huerta has said, "no matter if you lack a formal education, we can do things, we can change things. The secret is taking responsibility."

Fluency (from *Taking the Lead*, p. 736)

PRACTICE Have partners echo-read the passage. One partner reads a sentence, and the other echoes. Then they switch roles. Direct students to help their partners by reminding them to read with lively expression—in a way that shows feeling and keeps listeners interested.

DAILY FLUENCY Students will practice fluency using **Practice Book** page 248 or the **Fluency Solutions Audio CD**. The passage is recorded at a slow, practice speed and a faster, fluent speed.

Quick Check

Can students read fluently with expression?

During **Small Group Instruction**

If No → **Approaching Level** Use the Fluency lesson and model, p. 741U.

If Yes → **On Level** See Fluency, p. 741X.

Beyond Level See Fluency, p. 741BB.

 **Comprehension**

REVIEW SKILL
CAUSE AND EFFECT

EXPLAIN/MODEL

Remind students that authors of expository texts sometimes use a cause-and-effect text structure. They do so to explain why something happens, the results of what happens, or both.

- The **cause** is what makes something happen. The **effect** is what happens—the result of the cause.

- Explain that signal words such as *because* or *since* may explicitly signal a cause-and-effect relationship. However, cause and effect may be implicit in the organization of information.

- Thinking about cause-and-effect relationships helps good readers understand why things happen, and what can happen when certain events take place. Point out that the effect of one action or event can in turn become the cause of another action or event.

Discuss with students how to identify cause-and-effect relationships in an expository selection. Have students review the section subtitled "Law and Order" on page 735 of *Taking the Lead*. Model asking questions such as: *What did Huerta do because many farmworkers could not read or understand English?*

 #### PRACTICE/APPLY

Have students work with partners or in small groups to identify causes and effects in the "Doing More" section of *Taking the Lead*, on pages 735–736.

- Read the first paragraph. What did Huerta and Chávez do because they wanted to organize farmworkers? (They formed the National Farm Workers Association.)

- Read the second paragraph. What was one effect, or result, of the meetings that Huerta organized? (She saved the farmworkers' jobs.)

- Read the third paragraph. Why did the National Farm Workers Service Center build 4,200 homes? (Many working families did not have an affordable place to live.)

Remind partners to support their answers with evidence from the text. Have partners share their answers with the class.

PRACTICE BOOK See **Practice Book** page 249 for Using Multiple Text Features.

Objective

- Identify and describe cause-and-effect relationships

✓ **Skills Trace**

Cause and Effect	
Introduce	203A–203B
Practice/ Apply	204–219; Practice Book, 75–76
Reteach/ Review	225M–225Z, 707A–B, 708–723, 729M–729Z; Practice Book, 237–238
Assess	Weekly Tests; Units 2, 6 Tests
Maintain	251B, 333B, 737B

Objectives

- Identify purposes of functional documents
- Use functional documents

Materials

- Transparency 6
- Practice Book, p. 250

Research
Study Skills

 **Use Functional Documents**

EXPLAIN

Tell students that **functional documents** are documents with various specific functions or uses. You can *find* information in some kinds of functional documents. You can *give* information in others. Point out that some functional documents are available online. Others accompany a product to show buyers procedures for using or assembling the product. Some functional documents are posted in public places. To obtain other functional documents, you need to contact or visit the organization that publishes or distributes that particular document.

- Newsletters, e-mail messages, posters, menus, surveys, and instructional manuals all provide information that can help you do things.

- Flyers, posters, and schedules are put in public places to give you information about dates, times, and places of events. They often contain persuasive language to influence readers to attend the events.

- Forms, including applications, request information from you, such as your name and address. They have spaces or boxes for recording that information. To fill in a form, you may need to put an "X" in a box, fill in a circle, write words or sentences, or sign your name. Forms are required to join an organization, get a driver's license, or apply for a job.

- To complete a form, you should first listen attentively to any oral instructions that explain how to fill in and return the document. Next you should read through the form to make sure that you understand it. Then you should follow the directions carefully to record the information. When you finish, check to make sure that the form is complete. Then follow the directions for submitting it.

Ned's Pet Store and Shelter
14 Bernadino Street • Las Vegas, New Mexico
Volunteer Application
Thanks for your interest in being a volunteer at Ned's Pet Store and Shelter!
Please fill out each item listed below. Be sure to print clearly.

Last name: _Rivera_ First Name: _Jaime_
Address: _1079 Alameda Avenue_
City: _Las Vegas_ State: _NM_ Zip Code: _87701_
Telephone number: _505-843-6039_

Do you currently go to school? ☑ yes ☐ no
Name of School: _Valley Elementary School_
Grade: _7_

Do you now own or care for any of the following pets?
☐ cat ☑ dog ☐ bird ☐ turtle or fish
☐ snake ☐ horse ☐ sheep ☑ goat
Briefly describe your experiences in caring for animals: **I feed my two dogs, brush them, and take them for walks. I feed our goats and help take care of them.**

What times and days would you be available to volunteer? Check the boxes that apply.
☐ mornings ☐ afternoons
☑ some weekdays ☑ Saturday or Sunday

Please sign your name below. Volunteers under the age of 16 must also include a signature from a parent or guardian.
Jaime Rivera
Signature
Robert S. Rivera
Parent or Guardian's Signature

Study Skills Transparency

Think Aloud Jaime wants to volunteer at Ned's Pet Store and Shelter. Let's look at the form that he filled out. He printed his last name followed by his first name, and he included his address and telephone number. He didn't check the boxes for "sheep" and some other animals because he has not taken care of those animals. Jaime checked "some weekdays" and "Saturday or Sunday" because he can work on weekends and on weekdays after school and during the summer. He signed his name and had his father sign, too, because Jaime is under the age of 16.

PRACTICE/APPLY

- Ask students to write the information that they would include when filling in the same form. Then have students work with partners to give step-by-step oral instructions for how to fill in this form. Remind students to explain what to do on all sections.

- Give students time to explore other functional documents. Have them collect other forms, such as online applications, and booklets, such as manuals that come with video games. Discuss why it is important to follow the directions on functional documents precisely.

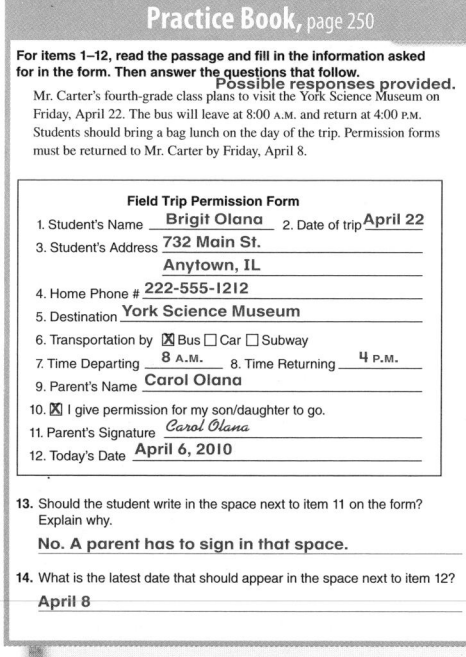

Practice Book, page 250

For items 1–12, read the passage and fill in the information asked for in the form. Then answer the questions that follow.
Possible responses provided.
Mr. Carter's fourth-grade class plans to visit the York Science Museum on Friday, April 22. The bus will leave at 8:00 A.M. and return at 4:00 P.M. Students should bring a bag lunch on the day of the trip. Permission forms must be returned to Mr. Carter by Friday, April 8.

Field Trip Permission Form
1. Student's Name _Brigit Olana_ 2. Date of trip _April 22_
3. Student's Address _732 Main St._
Anytown, IL
4. Home Phone # _222-555-1212_
5. Destination _York Science Museum_
6. Transportation by ☒ Bus ☐ Car ☐ Subway
7. Time Departing _8 A.M._ 8. Time Returning _4 P.M._
9. Parent's Name _Carol Olana_
10. ☒ I give permission for my son/daughter to go.
11. Parent's Signature _Carol Olana_
12. Today's Date _April 6, 2010_

13. Should the student write in the space next to item 11 on the form? Explain why.
No. A parent has to sign in that space.

14. What is the latest date that should appear in the space next to item 12?
April 8

Approaching Reproducible, page 250
Beyond Reproducible, page 250

Answering Questions:

EXPLAIN

Good test takers know how to answer the question that is asked.

- **Read the selection**.
- **Read** the **question** and all the **answers**.
- **Paraphrase** the question. Put it into your own words to make sure you understand what the question is asking.
- **Reread** or **scan** the selection to determine the best answer.
- Some answers are **stated**. An answer stated in one place is **right there**. When an answer is in two places, **think and search** to locate and combine the information.
- Sometimes the answer is **not stated**. **Connect** clues and evidence from the selection or **analyze** the text evidence to determine the answer.

MODEL

Remind students not to write in their books but to record their answers on a separate sheet of paper.

Question 1 Read the question and all of the answer choices.

Think Aloud First, I rephrase this sentence into the question, "What did Keagan Bolibol invent?" I can **locate** the answer to this question in the text. Paragraph 3 says she invented the "Problem Pad." The best answer is B. **RIGHT THERE**

Right There answers are found in one place in the text.
Think and Search answers are found in more than one place.
Author and Me answers ask the reader to look for clues.

Keagan Bolibol won $25,000 for her invention. ▶

❶ For every problem, there is a solution. That could be why more and more invention contests keep popping up. The contests offer big prizes to people who can invent clever gadgets that make life easier.

❷ Many contests give inventors a specific problem to solve. One contest challenges people to create a new office product. Another contest asks entrants to come up with an invention for pets. Even the U.S. government holds invention contests. A Department of Defense competition is looking for inventions that will lighten the equipment load soldiers carry.

There are even invention contests ❸ for kids. One contest asks students to invent something to make school life easier. Keagan Bolibol, 10, from Woodinville, Washington, saw her homework was getting sloppy, so she invented the Problem Pad. This dry-erase page lets kids work out homework problems without messing up a notebook. She won $25,000 for her solution!

Students at Adobe Bluffs ❹ Elementary School in San Diego came up with a new way to put out fires. Their solution uses chemicals, so it doesn't cause water damage. Thomas Edison would have been proud of all these young inventors!

738

Answering Questions

QAR Strategies

A good reader thinks about **question-answer relationships** and different ways to reread a text to answer questions.

Right There: The answer is stated in the text. You can locate the answer in one place.

Think and Search: The reader combines information stated in different parts of the text to find the answer.

Author and Me: The answer is not directly stated. The reader must infer the answer by finding clues in the text.

Use "Building a Better Gadget" to answer questions 1–4.

1 Keagan Bolibol invented —

A a new office product
B the Problem Pad
C a chemical solution
D a pet gadget

2 Which of the following is a fact?

F The U.S. government should not have invention contests.
G Thomas Edison would have been proud.
H One student won $25,000 for her invention.
J Students at Adobe Bluffs Elementary School are creative.

3 Paragraph 2 is mainly about —

A invention contests that ask inventors to solve a specific problem
B inventors who want to make more money from their inventions
C the U.S. government wanting to find jobs for inventors
D students who want to find ways to make school life easier

4 Which is the best summary of the selection?

F There are invention contests for kids. Keagan Bolibol won a large prize for her invention. Kids at an elementary school in San Diego invented something that puts out fires. Thomas Edison would have been proud of these kids.
G The U.S. government wants people to make inventions that help soldiers. They have an invention contest. They don't want soldiers to have to carry so much heavy equipment. Another contest helps pets.
H Keagan Bolibol won $25,000 for her invention. There are lots of different kinds of invention contests. Some people win big prizes like Keagan. One contest wants people to invent office products.
J There are many different invention contests. Some contests ask people to solve a specific problem, such as creating an invention for pets. There are also contests for kids. One girl won $25,000 for her invention.

739

GUIDED PRACTICE

Question 2 Read the question and all of the answer choices. Ask: *What evidence can you* **locate** *to support one of the answer choices?* (Paragraph 3 says a student won $25,000 for her Problem Pad.) *What is the best answer?* (H) RIGHT THERE

APPLY

Have students answer questions 3 and 4.

Question 3 After students have found an answer, ask: *How can you rephrase the sentence to make it into a question?* (What is paragraph 2 mainly about?) *What information did you* **connect** *to find the* **unstated** *answer?* (There are many invention contests, such as one that asks people to invent a new office product and one where people create inventions for pets.) *What is the main idea?* (There are many different invention contests. The best answer is A.) AUTHOR AND ME

Question 4 After students have found an answer, ask: *What details can you* **connect** *to include in a good summary?* (There are many different invention contests. Some contests ask people to solve a specific problem, such as creating an invention for pets. There are also contests for kids. One girl won $25,000 for her invention.) *What is the best answer?* (Answer J is the best answer.) AUTHOR AND ME

Monitor Comprehension

Self-Monitoring for Reading Comprehension

Ask yourself:

• Am I determining my answer by using personal experience instead of real proof from the selection?
• Am I adding information that is not connected to the selection to determine my answer?
• Can I prove my answer with text evidence?
• Is there a logical connection between my answer and the text evidence I am using to prove my answer?

Writing Prompt

EXPLAIN

Review with students that they will often be asked to write to a prompt when taking a test. The prompt is a writing assignment. It provides the context for what you are supposed to write about on the test.

Usually the prompt will provide a **topic** to write about. Sometimes it will give the **purpose** and **genre** or writing mode. If the prompt does not give this information, you need to choose an appropriate purpose and genre.

- You can write to entertain. (imaginative or personal narrative)
- You can write to explain or inform. (expository or procedural)
- You can write to influence. (persuasive)

MODEL

Determine the Topic and Purpose
Read the prompt on page 740 of the **Student Book**. Ask, *What is the topic of this composition?* (a person whom the student thinks is interesting) Ask: *What is the purpose of this piece*? (Students might write about an interesting person to inform, entertain, or even to influence their readers.)

Determine the Genre or Writing Mode Read the sample composition with students. Point out that this student chose to write an expository composition that provides information. Draw students' attention to the hints in the bubbles. Note that this student established a central idea in a topic sentence.

Writing: Expository

✏️ Write to a Prompt

> Write a composition about a person that you think is interesting.

> Think about the purpose of your composition.

> As you write, think about what makes an effective sentence.

Below, see how one student begins a response to the prompt above.

> The writer used specific details to support her opinion.

Dolores Huerta has worked hard to get equal rights for all people. Without her, life would be very different for many people today, especially children.

As the author says in "Taking the Lead," Huerta worried about farmworker children who came to school hungry and without shoes. Instead of trying to teach them, she worked for the rights of their parents. She knew that if their parents earned equal pay in the fields and could vote on important issues, their children would have better lives and more opportunities.

740

Writing Prompt

Respond in writing to the prompt below. Review the hints below before and after you write.

> Write a composition about a person who made a difference to your family or your community.

Writing Hints

- ☑ Remember to write about a person who made a difference. Think about genre.
- ☑ Plan your writing by organizing your ideas.
- ☑ Include important details to support your ideas.
- ☑ Check that each sentence you write helps the reader to understand your ideas.
- ☑ Review and edit your writing.
- ☑ Use correct spelling, grammar, and punctuation.

741

PRACTICE

Topic Have students read the writing prompt on **Student Book** page 741 and restate the topic.

Purpose Students are asked to give information about a specific individual and to explain ways that he or she made a difference.

Genre or Writing Mode This is an expository prompt. Students are asked to write a composition that informs and explains.

APPLY

Writing Prompt Students can practice writing from the prompt, simulating a test-taking situation. Distribute paper for students' responses.

Tell students: *You may use scrap paper to plan your composition before you begin to write. Use the Writing Hints to make sure you follow the necessary steps for responding to the prompt.*

For a guided writing process lesson, see pages 741A–741F.

4-POINT SCORING RUBRIC

④ Excellent	③ Good	② Fair	① Unsatisfactory
Focus and Coherence Sustained focus shows sense of completeness and how ideas are related.	**Focus and Coherence** Focus generally shows sense of completeness and clear relationship between ideas.	**Focus and Coherence** Somewhat focused paragraphs and/or composition has some sense of completeness but may shift quickly from idea to idea.	**Focus and Coherence** Weak connection to prompt and abrupt shifts from idea to idea show lack of focus and little or no sense of completeness.
Organization Logical progression of thought, with meaningful transitions and effective presentation of ideas.	**Organization** Generally logical progression of thought, with mostly meaningful transitions and generally effective organizational strategy.	**Organization** Progression of thought may not be completely logical and requires more meaningful transitions; organizational strategy is not effective.	**Organization** Progression of thought is not logical, and transitions are minimal or lacking; no evidence of organizational strategy.
Development of Ideas/Word Choice Thorough, insightful, and specific development of ideas shows interesting connections and willingness to take compositional risks.	**Development of Ideas/Word Choice** Development of ideas may be thoughtful but shows little evidence of willingness to take compositional risks.	**Development of Ideas/Word Choice** Development of ideas, using lists or brief explanations, is superficial, inconsistent, or contrived.	**Development of Ideas/Word Choice** Development of ideas is general or vague.
Voice Authentic and original writing expresses unique perspective.	**Voice** Mostly authentic and original writing generally expresses unique perspective.	**Voice** Shows some authenticity or originality but has difficulty expressing unique perspective.	**Voice** Shows little or no sense of individual voice.
Conventions/Sentence Fluency Demonstrates consistent command of spelling, capitalization, punctuation, grammar, usage, and sentence structure.	**Conventions/Sentence Fluency** Generally demonstrates good command of spelling, capitalization, punctuation, grammar, usage, and sentence structure.	**Conventions/Sentence Fluency** Demonstrates limited command of spelling, capitalization, punctuation, grammar, usage, and sentence structure.	**Conventions/Sentence Fluency** Demonstrates little or no command of spelling, capitalization, punctuation, grammar, usage, and sentence structure.

Write

WHOLE GROUP

WRITING WORKSHOP
• Research Report

Professional Development
GRADES 3–6

Writing Guide

Macmillan/McGraw-Hill

UNIT 6
Expository Writing

WEEK 1	**Strong Sentences/Trait: Ideas** Supporting Details
WEEK 2	**Strong Paragraphs/Trait: Ideas** Main Idea and Details
WEEK 3	**Research Report**
	• Plan/Prewrite, 741A
	• Draft, 741B
	• Revise, 741C–741D
	• Minilessons Organization: Paragraphs Ideas: Writing from Notes
	• Conferencing Routine, 741E
	• Edit/Proofread, 741F
	• Publish, 741F
WEEK 4	**Strong Sentences/Trait: Sentence Fluency** Transition Words and Phrases
WEEK 5	**Strong Paragraphs/Trait: Organization** Writing a Conclusion
WEEK 6	**Research Report**

Research Report

 **Plan/Prewrite**

TEACH/MODEL

Define the Genre Tell students that a research report is a type of expository writing that gives information about a specific topic. Discuss the features of a research report.

 Transparency 88

Features of a Research Report

• It has a clear **topic** and answers questions about the topic.

• It starts with an **introduction** and ends with a **conclusion**.

• It includes **main ideas** that tell about the topic and are often stated in **topic sentences**.

• It includes **supporting details** that give facts, examples, or explanations about the main ideas.

• It uses **transition words and phrases** to connect ideas.

• It presents information from **reliable sources** and lists the sources in a **bibliography**.

Writing Transparency

Set the Purpose Explain that students are going to take a Writer's Notebook entry and turn it into a research report. Remind them that they have already been working on many different pieces of writing to add supporting details, narrow topics, and create paragraphs. In a few moments, they are going to look at an example of a research report. The writer started out with a journal entry and revised it to make a research report that gives information about a topic. Point out that the writer had to find information in reliable sources, take notes on that information, paraphrase the information into main ideas and supporting details, and write the report.

Consider the Audience In a research report, one of the writer's purposes is to give information about a topic that will be clear and interesting for the reader. Before writing, the writer should think about who the audience is and what they might want to know about the topic.

Discuss the Student Sample

Student Sample Display **Writing Transparencies 89, 90,** and **91**. Read the journal entry and the research report aloud. Point out that the writer chose a journal entry about coral reefs and researched facts about coral reefs to include in her report. On chart paper or the board, write students' ideas about why this is a strong research report.

Ask the following:

- *What is the topic?* (coral reefs)

- *Which paragraph is the introduction?* (the first)

- *What is the main idea of the second paragraph?* (A coral reef is made up of animals called coral.)

- *What supporting details give facts about the main idea?* (Responses should be facts from the second paragraph.)

- *What conclusion does the writer draw?* (People should save the coral reefs.)

 **Select a Journal Entry** Students can select one or two entries from their Writer's Notebooks. See Selecting Journal Entries for guidance on how to help students identify appropriate journal entries that they will take through the writing process.

Use a Graphic Organizer Students can also select new topics to write about. Have students work in pairs to discuss ideas for research reports. Suggest they fill out the first two columns of a KWL chart as they explore possible topics.

Organize Your Ideas Once students have chosen their topics, they should use reliable sources to research, and take notes on what they find. They can then complete an outline to help map out their reports. Show students Selena's outline on **Transparency 92**. Discuss the use of Roman numbers for main ideas and capital letters for supporting details.

 Draft

Before writing, students should review their outlines. Explain that they should write one paragraph for each main section of their outline. As they write, students should consult their notes for supporting details. They should remember to paraphrase any information they use in their writing to avoid plagiarizing someone else's exact words.

Have students begin their drafts. Prompt students to think about how the writer of the sample organized her report into paragraphs that had main ideas and supporting details.

Objectives

- Define genre of research report
- Plan/prewrite a draft
- Develop a draft

Materials

- Writer's Notebooks
- Writing Transparencies 88–92

Selecting Journal Entries

This quick classroom routine encourages students to reread their work with a purpose and make some judgments about their own writing.

1. Read each student's Writer's Notebook, select two of the strongest entries from recent student writing, and flag each of them with a self-stick note.

2. Explain that you have posted a self-stick note on two pieces that you thought were strong. The student's job is to reread them and choose one of the pieces for you to give an individual Revision Assignment. Give the student a basis for choosing the entry, and post the criteria. For example:

☑ Choose a piece with a topic you'd like to learn more about by doing research.

☑ Choose a piece with a topic that readers will enjoy learning about.

☑ After deciding on a piece, write a big check mark (√) on the self-stick note attached to the entry that you want me to read.

Objectives

- Craft a new introduction for a research report
- Revise a draft

Materials

- Writer's Notebooks
- Writing Transparencies 88, 90, 93, 94

ELL

Questions Explain that questions are one way to grab readers' interest and attention. Write statements from students' introductions. Help students rephrase the statements as questions.

Teacher-to-Teacher

The amount of time that you have and the available resources for students to complete the research will affect the length of this piece of research writing. The priority is to break down the skills that a student needs to practice and to be certain that the student is demonstrating that he/she can take notes and use those notes to write clear sentences.

Research Report

Minilesson 1: Organization

TEACH/MODEL

Set the Purpose/Write an Introduction Remind students that a research report has an introduction that presents the topic to the readers. Explain that students will revise their introductions to better grab readers' interest.

Revise the Introduction Display **Writing Transparency 90**. Read aloud the introduction. Then display the revised introduction on **Writing Transparency 93**.

Ask: *How did Selena's revision help grab readers' interest?* (Selena used descriptive details and figurative language to draw the reader in to her report.)

 Revise

PRACTICE/APPLY

Review the traits of a research report on **Writing Transparency 88**. Explain to students that they are going to look at the introductions in their own research reports to add more details that will grab the readers' interest. Ask students to follow the directions on **Writing Transparency 94**.

 Transparency 94

1. Reread your research report.
2. Circle the introduction.
3. At the bottom of the report, rewrite the introduction so that it grabs readers' attention and draws them in.

Writing Transparency

Allow students time to work individually. Ask them to share their original and revised introductions. Point out examples of descriptive details, and compliment students on their efforts.

Summarize Learning Discuss the following: *When you write a research report, you include an introduction. The introduction presents your topic. It should also grab readers' interest. What are some descriptive details that you used in your introduction? What words and phrases did you use to draw your readers in?*

Research Report

Minilesson 2: Organization

TEACH/MODEL

Set the Purpose/Write from Notes Remind students that good writers use reliable sources to find information for research reports. They take notes about what they read by writing down key words and phrases. Writers refer to these notes and paraphrase the information when they write their reports. Display **Writing Transparency 95**. Explain that these are the notes Selena took when researching information for the coral reef report.

Transparency 95

What are coral reefs made from?
• made up of millions of corals
• corals = small animals
• top layer = live coral
• bottom layer = skeletons of hard coral

What kinds of corals are there?
• more than 2,500 kinds
• shapes: trees, mushrooms, fans, lace
• colors: pink, yellow, orange, purple

Writing Transparency

Compare the notes with paragraphs 2 and 3 on **Transparency 90**. Point out how the writer turned the questions into main ideas, or topic sentences, and the other notes into supporting details.

Revise

PRACTICE/APPLY

Have students go back to their own research reports. Encourage them to find additional information to add to their reports. Have them take notes on the information by writing key words and phrases. Then ask them to turn their notes into additional main ideas and supporting details for their research report. Remind them to paraphrase, or use their own words.

Summarize Learning Discuss the following: *When you take notes, you should write down key words and phrases. When you use your notes to write the main ideas or details for your report, you should always paraphrase, or use your own words. Why do you think it is important to paraphrase?*

Objective

• Write supporting details from notes

Materials

• Writer's Notebooks
• Writing Transparencies 90, 95, 96
• Teacher's Resource Book, p. 205

CREATING RUBRICS

Teacher-Developed Rubric

As a follow-up, display **Transparency 96**. Have students refer to **Teacher's Resource Book** page 205. Work with students to fill in the rubric for this week's writing. Tell students that you will use this rubric to evaluate their completed pieces. They should refer to the rubric as they write, revise, and proofread.

ON YOUR OWN **Teacher's Resource Book,** page 205

Writing Rubric			
4 Excellent	**3 Good**	**2 Fair**	**1 Unsatisfactory**
Focus and Coherence	Focus and Coherence	Focus and Coherence	Focus and Coherence
Organization	Organization	Organization	Organization
Development of Ideas/ Word Choice	Development of Ideas/ Word Choice	Development of Ideas/ Word Choice	Development of Ideas/ Word Choice
Voice	Voice	Voice	Voice
Conventions/Sentence Fluency	Conventions/Sentence Fluency	Conventions/Sentence Fluency	Conventions/Sentence Fluency
Presentation	Presentation	Presentation	Presentation

Write

Objective

- Meet with the teacher to discuss writing and receive revision assignments

Materials

- Writer's Notebooks

Peer Review

Think, Pair, Share Ask students to read their revised drafts aloud to partners. Suggest that listeners restate the main idea and supporting details of each paragraph. Listeners should point out details that do not support the main idea or details they think should be added. Encourage writers to use their partners' input when revising their drafts.

Flexible Pairing Option Consider pairing students who do not know each other well or do not regularly work together.

Research Proven Writing Approach

The Writers' Express®
Immediate Impact. Lasting Transformation.   wex.org

Conferencing Routine

Dynamic Feedback System

Step 1 Read and appreciate the writing.

Step 2 Notice how the student uses the targeted skill. (e.g., write an introduction: Ask: *How does the introduction help grab your interest and attention?*)

Step 3 Write comments that show how the writing has an impact on you. Direct your comments to those places in the piece where the student has used the targeted skill.

Step 4 Meet with and give the student a revision assignment.

Write Effective Comments

Research Report At least one of your comments should highlight the way the student uses the skills related to the genre. Here are some sample comments to get you started. Once you're comfortable, you can craft your own comments to be more specific to an entry.

- *Your introduction caught my interest and made me keep reading.*

- *What great supporting details these are! They help me understand the main idea.*

- *You did a good job of putting this in your own words.*

- *This paragraph confuses me. Do these details support the main idea?*

Revision Assignments

Research Report Below are examples of effective revision assignments. Use them to get started.

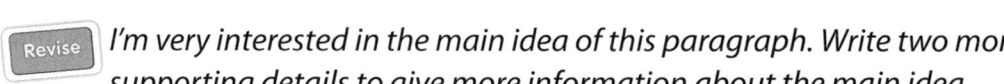 *I'm very interested in the main idea of this paragraph. Write two more supporting details to give more information about the main idea.*

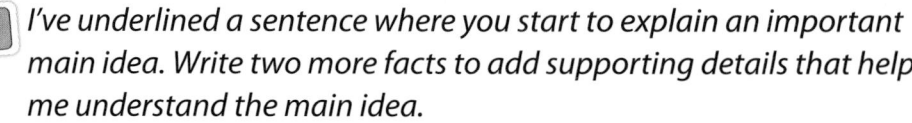 *I've underlined a sentence where you start to explain an important main idea. Write two more facts to add supporting details that help me understand the main idea.*

Research Report

 ## Edit/Proofread: Conventions

During the editing process, students should proofread their own work for spelling, grammar, and punctuation. Remind students to

- check for correct use of adverbs to show frequency and intensity;
- make sure that there are no double negatives;
- check for proper use of commas and end punctuation;
- read their writing aloud and check for errors in syntax.

Use the Grammar, Mechanics, and Spelling lessons on pages 741I–741L for minilessons on conventions with which students may have difficulty.

Publish and Share

Ask students to write or type a final copy of their research reports. Remind them to use their best handwriting to correctly form letters. Model for them how to create documents with appropriate spacing between words, sentences, paragraphs, and correct margins.

It is important to post students' work. Post examples of strong introductions, main ideas, and supporting details.

Have students publish their research reports in a class reference book. They can draw pictures or use photographs to illustrate their reports.

Presentations Ask students to present their research reports to the class. Encourage listeners to ask questions for the presenter to answer.

Objectives

- Edit drafts for grammar, mechanics, and spelling
- Publish a written work for a specific purpose

WRITING RUBRICS

Evaluate Students' Writing Use the rubric on page 807G. Review your evaluation with each student. Refer to the rubric you created with students to clearly identify strengths in their writing and areas on which they should focus

5-Day Vocabulary

Connect Language Arts

WHOLE GROUP

✔ **VOCABULARY**
- Tested Words

✔ **SPELLING**
- Prefixes

✔ **GRAMMAR**
- Negatives

SMALL GROUP

- Differentiated Instruction, pp. 741M–741LL

ON YOUR OWN — **Practice Book,** page 251

Many English words are formed by adding word parts, such as prefixes and suffixes, to a basic word, or root word. Many words have **roots** that come from **Latin** or **Greek**.

- Words that have the Latin root *loc* have to do with a place.
- Words that have the Greek root *phon* have to do with sound.
- Words that have the Greek root *graph* have to do with writing.

English also borrows words from many other languages. For example, the word *zero* comes from Arabic and the word *nickel* comes from German.

A. Complete each sentence with a word from the box that can take the place of the underlined words.

| graphic | relocate | location | telephone |

1. The committee met to choose a <u>place</u> for the new community center. ___location___

2. Lee included a <u>diagram</u> in her report to illustrate one of the ideas she wrote about. ___graphic___

3. One way people communicate is by calling one another on <u>a device that transmits sound</u>. ___telephone___

4. Some people <u>move to a different place</u> when there is a war in their homeland. ___relocate___

B. Use a dictionary to find what language this word comes from.

5. canyon ___Spanish___

Approaching Reproducible, page 251

Beyond Reproducible, page 251

Build Robust Vocabulary

Day 1 Teach/Practice

CONNECT TO WORDS

- Practice this week's vocabulary words using the following prompts:

1. What would you like to be doing two *decades* from now?

2. What things can you do to be *active* in your community?

3. How might a heavy snowfall *transform* your neighborhood?

4. Have you ever been a *volunteer* for an organization? Explain.

5. What rights do people have that might be *violated* by others?

ACADEMIC VOCABULARY

- Review the important academic words for the week. These words include *generate questions, fact, opinion, verify, cause, effect, Greek, Latin, and other linguistic roots, functional documents.*

- Write each word on the board. Define each using student-friendly language, and ask students to select the word you are defining. Then point to words in random order for students to define.

Day 2 Review

CONNECT TO WORDS

- Review the definitions of this week's vocabulary words using **Student Book** pages 732–733. Discuss each word using the following prompts:

1. Which number is the same as five *decades*? Ten *decades*?

2. Are you *active* when you sit still or when you move around?

3. For what reason might you *transform* your room?

4. Does a *volunteer* work for free or get paid a salary?

5. How do you feel if someone has *violated* your trust?

LATIN, GREEK, AND OTHER ROOTS

- Remind students that many words in English have Greek or Latin roots. Other words have roots derived from languages from all over the world. Knowing the meaning of these roots can help readers figure out the meaning of unknown words.

- Display **Transparency 55**. Point out the Latin and Greek roots and their meanings. Then have students read the first sentence. Model how to use the meaning of the Greek roots *geo* and *logy* to define *geology*.

- Have students use the Latin or Greek root in the other underlined words to help figure out their meanings.

- Have partners use a dictionary to list other words with these Greek and Latin roots. Have pairs compare lists and use each other's words in sentences.

Day 3 · Reinforce

CONNECT TO WORDS

- In their Writer's Notebooks, ask students to create Word Squares for each vocabulary word. In the first square, students write the word. (Example: *volunteer*)

- In the second square, students write their own definition of the word and any related words, such as synonyms. (Example: *helper, unpaid worker*)

- In the third square, students draw a simple illustration that will help them remember the word. (Example: a drawing of a child and an adult cleaning up a beach)

- In the fourth square, students write nonexamples, including antonyms for the word. (Example: *paid worker, employee*)

RELATED WORDS

- Help students generate words related to *active*. The classification of synonyms and related words can help improve students' vocabularies.

- Begin a word web on the board. Write *active* in the center.

- Have students brainstorm words that they associate with *active*. Record related words around the center circle. Tell students to use a thesaurus to find synonyms. Responses might include *busy, energetic, lively,* and *sports*.

- Continue with words belonging to the same word family, such as *activate, activity,* and *activation*.

Day 4 · Extend

CONNECT TO WORDS

- Review this week's vocabulary using the following sentence stems. Have students orally complete each one.

  1. Over the past decade, my family has _____.

  2. Being an active person means that I _____.

  3. It is important to be a volunteer because _____.

  4. I would like to transform _____ because _____.

  5. The workers' rights were violated when _____.

MORPHOLOGY

- Use the additional selection word *organizer* as a springboard for students to learn other words. Tell students that learning about suffixes can raise their word consciousness.

- Write *organizer* on the board. Underline -*er*. Explain that when -*er* appears at the end of a word, it often means "one who." An *organizer* is a person who organizes others—that is, someone who helps them meet and get things done.

- Write *worker, leader,* and *swimmer*. Have students underline -*er* in each.

- Tell students to use the word parts to define each word. (*Worker* means "one who works." *Leader* means "one who leads." *Swimmer* means "one who swims.")

- Point out the letters -*er* at the end of a word do not always mean "one who," as in *steer*, *bitter,* and *better*.

Day 5 · Assess and Reteach

POSTTEST

- Display **Transparency 56**. Have students complete the cloze sentences using one of this week's vocabulary words.

- Note how quickly and accurately students can complete this task. During Small Group time, work with students who make errors or require too much time to complete this task.

CONNECT TO WRITING

- Have students write sentences in their Writer's Notebooks using this week's vocabulary. Tell them to write sentences that provide information they learned from this week's readings.

- **ELL** Provide the Day 4 sentence stems for students needing extra support.

Go to pages T14–T15 for **Differentiated Spelling Lists**.

Prefixes

Spelling Words

discourage	mislead	unable
disappoint	misstep	unplug
disbelief	misnumber	uncertain
distrust	nonfat	uncomfortable
disloyal	nonfiction	uncover
misplace	nonsense	unclean
mislabel	nonstop	

Review prince, weighed, bolder
Challenge mishap, unravel

Dictation Sentences

1. Bad news did not <u>discourage</u> her.
2. My dog will never <u>disappoint</u> me.
3. He stood there in total <u>disbelief</u>.
4. Do you <u>distrust</u> the girl who took your pen?
5. Some fans were being <u>disloyal</u>.
6. Did you <u>misplace</u> your gloves?
7. I did not <u>mislabel</u> the jar.
8. My compass will not <u>mislead</u> me.
9. I tried not to <u>misstep</u>.
10. She was careful not to <u>misnumber</u> the list.
11. The <u>nonfat</u> milk is healthier.
12. <u>Nonfiction</u> books include facts.
13. The baby talk was all <u>nonsense</u>.
14. We are taking a <u>nonstop</u> flight.
15. Ned was <u>unable</u> to fix the TV.
16. <u>Unplug</u> the iron after using it.
17. I felt <u>uncertain</u> about my answer.
18. This is a very <u>uncomfortable</u> chair.
19. The cook will <u>uncover</u> the dish.
20. The basement was <u>unclean</u>.

Review/Challenge Words

1. Who married the <u>prince</u>?
2. The butcher <u>weighed</u> the meat.
3. That is a much <u>bolder</u> thing to say.
4. Breaking the vase was a <u>mishap</u>.
5. <u>Unravel</u> the garden hose.

Day 1 — Pretest

ASSESS PRIOR KNOWLEDGE

- Model for students how to spell the word *discourage*. Segment the word syllable by syllable, then determine that the prefix *dis-* is added to the base word *courage*. Point out that the prefix *dis-* means "the opposite of" or "not."

- Use the Dictation Sentences. Say the underlined word, read the sentence, and repeat the word. Have students write the words.

- Have students self-correct their tests. Point out that adding *dis-, mis-, non-,* or *un-* does not change the spelling of the base word.

- Have students cut apart the **Spelling Word Cards BLM** on **Teacher's Resource Book** page 71 and figure out a way to sort them. Have them save the cards for use throughout the week.

Day 2 — Word Sorts and Review

SPIRAL REVIEW

Review homophones. Dictate these homophone pairs: *weighed/wade; bolder/boulder;* and *prince/prints*. Have students write each word correctly in a sentence. Also have students spell and use common homophones trios, such as *they're, their, there* and *to, two, too.*

WORD SORTS

- Have students take turns sorting the spelling words and explaining how they sorted them. When students have finished the sort, discuss any challenging spellings.

- Review the spelling words, pointing out the prefixes. Use the cards on the Spelling Word Cards BLM. Write the key words *disbelief, mislead, nonsense,* and *unplug* on the board. Model how to sort words by prefix type. Place one or two cards beneath the correct key words.

ON YOUR OWN — Phonics/Spelling, page 163–164

Fold back the paper along the dotted line. Use the blanks to write each word as it is read aloud. When you finish the test, unfold the paper. Use the list at the right to correct any spelling mistakes.

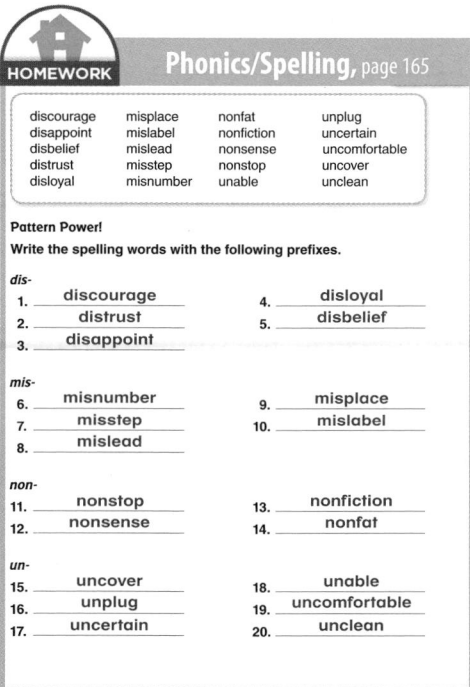

1.	1. discourage
2.	2. disappoint
3.	3. disbelief
4.	4. distrust
5.	5. disloyal
6.	6. misplace
7.	7. mislabel
8.	8. mislead
9.	9. misstep
10.	10. misnumber
11.	11. nonfat
12.	12. nonfiction
13.	13. nonsense
14.	14. nonstop
15.	15. unable
16.	16. unplug
17.	17. uncertain
18.	18. uncomfortabl
19.	19. uncover
20.	20. unclean
Review Words 21.	21. prince
22.	22. weighed
23.	23. bolder
Challenge Words 24.	24. mishap
25.	25. unravel

HOMEWORK — Phonics/Spelling, page 165

discourage	misplace	nonfat	unplug
disappoint	mislabel	nonfiction	uncertain
disbelief	mislead	nonsense	uncomfortable
distrust	misstep	nonstop	uncover
disloyal	misnumber	unable	unclean

Pattern Power!
Write the spelling words with the following prefixes.

dis-
1. discourage
2. distrust
3. disappoint
4. disloyal
5. disbelief

mis-
6. misnumber
7. misstep
8. mislead
9. misplace
10. mislabel

non-
11. nonstop
12. nonsense
13. nonfiction
14. nonfat

un-
15. uncover
16. unplug
17. uncertain
18. unable
19. uncomfortable
20. unclean

Day 3 — Word Meanings

ANALOGIES

Write these analogies on the board. Have students copy them into their Writer's Notebooks and complete them with a Spelling Word.

1. *Find* is to *discover* as *lose* is to _____. (misplace)

2. *Jump* is to *hop* as *trip* is to _____. (misstep)

3. *Storybook* is to *fiction* as *science book* is to _____. (nonfiction)

4. *Happy* is to *sad* as *sure* is to _____. (uncertain)

5. *Relaxed* is to *calm* as *anxious* is to _____. (uncomfortable)

Challenge students to come up with other analogies using Spelling Words, Review Words, or Challenge Words, leaving blank spaces for those words. Have partners trade papers and fill in the missing word in each analogy.

Day 4 — Proofread

PROOFREAD AND WRITE

Write these sentences on the board. Have students circle and correct each misspelled word.

1. Taylor was unnable to stop talking non-sense. (unable, nonsense)

2. I was uncertin about my dance partner and feared he would make me mistep. (uncertain, misstep)

3. Sam looked on in dissbelief as the alien held up a nunfiction book. (disbelief, nonfiction)

4. I did not want to dissapoint my teacher, so I was certain not to missnumbur my paper. (*disappoint, misnumber*)

Error Correction Remind students that the base word will remain the same when adding a prefix to it. When spelling, students should remove the prefix, spell the base word, and then add the prefix to the beginning of the word.

Day 5 — Assess and Reteach

POSTTEST

Use the Dictation Sentences on page 741I for the Posttest.

If students have difficulty with any words in the lesson, have them place the words on a list called *Spelling Words I Want to Remember* in their Writer's Notebooks. Look for students' use of these words in their writings.

Challenge students to create a list of words they find with the prefixes dis-, *pre-, un-, mis-* and *non-*.

Use this week's words to do a final review of these types of words if they remain troublesome for students: words with double consonants in the middle (*disappoint*), words with alternative spellings of *sh* (*nonfiction*), words with silent letters (*weighed*), homophones (*prince/prints*). Remind students to use print and electronic resources to help check the spellings.

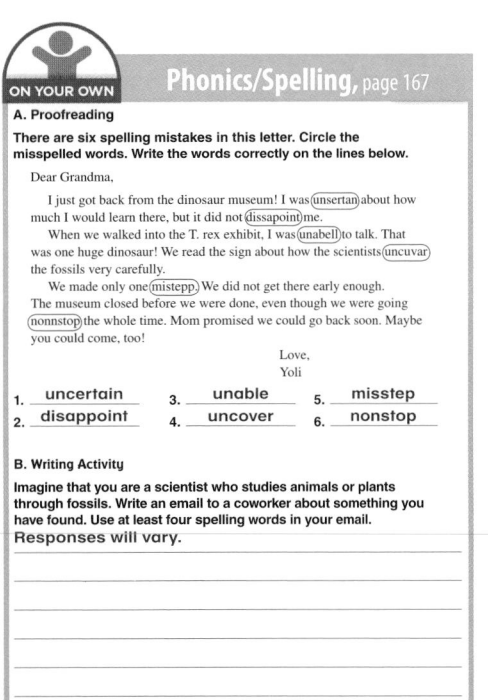

HOMEWORK — **Phonics/Spelling,** page 166

discourage	misplace	nonfat	unplug
disappoint	mislabel	nonfiction	uncertain
disbelief	mislead	nonsense	uncomfortable
distrust	misstep	nonstop	uncover
disloyal	misnumber	unable	unclean

What's the Word?
Complete each sentence with a spelling word.

1. Be careful not to **mislabel** the bags of fossils.
2. We were **uncertain** if the dig would be successful.
3. She removed the layer of soil to **uncover** the fossil below.
4. Not finding anything does not **discourage** fossil hunters.
5. I hope you did not **misplace** your notes on the dig.
6. If you work hard, you will not **disappoint** your boss.

Prefixes
A prefix occurs at the beginning of a word. A prefix gives a word a different meaning. Read the meanings for the prefixes in your spelling words. Notice that all of the prefixes share the meaning "the opposite of."

dis- "not" or "the opposite of"
non- "without" or "the opposite of"
un- "not" or "the opposite of"
mis- "wrong," "badly" or "the opposite of"

Write the spelling word that matches each meaning below.

7. without fat — **nonfat**
8. opposite of loyal — **disloyal**
9. a wrong step — **misstep**
10. not clean — **unclean**

ON YOUR OWN — **Phonics/Spelling,** page 167

A. Proofreading
There are six spelling mistakes in this letter. Circle the misspelled words. Write the words correctly on the lines below.

Dear Grandma,

   I just got back from the dinosaur museum! I was (unsertan) about how much I would learn there, but it did not (dissapoint) me.
   When we walked into the T. rex exhibit, I was (unabell) to talk. That was one huge dinosaur! We read the sign about how the scientists (uncuvar) the fossils very carefully.
   We made only one (mistepp.) We did not get there early enough. The museum closed before we were done, even though we were going (nonstop) the whole time. Mom promised we could go back soon. Maybe you could come, too!

                                       Love,
                                       Yoli

1. uncertain   3. unable   5. misstep
2. disappoint   4. uncover   6. nonstop

B. Writing Activity
Imagine that you are a scientist who studies animals or plants through fossils. Write an email to a coworker about something you have found. Use at least four spelling words in your email.
Responses will vary.

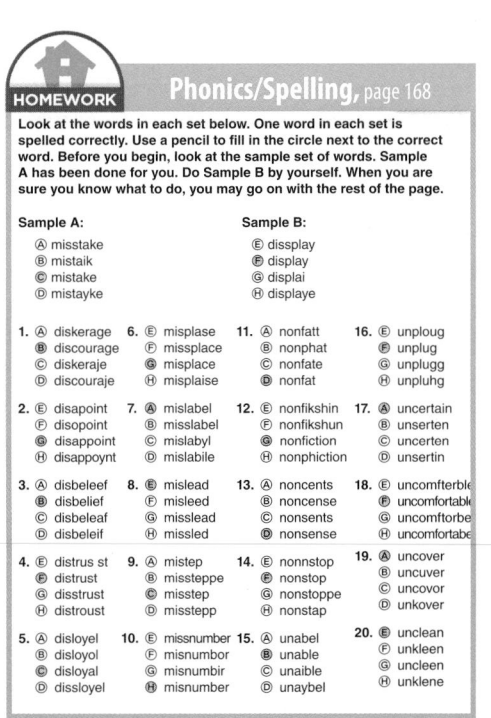

HOMEWORK — **Phonics/Spelling,** page 168

Look at the words in each set below. One word in each set is spelled correctly. Use a pencil to fill in the circle next to the correct word. Before you begin, look at the sample set of words. Sample A has been done for you. Do Sample B by yourself. When you are sure you know what to do, you may go on with the rest of the page.

Sample A:
- Ⓐ misstake
- ⬤ mistaik
- Ⓒ mistake
- Ⓓ mistayke

Sample B:
- Ⓔ dissplay
- ⬤ display
- Ⓖ displai
- Ⓗ displaye

1.
- Ⓐ diskerage
- Ⓑ discourage
- Ⓒ diskeraje
- Ⓓ discouraje

2.
- Ⓔ disapoint
- Ⓕ disopoint
- Ⓖ disappoint
- Ⓗ disappoynt

3.
- Ⓐ disbeleef
- Ⓑ disbelief
- Ⓒ disbeleaf
- Ⓓ disbeleif

4.
- Ⓔ distrus st
- Ⓕ distrust
- Ⓖ disstrust
- Ⓗ distroust

5.
- Ⓐ disloyel
- Ⓑ disloyol
- Ⓒ disloyal
- Ⓓ dissloyel

6.
- Ⓔ misplase
- Ⓕ missplace
- Ⓖ misplace
- Ⓗ misplaise

7.
- Ⓐ mislabel
- Ⓑ misslabel
- Ⓒ mislabyl
- Ⓓ mislabile

8.
- Ⓔ mislead
- Ⓕ mislead
- Ⓖ misslead
- Ⓗ missled

9.
- Ⓐ mistep
- Ⓑ missteppe
- Ⓒ misstep
- Ⓓ misstepp

10.
- Ⓔ missnumber
- Ⓕ misnumbor
- Ⓖ misnumbir
- Ⓗ misnumber

11.
- Ⓐ nonfatt
- Ⓑ nonphat
- Ⓒ nonfate
- Ⓓ nonfat

12.
- Ⓔ nonfikshin
- Ⓕ nonfikshun
- Ⓖ nonfiction
- Ⓗ nonphiction

13.
- Ⓐ noncents
- Ⓑ noncense
- Ⓒ nonsents
- Ⓓ nonsense

14.
- Ⓔ nonnstop
- Ⓕ nonstop
- Ⓖ nonstoppe
- Ⓗ nonstap

15.
- Ⓐ unabel
- Ⓑ unable
- Ⓒ unaible
- Ⓓ unaybel

16.
- Ⓔ unploug
- Ⓕ unplug
- Ⓖ unplugg
- Ⓗ unpluhg

17.
- Ⓐ uncertain
- Ⓑ unserten
- Ⓒ uncerten
- Ⓓ unsertin

18.
- Ⓔ uncomfterble
- Ⓕ uncomfortable
- Ⓖ uncomftorbe
- Ⓗ uncomfortabe

19.
- Ⓐ uncover
- Ⓑ uncuver
- Ⓒ uncovor
- Ⓓ unkover

20.
- Ⓔ unclean
- Ⓕ unkleen
- Ⓖ uncleen
- Ⓗ unklene

5-Day Grammar

Daily Language Activities

Write these sentences on the board.

DAY 1
We cant' go bike riding. We have to wait for the rain to stop maybe your mom can drive we. (1: can't; 2: stop. Maybe; 3: us.)

DAY 2
I not want a ticket for that movie. I like not scary movies. (1: do not want; 2: do not like scary movies.)

DAY 3
I cann't come to your house. I have'ent studied enough for my math Test. (1: can't; 2: haven't; 3: test.)

DAY 4
Mom don't want to listen to no loud music. I'm unsertain what station would be better. (1: Mom doesn't want; 2: listen to (any) loud music.; 3: uncertain)

DAY 5
I didn't not do good on my project. I didn't write neat? (1: didn't do; 2: well; 3: neatly.)

 # Negatives

Day 1 Introduce the Concept

INTRODUCE NEGATIVES

- A **negative** is a statement that means "no," or the opposite of its regular meaning. Most statements can be changed to a negative form: *I want those shoes. I do not want those shoes.*

- If a sentence has a form of *be* as a main or helping verb, just add *not* to make it negative: *He is my brother. He is not my brother.*

- Use the **Teach/Model/Apply** routine and the English Language Learner supports on the transparency to provide additional instruction and guided practice.

Day 2 Teach the Concept

REVIEW NEGATIVES

Review with students that negatives mean "no" or the opposite of the usual meaning. Review how to change different statements with forms of *be* into negatives.

INTRODUCE NEGATIVES WITH HELPING VERBS

- Many verbs with *not* can be made into contractions. The apostrophe takes the place of the *o* in *not*: *haven't, doesn't*. Some contractions have special spellings: *won't* for *will not, can't* for *cannot*.

- There are other negative words that can be used in sentences, such as *never, no one, nothing, no: I have no shoes. I do not have shoes.*

 See Grammar Transparency 136 for modeling and guided practice.

 See Grammar Transparency 137 for modeling and guided practice.

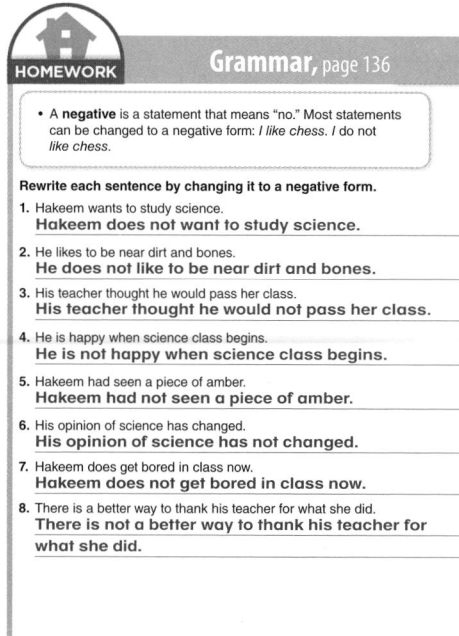

HOMEWORK — **Grammar,** page 136

- A **negative** is a statement that means "no." Most statements can be changed to a negative form: *I like chess. I do not like chess.*

Rewrite each sentence by changing it to a negative form.

1. Hakeem wants to study science.
   Hakeem does not want to study science.

2. He likes to be near dirt and bones.
   He does not like to be near dirt and bones.

3. His teacher thought he would pass her class.
   His teacher thought he would not pass her class.

4. He is happy when science class begins.
   He is not happy when science class begins.

5. Hakeem had seen a piece of amber.
   Hakeem had not seen a piece of amber.

6. His opinion of science has changed.
   His opinion of science has not changed.

7. Hakeem does get bored in class now.
   Hakeem does not get bored in class now.

8. There is a better way to thank his teacher for what she did.
   There is not a better way to thank his teacher for what she did.

ON YOUR OWN — **Grammar,** page 137

- A **negative** is a word that means "no."
- Many verbs with *not* can be made into contractions.

Rewrite each sentence by replacing the verb and *not* with a contraction.

1. Imagine if we did not know anything about dinosaurs.
   Imagine if we didn't know about dinosaurs.

2. What if there was not a place you could go to see their bones?
   What if there wasn't a place you could go to see their bones?

3. A long time ago, people were not interested in studying dinosaurs.
   A long time ago, people weren't interested in studying dinosaurs.

4. There was not any effort made to keep bones and other items that were found.
   There wasn't any effort made to keep bones and other items that were found.

5. We did not have ways to know how these animals lived. **We didn't have ways to know how these animals lived.**

6. There were not museums like there are today.
   There weren't museums like there are today.

7. Years ago, there was not anyone who wanted to search for dinosaurs.
   Years ago, there wasn't anyone who wanted to search for dinosaurs.

Day 3 — Review and Practice

REVIEW NEGATIVES WITH VERBS

Review how to change statements containing different types of verbs into negative statements. Have students name other negative words.

MECHANICS AND USAGE: CORRECTING DOUBLE NEGATIVES

- Never use two negatives in one sentence. This error is called a *double negative*: I don't *know* nobody *on the team*.

- There is often more than one way to correct a double negative. You can take out one negative word, or you can change one of the negative words to a positive word: *I don't know* anybody *on the team*. I know nobody *on the team*.

 See Grammar Transparency 138 for modeling and guided practice.

HOMEWORK **Grammar,** page 138

- Do not use two negatives in the same sentence.
- You can fix a sentence with two negatives by removing one.
- You can correct a sentence with two negatives by changing one negative to a positive word.

Rewrite each sentence below by dropping a negative or changing one negative to a positive word. **Possible responses are given.**

1. I haven't found nothing in this area yet.
   I haven't found anything in this area yet.

2. Our team didn't waste no time finding the skeleton.
   Our team didn't waste time finding the skeleton.

3. Don't never go out in the bright sun without putting on a hat.
   Don't ever go out in the bright sun without putting on a hat.

4. There isn't no place to find dinosaur bones here.
   There isn't any place to find dinosaur bones here.

5. I wouldn't never want to see a dinosaur in real life.
   I wouldn't want to see a dinosaur in real life.

6. Doesn't no one know about the oldest fossil ever found?
   Doesn't anyone know about the oldest fossil ever found?

7. The team couldn't find the sunken ship nowhere.
   The team couldn't find the sunken ship anywhere.

8. Iris didn't put no labels on the stones she found.
   Iris didn't put labels on the stones she found.

Day 4 — Review and Proofread

REVIEW HOW TO USE NEGATIVES

Have students practice using negatives. Have one student describe something that he or she does. Have a second student turn that sentence into a negative. Discuss different ways the statement can be made negative. Review correcting double negatives.

PROOFREAD

Have students correct errors in the following sentences.

1. I don't like no red shoes. (don't like red)

2. We willn't ride our bikes today. (won't ride or will not ride)

3. Those glasses do not be new. (are not new)

4. They are not like nobody I know. (are not like anybody; are like nobody)

 See Grammar Transparency 139 for modeling and guided practice.

ON YOUR OWN **Grammar,** page 139

A. Read the personal essay below. Underline the sentences that contain two negatives.

The New Kid in Class

Last month, I started going to a new school. I didn't know nobody at this school. At first, I thought there wasn't no way I would be comfortable here.

The teacher introduced me to the class. I had to tell them a little about myself. Everyone was laughing at me. I didn't have no idea what to say. I told the class about how I'd seen a real bear far off in the woods.

Instead of laughing at me, the students were all listening to me. They asked me lots of questions. I still don't know if I'll get used to this new school, but my first day didn't turn out so bad.

B. Rewrite the personal essay, correcting the sentences that contain two negatives.

Last month, I started going to a new school. I didn't know anybody at this school. At first, I thought there was no way I would be comfortable here.

The teacher introduced me to the class. I had to tell them a little about myself. Everyone was laughing at me. I didn't have any idea what to say. I told the class about how I'd seen a real bear far off in the woods.

Instead of laughing at me, the students were all listening to me. They asked me lots of questions. I still don't know if I'll get used to this new school, but my first day didn't turn out so bad.

Day 5 — Assess and Reteach

ASSESS

Use the Daily Language Activity or **Grammar Practice Book** page 140 for assessment.

RETEACH

Use **Grammar Practice Book** page 140 and selected pages from the **Grammar and Writing Handbook** for additional reteaching.

Check students' writing for use of the skill and listen for it in their speaking. Assign Grammar Revision Assignments in their Writer's Notebooks as needed.

 See Grammar Transparency 140 for modeling and guided practice.

HOMEWORK **Grammar,** page 140

A. Each numbered sentence contains two negatives. Circle the answer choice that best revises it.

1. Sue can't think of nothing more exciting than finding fossils.
   a. Sue can think of anything more exciting than finding fossils.
   b. Sue can't not think of anything more exciting than finding fossils.
   c. Sue can't think of anything more exciting than finding fossils.
   d. Sue can think of nothing no more exciting than finding fossils.

2. No one nowhere had found a dinosaur smaller than this one.
   a. No one never had found a dinosaur smaller than this one.
   b. No one anywhere had found a dinosaur smaller than this one.
   c. Not no one anywhere had found a dinosaur smaller than this one.
   d. Nobody nowhere had found a dinosaur smaller than this one.

3. Isn't amber not always a golden color?
   a. Isn't any amber always a golden color?
   b. Is amber never no golden color?
   c. Is amber always no golden color?
   d. Isn't amber always a golden color?

4. That sunken ship isn't nowhere near here.
   a. That sunken ship is anywhere near here.
   b. That sunken ship isn't not nowhere near here.
   c. That sunken ship isn't nowhere ever near here.
   d. That sunken ship is nowhere near here.

5. Scientists didn't have no equipment to explore the tops of rainforest trees.
   a. Scientists didn't have any equipment to explore the tops of rainforest trees.
   b. Scientists did have no equipment to explore the tops of rainforest trees.
   c. Scientists didn't never have equipment to explore the tops of rainforest trees.
   d. Scientists didn't have equipment to not explore the tops of rainforest trees.

6. Nobody never knew that the lost city was right under them.
   a. Nobody not never knew that the lost city was right under them.
   b. Nobody didn't never know that the lost city was right under them.
   c. Nobody ever knew that the lost city was right under them.
   d. No one never knew that the lost city was right under them.

Daily Planner

DAY 1	• Prepare to Read • Academic Language • Vocabulary (Preteach)
DAY 2	• Comprehension • Leveled Reader Lesson 1
DAY 3	• Phonics/Decoding • Leveled Reader Lesson 2
DAY 4	• Phonics/Decoding • Vocabulary (Review) • Leveled Reader Lesson 3
DAY 5	• High-Frequency Words • Fluency • Self-Selected Reading

Interactive Student Book

If you wish to preteach the main selection, use StudentWorks Plus for:

- Vocabulary Preteaching
- Word-by-Word Highlighting
- Think Aloud Prompts

Academic Language

Academic words include those harder Tier 2 words that appear in much of students' reading materials as well as the language of instruction. The words chosen for instruction were selected from the **Living Word Vocabulary** list and Avril Coxhead's list of **High-Incidence Academic Words**.

Approaching Level

Prepare to Read

Objective   Preview *Taking the Lead*
Materials   • **StudentWorks Plus**   • self-stick notes

PREVIEW THE MAIN SELECTION

- Have students preview *Taking The Lead* using **StudentWorks Plus**, the interactive eBook. This version of the Student Book contains oral summaries in multiple languages, story recording, word-by-word highlighting, Think Aloud prompts, and comprehension-monitoring questions.

- Remind students that listening carefully to and following along with the word-by-word reading will help them prepare for the reading of the selection with the class. Ask students to place self-stick notes on any challenging words or places that confuse them. Discuss these with students prior to the reading of the selection with the rest of the class.

- Tell students to write three or four sentences in their Writer's Notebooks telling what they learned about the work of Dolores Huerta.

Academic Language

Objective   Teach academic language
Materials   • none

PRETEACH LANGUAGE OF INSTRUCTION

Tell students that there are many important lesson words you will be using this week. You want them to become familiar with these words *before* the lessons. These words also appear in the directions of the tests they will be taking this year.

Preteach the following academic words: *fact, opinion, verify, generate questions, biography, Latin, Greek, and other linguistic roots.*

- Define each word using student-friendly language. Tell students that a *fact* is something that can be proven true and an *opinion* is what someone feels or believes. For example, *rainy weather* is a fact, but *rainy weather is fun* is an opinion.

- In addition, relate each word to known words. For example, connect *generate* to *make; biography* to *life story; verify* to *prove* or *confirm;* and *root* to *basic meaning.*

- Highlight these words when used throughout the week and reinforce their meanings.

Approaching Level

Phonics/Decoding

Objective Decode words with prefixes

Materials
- **Approaching Reproducible**, p. 244
- **Sound-Spelling WorkBoard**
- **Word-Building Cards**

Sound-Spelling WorkBoard

PHONICS MAINTENANCE

Tier 2

- Distribute a **Sound-Spelling WorkBoard** to each student. Say a syllable or prefix previously taught, including open syllables, vowel-team syllables, and the prefixes *un-* and *dis-*. Have students find the **Word-Building Card** on the board for each syllable or prefix.

- Review the spelling(s) for each sound by providing a sample word containing that spelling. Guide students to write the word on the board. Model how to segment the word and write the spelling for each sound, as needed. In addition, point out spelling hints, such as that adding a prefix does not change the spelling of the base word.

- Dictate the following words for students to spell: *agree, sturdy, circle, stable, feelings, uneven, disconnect*. Write the words on the board and have students self-correct their work.

RETEACH SKILL

Prefixes Display the Word-Building Cards for the prefixes *dis-, mis-, non-,* and *un-*. Model how to decode a word containing each prefix; then guide students as they decode the remaining words.

- Write the words below on the board. Model how to decode the first word in each row, then guide students as they decode the remaining words. For the multisyllabic words, divide the words into syllables using the syllable-scoop technique to help students read one syllable at a time.

- When completed, point to the words in random order for students to chorally read. Repeat several times.

uncut	unblock	uncap	unable	unfair	unfairness
nonstop	nonslip	nonliving	nondrip	nonsense	nonsensical
dislike	displace	distaste	discount	disgraced	distrusted
misdeed	misfile	mislead	misspell	misjudge	misspelling

Approaching Reproducible, page 244

A **prefix** is a word part that can be added to the beginning of a base word. A prefix changes the meaning of the word. The prefixes **dis-, non-,** and **un-** mean "the opposite of" or "without." The prefix **mis-** means "badly" or "incorrectly."

disrespect = without respect   *unhappy* = opposite of happy
nonstop = without a stop   *misbehave* = behave badly

Answer each question with a word from the box that has the same meaning as the underlined words.

| uncovered | disappeared | unbelievable |
| nonfiction | misjudge | disagree |

1. What is the most the opposite of believable thing someone has told you about dinosaurs? **unbelievable**

2. What should you do if you do not agree with something you have read? **disagree**

3. What kind of not fiction book do you like to read? **nonfiction**

4. What would you do if you opposite of covered a fossil in your yard? **uncovered**

5. Why do you think the dinosaurs opposite of appeared? **disappeared**

6. What might happen if you incorrectly judge your location? **misjudge**

Approaching Level

Vocabulary

Objective Preteach selection vocabulary

Materials
- **Visual Vocabulary Resources**   • **Vocabulary Cards**
- **Approaching Reproducible**, p. 245

 **PRETEACH KEY VOCABULARY**

Tier 2

Introduce the Words Use the **Visual Vocabulary Resources** to preteach the key selection words *decades, active, volunteer, transform,* and *violated*. Use the following routine, which appears in detail on the cards.

- Define the word in English, and provide the example given.

- Define the word in Spanish, if appropriate, and indicate if the word is a cognate.

- Display the picture, and explain how it illustrates or demonstrates the word.

- Then engage students in structured partner-talk about the image, using the key word.

- Ask students to chorally say the word three times.

- Point out any known sound-spellings or focus on a key aspect of phonemic awareness related to the word.

- You may wish to also distribute copies of the Vocabulary Glossary in the **ELL Resource Book**.

REVIEW PREVIOUSLY TAUGHT VOCABULARY

Display the **Vocabulary Cards** from the previous four weeks. Say the meanings of each word, one by one, and have students identify them. Then point to words in random order for students to provide definitions and related words they know.

Context Clues Remind students that context clues are clues within the text that help a reader figure out what an unfamiliar or multiple-meaning word means. These clues may include sentence structure clues, synonyms or antonyms, definitions, descriptions, or examples. Have students write a context sentence for each vocabulary word. For example, *With some paint and curtains, we were able to transform the* dreary *basement into a nice, cheerful room.*

Approaching Reproducible, page 245

A. Read each clue. Find the correct vocabulary word in the box and write it on the line next to the clue.

decades	active	transform	volunteer	violated

1. a person who gives time or services without pay   **volunteer**
2. to change into another form   **transform**
3. being involved   **active**
4. periods of ten years   **decades**
5. broke or did harm to   **violated**

B. Choose the vocabulary word from the box that best completes each sentence.

6. Jonah is   **active**   in a community service organization.
7. If someone does not do what he or she promised to do, your trust in that person may be   **violated**.
8. My grandmother has worked for women's rights for many   **decades**.
9. Elena is a   **volunteer**   at the local hospital.
10. Cleaning up a park and planting trees can   **transform**   its appearance.

Approaching Level

Vocabulary

Objective Review vocabulary and high-frequency words
Materials • **Vocabulary Cards** • **High-Frequency Word Cards**

REVIEW VOCABULARY

Review Words Display the **Vocabulary Cards** *decades, active, volunteer, transform,* and *violated.* Point to each word, read it aloud, and have students chorally repeat.

Then provide the following word sets. Have students name the word in each set that is not related to the other words:

- decades, ten, years, money
- active, energetic, unmoving, lively
- volunteer, unpaid, employee, helper
- transform, same, alter, change
- violated, mistreated, protected, hurt

HIGH-FREQUENCY WORDS

Top 250 Words The ability to read accurately and effortlessly the most frequently used words in written English will help students develop reading fluency. Display **High-Frequency Word Cards** 221–230. Then do the following:

- Display one card at a time, and ask students to chorally state each word.
- Have students spell each word aloud.
- Ask students to write each word in their Writer's Notebooks as they state aloud each letter. Then have them read the word again.
- When completed, quickly flip through the word card set as students chorally read the words.
- Provide opportunities for students to use the words in speaking and writing. For example, provide sentence starters, such as *Yesterday I <u>went</u> to* _____, for oral and written practice. Or ask a question, such as *Which words can be used at the beginning of a question?* (when pointing to the *what* and *when* word cards), and have students use those words to ask questions.
- Continue the routine throughout the week.

Tier 2

ELL

Practice Vocabulary Pair students of different proficiency. Orally model the vocabulary in sentences. For example: *My parents want to transform the garage into a new bedroom.* On the board, provide sentence frames for pairs to copy and complete using the vocabulary. For example: *My* _____ *grandmother loves to dance and swim.* (active)

Word Webs

Have students create Word Webs in their Writer's Notebooks for each vocabulary word. Write the related words provided, and ask students to add other words, phrases, and illustrations.

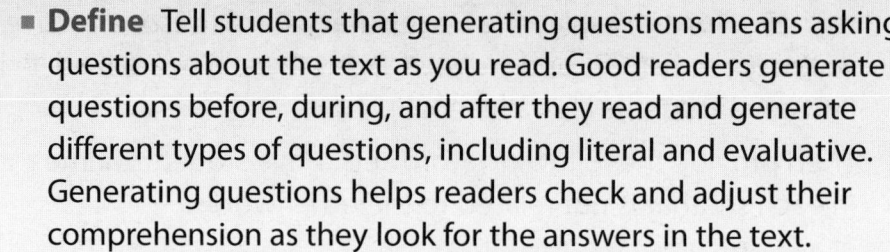

Student Book

Approaching Level
Comprehension

Tier 2

Objective Reteach generate questions and fact and opinion

Materials • **Student Book:** "A Fight Against Injustice"

RETEACH THE STRATEGY: GENERATE QUESTIONS

- **Define** Tell students that generating questions means asking questions about the text as you read. Good readers generate questions before, during, and after they read and generate different types of questions, including literal and evaluative. Generating questions helps readers check and adjust their comprehension as they look for the answers in the text.

- **Relate to Real Life** Have students imagine that their friend is throwing them a surprise party and they want to know where the party will be. They might ask: *Is the party outdoors? Is it at night? Will people need to wear sneakers or any special clothing?* Explain that these are questions that are being generated to gather information. Similarly, students can generate questions to gather information on what they are reading.

- **Set Purposes** Remind students that good readers generate questions as they read, then look for the answers as they continue reading. If they can't find the answer, they can look back and reread.

RETEACH THE SKILL: FACT AND OPINION

- **Define** Tell students that a fact is something that can be proven to be true. An opinion is something that someone thinks or believes. Words like *I believe* or *I think* can signify opinions.

- **Relate to Real Life** Ask students to tell about a book they have recently read. Ask: Who were the main characters? Did you like the book? What was your favorite part? Point out that when they name the characters from the book, they are giving facts. When they tell about their favorite part, or if they liked the book, they are giving an opinion. Other people might have different opinions about the same book.

- **Set Purposes** Remind students that good readers distinguish between fact and opinion as they read. This helps them to better comprehend the information in a text.

- **Apply** Work with students to identify facts and opinions in "A Fight Against Injustice." Then work with students to generate questions about the work of LULAC. If students are unable to do so, have them use a self-correction strategy, such as rereading for key facts. Students will apply this strategy and skill to a simpler text as they read *Charles Drew*.

Corrective Feedback

Remind students that a fact is something that can be verified, or proven to be true, and an opinion is what someone believes. Give a pair of statements such as: *I take the bus to school in the mornings. Taking the bus is the best way to get to school.* Have students note that the first statement is a fact, while the second is an opinion. Have students state facts and opinions for their classmates to identify.

Discuss how facts can be verified, such as by asking an expert, using an online reference source, or checking in a reliable book on the topic.

Approaching Level

Leveled Reader Lesson 1

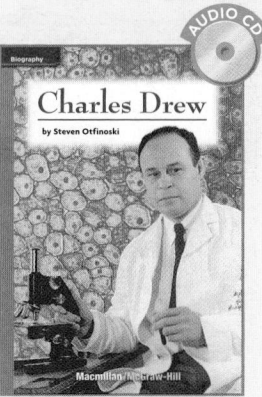

Leveled Reader

Objective   Read to apply skills and strategies

Materials   • **Leveled Reader:** *Charles Drew*

BEFORE READING

Preview and Predict   Have students read the title and preview the first chapter. Ask students to make predictions about what they may learn in the chapter. Students should note any questions they have before they read.

 **Review the Vocabulary Words**   Have students read the vocabulary words on the inside front cover. Briefly define each and ask students to state related words they have learned.

Set a Purpose for Reading   *Let's read to find out who Charles Drew was and why he is important today.*

DURING READING

 **STRATEGY**

GENERATE QUESTIONS

Remind students that when generating questions can help focus their reading, as they look closely at the text to find the answers.

 **SKILL**

FACT AND OPINION

Remind students to look for facts, which can be proven to be true, and opinions, which state the author's beliefs, as they read. Read Chapter 1 with students. Help students complete a Fact and Opinion Chart. Have them describe how they could check each fact they list.

As you read, help students decode unknown words. In addition, ask open-ended questions to facilitate rich discussion, such as *What facts is the author telling us about Charles Drew?* Build on students' responses to help them develop a deeper understanding of the text.

Stop after every two pages, and have students identify facts and opinions in the text before reading on. If they struggle, help students reread the difficult pages or passages. Then model identifying a fact or opinion about a concept in the chapter.

AFTER READING

Discuss the information that students learned about Charles Drew. Ask: *What opinions do you have about Drew?*

 **Digital Learning**

Use the **Leveled Reader Audio CD** for fluency building *after* students read the book with your support during Small Group time.

Leveled Reader

Approaching Level

Leveled Reader Lesson 2

Objective	Reread to apply skills and strategies and develop fluency
Materials	• **Leveled Reader:** *Charles Drew*
	• **Approaching Reproducible**, p. 248

BEFORE READING

 **Review the Strategy and Skill** Review students' completed Fact and Opinion Charts from the first read. Remind students that a fact can be proven to be true and an opinion is what someone believes. Remind students to generate questions to help comprehend what they read.

Review the Vocabulary Words Have students search the book for each vocabulary word. Ask students to read aloud the sentence containing the word and state the word's definition or provide related words. Point out any words with common roots from Latin, Greek, or other languages.

Set a Purpose for Reading *Let's reread to check our understanding of the information in the book and to work on our reading fluency.*

DURING READING

Reread *Charles Drew* with students. Have them read silently two pages at a time, or read aloud to a partner. Stop and have students identify facts or make at least one opinion before they read the next two pages. Model oral generalizations, as needed.

AFTER READING

Check Comprehension Have partners complete the Comprehension Check on page 16. Review students' answers. Help students find evidence for their answers in the text.

MODEL FLUENCY

Model reading the fluency passage on **Approaching Reproducible** page 248. Tell students to pay close attention to your expression—that is, the way in which you show feeling and interest by how you read. Then read one sentence at a time and have students echo-read the sentences, copying your expression.

During independent reading time, have students work with a partner using the fluency passage. One student reads aloud while the other repeats each sentence back. If students need additional support, have them listen to the "practice speed" version of the passage on the **Fluency Solutions Audio CD**.

Approaching Reproducible, page 248

As I read, I will pay attention to expression.

	Pompeii was buried under eight to ten feet of ash and
11	rock. Only the tops of some buildings could be seen.
21	People who had escaped came back to search through the
31	rubble and find their homes.
36	Over time, people stopped searching for their homes.
44	Pompeii became a forgotten city, lost in ash and rock.
54	Hundreds of years passed. The whole city of Pompeii
63	was now covered with debris. People never guessed that
72	a lost city was buried near the smoking volcano.
81	In 1710, a well digger stumbled upon the remains of
90	a building in a nearby town. Soon people began to realize
101	that this was the ancient city of Pompeii. Explorers and
111	scientists began to dig up the lost city. As they inspected
122	the ruins, they found vases, statues, and parts of homes. 132

Comprehension Check Possible responses provided.

1. Why were people interested in Pompeii? **Cause and Effect Scientists wanted to learn about it.**

2. How was Pompeii found again? **Cause and Effect A well digger stumbled upon some remains and people soon realized that they must be from Pompeii.**

	Words Read	−	Number of Errors	=	Words Correct Score
First Read		−		=	
Second Read		−		=	

Approaching Level

Leveled Reader Lesson 3

Objective Build fluency

Materials
- **Leveled Reader:** *Charles Drew*
- **Approaching Reproducible**, p. 248

FOCUS ON FLUENCY

Timed Reading Tell students that they will be doing a final timed reading of the fluency passage on **Approaching Reproducible** page 248 that they have been practicing. With each student, follow these directions:

- Place the passage facedown.
- When you say "Go," the student begins reading the passage aloud.
- When you say "Stop," the student stops reading the passage.

As they read, note words students mispronounce and their overall expression. Stop after one minute. Help students record and graph the number of words they read correctly.

REREAD PREVIOUSLY READ BOOKS

- Distribute copies of the past six **Leveled Readers**. Have students select two to reread. Tell students that rereading these books will help them develop their skills. The more times they read the same words, the quicker they will learn these words. This will make the reading of other books easier.

- Circulate and listen in as students read. Stop students periodically and ask them how they are figuring out difficult words and how they are monitoring their comprehension. Note students who need additional work with specific decoding or comprehension skills.

- Encourage students to read other previously read Leveled Readers during independent reading time or for homework.

Meet Grade-Level Expectations

As an alternative to this day's lesson, guide students through a reading of the On-Level Leveled Reader. See page 741Y. Since both books contain the same vocabulary, phonics, and comprehension skills, the scaffolding you provided will help most students gain access to this more challenging text.

Book Talk

Bringing Groups Together Students will work with peers of various language and reading abilities to discuss this week's Leveled Readers. Refer to page 160 in the **Teacher's Resource Book** for more about how to conduct a Book Talk.

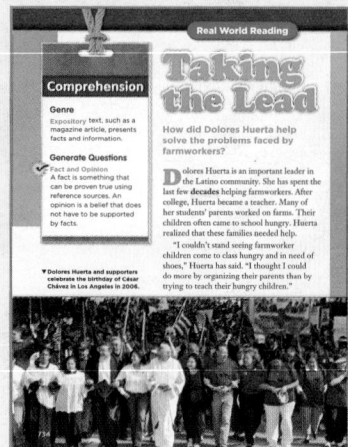

Student Book

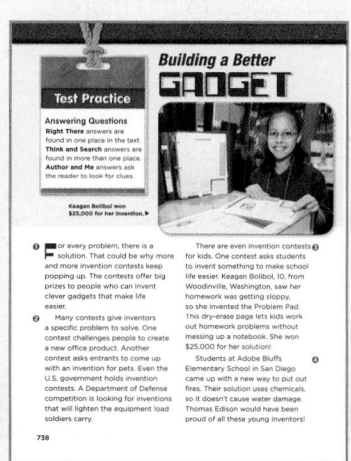

Student Book

Decodable Text

Use the decodable stories in the **Teacher's Resource Book** to help students build fluency with basic decoding patterns.

Approaching Level

Fluency

Objectives	Reread selections to develop fluency; develop speaking skills
Materials	• **Student Book:** *Taking the Lead,* "Building a Better Gadget"

REREAD FOR FLUENCY

- Have students reread a portion of *Taking the Lead.* Suggest that they focus on their favorite passage from the selection. Work with students to read the pages with appropriate expression.

- Provide time for students to read their sections of text to you. Comment on their expression and provide corrective feedback by modeling proper fluency.

DEVELOP SPEAKING/LISTENING SKILLS

- Have students practice reading the article "Building a Better Gadget."

- Work with students to read with appropriate expression. Model reading a few sentences at a time. Emphasize the way you use your voice to keep the text lively, to keep the listeners interested, and to call attention to details. Have students repeat.

- Provide time for students to read aloud one paragraph of the selection to partners. Have students name the ways their partner expressed feeling and interest with his or her voice.

- Have students orally summarize the part of the article about Keagan Bolibol. Ask them to include the most significant details in the article, using appropriate expression.

Approaching Level

Self-Selected Reading

Objective Read independently to generate questions and distinguish fact from opinion

Materials • **Leveled Classroom Library** • other nonfiction books

APPLY SKILLS AND STRATEGIES TO INDEPENDENT READING

■ **Read Independently** Have students choose a nonfiction book for sustained silent reading. (See the **Theme Bibliography** on pages T8–T9 for suggestions.) Remind them that a fact is something that can be proven to be true, while an opinion is something someone thinks or believes. Have students read their books and record facts and opinions on a Fact and Opinion Chart. Alternatively, have students choose a **Leveled Classroom Library** book and sequence and summarize the main events of the plot.

■ **Show Evidence of Reading** While reading, students may generate a reading log or journal. After reading, have students use their Fact and Opinion Charts to write or orally state a summary of the book, maintaining meaning and logical order. Provide time for students to share their summaries and comments through Book Talks. Ask: *Did you like this book? Would you recommend it to a classmate? Why or why not?*

Approaching

Leveled Classroom Library
See Leveled Classroom
Library lessons on pages T2–T7.

Daily Planner

DAY 1	• Vocabulary • Phonics
DAY 2	• Leveled Reader Lesson 1
DAY 3	• Leveled Reader Lesson 2
DAY 4	• Fluency
DAY 5	• Self-Selected Reading

ELL

Practice Vocabulary Pair ELL students with native speakers. On the board, provide sentence frames for pairs to copy and complete using the vocabulary and additional words when necessary. For example: *My father is a _____ at a community center where he _____ the basketball team.* (volunteer; coaches)

Sound-Spelling WorkBoard

On Level

Vocabulary

Objective   Review vocabulary

Materials   • **Vocabulary Cards**

REVIEW PREVIOUSLY TAUGHT WORDS

Review the Words Display the **Vocabulary Cards** for *decades, active, volunteer, transform,* and *violated.* Point to each word, read it aloud, and have students chorally repeat.

Then provide the following Yes/No questions. Ask students to answer each question, justifying their answer. Allow other students to respond. Use the discussions to determine each student's depth of word knowledge.

- When you count *decades,* do you count by minutes?
- Are *active* people busy?
- Is your teacher a *volunteer*?
- Can you *transform* an empty lot into a park quickly?
- If someone *violated* your privacy, would you be upset?

Phonics/Word Study

Objective   Decode words with prefixes

Materials   • **Word-Building Cards**   • **Sound-Spelling WorkBoards**

RETEACH SKILL

- **Words with Prefixes** Display the **Word-Building Cards** for prefixes. Remind students that a prefix is a group of letters added to the beginning of a word to make a new word. The prefixes *dis-, non-,* and *un-* mean "not." The prefix *mis-* means "bad" or "wrong."

- Write the words below on the board. If necessary, divide the words into syllables using the syllable-scoop technique to help students read one syllable at a time. When completed, point to the words in random order for students to chorally read.

unable	uncertain	uncrowded	unlucky
nonactive	nonbeing	noncentral	nontoxic
misspeak	misadjust	misconnect	mislocate
disable	disobey	disorder	discolored

- **Spelling** Dictate the following words for students to spell: *disconnect, nonstop, misdeed, unwrap.* Model how to segment words, such as spelling a word syllable by syllable.

On Level

Fluency

Objectives Reread selections to develop fluency; develop speaking skills
Materials • **Student Book:** *Taking the Lead,* "Building a Better Gadget"

REREAD FOR FLUENCY

- Have students reread *Taking the Lead.* Work with students to read with appropriate expression. Model as needed.

- Provide time for students to read a section of text to you. Comment on their expression and provide corrective feedback.

DEVELOP SPEAKING/LISTENING SKILLS

- Have students practice reading the article "Building a Better Gadget."

- Work with students to read with appropriate expression. Model reading a few sentences at a time. Emphasize the way you call attention to details and use your voice to keep the text interesting to the listeners. Have students repeat.

- Provide time for students to read aloud the article to the class. Have students explain how the reader expressed feeling and interest with his or her voice.

- Have students retell the part of the article about Keagan Bolibol as a brief narrative from her point of view. Ask them to emphasize the main points in the article by imagining what might have motivated Keagan to enter the contest.

Self-Selected Reading

Objective Read independently to distinguish fact from opinion
Materials • **Leveled Classroom Library** • other nonfiction books

APPLY SKILLS AND STRATEGIES TO INDEPENDENT READING

- **Read Independently** Have students choose a nonfiction book for sustained silent reading. (See the **Theme Bibliography** on pages T8–T9 for book suggestions.) Tell students to read their books and record facts and opinions on a Fact and Opinion Chart. Alternatively, students can read a **Leveled Classroom Library** book.

- **Show Evidence of Reading** While reading, students may generate a reading log or journal. After reading, have students use their Fact and Opinion Charts to write a summary of the book, maintaining meaning and logical order. Provide time for students to share their summaries and comments through Book Talks. Ask: *Would you recommend this book to a classmate? Why or why not?*

Student Book

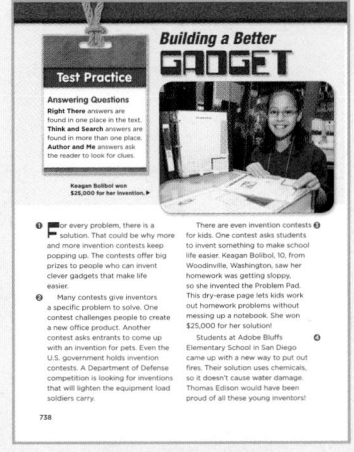

Student Book

On Level

Leveled Classroom Library
See Leveled Classroom Library lessons on pages T2–T7.

Leveled Reader

On Level

Leveled Reader Lesson 1

Objective   Read to apply strategies and skills
Materials   • **Leveled Reader:** *Marie Curie*

BEFORE READING

Preview and Predict   Have students read the title and preview the book by reading the chapter titles and looking at the photographs. Tell students to predict what this book is about and the types of information they might learn.

Review the Vocabulary Words   Have students read the vocabulary words on the inside front cover. Tell students to state related words they have learned. Review definitions, as needed.

Set a Purpose for Reading   *Let's read to find out who Marie Curie was and why we are learning about her today.*

DURING READING

STRATEGY
GENERATE QUESTIONS

Remind students that generating questions can help them to comprehend what they are reading. It also allows them to check and adjust their comprehension as needed.

SKILL
FACT AND OPINION

Remind students that a fact is something that can be proved true and an opinion is what someone believes. An author might add their opinions when writing a text. Readers need to distinguish between facts and opinions as they read a text.

Read Chapter 1 with students. Ask open-ended questions to facilitate rich discussion, such as *What facts does the author give about Marie Curie and her achievements?* Build on students' responses to help them develop a deeper understanding of the text. Have students fill in a Fact and Opinion Chart as they read.

Latin, Greek, and Other Linguistic Roots   As they read, have students point out this week's new vocabulary words and find the meanings of any words with Latin or Greek roots that they notice.

AFTER READING

Ask: *What facts and opinions did the author provide? How does that information help you generate and answer questions about the text?* Have students identify text details that support their answers.

On Level

Leveled Reader Lesson 2

Objective Reread to apply skills and strategies and develop fluency
Materials • **Leveled Reader:** *Marie Curie*
• **Practice Book,** p. 248

Leveled Reader

BEFORE READING

Review the Strategy and Skill Review students' completed Fact and Opinion Charts from the first read. Remind students that they should generate questions before, during, and after they read.

A fact is something that can be proven to be true. An opinion is something that someone thinks or believes. Distinguishing between fact and opinion can help students find the answers to the questions they generate as they read. If students' Fact and Opinion Charts are incomplete, provide a model chart or use a student chart and revise it as a group. Have students copy the revised chart in their Writer's Notebooks.

Set a Purpose for Reading *Let's reread to check our understanding of the information in the book and to work on our reading fluency.*

DURING READING

Reread *Marie Curie* with students. Have them read silently two pages at a time or read aloud to a partner. Stop and have students identify facts and opinions in the text and generate questions before they read the next two pages. Model generating questions, as needed.

AFTER READING

Check Comprehension Have partners complete the Comprehension Check on page 20. Review students' answers. Help students find evidence for their answers in the text.

MODEL FLUENCY

Model reading the fluency passage on **Practice Book** page 248. Tell students to pay close attention to your expression—that is, the way in which you show feeling and interest by how you read. Then read one sentence at a time and have students echo-read the sentences, copying your expression.

During independent reading time, have students work with a partner using the fluency passage. One student reads aloud while the other repeats each sentence back. If students need additional support, have them listen to the "practice speed" version of the passage on the **Fluency Solutions Audio CD**.

Book Talk

Bringing Groups Together Students will work with peers of various language and reading abilities to discuss this week's **Leveled Readers**. Refer to page 160 in the **Teacher's Resource Book** for more about how to conduct a Book Talk.

Practice Book, page 248

As I read, I will pay attention to expression.

	Thousands of years ago, pharaohs ruled the great kingdom
9	of Egypt. When pharaohs died, they were buried in tombs
19	with their treasures. One of these pharaohs was very young.
29	His name was King Tutankhamen (TOOT-ahngk-ah-muhn).
34	The entrance to Tutankhamen's tomb was well hidden.
42	The Egyptians built tombs that were hard to find and even
53	harder to enter. They made secret entrances and false passages.
63	Soon after the king was buried, robbers broke into the
73	tomb and took some of the treasures. The tomb was then
84	resealed. It stayed buried in the sand for thousands of years.
95	In the early 1900s, an Englishman named Lord Carnarvon
103	began the search for this pharoah's tomb. Carnarvon believed
112	that the king was buried in the Valley of the Kings.
123	In 1907, Carnarvon began working with a man named
131	Howard Carter. Carter was an artist for paleontologists.
139	He made drawings of the fossils and other findings. Carter
149	and Carnarvon began a search for King Tutankhamen's
157	tomb. It was a search that would last for many years. 168

Comprehension Check Possible responses provided.

1. How do you know that King Tutankhamen's tomb was hard to find? **Main Idea and Details** You know the tomb was hard to find because Carnarvon and Carter's search took many years.

2. Why did the Egyptians build tombs that were hard to find? **Cause and Effect** The Egyptians built tombs that were hard to find to make it more difficult for robbers to steal from the tombs.

	Words Read	−	Number of Errors	=	Words Correct Score
First Read		−		=	
Second Read		−		=	

Daily Planner

DAY 1	• Leveled Reader Lesson 1
DAY 2	• Leveled Reader Lesson 2
DAY 3	• Phonics
DAY 4	• Vocabulary • Fluency
DAY 5	• Self-Selected Reading

Beyond Level

Phonics/Word Study

Objective	Decode multisyllabic words with prefixes
Materials	• none

EXTEND/ACCELERATE

- **Read Multisyllabic Words with Prefixes** Write the words below on the board. Challenge students to read the words, using known word parts. When completed, point to the words in random order for students to chorally read.

unbearable	uncomfortable	unfamiliar	unthinkable
nonperfect	nonessential	nonrealistic	nonwashable
disappoint	disapprove	dismantle	disconnected
misadvise	miscalculated	misunderstood	mispronounce

- **Define the Words** Tell students to use their knowledge of word parts to figure out the meanings of the above words. Then have partners find the words in a dictionary and confirm or revise the meanings. Challenge students to use these words in this week's writing assignments.

- **Spell Words with Prefixes** Dictate the following words for students to spell: *misidentify, nonstick, dishonest, untangle*. Write the words for students to self-correct.

Vocabulary

Objectives	Review biographies; compare biographies
Materials	• **Student Book:** *Taking the Lead* • biographies

ENRICH VOCABULARY

- **Review Biographies** Remind students that a biography tells a true story about the events in a real person's life. Sometimes, authors write shorter sketches about a person's life. These include only a few important events. Have students recount what they have learned by reading biographies and biographical sketches this week.

- **Compare Biographies** Have students select another biography or biographical sketch from the **Leveled Classroom Library** or other sources to read. As they read, remind students to look for the elements of a biography. Tell students to orally summarize the main events of one of the biographies or sketches. Have students also look for any words with common Latin or Greek or other linguistic roots that they may encounter as they read.

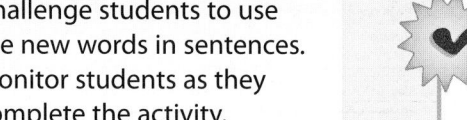

ELL

Self-Monitor Vocabulary
Have student pairs of different proficiency identify and define unfamiliar words from the main selection using a dictionary. Challenge students to use the new words in sentences. Monitor students as they complete the activity.

Beyond Level

Fluency

Objectives   Reread selections to develop fluency; develop speaking skills

Materials   • **Student Book:** *Taking the Lead,* "Building a Better Gadget"

REREAD FOR FLUENCY

■ Have students reread *Taking the Lead*. Work with students to read the book with appropriate expression.

■ Provide time for students to read a section of text to you. Comment on their expression and provide corrective feedback by modeling proper fluency.

DEVELOP SPEAKING/LISTENING SKILLS

■ Have students practice reading the article "Building a Better Gadget."

■ Work with students to read with appropriate expression. Model reading two paragraphs at a time. Emphasize the way you call attention to details and use your voice to keep the text interesting for listeners. Have students repeat.

■ Provide time for students to read the article aloud to the class. Have students explain how the reader expressed feeling and interest with his or her voice.

Student Book

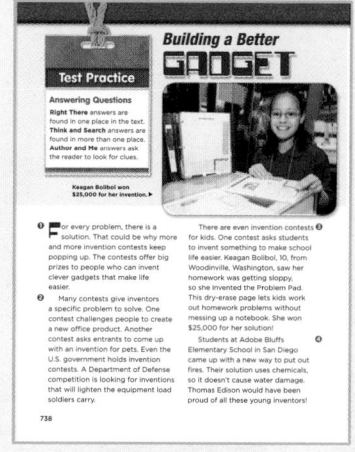

Student Book

Self-Selected Reading

Objective   Read independently to distinguish fact from opinion

Materials   • **Leveled Classroom Library**   • other nonfiction books

APPLY SKILLS AND STRATEGIES TO INDEPENDENT READING

■ **Read Independently** Have students choose a nonfiction book for sustained silent reading. (See the **Theme Bibliography** on pages T8–T9 for book suggestions.) Have students read their books and record facts and opinions on a Fact and Opinion Chart.

■ **Show Evidence of Reading** While reading, students may generate a reading log or journal. After reading, tell students to use their Fact and Opinion Charts to summarize the book, maintaining meaning and logical order. Provide time for students to share their summaries and comments through Book Talks. Ask: *Did the author state his or her main ideas clearly and accurately?*

■ **Evaluate** Have students trade Fact and Opinion Charts with a partner. Ask them to take turns presenting information from the chart. One student reads, while the other student tells if the statement is a fact or an opinion. Students should then list the words in the text that told them a statement was an opinion.

Gifted & Talented

Beyond

Leveled Classroom Library
See Leveled Classroom
Library lessons on pages T2–T7.

Leveled Reader

Beyond Level

Leveled Reader Lesson 1

Objective	Read to apply strategies and skills
Materials	• **Leveled Reader:** *Dr. Jonas Salk*

BEFORE READING

Preview and Predict Have students preview the book by reading the title and chapter titles and looking at the photographs. Tell students to predict what they think this book is about and the types of information they might learn.

Review the Vocabulary Words Have students read the vocabulary words on the inside front cover. Prompt students to state each definition and any related words they have learned.

Set a Purpose for Reading *Let's read to find out who Dr. Jonas Salk was and why he is important today.*

DURING READING

STRATEGY
GENERATE QUESTIONS

Tell students to define the word *generate*. Remind students that when they generate questions, they look for the answers later in the text. Generating questions helps students pay attention to details as they read, which helps with comprehension.

SKILL
FACT AND OPINION

Have students define the terms *fact* and *opinion*. Remind students that a fact is something that can be proven to be true. An opinion is something that someone believes.

Read the book with students. Ask open-ended questions to facilitate rich discussion, such as *How does the author present his opinions? How would you have stated them instead?* Build on students' responses to help them develop a deeper understanding of the text. Have students fill in Fact and Opinion Charts as they read.

AFTER READING

Check Comprehension Ask students to discuss the questions they generated while reading *Dr. Jonas Salk*. Have students identify where in the text they found their answers.

Analyze Have students imagine that they are interviewing Dr. Jonas Salk. Ask them to create a list of questions to ask him, and then search for the answers in the book. Tell them to make sure they are using facts from the book in their answers, and not opinions.

Beyond Level

Leveled Reader Lesson 2

Objective Reread to apply skills and strategies and develop fluency
Materials • **Leveled Reader:** *Dr. Jonas Salk* • **Beyond Reproducible,** p. 248

BEFORE READING

Review the Strategy and Skill Review students' completed Fact and Opinion Charts from the first read.

Remind students that a fact can be proven to be true, while an opinion is what someone believes. Separating fact from opinion can help a reader find answers to the questions they generate while they read. If students' Fact and Opinion Charts are incomplete, provide a model chart or use a student chart and revise it as a group. Have students copy the revised chart in their Writer's Notebooks.

Set a Purpose for Reading *Let's reread to check our understanding of the information in the book and work on our reading fluency.*

DURING READING

Have students reread *Dr. Jonas Salk* silently or with a partner. If reading in pairs, prompt students to stop every two pages and ask their partner probing questions.

AFTER READING

Check Comprehension Have students independently complete the Comprehension Check on page 24. Review students' answers. Help students find evidence for their answers in the text.

Synthesize Have students write facts and opinions from this week's readings on slips of paper. Tell them to give the papers to a partner to sort. Discuss what clues the students found on each paper that led them to categorize the information as fact or opinion.

MODEL FLUENCY

Model reading the fluency passage on **Beyond Reproducible** page 248. Tell students to pay close attention to your expression—that is, the way in which you show feeling and interest by how you read. Then read one sentence at a time and have students echo-read the sentences, copying your expression.

During independent reading time, have students work with a partner using the fluency passage. One student reads aloud while the other repeats each sentence back. Students can check their fluency by reading along with the "expert speed" version of the passage on the **Fluency Solutions Audio CD**.

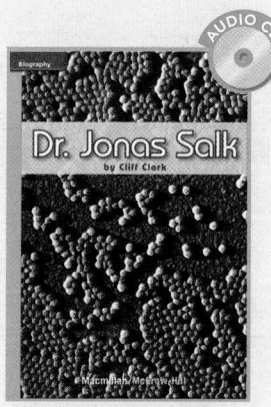

Leveled Reader

Book Talk

Bringing Groups Together Students will work with peers of various language and reading abilities to discuss this week's **Leveled Readers**. Refer to page 162 in the **Teacher's Resource Book** for more about how to conduct a Book Talk.

Beyond Reproducible, page 248

As I read, I will pay attention to expression.

	The auction was about to begin. For years, many people had waited
12	anxiously for this day. On October 4, 1997, in New York City, a
23	Tyrannosaurus rex named Sue came into the room and was put up for sale.
37	Well, really just her skull came into the room. Dinosaur Sue's skull
49	was 5 feet (1.5 m) long and weighed 600 pounds (272 kg). It looked
59	like a big boulder. But it was much more valuable than that.
71	Dinosaur Sue caused a lot of excitement when she was discovered by
83	fossil hunter Sue Hendrickson in 1990. Fossil hunters search for fossils.
93	Fossils are hardened remains of plants or animals that lived long ago.
105	Many fossil hunters search for dinosaur remains. The fossils of Dinosaur
116	Sue were carefully removed from their home in South Dakota, where
127	they had rested for 67 million years, and were put in storage.
138	Seven years later, Sue was sold and was finally ready to move to her new
153	home. The Field Museum in Chicago had shocked everyone by bidding
164	nearly $8.4 million for Sue at the auction.
171	Dinosaur Sue lived during a period of Earth's history called the
182	Mesozoic (mez-uh-ZOH-ik) era. 184

Comprehension Check Possible responses provided.

1. When did Dinosaur Sue live? **Main Idea and Details** Dinosaur Sue lived during the Mesozoic era.

2. Why did Dinosaur Sue cause a lot of excitement? **Cause and Effect** The dinosaur was very large and valuable, and people had waited a long time for the auction.

	Words Read	−	Number of Errors	=	Words Correct Score
First Read		−		=	
Second Read		−		=	

Daily Planner

DAY 1	• Build Background Knowledge • Vocabulary
DAY 2	• Vocabulary • Access to Core Content *Taking the Lead*
DAY 3	• Vocabulary • Grammar • Access to Core Content *Taking the Lead*
DAY 4	• Vocabulary • Writing/Spelling • Leveled Reader *Marie Curie*
DAY 5	• Vocabulary • Leveled Reader *Marie Curie* • Self-Selected Reading

StudentWorks Plus
Interactive Student Book

Use StudentWorks Plus for:
- Vocabulary preteaching
- Word-by-word highlighting
- Think Aloud prompts

Cognates

Help students identify similarities and differences in pronunciation and spelling between English and Spanish cognates.

coordinate	*coordinar*
strategy	*estrategia*
decades	*décadas*
active	*activo*
transform	*transformar*
coordinate	*coordinar*
opinion	*opinión*
negatives	*negativos*

ELL   ENGLISH LANGUAGE LEARNERS

Prepare to Read

Content Objective Explore solving problems to improve lives
Language Objective Use key words to talk about people who solve problems
Materials • StudentWorks Plus

BUILD BACKGROUND KNOWLEDGE

All Language Levels

- Have students preview *Taking the Lead* using **StudentWorks Plus**, which contains oral summaries in multiple languages, online multilingual glossaries, word-by-word highlighting, and questions that assess and build comprehension.

- Students can build their word-reading fluency by reading along as the text is read or by listening during the first reading and, at the end of each paragraph, returning to the beginning of the paragraph and reading along.

- Students can build their comprehension by reviewing the definitions of key words in the online glossary and by answering the comprehension questions. When appropriate, the text required to answer the question is highlighted to provide students with additional support and scaffolding.

- After reading, ask students to respond to these questions: *Who is someone who has made a difference in your community? What did he or she do?*

Academic Language

Language Objective Use academic language in classroom conversations

All Language Levels

- This week's academic words are **boldfaced** throughout the lesson. Define the word in context, and provide a clear example from the selection. Then ask students to generate an example or a word with a similar meaning.

Academic Language Used in Whole Group Instruction

Theme Words	Key Selection Words	Strategy and Skill Words
coordinate **strategy** **improvements**	**decades** **active** **transform** **volunteer** **violated**	**generate questions** **fact** **opinion** **negatives** **Latin and Greek roots**

ELL   ENGLISH LANGUAGE LEARNERS

Vocabulary

Language Objective Demonstrate understanding and use of key words by describing a problem solver

Materials • **Visual Vocabulary Resources**
          • **ELL Resource Book**

PRETEACH KEY VOCABULARY

Use the **Visual Vocabulary Resources** to preteach the key selection words *decades, active, transform, volunteer,* and *violated.* Focus on two words per day. Use the following routine, which appears in detail on the cards.

Beginning/Intermediate

- Point out any known sound-spellings, or focus on a key aspect of phonemic awareness related to the word.

All Language Levels

- Define the word in English, and provide the example given.

- Define the word in Spanish, if appropriate, and indicate if the word is a cognate.

- Display the picture, and explain how it illustrates the word. Engage students in structured activity, using the key word.

- Ask students to chorally say the word three times.

- Distribute copies of the Vocabulary Glossary in the **ELL Resource Book** on page 316.

PRETEACH FUNCTION WORDS AND PHRASES

All Language Levels

Use the Visual Vocabulary Resources to preteach the function words and phrases *often, over the years, no matter,* and *set up.* Focus on one word or phrase per day. Use the detailed routine on the cards.

- Define the word in English and, if appropriate, in Spanish. Point out if the word is a cognate.

- Refer to the picture and engage students in talk about the word. For example, students will partner-talk using sentence frames.

- Ask students to chorally repeat the word three times.

TEACH BASIC WORDS

Beginning/Intermediate

Use the Visual Vocabulary Resources to teach the basic words *workers, jobs, leader, community, group,* and *organization.* Teach these "organized labor" words using the routine provided on the card.

Visual Vocabulary Resources

ELL Resource Book, page 316

Use the word chart to study this week's vocabulary words.
Write a sentence using each word in your writer's notebook.

Word	Context Sentence	Illustration
decades	Sometimes it takes <u>decades</u> for things to change.	*1930's 1940's 1950's* How old will you be two decades from now?
volunteers	The <u>volunteers</u> work with the children for free.	
transform	Cold temperatures can <u>transform</u> the water in the pond into ice.	What is another word for *transform*?
violated	He got a ticket because he <u>violated</u> the parking rules.	
active	I played an <u>active</u> role in the game.	

ELL Resource Book

ELL ENGLISH LANGUAGE LEARNERS

Access to Core Content

Content Objective Read grade-level text
Language Objective Discuss text, using key words and sentence frames
Materials • ELL Resource Book, pp. 314–315

PRETEACH MAIN SELECTION (PAGES 734–737)

All Language Levels

Use the Interactive Question-Response Guide on **ELL Resource Book** pages 314–315 to introduce students to *Taking the Lead.* Preteach half of the selection on **Day 2** and half on **Day 3**.

- Use the prompts provided in the guide to develop meaning and vocabulary. Use the partner-talk and whole-class responses to engage students and increase student-talk.

- When completed, have partners reread the story.

Beginning	Intermediate	Advanced
Use Visuals During the Interactive Reading, select a few photographs. State facts or opinions about the photographs. Help students retell your statements. Then have them identify the statements as facts or opinions.	**Describe** During the Interactive Reading, select a few lines of text that include facts. After you have read and explained it, have students retell the facts in the text.	**Discuss** During the Interactive Reading, select a passage that include facts and opinions. After you have read and explained it, have students retell the facts. Then have students discuss whether they agree or disagree with the opinions.

ELL ENGLISH LANGUAGE LEARNERS

Fluency

Content Objectives Reread selections to develop fluency; develop speaking skills

Language Objective Tell a partner what a selection is about

Materials • **Student Book**: *Taking the Lead,* "Building a Better Gadget"
• **Teacher's Resource Book**

REREAD FOR FLUENCY

Beginning

- Have students read the decodable passages in the **Teacher's Resource Book**, pages 34–35.

Intermediate/Advanced

- Have students reread a portion of *Taking the Lead.* Work with students to read the pages with expression. For example, read each sentence of the first paragraph and have students echo. Then have students continue by chorally reading additional paragraphs. Remind students to read in a lively, involved way, using appropriate emotion in their voices.

- Provide time for students to read their sections of text to you. Comment on their expression, and provide corrective feedback by modeling proper fluency.

DEVELOP SPEAKING/LISTENING SKILLS

All Language Levels

- Have students practice reading the article "Building a Better Gadget." Work with them to read with expression.

- Provide time for students to read the article aloud to a partner. Have students tell their partner about the article. Provide the sentence frame *The article was about ____.*

Self-Selected Reading

Content Objective Read independently

Language Objective Orally retell information learned

Materials • **Leveled Classroom Library** • other nonfiction books

APPLY SKILLS AND STRATEGIES TO INDEPENDENT READING

All Language Levels

- Have students choose a nonfiction book or **Leveled Classroom Library** book for independent reading. (See the Theme Bibliography on pages T8–T9 for book suggestions.)

- After reading, tell students to orally summarize and share their reactions to the book with classmates. Ask: *Would you recommend this book to a classmate? Why or why not?*

Student Book

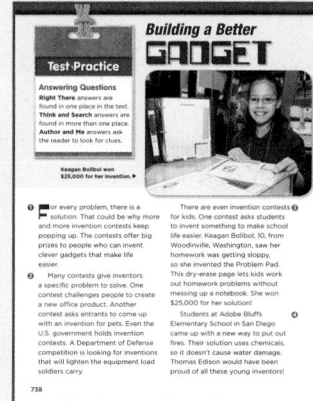

Leveled Classroom Library
See Leveled Classroom
Library Lessons on pages T2–T7.

Transfer Skills

Negatives Spanish requires double negatives in many types of sentences. Therefore, Spanish-speaking students may introduce double negatives in English, such as *I don't like nothing*. These students will benefit from extra practice in the form of games or guided writing. During conversations, model the correct use of negatives by restating what students say. See language transfers on pages T16–T31.

Corrective Feedback

During whole group grammar lessons, follow the routine on the **Grammar Transparencies** to provide students with extra support. This routine includes completing the items with English Language Learners while other students work independently, having students reread the sentences with partners to build fluency, and providing a generative task, such as writing a new sentence using the skill.

ELL ENGLISH LANGUAGE LEARNERS

Grammar

Content Objective Identify negatives
Language Objective Speak in complete sentences, using sentence frames

NEGATIVES

Beginning/Intermediate

- Remind students that a negative is a statement that means "no" or the opposite of its regular meaning, and that we can change statements to a negative form using words *no, not, never, nobody*, and *isn't*. For example: *I want those shoes. I do not want those shoes*. Remind students that it is incorrect to use two negative words in the same sentence, as in *I don't want no dessert*.

All Language Levels

- Review how to form negatives. Write below sentences on the board. Have students underline the negative in each sentence. Have them say: *The negative word is ___.*

  Some laws were <u>not</u> fair for farmworkers.

  Farmworkers <u>didn't</u> get paid enough.

  Many families had <u>no</u> homes.

  Some children <u>never</u> went to school.

PEER DISCUSSION STARTERS

All Language Levels

- Write the following sentences on the board:

  Dolores Huerta helped farmworkers by ___.
  Huerta believed that ___.

- Pair students and have them complete each sentence frame. Have them expand on their sentences by providing as many details as they can from this week's readings. Circulate, listen in, and take note of each student's language use and proficiency.

Beginning	Intermediate	Advanced
Use Visuals Describe the photographs in *Taking the Lead* to students using negatives. Ask: *What do you see?* Help them point and form sentences using negatives.	**Describe** Ask students to describe the photographs in *Taking the Lead* using negatives. Have them use complete sentences. Model sentences as needed.	**Discuss** Ask students to describe the photographs using negatives. Encourage them to use adjectives and adverbs in their descriptions.

ELL ENGLISH LANGUAGE LEARNERS

Writing/Spelling

Content Objective Spell words correctly
Language Objective Write in complete sentences, using sentence frames

All Language Levels

■ Write the key vocabulary words on the board: *decades, active, transform, volunteer, violated.* Have students copy each word on their **WorkBoards**. Help them say each word and then write a sentence for it. Provide sentence starters such as:

People who live for many decades have ___.

To become active in your community, you can ___.

You can transform your bedroom by ___.

Volunteers are important because ___.

She violated the rules when she ___.

Beginning/Intermediate

■ Help students spell words using their growing knowledge of English sound-spelling relationships. Model how to segment the word students are trying to spell, and attach a spelling to each sound (or spellings to each syllable if a multisyllabic word). Use the Sound-Spelling Cards to reinforce the spellings for each English sound.

Advanced

■ Dictate the following words for students to spell: *unfair, dislike, mislead, nonstop, unkind, misbehave, nontoxic, disappear.* Use the Sound-Spelling Cards to guide students as they spell each word.

■ When completed, review the meanings of words that can be easily demonstrated or explained. Use actions, gestures, and available pictures.

Sound-Spelling WorkBoard

Phonics/Word Study

For English Language Learners who need more practice with this week's phonics/spelling skill, see the Approaching Level lesson on page 741N. Focus on minimal contrasts, articulation, and those sounds that do not transfer from the student's first language to English. See language transfers on pages T16–T31.

Leveled Reader

Leveled Reader

Content Objective Read to apply skills and strategies

Language Objective Retell information, using complete sentences

Materials • **Leveled Reader**: *Marie Curie*
- **ELL Resource Book,** p. 317
- **Visual Vocabulary Resources,** pp. 511–516

BEFORE READING

All Language Levels

- **Preview** Read the title *Marie Curie*. Ask: *What's the title? Say it again.* Repeat with the author's name. Then page through the photographs. Use simple language to tell about each page. Follow up with questions, such as *What did Marie Curie discover? What do you think it was like to make a new discovery?*

- **Review Skills** Use the inside front cover to review the comprehension skill and vocabulary words.

- **Set a Purpose** Say: *Let's read to find out about a scientist who helped to change medical science.*

DURING READING

All Language Levels

- Have students read each page aloud using the differentiated suggestions. Provide corrective feedback, such as modeling how to blend a decodable word or clarifying meaning by using techniques from the Interactive Question-Response Guide.

- **Retell** After every two pages, ask students to state the main ideas they have learned so far. Help them to complete the Fact and Opinion Chart. Restate students' comments when they have difficulty using story-specific words. Provide differentiated sentence frames to support students' responses and engage students in partner-talk where appropriate.

Vocabulary

Preteach Vocabulary Use the routine in the **Visual Vocabulary Resources**, pages 511–516, to preteach the ELL Vocabulary listed in the inside front cover of the Leveled Reader.

Beginning	Intermediate	Advanced
Echo-Read Have students echo-read after you.	**Choral-Read** Have students chorally read with you.	**Choral-Read** Have students chorally read.
Check Comprehension Point to pictures and ask questions, such as *Do you see an X-ray? Point to it. What do x-rays show?*	**Check Comprehension** Ask questions/prompts, such as *What award did Marie Curie win? What did she do to receive the Nobel Prize?*	**Check Comprehension** Ask: *How did Marie Curie's invention help French soldiers during World War I? Read sentences that explain this idea.*

AFTER READING

Use the chart below and **Think and Compare** questions in the Leveled Reader to determine students' progress.

Think and Compare	Beginning	Intermediate	Advanced
1 Reread the Introduction on page 2. Find one opinion. Then find a fact. (*Fact and Opinion*)	Possible responses: Nonverbal response. Opinion: Story will amaze me. Fact: Win Nobel Prize.	Possible responses: One opinion is that I will be amazed by the story. One fact is that Marie Curie won two Nobel Prizes.	Possible responses: One opinion is that I will be amazed by Marie Curie's story. One fact is that she was the first woman to win a Nobel Prize.
2 Do you think Marie showed wisdom when she worked with radium without knowing its dangers? Explain your answer. (*Analyze*)	Possible responses: Nonverbal response. No. Got sick. Need to be careful.	Possible responses: No, she was not smart. The radium made her sick. She needed to be careful.	Possible responses: No, she was not wise to work with radium because the radium made her very sick. She should have been more careful.
3 Marie was a role model for women in her day. Who is a good role model for woman today? Explain your choice. (*Synthesize*)	Possible responses: Nonverbal response. Hillary Clinton. She is a leader.	Possible responses: Hillary Clinton is a role model. She is a leader.	Possible responses: Hillary Clinton is a good role model because she is a leader. She was the first woman to run for President.

BOOK TALK

Develop Listening and Speaking Skills Distribute copies of **ELL Resource Book**, page 317, and form small groups. Help students determine the leader to discuss the Book Talk questions. Tell students to remember the following while engaged in the activity:

- Share information in cooperative learning interactions. Remind students to work with their partners to retell the story and complete any activities. Ask: *What happened next in the story?*

- Express opinions, ideas, and feelings on a variety of social and academic topics. Ask: *What do you think about the characters in the story?*

- Use high-frequency English words to describe people, places, and objects.

ELL Resource Book

Book Talk

Bringing Groups Together Students will work with peers of varying language abilities to discuss the questions for the Book Talk activity. Form groups so that students who read Beyond Level, On Level, Approaching Level, and English Language Learner Leveled Readers are in the same group for the activity.

Progress Monitoring

Weekly Assessment

ASSESSED SKILLS

- Vocabulary: Vocabulary Words, Latin, Greek, and Other Linguistic Roots
- Comprehension: Fact and Opinion
- Grammar: Negatives
- Phonics/Spelling: Prefixes

Selection Test for Taking the Lead *Also Available*

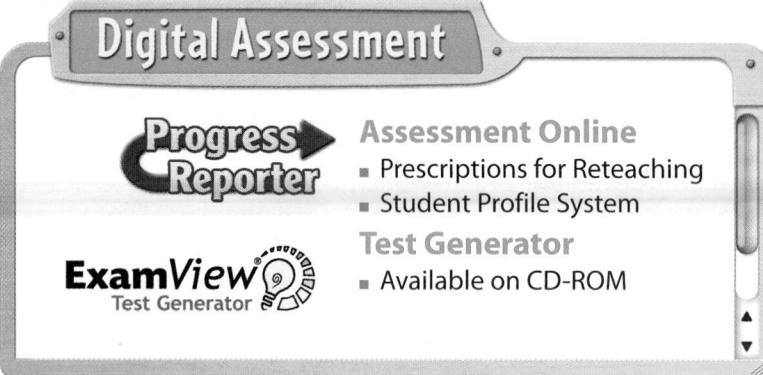

Digital Assessment

Progress Reporter

Assessment Online
- Prescriptions for Reteaching
- Student Profile System

ExamView Test Generator

Test Generator
- Available on CD-ROM

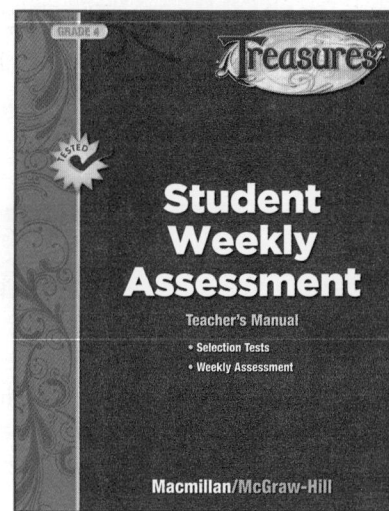

GRADE 4

Treasures

Student Weekly Assessment

Teacher's Manual
- Selection Tests
- Weekly Assessment

Macmillan/McGraw-Hill

**Weekly Assessment
Unit 6 Week 3**

Fluency Assessment

Assess fluency for one group of students per week. Use the Oral Fluency Record Sheet to track the number of words read correctly. Fluency goal for all students: **113–133 words correct per minute (WCPM)**.

Approaching Level	Weeks 1, 3, 5
On Level	Weeks 2, 4
Beyond Level	Week 6

GRADES 1–6

Treasures

Fluency Assessment

Macmillan/McGraw-Hill

Fluency Assessment

Diagnose	IF...	Prescribe
VOCABULARY WORDS **VOCABULARY STRATEGY** Latin, Greek, and Other Linguistic Roots	0–2 items correct . . .	See **Vocabulary Intervention Teacher's Edition.** **LOG ON** ▶ Online Practice: Go to www.macmillanmh.com. 💿 Vocabulary PuzzleMaker
COMPREHENSION Skill: Fact and Opinion	0–3 items correct . . .	See **Comprehension Intervention Teacher's Edition.** 🌀 *SPIRAL REVIEW* See Fact and Opinion lesson in Unit 6 Week 4, page 769B.
GRAMMAR Negatives	0–1 items correct . . .	See **Writing and Grammar Intervention Teacher's Edition.**
PHONICS AND SPELLING Prefixes	0–1 items correct . . .	**LOG ON** ▶ Online Practice: Go to www.macmillanmh.com. See **Phonics Intervention Teacher's Edition.**
FLUENCY	109–112 WCPM	💿 Fluency Solutions Audio CD
	0–108 WCPM	See **Fluency Intervention Teacher's Edition.**

Response to Intervention

To place students in Tier 2 or Tier 3 Intervention use the *Diagnostic Assessment*.

- Phonics
- Vocabulary
- Comprehension
- Fluency
- Writing and Grammar

Week 4 ★ At a Glance

Priority Skills and Concepts

Comprehension
- **Strategy:** Generate Questions
- **Skill:** Draw Conclusions
- Fact and Opinion
- **Genre:** Poetry, Biography

Robust Vocabulary
- **Selection Vocabulary:** *technique, foolishness, inspire, evaporate, magnify, annual*
- **Strategy:** Multiple-Meaning Words

Fluency
- Accuracy

Phonics/Spelling
- **Word Study:** Suffixes, Multisyllabic Words
- **Spelling Words:** *spotless, sunny, furry, really, hairy, barely, tasteless, handful, lifeless, illness, hopefully, happiness, goodness, sorrowful, gently, sickness, joyfully, aimless, breathless, certainly*
- *disappoint, nonfat, misnumber*

Grammar/Mechanics
- Prepositions
- Review Using Quotations

Writing
- **Trait:** Sentence Fluency
- Transition Words and Phrases

Key

 Tested in program    Review Skill

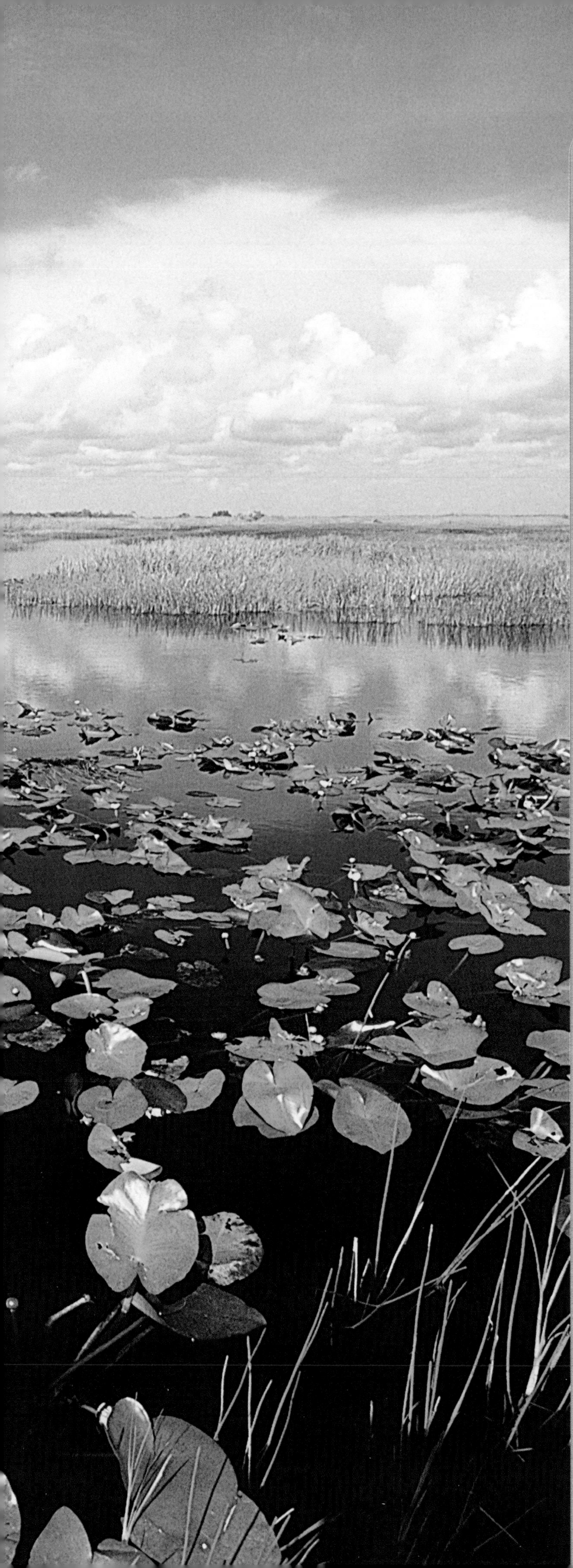

Digital solutions to help plan and implement instruction

☑ Teacher Resources

 **LOG ON** ▶

ONLINE www.macmillanmh.com

▶ **Teacher's Edition**
- Lesson Planner and Resources also on CD-ROM

 TeacherWorks^Plus

▶ **Formative Assessment**
- ExamView® on CD-ROM also available

 Progress Reporter

▶ **Instructional Resources**
- Unit Videos
- Classroom Presentation Toolkit

VIDEO

▶ **Professional Development**
- Video Library

 Professional Development

☑ Student Resources

 **LOG ON** ▶

ONLINE www.macmillanmh.com

▶ **Interactive Student Book**

StudentWorks^Plus

▶ **Leveled Reader Database**

▶ **Activities**
- Research Toolkit
- Oral Language Activities
- Vocabulary/Spelling Activities

 Listening Library
- Recordings of Student Books and Leveled Readers

 Fluency Solutions
- Fluency Modeling and Practice

Weekly Literature

Theme: Step By Step

StudentWorks Plus
LOG ON
Interactive Student Book

- Word-by-Word Reading
- Summaries in Multiple Languages
- Comprehension Questions

SNOWFLAKE BENTLEY
By Jacqueline Briggs Martin
Illustrated by Mary Azarian

Main Selection
Genre Biography

Let It Snow
by Cynthia Robey

Preteach Vocabulary and Comprehension
Genre Expository

HAIKU

Paired Selection
Genre Poetry

Support Literature

Treasures
INTERACTIVE
Read-Aloud
ANTHOLOGY with PLAYS
Macmillan/McGraw-Hill

Interactive Read-Aloud Anthology
- Listening Comprehension
- Robust Vocabulary
- Readers Theater Plays for Fluency

Resources for Differentiated Instruction

Leveled Readers: Science

GR Levels O–V

Genre	Expository

- Same Theme
- Same Vocabulary
- Same Comprehension Skills

Q

S

Approaching Level

On Level

V

O

Beyond Level

ELL

Leveled Reader Database
Go to **www.macmillanmh.com**.

Leveled Practice

Approaching Reproducibles	Practice Book	Beyond Reproducibles	English Language Learner Practice Book
Approaching	**On Level**	**Beyond**	**ELL**

Leveled Classroom Library

Approaching   **On Level**   **Beyond**

Response to Intervention

Tier 2

- Phonics
- Vocabulary
- Comprehension
- Fluency
- Writing and Grammar

Tier 3

Assessment

Time For Kids
- TFK Teacher's Manual
- Apply Answering Question Strategies

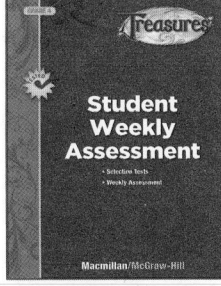
Student Weekly Assessment

Unit Assessment

Benchmark Assessment

Weekly Assessment   Unit Assessment   Benchmark Assessment

 HOME-SCHOOL CONNECTION

- Family letters in English and Spanish
- Take-Home Stories and activities

Home-School Connection

Online Homework
www.macmillanmh.com

Go to **www.macmillanmh.com** for **Online Lesson Planner**

TeacherWorks Plus™
All-In-One Planner and Resource Center

Professional Development
Video Library

Snowflake Bentley,
pp. 746–767

WHOLE GROUP

ORAL LANGUAGE
- **Listening Comprehension**
- **Speaking/Viewing**

WORD STUDY
- **Vocabulary**
- **Phonics/Word Study**
- **Spelling**

READING
- **Comprehension**
- **Fluency**

LANGUAGE ARTS
- **Writing**
- **Grammar**

ASSESSMENT
- **Informal/Formal**

DAY 1

Listening/Speaking/Viewing
❓ Focus Question What steps are the scientists in the photo taking to find a solution?
Build Background, 742
Read Aloud: "Water Dance," 743A–743B

✔ **Vocabulary**
technique, foolishness, inspire, evaporate, magnify, annual, 745, 773C
Practice Book, 254
Strategy: Multiple-Meaning Words, 744

✔ **Spelling** Pretest: Suffixes, 773E
Phonics/Spelling Book, 169–170

Let It Snow

Read "Let It Snow," 744–745

Student Book

✔ **Comprehension,** 745A–745B
Strategy: Generate Questions

Skill: Draw Conclusions
Practice Book, 255

Fluency Model Fluency, 743B

Writing
Daily Writing Write a short report describing the characteristics of your favorite climate.

✔ **Trait:** Sentence Fluency
Transition Words and Phrases, 771A–771B

✔ **Grammar** Daily Language Activities, 773G
Prepositions, 773G
Grammar Practice Book, 141

Quick Check Vocabulary, 744
Comprehension, 745B

DAY 2

Listening/Speaking
❓ Focus Question What did Snowflake Bentley give to the world?

Vocabulary
Review Vocabulary Words, Multiple-Meaning Words, 746, 773C
Practice Book, 260

✔ **Morphology**
Suffixes, 743C–743D
Practice Book, 253

Spelling Word Sorts, 773E
Phonics/Spelling Book, 171

Read *Snowflake Bentley,* 746–767

Student Book

✔ **Comprehension,** 746–767
Strategy: Generate Questions

Skill: Draw Conclusions
Practice Book, 256

✔ **Fluency** Repeated Reading: Accuracy, 769A

Writing
Daily Writing Write a journal entry about what you would do on a snow day from school.

✔ **Reading/Writing Connection,** 772–773

Grammar Daily Language Activities, 773G
Prepositions, 773G
Grammar Practice Book, 142

Quick Check Morphology, 743D
Comprehension, 767

SMALL GROUP Lesson Plan ▶ Differentiated Instruction 742G–742H

Priority Skills

Vocabulary	Comprehension	Writing	Science
Vocabulary Words Multiple-Meaning Words	**Strategy:** Generate Questions **Skill:** Draw Conclusions	Trait: Sentence Fluency Transition Words and Phrases	Knows that matter has physical properties

DAY 3

Listening/Speaking

? Focus Question How is the information about snow in "Let It Snow" the same as in *Snowflake Bentley*? How is the information different?

Summarize, 769

Vocabulary

Review Words, Related Words, 773D

Spelling Word Meanings, 773F
Phonics/Spelling Book, 172

Read *Snowflake Bentley,* 746–767

Student Book

Comprehension
Comprehension Check, 769

Review Skill: Fact and Opinion, 769B
Practice Book, 258

Fluency Repeated Reading: Accuracy, 769A
Practice Book, 257

Writing

 Daily Writing Write a short dialogue describing snow to a person who has never seen it.

Trait: Sentence Fluency
Transition Words and Phrases, 773A

Grammar Daily Language Activities, 773G
Mechanics and Usage, 773H
Grammar Practice Book, 143

 Quick Check Fluency, 769A

DAY 4

Listening/Speaking/Viewing

? Focus Question How do these poems make you feel about snow? How did you feel about it when you read *Snowflake Bentley*? Compare the two feelings.

Vocabulary

Review Words, Morphology, 773D

Spelling Proofread, 773F
Phonics/Spelling Book, 173

Read Haiku, 770–771

Student Book

Comprehension
Poetry: Haiku

Literary Elements: Imagery and Metaphor, 770
Practice Book, 259

Fluency Repeated Reading: Accuracy, 769A

Writing

 Daily Writing Write a poem about rain. Use interesting words to describe details.

Trait: Ideas
Adding Information, 773A

Grammar Daily Language Activities, 773G
Prepositions, 773H
Grammar Practice Book, 144

 Quick Check Vocabulary, 773D

DAY 5
Review and Assess

Listening/Speaking/Viewing

? Focus Question Summarize the life of a snowflake, from the time it forms high in the clouds to the moment it melts on the tip of your tongue.

Vocabulary

Assess Words, Connect to Writing, 773D

Spelling Posttest, 773F
Phonics/Spelling Book, 174

Read Self-Selected Reading, 742K
Practice Book, 261

Student Book

Comprehension
Connect and Compare, 771

Fluency Practice, 742K

Writing

 Daily Writing Write a weather report about an upcoming blizzard.

Conferencing, 773B

Grammar Daily Language Activities, 773G
Prepositions, 773H
Grammar Practice Book, 145

Weekly Assessment, 773II–773JJ

Differentiated Instruction

What do I do in small groups?

Teacher-Led Small Groups

Independent Activities

Focus on Skills

IF... students need additional instruction, practice, or extension based on your **Quick Check** observations for the following priority skills

 Phonics/Word Study
Suffixes

 Vocabulary Words
technique, foolishness, inspire, evaporate, magnify, annual
Strategy: Multiple-Meaning Words

 Comprehension
Strategy: Generate Questions
Skill: Draw Conclusions

 Fluency

THEN...

Approaching **ELL**	Preteach and Reteach Skills
On Level	Practice
Beyond	Enrich and Accelerate Learning

 **LOG ON** ▶ **Suggested Small Group Lesson Plan**

	DAY 1	**DAY 2**
Approaching Level **Tier 2** • **Preteach/Reteach** **Tier 2 Instruction**	• Prepare to Read, 773I • Academic Language, 773I • Preteach Vocabulary, 773K	• Comprehension, 773M Generate Questions/Draw Conclusions **ELL** • Leveled Reader Lesson 1, 773N
On Level • **Practice**	• Vocabulary, 773S • Phonics, 773S Suffixes **ELL**	• Leveled Reader Lesson 1, 773U
Beyond Level • **Extend/Accelerate** **Gifted and Talented**	• Leveled Reader Lesson 1, 773Y • Analyze Information, 773Y	• Leveled Reader Lesson 2, 773Z • Synthesize Information, 773Z
ELL • **Build English Language Proficiency** • See **ELL** in other levels.	• Prepare to Read, 773AA • Academic Language, 773AA • Preteach Vocabulary, 773BB	• Vocabulary, 773BB • Preteach Main Selection, 773CC

Small Group

Focus on Leveled Readers

Leveled Reader Library

Levels Q–V

Q — **Amazing Stuff! Materials at Work** by Mary Kay Carson
Approaching

S — **Amazing Stuff! Materials at Work** by Mary Kay Carson
On Level

V — **Amazing Stuff! Materials at Work** by Mary Kay Carson
Beyond

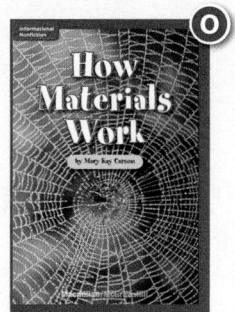
O — **How Materials Work** by Mary Kay Carson
ELL

Manipulatives

Sound-Spelling WorkBoards

Sound-Spelling Cards

Science

Teacher's Annotated Edition

The student knows that matter has physical properties.

about / **today**
High-Frequency Word Cards

Additional Leveled Readers

LOG ON ▶ **Leveled Reader Database**
www.macmillanmh.com

Search by

- Comprehension Skill
- Content Area
- Genre
- Text Feature

- Guided Reading Level
- Reading Recovery Level
- Lexile Score
- Benchmark Level

Subscription also available.

Visual Vocabulary Resources

DAY 3

- Phonics Maintenance, 773J
  Suffixes **ELL**
- Leveled Reader Lesson 2, 773O

- Leveled Reader Lesson 2, 773V

- Phonics, 773W
  Suffixes **ELL**

- Vocabulary, 773BB
- Grammar, 773EE

DAY 4

- Reteach Phonics Skill, 773J
  Suffixes **ELL**
- Review Vocabulary, 773L
- Leveled Reader Lesson 3, 773P

- Fluency, 773T

- Vocabulary, 773W
- Compare Haiku, 773W
- Fluency, 773X

- Vocabulary, 773BB
- Writing/Spelling, 773FF
- Preteach Paired Selection, 773CC
- Fluency, 773DD
- Leveled Reader, 773GG

DAY 5

- High-Frequency Words, 773L
- Fluency, 773Q
- Self-Selected Independent Reading, 773R
- Book Talk, 773P

- Self-Selected Independent Reading, 773T
- Book Talk, 773V

- Self-Selected Independent Reading, 773X
- Evaluate Information, 773X
- Book Talk, 773Z

- Vocabulary, 773BB
- Leveled Reader, 773GG
- Self-Selected Independent Reading, 773DD
- Book Talk, 773HH

Managing the Class

What do I do with the rest of my class?

Teacher-Led Small Groups

Independent Activities

- Practice Book and Reproducibles
- ELL Practice Book
- Leveled Reader Activities
- Literacy Workstations
- Online Activities

Classroom Management Tools

Weekly Contract

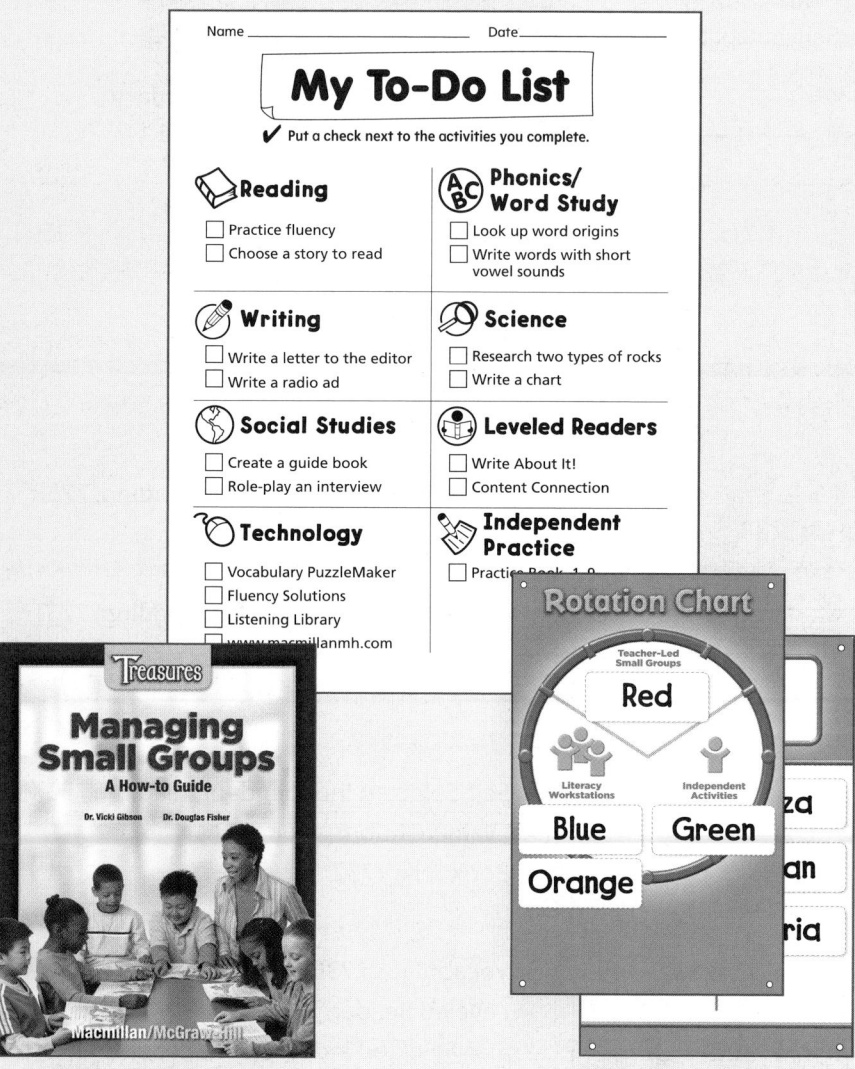

Name _____ Date _____

My To-Do List

✔ Put a check next to the activities you complete.

Reading
- [ ] Practice fluency
- [ ] Choose a story to read

Phonics/Word Study
- [ ] Look up word origins
- [ ] Write words with short vowel sounds

Writing
- [ ] Write a letter to the editor
- [ ] Write a radio ad

Science
- [ ] Research two types of rocks
- [ ] Write a chart

Social Studies
- [ ] Create a guide book
- [ ] Role-play an interview

Leveled Readers
- [ ] Write About It!
- [ ] Content Connection

Technology
- [ ] Vocabulary PuzzleMaker
- [ ] Fluency Solutions
- [ ] Listening Library
- [ ] www.macmillanmh.com

Independent Practice
- [ ] Practice Book 1–8

How-to Guide

Treasures
Managing Small Groups
A How-to Guide
Dr. Vicki Gibson   Dr. Douglas Fisher
Macmillan/McGraw-Hill

Rotation Chart

Rotation Chart
Teacher-Led Small Groups
Red
Literacy Workstations   Independent Activities
Blue   Green
Orange

Digital Learning

LOG ON
StudentWorks Plus
Interactive Student Book

StudentWorks Plus Online
- Summaries in Multiple Languages
- Word-by-Word Reading
- Comprehension Questions

Meet the Author/Illustrator

Print   Close Window

Rosalyn Schanzer
- As a child, Rosalyn loved reading stories about horses.
- She lives with her husband, her two children, and her dog named Jones.
- Rosalyn worked for years illustrating other people's books before finally deciding to write her own.

Other books by Rosalyn Schanzer
- Schanzer, Rosalyn. *Escaping to America: A True Story*. New York: HarperCollins, 2000.
- Schanzer, Rosalyn. *Gold Fever*. Washington, D.C.: National Geographic Society, 1999.

- Other Books by the Author or Illustrator

Leveled Practice

Treasures
Practice Book
- Practice
- Vocabulary
- Fluency
- Comprehension
- Writing
Macmillan/McGraw-Hill

Treasures
English Language Learner Practice Book
Macmillan/McGraw-Hill

On Level   **ELL**

Also Available:
Approaching Reproducible
Beyond Reproducible

Independent Activities

Oral Language Activities

- Focus on Vocabulary and Concepts
- English Language Learner Support

Vocabulary/Spelling Activities

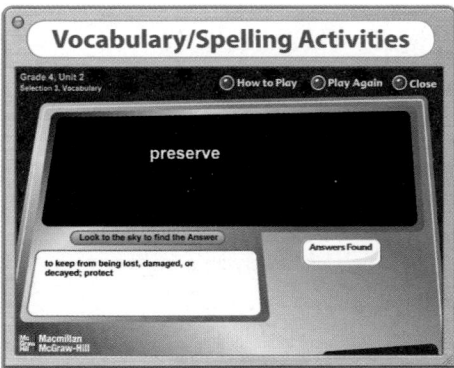

- Differentiated Lists and Activities

Leveled Reader Database

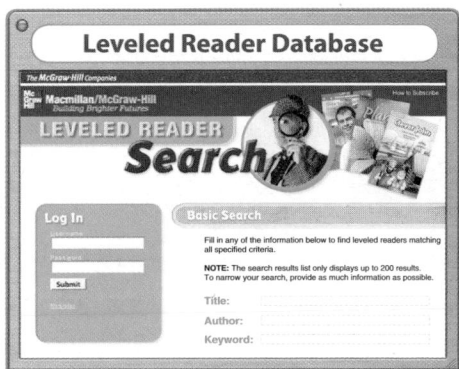

- Leveled Reader Database
- Search titles by level, skill, content area, and more

Research Toolkit

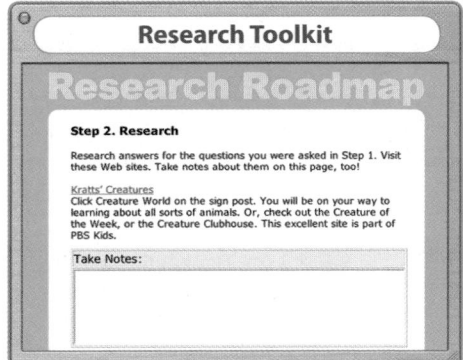

- Research Roadmap
- Research and Presentation Tools
- Theme Launcher Video
- Links to Science and Social Studies

Available on CD

LISTENING LIBRARY
Recordings of selections
- Main Selections
- Paired Selections
- Leveled Readers

VOCABULARY PUZZLEMAKER

FLUENCY SOLUTIONS
Recorded passages at two speeds for modeling and practicing fluency

Leveled Reader Activities

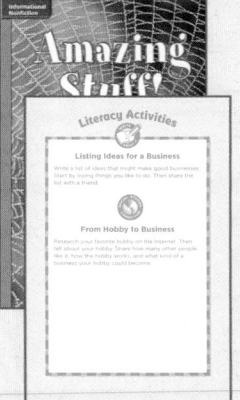

Approaching　　**On Level**　　**Beyond**　　**ELL**

See inside cover of all Leveled Readers.

Literacy Workstations

See lessons on pages 742K–742L.

Managing the Class

What do I do with the rest of my class?

Reading

Objectives

- Develop fluency through partner-reading
- Read independently for a sustained period of time; use **Practice Book** page 261 for Reading Strategies and Reading Log

---

Reading — Fluency
20 Minutes

- Select a paragraph from the Fluency passage on page 257 of your Practice Book.
- With a partner, take turns reading the passage. Vary your reading rate as you read each sentence.

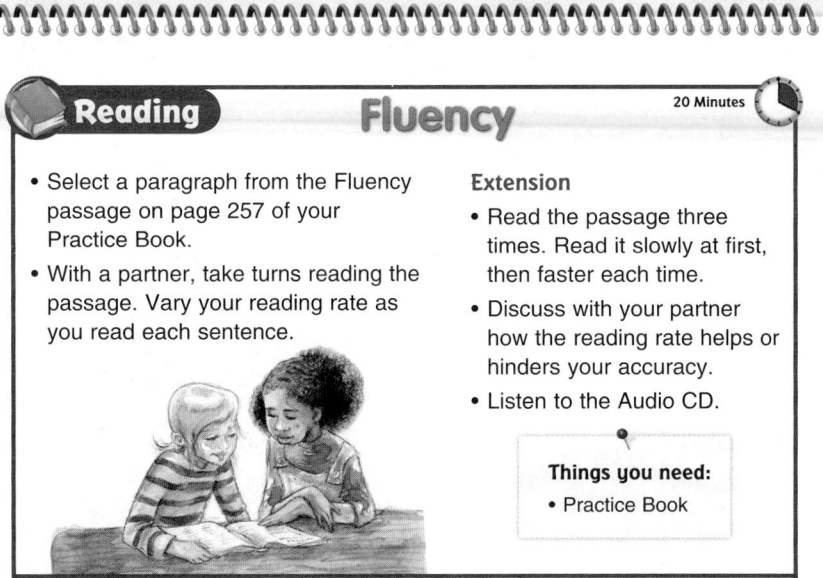

Extension

- Read the passage three times. Read it slowly at first, then faster each time.
- Discuss with your partner how the reading rate helps or hinders your accuracy.
- Listen to the Audio CD.

> **Things you need:**
> - Practice Book

Fluency Solutions
Listening Library

(57)

Reading — Independent Reading
20 Minutes

- Read a nonfiction article about a scientific experiment. As you read, take notes.
- Remember to make sure you know what is happening in the article. Use what you have learned about asking questions and rereading to check your comprehension.

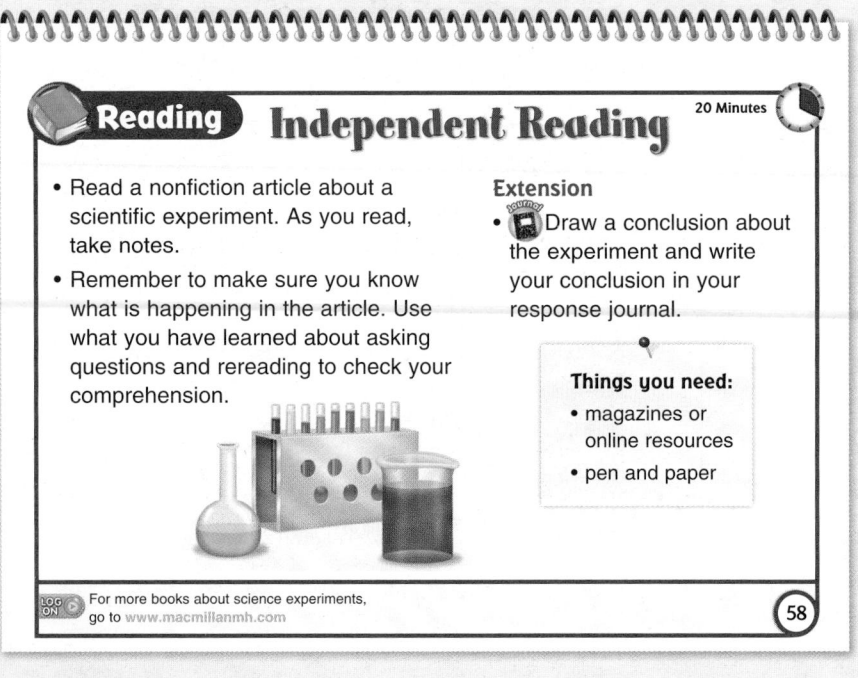

Extension

- Draw a conclusion about the experiment and write your conclusion in your response journal.

> **Things you need:**
> - magazines or online resources
> - pen and paper

For more books about science experiments, go to www.macmillanmh.com

(58)

Phonics/Word Study

Objectives

- Find definitions in a dictionary
- Write sentences illustrating multiple meanings
- Create words using word endings

Phonics/Word Study — Multiple-Meaning Words
20 Minutes

- Look up the word *magnify* in the dictionary.
- Write two meanings for this word.
- Write one sentence for each meaning.
- Repeat this activity, using the words *change* and *cast*.

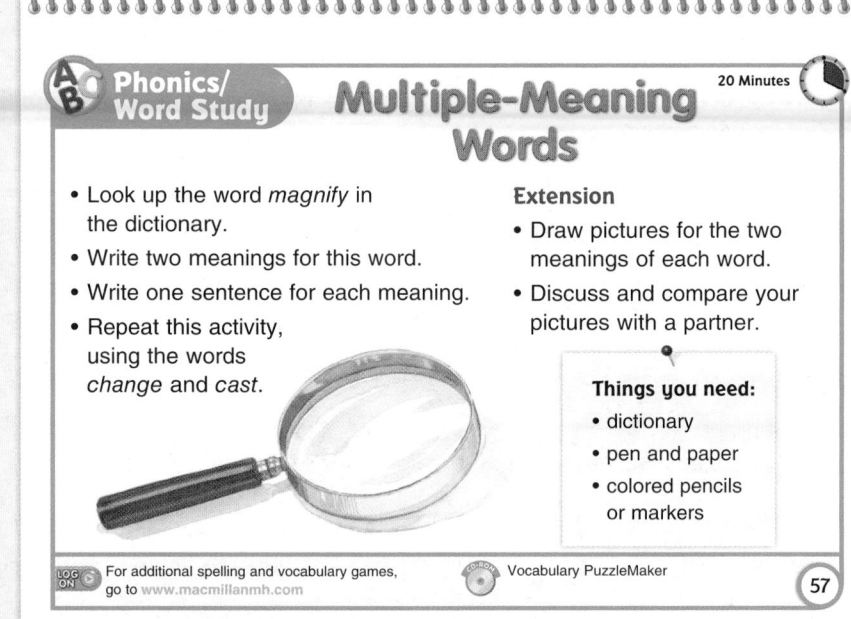

Extension

- Draw pictures for the two meanings of each word.
- Discuss and compare your pictures with a partner.

> **Things you need:**
> - dictionary
> - pen and paper
> - colored pencils or markers

For additional spelling and vocabulary games, go to www.macmillanmh.com

Vocabulary PuzzleMaker

(57)

Phonics/Word Study — Suffixes
20 Minutes

- Create a five-layered, Layered Book Foldable®.
- Write *Suffixes* at the top.
- On the layers, write the suffixes: *-y, -ly, -ful, -less, -ness*.
- Write these base words with its correct suffix on each layer: *bare, hair, success, joy, good,* and *taste*.
- Add more words using these suffixes to each layer.

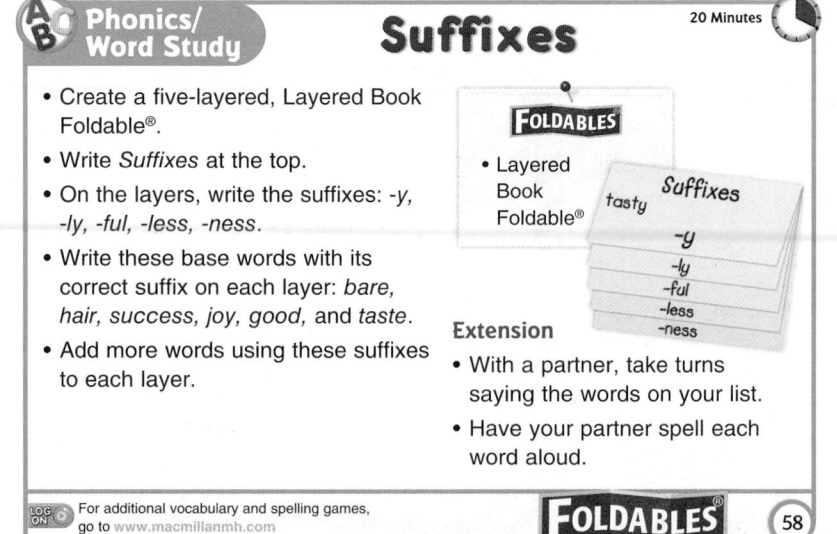

FOLDABLES

- Layered Book Foldable®

Extension

- With a partner, take turns saying the words on your list.
- Have your partner spell each word aloud.

For additional vocabulary and spelling games, go to www.macmillanmh.com

FOLDABLES®

(58)

Literacy Workstations

Literacy Workstation Flip Charts

Writing

Objectives

- Write a book review
- Write a paragraph about how to save money

Content Literacy

Objectives

- Research information about snow
- Write a poem from your research
- Research rainfall and snowfall in your state and make a chart

---

Writing — A Book Review
20 Minutes

- Choose a book of poetry that you especially like. Write a book review that will make others want to read this book.
- Include a strong topic sentence that will grab the reader's attention.
- Write a brief summary about the kinds of poems included in this book.
- Support your recommendation with examples of poems from the book.

Extension

- Make a book cover for your book review.
- Include pictures that tell something about the book of poetry.

Things you need:
- poetry books
- pen and paper
- colored pencils

57

Science — It's Snowing!
20 Minutes

- Use a science book or the Internet to find out why it snows.
- Where does the most snow fall in the United States? Why?
- Write a summary of the facts that you learn.

Extension

- Turn your facts about snow into a poem.
- Use a metaphor to write a fresh comparison about snow—for example, *The falling crystal flakes are powder on my face.*

Facts About Snow

Things you need:
- science book or online resources
- pen and paper

57

Writing — MONEY MATTERS
20 Minutes

- Write a short paragraph about how people can save money. Include a clear topic sentence and supporting details.
- Make sure to include facts and examples in your paragraph.

Extension

- Exchange papers with a partner.
- Identify the topic sentence and supporting details in your partner's paragraph.
- Tell what parts are clear and what parts are hard to understand.

Things you need:
- pen and paper

58

Social Studies — Rain and Snow
20 Minutes

- Use a geography book or an almanac to learn more about the climate of your state.
- Find out how many inches of rain and snow your state receives annually.
- On a piece of paper, write the number of inches for three years in a row.

Extension

- Use figurative language, such as similes and metaphors, to describe how dry or wet your state is. For example, if you live in a dry state, you might write that your state is as dry as dust.

	2008	2009	2010
Inches of Snow	12	8	4
Inches of Rain	22	28	31

Things you need:
- geography book
- pen and paper

58

742

Prepare

WHOLE GROUP

ORAL LANGUAGE
- Build Background
- Connect to Theme
- Read Aloud

✔ **PHONICS/WORD STUDY**
- Suffixes

✔ **VOCABULARY**
- Multiple-Meaning Words
- Teach Words

✔ **COMPREHENSION**
- Strategy: Generate Questions
- Skill: Draw Conclusions

SMALL GROUP

- Differentiated Instruction, pp. 773I–773HH

Oral Language

Build Background

ACCESS PRIOR KNOWLEDGE

Share the following information: The people in this photograph are scientists. They have used string to divide the land you see into smaller areas. The scientists are using a bucket and tools called pickaxes in order to gather rocks and soil so that they may observe them more closely and conduct experiments on them. Scientists work step by step to collect and analyze information.

Write the following words on the board, and briefly define each using the **Define/Example/Ask** routine: **scientist** (an expert who works in an area of science), **observe** (watch closely), **conduct** (perform).

FOCUS QUESTION Ask students to read "Talk About It" on **Student Book** page 743. Then have students turn to a partner and describe the photo. Ask:

- What types of experiments do you think the scientists will conduct on the rocks and soil they gathered?

- Have you ever conducted an experiment? Explain.

Talk About It

What steps are these scientists taking to find a solution?

LOG ON ▶ **VIEW IT**

Oral Language Activities
Step by Step
www.macmillanmh.com

743

Use the Picture Prompt

BUILD WRITING FLUENCY

Have students write in their Writer's Notebooks about an experiment they observed. They should write as much as they can for 15 minutes. Meet with individuals during Writing Conference time to provide feedback and revision assignments. Prior to meeting, students should self-correct any errors they find.

Connect to the Unit Theme

DISCUSS THE BIG IDEA

Scientists can solve problems using observation and trial-and-error experimentation.

Ask students what they have learned so far in this unit about solving problems.

- What effective methods for solving problems have we read about so far? Did any of these methods involve conducting an experiment?

- How could you use observations and experiments to solve problems?

USE THEME FOLDABLES

Write the **Big Idea** statement on the board. Ask students to copy it on their Unit Theme Foldables. Remind them to add details as they complete this week's readings.

Dinah Zike's
FOLDABLES®
Study Organizer

Unit Theme
Week 1
Week 2
Week 3
Week 4
Week 5

Layered Book

Read Aloud

Read "Water Dance"

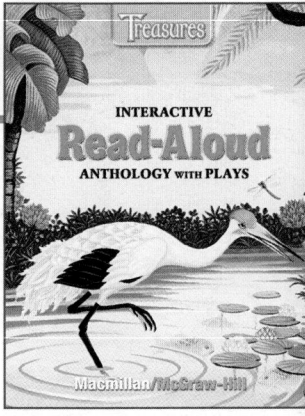

Read Aloud

GENRE: Literary Text/Poetry

Review key characteristics of a **poem**:

- Poems are written in lines, with carefully chosen line breaks. Distinct groups of lines are called stanzas.

- Free verse poems do not have a regular rhyming pattern or standard line lengths.

- Poems may use figurative language such as metaphors, similes, and personification. Personification is a literary device in which animals or objects are given human feelings, thoughts, or attitudes.

FOCUS ON VOCABULARY

Introduce the following words, using the **Define/Example/Ask** routine. Tell students that knowing these words will help them understand the imagery in the poem.

Vocabulary Routine

Use the routines below to discuss the meaning of each word.

Define: To **cascade** means to fall in a tumbling motion.
Example: I watched the water cascade over the dishes in the sink.
Ask: Where can you watch water cascade over something?

Define: **Palisades** are cliffs in a line along a river.
Example: We saw the palisades towering over the river below.
Ask: Why should you be careful if you are on palisades?

Define: To **drench** means to soak with water.
Example: The rain will drench us if we don't use our umbrellas.
Ask: When might you want to drench yourself?

LISTENING FOR A PURPOSE

Ask students to listen carefully as you read "Water Dance" on **Read-Aloud Anthology** pages 62–65. Use the Think Alouds and Genre Study provided.

ELL **Interactive Reading** Build students' oral language by engaging them in talk about the poem's basic meaning.

- Point to the title of the poem on page 62. Say: *Water can move in so many different ways. The title might be a way of describing how water moves. Let's read the poem to find out.*

- After the second stanza, say: *This poem is written like a riddle. Turn to a partner and explain how this poem is like a riddle.*

- After the fifth stanza, ask: *What are some ways in which the poet uses personification? Who or what is the narrator of this poem?*

- After the last stanza, ask: *Why is the title of the poem "Water Dance"?*

Think/Pair/Share Use **Copying Master 4**, "I figured out ___ because …," to prompt students to share something they noticed about the structure, word choice, or imagery of the poem. When completed, have students turn to a partner and orally summarize and generate questions about the poem.

RESPOND TO THE POEM

Ask students the Think and Respond questions on page 65. Then have students generate a list of words that are related to how water moves. Have them use the words to create imagery, such as metaphors, similes, or other figurative language, that might fit in this poem.

Model Fluency

Reread the poem. Tell students that this time you want them to focus on one aspect of how you read—your **accuracy**.

Explain that good readers read accurately. They pronounce each word correctly, and they do not skip words or sentences or change the words the author wrote. Model an example:

Think Aloud Listen as I read the third stanza of the poem. First I'm going to read the stanza accurately: *At the foot of the mountains,/I leap from a stone cliff./Spiraling./Plunging./I am the waterfall.* Now listen as I read it again and skip a word: *At the foot of the mountains,/I leap from a stone./Spiraling./Plunging./I am the waterfall.* Did you notice how the image of the waterfall was not as clear or powerful without the word *cliff*? Now you try. Repeat each line after me, making sure to read all of the words accurately the same way that I do.

Establish Fluency Focus Remind students that you will be listening for this same quality in their reading throughout the week. You will help them improve their reading by giving them multiple opportunities to read the same text in order to improve their accuracy.

Objective

- Decode multisyllabic words with suffixes

Materials

- Practice Book, p. 253
- Transparency 29
- Word-Building Cards
- Teacher's Resource Book, p. 148

ELL

Additional Practice To introduce suffixes, write simple word pairs such as *rest/restless, help/helpful, kind/kindness, rain/rainy,* and *quick/quickly.* Write sentences for the words in each word pair, and discuss how the suffix changes the meaning of the words and their parts of speech. Use the Approaching Level lesson on page 773J for additional practice. See language transfers on pages T16–T31.

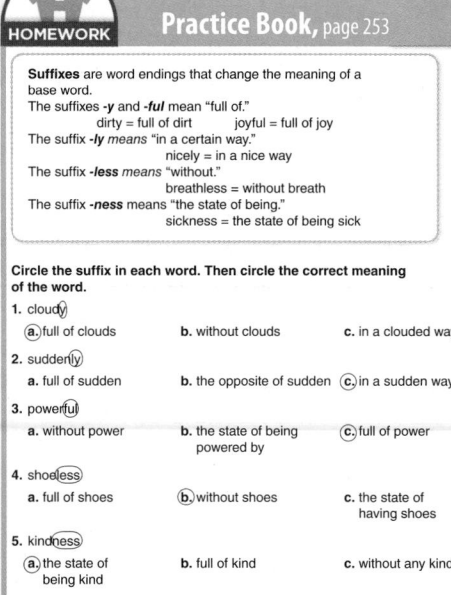

HOMEWORK

Practice Book, page 253

Suffixes are word endings that change the meaning of a base word.
The suffixes **-y** and **-ful** mean "full of."
    dirty = full of dirt   joyful = full of joy
The suffix **-ly** means "in a certain way."
    nicely = in a nice way
The suffix **-less** means "without."
    breathless = without breath
The suffix **-ness** means "the state of being."
    sickness = the state of being sick

Circle the suffix in each word. Then circle the correct meaning of the word.

1. cloud(y)
   a. full of clouds b. without clouds c. in a clouded way
2. sudden(ly)
   a. full of sudden b. the opposite of sudden (c.) in a sudden way
3. power(ful)
   a. without power b. the state of being powered by (c.) full of power
4. shoe(less)
   a. full of shoes (b.) without shoes c. the state of having shoes
5. kind(ness)
   (a.) the state of being kind b. full of kind c. without any kind
6. loud(ly)
   a. without loud b. full of loud (c.) in a loud way

Approaching Reproducible, page 253

Beyond Reproducible, page 253

Morphology

 **Suffixes**

EXPLAIN/MODEL

Explain that a suffix is a letter or group of letters added to the end of a base word. A suffix changes the meaning of the base word. It can also change the word's part of speech. Introduce these common suffixes. Write each suffix and sample word on the board. Explain that the spelling of the base word may change when a suffix is added (penny/penniless). Read and define the suffix. Then use the suffix's meaning to model how to determine the meaning of the words.

- **-less** "lacking"; turns a noun into an adjective
  The kitchen is <u>spotless</u>.
- **-ful** "having the quality of, as much as can be held by"; may make a noun into an adjective (or the word may remain a noun)
  The sunset was <u>beautiful</u>.   I had a <u>handful</u> of cherries.
- **-ness** "the quality or state of"; turns an adjective into a noun
  I will never forget your <u>kindness</u>.
- **-ment** "the state, action, or result of"; turns a verb into a noun
  I used the proper <u>equipment</u> to play soccer.
- **-y, -ly** "in a certain way, like"; makes the base word an adjective, an adverb, or a noun
  The teacher told the students to clean their <u>messy</u> desks.
  The river moved <u>rapidly</u> after the heavy rain.
  <u>Honesty</u> is important to our family.

Think Aloud Look at the first underlined word: *spotless.* I see the base word *spot.* The end, or suffix, of the word is *-less.* I put the two parts together to get *spotless,* or lacking spots.

PRACTICE/APPLY

Read the Words Display **Transparency 29**. Help students underline the suffix, define it, then use its meaning to determine the meaning of the whole word.

breathless	mindless	timeless	weightless
mouthful	mindful	rightful	wonderful
fondness	happiness	calmness	darkness
treatment	argument	statement	commitment
mousy	catchy	crafty	modesty
swiftly	graciously	superbly	finally

Phonics Transparency 29

Read Multisyllabic Words

TRANSITION TO LONGER WORDS Display the suffixes and words below. Point out some words have more than one suffix. Have students read the suffix in the first column and underline the suffix in the words in the second column. In the third column have students underline the first suffix and circle the second. Remind them adding suffixes can change spellings. Model how to read each word and determine its meaning. Lastly have students read the words chorally as you point them out in random order and at varying speeds.

less	thoughtless	thoughtlessness
ful	respectful	respectfully
ness	business	businessless
ment	development	developmentally
y	speedy	speedily
ly	lovely	loveliness

Phonics Transparency 29

BUILD WORDS Use **Word-Building Cards** *care, fear, end, pain, use, thought, truth, bright, sad, tight, less, ful, ly, ness.* Display the cards. Have students use the word parts to build as many multisyllabic words with suffixes as possible. These and other words can be formed: *careless, carelessly, carefully, fearful, fearlessly, endlessly, painful, useless, useful, thoughtlessly, thoughtfully, truthful, sadness.*

APPLY DECODING STRATEGY Guide students to use the Decoding Strategy to decode *meaningfully, silliness, selfishness, uncontrollably,* and *warily.* Write each word. Remind students to look for common word parts, such as suffixes, in step 1 of the Decoding Strategy procedure. Conclude by discussing the meaning of each word.

Build Fluency

SPEED DRILL Distribute copies of the **Suffixes Speed Drill** on **Teacher's Resource Book** page 148. Use the Speed Drill routine to help students become fluent reading words with these suffixes.

Quick Check

Can students read words with suffixes?

During **Small Group Instruction**

Tier 2

If No → **Approaching Level** Reteach the skill using the lesson on p. 773J.

If Yes → **On Level** Consolidate the learning using p. 773S.

Beyond Level Extend the learning using p. 773W.

Decoding Strategy

Decoding Strategy Chart

Step 1	Look for word parts (prefixes) at the beginning of the word.
Step 2	Look for word parts (suffixes) at the end of the word.
Step 3	In the base word, look for familiar spelling patterns. Think about the six syllable-spelling patterns you have learned.
Step 4	Sound out and blend together the word parts.
Step 5	Say the word parts fast. Adjust your pronunciation as needed. Ask yourself: "Is this a word I have heard before?" Then read the word in the sentence and ask: "Does it make sense in this sentence?"

© Macmillan/McGraw-Hill

Vocabulary

STRATEGY
DICTIONARY

Multiple-Meaning Words Explain that sometimes words can have more than one meaning. Readers can figure out the meaning of a multiple-meaning word by looking closely at how the word is used and by using context clues in sentences before and after the sentence with that word. Students may also use a dictionary for help.

Model analyzing the multiple-meaning word *annual* on page 744.

Think Aloud When I read the word *annual* in the first paragraph, I think about my mother's garden. I know that some of the flowers there are called "annuals," but that meaning does not make sense here. I check the dictionary and learn that *annual* can also mean "happening or returning once a year," such as an annual holiday or an annual checkup. Judging from the context, I think that is the way the word is being used in the first paragraph.

Ask students to find and discuss different meanings of the word *negative* in a dictionary. Then have them tell what *negatives* means in the last paragraph of the "Studying Snowflakes" section on page 745.

Read "Let It Snow"

As you read "Let It Snow" with students, have them identify clues that reveal the meanings of the highlighted words. Tell students they will read these words again in *Snowflake Bentley.*

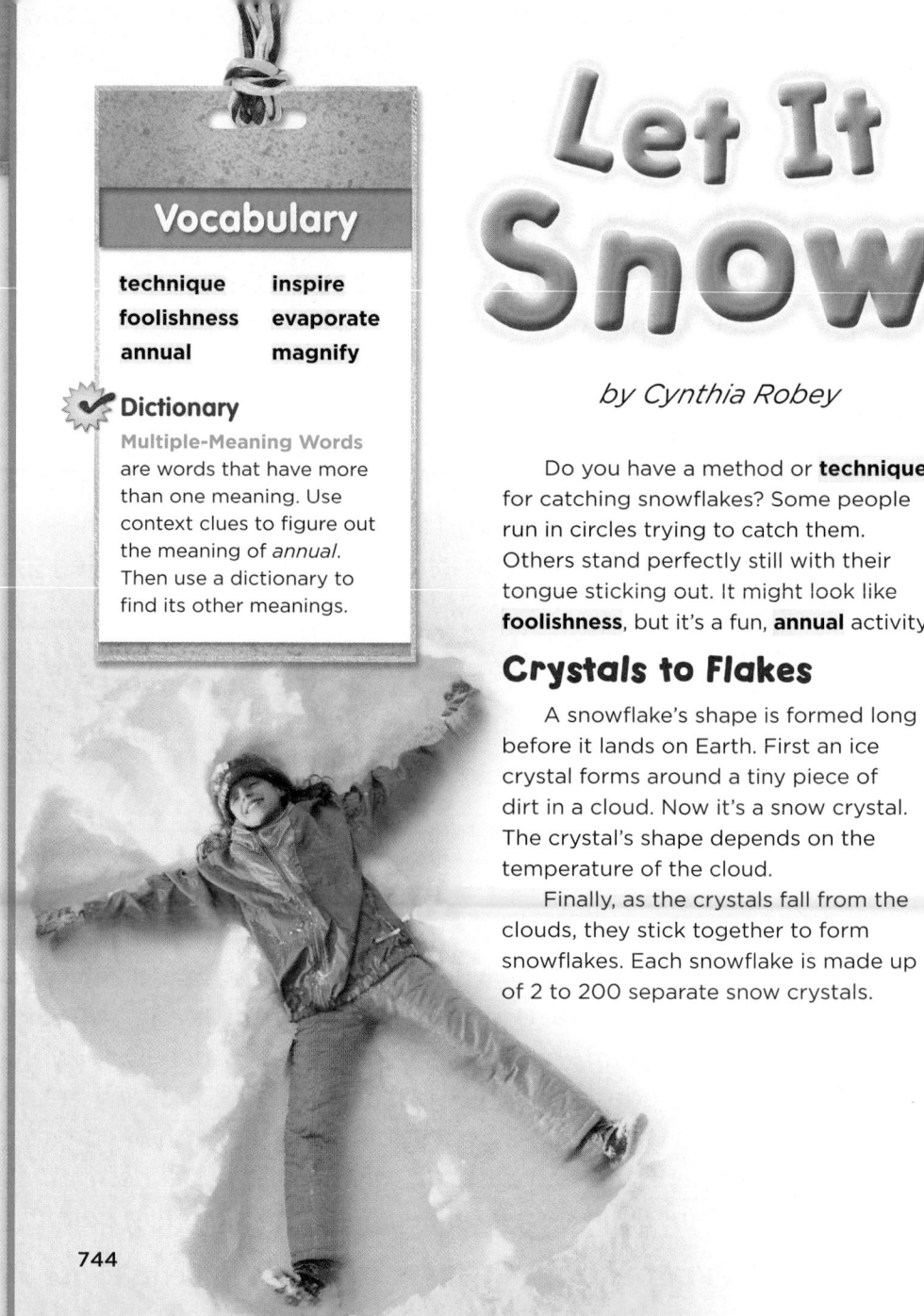

Vocabulary

technique	inspire
foolishness	evaporate
annual	magnify

Dictionary

Multiple-Meaning Words are words that have more than one meaning. Use context clues to figure out the meaning of *annual*. Then use a dictionary to find its other meanings.

Let It Snow

by Cynthia Robey

Do you have a method or **technique** for catching snowflakes? Some people run in circles trying to catch them. Others stand perfectly still with their tongue sticking out. It might look like **foolishness**, but it's a fun, **annual** activity!

Crystals to Flakes

A snowflake's shape is formed long before it lands on Earth. First an ice crystal forms around a tiny piece of dirt in a cloud. Now it's a snow crystal. The crystal's shape depends on the temperature of the cloud.

Finally, as the crystals fall from the clouds, they stick together to form snowflakes. Each snowflake is made up of 2 to 200 separate snow crystals.

744

Quick Check

Can students identify word meanings?

During **Small Group Instruction**

Tier 2

If No → **Approaching Level** Reteach the words using the Vocabulary lesson, pp. 773K–773L.

If Yes → **On Level** Consolidate the learning using p. 773S.

Gifted Talented

Beyond Level Extend the learning using p. 773W.

Studying Snowflakes

Snow crystals form into one of seven shapes. You probably know the stellar crystal best. These star-shape crystals are not the most common, but they're the kind that **inspire** the work of most artists.

How can you study snowflakes before they **evaporate** and disappear? First, go outside when it's not windy and about 25°F. Second, bring a piece of dark cloth with you. This will make it easier to see the crystals. Finally, you will need to use a microscope that will **magnify** and enlarge the crystal so that you can get a good look at it.

Wilson "Snowflake" Bentley learned how to make the crystals show up in photographs. He cut away the dark parts of the negatives to make them visible.

Dangerous Snowflakes

If conditions are just right, beautiful snowflakes can turn into a dangerous storm called a blizzard. In blizzards, strong winds can blow the snow around. This causes "whiteout" conditions, making it very difficult to see where you are going.

Always pay attention to the weather. That way you can safely catch and study all the snowflakes you want.

Reread for **Comprehension**

Generate Questions
Draw Conclusions When you draw conclusions, you think about two or more facts or details an author presents. You add to this your own experience that is connected to this information to arrive at a new understanding about a text or story. Generating questions as you read can help you to draw conclusions, and identify the devices authors use to present information. Reread the selection and use your Conclusions Chart to help you understand how snowflakes are formed.

Text Clues	Conclusion

 **LEARN IT** Comprehension
www.macmillanmh.com

745

Vocabulary

TEACH WORDS

Introduce each word using the **Define/Example/Ask** routine. Model reading each word using the syllable-scoop technique.

> ### Vocabulary Routine
>
> **Define:** A **technique** is a certain way to do something that requires skill.
> **Example:** The artist has a special technique for painting portraits.
> **Ask:** Name activities for which people might develop a technique. EXAMPLE

- If you act with **foolishness**, you are acting unwisely. *Many think it is foolishness to try to travel through time.* What are some other examples of foolishness? EXAMPLE

- If you **inspire** people, it means you encourage them to do something or to change. *Better grades inspire me to do my homework.* How could you inspire a classmate to try something new? EXPLANATION

- To **evaporate** is to change from a liquid to a gas or vapor. *In science class, we saw the boiling water evaporate into the air.* What other things might evaporate? PRIOR KNOWLEDGE

- To **magnify** something means to make it appear larger. *We had to magnify the plant cell several times in order to see it.* What is an antonym for *magnify*? ANTONYM

- Something **annual** happens every year. *My town has an annual festival to celebrate the harvest.* How are the words *annual* and *daily* alike? How are they different? COMPARE AND CONTRAST

ELL

Preteach Vocabulary See pages 773BB and 773K to preteach the vocabulary words to **ELL** and **Approaching Level** students. Use the **Visual Vocabulary Resources** to demonstrate and discuss each word. To further reinforce concepts, have students complete page 332 in the **ELL Resource Book**.

HOMEWORK — **Practice Book,** page 254

A. Choose a word in the box to replace the underlined word or words in each sentence.

technique	foolishness	inspire
evaporate	magnify	annual

1. Lucky for him, Bentley's mother never said, "Stop this silliness! Come in out of the storm at once!" __foolishness__

2. Bentley had to develop a special method to photograph snowflakes. __technique__

3. The newspaper held an occurring-every-year photo contest. __annual__

4. Bentley had to work fast to make sure a snowflake didn't dry up. __evaporate__ Possible responses provided.

B. Use each word correctly in a sentence.

5. magnify __Bentley was able to *magnify* his snowflakes to show more detail.__

6. inspire __Encouraging words can *inspire* us to try harder.__

Approaching Reproducible, page 254
Beyond Reproducible, page 254

Objectives
- Generate questions
- Draw conclusions
- Use academic language: *generate questions, conclusions*

Materials
- Transparencies 4, 29a, 29b
- Practice Book, p. 255

Skills Trace

Draw Conclusions

Introduce	295A–295B
Practice/ Apply	296–319; Practice Book, 102–103
Reteach/ Review	325M–325Z, 477A–477B, 478–497, 503M–503Z; Practice Book, 165–166
Assess	Weekly Tests; Units 3, 4, 6 Tests
Maintain	361B, 745A–745B, 746–769, 773M–773Z, 797B

ELL

Academic Language
Preteach the following academic language words to **ELL** and **Approaching Level** students during Small Group time: *generate questions, draw conclusions.* See pages 773AA and 773I.

Reread for
Comprehension

STRATEGY
GENERATE QUESTIONS

What Is It? Good readers **generate questions** about a selection as they read. Questions such as *Do I understand what is happening here? What does this word or phrase mean? Why has the author included this information?* help to ensure their comprehension.

Why Is It Important? Looking for the answers to these and other literal, evaluative, and interpretive questions can help readers improve their comprehension and draw conclusions, arriving at a new understanding of a text or story.

SKILL
DRAW CONCLUSIONS

What Is It? Explain that when you **draw conclusions** you use logical reasoning to consider two or more pieces of information in order to reach a new understanding about characters or events in a story.

Why Is It Important? Drawing conclusions will help students get more information and ideas from a story. It can help them recognize the varied structural patterns and features of literary nonfiction, including how authors present major events in a person's life.

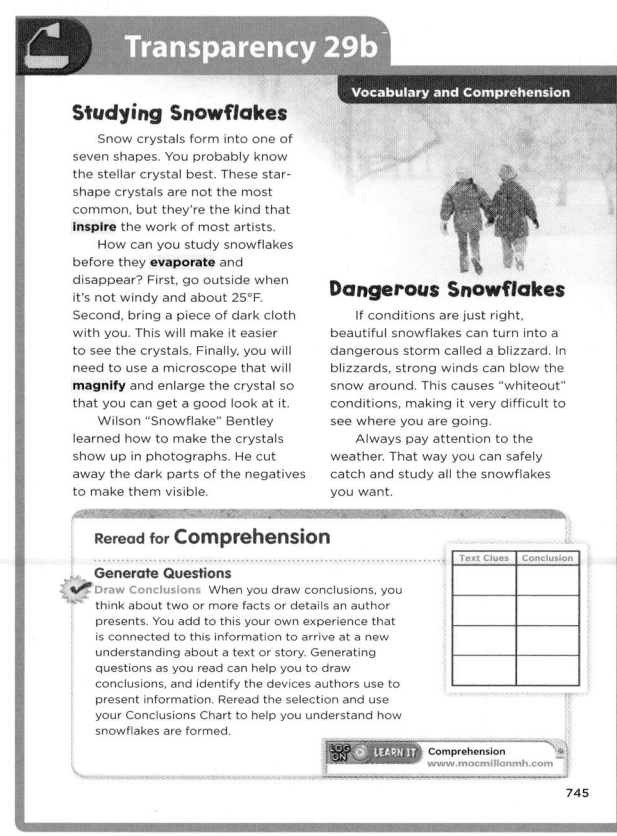

Student Book pages 744–745 available on Comprehension Transparencies 29a and 29b

■ To draw conclusions, tell students to look for two or more facts or details the author provides about a character or event. They should then think and ask themselves questions about what they know concerning a similar situation: *Did something like this happen to them or someone they know? Have they read about something like this before?* Based on these facts and their own related prior knowledge, they can use logical reasoning to draw a conclusion.

MODEL

How Do I Use It? Read aloud the first paragraph of "Let It Snow" on **Student Book** page 744. Use **Transparency 4** to record text clues and conclusions on a Conclusions Chart.

Think Aloud I can draw conclusions from details the author gives and my own prior knowledge. The author states that catching snowflakes is an annual activity. I know that things that happen annually happen once a year or around the same time each year. I know that snow usually falls in winter, so I can conclude that catching snowflakes is a wintertime activity. I will add this information to my Conclusions Chart.

GUIDED PRACTICE

Tell students to read the "Crystals to Flakes" section and draw a conclusion about the size of snowflakes. (The author states that snowflakes can be made up of 2 to 200 crystals. I can conclude that snowflakes can be different sizes depending on the number of crystals.) Have students read the "Studying Snowflakes" section to draw a conclusion about how temperature affects viewing snowflakes. (The author states that 25 degrees is a good temperature for viewing snowflakes. Even though I know that water freezes at 32 degrees, I can conclude that 32 degrees is not cold enough for viewing snowflakes.) Add this information to the Conclusions Chart.

APPLY

Tell students to draw conclusions about the "Dangerous Snowflakes" section. Have them add this information to complete the Conclusions Chart.

Quick Check

Can students draw conclusions from information in a text?

During **Small Group Instruction**

Tier 2

If No → **Approaching Level** Reteach the skill using the Comprehension lesson, pp. 773M–773P.

If Yes → **On Level** Consolidate the learning using pp. 773U–773V.

Beyond Level Extend the learning using pp. 773Y–773Z.

Transparency 4

Conclusions Chart

Text Clues	Conclusion
Catching snowflakes is an annual activity.	Catching snowflakes happens in the winter.
Snowflakes have different numbers of crystals.	Snowflakes can be different sizes.
You should view snowflakes at about 25 degrees.	32 degrees is too warm to view snowflakes.
Blizzards cause "whiteout" conditions.	You should not view snowflakes in a blizzard.

Graphic Organizer Transparency

HOMEWORK **Practice Book,** page 255

To **draw a conclusion**, use information from the selection and your own prior experience connected to the reading selection.

Read the passage. Then read the conclusions. Support each one with evidence from the text.

My science project was due on Wednesday, but things had not gone as planned. I was trying to train my dog, Snowball, not to bark when someone came through the door. I had thought that giving Snowball a treat when she stopped barking would teach her to sit quietly. I'd repeated the procedure each day for two weeks and recorded the results. Snowball was still barking.

I talked to my teacher, Mrs. Gomez, about my problem. "Hmm," she said. "From what you've written in your notebook, it looks like the two times when Snowball did sit quietly, you also used a firm voice and then patted her head." "You're right!" I exclaimed. "I know exactly what to do."

On Wednesday, the students in Mrs. Gomez's class turned in their reports. I was last. "Thanks for your help, Mrs. Gomez," I said. "I guess in science, just like everything else, it's really important to keep on trying."

1. The author's dog Snowball sometimes misbehaves. He barks whenever a stranger approaches.

2. The author would like to improve Snowball's behavior. He tries an experiment in which he rewards Snowball with a treat whenever she behaves.

3. The author's experiment fails. Despite his efforts, after two weeks, Snowball is still barking.

4. The author is concerned about his science experiment. He goes to Mrs. Gomez for advice.

Approaching Reproducible, page 255
Beyond Reproducible, page 255

Read

WHOLE GROUP

✓ **MAIN SELECTION**
- *Snowflake Bentley*
- Skill: Draw Conclusions

✓ **PAIRED SELECTION**
- Literary Text/Poetry: "Haiku"
- Literary Elements: Imagery and Metaphor

SMALL GROUP

- Differentiated Instruction, pp. 773I–773HH

Main Selection

GENRE: Literary Nonfiction/Biography

Have a student read the definition of Biography on **Student Book** page 746. Point out that a biography is a type of literary nonfiction. Students should look for facts, details, and events of a real person's life as written by another person.

STRATEGY
GENERATE QUESTIONS

Tell students that they can generate questions to check their understanding of a selection and to clarify meaning as they read.

SKILL
DRAW CONCLUSIONS

Explain that students can draw conclusions by using text clues and prior knowledge related to the text to form a new understanding of what they are reading.

Comprehension

Genre

A **Biography** is a story about the life of a real person written by someone else.

Generate Questions

✓ **Draw Conclusions**
As you read, fill in your Conclusions Chart.

Text Clues	Conclusion

Read to Find Out

What did Snowflake Bentley give to the world?

Vocabulary

Vocabulary Words Review the tested words while reading: **technique, foolishness, annual, inspire, evaporate,** and **magnify**.

Additional Selection Words Students may be unfamiliar with these words. Pronounce the words, give student-friendly explanations as needed, and help students use previously taught vocabulary strategies: context clues, dictionary, word parts.

intricate (p. 751): having many complex parts

molecules (p. 758): particles of matter made up of atoms

pneumonia (p. 765): a disease of the lungs that can cause fever, chills, cough, and difficulty breathing

grandeur (p. 766): the state or quality of being magnificent or great

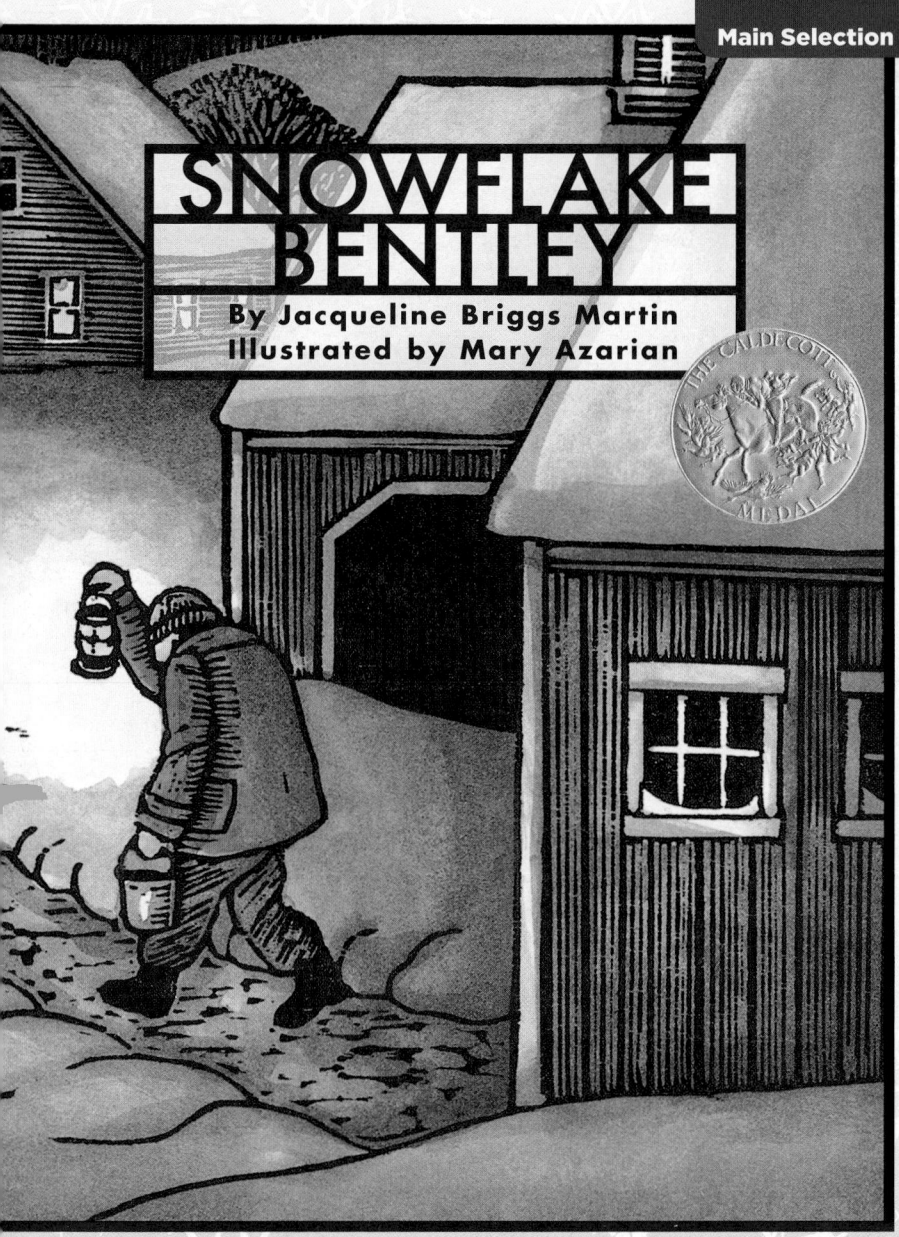

SNOWFLAKE BENTLEY

By Jacqueline Briggs Martin

Illustrated by Mary Azarian

747

Read the Main Selection

Preteach	Read Together	Read Independently
Have Approaching Level students and English Language Learners listen to the selection on **StudentWorks Plus**, the interactive e-Book, before reading with the class.	Use the prompts to guide comprehension and model how to complete the graphic organizer. Have students use **Think/Pair/Share** to discuss the selection.	If students can read the selection independently, have them read and complete the graphic organizer. Suggest that they use their purposes to choose their reading strategies.

StudentWorks Plus
Interactive Student Book

Preview and Predict

QUICK WRITE Tell students to read the title, preview the illustrations, think about the genre, and make predictions about the story. Students may also include their own knowledge about snowflakes.

Set Purposes

FOCUS QUESTION Discuss the "Read to Find Out" question on **Student Book** page 746. Remind students to look for the answer as they read.

Point out the Conclusions Chart in the Student Book and on **Practice Book** page 256. Explain that students will fill it in as they read.

Read *Snowflake Bentley*

Use the questions and Think Alouds to support instruction about the comprehension strategy and skill.

Practice Book, page 256

As you read *Snowflake Bentley*, fill in the Conclusions Chart.

Text Clues	Conclusion

How does the information you wrote in your Conclusions Chart help you answer your questions about *Snowflake Bentley*?

Approaching Reproducible, page 256
Beyond Reproducible, page 256

Develop Comprehension

1 STRATEGY
GENERATE QUESTIONS

Teacher Think Aloud I can improve my reading comprehension by **generating questions** as I read and looking for the answers. I know that this is a biography of Wilson, or "Willie," Bentley, and that the title of the selection is *Snowflake Bentley*. So I ask myself, *Why was a biography written about Willie Bentley? What did he accomplish? Why has the author included all this information about Willie's love for snow?* I will have to read further to find out. At the end of page 749, I read that Willie could not share snowflakes because he could not save them. Will Willie learn how to save the snowflakes? Will that be his accomplishment? I will read on to find out.

Wilson Bentley was born February 9, 1865, on a farm in Jericho, Vermont, between Lake Champlain and Mount Mansfield, in the heart of the "snowbelt," where the **annual** snowfall is about 120 inches.

In the days when farmers worked with ox and sled and cut the dark with lantern light, there lived a boy who loved snow more than anything else in the world.

Willie Bentley's happiest days were snowstorm days. He watched snowflakes fall on his mittens, on the dried grass of Vermont farm fields, on the dark metal handle of the barn door. He said snow was as beautiful as butterflies, or apple blossoms.

748

Monitor Comprehension

Monitor and Clarify: *Self-Correct*

Explain Students may need to pause at times to check the conclusions they have drawn during reading. To correct inaccurate conclusions they may have formed, they can generate questions. For example, they can ask themselves *Why?* or *How?* questions.

Discuss If students have drawn the conclusion that Willie loved the winter, ask: *How did you come to that conclusion?* (Willie loved the snow, and snow usually falls during the winter.)

Apply Have students explain why a conclusion that Willie wanted to study snowflakes needs to be self-corrected. (Willie loved watching snow, but the author does not state that he loved studying it. We may find out later that he studied snow, but we do not have enough information now to draw that conclusion.)

Willie's mother was his teacher until he was fourteen years old. He attended school for only a few years. "She had a set of encyclopedias," Willie said. "I read them all."

He could net butterflies and show them to his older brother, Charlie. He could pick apple blossoms and take them to his mother. But he could not share snowflakes because he could not save them.

Develop Comprehension

2 GENRE: Literary Nonfiction/Biography

What clues on pages 748 and 749 tell you that this selection is a **biography**? (The selection is about Willie Bentley, who was a real person. The author includes details about Willie, such as when and where he was born and grew up, and other facts about him and his family. We will probably learn more about his life as we continue to read.)

Phonics/Word Study

APPLY DECODING SKILLS While reading, point out words with the sound/spelling patterns, syllable types, and word parts students have recently learned. Help students blend these words. You may wish to focus on selection words with suffixes: *beautiful, wonderful, clearly,* and *photography.*

ELL   ENGLISH LANGUAGE LEARNERS

Beginning

Access Content Preteach story content, build language, and develop meaning using the Interactive Question-Response Guide in the **ELL Resource Book**, pages 318–329. Give ample time for students to respond. They may point or use words or short phrases to respond.

Intermediate

Describe Preteach story content, build language, and develop meaning using the Interactive Question-Response Guide in the ELL Resource Book, pages 318–329. Have students respond in complete sentences. Repeat their responses, correcting pronunciation or grammar as needed.

Advanced

Explain Complete the Intermediate task with students. Elicit details from students for their responses.

Develop Comprehension

3 SKILL
DRAW CONCLUSIONS

What **conclusion** can you **draw** about Willie based on the facts that he used the old microscope his mother gave him, and was catching single snowflakes for study rather than building forts and throwing snowballs like other children his age? (Willie is unusually curious, determined, and motivated for someone his age.) Add this information to your Conclusions Chart.

Text Clues	Conclusion
While other children played in the snow, Willie caught and studied snowflakes.	Willie was unusually curious, determined, and motivated for someone his age.

4 FACT AND OPINION

Find one **opinion** and one **fact** in the sidebar on page 751. (Opinion: The snowflakes were masterpieces of design. Fact: sample answer: Most crystals had six branches.) How could you verify what is fact? (We could verify facts by finding Willie Bentley's research and looking at the results.)

From his boyhood on he studied all forms of moisture. He kept a record of the weather and did many experiments with raindrops.

3

When his mother gave him an old microscope, he used it to look at flowers, raindrops, and blades of grass. Best of all, he used it to look at snow.

While other children built forts and pelted snowballs at roosting crows, Willie was catching single snowflakes. Day after stormy day he studied the icy crystals.

750

Vocabulary

Word Structure Clues: *Greek Roots*

Explain/Model Remind students that base words or roots are the smallest meaningful parts into which words can be broken down. List some common Greek roots, such as *micro,* "small"; *scope,* "instrument for viewing"; *tele,* "distance"; and *phone,* "sound."

Think Aloud If I know that *micro* means "small" and *scope* means "instrument for viewing," I can figure out that *microscope* means "an instrument for viewing small things."

Practice/Apply Ask students what other words they can think of with these Greek roots. (Examples: *microphone, telephone, telegraph, phonics*) Discuss their meanings.

He learned that most crystals had six branches (though a few had three). For each snowflake the six branches were alike. "I found that snowflakes were masterpieces of design," he said. "No one design was ever repeated. When a snowflake melted . . . just that much beauty was gone, without leaving any record behind." **4**

Starting at age fifteen he drew a hundred snow crystals each winter for three winters. **5** **6**

Their intricate patterns were even more beautiful than he had imagined. He expected to find whole flakes that were the same, that were copies of each other. But he never did.

Willie decided he must find a way to save snowflakes so others could see their wonderful designs. For three winters he tried drawing snow crystals. They always melted before he could finish.

751

Develop Comprehension

5 **STRATEGY**
DICTIONARY

A **multiple-meaning word** is a word that has several different meanings. Readers need to determine which meaning best fits the context of the story. What context clues reveal the correct meaning for the way the author uses the word *crystal* on pages 750 and 751? (Through his microscope, Willie saw that the crystals had "intricate patterns." He learned that each crystal had either three or six branches that were alike. The correct definition for *crystal* in this case is a solid body with flat surfaces, whose atoms repeat in a pattern.)

6 **CAUSE AND EFFECT**

What **caused** Willie to spend so much time trying to draw snowflakes? (He was fascinated by the fact that snowflakes are so beautiful, and are all unique. He was sorry that there was no record of their beauty after they melted. He wanted to share their beauty with others.)

Develop Comprehension

7 MAKE INFERENCES

Do you think that a camera with its own microscope was common when Willie was young? Why or why not? (A camera with its own microscope was probably very uncommon, because only scientists doing special kinds of work would have a need for such a camera. Also, WIllie was born in 1865, so his parents buy him this camera in 1882, when cameras themselves were still somewhat new. Very few people had them, let alone with a microscope.)

8 SKILL
DRAW CONCLUSIONS

Although his father says that fussing with snow is "foolishness," what can you conclude about Willie's parents and their feelings for the work their son is trying to do? (Based on the fact that Willie's parents spend their savings to buy him a special camera and that the camera costs more than his father's herd of cows, they must have believed in the work he was doing.) Add this information to your Conclusions Chart.

Text Clues	Conclusion
While other children played in the snow, Willie caught and studied snowflakes.	Willie was unusually curious, determined, and motivated for someone his age.
Willie's father thinks fussing with snow is foolishness, but his parents spend their life savings to buy him a special camera.	Willie's parents believe the work he is trying to do with snowflakes is worthwhile and important.

The camera made images on large glass negatives. Its microscope could **magnify** a tiny crystal from sixty-four to 3,600 times its actual size.

7

8

When he was sixteen, Willie read of a camera with its own microscope. "If I had that camera I could photograph snowflakes," he told his mother.

Willie's mother knew he would not be happy until he could share what he had seen.

"Fussing with snow is just **foolishness**," his father said. Still, he loved his son.

752

When Willie was seventeen his parents spent their savings and bought the camera.

It was taller than a newborn calf, and cost as much as his father's herd of ten cows. Willie was sure it was the best of all cameras.

753

Develop Comprehension

9 MONITOR AND CLARIFY: SELF-CORRECT

The author includes many details about the camera on pages 752 and 753. What can you do to **monitor** and **self-correct** your comprehension of the details about the camera? (To monitor and self-correct as I read, I can ask myself questions such as, "How large is the camera?" and "What special features does the camera have?" I have to make sure that I read the regular text as well as the captions to get all of the correct details.)

Develop Comprehension

10 ANALYZE TEXT FEATURES

Look at the information the author provides in the sidebar on page 755. How is the information in this sidebar text different from the information in the main body of the text? (In the sidebar on this page, the author provides detailed information about the steps Willie took to finally achieve results with his camera. In the main body of the text, she describes the events that took place without providing the details.) **Why is it important to read the information in the sidebars of this selection?** (Without reading the sidebars, readers would not know exactly what Willie did to achieve his results.)

Even so his first pictures were failures—no better than shadows. Yet he would not quit. Mistake by mistake, snowflake by snowflake, Willie worked through every storm.

Winter ended, the snow melted, and he had no good pictures.

10

11

754

Author's Craft: *Nonfiction Text Structures*

Explain Authors use certain common text structures for conveying information and describing implicit and explicit relationships among ideas. These structures include cause and effect, sequence, and compare and contrast.

Discuss Review the text structures with students. Have students point out examples of cause and effect, sequence, or compare and contrast in *Snowflake Bentley*.

Apply Have students write paragraphs using one of the structures discussed. Ask them to read their paragraphs aloud to the class. Classmates will identify which structures students have used.

Willie's experiment: He used a very small lens opening, which let only a little light reach the negative, but he kept the lens open for several seconds—up to a minute and a half.

He learned, too, that he could make the snow crystals show up more clearly by using a sharp knife to cut away all the dark parts of the negative around the crystals. This etching meant extra hours of work for each photograph, but Willie didn't mind.

He waited for another season of snow. One day, in the second winter, he tried a new experiment. And it worked!

Willie had figured out how to photograph snowflakes! "Now everyone can see the great beauty in a tiny crystal," he said.

Develop Comprehension

11 SKILL
DRAW CONCLUSIONS

 The author uses repetition on page 754, writing, *Mistake by mistake, snowflake by snowflake, Willie worked through every storm*. What **conclusion** can you draw from the author's use of this literary device? Add the text clues and conclusion to your Conclusions Chart. (By repeating these words, the author creates the feeling of time passing slowly, and Willie working painstakingly. He is determined to succeed.) How does this literary device help readers identify that this is a major event in Willie's life? (By emphasizing the time it took Willie to be successful, it shows how determined he was, and why his eventual success was so important.)

Text Clues	Conclusion
While other children played in the snow, Willie caught and studied snowflakes.	Willie was unusually curious, determined, and motivated for someone his age.
Willie's father thinks fussing with snow is foolishness, but his parents spend their life savings to buy him a special camera.	Willie's parents believe the work he is trying to do with snowflakes is worthwhile and important.
Willie would not quit. Mistake by mistake, snowflake by snowflake, he worked through every storm.	The repetition creates the feeling of time going slowly and Willie working painstakingly. He is determined to succeed.

Develop Comprehension

12 FIGURATIVE LANGUAGE: METAPHOR

What **metaphors** can you find in the sidebar text on page 756? What things are being compared? (The last sentence contains two metaphors. Willie compares a snowstorm to a gift and winter to a king.) How do these metaphors help you understand Willie's character? (Many people would think a snowstorm was a problem, but Willie was glad when it snowed. He thought winter was powerful and majestic, just like a king.)

13 AUTHOR'S CRAFT: DIALOGUE

What does the **dialogue** spoken by the neighbors reveal about how they viewed Willie's photographs? (The neighbors said that snow "is as common as dirt" and that taking pictures of it was unnecessary. The neighbors probably felt that Willie was wasting his time by taking pictures of snow because they could see snow every day just by looking outside.)

The best snowstorm of his life occurred on Valentine's Day in 1928. He made over a hundred photographs during the two-day storm. He called the storm a gift from King Winter.

 12

 13

But in those days no one cared. Neighbors laughed at the idea of photographing snow.

"Snow in Vermont is as common as dirt," they said. "We don't need pictures."

Willie said the photographs would be his gift to the world.

756

Comprehension/Writing

Text Features: *Parts of a Newspaper*

Explain Newspapers offer different kinds of information. They can tell readers if a snowstorm is predicted, teach them about interesting people, such as Snowflake Bentley, or inform them about current events in other parts of the world.

Discuss Bring in newspapers and have students leaf through them, identifying the various sections and the kinds of information they contain. Discuss the difference between a news article and an editorial. Have students explain how much they think newspapers influence their readers. Ask, *Should people believe everything they read in the paper? Why or why not?*

Apply Have students choose a newspaper article or editorial. Ask them to summarize the article and give their opinion about it. Remind students that the title of a newspaper should be italicized, while the title of an article should be written in quotation marks.

While other farmers sat by the fire or rode to town with horse and sleigh, Willie studied snowstorms. He stood at the shed door and held out a black tray to catch the flakes.

When he found only jumbled, broken crystals, he brushed the tray clean with a turkey feather and held it out again.

14

757

Text Evidence

Draw Conclusions

Remind students that when they answer a question about a selection they will often need to find evidence in the text to support their answer. Reread question 14 aloud. Then ask, *What questions can you raise to help you conclude how the author's use of a literary device, such as a simile, can help you reach a conclusion about the subject of a biography?* (Why did Willie's neighbors think that they didn't need pictures of snow, because it was as common as "dirt"? What does this tell me about how far Willie had progressed with his work?) *Where in the text would you look to find information to answer these questions? Point to the information when you find it.* (Students would want to return to the previous page and Willie's statement that "everyone can see the great beauty in a crystal," and on this page, that the photographs *would be* his "gift to the world," to conclude that Bentley had not shared his photos with anyone yet.

Develop Comprehension

14 **SKILL**
DRAW CONCLUSIONS

 Identify the simile the author uses to reveal what Willie's neighbors think about his work. (They say snow in Vermont is as common as dirt and they don't need pictures of it.) How does Willie respond to their attitude? (He says his photographs will be his gift to the world.) What conclusion can you draw about Willie based on his attitude? Add this information to your Conclusions Chart. (Willie doesn't care what other people think and has faith in himself and his work.)

Text Clues	Conclusion
While other children played in the snow, Willie caught and studied snowflakes.	Willie was unusually curious, determined, and motivated for someone his age.
Willie's father thinks fussing with snow is foolishness, but his parents spend their life savings to buy him a special camera.	Willie's parents believe the work he is trying to do with snowflakes is worthwhile and important.
Willie would not quit. Mistake by mistake, snowflake by snowflake, he worked through every storm.	The repetition creates the feeling of time going slowly and Willie working painstakingly. He is determined to succeed.
The neighbors did not understand why Willie was interested in snow, when it was so common.	He doesn't care what other people think, and is sure that one day his work will be appreciated.

Develop Comprehension

 FACT AND OPINION

 Does the information in the sidebar on page 758 give you **facts** or **opinions**? (facts) Explain your answer. (It reveals the science behind snowflakes. This is not information that someone believes or feels, but facts that can be checked in a source.)

16 STRATEGY
GENERATE QUESTIONS

Teacher Think Aloud Seeing how difficult it was to take pictures of the snowflakes helps me **generate questions**. For example, did Willie find out so much information about snowflakes only through the photographs he took, or did he also learn about them through all the effort he put in to taking the photographs? What do you think? What are some other questions you can generate?

PARTNERS Prompt students to apply the strategy in a Think Aloud.

Student Think Aloud I think it was a combination of both. I also wonder how Willie had so much patience. How could he wait so long for just the right crystal? Maybe his successes kept him going. When he successfully photographed a snowflake, it might have encouraged him to continue.

He learned that each snowflake begins as a speck, much too tiny to be seen. Little bits—molecules—of water attach to the speck to form its branches. As the crystal grows, the branches come together and trap small quantities of air.

He waited hours for just the right crystal and didn't notice the cold.

If the shed were warm the snow would melt. If he breathed on the black tray the snow would melt. If he twitched a muscle as he held the snow crystal on the long wooden pick the snowflake would break. He had to work fast or the snowflake would **evaporate** before he could slide it into place and take its picture. Some winters he was able to make only a few dozen good pictures.

Some winters he made hundreds.

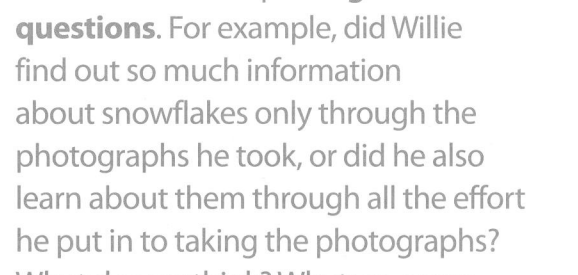 **Draw Conclusions**
Think about what you have read so far. What conclusions can you draw about Willie?

Many things affect the way these crystal branches grow. A little more cold, a bit less wind, or a bit more moisture will mean different-shaped branches. Willie said that was why, in all his pictures, he never found two snowflakes alike.

18

759

Develop Comprehension

17 **SKILL**
DRAW CONCLUSIONS

 Think about what you have read so far. What **conclusions** can you **draw** about Willie? What kind of person is he? Use your Conclusions Chart to support your answer. (Willie is very curious and interested in learning more about snow. He is clever when he finds new ways to try to study snow more closely. He works hard and never quits despite the fact that he does not have much support from his neighbors.)

18 **SELF-SELECTED STRATEGY USE**

What strategies have you used to help you understand the selection? Where did you use them? How did they help?

RETURN TO PREDICTIONS AND PURPOSES

 Have students respond to the selection by confirming or revising their predictions and purposes for reading. Ask them to revise or write additional questions to help focus their attention as they continue to read the selection.

Stop here if you wish to read this selection over two days.

Develop Comprehension

19 SETTING

How does the place where he lived affect Willie and his interests? (Willie lives on a farm surrounded by nature. He is able to use nature as the main subject of his photographs because he can find different elements of nature right on his farm.) If Willie had lived in the city, how might that have affected his interests? (Willie still might have enjoyed photography, but he would probably choose different subjects for his pictures. He could still take photos of snow, but he might have also taken photos of people and buildings.)

Willie's nieces and nephews lived on one side of the farmhouse that Willie shared with his brother Charlie. Willie often played the piano as they sang and shared stories and games with them.

19
20

Willie so loved the beauty of nature he took pictures in all seasons.

In the summer his nieces and nephews rubbed coat hangers with sticky pitch from spruce trees. Then Willie could use them to pick up spider webs jeweled with water drops and take their pictures.

On fall nights he would gently tie a grasshopper to a flower so he could find it in the morning and photograph the dew-covered insect.

760

ELL ENGLISH LANGUAGE LEARNERS

STRATEGIES FOR EXTRA SUPPORT

Question 19 SETTING

Use Illustrations Have students look at the illustration on page 761. Tell students to use the illustration to say what they can about how it reflects the setting of the biography. (The illustration shows grass, flowers, and a grasshopper. The setting is in an area that is surrounded by nature.) Have students explain how the illustration shows what type of person Willie is. (He looks happy and seems very interested. This shows how much he loved being a part of nature.)

761

Develop Comprehension

20 SKILL
DRAW CONCLUSIONS

 What **conclusion** can you **draw** about the relationship Willie had with his nieces and nephews? (The author states that Willie shared music, stories, and games with his nieces and nephews. They also helped Willie when he wanted to take photos of spider webs. Willie and his nieces and nephews cared for each other very much and enjoyed spending time together.)

Develop Comprehension

21 MAKE INFERENCES

How and why did people's attitudes toward Willie Bentley change? Use evidence from the text to support your **inference**. (When people began to see how beautiful Willie Bentley's crystal pictures were, they realized that his work was worthwhile and not foolish. They enjoyed watching slideshows of the crystals, and people bought copies of his pictures. People from all over began to learn of his work. Artists and universities bought his photographs. Willie Bentley and his work became well known and respected.)

But his snow crystal pictures were always his favorites. He gave copies away or sold them for a few cents. He made special pictures as gifts for birthdays.

762

Listening/Speaking

Point out that Snowflake Bentley experimented until he found a way to photograph snowflakes. His technique became known as microphotography.

Have students think of a skill that they can teach others, such as how to perform a magic trick, play a game, or make a paper airplane. Students should teach their skill to the class, giving precise directions and instructions. Remind students to use details, examples, anecdotes, or experiences to explain or clarify information. Listeners should explain whether the directions were clear and complete.

Many colleges and universities bought lantern slide copies of his photographs and added to their collections each year. Artists and designers used the photographs to **inspire** their own work.

21

22

He held evening slide shows on the lawns of his friends. Children and adults sat on the grass and watched while Willie projected his slides onto a sheet hung over a clothesline.

Develop Comprehension

22 **STRATEGY**
DICTIONARY

 What are some **multiple meanings** of the word *slide?* (to pass along a surface; a small plate of glass for use with a microscope; a piece of equipment in a playground) What context clues reveal the correct meaning of *slide* that the author uses on page 763? (Willie invited people to "slide shows" where they could view his pictures projected onto a sheet. Some colleges bought copies of the slides that Willie had created. The correct definition for *slide* in this case is a small plastic or glass sheet that has a picture on it.)

Develop Comprehension

23 FACT AND OPINION

In the sidebar on page 764, what **opinion** does the author share? What **facts** does the author include? (The author says that people who want to learn about snow crystals start by using *Snow Crystals* by Wilson Bentley. This is an opinion. There is no way to check whether *everyone* who wants to learn about snow crystals starts with Willie's book. The facts tell the amount of money Willie earned and spent.)

Even today, those who want to learn about snow crystals begin with Wilson Bentley's book, *Snow Crystals*.

By 1926 he had spent $15,000 on his work and received $4,000 from the sale of photographs and slides. **23**

764

Comprehension/Writing

Compare and Contrast: *Caldecott Winners*

Explain *Snowflake Bentley* won one of the most prestigious awards in children's literature, the Caldecott Medal, for its illustrations. The award is given once a year and has been awarded to many different kinds of books.

Discuss Have students research other books that have won the Caldecott Medal and then compare and contrast them with *Snowflake Bentley*. Partners should discuss connections among the books, such as how fiction and nonfiction books treat similar topics or ideas.

Apply Have partners summarize their findings and present them to the class. Remind students to support their ideas with text evidence.

He wrote about snow and published his pictures in magazines. He gave speeches about snow to faraway scholars and neighborhood skywatchers. "You are doing great work," said a professor from Wisconsin.

The little farmer came to be known as the world's expert on snow, "the Snowflake Man." But he never grew rich. He spent every penny on his pictures.

Willie said there were treasures in snow. "I can't afford to miss a single snowstorm," he told a friend. "I never know when I will find some wonderful prize."

Other scientists raised money so Willie could gather his best photographs in a book. When he was sixty-six years old Willie's book—his gift to the world—was published. Still, he was not ready to quit.

Less than a month after turning the first page on his book, Willie walked six miles home in a blizzard to make more pictures. He became ill with pneumonia after that walk and died two weeks later. **24**

Develop Comprehension

24 MAIN IDEA AND DETAILS

What are some important **details** on this page? (Willie wrote about snow, published his photographs, and gave speeches. He spent more money making his photographs than he made from selling them. He believed he should not miss a single snowstorm. Even after he published his book, he did not stop taking photographs. He risked his health to take pictures during a blizzard.) What do these details have in common? (They show how dedicated Willie Bentley was to his work.) What is the **main idea** of the information on this page? (Willie Bentley was unusually dedicated to his work, photographing snowflakes and sharing his findings with others.)

Develop Comprehension

25 STRATEGY
GENERATE QUESTIONS

What **questions** can you **generate** and answer to further discover what people thought about Willie Bentley?

Student Think Aloud Why did people build a monument for Willie? They were proud of him. They liked him as a person, and were impressed and delighted by the work he had done. What do we learn from the fact that the neighborhood children grew up to tell stories about Willie Bentley? They were proud to have known him. Why did they set up a museum in his honor? They wanted others to learn about Willie Bentley's discoveries.

26 SKILL
DRAW CONCLUSIONS

What happened to Willie and his work over time? **Draw** a **conclusion** to explain how people changed their opinions of Willie and his work. (A monument and museum were built in honor of Willie. People, including his former neighbors, read his book and shared stories about his life. A conclusion is that although people did not support him at first, they eventually began to respect him for his hard work and achievements.) Add this information to your Conclusions Chart.

Text Clues	Conclusion
A monument and museum were built to honor Willie. People talked about his book and his life.	Willie finally earned the respect he had always deserved.

A monument was built for Willie in the center of town. The girls and boys who had been his neighbors grew up and told their sons and daughters the story of the man who loved snow. Forty years after Wilson Bentley's death, children in his village worked to set up a museum in honor of the farmer-scientist.

And his book has taken the delicate snow crystals that once blew across Vermont, past mountains, over the earth. Neighbors and strangers have come to know of the icy wonders that land on their own mittens—thanks to Snowflake Bentley.

The plaque on the monument says "SNOWFLAKE" BENTLEY Jericho's world famous snowflake authority

For fifty years Wilson A. Bentley, a simple farmer, developed his **technique** of micro-photography to reveal to the world the grandeur and mystery of the snowflake—its universal hexagonal shape and its infinite number of lovely designs.

25

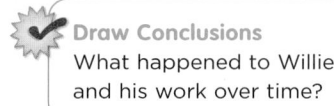

Draw Conclusions
What happened to Willie and his work over time?

26

Develop Comprehension

RETURN TO PREDICTIONS AND PURPOSES

Review students' predictions and purposes. Were they correct? Did they identify what the world gave to Snowflake Bentley? (the chance to study the snowflakes he loved) Did they identify what he gave to the world? (the chance to see the beauty of snowflakes)

REVIEW READING STRATEGIES

- **Generate Questions** In what ways did generating questions help you to understand the selection?

- **Monitor and Clarify: Self-Correct** Do you understand the strategy of self-correcting in order to monitor your comprehension? When might you use it again?

- **Decoding** What difficult words did you encounter? How did the Reading Multisyllabic Words Strategy help you sound out these words?

- **Self-Selected Strategy Use** What strategies did you use to make sense of what you read? Where? How were these strategies helpful?

 **PERSONAL RESPONSE**

Have students use what they have learned about Snowflake Bentley to write a paragraph about him that might appear on a plaque in his museum.

Quick Check

Can students draw conclusions based on text evidence?

During **Small Group Instruction**

If No → **Approaching Level** Reteach the skill and have students apply it to a simpler text. Use Leveled Reader lessons, pp. 773N–773P.

If Yes → **On Level** Have students apply the skill to a new text to consolidate learning. Use Leveled Reader lessons, pp. 773U–773V.

Beyond Level Have students apply the skill to a more complex text to extend learning. Use Leveled Reader lessons, pp. 773Y–773Z.

Author and Illustrator

SNAPSHOTS OF JACQUELINE AND MARY

Have students read the biographies of the author and the illustrator. Ask:

- Where did Jacqueline Briggs Martin get ideas for this story?

- How does Mary Azarian's choice of woodcut illustrations suit the theme and content of the story?

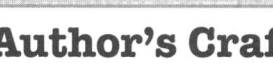

WRITE ABOUT IT

Author's Craft: Dialogue
Remind students that the author often uses dialogue to reveal more about characters. Have students reread pages 752 and 753 and then write a dialogue between Willie's mother and father about buying the special camera for Willie. Remind them to use proper punctuation.

Author's Purpose

Remind students that authors who write to inform often present facts and details about a topic or person. Suggest that students use their Conclusions Charts to help them find clues that reveal Jacqueline Briggs Martin's purpose for writing. Have them explain whether the purpose is stated or implied.

SNAPSHOTS OF JACQUELINE AND MARY

Jacqueline Briggs Martin began to write this story after she saw a snowflake and thought about an article she had read about a man who loved snow. Jacqueline saw lots of snow when she was growing up. She lived on a farm in Maine where she enjoyed nature, stories, and history.

Other books illustrated by Mary Azarian

Mary Azarian has also seen a lot of snow. Just like Wilson Bentley, she lives on a farm in Vermont. Mary used her experiences on the farm to create her woodcut illustrations.

LOG ON ▶ FIND OUT

Author Jacqueline Briggs Martin
Illustrator Mary Azarian
www.macmillanmh.com

Author's Purpose

Why did Jacqueline Briggs Martin write *Snowflake Bentley*? Was her purpose for writing this biography stated or implied? Explain using details from the selection.

Author's Craft

Dialogue

- One way writers help their readers understand the characters is by providing clues about them in what the characters say. Sometimes writers will use dialogue to sketch a character. Example: "Fussing with snow is just foolishness." (p. 752) From this line we know that Willie's father didn't completely share his son's belief that photographing snowflakes was worthwhile.

- Have students find and discuss other examples of dialogue, such as "I never know when I will find some wonderful prize." (p. 765)

- Discuss how the dialogue reveals each character and how the author's word choice helps her achieve that purpose.

Comprehension Check

Summarize

To summarize *Snowflake Bentley* use the most important details from the selection. Information from your Conclusions Chart may help you.

Text Clues	Conclusion

Think and Compare

1. What did Willie want when he was sixteen that would **magnify** tiny crystals? Details

2. Why was it that some years Willie was able to make only a few dozen good snowflake pictures? Cause and Effect

3. What can you conclude about Wilson Bentley's decision to make photographing snowflakes his life's work? Explain using details from the story. Generate Questions: Draw Conclusions

4. Reread pages 752–753. How does the author show the reader how Willie's parents feel about him? Use details from the selection to explain your answer. Author's Purpose

5. Read "Let It Snow" on pages 744–745. How is the information about snow in that selection the same as in *Snowflake Bentley*? How is it different? Explain using details from both selections. Reading/Writing Across Texts

769

Make Connections

Text-to-Self Have students respond to the following question to make connections to their own lives. Use the Think Aloud to model a response. *If you could spend your life studying one thing in nature, what would it be? What technique would you use to study it and why?*

Think Aloud: I would study rocks from all different places. Like Willie Bentley, I'd photograph them and use a microscope to look at pieces of rock. I would do experiments to see what they are made of and to learn more about them.

Text-to-World Have students respond to the question below to make connections to the world. Use the Think Aloud to model a response. *Why is it important to study the world—even at the microscopic level?* Use story details to explain.

Think Aloud: Studying the world can help you discover something new, like Snowflake Bentley's snowflakes. It may also help you appreciate all the things the world has to offer, great and small.

 **Comprehension Check**

SUMMARIZE

Have partners summarize *Snowflake Bentley*. Remind them to use their Conclusions Charts to help them organize their summaries.

THINK AND COMPARE
Text Evidence

1. **Details** <u>Answer stated in text</u> Willie wanted a camera with its own microscope. LOCATE

2. **Cause and Effect** <u>Answer stated in text</u> It was difficult to photograph the snowflakes. They melted, broke, and evaporated easily. COMBINE

3. **Generate Questions: Draw Conclusions** <u>Answer</u> He is so fascinated by the snowflakes, he wants to share them with others. <u>Evidence</u> He gives and sells snowflake photos, shows them in slide shows, publishes them, and writes a book about them. CONNECT

4. **Author's Purpose** <u>Answer</u> The author shows us through words and action that his parents love him and want him to be happy. <u>Evidence</u> His parents spend their savings to buy him the camera. His father says "fussing with snow" is foolishness, but the author writes that "still, he loved his son." Willie's mother knows Willie will not be happy until he can share his discoveries. ANALYZE

5. **Text-to-Text** "Let It Snow" teaches about snowflakes and Bentley's photography method. *Snowflake Bentley* teaches us about Bentley's life, details about his experiments, and how he became famous for his snowflake photographs.

Objectives

- Read fluently with accuracy
- Rate: 113–133 WCPM

Materials

- Transparency 29
- Practice Book, p. 257
- Fluency Solutions Audio CD

ELL

Develop Fluency Review the meaning of the passage with students. You may want to focus on words such as *breathed*, *twitched*, and *evaporate*, and practice saying them before reading. Students may also echo-read the passage.

Practice Book, page 257

As I read, I will focus on reading accurately.

	Tornadoes begin with warm, humid air. Humid air is air
10	that holds a lot of moisture. This humid air meets up with
22	colder air. As the air masses come together, the warm air
33	rises. As the warm air moves upward, it holds more and
44	more moisture. Huge, dark clouds called thunderheads begin
52	to develop. These clouds can spread as wide as 100 miles
62	(161 km) across the sky. There is so much moisture in the
73	clouds that it can't just **evaporate** into the air. So it falls as
86	rain. The thunderheads produce giant storms with thunder
94	and lightning. These storms are called supercells.
101	Winds high up in the storm clouds blow faster than the
112	winds lower down. The winds also blow in different
121	directions. This causes the air to spin. Then, as the winds
132	spin, they form a long funnel cloud. However, one last
142	thing needs to happen for the funnel cloud to become a
153	tornado. It needs to touch the ground. 160

Comprehension Check

1. Describe the conditions needed to form a thunderhead. **Main Idea and Details** The conditions needed to form a thundercloud include warm, humid air meeting cold air and the warmer air rising.

2. What is the author's purpose? **Author's Purpose** The author's purpose is to inform readers about how tornadoes are formed.

	Words Read	−	Number of Errors	=	Words Correct Score
First Read		−		=	
Second Read		−		=	

Approaching Reproducible, page 257

Beyond Reproducible, page 257

Fluency

Repeated Reading: Accuracy

EXPLAIN/MODEL Model reading **Transparency 29** for students fluently and accurately. Remind students that when they read accurately, they pronounce each word correctly. They avoid skipping or mispronouncing words, which can confuse listeners as well as themselves.

 Transparency 29

> He waited hours for just the right crystal and didn't notice the cold.
>
> If the shed were warm the snow would melt. If he breathed on the black tray the snow would melt. If he twitched a muscle as he held the snow crystal on the long wooden pick the snowflake would break. He had to work fast or the snowflake would evaporate before he could slide it into place and take its picture. Some winters he was able to make only a few dozen good pictures.
>
> Some winters he made hundreds.

Fluency (from *Snowflake Bentley*, p. 758)

PRACTICE Reread the first two sentences with students. Divide the class into two groups. Have the groups alternate reading the sentences chorally with accuracy. Remind students that reading accurately will help them demonstrate their comprehension.

 DAILY FLUENCY Students will practice fluency using **Practice Book** page 257 or the **Fluency Solutions Audio CD**. The passage is recorded at a slow practice speed and a faster fluent speed.

Quick Check

Can students read fluently and accurately?

During **Small Group Instruction**

If No → **Approaching Level** Use the Fluency lesson and model, p. 773Q.

If Yes → **On Level** See Fluency, p. 773T.

Beyond Level See Fluency, p. 773X.

Comprehension

REVIEW SKILL
FACT AND OPINION

EXPLAIN/MODEL

- Remind students that a **fact** is a statement that can be proven true. Have students explain how readers can **verify**, or check, the accuracy of an author's facts, such as by using reference materials.

- An **opinion** is a thought or feeling about something. It states a point of view that is not necessarily based on facts.

- Good readers distinguish between fact and opinion as they read. Nonfiction articles always contain facts but may also contain opinions of the author or others on the topic.

Review distinguishing facts from opinions by looking at "Let It Snow" with students, on **Student Book** page 744. Read the first paragraph of the section "Crystals to Flakes." Ask: *Does this paragraph tell us facts or opinions?* Explain that it tells facts. It gives scientific information that can be verified. Have students go through the rest of the text identifying facts and/or opinions. Have them determine whether the article is based more on fact or opinion. (fact)

PRACTICE/APPLY

Have students work with partners or in cooperative groups. Ask them to use the following questions to discuss distinguishing facts from opinions in *Snowflake Bentley*.

- Reread the first page of the selection and find an opinion relating to Willie's childhood. (Sample answer: Willie loved snow more than anything else in the world.)

- How do you know this is not a fact? (This is not information that can be verified. We know that Willie loved snow, but we cannot know if he loved it more than anything else in the world.)

- What kind of information is more commonly found in the selection's sidebars—facts or opinions? Give an example. (facts; In one sidebar we learn that Willie's camera could magnify a tiny crystal from 64 to 3,600 times its actual size.)

Have partners share their answers with the class. Then have students work together to make a class chart listing the facts and opinions in the selection. Discuss various ways that the facts in the chart could be checked.

PRACTICE BOOK See **Practice Book** page 258 for Sensory Language.

Objectives

- Distinguish facts from opinions in expository texts
- Explain how to verify facts

Skills Trace

Fact and Opinion

Introduce	329A–329B
Practice/Apply	330–333; Practice Book, 111–112
Reteach/Review	337Q–337DD, 733A–733B, 734–737, 741Q–741DD; Practice Book, 246–247
Assess	Weekly Tests; Units 3, 6 Tests
Maintain	455B, 527B, 769B

Paired Selection

GENRE: Literary Text/Poetry

Have students read the bookmark on **Student Book** page 770. Explain that a haiku

- is a traditional Japanese form of poetry;
- often focuses on an aspect of nature;
- has three short lines—the first and third lines usually have the same number of syllables.

Literary Elements:
Imagery and Metaphor

EXPLAIN/MODEL Writers may use imagery and metaphor to make their writing more interesting and imaginative for the reader.

- **Imagery** uses descriptive words or phrases to help create a picture in the reader's mind.

- A **metaphor** compares two things that do not seem alike, without using the words *like* or *as*. An example is *The storm was a beast*.

Explain that Matsuo Basho uses imagery in his haiku to help the reader see and hear what the world is like in winter.

APPLY Tell partners to take turns reciting all four haiku. Point out how each author uses imagery. Have students write a haiku using imagery similar to that of the two authors.

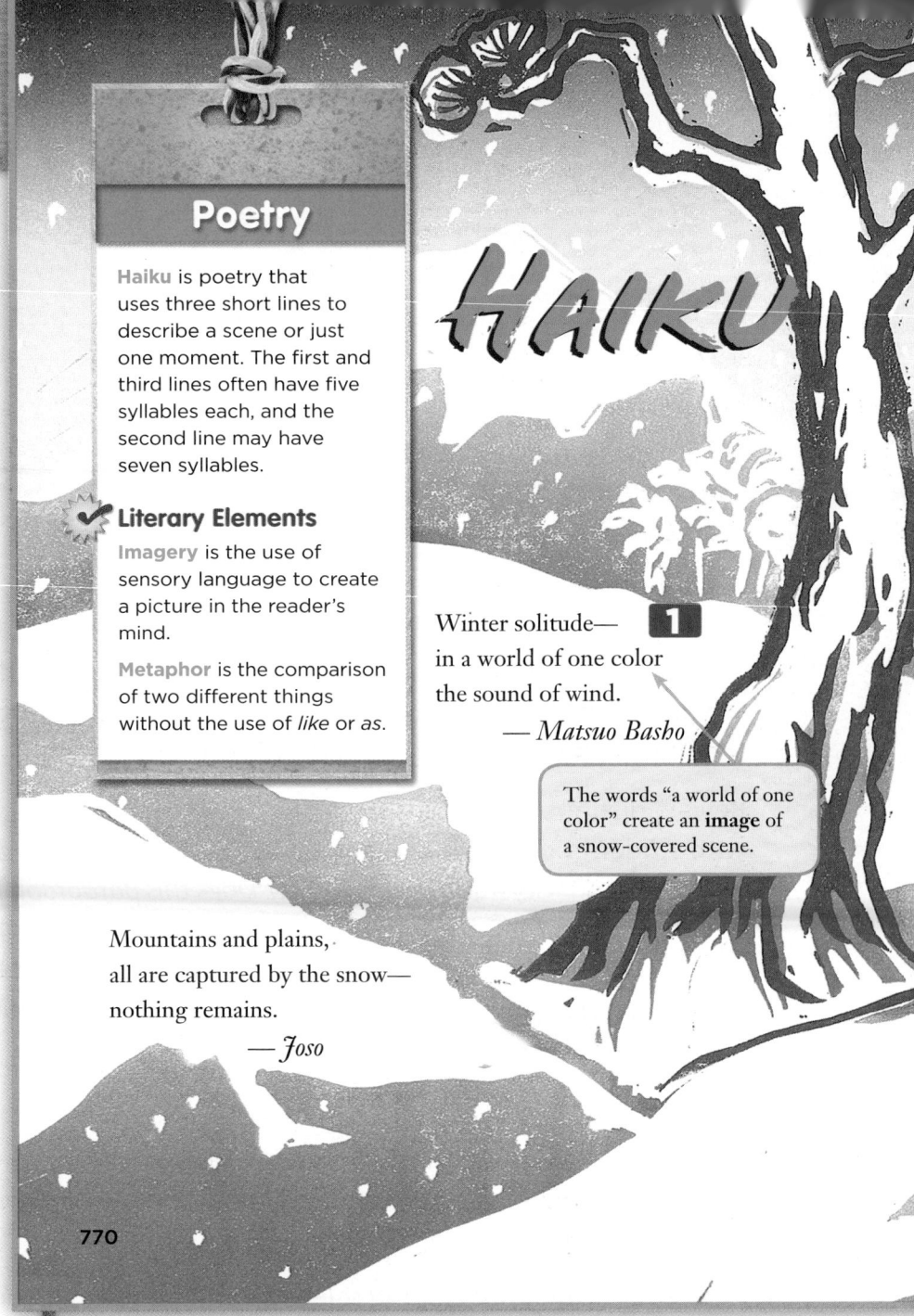

Poetry

Haiku is poetry that uses three short lines to describe a scene or just one moment. The first and third lines often have five syllables each, and the second line may have seven syllables.

✔ Literary Elements

Imagery is the use of sensory language to create a picture in the reader's mind.

Metaphor is the comparison of two different things without the use of *like* or *as*.

Winter solitude—
in a world of one color
the sound of wind.
— *Matsuo Basho*

The words "a world of one color" create an **image** of a snow-covered scene.

Mountains and plains,
all are captured by the snow—
nothing remains.
— *Joso*

770

Comprehension/Writing

Poetry: *Sensory Language*

Explain When authors write poetry, they often include figurative and sensory language to add interest or beauty to their poems and to help create mental images in the minds of readers.

Discuss Point out that the phrase *in a world of one color* on page 770 appeals to one's sense of sight, while *the sound of wind* appeals to one's sense of hearing. Have students point out the metaphors used and identify which two things are being compared.

Apply Have students write a haiku about something in nature. Remind them that haikus are comprised of three lines. The first and third lines often have five syllables, while the second line often has seven. Tell students to use sensory language in their haikus and to include a metaphor.

Poetry

No sky at all;
no earth at all—and still
the snowflakes fall....
— *Hashin*

The snow is melting
and the village is flooded
with children.
— *Kobayashi Issa* 2

Children do not really
flood the village. This
metaphor compares
children running
through the streets to
an overflow of water. 3

Connect and Compare

1. In the haiku by Joso, what phrase tells the reader that the poet thinks of the snow as an invader? **Metaphor**

2. Compare the three haiku by Joso, Basho, and Hashin. How do these poets feel about snow? Use details from the haiku in your answer. **Analyze**

3. Compare the poets' feelings about snow to Willie's feelings about snow in *Snowflake Bentley*. How are they alike and different? **Reading/Writing Across Texts**

4. Think of a metaphor that compares two different things. Now use the metaphor to write a haiku. Include sensory language in your haiku. **Apply**

771

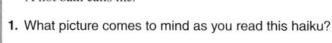
Read
Paired Selection

Read Haiku

As students read, remind them to apply what they have learned about imagery and metaphors.

1 LITERARY ELEMENTS: IMAGERY

 What picture is created by the imagery in the haiku by Basho? (The land is white with snow, and wind is blowing.)

2 LITERARY ELEMENT: METAPHOR

 Why do you think Kobayashi Issa chose to use a metaphor in his haiku? (By making an unusual and interesting comparison, he helps readers form a mental image of what he is expressing.)

3 MOOD

Which poem seems to have the happiest mood? Why? (the poem by Issa; the image is lively and hopeful.)

Connect and Compare

1. *Mountains and plains, all are* captured *by the snow.* METAPHOR

2. The poems describe snow covering land. The poets think that snow transforms the earth. They say land is *captured*, there is no sky or earth, and that the world is *one color.* ANALYZE

3. **FOCUS QUESTION** In *Snowflake Bentley*, Bentley loves snow and is fascinated by it. The poets are also fascinated by the snow, but we do not know if they like it or not. READING/ WRITING ACROSS TEXTS

4. Students' poems should reflect proper haiku form and contain metaphors. For additional support, see the Comprehension/Writing lesson on page 770. APPLY

Write

WHOLE GROUP

WRITING WORKSHOP
- Developing Expository Writing
- Trait: Sentence Fluency
- Transition Words and Phrases

Professional Development
GRADES 3–6

Writing Guide

Macmillan/McGraw-Hill

Trait: Sentence Fluency

Strong Sentences: Transition Words and Phrases

TEACH/MODEL Tell students that good writers use **transition words and phrases** to connect ideas and create strong sentences. Explain that transition words and phrases help readers connect information within paragraphs and from one paragraph to the next.

Write the following transition words and phrases on the board. Explain that they are examples of transitions that are often used in expository writing. Have students brainstorm additional transition words and phrases, such as time-order transitions. Point out that transition words and phrases like *therefore* and *as a result* are often used to indicate a conclusion.

actually	finally	nevertheless
also	for example	since
although	in addition	so
as a result	in fact	therefore
because	in other words	though

Write the following sentences and read them aloud.

> Although it was raining yesterday, it is snowing today. In fact, the temperature dropped 20 degrees overnight. As a result, my driveway is covered in snow and ice. Nevertheless, I still have to go to school. For that reason, I cannot shovel right now. The snow will be waiting for me when I get home, though.

Have students identify the transition words or phrases. Discuss the information or ideas that are being connected. Point out that without the transition words the paragraph would be harder to understand.

Teacher Write Aloud

PRACTICE/APPLY Further explore with students the use of transition words and phrases. Remind them that transition words connect information within a paragraph or main ideas between paragraphs. Write the sentences below on the board. Then complete the Teacher Think Aloud.

> Rain is important to Earth.
> Rain is a source of fresh water.
> All living things need water.
> Trees need water to live.
> My flowers need water to grow.
> I need water to drink and be healthy.
> I don't mind when it rains.

Teacher Think Aloud Each of these sentences gives a detail about rain. They support the main idea that rain is important. When I read the sentences by themselves like this, it's hard to connect all the ideas. If I rewrite the sentences in paragraph form and add transition words and phrases, that will help make the ideas clearer. Let's add transitions to create stronger sentences.

Complete the Think Aloud by brainstorming transition words that help connect the information. Write students' responses. Choose transition words to add, and write a paragraph like the following one. Stop to discuss how the transition words help connect information, and point out the use of *For all these reasons* to indicate a conclusion.

> Rain is important to Earth. That's because rain is a source of fresh water. It's a fact that all living things need water. Trees, for example, need water to grow. My flowers do, too. Like trees and flowers, I need water to quench my thirst and keep me healthy. For all these reasons, I don't mind when it rains.

 **Draft** Display the Writing Prompt on **Writing Transparency 97**. Remind students to use transition words and phrases to connect information. Circulate and provide Over-the-Shoulder Conferences as students work.

Objective
- Write sentences with transition words and phrases

Materials
- Writer's Notebooks
- Writing Transparency 97

 **Daily Journal Prompts**

Focus on Transition Words and Phrases

Use these and other prompts for independent daily journal writing.

- Write about a moment when one thing happened to you as a result of something else.

- Write about a moment when you got caught outside in bad weather.

- Write about a moment when you explained something to a friend.

- Write about a moment when something unexpected happened to you.

 Transparency 97

Write about your favorite type of weather. Use supporting details to describe the weather. Use transition words to connect details or ideas.

Writing Transparency

Reading and Writing Connection

✔ Trait: Sentence Fluency

TRANSITION WORDS AND PHRASES

Remind students that, for writing to sound smooth and natural, the relationship among the ideas should be clear. Adding transition words and phrases can help writers connect ideas with strong sentences that flow smoothly.

Read the Passage

Use the example from *Snowflake Bentley* to show how the author uses transition words and phrases to connect ideas.

- Have students read the bookmark. Explain that transition words and phrases make writing flow more smoothly because they connect the information and ideas.

   Ask: *When have you been really determined to do something?*

- Have students chorally read the excerpt from *Snowflake Bentley*. Direct their attention to the callout. Have students identify and discuss the transition words and phrases the author uses to connect ideas.

   Ask: *Which transition words and phrases help make Willie's problem clear? Which transition words help you understand the passage of time?*

Reading and Writing Connection

Writing

✶ **Trait: Sentence Fluency**
Good writers use **transition words and phrases** to connect their ideas and to make their writing flow smoothly.

Read the passage below from *Snowflake Bentley*. Notice how the author uses transition words to connect ideas.

An excerpt from *Snowflake Bentley*

The author uses transition words to connect supporting details within paragraphs and ideas between paragraphs.

When Willie was seventeen his parents spent their savings and bought the camera.... Willie was sure it was the best of all cameras.

Even so his first pictures were failures.... Mistake by mistake, snowflake by snowflake, Willie worked through every storm.

Winter ended, the snow melted, and he had no good pictures.... One day, in the second winter, he tried a new experiment. And it worked!

Respond to the Selection

Have students write a response to the selection.

✓ **Engagement** Help students deepen their connection to the text and discover their own perspective.

- *Focus on a moment when you were determined to do something difficult.*

✓ **Response** Help students explore more deeply their reactions to particular passages in the reading.

- *Focus on a moment in the text when you could really feel Willie's determination. Use text evidence in your writing.*

✓ **Literary Analysis** Help students deepen their connection to the text and discover their own perspective.

- *Focus on other places in the story where the author uses transition words. Use text evidence in your writing.*

Read and Find

Read Caitlin's writing below. What transition words does she use to connect ideas? Use the checklist below to help you.

Polar Bears
by Caitlin K.

Polar bears are big. In fact, they are the biggest predators on land. Even though their fur is white, they have black noses and black skin. Polar bears have two kinds of fur. Guard hairs keep them dry, and thick fur next to their skin keeps them warm. In addition to their fur, they have a thick layer of fat.

Although polar bears are land animals, they spend a lot of time in the water. That's because these strong swimmers hunt for seals.

Read about polar bears.

Writer's Checklist

✓ Does the author use transition words?

✓ Do the transition words connect information and ideas?

☑ Do the **transition words** make the writing flow more smoothly?

773

Read the Student Model

Have students chorally read the student model at the top of **Student Book** page 773. Discuss how this student writer used transition words and phrases to connect ideas. Use the Writer's Checklist.

Journal Prompt

Draft Write the following prompt on the board. Have students write a response to the prompt.

> *Think about a moment when you worked really hard because you were determined to figure something out. Write about that moment. Be sure to use transition words.*

Tell students that you will be reading and commenting on their writing during Writing Conference time.

Model how to use the Writer's Checklist so students can write and revise their work. Then ask:

- *What is the moment you chose?*
- *What transition words did you use? Will readers be able to use the transition words to make connections and to figure out a conclusion? If not, what transition words could you add?*

Write

Objectives

- Add transition words
- Add information
- Write strong sentences

Materials

- Writer's Notebooks
- Teacher's Resource Book, p. 206

ELL

Use Transition Words Write some transition words and phrases on the board. Review the words and their meanings. Then say sentence frames and have students complete the sentences with transition words. Discuss how different transition words change the meaning of each sentence.

HOMEWORK Teacher's Resource Book, page 206

Read the paragraph. Circle five transition words or phrases.

Do you know that there is more than one kind of seal? In fact, there are two kinds. A true seal has no ear flaps on the outside of its head. On the other hand, an eared seal does have ear flaps. Both kinds of seals are mammals. Even though they spend most of the time in the water, they need to come up for air. In addition, seals swim in the cold waters of Antarctica or the Arctic. As a result, they have a thick layer of blubber to keep them warm.

Now choose three of the transition words or phrases. Use them in sentences.

1. _____

2. _____

3. _____

Minilessons

Minilesson 1 | Sentence Fluency/Transition Words and Phrases

TEACH/MODEL

Remind students that they have been working on identifying and using transition words and phrases, including those that indicate a conclusion. Today they will practice that again. Have students read the directions on **Teacher's Resource Book** page 206.

PRACTICE/APPLY

Have students work independently to identify and circle the transition words and phrases in the paragraph. Then have them use three of them in sentences of their own. When they are finished, ask students to share their work during Sharing Circle. Have students identify the transition words and phrases.

Minilesson 2 | Ideas/Adding Information

TEACH/MODEL

Explain that when good writers revise their writing, they evaluate it, or look at it carefully to make sure everything is accurate and that the writing is clear. They also check for completeness. Is there additional information that would help readers better understand the topic? Good writers often add information to make their writing more accurate or complete. Write the following sentences and paragraph. Discuss how the writer revised the sentences by adding information.

> My friends and I went to the zoo. I saw seals.
>
> On Saturday, my friends and I went to the zoo. Although we saw many animals, the seals were my favorite. In fact, I liked them so much that I am writing my research report about seals.

PRACTICE/APPLY

Write the following sentences. In their Writer's Notebooks, have students revise the sentences by adding information to make the writing more complete and accurate.

> My friends and I saw lions. They were big.

Conferencing Routine

Dynamic Feedback System

 Step 1 Read and appreciate the writing.

 Step 2 Notice how the student uses the targeted skill. (e.g., transition words and phrases: Ask: *How did the writer use transition words and phrases to connect ideas?*)

 Step 3 Write comments that show how the writing has an impact on you. Direct your comments to those places in the piece where the student has used the targeted skill.

 Step 4 Meet with and give the student a revision assignment.

Write Effective Comments

Sentence Fluency At least one of your comments should highlight the way the student uses **transition words and phrases**. Here are some sample comments.

- I like the way you use transition words. Your writing flows smoothly.

- I'm confused here. How do the ideas connect to each other?

- What a great job you've done connecting your ideas and details.

Revision Assignments

Sentence Fluency Here are some examples of effective revision assignments for transition words and phrases.

 - ***Reread your entry.*** *Find a place in your writing where you think transition words that indicate a conclusion would clarify your writing. Add the transition words.*

 - **[Underline a section.]** Mark a specific section of a student's writing and ask the student to revise it in a specific way.

 - **[Underline a section.]** *Read the part that I underlined. How would transition words make your writing flow more smoothly? Write two sentences, using transition words.*

Teacher-to-Teacher

Over-the-Shoulder Conferences

Use these quick, focused opportunities to comment while students are writing.

- **Step 1** Quietly move close enough to a student that you can read the journal entry he or she is writing.

- **Step 2** Read part of what you see. You don't need to start from the beginning or read the entire piece.

- **Step 3** Show the student a spot in the writing where he or she is using a particular skill or describing something that piques your interest.

- **Step 4** Whisper a sentence or two about why you noticed that spot in the writing, and ask a question that will nudge the student to add transition words and phrases.

- **Step 5** Move on to the next student. Select students strategically. You should see 12–15 students in a 15-minute period.

Research Proven Writing Approach

The Writers' Express
Immediate Impact. Lasting Transformation.   wex.org

Connect
Language Arts

Practice Book, page 260

Multiple-meaning words have more than one meaning. You can use the dictionary to find the meanings, and then use context clues to choose the correct meaning being used in a sentence.

Each of the following words has more than one meaning. Write a sentence for each meaning of the word.
Possible responses provided.

1. content Jocelyn was *content* with her new job.
   content The *content* of the lesson was challenging.

2. paddle Grab the *paddle* so we can play table tennis.
   paddle Elliott had to *paddle* across the stream.

3. object The art *object* was based on a design of a piano.
   object The prosecutor had to *object* to the motion.

4. conductor Metal is a *conductor* of heat.
   conductor Mr. Strand is the *conductor* of an orchestra.

5. fine We saw a *fine* painting at the art museum.
   fine My mother had to pay a *fine* for parking illegally.

6. content Jocelyn was content with her new job.
   content The content of the lesson was challenging.

Approaching Reproducible, page 260

Beyond Reproducible, page 260

Build Robust Vocabulary

Day 1 — Teach/Practice

CONNECT TO WORDS

- Practice this week's vocabulary words using the following prompts:

1. How can you learn a new *technique* for an activity?

2. What activity might be considered *foolishness* by your parents?

3. What could you do to *inspire* a friend to reach a goal?

4. When might you want puddles outside to *evaporate*?

5. Why would you want to *magnify* an insect's wing?

6. Are most holidays *annual*? Explain.

ACADEMIC VOCABULARY

- Review the important academic vocabulary words for the week. These words include: *generate questions, conclusions, fact, opinion, verify, poetry, haiku, accuracy.*

- Write each word on the board. Define each using student-friendly language and ask students to select the word you are defining. Then point to words in random order for students to define.

Day 2 — Review

CONNECT TO WORDS

- Review the definitions of this week's vocabulary words using **Student Book** pages 744–745. Discuss each word using the following prompts:

1. For what school activities would you need a *technique*?

2. When is acting with *foolishness* inappropriate?

3. Who might *inspire* you to study more?

4. In what type of weather does water *evaporate* fastest?

5. What things in nature would you want to *magnify*?

6. When might an *annual* local fair take place?

MULTIPLE-MEANING WORDS

- Remind students that some words have multiple meanings. Students can use context clues and/or a dictionary to figure out the correct meanings of these words.

- Display **Transparency 57**. Read the first pair of sentences and model how to figure out the meanings of the words in italics.

- Have students define the italicized words in the remaining sentences. Students can use a dictionary as well as context clues.

- Have students use other words with multiple meanings to write sentence pairs in their Writer's Notebooks. Direct them to use this week's vocabulary words as well.

Day 3 Reinforce

CONNECT TO WORDS

- Ask students to create Word Squares for each word in their Writer's Notebooks.

- In the first square, students write the word. (Example: *foolishness*)

- In the second square, students write their own definition of the word and any related words, such as synonyms. (Example: *silliness, tomfoolery, horseplay*)

- In the third square, students draw a simple illustration that will help them remember the word. (Example: drawing of a child throwing a paper airplane during class)

- In the fourth square, students write nonexamples, including antonyms for the word. (Example: *seriousness, sternness, solemnity*)

RELATED WORDS

- Help students generate words related to *annual*. The classification of related words can help improve students' vocabularies.

- Draw three columns on the board. One column is headed "Annual Activities"; the second column is headed "Weekly Activities"; the third column is headed "Daily Activities."

- Have students list activities in which they take part, in each column. Have students include activities from home and school. Students should include the time of year, week, or day that they do each activity. They can use a dictionary or thesaurus to help them generate words.

Day 4 Extend

CONNECT TO WORDS

- Review this week's vocabulary using the following sentence stems. Have students orally complete each one.

  1. I improved my technique for_____ by _____.

  2. The teacher felt it was foolishness when we _____.

  3. I inspire others to _____ by _____.

  4. I watched the water evaporate when _____.

  5. I had to magnify the _____ to see it clearly.

  6. In my family, annual events include _____.

MORPHOLOGY

- Use the selection word *solitude* as a springboard for students to learn other words. Tell students that learning Latin roots and suffixes can help raise their word consciousness.

- Write the word *solitude* on the board. Underline *sol-*. Explain that *sol-* comes from the Latin *solus* meaning "alone." The suffix *-tude*, also rooted in Latin, means "the state, condition, or quality of." So, *solitude* is the state of being alone.

- Write the words *solo* and *solitaire* on the board. Have students underline *sol-* in each word.

- Use the word parts to define each word. Explain that *solo* means "alone" or refers to a musical piece played or sung by one person. *Solitaire* often refers to a card game played by one person.

Day 5 Assess and Reteach

POSTTEST

- Display **Transparency 58**. Have students complete the cloze sentences using one of this week's vocabulary words.

- Note how quickly and accurately students can complete this task. Work with students who make errors or require too much time to complete this task during Small Group time.

CONNECT TO WRITING

- Have students write sentences in their Writer's Notebooks using this week's vocabulary. Tell students to write sentences that provide information they learned from this week's readings.

- **ELL** Provide the Day 4 sentence stems for students needing extra support.

5-Day Spelling

Go to pages T14–T15 for **Differentiated Spelling Lists**.

✓ Suffixes

Spelling Words

spotless	handful	gently
sunny	lifeless	sickness
furry	illness	joyfully
really	hopefully	aimless
hairy	happiness	breathless
barely	goodness	certainly
tasteless	sorrowful	

Review disappoint, nonfat, misnumber
Challenge superbly, successful

Dictation Sentences

1. The dishes were <u>spotless</u>.
2. The forecast was <u>sunny</u>.
3. That little kitten is very <u>furry</u>.
4. I am <u>really</u> lucky to be chosen.
5. The dog is small but <u>hairy</u>.
6. I have <u>barely</u> enough time.
7. The dinner was <u>tasteless</u>.
8. I took a <u>handful</u> of peanuts.
9. The dry land seemed <u>lifeless</u>.
10. He recovered from a long <u>illness</u>.
11. <u>Hopefully</u> we will win the car!
12. Her smile showed her <u>happiness</u>.
13. He proved his <u>goodness</u> by offering to help.
14. The song's mood was <u>sorrowful</u>.
15. We **gently** played with the puppy.
16. <u>Sickness</u> kept me out of school.
17. The chorus sang <u>joyfully</u>.
18. I had a day of <u>aimless</u> wandering.
19. The race left me <u>breathless</u>.
20. I <u>certainly</u> hope you win.

Review/Challenge Words

1. They never <u>disappoint</u> their fans.
2. We buy <u>nonfat</u> yogurt.
3. Do not <u>misnumber</u> the papers or they will get out of order.
4. She played the piano <u>superbly</u>.
5. The charity auction was <u>successful</u>.

Word in **bold** is from the main selection.

Day 1 Pretest

ASSESS PRIOR KNOWLEDGE

- Model for students how to spell the word *spotless*. Segment the word syllable by syllable, then attach a spelling to each syllable. Point out that -*less* is a suffix that means "without" and makes the word an adjective. The suffix -*less* first came into English from German.

- Use the Dictation Sentences. Say the underlined word, read the sentence, and repeat the word. Have students write the words.

- Have students self-correct their tests. Point out that suffixes always end a word.

- Have students cut apart the **Spelling Word Cards BLM** on **Teacher's Resource Book** page 72 and figure out a way to sort them. Have them save the cards for use throughout the week.

Day 2 Word Sorts and Review

SPIRAL REVIEW

Review prefixes. Write *disappoint*, *nonfat*, and *misnumber* on the board. Have students identify other words with the same prefixes.

WORD SORTS

- Have students take turns sorting the spelling words and explaining how they sorted them. When they have finished, discuss words that have base words that are homophones, such as *hairy* and *barely*.

- Review the spelling words, pointing out the suffixes. Use the cards on the Spelling Word Cards BLM. Write the key words *sunny*, *really*, *tasteless*, *handful*, and *happiness* on the board. Model sorting words by suffix type. Place one or two cards beneath the correct key words.

ON YOUR OWN — **Phonics/Spelling,** pages 169–170

Fold back the paper along the dotted line. Use the blanks to write each word as it is read aloud. When you finish the test, unfold the paper. Use the list at the right to correct any spelling mistakes.

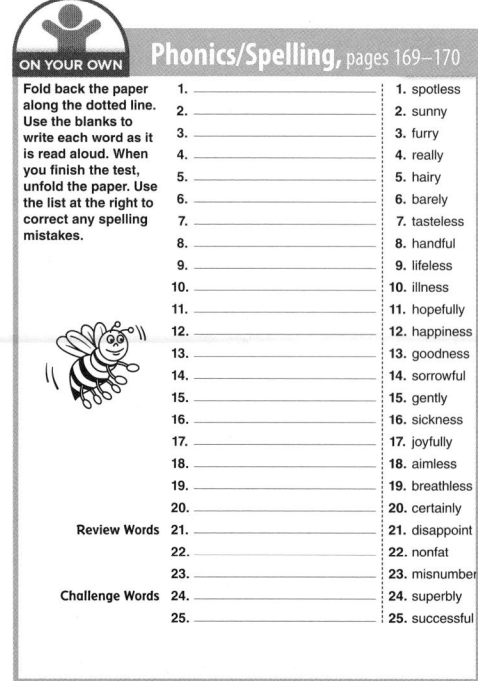

1.	1. spotless
2.	2. sunny
3.	3. furry
4.	4. really
5.	5. hairy
6.	6. barely
7.	7. tasteless
8.	8. handful
9.	9. lifeless
10.	10. illness
11.	11. hopefully
12.	12. happiness
13.	13. goodness
14.	14. sorrowful
15.	15. gently
16.	16. sickness
17.	17. joyfully
18.	18. aimless
19.	19. breathless
20.	20. certainly
Review Words 21.	21. disappoint
22.	22. nonfat
23.	23. misnumber
Challenge Words 24.	24. superbly
25.	25. successful

HOMEWORK — **Phonics/Spelling,** page 171

aimless	sickness	goodness	tasteless	certainly
barely	gently	hairy	joyfully	really
breathless	illness	handful	lifeless	sorrowful
hopefully	furry	happiness	spotless	sunny

Pattern Power!
Sort the spelling words by writing them under the correct suffix.

-less
1. aimless
2. breathless
3. tasteless
4. lifeless
5. spotless

-ly
6. barely
7. gently
8. hopefully
9. certainly
10. really
11. joyfully

-ness
12. illness
13. sickness
14. goodness
15. happiness

-y
16. hairy
17. furry
18. sunny

-ful
19. handful
20. sorrowful

ANTONYMS

Read each spelling word below. Ask students to copy the words into their Writer's Notebooks, and then write the spelling word that means the opposite.

1. sadness (*happiness*)
2. dirty (*spotless*)
3. roughly (*gently*)
4. joyful (*sorrowful*)
5. rainy (*sunny*)

Challenge students to come up with other words that are opposites of spelling, review, or challenge words. Have them write the antonym pairs in a list.

Have partners write an analogy for each antonym pair, leaving a blank space where one antonym of a pair should go. Ask them to exchange papers and fill in the blanks.

PROOFREAD AND WRITE

Write these sentences on the board, including the misspelled words. Have students proofread, circle each misspelled word, and write the words correctly.

1. The holiday was certinly celebrated joyfuly. (*certainly, joyfully*)
2. She was breathles but full of happyness after the game. (*breathless, happiness*)
3. I grabbed a handfull of taistless candy to give to my brother. (*handful, tasteless*)

Error Correction Remind students to watch for spelling changes when they add a suffix to a word ending in *y*, such as *happy*. Give examples of words with suffixes after a *y* where the spelling does *not* change, such as *enjoyment*.

POSTTEST

Use the Dictation Sentences on page 773E for the Posttest.

If students have difficulty with any words in the lesson, have them place the words on a list called *Spelling Words I Want to Remember* in their Writer's Notebooks. Look for students' use of these words in their writings.

Challenge student partners to find words for each suffix on the list and add them in their Writer's Notebooks.

Remind students that, like prefixes and roots, suffixes may be derived from Latin (such as *-er*) or Greek (such as *-ology*) or have other linguistic roots (such as *-ful,* derived from Old English, and *-ness,* derived from German). The way suffixes are spelled often reflects their origins. Discuss how learning common suffixes can help students understand and spell words.

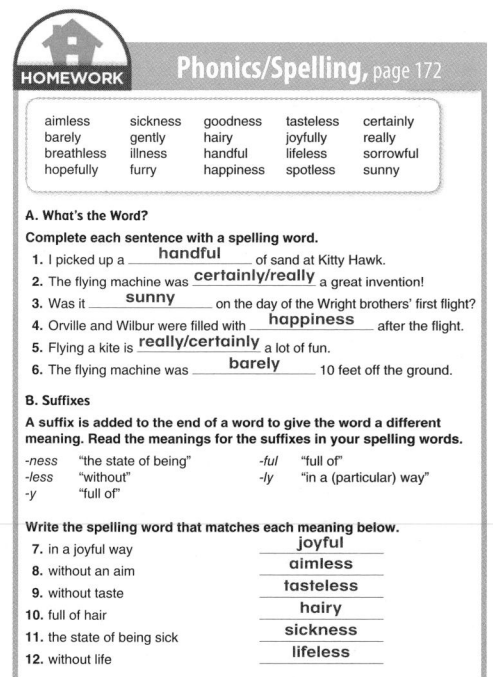

Prepositions

Daily Language Activities

Write the sentences on the board.

DAY 1
I watched the airplanes close. They came in for landings slow. Airplane food could probably be gooder. (1: closely; 2: slowly; 3: better)

DAY 2
Mom listened at the announcement more close than Dad. The announcement was not nothing important. (1: listened to; 2: closely; 3: nothing important *or* not anything important)

DAY 3
We went with the store to bye new clothes. The employee asked How can I help you today! (1: to the store; 2: buy; 3: asked, "How; 4: today?")

DAY 4
Brethless, I looked out the window. I could tell that it certainlly would be a suny day. (1: Breathless; 2: certainly; 3: sunny)

DAY 5
The coach said, "we realy can't have no quitters on this team. (1: "We; 2: really; 3: can't have any *or* can have no; 4: team.")

ELL

Demonstrate Examples
Review prepositions by acting out sentences such as: *Hold the book (over/under) the desk; (Give the book to/Take the book from) Jaime.* Suggest that students keep illustrated lists of prepositions to help them learn the meanings of these words.

Day 1 Introduce the Concept

INTRODUCE PREPOSITIONS

Present the following:

- A **preposition** is a word that shows the relationship between a noun or a pronoun and another word in a sentence.

- Common prepositions include *in, on, at, over, under, to, from, for, with, by, of, into, before, after*, and *during*.

- The noun or the pronoun that follows a preposition is the **object** of the preposition: *Someday I will fly to the* moon. *Will you go with* me?

- The word *to* is not always a preposition. The word *to* followed by a verb forms an **infinitive**: *to begin* (infinitive); *to* the store (preposition). Both prepositions and infinitives can be used to help embed subordinating ideas in sentences.

See Grammar Transparency 141 for modeling and guided practice.

HOMEWORK **Grammar,** page 141

- A **preposition** comes before a noun or pronoun and relates that noun or pronoun to another word in a sentence.
- Common prepositions are *about, above, across, after, around, at, before, behind, by, down, during, for, from, in, into, near, of, on, over, to, under,* and *with.*

Possible responses below.
Complete each sentence by adding a preposition.

1. Papa brought home a little flying machine ___for___ the kids.
2. Mama never complained ___about___ Orv and Will's messes.
3. The two older brothers did not agree ___with___ Orv and Will's activities.
4. Only the family knew ___of___ Orv and Will's plans.
5. There was no place ___near___ their home where they could fly a plane.
6. Flying ___over___ Kitty Hawk grounds was a good idea.
7. Orv and Will's plane flew ___over___ the ground.
8. Katherine took her first ride almost six years ___after___ the first flight.
9. Riding ___in___ an early plane was dangerous.
10. I like the wind ___in___ my hair.
11. The plane landed ___near___ the field.
12. He left the plans ___on___ the floor.

Day 2 Teach the Concept

REVIEW PREPOSITIONS

Review with students how to recognize prepositions and what they do in a sentence.

INTRODUCE PREPOSITIONAL PHRASES

Present the following:

- A **prepositional phrase** is a group of words that includes a preposition, the object of the preposition, and any words in between, such as *at the mall* and *by the tree*.

- Prepositions and prepositional phrases may convey location, time, or direction or may provide details.

- When a pronoun follows a preposition, it should be an object pronoun such as *me, you, him, her, it, us*, and *them*: *Between* you *and* me, *this is my first flight.*

See Grammar Transparency 142 for modeling and guided practice.

ON YOUR OWN **Grammar,** page 142

- A **prepositional phrase** is a group of words that begins with a **preposition** and ends with a noun or pronoun. Prepositional phrases can convey location, time, or direction.
- When a pronoun follows a preposition, it should be an object pronoun, such as *me, you, him, her, it, us,* or *them.*

A. Underline the prepositional phrases in the following sentences.

1. When they finished their first plane, Orv and Katherine went on a camping trip.
2. Will flew the plane over a group of boys.
3. Katherine helped her brothers by managing their shop.
4. In their letters, they told her everything they were doing.
5. Will said that Kitty Hawk was a safe place for practice.
6. The world had never before seen a craft fly in the air.
7. First, they controlled their aircraft from the ground.
8. They came home to Dayton with a new idea.
9. Orv and Will worked from day to night.
10. They had their friend Charlie build an engine for their new aircraft.

B. Write an object pronoun on the line to complete each sentence.

11. Orv and Will thanked their sister and spoke highly about ___her___ to reporters.
12. The ground seemed very far away when they flew above ___it___

Day 3 Review and Practice

REVIEW PREPOSITIONAL PHRASES

Review identifying prepositional phrases. Remind students to use object pronouns in prepositional phrases.

MECHANICS AND USAGE: REVIEW USING QUOTATIONS

- Use quotation marks before and after both someone's exact words and the titles of short works, such as songs, poems, and articles.

- Within a quotation, capitalize the first word of each sentence.

- If a quotation ends in a statement, punctuation goes before the last quotation mark. If the quotation is a statement or command, and the sentence continues after the quotation ends, a comma inside the last quotation mark closes the quotation.

See Grammar Transparency 143 for modeling and guided practice.

Grammar, page 143

HOMEWORK

- Use quotation marks at the beginning and end of a person's exact words. Begin a quotation with a capital letter.
- Begin a new paragraph each time a new person speaks.
- Use quotation marks for the titles of short works.

Rewrite this passage correctly. Add quotation marks and capital letters where needed. Begin new paragraphs whenever necessary.

what are you making, Rashid? I'm making a paper airplane, Papa, but I can't get it to fly, said Rashid. it looks good, but maybe you need to make the wings longer, his father answered. okay, Papa, what else? well, your grandmother used to open a little space in the middle of the plane for air to travel through. now, let's see what happens. Hey, it's flying, Papa! yelled Rashid.

"What are you making, Rashid?"

"I'm making a paper airplane, Papa, but I can't get it to fly," said Rashid.

"It looks good, but maybe you need to make the wings longer," his father answered.

"Okay, Papa, what else?"

"Well, your grandmother used to open a little space in the middle of the plane for air to travel through. Now let's see what happens."

"Hey, it's flying, Papa!" yelled Rashid.

Day 4 Review and Proofread

REVIEW PREPOSITIONS AND QUOTATION MARKS

Have students give examples of prepositions and prepositional phrases. Remind students that prepositions and prepositional phrases can describe location, time, or direction or can provide other details. Also review using quotation marks.

PROOFREAD

Have students correct errors in the following sentences.

1. Will's sister wrote "Will made many messes," (1: wrote,; 2: messes.")

2. "What are you making," asked Mama. (making?")

3. "I left your shirt in the washing machine", said Glenn. (machine,")

4. The bear's lived deep at the cave. (1: bears; 2: in)

See Grammar Transparency 144 for modeling and guided practice.

Grammar, page 144

ON YOUR OWN

Read the interview below. Then rewrite each line by switching the preposition in each underlined phrase with the correct one from another sentence.

1. "Captain Reilly, what do you like most inside exploring space?"
   "Captain Reilly, what do you like most about exploring space?"

2. "I like the feeling that I am about another world. It's exciting."
   "I like the feeling that I am in another world. It's exciting."

3. "What is your job to the space shuttle?"
   "What is your job inside the space shuttle?"

4. "I help the other crew members with repairs from the ship."
   "I help the other crew members with repairs to the ship."

5. "What can kids learn for exploring space?"
   "What can kids learn from exploring space?"

6. "Exploring space can help kids above their science and math classes."
   "Exploring space can help kids with their science and math classes."

7. "Do you have any advice in our audience?"
   "Do you have any advice for our audience?"

8. "Yes. There is a whole world with you, kids. Discover it!"
   "Yes. There is a whole world above you, kids. Discover it!"

Day 5 Assess and Reteach

ASSESS

Use the Daily Language Activity and **Grammar Practice Book** page 145 for assessment.

RETEACH

Use Grammar Practice Book page 145 and selected pages from the **Grammar and Writing Handbook** for additional reteaching. Remind students of the importance of using prepositions and prepositional phrases correctly as they speak and write.

Check students' writing for use of the skill and listen for it in their speaking. Assign Grammar Revision Assignments in their Writer's Notebooks as needed.

See Grammar Transparency 145 for modeling and guided practice.

Grammar, page 145

HOMEWORK

A. Complete each sentence below by writing the missing preposition.

1. Papa tossed the flying machine ___in; into___ the air.

2. Reuchlin and Lorin looked down ___on; upon___ Orv and Will's new hobby.

3. Will sold kites to the other kids ___at; in___ school.

4. Orv and Will built their first craft ___inside___ the bicycle shop.

5. However, the *Flyer* was so big, they had to build it ___outside___ the shop.

6. They tacked their plans ___to; on___ the wall.

7. He hopped ___onto___ the plane's body.

B. Underline the prepositional phrase in each of the sentences below.

8. Orv and Will took weeks preparing for their first flight.

9. On December 14, 1903, the *Flyer* rattled down the track.

10. Will flew the aircraft fifteen feet above ground.

11. Orv watched the flight from the ground.

12. One day, human beings would fly around the world.

13. They kept the plans in a safe place.

14. The crowd stood in place.

15. The plane stayed above the ground.

Daily Planner

DAY 1	• Prepare to Read • Academic Language • Vocabulary (Preteach)
DAY 2	• Comprehension • Leveled Reader Lesson 1
DAY 3	• Phonics/Decoding • Leveled Reader Lesson 2
DAY 4	• Phonics/Decoding • Vocabulary (Review) • Leveled Reader Lesson 3
DAY 5	• High-Frequency Words • Fluency • Self-Selected Reading

StudentWorks Plus
Interactive Student Book

If you wish to preteach the main selection, use StudentWorks Plus for:
• Vocabulary Preteaching
• Word-by-Word Highlighting
• Think Aloud Prompts

Academic Language

Academic words include those harder Tier 2 words that appear in much of students' reading materials as well as the language of instruction. The words chosen for instruction were selected from the **Living Word Vocabulary** list and Avril Coxhead's list of **High-Incidence Academic Words**.

Approaching Level

Prepare to Read

Objective Preview *Snowflake Bentley*
Materials • **StudentWorks Plus** • self-stick notes

PREVIEW THE MAIN SELECTION

■ Have students preview *Snowflake Bentley* using **StudentWorks Plus**. This version of the selection contains oral summaries in multiple languages, story recording, word-by-word highlighting, Think Aloud prompts and comprehension-monitoring questions.

■ Remind students that listening carefully to and following along with the word-by-word reading will help them prepare for the reading of the selection with the class. Ask students to place self-stick notes on any challenging words or places that confuse them. Discuss the confusing items with students prior to the reading of the selection with the rest of the class.

■ Tell students to write three or four sentences in their Writer's Notebooks telling what they learned about studying snowflakes.

Academic Language

Objective Teach academic language
Materials • none

PRETEACH LANGUAGE OF INSTRUCTION

Tell students that there are many important lesson words you will be using this week. You want them to become familiar with these words *before* the lessons. These words also appear in the directions of the tests they will be taking this year.

Preteach the following academic words and phrases: *biography, draw conclusions, generate questions, multiple-meaning words, imagery, metaphor,* and *haiku.*

■ Define each word using student-friendly language. Explain that a *biography* is a story of a real person written by someone else. Explain the root *bio* means "life" and the root *graph* means "write." Underline *bio* and *graph* in *biography* to help students remember.

■ In addition, relate each word to known words. Connect, for example, *multiple-meaning words* with *more than one meaning*; *imagery* to *an image, or picture, created in your mind as you read a description*; and *haiku* to *a poem with three short lines that usually describes something in nature.*

■ Highlight these words when used throughout the week, and reinforce their meanings.

Approaching Level

Phonics/Decoding

Objective Decode words with suffixes

Materials
- **Approaching Reproducible,** p. 253
- **Word-Building Cards**
- **Sound-Spelling WorkBoards**

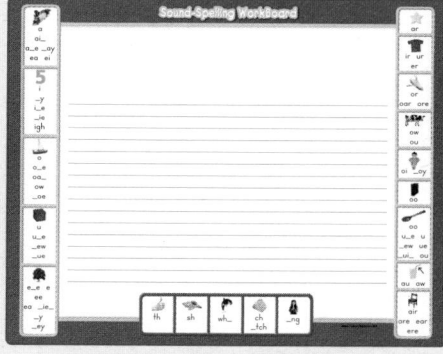

Sound-Spelling WorkBoard

PHONICS MAINTENANCE

Tier 2

- Distribute a **WorkBoard** to each student. Say a homophone pair, prefix, or suffix that was previously taught, such as *which/ witch*, the prefix *un-*, or the suffix *-able*. Have students look for the **Word-Building Cards** for these syllables.

- Review the spelling for each prefix or suffix and for homophones by providing sample words and, in the case of homophones, word pairs. Guide students to write the word. Model how to segment the word and write the spelling for each sound or syllable, as needed. In addition, point out spelling hints, such as that suffixes form their own syllable and sometimes change the spelling of the base words.

- Dictate the following words for students to spell: *scent, sent, cent, unhappy, distrust, fixable, action, refusal*. Write each word on the board, and have students self-correct their work.

RETEACH SKILL

Suffixes Write the suffixes *-ly, -y, -ful, -less, -ness,* and *-ment* on the board, and review the spelling for each. Provide a sample word and discuss the meaning of the suffix and the word's meaning.

- Write the words below on the board. Model how to decode the first word in each row, and then guide students as they decode the remaining words. Since the words are all multisyllabic, divide the words into syllables using the syllable-scoop technique to help students read one syllable at a time.

- When completed, point to the words in random order for students to chorally read. Repeat several times.

safely	brightly	bravely	strongly	strangely	scarcely
grassy	classy	crazy	crafty	rusty	trusty
careful	colorful	cheerful	fearful	tearful	thankful
harmless	hairless	homeless	hopeless	shoeless	shapeless
darkness	dimness	thinness	illness	kindness	wildness
statement	treatment		amazement		improvement

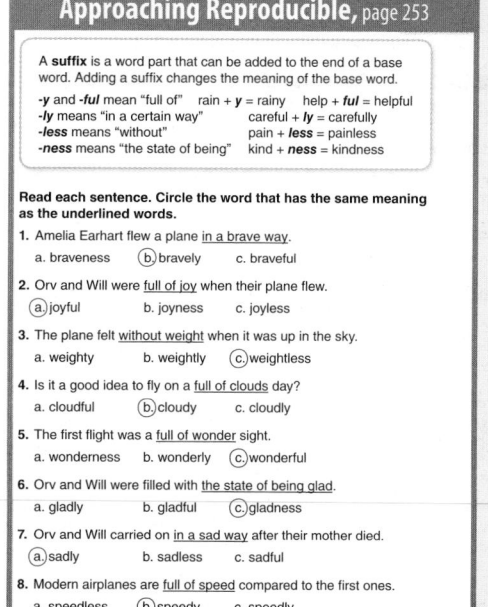

Approaching Reproducible, page 253

A **suffix** is a word part that can be added to the end of a base word. Adding a suffix changes the meaning of the base word.

-y and **-ful** mean "full of" rain + **y** = rainy help + **ful** = helpful
-ly means "in a certain way" careful + **ly** = carefully
-less means "without" pain + **less** = painless
-ness means "the state of being" kind + **ness** = kindness

Read each sentence. Circle the word that has the same meaning as the underlined words.

1. Amelia Earhart flew a plane <u>in a brave way</u>.
   a. braveness   (b) bravely   c. braveful

2. Orv and Will were <u>full of joy</u> when their plane flew.
   (a) joyful   b. joyness   c. joyless

3. The plane felt <u>without weight</u> when it was up in the sky.
   a. weighty   b. weightly   (c) weightless

4. Is it a good idea to fly on a <u>full of clouds</u> day?
   a. cloudful   (b) cloudy   c. cloudly

5. The first flight was a <u>full of wonder</u> sight.
   a. wonderness   b. wonderly   (c) wonderful

6. Orv and Will were filled with <u>the state of being glad</u>.
   a. gladly   b. gladful   (c) gladness

7. Orv and Will carried on <u>in a sad way</u> after their mother died.
   (a) sadly   b. sadless   c. sadful

8. Modern airplanes are <u>full of speed</u> compared to the first ones.
   a. speedless   (b) speedy   c. speedly

Approaching Level
Vocabulary

Objective   Preteach selection vocabulary
Materials   • **Visual Vocabulary Resources**   • **Vocabulary Cards**
           • **Approaching Reproducible,** p. 254

PRETEACH KEY VOCABULARY

Tier 2

Introduce the Words Use the **Visual Vocabulary Resources** to preteach the key selection words *technique, foolishness, inspire, evaporate, magnify, annual.* Use the following routine, which appears in detail on the cards.

- Define the word in English, and provide the example given.

- Define the word in Spanish, if appropriate, and indicate if the word is a cognate.

- Display the picture, and explain how it illustrates or demonstrates the word.

- Then engage students in structured partner-talk about the image, using the key word.

- Ask students to chorally say the word three times.

- Point out any known sound-spellings or focus on a key aspect of phonemic awareness related to the word.

- You may wish to also distribute copies of the Vocabulary Glossary in the **ELL Resource Book**.

REVIEW PREVIOUSLY TAUGHT VOCABULARY

Display the **Vocabulary Cards** from the previous four weeks. Say the meanings of the words, one by one, and have students identify them. Then point to words in random order for students to provide definitions and related words they know.

Context Clues Remind students that context clues are clues within the text that help a reader figure out what a word means. Have students write a context sentence for each vocabulary word. For example, *I was* annoyed *at my brother, because he kept teasing me.*

Approaching Reproducible, page 254

A. Read each clue. Then write the correct word from the box.

| technique | foolishness | inspire |
| evaporate | magnify | annual |

1. a way of doing something   __technique__
2. to make something look bigger   __magnify__
3. silliness   __foolishness__
4. to encourage someone   __inspire__
5. happening every year   __annual__
6. to change from water into vapor   __evaporate__

B. Now choose four of the words and use each in a sentence below. Possible responses provided.

7. It was *foolishness* to think I could eat just one cookie.

8. Simon invented a new *technique* for fixing flat tires.

9. We had to *magnify* and draw the veins in a leaf.

10. Our *annual* school party was cancelled because of the snow.

Approaching Level

Vocabulary

Objective   Review vocabulary and high-frequency words
Materials   • **Vocabulary Cards**   • **High-Frequency Word Cards**

✔ REVIEW VOCABULARY

Review Words   Display the **Vocabulary Cards** for *technique, foolishness, inspire, evaporate, magnify,* and *annual*. Point to each word, read it aloud, and have students chorally repeat.

Then provide the following *If* questions. Tell students to answer each question. Discuss the responses to determine students' understanding.

- If you wanted to improve your painting *technique*, would you be more likely to take painting lessons or buy an easel?

- If an idea shows *foolishness*, would you agree or disagree with it?

- If you *inspire* someone, would you encourage or discourage that person?

- If you let water in a cup *evaporate*, would there be less or more water than before?

- If you *magnify* something, would it look smaller or larger?

- If you researched *annual* rainfall, would you find out how much fell in the last year or in the last month?

HIGH-FREQUENCY WORDS

Tier 2

Top 250 Words   The ability to read accurately and effortlessly the most frequently used words in written English will help students develop reading fluency. Display **High-Frequency Word Cards** 231–240. Then do the following:

- Display one card at a time, and ask students to chorally state each word.

- Have students spell each word aloud.

- Tell students to write each word in their Writer's Notebooks as they state aloud each letter. Then have them read the word again.

- When completed, quickly flip through the Word Card set as students chorally read the words.

- Provide opportunities for students to use the words in speaking and writing. For example, provide sentence starters, such as *I will _____ with _____,* for oral and written practice. Or point to a Word Card and ask a question, such as *What other words can be used to begin a question?* (when pointing to the *who* Word Card)

- Continue the routine throughout the week.

ELL

Practice Vocabulary   Pair students of different proficiency. Orally model the vocabulary in sentences. For example: *My teammates inspire me to be a better player.* On the board, provide sentence frames for pairs to copy and complete using the vocabulary. For example: *We learned the _____ to create a Web page.* (*technique*)

Word Webs

Have students create word webs in their Writer's Notebooks for each vocabulary word. Write the related words provided, and ask students to add other words, phrases, and illustrations.

Let It Snow
by Cynthia Robey

Student Book

Approaching Level

Comprehension

Objective   Reteach generate questions and draw conclusions

Materials   • **Student Book:** "Let It Snow"

RETEACH STRATEGY: GENERATE QUESTIONS

Tier 2

- **Define** Tell students that generating questions means asking questions about what you are reading. You then look for clues to help figure out answers to your questions. Generating questions helps you monitor your comprehension and figure out information the author does not state directly.

- **Relate to Real Life** Ask students to imagine they have a friend who has not returned their phone call. The friend also passed them in the hallway without saying hello. Say: *What questions can you ask to help you figure out why your friend is acting this way?* Have students brainstorm a list of questions. Write them on the board.

- **Set Purposes** Remind students that good readers generate questions about a story before, during, and after reading. Then they look for story clues to help them answer those questions. Asking and answering questions helps them figure out information and better understand a text.

RETEACH SKILL: DRAW CONCLUSIONS

- **Define** Tell students that when you draw conclusions, you use information in the text and your own experiences related to the text to come to a reasonable decision about information in the text.

- **Relate to Real Life** Have students imagine hikers who go out on a trail in a cold climate without proper clothing and without a map. Based on this information and their own experiences with hiking and cold weather, what reasonable conclusion can they draw about the hikers?

- **Set Purposes** Remind students that good readers draw conclusions as they read. This helps readers get more information and ideas from the text.

- **Apply** Work with students to generate questions about selected portions of the text in "Let It Snow." Then use their answers to these questions to draw conclusions about the text. Students will apply this strategy and skill to a simpler text as they read *Amazing Stuff!*

Corrective Feedback

Explain that good readers stop and monitor their comprehension as they read. Read each paragraph with students. Ask: *What is this paragraph mostly about?* Explain that there are several strategies you can use when having trouble identifying the most important ideas. Model asking questions about the text and rereading to find answers. Also model paraphrasing the text to assure understanding and reading more slowly to find answers to your questions.

Approaching Level

Leveled Reader Lesson 1

Leveled Reader

Objective   Read to apply skills and strategies

Materials   • **Leveled Reader:** *Amazing Stuff!*

BEFORE READING

Preview and Predict Have students read the title and preview the first chapter. Tell students to make predictions about the content of this section. Explain that connecting new information with what they already know will help them draw conclusions as they read.

 **Review Vocabulary Words** Have students read the vocabulary words on the inside front cover. Briefly define each and have students state related words they have learned.

Set a Purpose for Reading *Let's read to find out about different materials and their properties.*

DURING READING

 **STRATEGY**
GENERATE QUESTIONS

Remind students that generating questions means asking questions about the text and looking for clues to help them answer the questions.

SKILL
DRAW CONCLUSIONS

Remind students to use information in the text and their own experiences related to the text to draw conclusions. Read Chapter 1 with students. Help them complete a Conclusions Chart.

As you read, help students decode unknown words. In addition, ask open-ended questions to facilitate rich discussion, such as *What is the author telling us about the states of matter?* and *What does the author want us to learn about different materials?* Build on students' responses to help them develop a deeper understanding of the text.

Stop after every two pages, and tell students to generate questions and draw conclusions before reading on. If they struggle, help students reread the difficult pages or passages. Then model generating questions and drawing conclusions.

AFTER READING

Have students compare what they learned in *Snowflake Bentley* to what they learned in *Amazing Stuff!* Ask, *Are there any similarities between these two books? If so, what are they?*

Digital Learning

Use the **Leveled Reader Audio CD** for fluency building *after* students read the book with your support during Small Group time.

Leveled Reader

Approaching Level

 **Leveled Reader Lesson 2**

Objective	Reread to apply skills and strategies and develop fluency
Materials	• **Leveled Reader:** *Amazing Stuff!*
	• **Approaching Reproducible,** p. 257

BEFORE READING

 **Review the Strategy and Skill** Review students' completed Conclusions Charts from the first read. Remind students that they can use information in the text and their own experiences related to the text to draw conclusions about what they read.

Review Vocabulary Words Have students search the book for each vocabulary word. Tell students to read aloud the sentence containing the word and state the word's definition or provide related words. Point out any multiple-meaning words that are provided in the text.

Set Purposes for Reading *Let's reread to check our understanding of the information in the book and to work on our reading fluency.*

DURING READING

Reread *Amazing Stuff!* with students. Have them read silently two pages at a time, or read aloud to a partner. Stop and have students generate questions and draw conclusions before reading the next two pages. Model generating questions and drawing conclusions, as needed.

AFTER READING

Check Comprehension Have partners complete the Comprehension Check on page 20. Review students' answers. Help students find evidence for their answers in the text.

MODEL FLUENCY

Model reading the fluency passage on **Approaching Reproducible** page 257. Tell students to pay close attention to your accuracy as you read. Then read one sentence at a time and have students echo-read the sentences, copying your accuracy.

During independent reading time, have students work with a partner using the fluency passage. One student reads aloud while the other repeats each sentence back. If students need additional support, have them listen to the "practice speed" version of the passage on the **Fluency Solutions Audio CD**.

Approaching Reproducible, page 257

As I read, I will focus on reading accurately.

	Hurricanes are huge, powerful storms. High-speed
6	winds move around and around in a circle. Winds travel as
17	fast as 200 miles per hour (300 km/h). Hurricanes also
25	hold a lot of rain. They can be miles wide. Hurricane
36	damage can cover a large area.
42	Three things are needed for a hurricane to form. The
52	first is warm ocean water. The second is a lot of humid air.
65	The third is winds that blow in a circular pattern. These
76	three things often come together in late summer and early
86	fall. That time is known as hurricane season.
94	Storms begin forming over warm ocean water. These
102	storms **magnify** and grow stronger. Hurricanes can stay
110	out in the ocean and do little harm. But when they leave
122	the ocean and move onto land, they can become deadly. 132

Comprehension Check

1. In your own words, tell how a hurricane is formed. **Main Idea and Details** A storm forms over warm ocean water. The winds begin to blow in a circular pattern.

2. What is the author's purpose in writing this passage? **Author's Purpose** The author's purpose is to give the reader facts about what hurricanes are and how they form.

	Words Read	−	Number of Errors	=	Words Correct Score
First Read		−		=	
Second Read		−		=	

Approaching Level

Leveled Reader Lesson 3

Objective   Build fluency

Materials
- **Leveled Reader:** *Amazing Stuff!*
- **Approaching Reproducible,** p. 257

✓ FOCUS ON FLUENCY

Timed Reading   Tell students that they will be doing a final timed reading of the fluency passage on **Approaching Reproducible** page 257 that they have been practicing. With each student, follow these directions:

- Place the passage facedown.

- When you say "Go," the student begins reading the passage aloud.

- When you say "Stop," the student stops reading the passage.

As they read, note words students mispronounce and their overall accuracy. Stop after one minute. Help students record and graph the number of words they read correctly.

REREAD PREVIOUSLY READ BOOKS

- Distribute copies of the past six **Leveled Readers**. Have students select two to reread. Tell students that rereading these books will help them develop their skills. The more times they read the same words, the quicker they will learn these words. This will make the reading of other books easier.

- Circulate and listen in as students read. Stop students periodically and ask them how they are figuring out difficult words and how they are generating questions. Note students who need additional work with specific decoding or comprehension skills.

- Encourage students to read other previously read Leveled Readers during independent reading time or for homework.

Meet Grade-Level Expectations

As an alternative to this day's lesson, guide students through a reading of the On Level Leveled Reader. See page 773U. Since both books contain the same vocabulary, phonics, and comprehension skills, the scaffolding you provided will help most students gain access to this more challenging text.

Book Talk

Bringing Groups Together Students will work with peers of various language and reading abilities to discuss this week's Leveled Readers. Refer to page 162 in the **Teacher's Resource Book** for more about how to conduct a Book Talk.

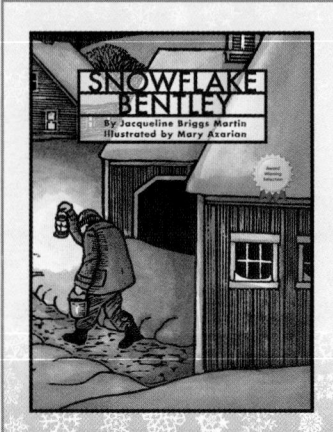

Student Book

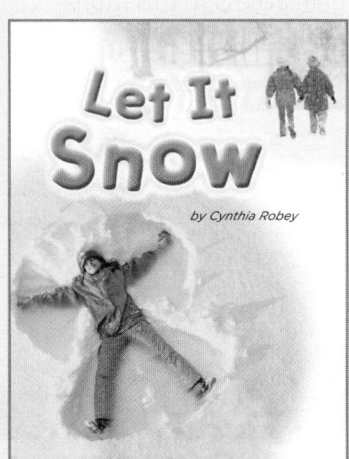

Student Book

Approaching Level

Fluency

Objectives Reread selections to develop fluency; develop speaking skills

Materials • **Student Book:** *Snowflake Bentley*, "Let It Snow"

REREAD FOR FLUENCY

- Have students reread a portion of *Snowflake Bentley*. Suggest that they focus on two to four of their favorite pages from the selection. Work with students to read the pages with accuracy.

- Provide time for students to read their sections of text to you. Comment on their accuracy, and provide corrective feedback by modeling proper fluency.

DEVELOP SPEAKING/LISTENING SKILLS

- Have students practice reading the selection "Let It Snow."

- Work with students to read with accuracy. Model reading a few lines at a time. Emphasize pronouncing words correctly and pausing at punctuation. Have students repeat.

- Provide time for students to read the introduction to the article aloud to partners. Tell students to name places where their partner read difficult words with accuracy and followed punctuation.

- Challenge students to prepare an organized oral presentation with an effective introduction and conclusion to retell the information in one section of the article.

Approaching Level

Self-Selected Reading

Objective Read independently to generate questions and draw conclusions

Materials • **Leveld Classroom Library** • other informational books

APPLY SKILLS AND STRATEGIES TO INDEPENDENT READING

- **Read Independently** Have students choose a **Leveled Classroom Library** book or an informational book for sustained silent reading. (See the **Theme Bibliography** on page T8–T9 for book suggestions.) Remind them that when they draw conclusions, they use clues the author gives and what they already know related to the text to figure out things that the author does not say directly. Have students read their books and record their conclusions on a Conclusions Chart.

- **Show Evidence of Reading** While reading, students may generate a reading log or journal. After reading, have students use their Conclusions Charts and logs to paraphrase the content of the book, maintaining meaning and logical order. They may write or orally state a summary of the book. Ask students to share their summaries and reactions to the book while participating in Book Talks. Ask: *Would you recommend this book to a classmate? Why or why not?*

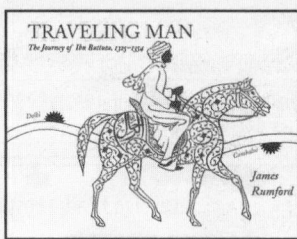

Approaching

Leveled Classroom Library
See Leveled Classroom
Library lessons on pages T2–T7.

Daily Planner

DAY 1	• Vocabulary • Phonics
DAY 2	• Leveled Reader Lesson 1
DAY 3	• Leveled Reader Lesson 2
DAY 4	• Fluency
DAY 5	• Self-Selected Reading

ELL

Practice Vocabulary Pair ELL students with native speakers. On the board, provide sentence frames for pairs to copy and complete using the vocabulary and additional words when necessary. For example: *My ____ always support me and ____ me to try new things.* (*parents; inspire*)

Sound-Spelling WorkBoard

On Level

Vocabulary

Objective Review vocabulary
Materials • **Vocabulary Cards**

REVIEW PREVIOUSLY TAUGHT WORDS

Review the Words Display the **Vocabulary Cards** for *technique, foolishness, inspire, evaporate, magnify*, and *annual*. Point to each word, read it aloud, and have students chorally repeat.

Then provide the following prompts. Allow several students to respond to each prompt.

Have students describe a time when

- they learned a new *technique* for doing something;
- they thought someone's actions showed *foolishness*;
- someone said something to *inspire* them;
- they knew that a liquid would *evaporate*;
- they wished they could *magnify* something;
- they took part in an *annual* fair, festival, or other activity.

Phonics/Word Study

Objective Decode multisyllabic words with suffixes
Materials • **Word-Building Cards** • **Sound-Spelling Workboards**

RETEACH SKILL

- **Words with Suffixes** Point to the suffixes *-ly, -y, -ful, -less, -ness*, and *-ment* on the **Word-Building Cards**, and review the spellings and rules for adding a suffix to a base word. Provide a sample word for each suffix and discuss its meaning.

- Write the words below on the board. If necessary, divide the words into syllables using the syllable-scoop technique to help students read one syllable at a time. When completed, point to the words in random order for students to chorally read.

funny	furry	honesty	honestly	hungrily
sadness	shyness	ugliness	careless	cheerless
helpful	helpfully	hopefulness	fulfillment	agreement

- **Spelling** Dictate the following words for students to spell on their **WorkBoards**: *beautiful, breathless, foolishness, clearly, icy, arrangement*. Model how to segment words, such as spelling a word syllable by syllable.

On Level

Fluency

Objectives   Reread selections to develop fluency; develop speaking skills
Materials   • **Student Book:** *Snowflake Bentley*, "Let It Snow"

REREAD FOR FLUENCY

- Ask students to reread *Snowflake Bentley*, focusing on two to four of their favorite pages. Work with them on reading with accuracy.

- Have students read their sections of text to you. Comment on their accuracy. Provide corrective feedback by modeling proper fluency.

DEVELOP SPEAKING/LISTENING SKILLS

- Have students practice reading "Let It Snow."

- Work with students to read with accuracy. Model reading a few sentences at a time. Emphasize pronouncing words correctly and pausing appropriately for punctuation. Have students repeat.

- Provide time for students to read the first page aloud to partners. Tell students to name places in which their partner read difficult words with accuracy and followed punctuation.

- Tell students to think of a way they might study an aspect of weather such as rainfall or the temperature. Have them create and orally share a brief step-by-step routine for the method that they choose. Remind them to be accurate as they speak.

Self-Selected Reading

Objective   Read independently to draw conclusions
Materials   • **Leveled Classroom Library**   • other informational books

APPLY SKILLS AND STRATEGIES TO INDEPENDENT READING

- **Read Independently** Have students choose an informational book or a **Leveled Classroom Library** book for sustained silent reading. (See the **Theme Bibliography** on pages T8–T9 for book suggestions.) Remind them that drawing conclusions helps them figure out information the author does not state directly. As students read their books they should create a Conclusions Chart.

- **Show Evidence of Reading** While reading, students may generate a reading log or journal. After reading, have students use their Conclusions Charts and logs to paraphrase the content of the book, maintaining meaning and logical order. They may write or orally state a summary of the book. Ask students to share their summaries and reactions to the book while participating in Book Talks. Ask: *Would you recommend this book to a classmate? Explain.*

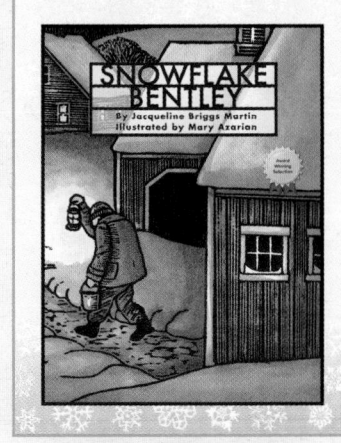

Student Book

Student Book

On Level
Leveled Classroom Library
See Leveled Classroom
Library lessons on pages T2–T7.

Leveled Reader

On Level

Leveled Reader Lesson 1

Objective Read to apply strategies and skills
Materials • **Leveled Reader:** *Amazing Stuff!*

BEFORE READING

Preview and Predict Have students read the title and preview the chapter headings and photographs. Have students think about what they know about different materials and what they think they will learn. Explain that connecting new information with information they already know will help them draw conclusions as they read.

Review Vocabulary Words Have students read the vocabulary words on the inside front cover. Have students state related words they have learned. Review definitions, as needed.

Set a Purpose for Reading *Let's read to find out about different materials and their properties.*

DURING READING

STRATEGY
GENERATE QUESTIONS

Remind students that generating questions can help them monitor their comprehension as they read, and help them uncover details that the author does not state directly.

SKILL
DRAW CONCLUSIONS

Remind students to use information in the text and their own related experiences to draw conclusions about what they read.

Read Chapter 1 with students. Ask open-ended questions to facilitate rich discussion, such as *What is the author telling us about different materials and their properties?* Build on students' responses to help them develop a deeper understanding of the text. Have them fill in a Conclusions Chart as they read.

Multiple-Meaning Words As they read, have students point out this week's new vocabulary words and any words with multiple meanings that they come across. Have them use context clues or a dictionary to determine the meanings.

AFTER READING

Have students compare *Snowflake Bentley* to *Amazing Stuff!* Ask: *Are there any similarities between these two books? Explain your answer.* Ask students if they can figure out the properties of snow.

On Level

Leveled Reader Library

Leveled Reader Lesson 2

Objective Reread to apply skills and strategies and develop fluency

Materials
- **Leveled Reader:** *Amazing Stuff!*
- **Practice Book,** p. 257

BEFORE READING

Review the Strategy and Skill Review students' completed Conclusions Charts from the first read. Remind students that they can use information in the text and their own experiences related to the text to draw conclusions about what they read.

Drawing conclusions requires students to combine what they learn from the book with information they already know that is related to the information in the book. If students' Conclusion Charts are incomplete or inaccurate, provide a model or use a student's chart and revise it as a group. Have students copy the revised Conclusions Chart in their Writer's Notebooks.

Set Purposes for Reading *Let's reread to check our understanding of the information in the book and to work on our reading fluency.*

DURING READING

Reread *Amazing Stuff!* with students. Have them read two pages at a time, silently, or read aloud to a partner. Stop and have students ask and answer questions about what they read before reading the next two pages. Model generating different types of questions as needed, such as literal questions about details, interpretive questions about meaning, and evaluative questions to make judgments.

AFTER READING

Check Comprehension Have partners complete the Comprehension Check on page 20. Review students' answers. Help students find evidence for their answers in the text.

MODEL FLUENCY

Model reading the fluency passage on **Practice Book** page 257. Tell students to pay close attention to your accuracy as you read. Then read one sentence at a time and have students echo-read the sentences, copying your accuracy.

During independent reading time, have students work with a partner using the fluency passage. One student reads aloud while the other repeats each sentence back. If students need additional support, have them listen to the "practice speed" version of the passage on the **Fluency Solutions Audio CD**.

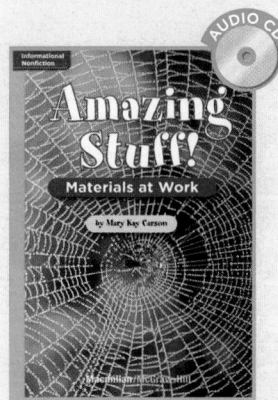

Leveled Reader

Book Talk

Bringing Groups Together Students will work with peers of various language and reading abilities to discuss this week's **Leveled Readers**. Refer to page 162 in the **Teacher's Resource Book** for more about how to conduct a Book Talk.

Practice Book, page 257

As I read, I will focus on reading accurately.

	Tornadoes begin with warm, humid air. Humid air is air
10	that holds a lot of moisture. This humid air meets up with
22	colder air. As the air masses come together, the warm air
33	rises. As the warm air moves upward, it holds more and
44	more moisture. Huge, dark clouds called thunderheads begin
52	to develop. These clouds can spread as wide as 100 miles
62	(161 km) across the sky. There is so much moisture in the
73	clouds that it can't just **evaporate** into the air. So it falls as
86	rain. The thunderheads produce giant storms with thunder
94	and lightning. These storms are called supercells.
101	Winds high up in the storm clouds blow faster than the
112	winds lower down. The winds also blow in different
121	directions. This causes the air to spin. Then, as the winds
132	spin, they form a long funnel cloud. However, one last
142	thing needs to happen for the funnel cloud to become a
153	tornado. It needs to touch the ground. 160

Comprehension Check

1. Describe the conditions needed to form a thunderhead. **Main Idea and Details** The conditions needed to form a thundercloud include warm, humid air meeting cold air and the warmer air rising.

2. What is the author's purpose? **Author's Purpose** The author's purpose is to inform readers about how tornadoes are formed.

	Words Read	−	Number of Errors	=	Words Correct Score
First Read		−		=	
Second Read		−		=	

Daily Planner

DAY 1	• Leveled Reader Lesson 1
DAY 2	• Leveled Reader Lesson 2
DAY 3	• Phonics
DAY 4	• Vocabulary • Fluency
DAY 5	• Self-Selected Reading

ELL

Self-Monitor Vocabulary
Have student pairs of different proficiency identify and define unfamiliar words from the main selection using a dictionary. Challenge students to use the new words in sentences. Monitor students as they complete the activity.

Beyond Level

Phonics/Word Study

Objective	Decode multisyllabic words with suffixes
Materials	• **Sound-Spelling WorkBoards**

EXTEND/ACCELERATE

- **Read Multisyllabic Words with Suffixes** Write the words below on the board. Challenge students to read the words, using known word parts. When completed, point to the words in random order for students to chorally read.

glittery	peppery	sugary	powdery
completely	incompletely	competently	creatively
forgetfulness	pleasantness	humorless	penniless
beautiful	successful	overstatement	environment

- **Define Words** Have students use their knowledge of word parts to figure out the meanings of the above words. Then have partners find the words in a dictionary and confirm or revise the meanings. Challenge students to use these words in this week's writing assignments.

- **Spell Words with Suffixes** Dictate the following words for students to spell on their **WorkBoards**: *syrupy, colorful, playfully, unhappiness, colorless, entanglement*. Write the words for students to self-correct.

Vocabulary

Objectives	Review imagery; compare haiku
Materials	• examples of haiku

ENRICH VOCABULARY

- **Review Imagery** Remind students that the authors of the poems in the selection "Haiku" used descriptive words and phrases to help the reader picture something in nature. Brainstorm a list of things in nature. Then brainstorm words and phrases, including figurative language such as metaphors, that create an image of each object in the readers' minds.

- **Compare Haiku** Remind students that a haiku is a poem with three short lines. Gather several haiku and have students read them and compare the imagery and figurative language in each. Then have students write their own haiku using vivid imagery and metaphors.

Beyond Level

Fluency

Objectives   Reread selections to develop fluency; develop speaking skills
Materials   • **Student Book:** *Snowflake Bentley*, "Let It Snow"

REREAD FOR FLUENCY

- Have students reread a portion of *Snowflake Bentley*. Suggest that they focus on two to four of their favorite pages from the selection. Work with students on reading the pages with accuracy.

- Have students read a section of text to you. Comment on their accuracy. Provide corrective feedback by modeling proper fluency.

DEVELOP SPEAKING/LISTENING SKILLS

- Have students practice reading "Let It Snow."

- Work with students to read with accuracy. Model reading a few sentences at a time. Emphasize pronouncing words correctly and pausing appropriately for punctuation. Have students repeat.

- Provide time for students to read the selection aloud to partners. Tell students to name places in which their partner read difficult words with accuracy and properly observed punctuation.

- Have students think of an anecdote or personal experience related to "Let It Snow" and include it in a summary of the story.

Self-Selected Reading

Objective   Read independently to generate questions and draw conclusions
Materials   • **Leveled Classroom Library**   • other informational books

APPLY SKILLS AND STRATEGIES TO INDEPENDENT READING

- **Read Independently**   Have students choose an informational book for sustained silent reading. (See the **Theme Bibliography** on pages T8–T9 for book suggestions.) Have students read their books and record their conclusions on a Conclusions Chart.

- **Show Evidence of Reading**   While reading, students may generate a reading log or journal. After reading, have them use their Conclusions Charts and logs to paraphrase the content of the book, maintaining meaning and logical order. They may write or state a summary of the book. Have them share their summaries and reactions to the book while participating in Book Talks. Ask: *Would you use this book as a reference for an oral report? Explain.*

- **Evaluate**   Challenge students to discuss how their self-selected books relate to the weekly theme, Step by Step. Have them present their conclusions to the class.

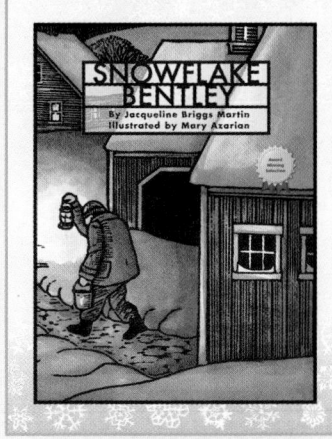

Student Book

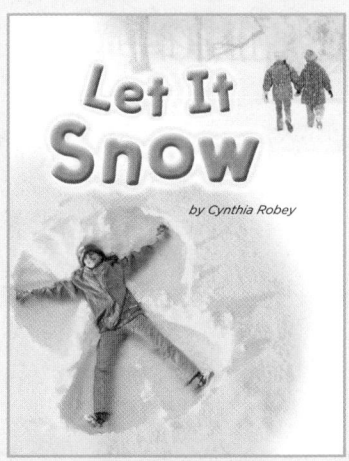

Student Book

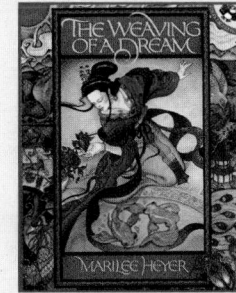

Beyond

Leveled Classroom Library
See Leveled Classroom
Library lessons on pages T2–T7.

Leveled Reader

Beyond Level

Leveled Reader Lesson 1

Objective	Read to apply strategies and skills
Materials	• **Leveled Reader:** *Amazing Stuff!*

BEFORE READING

Preview and Predict Have students read the title and preview the book. Tell students to make predictions about the content of the selection. Have students consider what they already know about matter and what they think they will learn. Explain that connecting new information with prior knowledge related to the topic will help them draw conclusions as they read.

 **Review Vocabulary Words** Have students read the vocabulary words on the inside front cover. Tell students to state related words they have learned. Review definitions, as needed.

Set a Purpose for Reading *Let's read to find out about different materials and their properties and about matter.*

DURING READING

 **STRATEGY**
GENERATE QUESTIONS

Ask students to define the term *generate questions*. Remind them to ask and answer questions about the text as they read.

 **SKILL**
DRAW CONCLUSIONS

Have students define what it means to draw conclusions. Remind them to combine the information they learn from the text with prior knowledge related to the text in order to draw conclusions.

Read the book with students. Ask open-ended questions to facilitate rich discussion, such as *What is the author telling us about matter? What does she want us to know about materials?* Build on students' responses to help them develop a deeper understanding of the text. Have students fill in a Conclusions Chart independently as they read.

AFTER READING

Compare Have students compare the information described in this book with information they learned in another science book. Ask: *In what ways are the books similar and different?*

Analyze Have students choose two types of materials and consider their various properties. Instruct students to list similarities and differences between the two materials and create a poster illustrating their findings.

Gifted Talented

Beyond Level

 **Leveled Reader Lesson 2**

Objective	Reread to apply skills and strategies and develop fluency
Materials	• **Leveled Reader:** *Amazing Stuff!*
	• **Beyond Reproducible,** p. 257

BEFORE READING

 **Review the Strategy and Skill** Review students' completed Conclusions Charts from the first read. Remind students that they can use information in the text and their own experiences related to the text to draw conclusions about what they read.

Drawing conclusions requires students to combine information they learn from the book with prior knowledge related to the text. If students' Conclusions Charts are incomplete or inaccurate, provide a model or use a student's chart and revise it as a group. Have students copy the revised Conclusions Chart in their Writer's Notebooks.

Set Purposes for Reading *Let's reread to check our understanding of the information in the book and to work on our reading fluency.*

DURING READING

Have students reread *Amazing Stuff!* silently or with a partner. If reading in pairs, prompt students to stop every two pages to ask and answer questions in order to help each other draw conclusions.

AFTER READING

Check Comprehension Have partners complete the Comprehension Check on page 20. Review students' answers. Help students find evidence for their answers in the text.

Synthesize Ask students to choose a material to research. Then have them make a pamphlet explaining what they learned about the material. They should address such questions as these: *What are its properties? Does it have high or low density? What are its uses?*

MODEL FLUENCY

Model reading the fluency passage on **Beyond Reproducible** page 257. Tell students to pay close attention to your accuracy as you read. Then read one sentence at a time and have students echo-read the sentences, copying your accuracy.

During independent reading time, have students work with a partner using the fluency passage. One student reads aloud while the other repeats each sentence back. If students need additional support, have them listen to the "expert speed" version of the passage on the **Fluency Solutions Audio CD**.

Leveled Reader

Book Talk

Bringing Groups Together Students will work with peers of various language and reading abilities to discuss this week's **Leveled Readers.** Refer to page 162 in the **Teacher's Resource Book** for more about how to conduct a Book Talk.

Beyond Reproducible, page 257

As I read, I will focus on reading accurately.

	Rain is liquid precipitation that falls in drops from the clouds. The
12	water from oceans, lakes, rivers, and even small puddles **evaporates**. It
23	goes back into the air as a gas, called water vapor. When the air gets
38	cold enough, the vapor turns back into a liquid and forms tiny water
51	droplets. These droplets aren't heavy enough to fall from the sky. They
63	stay up in the air and millions of them join together to form a cloud. As
79	more water droplets gather together, they become heavy enough to fall
90	to the ground as rain. Over time, the rain will make its way back to the
106	oceans and other bodies of water. Then the water cycle will begin all
119	over again.
121	When rain falls, it usually soaks into the ground or flows into rivers
134	and streams. But too much rain can create a lot of damage. It can make
149	rivers and streams overflow. That can create floods that destroy homes
160	and property. Dams can get so full that they break and wipe out whole
174	cities. 175

Comprehension Check

1. What are the steps of the water cycle? **Main Idea and Details** Water vapor forms clouds. The vapor cools, and falls to Earth as rain. When water evaporates, the cycle starts over again.

2. What is the author's purpose in writing about the water cycle? **Author's Purpose** The author's purpose is to inform readers about how the water cycle works and how it can occasionally cause damage.

	Words Read	−	Number of Errors	=	Words Correct Score
First Read		−		=	
Second Read		−		=	

Daily Planner

DAY 1	• Build Background Knowledge • Vocabulary
DAY 2	• Vocabulary • Access to Core Content *Snowflake Bentley*
DAY 3	• Vocabulary • Grammar • Access to Core Content *Snowflake Bentley*
DAY 4	• Vocabulary • Writing/Spelling • Access to Core Content "Haiku" • Leveled Reader *How Materials Work*
DAY 5	• Vocabulary • Leveled Reader *How Materials Work* • Self-Selected Reading

Interactive Student Book

Use StudentWorks Plus for:
- Vocabulary Preteaching
- Word-by-Word Highlighting
- Think Aloud Prompts

Cognates

Help students identify similarities and differences in pronunciation and spelling between English and Spanish cognates.

observe	*observar*
conduct	*conducir*
technique	*técnica*
inspire	*inspirar*
evaporate	*evaporar*
annual	*anual*
preposition	*preposiciones*

ELL ENGLISH LANGUAGE LEARNERS

Prepare to Read

Content Objective Describe the life and work of Wilson Bentley
Language Objective Use key words to talk about Wilson Bentley
Materials • StudentWorks Plus

BUILD BACKGROUND KNOWLEDGE

All Language Levels

- Have students preview *Snowflake Bentley* using **StudentWorks Plus**, which contains oral summaries in multiple languages, online multilingual glossaries, word-by-word highlighting, and questions that assess and build comprehension.

- Students can build their word-reading fluency by reading along as the text is read or by listening during the first reading and, at the end of each paragraph, returning to the beginning of the paragraph and reading along.

- Students can build their comprehension by reviewing the definitions of key words in the online glossary and by answering the comprehension questions. When appropriate, the text required to answer the question is highlighted to provide students with additional support and scaffolding.

- After reading, ask students to respond to these questions: *What things are you interested in? How can you learn about them?*

Academic Language

Language Objective Use academic language in classroom conversations

All Language Levels

- This week's academic words are **boldfaced** throughout the lesson. Define the word in context, and provide a clear example from the selection. Then ask students to generate an example or a word with a similar meaning.

Academic Language Used in Whole Group Instruction

Theme Words	Key Selection Words	Strategy and Skill Words
scientist **observe** **conduct**	**technique** **foolishness** **inspire** **evaporate** **magnify** **annual**	**generate questions** **draw conclusions** **multiple-meaning words** **prepositions** **prepositional phrases**

Vocabulary

Language Objective Demonstrate understanding and use of key words by describing Wilson Bentley

Materials • **Visual Vocabulary Resources**
  • **ELL Resource Book**

Visual Vocabulary Resources

PRETEACH KEY VOCABULARY

Use the **Visual Vocabulary Resources** to preteach the key selection words *technique, foolishness, inspire, evaporate, magnify,* and *annual*. Focus on two words per day. Use the following routine, which appears in detail on the cards.

Beginning/Intermediate

- Point out any known sound-spellings, or focus on a key aspect of phonemic awareness related to the word.

All Language Levels

- Define the word in English, and provide the example given.

- Define the word in Spanish, if appropriate, and indicate if the word is a cognate.

- Display the picture, and explain how it illustrates the word. Engage students in a structured activity, using the key word.

- Ask students to chorally say the word three times.

- Distribute copies of the Vocabulary Glossary, **ELL Resource Book** page 332.

PRETEACH FUNCTION WORDS AND PHRASES

All Language Levels

Use the Visual Vocabulary Resources to preteach the function words and phrases *no better than, kept a record, gave away,* and *gather in a book*. Focus on one word or phrase per day. Use the detailed routine on the cards.

- Define the word in English and, if appropriate, in Spanish. Point out if the word is a cognate.

- Refer to the picture and engage students in talk about the word. For example, students will partner-talk using sentence frames.

- Ask students to chorally repeat the word three times.

TEACH BASIC WORDS

Use the Visual Vocabulary Resources to teach the basic words *snowflake, crystals, sleigh, raindrop, mittens,* and *snowstorm*. Teach these "weather" words using the routine provided on the card.

ELL Resource Book, page 332

Use the word chart to study this week's vocabulary words.
Write a sentence using each word in your writer's notebook.

Word	Context Sentence	Illustration
technique	I developed a <u>technique</u> for blowing a giant soap bubble.	
foolishness	Blowing soap bubbles may look like <u>foolishness</u>, but it's my science project.	
inspire	The beautiful flowers <u>inspired</u> me to paint.	
evaporate	Over time, water will <u>evaporate</u> into the air.	
magnify	Mom's glasses <u>magnify</u> the words on the page.	
annual	The <u>annual</u> snow festival is held in February. What annual events does your family celebrate?	

ELL Resource Book

ELL ENGLISH LANGUAGE LEARNERS

Access to Core Content

Content Objective Read grade-level text

Language Objective Discuss text, using key words and sentence frames

Materials • **ELL Resource Book,** pp. 318–331

PRETEACH MAIN SELECTION (PAGES 746–767)

All Language Levels

Use the Interactive Question-Response Guide on **ELL Resource Book** pages 318–329 to introduce students to *Snowflake Bentley*. Preteach half of the selection on Day 2 and half on Day 3.

- Use the prompts provided in the guide to develop meaning and vocabulary. Use the partner-talk and whole-class responses to engage students and increase student talk.

- When completed, have partners reread the story.

PRETEACH PAIRED SELECTION (PAGES 770–771)

All Language Levels

Use the Interactive Question-Response Guide on ELL Resource Book pages 330–331 to preview the paired selection, "Haiku." Preteach the selection on Day 4.

Beginning	Intermediate	Advanced
Use Visuals During the Interactive Reading, select several illustrations. Describe them and have students summarize what you said. Then help students draw conclusions based on the illustrations.	**Draw Conclusions** During the Interactive Reading, select a few lines of text. After you have read and explained it, have students draw conclusions based on the text. Provide an example as needed.	**Draw Conclusions** During the Interactive Reading, select a passage of text. After you have read and explained it, have students draw conclusions based on the passage.

ELL ENGLISH LANGUAGE LEARNERS

Fluency

Content Objectives Reread selections to develop fluency; develop speaking skills

Language Objective Tell a partner what a selection is about

Materials • **Student Book:** *Snowflake Bentley,* "Haiku"
• **Teacher's Resource Book**

✓ REREAD FOR FLUENCY

Beginning

■ Have students read the decodable passages on pages 36–37 in the **Teacher's Resource Book**.

Intermediate/Advanced

■ Have students reread two to four pages from *Snowflake Bentley.* Help them read with accuracy. For example, read the first paragraph and have students echo. Then have them chorally read additional paragraphs. Remind students to read every word and to pause appropriately when they see punctuation.

■ Provide time for students to read their sections of text to you. Comment on their accuracy, and provide corrective feedback by modeling proper fluency.

DEVELOP SPEAKING/LISTENING SKILLS

All Language Levels

■ Have students practice reading the poems in "Haiku." Work with them to read with accuracy.

■ Provide time for students to recite the poems. Have students tell their partner about their favorite haiku. Provide the sentence frame *I liked ___ because ___.*

Student Book

Self-Selected Reading

Content Objective Read independently

Language Objective Orally retell information learned

Materials • **Leveled Classroom Library** • other nonfiction books

APPLY SKILLS AND STRATEGIES TO INDEPENDENT READING

All Language Levels

■ Have students choose an informational book or **Leveled Classroom Library** book for independent reading. (See the **Theme Bibliography** on pages T8–T9 for book suggestions.)

■ After reading, ask students to orally summarize and share their reactions to the book with classmates. Ask: *Would you recommend this book to a classmate? Why or why not?*

Leveled Classroom Library
See Leveled Classroom
Library lessons on pages T2–T7.

Transfer Skills

Prepositions There are no exact equivalents of English prepositions in Cantonese, although there are words to mark location and movement. Students who speak this language may omit prepositions, saying, for example, *The snowflakes land mittens.* Model correct usage in additional examples, and have students repeat. Look for opportunities to point out how prepositions are used in the reading selections. See language transfers on pages T16–T31.

Corrective Feedback

During Whole Group grammar lessons, follow the routine on the **Grammar Transparencies** to provide students with extra support. This routine includes completing the items with English Language Learners while other students work independently, having students reread the sentences with partners to build fluency, and providing a generative task, such as writing a new sentence using the skill.

ELL ENGLISH LANGUAGE LEARNERS

Grammar

Content Objective Identify prepositions
Language Objective Speak in complete sentences, using sentence frames

✓ PREPOSITIONS

Beginning/Intermediate

- Review prepositions. Remind students that a preposition shows the relationship between a noun or pronoun and another word in a sentence. Write on the board: *in, on, at, over, under, to, from, for, with, by, into, before, after*. Use classroom objects to illustrate the meaning, as in *The book is on/in/under the desk.* Then write sentences on the board and underline the prepositions: *He looked at snowflakes. He placed it under the microscope.*

All Language Levels

- Review prepositions and prepositional phrases. Write the below sentences on the board. Have students underline the prepositions. Have them say: *The preposition is ___. The prepositional phrase is ___.*

  Snow falls from the sky.

  It lands on children's mittens.

  It is fun to play outside after a snowstorm.

  I like to slide down the hill.

PEER DISCUSSION STARTERS

All Language Levels

- Write the following sentences on the board:

  Willie Bentley was ___.   I learned that snowflakes ___.

- Have student pairs complete each sentence frame, expanding on their sentences by providing details from this week's readings. Circulate, listen in, and take note of each student's language use and proficiency.

Beginning	**Intermediate**	**Advanced**
Use Visuals Describe the illustrations in *Snowflake Bentley* to students. Ask: *What do you see?* Help them point and describe the objects using prepositions.	**Describe** Ask students to describe the illustrations in *Snowflake Bentley* using prepositions. Have them use complete sentences. Model sentences as needed.	**Describe** Ask students to describe the illustrations in *Snowflake Bentley* using prepositions and prepositional phrases.

ELL   ENGLISH LANGUAGE LEARNERS

Sound-Spelling WorkBoard

Writing/Spelling

Content Objective Spell words correctly

Language Objective Write in complete sentences, using sentence frames

All Language Levels

■ Write the key vocabulary words on the board: *technique, foolishness, inspire, evaporate, magnify, annual.* Have students copy each word on their **WorkBoards.** Help them say each word and then write a sentence for it. Provide sentence starters such as:

> *A good technique for waking up on time is* ___ .
>
> *An example of foolishness is* ___ .
>
> *A good coach can inspire a team to* ___ .
>
> *Something that will evaporate if you leave it in the sun is* ___ .
>
> *If you magnify it, you can see* ___ .
>
> *An annual event that I enjoy is* ___ .

Beginning/Intermediate

■ Help students spell words using their growing knowledge of English sound-spelling relationships. Model how to segment the word students are trying to spell, and attach a spelling to each sound (or spellings to each syllable if a multisyllabic word). Use the **Sound-Spelling Cards** to reinforce the spellings for each English sound.

Advanced

■ Dictate the following words for students to spell: *safely, darkness, rusty, careful, cheerful, homeless, kindness, rainy, closely, shapeless.* Use the Sound-Spelling Cards to guide students as they spell each word.

■ When completed, review the meanings of words that can be easily demonstrated or explained. Use actions, gestures, and available pictures.

Phonics/Word Study

For English Language Learners who need more practice with this week's phonics/spelling skill, see the Approaching Level lesson on page 773J. Focus on minimal contrasts, articulation, and those sounds that do not transfer from the student's first language to English. See language transfers on pages T16–T31.

Leveled Reader

ELL ENGLISH LANGUAGE LEARNERS

Leveled Reader

Content Objective Read to apply skills and strategies

Language Objective Retell information, using complete sentences

Materials • **Leveled Reader:** *How Materials Work*
  • **ELL Resource Book,** p. 333
  • **Visual Vocabulary Resources,** pp. 517–520

BEFORE READING

All Language Levels

■ **Preview** Read the title *How Materials Work*. Ask: *What's the title? Say it again*. Repeat with the author's name. Then look at the photographs in the book. Use simple language to tell about each page. Immediately follow up with questions, such as *What kinds of materials do you see? How do you use these materials?*

■ **Review Skills** Use the inside front cover to review the comprehension skill and vocabulary words.

■ **Set a Purpose** Say: *Let's read to find out how people use different types of materials.*

DURING READING

All Language Levels

■ Have students read each page aloud using the differentiated suggestions. Provide corrective feedback, such as modeling how to blend a decodable word or clarifying meaning by using techniques from the Interactive Question-Response Guide.

■ **Retell** After every two pages, ask students to state the main ideas they have learned so far. Help them to complete the Conclusions Chart. Restate students' comments when they have difficulty using story-specific words. Provide differentiated sentence frames to support students' responses and engage students in partner-talk where appropriate.

Vocabulary

Preteach Vocabulary Use the routine in the **Visual Vocabulary Resources**, pages 517–520, to preteach the ELL Vocabulary listed in the inside front cover of the **Leveled Reader**.

Beginning	Intermediate	Advanced
Echo-Read Have students echo-read after you.	**Choral-Read** Have students chorally read with you.	**Choral-Read** Have students chorally read.
Check Comprehension Point to pictures and ask questions, such as *What types of materials do you see? Point to them.*	**Check Comprehension** Ask questions/prompts, such as *Is this material solid? How does solid material change into liquid?*	**Check Comprehension** Ask: *How are solids and gases alike? How are they different? How does liquid change into gas?*

ELL ENGLISH LANGUAGE LEARNERS

AFTER READING

Use the chart below and Think and Compare questions in the **Leveled Reader** to determine students' progress.

Think and Compare	Beginning	Intermediate	Advanced
1 Reread Chapter 2. What can you conclude about how properties work well for a specific use? *(Draw Conclusions)*	Possible responses: Nonverbal response. Properties tell how to use.	Possible responses: Properties of the materials tell how to use the materials.	Possible responses: Properties of the materials determine how the materials can be used.
2 What do you think a good use of super-hard diamonds might be? Explain. *(Apply)*	Possible responses: Nonverbal response. Tools. Cut many things.	Possible responses: You can use diamonds in tools to cut things. It would cut lots of things.	Possible responses: You can use diamonds in cutting tools because they could cut many things easily.
3 Different materials are available around the world, but we have to understand their properties to best use them. Plan to build a home in your area. Tell what the best materials would be to use. *(Evaluate)*	Possible responses: Nonverbal response. Metal and stone. Very strong.	Possible responses: I would use metal and stone. These materials are very strong.	Possible responses: I would use metal and stones to build a home because they are strong materials. Metal can also be formed in different shapes.

BOOK TALK

Develop Listening and Speaking Skills Distribute copies of **ELL Resource Book** page 333 and form small groups. Help students determine the leader to discuss the Book Talk questions. Tell students to remember the following while engaged in the activity:

- Employ self-corrective techniques and monitor their own and other students' language production. Students should ask themselves: *What parts of this passage were confusing to me? Can my classmates help me clarify a word or sentence that I don't understand?*

ELL Resource Book

Book Talk

Bringing Groups Together Students will work with peers of varying language abilities to discuss the Book Talk questions. Form groups so that students who read Beyond Level, On Level, Approaching Level, and ELL Leveled Readers are in the same group for the activity.

Progress Monitoring

Weekly Assessment

ASSESSED SKILLS

- Vocabulary: Vocabulary Words, Multiple-Meaning Words
- Comprehension: Draw Conclusions
- Grammar: Prepositions
- Phonics/Spelling: Suffixes

Selection Test for* Snowflake Bentley *Also Available

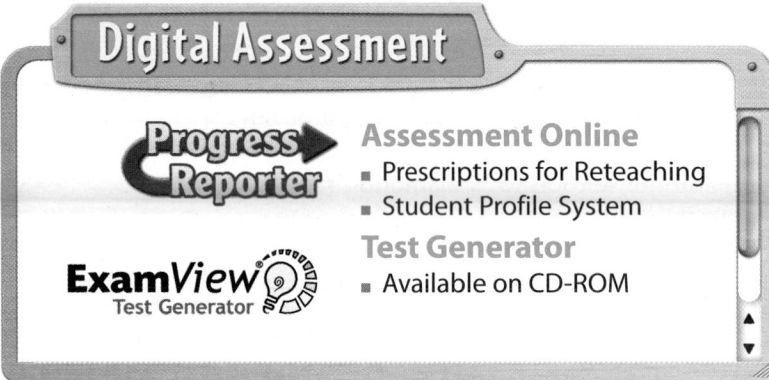

Digital Assessment

Assessment Online
- Prescriptions for Reteaching
- Student Profile System

Test Generator
- Available on CD-ROM

**Weekly Assessment
Unit 6 Week 4**

Fluency Assessment

Assess fluency for one group of students per week. Use the Oral Fluency Record Sheet to track the number of words read correctly. Fluency goal for all students: **113–133 words correct per minute (WCPM)**.

Approaching Level	Weeks 1, 3, 5
On Level	Weeks 2, 4
Beyond Level	Week 6

Fluency Assessment

Diagnose		Prescribe
Review the assessment answers with students. Have them correct their errors. Then provide additional instruction as needed.		
	IF...	**THEN...**
VOCABULARY WORDS VOCABULARY STRATEGY Multiple-Meaning Words	0–2 items correct . . .	See **Vocabulary Intervention Teacher's Edition.** Online Practice: Go to www.macmillanmh.com. Vocabulary PuzzleMaker
COMPREHENSION Skill: Draw Conclusions	0–3 items correct . . .	See **Comprehension Intervention Teacher's Edition.** See Draw Conclusions lesson in Unit 6 Week 5, page 797B.
GRAMMAR Prepositions	0–1 items correct . . .	See **Writing and Grammar Intervention Teacher's Edition.**
PHONICS AND SPELLING Suffixes	0–1 items correct . . .	Online Practice: Go to www.macmillanmh.com. See **Phonics Intervention Teacher's Edition.**
FLUENCY	109–112 WCPM	Fluency Solutions Audio CD
	0–108 WCPM	See **Fluency Intervention Teacher's Edition.**

Response to Intervention

To place students in Tier 2 or Tier 3 Intervention use the *Diagnostic Assessment*.

- Phonics
- Vocabulary
- Comprehension
- Fluency
- Writing and Grammar

Week 5 ★ At a Glance

Priority Skills and Concepts

 ### Comprehension
- **Strategy:** Generate Questions
- **Skill:** Author's Perspective
- Draw Conclusions
- **Genre:** Expository, Biography, Poetry

 ### Robust Vocabulary
- **Selection Vocabulary:** *hilarious, mischief, independence, dizzy, nowadays, came in handy*
- **Strategy:** Dictionary: Idioms

 ### Fluency
- **Rate and Accuracy**

 ### Phonics/Spelling
- **Word Study:** Prefixes and Suffixes, Multisyllabic Words
- **Spelling Words:** *unchanged, unnamed, restate, reverse, infrequent, invisible, prepaid, displease, action, establishment, oversized, prejudge, interstate, intersect, deflate, semiweekly, happily, kindness, finally, fearful*
- *really, handful, goodness*

 ### Grammar/Mechanics
- **Sentences Using Prepositions**
- **Combining Sentences**

 ### Writing
- **Trait: Organization**
- Writing a Conclusion

Key

 Tested in program    Review Skill

Digital Learning

Digital solutions to help plan and implement instruction

☑ Teacher Resources

LOG ON ▶

ONLINE www.macmillanmh.com

▶ **Teacher's Edition**
- Lesson Planner and Resources also on CD-ROM

TeacherWorks™ *Plus*

▶ **Formative Assessment**
- ExamView® on CD-ROM also available

Progress Reporter

▶ **Instructional Resources**
- Unit Videos
- Classroom Presentation Toolkit

VIDEO

▶ **Professional Development**
- Video Library

Professional Development

☑ Student Resources

LOG ON ▶

ONLINE www.macmillanmh.com

▶ **Interactive Student Book**

StudentWorks™ *Plus*

▶ **Leveled Reader Database**

▶ **Activities**
- Research Toolkit
- Oral Language Activities
- Vocabulary/Spelling Activities

 Listening Library
- Recordings of Student Books and Leveled Readers

 Fluency Solutions
- Fluency Modeling and Practice

Weekly Literature

Theme: Invent It

Student Book

LOG ON StudentWorks *Plus*

Interactive Student Book

- Word-by-Word Reading
- Summaries in Multiple Languages
- Comprehension Questions

Main Selection

Genre Biography

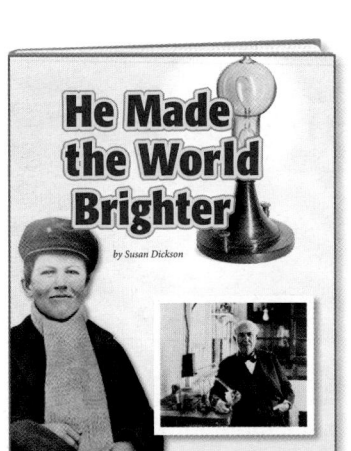

Preteach Vocabulary and Comprehension

Genre Biography

Paired Selection

Genre Poetry

Support Literature

Interactive Read-Aloud Anthology

- Listening Comprehension
- Robust Vocabulary
- Readers Theater Plays for Fluency

Resources for Differentiated Instruction

Leveled Readers

AUDIO CD

GR Levels O–U

Genre	Biography

- Same Theme
- Same Vocabulary
- Same Comprehension Skills

Who Invented It? by Lisa Benjamin
Macmillan/McGraw-Hill
Approaching Level (O)

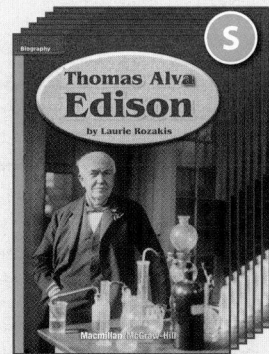
Thomas Alva Edison by Laurie Rozakis
Macmillan/McGraw-Hill
On Level (S)

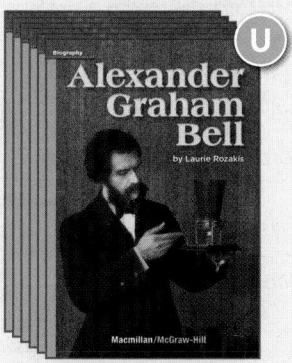
Alexander Graham Bell by Laurie Rozakis
Macmillan/McGraw-Hill
Beyond Level (U)

A Great Inventor by Laurie Rozakis
Macmillan/McGraw-Hill
ELL (Q)

Leveled Reader Database
Go to www.macmillanmh.com.

Leveled Practice

Approaching Reproducibles
Approaching

Practice Book
On Level

Beyond Reproducibles
Beyond

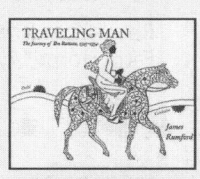
English Language Learner Practice Book
ELL

Leveled Classroom Library

TRAVELING MAN
Approaching

CLEVER TORTOISE — FRANCESCA MARTIN
On Level

THE WEAVING OF A DREAM
Beyond

Response to Intervention

Tier 2

- Phonics
- Vocabulary
- Comprehension
- Fluency
- Writing and Grammar

Tier 3

Assessment

TIME FOR KIDS
Macmillan/McGraw-Hill

Time For Kids

- TFK Teacher's Manual
- Apply Answering Question Strategies

Student Weekly Assessment
Macmillan/McGraw-Hill
Weekly Assessment

Unit Assessment
Includes Writing Prompts
Macmillan/McGraw-Hill
Unit Assessment

Benchmark Assessment
Macmillan/McGraw-Hill
Benchmark Assessment

HOME-SCHOOL CONNECTION

- Family letters in English and Spanish
- Take-Home Stories and activities

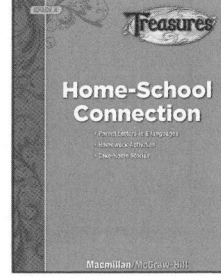
Home-School Connection
Macmillan/McGraw-Hill

Online Homework
www.macmillanmh.com

  # Suggested Lesson Plan

Go to **www.macmillanmh.com** for Online Lesson Planner

TeacherWorks™ Plus
All-In-One Planner and Resource Center

Professional Development Video Library

How Ben Franklin Stole the Lightning, pp. 778–795

WHOLE GROUP

ORAL LANGUAGE

- **Listening Comprehension**
- **Speaking/Viewing**

WORD STUDY

- **Vocabulary**
- **Phonics/Word Study**
- **Spelling**

READING

- **Comprehension**
- **Fluency**

LANGUAGE ARTS

- **Writing**
- **Grammar**

ASSESSMENT

- **Informal/Formal**

DAY 1

Listening/Speaking/Viewing
❓ **Focus Question** How does the invention in the photo make the worker's job a little easier?

Build Background, 774
Read Aloud: "What REA Service Means to Our Farm Home," 775A–775B

Vocabulary
hilarious, mischief, independence, came in handy, dizzy, nowadays, 777, 801C
Practice Book, 263
Strategy: Dictionary/Idioms, 776

Spelling Prefixes and Suffixes, 801E
Phonics/Spelling Book, 175–176

Read "He Made the World Brighter," 776–777

Comprehension, 777A–777B
Strategy: Generate Questions *Student Book*

Skill: Author's Perspective
Practice Book, 264

Fluency Model Fluency, 775B

Writing
Daily Writing Think about a problem you would like an invention to solve. Create a solution and describe your invention.
Trait: Organization
Writing a Conclusion, 799A–799B

Grammar Daily Language Activities, 801G
Sentences Using Prepositions, 801G
Grammar Practice Book, 146

Quick Check Vocabulary, 776
Comprehension, 777B

DAY 2

Listening/Speaking
❓ **Focus Question** What does the author think Ben Franklin's greatest achievement is?

Vocabulary
Review Words, Idioms, 778, 801C
Practice Book, 269

Morphology
Prefixes and Suffixes, 775C–775D
Practice Book, 262

Spelling Word Sorts, 801E
Phonics/Spelling Book, 177

Read *How Ben Franklin Stole the Lightning,* 778–795

Comprehension, 778–795
Strategy: Generate Questions *Student Book*

Skill: Author's Perspective
Practice Book, 265

Fluency Repeated Reading: Rate and Accuracy, 797A

Writing
Daily Writing Pick an invention and describe what life would be like without it.
Reading/Writing Connection, 800–801

Grammar Daily Language Activities, 801G
Sentences Using Prepositions, 801G
Grammar Practice Book, 147

Quick Check Morphology, 775D
Comprehension, 795

SMALL GROUP Lesson Plan ⟩ Differentiated Instruction 774G–774H

Priority Skills

Vocabulary	Comprehension	Writing	Science
Vocabulary Words Dictionary/Idioms	**Strategy:** Generate Questions **Skill:** Author's Perspective	Trait: Organization Writing a Conclusion	Conduct tests and draw conclusions about physical properties of matter

DAY 3

Listening/Speaking

❓ **Focus Question** How was Thomas Alva Edison like Ben Franklin? Use details from both selections to explain your answer.

Summarize, 797

Vocabulary

Review Words, Related Words, 801D

Spelling Word Meanings, 801F
Phonics/Spelling Book, 178

Read *How Ben Franklin Stole the Lightning,* 778–795

Student Book

Comprehension
Comprehension Check, 797

Review Skill: Draw Conclusions, 797B
Practice Book, 267

Fluency Repeated Reading: Rate and Accuracy, 797A
Practice Book, 266

Writing

Daily Writing Write a dialogue between Ben Franklin and Thomas Edison or a modern-day inventor.

Trait: Organization
Writing a Conclusion, 801A

Grammar Daily Language Activities, 801G
Mechanics and Usage, 801H
Grammar Practice Book, 148

Quick Check Fluency, 797A

DAY 4

Listening/Speaking/Viewing

❓ **Focus Question** How is the information presented in "Lightning Bolt" similar to the information in *How Ben Franklin Stole the Lightning*? In what ways is it similar?

Vocabulary

Review Words, Morphology, 801D

Spelling Proofread, 801F
Phonics/Spelling Book, 179

Read "Light Bulb" and "Lightning Bolt," 798–799

Student Book

Comprehension
Genre: Poetry

Literary Elements: Figurative Language and Alliteration, 798
Practice Book, 268

Fluency Repeated Reading: Rate and Accuracy, 797A

Writing

Daily Writing Has the electricity ever gone off in your home? Write a journal entry about what it was like or what you think it would be like.

Trait: Organization
Bibliography/Works Cited, 801A

Grammar Daily Language Activities, 801G
Sentences Using Prepositions, 801H
Grammar Practice Book, 149

Quick Check Vocabulary, 801D

DAY 5
Review and Assess

Listening/Speaking/Viewing

❓ **Focus Question** What were some of the basic household problems that Ben Franklin and Thomas Edison solved that make our lives easier today?

Vocabulary

Assess Words, Connect to Writing, 801D

Spelling Posttest, 801F
Phonics/Spelling Book, 180

Read Self-Selected Reading, 774K
Practice Book, 270

Student Book

Comprehension
Connect and Compare, 799

Fluency Practice, 774K

Writing

Daily Writing Suppose you have the chance to interview the inventor of your favorite appliance. What would you ask?

Conferencing, 801B

Grammar Daily Language Activities, 801G
Sentences Using Prepositions, 801H
Grammar Practice Book, 150

Weekly Assessment, 801II–801JJ

Differentiated Instruction

What do I do in small groups?

Teacher-Led Small Groups

Independent Activities

Focus on Skills

IF... students need additional instruction, practice, or extension based on your **Quick Check** observations for the following priority skills

 Phonics/Word Study
Prefixes and Suffixes

 Vocabulary Words
hilarious, mischief, independence, dizzy, nowadays, came in handy
Strategy: Dictionary/Idioms

 Comprehension
Strategy: Generate Questions
Skill: Author's Perspective

 **Fluency**

THEN... | **Approaching** **ELL** | Preteach and Reteach Skills
On Level | Practice
Beyond | Enrich and Accelerate Learning

 **Suggested Small Group Lesson Plan**

	DAY 1	DAY 2
Approaching Level • **Preteach/Reteach** Tier 2 **Tier 2 Instruction**	• Prepare to Read, 801I • Academic Language, 801I • Preteach Vocabulary, 801K	• Comprehension, 801M Generate Questions/Author's Perspective **ELL** • Leveled Reader Lesson 1, 801N
On Level • **Practice**	• Vocabulary, 801S • Phonics, 801S Prefixes and Suffixes **ELL**	• Leveled Reader Lesson 1, 801U
Beyond Level • **Extend/Accelerate** **Gifted and Talented**	• Leveled Reader Lesson 1, 801Y • Analyze Information, 801Y	• Leveled Reader Lesson 2, 801Z • Synthesize Information, 801Z
ELL • **Build English Language Proficiency** • See **ELL** in other levels.	• Prepare to Read, 801AA • Academic Language, 801AA • Preteach Vocabulary, 801BB	• Vocabulary, 801BB • Preteach Main Selection, 801CC

Small Group

Focus on Leveled Readers

Levels O–U

Approaching

On Level

Beyond

ELL

Additional Leveled Readers

LOG ON ▶ **Leveled Reader Database**
www.macmillanmh.com

Search by

- Comprehension Skill
- Content Area
- Genre
- Text Feature
- Guided Reading Level
- Reading Recovery Level
- Lexile Score
- Benchmark Level

Subscription also available.

Manipulatives

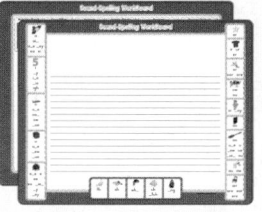

Sound-Spelling WorkBoards

Sound-Spelling Cards

High-Frequency Word Cards

Visual Vocabulary Resources

DAY 3

- Phonics Maintenance, 801J
  Prefixes and Suffixes **ELL**
- Leveled Reader Lesson 2, 801O

- Leveled Reader Lesson 2, 801V

- Phonics, 801W
  Prefixes and Suffixes **ELL**

- Vocabulary, 801BB
- Grammar, 801EE

DAY 4

- Reteach Phonics Skill, 801J
  Prefixes and Suffixes **ELL**
- Review Vocabulary, 801L
- Leveled Reader Lesson 3, 801P

- Fluency, 801T

- Vocabulary, 801W
- Compare Poems, 801W
- Fluency, 801X

- Vocabulary, 801BB
- Writing/Spelling, 801FF
- Preteach Paired Selection, 801CC
- Fluency, 801DD
- Leveled Reader, 801GG

DAY 5

- High-Frequency Words, 801L
- Fluency, 801Q
- Self-Selected Independent Reading, 801R
- Book Talk, 801P

- Self-Selected Independent Reading, 801T
- Book Talk, 801V

- Self-Selected Independent Reading, 801X
- Evaluate Information, 801X
- Book Talk, 801Z

- Vocabulary, 801BB
- Leveled Reader, 801GG
- Self-Selected Independent Reading, 801DD
- Book Talk, 801HH

Managing the Class

What do I do with the rest of my class?

- Practice Book and Reproducibles
- ELL Practice Book
- Leveled Reader Activities
- Literacy Workstations
- Online Activities

Classroom Management Tools

Weekly Contract

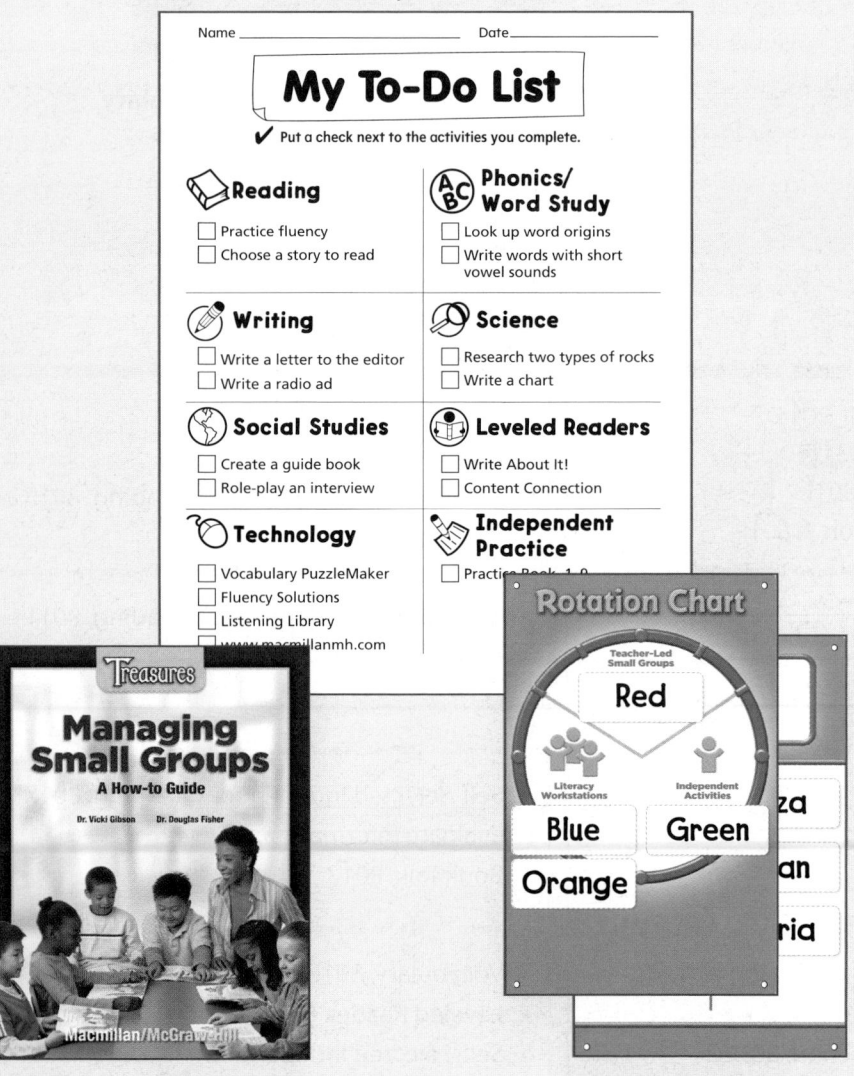

Name _____ Date _____

My To-Do List

✔ Put a check next to the activities you complete.

Reading
- [ ] Practice fluency
- [ ] Choose a story to read

Phonics/ Word Study
- [ ] Look up word origins
- [ ] Write words with short vowel sounds

Writing
- [ ] Write a letter to the editor
- [ ] Write a radio ad

Science
- [ ] Research two types of rocks
- [ ] Write a chart

Social Studies
- [ ] Create a guide book
- [ ] Role-play an interview

Leveled Readers
- [ ] Write About It!
- [ ] Content Connection

Technology
- [ ] Vocabulary PuzzleMaker
- [ ] Fluency Solutions
- [ ] Listening Library
- [ ] www.macmillanmh.com

Independent Practice
- [ ] Practice Book, 1–9

Treasures
Managing Small Groups
A How-to Guide
Dr. Vicki Gibson   Dr. Douglas Fisher
Macmillan/McGraw-Hill

How-to Guide

Rotation Chart
Teacher-Led Small Groups
Red
Literacy Workstations   Independent Activities
Blue   Green
Orange

Rotation Chart

Digital Learning

LOG ON ▶

StudentWorks Plus
Interactive Student Book

StudentWorks Plus Online
- Summaries in Multiple Languages
- Word-by-Word Reading
- Comprehension Questions

Meet the Author/Illustrator

Rosalyn Schanzer
- As a child, Rosalyn loved reading stories about horses.
- She lives with her husband, her two children, and her dog named Jones.
- Rosalyn worked for years illustrating other people's books before finally deciding to write her own.

Other books by Rosalyn Schanzer
- Schanzer, Rosalyn. *Escaping to America: A True Story.* New York: HarperCollins, 2000.
- Schanzer, Rosalyn. *Gold Fever.* Washington, D.C.: National Geographic Society, 1999.

- Other Books by the Author or Illustrator

Leveled Practice

Treasures
Practice Book
- Phonics
- Vocabulary
- Fluency
- Comprehension
- Writing
Macmillan/McGraw-Hill

On Level

Treasures
English Language Learner Practice Book
Macmillan/McGraw-Hill

ELL

Also Available:
Approaching Reproducible
Beyond Reproducible

Independent Activities

 **ONLINE INSTRUCTION** www.macmillanmh.com

Oral Language Activities

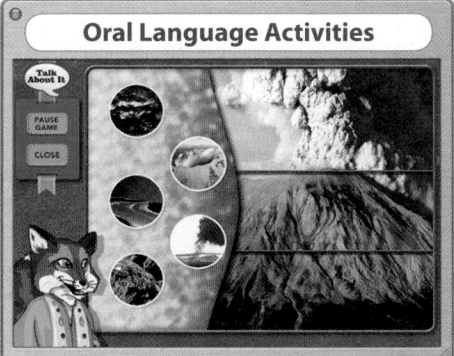

- Focus on Vocabulary and Concepts
- English Language Learner Support

Vocabulary/Spelling Activities

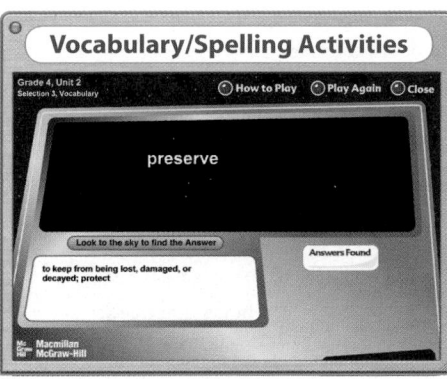

- Differentiated Lists and Activities

Leveled Reader Database

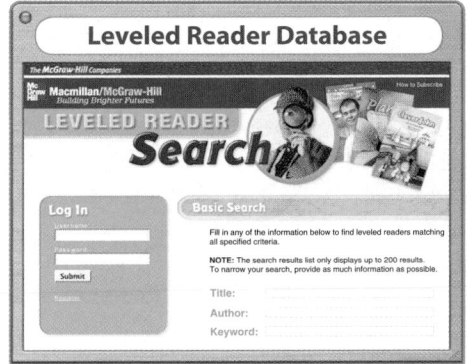

- Leveled Reader Database
- Search titles by level, skill, content area, and more

Research Toolkit

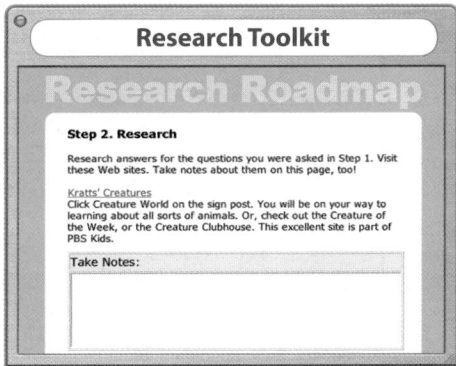

- Research Roadmap
- Research and Presentation Tools
- Theme Launcher Video
- Links to Science and Social Studies

Available on CD

LISTENING LIBRARY
Recordings of selections
- Main Selections
- Paired Selections
- Leveled Readers

VOCABULARY PUZZLEMAKER

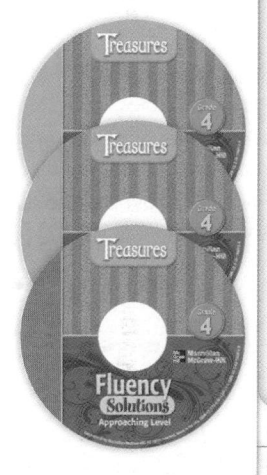

FLUENCY SOLUTIONS
Recorded passages at two speeds for modeling and practicing fluency

Leveled Reader Activities

Approaching

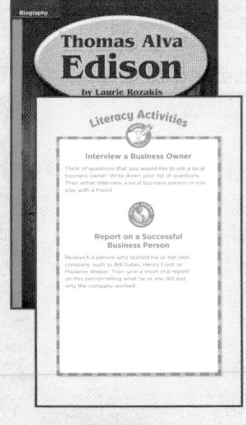

On Level

Beyond

ELL

See inside cover of all Leveled Readers.

Literacy Workstations

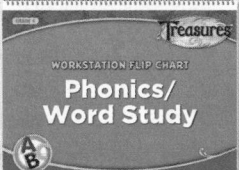

See lessons on pages 774K–774L.

Managing the Class

What do I do with the rest of my class?

Reading

Objectives

- Develop fluency through partner-reading
- Read independently for a sustained period of time; use **Practice Book** page 270 for Reading Strategies and Reading Log

---

Reading — Fluency
20 Minutes

- Select a paragraph from the Fluency passage on page 266 of your Practice Book.
- With a partner, take turns reading the sentences aloud. Focus on accuracy.
- Pause when you come to commas and end punctuation.

Extension

- Read the sentences again, pretending that they all end with exclamation points.
- Discuss how the passage sounds different.
- Listen to the Audio CD.

Things you need:
- Practice Book

Fluency Solutions
Listening Library

59

Reading — Independent Reading
20 Minutes

- Read the biography of a well-known scientist. As you read, think about a problem that the scientist was trying to solve and write down details for a solution. Note why the author thinks the scientist was important.

Extension

- Do you agree with the author's point of view about this scientist? Why or why not? Discuss with a partner.

Things you need:
- biographies
- pen and paper

For more about biographies
go to www.macmillanmh.com

60

Phonics/Word Study

Objectives

- Research idioms that feature certain words
- Identify and use idioms in sentences
- Sort words according to suffixes and prefixes

Phonics/Word Study — Idioms
20 Minutes

- Use a dictionary or do an online search to find idioms that feature the word *handy, mischief,* and *light.*
- Write a sentence for each word using the idiom.

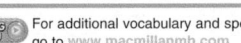

Extension

- Draw a picture of one of your idioms.
- Show your picture to a partner. Ask your partner to guess the idiom.

Things you need:
- dictionary or online resources
- pen and paper
- colored pencils or markers

For additional vocabulary and spelling games, go to www.macmillanmh.com   Vocabulary PuzzleMaker

59

Phonics/Word Study — Prefixes and Suffixes
20 Minutes

- Create a Four-Door Foldable®.
- Write these prefixes and suffixes on the outside tabs: *un-, re-, -ed, -ly.*
- Write these words on the correct inside tab: *unnamed, finally, restate, oversized, reverse,* and *happily.*
- Add more words with these prefixes and suffixes to your Foldable.

Extension

- Place the words from your Foldable in alphabetical order.

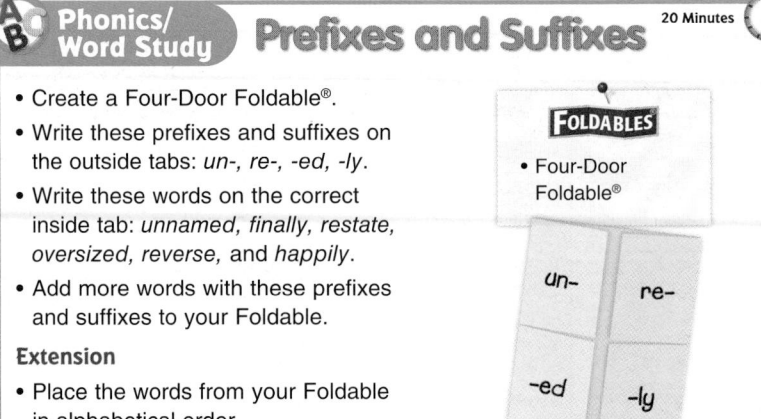

FOLDABLES
- Four-Door Foldable®

For additional vocabulary and spelling games, go to www.macmillanmh.com   **FOLDABLES®**

60

Literacy Workstations

Reading

Phonics/ Word Study

Writing

Science/ Social Studies

Literacy Workstation Flip Charts

Writing

Objectives

- Write a fictional narrative about being without electricity
- Write using a title, a beginning, middle, and an end
- Write a summary about an invention using sequence words

Content Literacy

Objectives

- Research information about the light bulb
- Make a time line
- List the pros and cons of putting wires underground

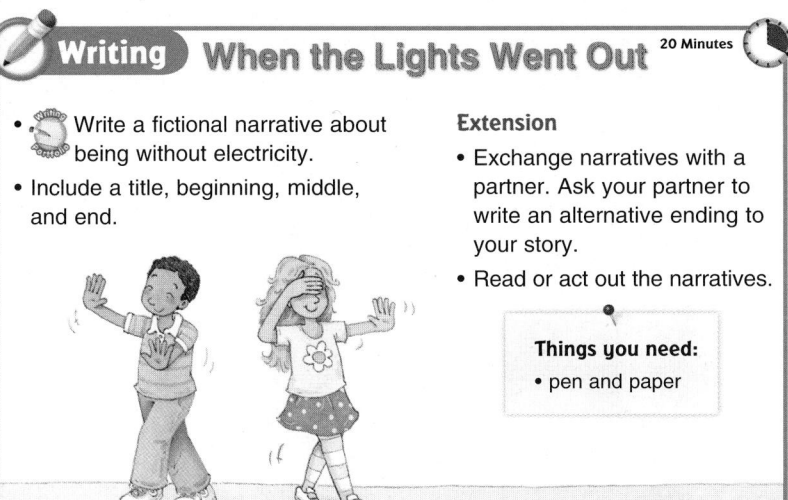

Writing — **When the Lights Went Out** — 20 Minutes

- Write a fictional narrative about being without electricity.
- Include a title, beginning, middle, and end.

Extension

- Exchange narratives with a partner. Ask your partner to write an alternative ending to your story.
- Read or act out the narratives.

Things you need:
- pen and paper

59

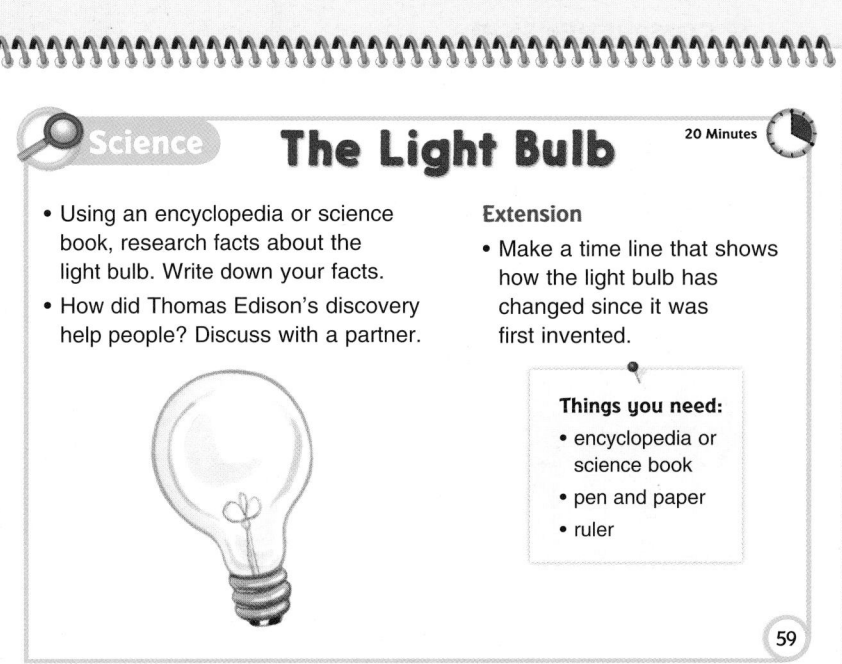

Science — **The Light Bulb** — 20 Minutes

- Using an encyclopedia or science book, research facts about the light bulb. Write down your facts.
- How did Thomas Edison's discovery help people? Discuss with a partner.

Extension

- Make a time line that shows how the light bulb has changed since it was first invented.

Things you need:
- encyclopedia or science book
- pen and paper
- ruler

59

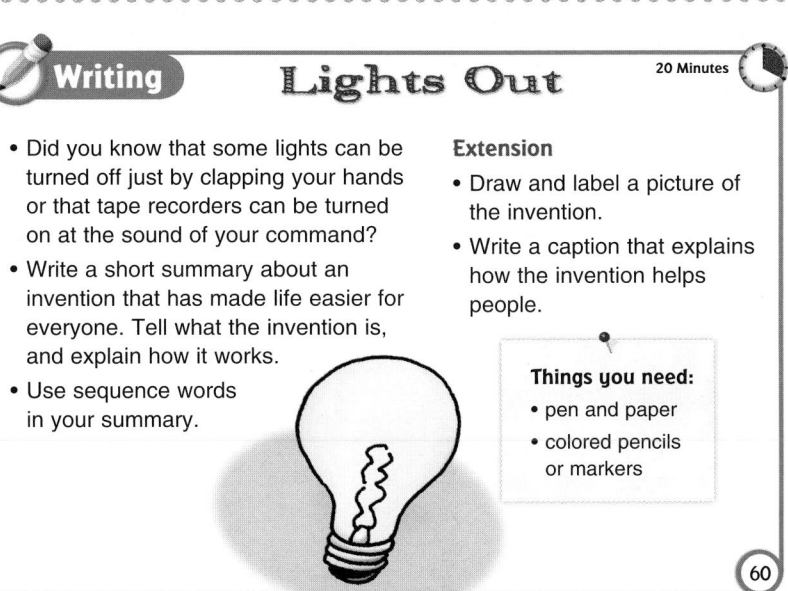

Writing — **Lights Out** — 20 Minutes

- Did you know that some lights can be turned off just by clapping your hands or that tape recorders can be turned on at the sound of your command?
- Write a short summary about an invention that has made life easier for everyone. Tell what the invention is, and explain how it works.
- Use sequence words in your summary.

Extension

- Draw and label a picture of the invention.
- Write a caption that explains how the invention helps people.

Things you need:
- pen and paper
- colored pencils or markers

60

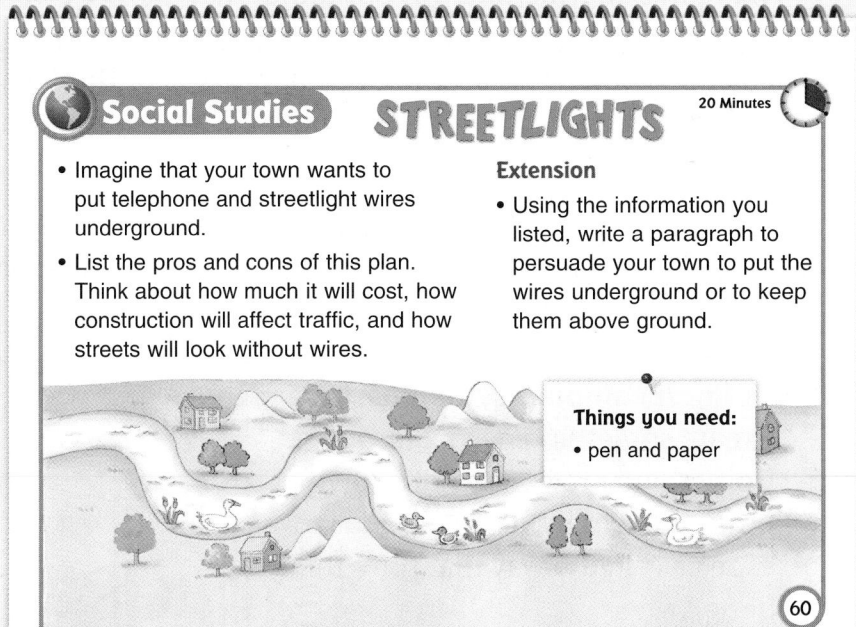

Social Studies — **STREETLIGHTS** — 20 Minutes

- Imagine that your town wants to put telephone and streetlight wires underground.
- List the pros and cons of this plan. Think about how much it will cost, how construction will affect traffic, and how streets will look without wires.

Extension

- Using the information you listed, write a paragraph to persuade your town to put the wires underground or to keep them above ground.

Things you need:
- pen and paper

60

Prepare

WHOLE GROUP

ORAL LANGUAGE
- Build Background
- Connect to Theme
- Read Aloud

✦ **PHONICS/WORD STUDY**
- Prefixes and Suffixes

✦ **VOCABULARY**
- Dictionary: Idioms
- Teach Words

✦ **COMPREHENSION**
- Strategy: Generate Questions
- Skill: Author's Perspective

SMALL GROUP

- Differentiated Instruction, pp. 801I–801HH

774

Oral Language

Build Background

ACCESS PRIOR KNOWLEDGE

Share this information: This photograph shows a mail carrier riding on a new electric scooter. This invention, or new product, helps him deliver mail more quickly and easily. Any tool or machine or other item we use was once new and innovative. It was an invention.

Write the following words on the board, and briefly define each using the **Define/Example/Ask** routine: **invent** (create something new), **discovery** (something previously not known), **innovative** (new, different, and better, especially in the way that something is done).

FOCUS QUESTION Ask students to read "Talk About It" on **Student Book** page 775. Then have them turn to a partner and describe the photo. Ask:

- How might being innovative lead to an important discovery?

- What steps do you think were taken to invent the scooter in the photo?

Invent It

Talk About It

How does this invention make this worker's job a little easier?

LOG ON ▶ VIEW IT

Oral Language Activities
Invent It
www.macmillanmh.com

775

ELL ENGLISH LANGUAGE LEARNERS

Beginning	Intermediate	Advanced
Use Visuals Tell students about the photograph. *The mail carrier is delivering mail. He is riding a new electric scooter. This scooter is a new invention.* Then ask students to tell you about the photograph. Repeat correct responses in a louder and slower voice so the rest of the class may hear.	**Describe** Ask students to tell you about the photograph. *How does the new scooter help the mail carrier? Is the scooter innovative? Why or why not?* Correct grammar and pronunciation in students' responses as needed.	**Discuss** Ask students to discuss machines and inventions they use that are innovative. Elicit details to support students' response.

Use the Picture Prompt

BUILD WRITING FLUENCY

Ask students to write in their Writer's Notebooks what they know about inventing products. Have them write as much as they can and as well as they can for 15 minutes. Meet with students during Writing Conference time to give feedback and revision assignments. Students should self-correct any errors they notice prior to the conference.

Connect to the Unit Theme

DISCUSS THE BIG IDEA

Problem solving can lead to inventions that improve our lives.

Discuss with students what they have learned so far in this unit about inventors and their inventions.

- What kinds of inventions have we read about so far? How are they alike? How are they different?

- How did problem solving lead the inventors to make their discoveries?

USE THEME FOLDABLES

Write the **Big Idea** statement on the board. Have students copy it on their Unit Theme Foldables and add details as they complete this week's readings.

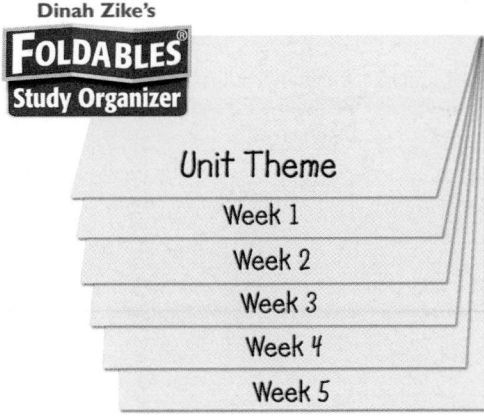

Dinah Zike's
FOLDABLES®
Study Organizer

Unit Theme
Week 1
Week 2
Week 3
Week 4
Week 5

Layered Book

Objectives

- Identify the characteristics of an essay
- Develop vocabulary
- Read sentences fluently, focusing on rate and accuracy

Materials

- Read-Aloud Anthology, pp. 40–43

Read Aloud

Read "What REA Service Means to Our Farm Home"

Read Aloud

GENRE: Informational Text/Persuasive

One type of informational text is an essay. Share these key characteristics of an **essay**:

- An essay is a short nonfiction work that expresses an author's opinions and point of view on a topic. A persuasive essay tries to influence readers to think or act a certain way.

- An essay contains facts and details that support the opinions.

- The author of an essay may describe his or her own experiences.

Explain that this essay is a **primary source**, or a firsthand account from an earlier era. The author describes how her family's life was changed when they first got electrical service in their rural home.

FOCUS ON VOCABULARY

Introduce the words, using the **Define/Example/Ask** routine. Knowing these words will help them to understand the essay.

Vocabulary Routine

Use the routines below to discuss the meaning of each word.

Define: A **cooperative** is a group of farmers who work together by sharing supplies.
Example: The farmer joined his local cooperative to save money on equipment for his farm.
Ask: What types of supplies might farmers in a cooperative share?

Define: **Sentiments** are feelings or opinions.
Example: The two friends shared the same sentiments about homework.
Ask: What are your sentiments about speaking in class?

Define: A **pike** is a road and is the short form of *turnpike*.
Example: Mr. Pundle drove ten miles down the pike to get to the store.
Ask: What pike is nearest to your house?

LISTENING FOR A PURPOSE

Ask students to listen carefully as you read "What REA Service Means to Our Farm Home" on **Read-Aloud Anthology** pages 40–43. Use the Think Alouds and genre study provided.

ELL Interactive Reading Build students' oral language by engaging them in discussion about the essay's basic meaning.

- Point to the picture of the woman in her home. Have students focus on the lamp and the vacuum cleaner. Explain that both require electricity to operate.

- After the first paragraph, say: *Turn to your partner and discuss what two items the author is comparing.*

- After the third paragraph, say: *Explain to your partner why the author's family might have switched to using electric machines.*

- After the last paragraph, say: *Tell your partner what it means to the author to have electric machines.*

Think/Pair/Share Use **Copying Master 1**, "I wonder...," to help students further comprehend what they read. Then have students turn to a partner and orally summarize the story, using their responses to guide them. Finally, have a few students share their summaries with the class.

RESPOND TO THE ESSAY

Ask students the **Think and Respond** questions on page 43. Have them generate a list of items they use daily that run on electricity. In groups, ask students to debate the importance of the items and how their lives would be different if they did not have them.

Model Fluency

Reread the essay. Tell students that this time you want them to focus on two aspects of how you read—your **rate** and **accuracy**.

Point out that you speed up in sections of the text that are exciting to add drama to your reading. You read at a rate, or pace, that allows you to read each word correctly, or accurately. Model an example.

Think Aloud Listen as I read the part where the author sums up how her life has changed due to electricity: "So you see I am thoroughly enjoying the many things that electricity had made possible, and I am enjoying life more because I have more time to spend visiting my friends, studying and reading, and doing the things that make life richer and fuller."
Did you notice how I read at a steady pace and read each word clearly and accurately? Now you try. Repeat each sentence after me, using the same rate and accuracy that I do.

Establish Fluency Focus Remind students that you will be listening for these same qualities in their reading throughout the week. You will help them improve their reading by adjusting their rate to add clarity and drama and to increase accuracy.

Readers Theater

BUILDING LISTENING AND SPEAKING SKILLS
Distribute copies of "The Camera in the Attic," **Read-Aloud Anthology** pages 203–219. Assign parts. Have students practice throughout the unit. Have students present the play or perform a dramatic reading at the end of the unit.

ELL

Discuss Genre Review the characteristics of an essay with students. Ask: *What kind of information can you find in an essay? What experience does that author write about in this essay? Why do you think the author wrote this essay?* Correct the meaning of students' responses as needed. Elicit details and specific information to support students' responses.

Objective

- Decode multisyllabic words with prefixes and suffixes

Materials

- Practice Book, p. 262
- Transparency 30
- Word-Building Cards
- Teacher's Resource Book, p. 149

ELL

Transfer Skills English and Spanish languages use suffixes and prefixes. Help students connect Spanish suffixes and prefixes to English ones. For example, prefixes *un-, non-, in-, and dis-* in English are similar to *in-, des-,* and *dis-* in Spanish; suffixes *-able, -ness, and -tion* in English are similar to *-ible, -able, -idad, -sión,* and *-ción* in Spanish. See language transfers on pages T16–T31.

Practice Book, page 262

A **prefix** is a word part that can be added to the beginning of a base word. A prefix changes the meaning of the word. The prefixes *dis-, non-,* and *un-* mean "the opposite of" or "without." The prefix *mis-* means "badly" or "incorrectly."

A. Underline the prefix in the following words. Then write the meaning of the word.

1. unusual ____not usual____
2. discontent ____not content____
3. misread ____read incorrectly____
4. nonsense ____the opposite of sense____
5. unafraid ____not afraid____

A **suffix** is a word part that can be added to the end of a base word. Adding a suffix changes the meaning of the base word.
-y and *-ful* mean "full of"   *-ly* means "in a certain way"
-less means "without"   *-ness* means "the state of being"

B. Circle the suffix in each word. Then write the meaning of the word.

6. joyful ____full of joy____
7. sadness ____the state of being sad____
8. quietly ____in a quiet way____
9. toothless ____without teeth____
10. speedy ____full of speed____

Approaching Reproducible, page 262

Beyond Reproducible, page 262

775C Unit 6 Week 5

Word Study

 **Prefixes and Suffixes**

EXPLAIN/MODEL

Remind students that a prefix is a group of letters added to the beginning of a word to make a new word and that a suffix is a group added to the end of a word to make a new word. Recognizing common prefixes and suffixes can help students decode words and understand their meanings.

In the previous two weeks, students learned some of the most common prefixes and suffixes. In this lesson, they will learn other frequently used prefixes and suffixes not previously covered. These include:

- **re-** as in *review*
- **in-, im-, ir-, il-** as in *immobile*
- **en-, em-** as in *enable*
- **semi-** as in *semisweet*
- **pre-** as in *premade*
- **-er, -or** as in *baker*
- **-ion, -tion, -ation, -ition** as in *presentation*
- **-ment** as in *fulfillment*
- **-ible, -able** as in *edible*

Write the sample words on the board, underline the prefix or suffix, and model pronouncing and defining each one.

Think Aloud Look at the first word I wrote: *r-e-v-i-e-w.* I see the prefix *re-.* Listen and watch as I sound out the word: /ri vū'/, *review.* (Run your finger under the word as you sound it out.) The prefix *re-* means "again," so *review* means "view again."

PRACTICE/APPLY

Read the Word List Display **Transparency 30.** The first two lines include words with prefixes and suffixes that students will encounter in the upcoming selections. Have students underline the prefix or suffix in each word. Then have them chorally read the words.

shopkeeper	inventions	traveler	firefighters
attention	incubate	owner	remove
rewind	embrace	inconvenience	amazement
preview	entangle	break	agreeable
irregular	credible	preoccupy	impossible

Phonics Transparency 30

Read Multisyllabic Words

TRANSITION TO LONGER WORDS Help students transition from reading short words containing prefixes and suffixes to longer multisyllabic words containing them. Have students read a word in the first column. Then model reading the longer word in the second column. Point out the added syllable(s), as well as the prefix or suffix, to help students gain awareness of these common word parts.

remediate	remediation	management	manageable
exception	exceptional	illogical	illogically
enroll	enrolling	computer	computation
engage	engagement	containment	containable
invoke	invocation	endear	endearment
excitement	excitable	prescribe	prescription

Phonics Transparency 30

BUILD WORDS Use **Word-Building Cards** *un, re, non, semi, dis, over, il, inter, pre, ness, ed, ment, ly, ible, able, tion*. Display the cards. Have students add the word parts to words they find in their **Student Book** to build as many multisyllabic words containing prefixes and suffixes as possible. Discuss the meaning of each new word formed.

APPLY DECODING STRATEGY Guide students in using the Decoding Strategy to decode: *recommitment, prerecordable, impatience, inexcusable, recollection, endangerment, unbelievable*. Write each word on the board. Have students look for familiar spellings in Steps 1 and 2 of the Decoding Strategy procedure.

Build Fluency

SPEED DRILL Distribute copies of the **Prefixes and Suffixes Speed Drill** on **Teacher's Resource Book** page 149. Use the Speed Drill routine to help students become fluent reading words with prefixes and suffixes.

Quick Check

Can students read words with prefixes and suffixes?

During **Small Group Instruction**

Tier 2

If No → | Approaching Level | Reteach the skill using the lesson on p. 801J.

If Yes → | On Level | Consolidate the learning using p. 801S.

| Beyond Level | Extend the learning using p. 801W.

DAILY Syllable Fluency

Use **Word-Building Cards** 311–322. Display one card at a time. Have students chorally read each common syllable. Repeat at varying speeds and in random order. Have students work with partners during independent time to write as many words as they can containing each syllable.

tel writ tors

Decoding Strategy

Decoding Strategy Chart

Step 1	Look for word parts (prefixes) at the beginning of the word.
Step 2	Look for word parts (suffixes) at the end of the word.
Step 3	In the base word, look for familiar spelling patterns. Think about the six syllable-spelling patterns you have learned.
Step 4	Sound out and blend together the word parts.
Step 5	Say the word parts fast. Adjust your pronunciation as needed. Ask yourself: "Is this a word I have heard before?" Then read the word in the sentence and ask: "Does it make sense in this sentence?"

© Macmillan/McGraw-Hill

Vocabulary

STRATEGY
DICTIONARY

Idioms Explain that words can take on different meanings when they are used in particular phrases. Idioms are groups of words that have a collective meaning different from that of each individual word separately. Readers can often use context clues in a sentence or in surrounding sentences to determine an idiom's meaning, or they can check a dictionary.

Ask students to read "Idioms" in the bookmark on **Student Book** page 776. Then model how to figure out the meaning of the idiom *came in handy*.

Think Aloud When I read the idiom "came in handy" on page 777, I ask myself, "How can something handy come in? What does the idiom mean?" I check a dictionary and find that "come in handy" means "proves to be useful." This phrase is in the past tense, so it means, "proved to be useful." Looking back at the passage, I see that this meaning makes sense.

Read "He Made the World Brighter"

As you read the passage with students, ask them to identify clues that reveal the meanings of the highlighted words. Tell students they will read these words again in *How Ben Franklin Stole the Lightning*.

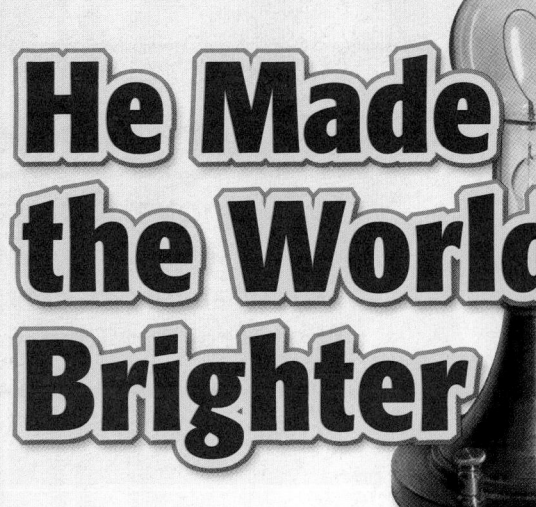

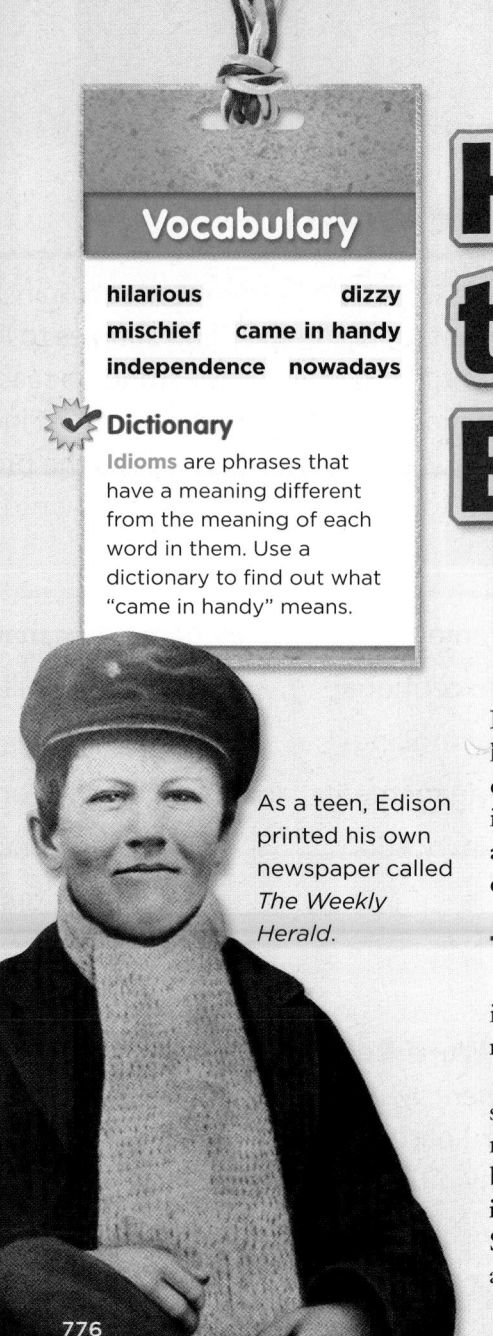

Vocabulary

hilarious	dizzy
mischief	came in handy
independence	nowadays

Dictionary

Idioms are phrases that have a meaning different from the meaning of each word in them. Use a dictionary to find out what "came in handy" means.

As a teen, Edison printed his own newspaper called *The Weekly Herald*.

776

He Made the World Brighter

by Susan Dickson

Thomas Edison was a poor student. **Hilarious**? It is funny when you know what he grew up to become. Even if his grades didn't show it, the mother of this future inventor was convinced he was smart. After a few disappointing months in school, she decided to teach Thomas herself at home.

Thomas's Childhood

Thomas Alva Edison was born in 1847 in Ohio. Although curious and prone to **mischief**, Thomas read whenever he could.

Thomas's first job, at thirteen, was selling newspapers. Back then that's when most boys started working. At sixteen he became a telegrapher. This gave Thomas **independence** and an opportunity to travel. Shortly after this, Edison decided to be an inventor.

Quick Check

Can students identify word meanings?

During **Small Group Instruction**

Tier 2

If No → **Approaching Level** Reteach the words using the Vocabulary lesson, pp. 801K–801L.

If Yes → **On Level** Consolidate the learning using p. 801S.

Gifted & Talented

Beyond Level Extend the learning using p. 801W.

The Young Inventor

Not everything Thomas invented was a success. In fact his first invention, an electric vote recorder, failed. Edison thought it would help count votes. No one else found it useful, but that didn't stop Edison.

Edison's Greatest Challenge

Back then gas was the best lighting source, but burning it was dirty and unhealthful. Gas could also be very dangerous. The idea of using electricity for lighting had been around for more than 50 years. But nobody had developed anything practical or safe.

Edison set out to solve this problem. He improved upon what others had learned about electricity. He tested thousands of ideas in a whirlwind of activity. Several men helped Edison with his experiments. By 1880 they had burned a light bulb

for more than 1,500 hours. They must have felt **dizzy** with excitement!

This was just the beginning. Edison's success led to the invention of an entire electric lighting system. That invention certainly **came in handy**! Many appliances and lights run on electricity **nowadays**. It is hard to imagine life without it. Next time you turn on your computer, think of Thomas Edison—and say "Thanks."

Edison with lamps he created

Reread for **Comprehension**

Generate Questions

Author's Perspective Authors have attitudes and opinions about the subjects they choose to write about. Asking questions about the way an author presents information about a subject can help you identify the author's perspective, or how the author feels about a subject. Use your Author's Perspective Map to find clues about the author's perspective.

Clue	Clue	Clue

↓ ↓ ↓

Author's Perspective

LOG ON ▶ LEARN IT Comprehension
www.macmillanmh.com

777

Vocabulary

TEACH WORDS

Introduce each word using the **Define/Example/Ask** routine. Model reading each word using the syllable-scoop technique.

Vocabulary Routine

Define: When a joke is **hilarious**, it makes you laugh a lot.
Example: We laughed at the hilarious antics of the pet monkey in the movie.
Ask: What is a synonym for *hilarious*?
SYNONYM

- **Mischief** is something amusing that may cause trouble. *My cat gets into mischief in my closet.* How can mischief cause trouble? EXPLANATION

- To gain **independence** is to gain freedom. *The American colonies won independence.* What is an antonym for *independence*? ANTONYM

- If something **came in handy**, it was useful to have nearby. *The extra batteries in my bag came in handy.* What are some everyday items that might come in handy? EXAMPLE

- Someone who feels **dizzy** finds it hard to keep his or her balance. *Angela felt dizzy when she got off the ride at the county fair.* Tell about a time when you felt dizzy. PRIOR KNOWLEDGE

- When something happens **nowadays**, it happens in the present time. *People use computers nowadays instead of typewriters.* How is life different nowadays from when your parents were your age? COMPARE AND CONTRAST

Preteach Vocabulary See pages 801BB and 801K to preteach the vocabulary words to **ELL** and Approaching Level students. Use the **Visual Vocabulary Resources** to demonstrate and discuss each word. To further reinforce concepts, have students complete page 346 in the **ELL Resource Book**.

HOMEWORK **Practice Book,** page 263

| hilarious | dizzy | nowadays |
| came in handy | mischief | independence |

Fill in the sentences below with words from the box. Then use the words in the blanks to complete the puzzle.

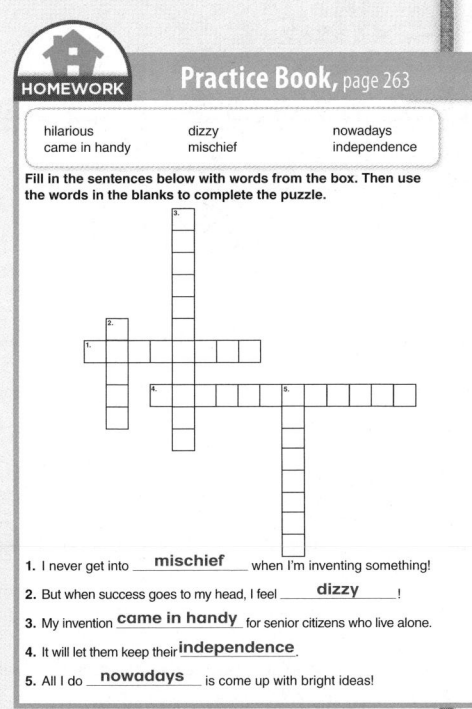

1. I never get into ___mischief___ when I'm inventing something!
2. But when success goes to my head, I feel ___dizzy___!
3. My invention ___came in handy___ for senior citizens who live alone.
4. It will let them keep their ___independence___
5. All I do ___nowadays___ is come up with bright ideas!

Approaching Reproducible, page 263
Beyond Reproducible, page 263

Objectives

- Generate questions
- Identify the author's perspective
- Use academic language: *generate, author's perspective*

Materials

- Transparencies 11, 30a, 30b
- Practice Book, p. 264

Skills Trace

Author's Perspective

Introduce	507A–507B
Practice/ Apply	508–527; Practice Book, 174–175
Reteach/ Review	531M–531Z; 777A–777B, 778–797, 801M–801Z; Practice Book, 264–265
Assess	Weekly Tests; Units 4, 6 Tests
Maintain	563B

ELL

Academic Language
Preteach the following academic language words to ELL and Approaching Level students during Small Group time: *generate questions, author's perspective.* See pages 801AA and 801I.

Reread for
Comprehension

STRATEGY
GENERATE QUESTIONS

What Is It? Explain that readers **generate questions** to help clarify information an author presents in a text. Readers can ask literal, interpretive, or evaluative questions such as *In what time period does the selection take place?* (literal), *What is the author's purpose?* (evaluative) and *Why is this information important?* (interpretive)

Why Is It Important? Generating questions is one way to become a critical reader. This strategy can produce answers that clarify misunderstandings, leading to a fuller comprehension of the text.

SKILL
AUTHOR'S PERSPECTIVE

What Is It? An **author's perspective** is his or her opinions about the subject matter of a selection, and how they are revealed in the text. Identifying an author's use of literary language in a biography can often help them recognize the author's perspective toward a subject.

Why Is It Important? Knowing how an author thinks about something can help readers make decisions about what to believe and what to check in another source.

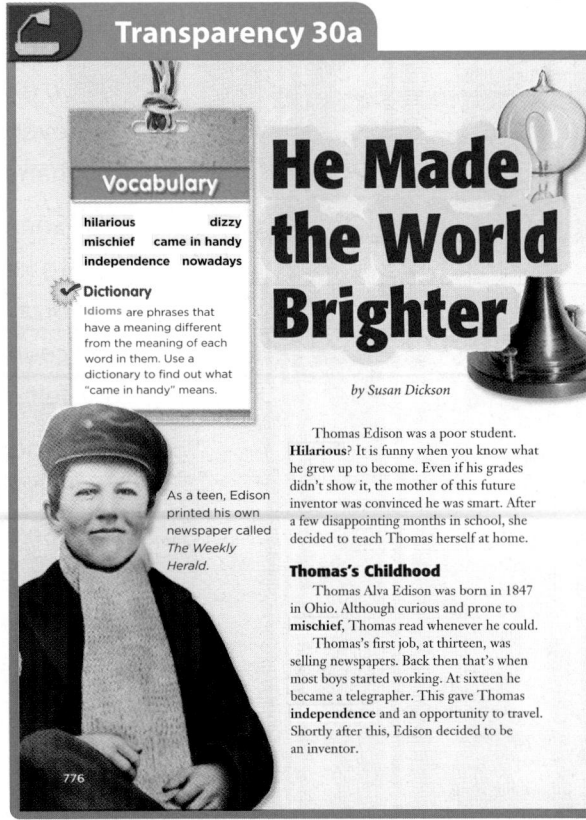

Transparency 30a

Vocabulary

hilarious	dizzy
mischief	came in handy
independence	nowadays

Dictionary
Idioms are phrases that have a meaning different from the meaning of each word in them. Use a dictionary to find out what "came in handy" means.

He Made the World Brighter

by Susan Dickson

As a teen, Edison printed his own newspaper called *The Weekly Herald.*

Thomas Edison was a poor student. **Hilarious**? It is funny when you know what he grew up to become. Even if his grades didn't show it, the mother of this future inventor was convinced he was smart. After a few disappointing months in school, she decided to teach Thomas herself at home.

Thomas's Childhood

Thomas Alva Edison was born in 1847 in Ohio. Although curious and prone to **mischief**, Thomas read whenever he could.

Thomas's first job, at thirteen, was selling newspapers. Back then that's when most boys started working. At sixteen he became a telegrapher. This gave Thomas **independence** and an opportunity to travel. Shortly after this, Edison decided to be an inventor.

776

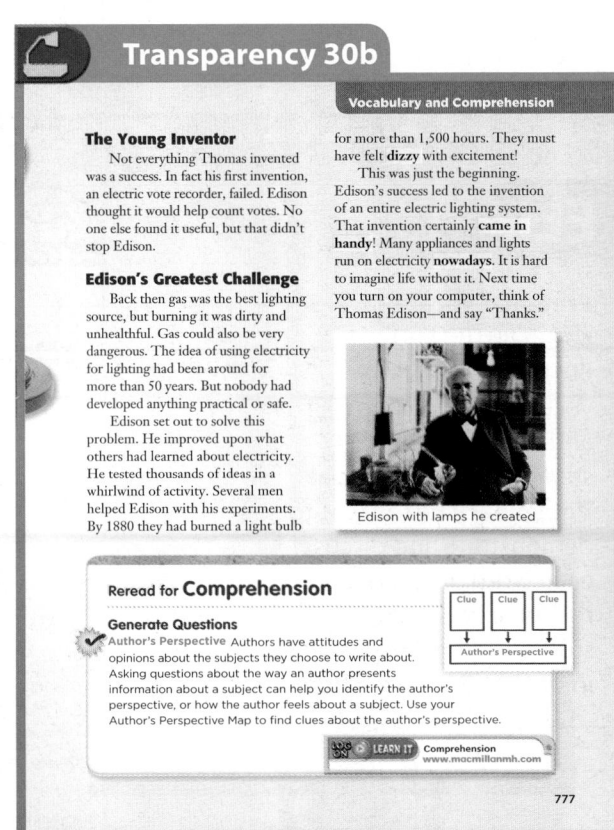

Transparency 30b

Vocabulary and Comprehension

The Young Inventor

Not everything Thomas invented was a success. In fact his first invention, an electric vote recorder, failed. Edison thought it would help count votes. No one else found it useful, but that didn't stop Edison.

Edison's Greatest Challenge

Back then gas was the best lighting source, but burning it was dirty and unhealthful. Gas could also be very dangerous. The idea of using electricity for lighting had been around for more than 50 years. But nobody had developed anything practical or safe.

Edison set out to solve this problem. He improved upon what others had learned about electricity. He tested thousands of ideas in a whirlwind of activity. Several men helped Edison with his experiments. By 1880 they had burned a light bulb

for more than 1,500 hours. They must have felt **dizzy** with excitement!

This was just the beginning. Edison's success led to the invention of an entire electric lighting system. That invention certainly **came in handy**! Many appliances and lights run on electricity **nowadays**. It is hard to imagine life without it. Next time you turn on your computer, think of Thomas Edison—and say "Thanks."

Edison with lamps he created

Reread for **Comprehension**

Generate Questions
Author's Perspective Authors have attitudes and opinions about the subjects they choose to write about. Asking questions about the way an author presents information about a subject can help you identify the author's perspective, or how the author feels about a subject. Use your Author's Perspective Map to find clues about the author's perspective.

Clue	Clue	Clue

Author's Perspective

LEARN IT Comprehension
www.macmillanmh.com

777

Student Book pages 776–777 available on Comprehension Transparencies 30a and 30b

- To identify the author's perspective, ask yourself, *What is the author's opinion of this? What clues in the selection reveal this opinion?* as you read. Then decide whether you agree or disagree.

- Think about techniques the author might use to convince you of something. For example, does the author use literary language or another literary device to influence readers' attitudes?

MODEL

How Do I Use It? Read the first two paragraphs of "He Made the World Brighter" on **Student Book** page 776.

Think Aloud In the first three paragraphs, the author says it is funny to think that Thomas Edison was a poor student, and that he was curious and prone to mischief. It seems that the author thinks Thomas Edison was a very smart person, and that his qualities of being curious and mischievous helped make him a great inventor. Is this the author's perspective on Edison? I will read on to find out.

GUIDED PRACTICE

- Have students read the first paragraph on page 777. Ask them what they learned about Edison's personality from this paragraph. (Edison did not give up.) Have them fill out the first Clue box in the Author's Perspective Map.

- Have students read "Edison's Greatest Challenge." Ask them what they learn about Edison, and the kind of worker he was, from the second paragraph. (He tested thousands of ideas. This shows that he was a very hard worker.) Have them fill out the second Clue box in the Author's Perspective Map.

- Help students identify Edison's major accomplishment. (Edison developed a safe way to use electricity for lighting, changing the way people live.) Have them record this idea in the remaining Clue box.

APPLY

Using the clues they have written on their charts, help students determine the author's perspective and include this information on the Author's Perspective Map.

Quick Check

Can students determine the author's perspective in a selection?

During **Small Group Instruction**

Tier 2

If No → **Approaching Level** Reteach the skill using the Comprehension lesson, pp. 801M–801P.

If Yes → **On Level** Consolidate the learning using pp. 801U–801V.

Beyond Level Extend the learning using pp. 801Y–801Z.

Transparency 9

Clue	Clue	Clue
Thomas Edison did not give up.	He tested thousands of ideas; he was a very hard worker.	Edison developed a safe way to use electricity for lighting, changing the way people live.

Author's Perspective
Edison, a hard working scientist who never gave up, helped develop a safe electrical lighting system, which changed the way people live.

Graphic Organizer Transparency

HOMEWORK

Practice Book, page 264

An **author's perspective** is his or her point of view. It may include the author's attitudes and opinions about a subject. The words *best, worst, should,* and *ought to* are often used to signal the author's opinion.

Read the passage. Then answer the questions that follow.

The Paralympic Games are great because they offer athletes with a disability the chance to compete on a world stage. In 1948, a sports competition was held for World War II veterans with spinal cord injuries. In 1960, after the Olympics in Rome, the first official Paralympic Summer Games took place. The first Paralympic Winter Games were played in 1976, and in that year, the competition was opened to athletes with disabilities other than spinal cord injuries.

Today, athletes who are visually impaired or blind, have amputated limbs, spinal cord injuries, or motor impairment due to stroke, brain injury, or cerebral palsy can enter the Paralympics. Furthermore, athletes are grouped by ability, not by medical classification.

1. Does the author of this passage have a strongly expressed point of view about the Paralympic Games? **yes**

2. Can you infer anything about the author's perspective from the passage? **I can infer that the author thinks the Paralympics Games are important.**

3. What word from the passage signals that the author is expressing an opinion? **great**

4. What type of information could the author add to the passage to express a clearer perspective on the Paralympic Games? **He or she could add a story about an athlete with a disability who the author admires.**

Approaching Reproducible, page 264
Beyond Reproducible, page 264

Read

WHOLE GROUP

✓ **MAIN SELECTION**
- *How Ben Franklin Stole the Lightning*
- Skill: Author's Perspective

✓ **PAIRED SELECTION**
- Literary Text/Poetry: "Light Bulb" and "Lightning Bolt"
- Literary Elements: Figurative Language and Alliteration

SMALL GROUP

- Differentiated Instruction, pp. 801I–801HH

Main Selection

GENRE: Literary Nonfiction/Biography

Have a student read the definition of Biography on **Student Book** page 778. As they read, students should look for real people and historical events.

STRATEGY
GENERATE QUESTIONS

Asking questions as they read will help students to check their understanding and focus on important ideas in the text. They should ask literal, interpretive, and evaluative questions.

SKILL
AUTHOR'S PERSPECTIVE

An author's perspective is how he or she feels about a subject. In a biography, students should look for any literary language or devices an author uses, as well as how the author presents major events in the person's life, to determine the author's perspective.

Comprehension

Genre

A **Biography** is a story about the life of a real person written by someone else.

Generate Questions

Author's Perspective
As you read, fill in your Author's Perspective Map.

Clue	Clue	Clue

→ **Author's Perspective**

Read to Find Out

What does the author think Ben Franklin's greatest achievement is?

778

Vocabulary

Vocabulary Words Review the tested vocabulary words while reading: **hilarious, mischief, independence, dizzy, nowadays, came in handy.**

Additional Selection Words Students may be unfamiliar with these words. Pronounce the words, give student-friendly explanations as needed, and help students use the previously taught vocabulary strategies: context clues, word parts, dictionary.

eclipse (p. 782): a shadow that moves across the sun or the moon

odometer (p. 785): a meter that tells how far a vehicle has traveled

scurvy (p. 787): a disease that causes weakness, joint pain, and dental problems

tyrants (p. 795): cruel or unfair rulers

Main Selection

Award Winning Author and Illustrator

How **BEN FRANKLIN** STOLE THE **LIGHTNING**

ROSALYN SCHANZER

779

Read the Main Selection

Preteach	Read Together	Read Independently
Have Approaching Level students and English Language Learners listen to the selection on **StudentWorks Plus**, the interactive e-Book, before reading with the class.	Use the prompts to guide comprehension and model how to complete the graphic organizer. Have students use **Think/Pair/Share** to discuss the selection.	If students can read the selection independently, have them read and complete the graphic organizer. Suggest that they use their purposes to choose their reading strategies.

StudentWorks Plus
Interactive Student Book

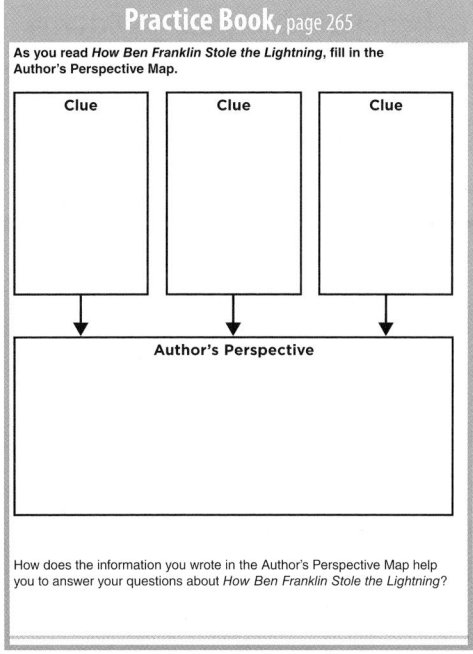

Preview and Predict

QUICK WRITE Ask students to read the title, preview the illustrations, and think about the genre. Students may also include what they already know about inventors and inventions.

Set Purposes

FOCUS QUESTION Discuss the "Read to Find Out" question on **Student Book** page 778. Remind students to look for the answer as they read. Point out the Author's Perspective Map in the Student Book and on **Practice Book** page 265. Explain that students will fill it in as they read.

Read *How Ben Franklin Stole the Lightning*

Use the questions and Think Alouds to support instruction for the comprehension strategy and skill.

Practice Book, page 265

As you read *How Ben Franklin Stole the Lightning*, fill in the Author's Perspective Map.

Clue	Clue	Clue

↓ ↓ ↓

Author's Perspective

How does the information you wrote in the Author's Perspective Map help you to answer your questions about *How Ben Franklin Stole the Lightning*?

Approaching Reproducible, page 265
Beyond Reproducible, page 265

Develop Comprehension

1 STRATEGY
GENERATE QUESTIONS

Teacher Think Aloud When I look at the illustration, I see a man with glasses and white hair engaging in many different activities. This must be Ben Franklin. I can ask **questions** before reading the selection. *How many activities is Ben Franklin taking part in?* He is shown writing, playing music, selling things, riding a horse, giving a speech, and so on. *Why does the drawing show Ben Franklin participating in all these different activities?* I think the selection will likely describe Ben Franklin as a man who did many different things.

2 AUTHOR'S CRAFT: A STRONG OPENING

Why do you think the author chose to begin this biography with the statement "It's true!"? (It grabs the reader's attention, making the reader curious about what comes next. It shows that what comes next will be based on facts.)

3 FACT AND OPINION

Identify two **facts** in the third paragraph. How can you determine that the information is a fact? (The information in the last two sentences can be checked in a reference book and is therefore factual.) What statements of **opinion** can you find in the paragraph? (The statements that Franklin could swim faster, argue better, and write funnier stories than other people.)

780

Monitor Comprehension

Monitor and Clarify: *Adjust Reading Rate*

Explain Tell students to adjust their reading rate depending upon what they are reading. If the text has a lot of facts, is difficult to understand, or has challenging vocabulary, they should read more slowly.

Discuss Model how to adjust your reading rate by rereading the second full paragraph on page 781 more slowly. Discuss how the slower rate helps you read, understand, and remember Ben Franklin's accomplishments. Then have students adjust their rate as they reread the paragraph.

Apply As they read the selection, have students adjust their rate to help them understand what they read.

t's true!

The great Benjamin Franklin really did steal lightning right out of the sky! And then he set out to tame the beast. It goes to figure, though, because he was a man who could do just about anything.

2

Why, Ben Franklin could swim faster, argue better, and write funnier stories than practically anyone in colonial America. He was a musician, a printer, a cartoonist, and a world traveler! What's more, he was a newspaper owner, a shopkeeper, a soldier, and a politician. He even helped to write the Declaration of **Independence** and the Constitution of the United States!

3

Ben was always coming up with newfangled ways to help folks out, too. He was the guy who started the first lending library in America. His post office was the first to deliver mail straight to people's houses.

4

781

Develop Comprehension

4 SKILL
AUTHOR'S PERSPECTIVE

What does the author want to share with readers about Benjamin Franklin? (She wants readers to know what a talented man Benjamin Franklin was. She says he could do just about anything, and gives examples of his accomplishments.) **What is interesting about the information the author provides in the second paragraph?** (It is basically just a paragraph of lists, explaining what Ben Franklin accomplished.) **Why did the author choose to write the paragraph this way?** (to stress that Ben Franklin had many interests and accomplished many things)

Phonics/Word Study

APPLY DECODING SKILLS While reading, point out words with the sound/spelling patterns, syllable types, and word parts students have recently learned. Help students blend these words. You may wish to focus on selection words with prefixes and suffixes, such as *politician, printer, practically,* and *inventions.*

ELL ENGLISH LANGUAGE LEARNERS

Beginning	**Intermediate**	**Advanced**
Access Content Preteach story content, build language, and develop meaning using the Interactive Question-Response Guide in the **ELL Resource Book**, pages 334–343. They may point or use short phrases to respond. Give ample time for students to respond.	**Describe** Preteach story content, build language , and develop meaning using the Interactive Question-Response Guide in the ELL Resource Book, pages 334–343. Have them respond in complete sentences. Correct the meaning of students' responses as needed.	**Explain** Complete the Intermediate task with students. Elicit details to support students' responses.

Develop Comprehension

5 AUTHOR'S PURPOSE

What was the **author's purpose** for indenting and placing spaces between each of the last three lines on page 782? (Each line ends with an exclamation point, so it shows that she is amazed by all the special things that Ben Franklin did. It is as if she is taking a breath between each one, because each of these things was so important.)

He also wrote almanacs that gave **hilarious** advice about life and told people when to plant crops, whether there might be an eclipse, and when the tides would be high or low.

5 And he helped to start a hospital!

A free academy!

A fire department!

782

Comprehension/Writing

Print Materials: *Almanacs*

Explain Tell students that the title of the almanac that Ben Franklin wrote was *Poor Richard's Almanac*. He published it annually, and it proved to be very popular.

Discuss Gather one or more almanacs to show students. Point out the various features of the almanac. Ask: *What features of this almanac might also have been in Franklin's almanacs?* (Possible answers: calendar, weather reports, astronomical information)

Apply Gather several newspapers and magazines for students to examine. Have them compare and contrast how these print materials are organized with the organization of almanacs. Review how to use the materials for research.

In colonial days, fire could break out at any time. And it was lightning that caused some of the worst fires. Whenever thunderstorms were brewing, they would ring the church bells for all they were worth, but it didn't do anybody a lick of good.

6

Of course, after Ben stole the lightning, there weren't nearly as many fires for firefighters to put out. "Now, why was that?" I hear you ask. "And how did he steal any lightning in the first place?" Well, it's a long story, but before we get to the answer, here's a hint. One of the things Benjamin Franklin liked to do best was to make inventions.

 **Author's Perspective**
What clues reveal how the author feels about Ben so far?

7

783

Comprehension

Literary Devices: *Imagery*

Explain When an author uses descriptive words and phrases to create vivid pictures or images in the reader's mind, he or she is making use of imagery.

Discuss Ask students to describe the pictures they see in their minds when they read the phrase *thunderstorms were brewing*. (clouds swirling around, wind blowing, sky getting darker)

Apply As they read the story, students should make note of other uses of imagery and figurative language. Encourage them to think about the author's purpose for using particular images, and how the author of a biography uses literary devices, such as imagery, to present major events in a person's life.

Develop Comprehension

6 **STRATEGY**
DICTIONARY

 One familiar example of an **idiom** is *hold your horses*, which means "slow down" or "be patient," not "hang on to actual horses." What do you think the idiom *for all they were worth* means? (with all the strength and energy they had)

7 **SKILL**
AUTHOR'S PERSPECTIVE

Think about the author's opinion of Ben Franklin, based on what you have read. What clues reveal how the author feels about Ben so far? (She wants readers to know what a talented man Benjamin Franklin was. She talks about his many different accomplishments.) Add this information to your Author's Perspective Map.

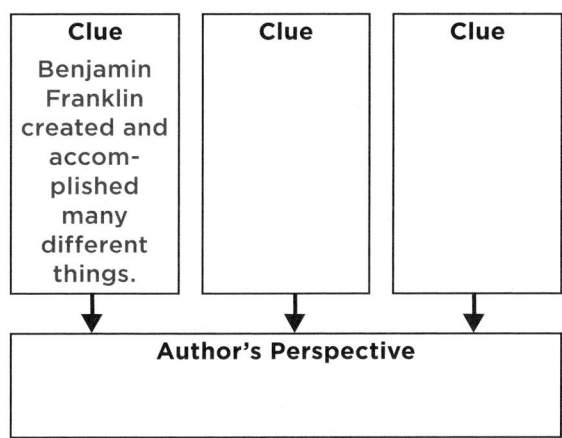

Clue	Clue	Clue
Benjamin Franklin created and accomplished many different things.		

Author's Perspective

Develop Comprehension

8 SKILL
AUTHOR'S PERSPECTIVE

What clues on this page reveal the **author's perspective** toward Ben Franklin? (The author describes Ben Franklin as a "born inventor" and that he "kept right on inventing better ways to do things the rest of his life.") Add this information to your Chart.

Clue	Clue	Clue
Benjamin Franklin created and accomplished many different things.	Ben Franklin made inventions to solve problems.	

↓ ↓ ↓

Author's Perspective

9 STRATEGY
DICTIONARY

How do context clues help you find the meaning of the **idiom** *lickety-split*? (The author talks about Ben wanting to swim faster, and says his next invention was a better way to go fast. *Lickety-split* means "very fast.")

10 MAKE PREDICTIONS

Based on what you have read so far, what **predictions** can you make about how Ben might use a kite later on? (He might use it to solve another problem. The title says he stole lightning and we see a picture of a kite. Maybe he will use a kite to "steal" lightning.)

8 Why, Ben was a born inventor. He loved to swim fast, but he wanted to go even faster. So one day when he was a mere lad of eleven, he got some wood and invented swim paddles for his hands and swim fins for his feet. Ben could go faster, all right, but the wood was pretty heavy, and his wrists got plumb worn out.

That's why his second invention was a better way to go fast. He lay on his back, held on to a kite string, **9** and let his kite pull him lickety-split across a big pond. (You might want to remember later on that Ben always **10** did like kites.)

Ben kept right on inventing better ways to do things for the rest of his life.

784

Text Evidence

Author's Perspective

Reread question 8 aloud to students. Then ask them where they would look to find clues that reveal the author's perspective, or how she feels, about Ben Franklin. (Words in the text that describe Franklin and his accomplishments.) If necessary, remind students that descriptive words and phrases can help readers find the author's perspective. Then ask, *What words in the text reveal the author's perspective? Point to them on the page.* (On page 784, the author writes that Franklin was "a born inventor," that his second invention was "a better way to go fast" in the water, and that he "kept right on inventing better ways to do things.") *What do these clues tell you about the author's perspective toward Ben Franklin and his accomplishments?* (The author reveals that she thinks Ben Franklin was a clever and resourceful inventor.)

Take books, for example. Ben read so many books that some of them sat on shelves way up high near the ceiling. So he invented the library chair. If he pulled up the seat, out popped some stairs to help him reach any books on high shelves. And in case climbing stairs made him **dizzy**, he invented a long wooden arm that could grab his books, too.

He also invented an odometer that told how far he had ridden to deliver the mail. And the first clock with a second hand. And he even thought up daylight saving time. Then he invented bifocals so older folks could see up close and far away without changing glasses.

785

Develop Comprehension

 MONITOR AND CLARIFY: ADJUST READING RATE

When there is a lot of factual information, as there is in the text on this page, **adjusting reading rate** helps readers understand and remember information. How might you adjust your reading rate to help you read page 785? (read more slowly) What is an odometer? (an invention that measures distance traveled) How does adjusting your reading rate help you understand what an odometer does? (Reading more slowly helps readers pay closer attention to the details about Ben's inventions, including the odometer. Although the author doesn't state specifically what it is, she does state that it told how far Ben had ridden, so it must be a device used to measure distances.)

Develop Comprehension

12 STRATEGY
DICTIONARY

What does the **idiom** *everybody and his brother and sister* mean? (It is a dramatic way of saying that everyone you can think of needed heat in winter.)

13 DRAW CONCLUSIONS

SPIRAL REVIEW

What **conclusions** can you draw about the glass armonica? (The author writes that people from all over Europe and America loved the glass armonica, which probably means that they also bought and owned their own armonicas. Even famous composers, such as Mozart and Beethoven, thought the armonica was a beautiful instrument, which is why they wrote music specifically for it. I can conclude that the armonica was a very popular and well-respected instrument. It was a very successful invention.)

14 COMPARE AND CONTRAST

Compare and contrast the invention of the Franklin stove and the glass armonica. Explain how they were similar and how they were different. (They were similar because both inventions were very clever and were devices many people were interested in using. They were different because while the stove was a necessity, providing warmth for people in cold weather, the glass armonica was used purely for enjoyment.)

12   Everybody and his brother and sister just had to find better ways to heat their houses in wintertime. So Ben came up with a Franklin stove that could warm up cold rooms faster and use a lot less wood than old-fashioned stoves and fireplaces.

   People all over Europe and America loved Ben's glass armonica. This instrument could spin wet glass bowls to make music that sounded like it came straight from **13** heaven. Mozart and Beethoven wrote music for it, and it was even played at a royal Italian wedding.

14   But as popular as warmer stoves and glass armonicas were, they aren't anywhere near as celebrated **nowadays** as the invention Ben made after he stole the lightning.

786

Comprehension

Procedural Text: *Following Directions*

Explain Remind students that procedural texts explain how to do something. Examples may include a cake recipe, instructions on building a model car, playing a game, or doing an experiment.

Discuss Write step-by-step directions for a simple activity, such as making a sandwich. Ask: *What are some important things to pay attention to as you read the directions?* (example: what materials you need; the sequence of events) *Why is it important to perform a science experiment according to the directions?* (If you do not, it may not work and could be dangerous.)

Apply Help students find directions for a simple experiment. Ask them to follow the directions and perform the experiment. Have them discuss their results with the class, sharing knowledge they have gained about following instructions.

Another hint about Ben's most famous invention is that it helped make life easier for everyone. His scientific ideas were helpful, too, and were often way ahead of their time. For example, he had a lot of ideas about health. He said that exercise and weight lifting help keep folks fit, but they have to work hard enough to sweat if they want to do any good.

He wrote that breathing fresh air and drinking lots of water are good for you. He was the guy who said "an apple a day keeps the doctor away."

And before anyone ever heard of vitamin C, he wrote that oranges, limes, and grapefruit give people healthy gums and skin. Sailors soon got wind of this idea. They began eating so many limes to stop getting sick from scurvy at sea that they became known as limeys.

787

Develop Comprehension

15 STRATEGY
GENERATE QUESTIONS

Teacher Think Aloud As I read, I **generate questions**. How did Ben come up with his ideas about health? He may have observed people's lifestyles and eating habits, and his body's own reactions. What does the author mean when she writes that Ben Franklin was "ahead of his time"? He figured things out before the rest of the world did. What other questions can you generate here?

Prompt students to apply the strategy in a Think Aloud.

Student Think Aloud How did Ben keep track of all the information he learned? What would he do with that information? He could compare it to new information as he learned it. He might compare and contrast what he learned to come up with new ideas for inventions.

16 SELF-SELECTED STRATEGY USE

What strategies have you used so far to help you? Where did you use them? Why? How did they help?

 **RETURN TO PREDICTIONS AND PURPOSES**

Have students respond to the selection by confirming or revising their predictions and purposes for reading. Have them revise or write additional questions to focus their attention.

Stop here if you wish to read this selection over two days.  STOP

Extra Support

Author's Perspective

If students are having difficulty, remind them that the author's perspective is his or her opinions and how they are revealed in the text. When the author describes Ben's inventions and scientific ideas as "helpful," and expresses the opinion that they were often way ahead of their time and helped make life easier for everyone, these opinions reflect the author's perspective. Have students reread the last paragraph on page 784. Then ask, *Is this statement a fact or the author's opinion?* (Opinion) *How does it reflect the author's perspective?* (The author feels that Ben was a great inventor, because she maintains he went on inventing better ways to do things for the rest of his life.)

Develop Comprehension

17 **GENRE:** Literary Text/Biography

A **biography** identifies the character traits of its subject. What did you find out about Ben Franklin when you read that he chased a "whirlwind," or a tornado, to find out how it works? (He was willing to put himself in danger in order to learn new things.) What makes a biography different from an autobiography? (An autobiography is written by the subject. A biography is written by someone else.)

Didn't the man ever stop to rest? Even when he was outside, Ben kept right on experimenting.

For instance, he often sailed to England and France to do business for America. As he crossed the Atlantic Ocean, he charted the Gulf Stream by taking its temperature. Once sailors knew the route of this fast, warm "river" in the cold ocean, they could travel between America and Europe in a shorter time than ever before.

He was probably the first person to write weather forecasts, too. Once he chased a roaring whirlwind by riding over the hills and forests of Maryland just to find out how it worked.

Ben had an old scientific trick that he liked to show people every chance he got. He used to store some oil inside a bamboo walking stick, and whenever he poured a few drops onto angry waves in a pond or lake, the water became smooth as glass!

17

788

Comprehension

Genres: *Biography, Autobiography, and Fiction*

Explain Remind students that biographies and autobiographies present the true stories of people's lives. Fictional stories may be based on real people and events, but the stories include made-up elements.

Discuss Writers often base their stories on real-life people and events, sometimes from their own lives. Discuss how students might use a real-life incident from their own lives as the basis of a fictional narrative.

Apply Have students research the life of a favorite fiction author and identify how the characters and events connect to that person's life. For example, students can compare and contrast the life of Laura Ingalls Wilder with events in the *Little House* books or connect the people and events that Betsy Byars describes in *The Moon and I* with characters and events from her fiction.

Meanwhile, over in Europe, people called "electricians" had started doing some tricks of their own. One trick was to raise a boy up near the ceiling with a bunch of silk cords, rub his feet with a glass "electric tube," and make sparks shoot out of his hands and face.

Another mean trick made the king of France laugh so hard he could hardly stop. His court electrician had run an electric charge through 180 soldiers of the guard, and they jerked to attention faster than they ever had in their entire lives.

But although people were doing lots of tricks with electricity, nobody had a clue about why or how it worked. So Benjamin Franklin decided to find out. He asked a British friend to send him an electric tube so that he could do some experiments.

In one experiment, he made a cork "electric spider" with thread for legs. It kept leaping back and forth between a wire and an electric tube just like it was alive.

Another time he asked a lady and gentleman to stand on some wax. One held an electric tube, the other held a wire, and when they tried to kiss, they got shocked by all the sparks shooting between their lips.

Ben even figured out how to light up a picture of a king in a golden frame. Anyone trying to remove the king's gold paper crown was in for a shock!

18 **19**

Develop Comprehension

18 SUMMARIZE

How would you **summarize** the kinds of tricks with electricity that are described on page 789? (Most made use of an "electric tube," and many involved someone getting shocked.)

19 DRAW CONCLUSIONS

 SPIRAL REVIEW

What **conclusions** can you draw about the work of early European "electricians"? Do you think they were aware of how important the discovery of electricity was? Use evidence from the text to draw your conclusion. (The European "electricians" did entertaining tricks with certain properties of electricity, like making a boy rise to the ceiling or forcing soldiers to stand at attention. But they did not have any ideas about how or why it worked, and did not seem interested in finding out. They seem unaware that electricity might be put to better use.)

 Social Studies

Connect to Content

INVENTORS

Tell students that many inventors and scientists have made discoveries and inventions that help people in many different ways. Have students identify famous inventors or scientists from their state.

Ask students to choose one of these people to research, and write a short biography of the person, including facts about his or her life, and information about what the person discovered or invented.

Develop Comprehension

20 PROBLEM AND SOLUTION

What steps did Ben Franklin take to begin **solving** the **problem** of fires caused by lightning? (He had the idea that lightning was electricity, so he decided to study it. He made a kite with a wire on top to attract lightning during a storm. He wanted to prove that lightning was electricity.)

Doing all these tricks gave Ben his idea for stealing lightning out of the sky. He believed that lightning was nothing more nor less than pure electricity. Now he set out to prove it.

First he made a silk kite with a wire on top to attract some lightning. Next he added a kite string, tied a key to the bottom, and knotted a silk ribbon below the key. Ben and his son William stood out of the rain inside the doorway of a shed on the side of a field. To keep from getting shocked, Ben held on to the dry silk ribbon. **20** Then he flew his kite straight up toward a big rain cloud.

790

Vocabulary

Dictionary: *Multiple-Meaning Words*

Explain/Model Explain that some words have more than one meaning. Tell students that they can determine the correct meaning of a multiple-meaning word by using context clues and/or a dictionary.

Think Aloud: I see the word *shed* in the second paragraph on page 790. I know that *shed* can be used as a noun or a verb. I read the sentence and find that it is being used as a noun here. I will use a dictionary to make sure I have the correct meaning. The meaning for *shed* that fits here is "a small structure for storage."

Practice/Apply Have students find *shocked* on page 790. Have them use context clues to try to determine the meaning. If they cannot figure out what it means, prompt them to use a dictionary. In this instance, *shocked* means "subjected to an electrical current."

For the longest time, nothing happened.

Just as Ben and William were about to give up, the hair on that wet kite string began to rise up and stand at attention. Ben put his knuckle near the key, and YIKES!!!! Out jumped a bright spark of genuine electricity!

Real lightning had traveled all the way down that kite string! Ben had stolen electric fire out of the heavens and proven that he was right.

21

(Of course, now we know that if the storm had been any stronger, the great inventor would have been toast.)

22

791

Develop Comprehension

21 SKILL
AUTHOR'S PERSPECTIVE

 The author says that "Ben had stolen electric fire out of the heavens." Is this a statement of scientific fact? Explain. (No. It is not to be taken literally. He did not really steal it. He gave the electricity a path to follow. Also, electricity is not fire, though it can cause a fire.) Why do you think the author uses this **image**? (It makes us realize the importance of this discovery, and how truly amazing it was.)

22 STRATEGY
DICTIONARY

 In the last sentence on page 791, what does the author mean when she uses the **idiom** "the great inventor would have been toast"? (He would have been killed by a more powerful bolt of lightning.) Why is this expression an idiom? (Franklin would not actually have been turned into toast.)

Develop Comprehension

23 | **STRATEGY**
DICTIONARY

What does the author mean by the **idiom** she includes in the phrase "Ben's practice from thinking up all those inventions *came in so handy*"? (Franklin remembered all the information he had learned in the past and was able to use it later.)

23

Finally! Here's the part of the story where Ben's practice from thinking up all those inventions **came in** so **handy**. Way back then, you remember, lightning was always setting fire to ships, houses, and church spires. Even the best fire departments couldn't keep entire towns from going up in smoke. So Ben decided to make his most famous invention of all—the lightning rod!

792

The whole idea was to pull lightning safely out of the sky before it could do any **mischief**. Ben showed people how to put a pointed iron rod on the tip-top of a roof or ship's mast and connect it to a wire leading all the way down under the ground or into water. Now the lightning could follow a safe path without burning up a thing.

> **Author's Perspective**
> Explain how the author feels about Ben's invention of the lightning rod.
>
> **24**

793

Develop Comprehension

24 SKILL
AUTHOR'S PERSPECTIVE

 Explain how the author feels about Ben's invention of the lightning rod. (She says the lightning rod is Ben's most famous invention. Like many of his other inventions, it solved a problem. It prevented lightning from setting buildings on fire. I can infer from this that the author thinks the lightning rod saved many lives.) Add this information to your Author's Perspective Map.

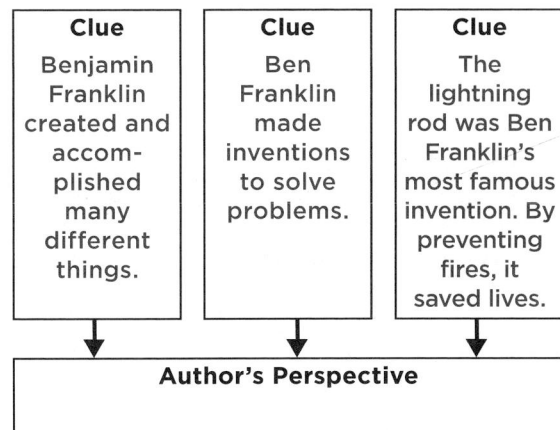

Clue	**Clue**	**Clue**
Benjamin Franklin created and accomplished many different things.	Ben Franklin made inventions to solve problems.	The lightning rod was Ben Franklin's most famous invention. By preventing fires, it saved lives.

Author's Perspective

ELL ENGLISH LANGUAGE LEARNERS

STRATEGIES FOR EXTRA SUPPORT

QUESTION 24 AUTHOR'S PERSPECTIVE

Help students clarify their understanding by retelling in their own words how the lightning rod helped people. Ask: *What was the problem with lightning?* (It struck buildings and set them on fire.) *What did Ben Franklin learn about lightning in his experiment with the kite?* (He learned that it is electricity and that he could attract it.) *Where does the lightning rod send the electricity it attracts?* (into the ground or water) *Why is this better?* (The lightning won't set buildings on fire or put people in danger.)

Develop Comprehension

25 STRATEGY
GENERATE QUESTIONS

 **Generate questions** to help you describe Ben Franklin's qualities.

Student Think Aloud What do we learn from Ben's electricity experiment? He used what he learned from his experiments to invent a lightning rod. Why does this make him special? It shows he was not only smart, but able to work at a problem until he found a solution. What else does it show about the kind of person he was? He wanted to help people and improve their lives.

26 SKILL
AUTHOR'S PERSPECTIVE

 What is the **author's perspective** on Ben Franklin? (He could do almost anything. He worked hard, and through his experiments, came up with many solutions to problems that people had at the time. With his lightning rod, he saved countless lives. He also helped make America a free nation. Ben Franklin made great contributions to the world.) Add this to your Author's Perspective Map.

Clue	Clue	Clue
Benjamin Franklin created and accomplished many different things.	Ben Franklin made inventions to solve problems.	The lightning rod was Ben Franklin's most famous invention. By preventing fires, it saved lives.

↓ ↓ ↓

Author's Perspective
The author admires Ben Franklin for his many contributions to the world.

This simple but brilliant invention worked beautifully. It saved more lives than anyone can count and made Ben Franklin a great hero.

Scientists from around the world lined up to give Ben medals and awards. But during his long life, he became much more than the master of lightning. Why, when America fought against Great Britain for the right to become a free nation, Ben convinced France to come help win the war, and when it was over, he helped convince Great Britain to sign the peace. He had helped in so many ways that the people of France honored him with a beautiful medallion. It says "He snatched the lightning from heaven and the scepter from tyrants."

And he did. **26**

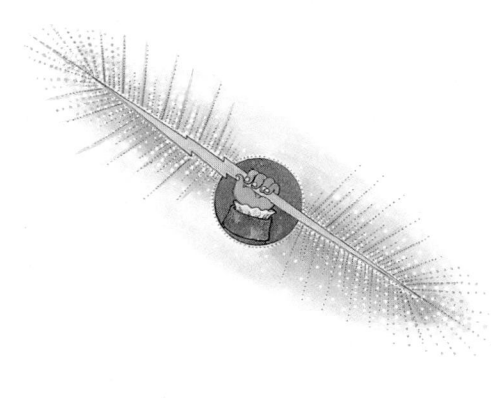

795

Quick Check

Can students identify the author's perspective?

During **Small Group Instruction**

If No → **Approaching Level** Reteach the skill and have students apply it to a simpler text. Use Leveled Reader lessons, pp. 801N–801P.

If Yes → **On Level** Have students apply the skill to a new text to consolidate learning. Use Leveled Reader lessons, pp. 801U–801V.

 Beyond Level Have students apply the skill to a more complex text to extend learning. Use Leveled Reader lessons, pp. 801Y–801Z.

Develop Comprehension

RETURN TO PREDICTIONS AND PURPOSES

Review students' predictions and purposes for reading. Did they find out who Ben Franklin was? (a curious person who invented things to help people.)

REVIEW READING STRATEGIES

- **Generate Questions** In what ways did generating different types of questions help you to understand the selection?

- **Monitor and Clarify: Adjust Reading Rate** Do you understand the strategy of adjusting your reading rate? When might you use it again?

- **Decoding** What difficult words did you encounter? How did the Reading Multisyllabic Words strategy help you sound out these words?

- **Self-Selected Strategy Use** What strategies did you use to make sense of what you read? Where? How were these strategies helpful?

RESPONSE TO LITERATURE

Have students write about a problem they solved, explaining what their solution was. Ask them to compare their solution to one of Ben Franklin's solutions.

Remind them to use correct grammar and spelling.

Author and Illustrator

MEET THE INVENTOR

Have students read the biography of the author and illustrator. Ask:

- Why did Rosalyn Schanzer think that going to Philadelphia would help her accuracy in this story?

- How does Rosalyn Schanzer show the personality of Ben Franklin in her drawings?

WRITE ABOUT IT

Author's Craft: Idioms

Have students brainstorm ideas for inventions they would like to see. Then ask them to write a descriptive paragraph about an original invention. They should include at least one idiom in their description.

Author's Purpose

Have students skim the selection to find clues about why Rosalyn Schanzer chose to focus on Franklin's inventions. Point out Franklin's life was so rich and diverse that she could have chosen several other focuses.

MEET THE INVENTOR

ROSALYN SCHANZER spent a lot of time in Philadelphia to write this piece. She visited the places where Ben Franklin lived and worked to make sure that her words and pictures would be accurate. Rosalyn probably would have gotten along really well with Ben. She is a great swimmer, just like he was. Once she even swam past sharks on a trip to Belize! Rosalyn also shares Ben's curiosity about the world. She's explored a jungle, visited an ancient city, and sailed a boat more than 800 miles.

Other books by Rosalyn Schanzer

Author Rosalyn Schanzer
www.macmillanmh.com

 Author's Purpose

Why did the author choose to focus on Benjamin Franklin's inventions? Use evidence from the text to support your answer.

796

 Author's Craft

Idioms

Rosalyn Schanzer plays with language. One literary device that she uses is idioms, or expressions that are not intended to be taken literally.

- For example: "It goes to figure, though, because he was a man who could do just about anything." (p. 781) *It goes to figure* means "it's not surprising." It is a playful way of saying this idea.

- Have students find and discuss other idioms in the story, such as "got wind of this idea" (p. 787) and "a lick of good." (p. 783)

- Ask students how idioms help make the story sound humorous and informal while providing factual information.

✔ Comprehension Check

Summarize

To summarize *How Ben Franklin Stole the Lightning* use the most important details from the selection. Information from your Author's Perspective Map may help you.

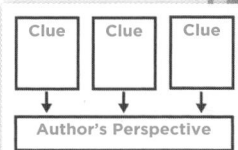

Think and Compare

1. What did Ben Franklin invent when he was eleven? Details

2. The text structure the author uses to present information on pages 790–791 is sequence. Is this text structure stated or implied? Explain using details from the selection to support your answer. Sequence

3. What do Ben Franklin's inventions tell about him? Use evidence from the text to explain your answer. Make Inferences

4. Why does the author believe that Ben Franklin was much more than an inventor, or "master of lightning"? Explain using details from the selection. Generate Questions: Author's Perspective

5. Read "He Made the World Brighter" on pages 776–777. How was Thomas Alva Edison like Ben Franklin? Use evidence from both selections to explain your answer. Reading/Writing Across Texts

797

Make Connections

Text-to-Self Have students respond to the following question to make connections to their own lives. Use the Think Aloud to model a response. *If you could improve on any of the inventions mentioned in the story, what would you do and why?*

Think Aloud: Ben Franklin created many inventions that helped people. His library chair was a chair that turned into a step stool to help people reach books on high shelves. I would make the library chair foldable, so it could be stored easily.

Text-to-World Have students respond to the following question to make connections to the world. *Do you think someone like Ben Franklin is ever bored?*

Think Aloud: Ben Franklin was constantly thinking up new ideas and inventions. He was always busy. I think that someone like Ben Franklin would be too busy to be bored.

Read
Respond

 ## Comprehension Check

SUMMARIZE

 Have partners summarize *How Ben Franklin Stole the Lightning* in their own words. Remind students to use their Author's Perspective Map to help them think about the biography.

THINK AND COMPARE
Text Evidence

1. **Details** Answer stated in text He invented swim paddles for his hands and swim fins for his feet. LOCATE

2. **Sequence** Answer stated in text It is stated, since the text uses signal words, such as *first, next,* and *then.* The text says: "First he made a silk kite . . . " and "Next he added a kite string . . ." COMBINE

3. **Make Inferences** Answer He enjoyed making people's lives easier and was a problem solver. Evidence The text tells how Ben was always devising ways to help people. It lists his many inventions and projects, which helped people in different ways, and solved problems. CONNECT

4. **Generate Questions: Author's Perspective** Answer She believes that because he accomplished so much in his life. Evidence He did many different things, from starting the first library and inventing the lightning rod, to helping establish the United States of America. ANALYZE

 5. **Text-to-Text** Both men were curious and hardworking inventors. Their most important discoveries had to do with electricity. Franklin made electricity in the form of lightning less dangerous. Edison used electricity to make light. COMPARE TEXTS

Objectives

- Read fluently with appropriate rate and accuracy
- 113–133 WCPM

Materials

- Transparency 30
- Fluency Solutions Audio CD
- Practice Book, p. 266

ELL

Develop Comprehension
Summarize the meaning of the passage. Show a picture or sketch of an odometer and hold up or draw a pair of bifocals. Ask students to name the inventions in the passage. Practice saying the names of the inventions with students. Echo-read the passage with students. Students may also read along with the **Fluency Solutions Audio CD**.

Practice Book, page 266

As I read, I will pay attention to my reading rate and accuracy.

	What would the world be like without light bulbs?
9	We have Thomas Edison to thank for that bright idea!
19	He also invented the phonograph and motion pictures.
27	Thomas Edison is the most famous American inventor.
35	He came up with more than 1,000 new devices. He worked
45	with electricity and technology to make our daily lives
54	better.
55	Find out how this one man changed history through his
65	inventions.
66	The 1800s have been called "The Age of Invention."
74	That is because many things were invented at that time.
84	It seemed like a whirlwind of inventions!
91	The first steamboat, steam-engine train, and airplane
98	were invented during this time. The telephone was invented
107	too. These inventions changed the way people lived and
116	worked. 117

Comprehension Check

1. How did Thomas Edison's inventions solve problems? **Problem and Solution** Thomas Edison worked with electricity and technology to make our daily lives better.
2. When the author says that Thomas Edison is the most famous American inventor, is this statement a fact or opinion? **Main Idea and Details** This is an opinion.

	Words Read	−	Number of Errors	=	Words Correct Score
First Read		−		=	
Second Read		−		=	

Approaching Reproducible, page 266

Beyond Reproducible, page 266

Fluency

Repeated Reading: Rate and Accuracy

EXPLAIN/MODEL Model how to read the text on **Transparency 30**. Explain that you adjust your rate, or tempo, to read steadily and with accuracy. Tell students that reading with accuracy and at an appropriate rate can increase their understanding as well as listeners' understanding of what they read.

Transparency 30

He also invented an odometer that told how far he had ridden to deliver the mail. And the first clock with a second hand. And he even thought up daylight saving time. Then he invented bifocals so older folks could see up close and far away without changing glasses.

Fluency (from *How Ben Franklin Stole the Lightning*, p. 785)

PRACTICE Have one student read a sentence, the next student join in, and then a third. Repeat until all students have read. When students reach the end of the passage, go back to the beginning and repeat until every student is reading.

DAILY FLUENCY Students will practice fluency using **Practice Book** page 266 or the **Fluency Solutions Audio CD**. The passage is recorded at a slow, practice speed and a faster, fluent speed.

Quick Check

Can students read fluently?

During **Small Group Instruction**

If No → Approaching Level   Reteach using the Fluency lesson and model, p. 801Q.

If Yes → On Level   Consolidate the learning using Fluency, p. 801T.

Beyond Level   Extend the learning using Fluency, p. 801X.

Comprehension

REVIEW SKILL
DRAW CONCLUSIONS

EXPLAIN/MODEL

Review that to **draw conclusions** students should form opinions and make judgments that go beyond the information the author states directly. Point out that conclusions should be supported by facts and details from the selection.

To help students draw conclusions while reading a biography, have them consider how the author presents major events in the person's life.

Discuss different types of conclusions that readers might draw after reading "He Made the World Brighter." For example, ask:

- Why might Thomas Edison have been a poor student?
- What was Thomas Edison's greatest invention? Explain.
- How might our lives be different without Edison's inventions?

PRACTICE/APPLY

Have students work in pairs to draw conclusions about Ben Franklin. Remind them to justify their conclusions with details from the text and to also use any prior knowledge related to the text.

- The author describes Ben Franklin as a "born inventor." What kind of personality must he have had? (Ever since he was little, he was inventing things. He must have been a smart, creative person with lots of energy. He must have loved solving problems and thinking of new ideas.)

- What was Ben Franklin's most important accomplishment? Explain. (Ben Franklin's most important accomplishment was probably inventing the lightning rod, because it saved countless lives and helped the world understand more about electricity.)

- Suppose Ben Franklin and Thomas Edison had lived at the same time. Would they have been more likely to be friends or rivals? Explain. (Sample answer: In "He Made the World Brighter" we see that Edison worked with others on his experiments. In the main selection we read that Franklin helped persuade France and Great Britain to act in certain ways. It seems that Franklin worked well with people. Based on this, I conclude that they probably would have been friends.)

PRACTICE BOOK See **Practice Book** page 267 for Using Illustrations.

Objective
- Draw and support conclusions based on selections

Skills Trace
Draw Conclusions

Introduce	295A–295B
Practice/Apply	296–319; Practice Book, 102–103
Reteach/Review	325M–325Z, 477A–477B, 478–497, 503M–503Z; Practice Book, 165–166
Assess	Weekly Tests; Units 3, 4, 6 Tests
Maintain	361B, 745A–745B, 746–769, 773M–773Z, 797B

Paired Selection

GENRE: Literary Text/Poetry

Have students read the bookmark on **Student Book** page 798. Explain that a concrete poem is a poem that

- has a shape or design that helps express the meaning or feeling of the poem
- may include figurative language

Literary Elements:
Figurative Language and Alliteration

EXPLAIN Tell students that figurative language and alliteration are two techniques that poets use to develop meaning.

- **Figurative language** includes similes, metaphors, and other words that create images in the reader's mind.

- **Alliteration** is the repetition of beginning consonant sounds, as in this sentence: _Poets paint precise pictures_.

PRACTICE/APPLY Discuss how figurative language and alliteration make a concrete poem more interesting. Point out how the author used figurative language to illustrate Edison's thoughts about electricity.

Have students take turns reciting the poems. Then discuss how the experience of listening to the poems read aloud is different from the experience of reading each poem on the page.

Poetry

A **Concrete Poem** has words and lines arranged in the shape of the thing it describes.

 Literary Elements

Figurative Language uses words to create mental images.

Alliteration is the repetition of the same consonant sound in a series of words.

> Edison didn't really squeeze his thoughts into a bulb. This example of **figurative language** helps the reader picture how hard Edison was thinking.

1

798

Light Bulb

Thomas Edison didn't hesitate to let ideas incubate, and try again, if they weren't right. One day to his intense delight, he **squeezed** his thoughts into a bulb and then turned on the light light light !!!

— _Joan Bransfield Graham_

Comprehension

Make Connections: _Reading Across Texts_

Explain Literary texts (such as poetry) and informational texts (such as biographies) present material in different ways.

Discuss Ask how a literary text would present the topic of a snowstorm. (It might use figurative language; describe the sound, feel, and look of the storm; describe how the people in the storm feel and act.) Ask how an informational text would present the same topic. (It might focus on facts and explain the science behind the storm, any records the storm broke, or damage it caused.)

Apply Have students tell how the authors of "He Made the World Brighter" and _How Ben Franklin Stole the Lightning_ presented the topics of light and electricity differently from the authors of "Light Bulb" and "Lightning Bolt."

Lightning Bolt

NEWS FLASH!

BEN FRANKLIN USES KITE & KEY TO UNLOCK ELECTRICITY!

2

This use of "kite" and "key" is an example of **alliteration**.

— *Joan Bransfield Graham*

Connect and Compare

1. Identify an example of figurative language in the poem "Lightning Bolt." **Figurative Language**

2. What do the shapes of these poems have to do with their topics? Explain. **Apply**

3. Compare the information presented in "Lightning Bolt" to the information in *How Ben Franklin Stole the Lightning*. In what ways is it similar? **Reading/Writing Across Texts**

> LOG ON ▶ **FIND OUT** **Poetry** Concrete Poem
> www.macmillanmh.com

799

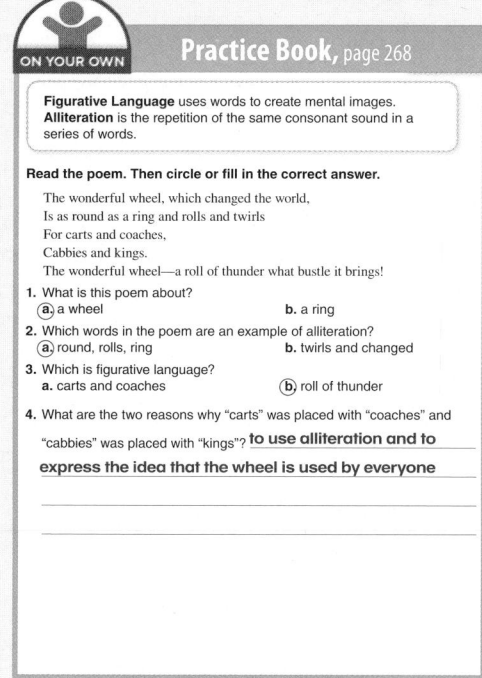

Approaching Reproducible, page 268

Beyond Reproducible, page 268

Read
Paired Selection

Read "Light Bulb" and "Lightning Bolt"

As students read, remind them to apply what they have learned about figurative language and alliteration.

1 **LITERARY ELEMENT: FIGURATIVE LANGUAGE**

What are two examples of **figurative language** in "Light Bulb"? (Two examples are "let ideas incubate" and "he squeezed his thoughts into a bulb.")

2 **COMPARE AND CONTRAST**

What similar idea connects the poems? (They are both about famous inventors and discovery.) How are the poems different? (Each poem is about a different inventor and invention. Each has a different shape.)

Connect and Compare

1. The words *FLASH* and *UNLOCK* show figurative language. The word *FLASH* creates an image of lightning in the sky. The word *UNLOCK* creates an image of opening a door to new knowledge. **FIGURATIVE LANGUAGE**

2. Each poem has a shape that mirrors its topic. "Light Bulb" is in the shape of a bulb, and "Lightning Bolt" is in the shape of lightning. **APPLY**

3. **FOCUS QUESTION** The information in "Lightning Bolt" and *How Ben Franklin Stole the Lightning* is similar in that both tell how Ben Franklin discovered the power of lightning. The poem gives its information in a concise way. The selection gives more detailed information about Ben Franklin. **READING/WRITING ACROSS TEXTS**

Write

WHOLE GROUP

✔ **WRITING WORKSHOP**
- Developing Expository Writing
- Trait: Organization
- Write a Conclusion

Professional Development
GRADES 3–6

Writing Guide

Macmillan/McGraw-Hill

UNIT 6
Developing Expository Writing

WEEK 1	**Strong Sentences/Trait: Ideas** Supporting Details
WEEK 2	**Strong Paragraphs/Trait: Ideas** Main Idea and Details
WEEK 3	**Research Report**
WEEK 4	**Strong Sentences/Trait: Sentence Fluency** Transition Words and Phrases

WEEK 5	**Strong Paragraphs/Trait: Organization**
	Writing a Conclusion, 799A
	• Reading/Writing Connection, 800
	• Minilessons, 801A
	   Organization: Writing a Conclusion
	   Conventions: Creating a Bibliography
	• Conferencing Routine, 801B

WEEK 6	**Research Report**

Trait: Organization
Strong Paragraphs: Writing a Conclusion

TEACH/MODEL Remind students that a paragraph has a topic sentence and supporting details. Explain that many paragraphs also have a concluding sentence. This sentence sums up the main idea and details in the paragraph. Point out that, in the same way, a research report ends with a **conclusion**. The conclusion is a strong paragraph that sums up the main ideas and details in the whole report. The writer often draws a conclusion based on the research in the report.

Tell students that good writers use strong words when they write a conclusion. The strong words help readers understand the conclusion the writer is drawing about the topic. Write this paragraph and read it aloud:

> Jackie Robinson was the first African American to play in the major leagues. Jackie Robinson opened the doors for African American baseball.

Explain that this paragraph is a conclusion to a research report about Jackie Robinson. Point out that although the writer sums up the topic and important ideas, he does not use strong words. The reader might not understand what conclusion the writer is drawing. Then write the following paragraph:

> Jackie Robinson was one of the greatest baseball players ever. He was the first African American baseball player in the major leagues. As a result of his courage and determination, the history of baseball was changed forever. Not only did Jackie Robinson earn the respect of fans and players, but he helped make baseball the national pastime that it is today.

Discuss how the strong words help readers clearly understand the conclusion about Jackie Robinson.

Teacher Write Aloud

PRACTICE/APPLY Further explore with students the concept of writing a conclusion. Remind them that a conclusion sums up the important ideas about a topic. Write the important ideas below from a report on Abraham Lincoln. Then complete the Teacher Think Aloud.

> • Abraham Lincoln was the sixteenth president of the United States.
> • He led the country during the Civil War, because he didn't want the United States to fall apart.
> • He believed that enslaved people should be free and signed the Emancipation Proclamation.

Teacher Think Aloud These sentences list the main ideas in a research report about Abraham Lincoln. I can use these main ideas to write a conclusion for a report.

Complete the Think Aloud by writing the following conclusion on the board. Stop to discuss how each sentence supports the concluding statement that Abraham Lincoln is still honored and respected today.

> Abraham Lincoln, the sixteenth president of the United States, had a huge influence on the history of the country. He led the country during the Civil War because he didn't want the United States to fall apart. He believed that enslaved people should be free and signed the Emancipation Proclamation. He was honest, courageous, and a great leader. As a result, he is still honored and respected today.

 **Draft** Display the writing prompt on **Writing Transparency 98**. Remind students to write a paragraph that includes a concluding statement. Circulate and provide Over-the-Shoulder Conferences as students work.

Objective

• Write supporting details

Materials

• Writer's Notebooks
• Writing Transparency 98

Daily Journal Prompts

Focus on Writing a Conclusion

Use these and other prompts for independent daily journal writing.

🖊 Write about a moment when you discovered something that surprised you or interested you about any topic.

🖊 Write about a moment when you watched a sports game.

🖊 Write about a moment when you shared information about your favorite athlete or entertainer.

🖊 Write about a moment when you told a friend about something you learned in school or on the news.

 Transparency 98

Write about a moment when you drew a conclusion about something that you saw or read.

Writing Transparency

Reading and Writing Connection

Trait: Organization

WRITING A CONCLUSION

Remind students that a concluding sentence or paragraph sums up ideas about the topic. A good writer includes a conclusion at the end of a research report. The writer uses strong words to summarize main ideas and draw a conclusion about the topic.

Read the Passage

Use the example from *How Ben Franklin Stole the Lightning* to show how the author uses a concluding sentence in a paragraph.

- Have students read the bookmark. Explain that an expository paragraph is a paragraph that gives information. The main idea is often stated in a topic sentence. Supporting details give information about the main idea. A concluding sentence sums up the information.

  Ask: *When have you shown a friend how to do something?*

- Then have students chorally read the excerpt from *How Ben Franklin Stole the Lightning*. Direct their attention to the callout. Have students discuss the main idea, the supporting details, and the concluding sentence.

  Ask: *What did you learn from the concluding sentence?*

Writing

✓ **Trait: Organization**
An expository paragraph often ends with a **concluding sentence** that sums up the author's ideas.

Reading and Writing Connection

Read the passage below. Notice how the author Rosalyn Schanzer uses a concluding sentence.

An excerpt from
How Ben Franklin Stole the Lightning

The author uses the last sentence as a concluding sentence to sum up ideas in the paragraph.

The whole idea was to pull lightning safely out of the sky before it could do any mischief. Ben showed people how to put a pointed iron rod on the tip-top of a roof or ship's mast and connect it to a wire leading all the way down under the ground or into water. Now the lightning could follow a safe path without burning up a thing.

800

Respond to the Selection

Have students write a response to the selection.

☑ **Engagement** Help students deepen their connection to the text and discover their own perspective.
- *Focus on a moment when you helped someone.*

☑ **Response** Help students explore more deeply their reactions to particular passages in the reading.
- *Focus on a moment in the story where you felt that Ben Franklin was a "hero." Use text evidence in your writing.*

☑ **Literary Analysis** Help students deepen their connection to the text and discover their own perspective.
- *Focus on a place in the selection where you think the author did a good job of summarizing ideas. Use text evidence in your writing.*

Read and Find

Read Reema's writing below. How did she conclude the paragraph? Use the checklist below to help you.

Painting
by Reema A.

Drawing sounded fine, but painting seemed weird to Shaheed. At first, he wouldn't paint at all. He didn't think he could do it. Then, for no good reason, he started. He looked around, saw a green tree, and painted a little blob of color. Then, he decided it looked like more than a blob. A few more strokes and Shaheed's picture was coming together. He could express himself without words—using shapes and colors to do it.

Read about the art of painting.

Writer's Checklist

✓ Does the paragraph have a main idea? What is it?

✓ What supporting details give information about the main idea?

☑ Does the paragraph have a **concluding sentence**? What is it?

801

Read the Student Model

Have students chorally read the student model at the top of **Student Book** page 801. Discuss how this student writer used a concluding sentence to sum up information in the paragraph. Use the Writer's Checklist.

Journal Prompt

Draft Write the following prompt on the board. Have students write a response to the prompt.

Write about a moment when you helped someone solve a problem.

Tell students that you will be reading and commenting on their writing during Writing Conference time.

Model how to use the Writer's Checklist so students can write and revise their work. Then ask:

- *What is the moment you chose?*

- *What supporting details did you write to show how you helped? Did you write a concluding sentence? If not, what conclusion could you add?*

ELL ENGLISH LANGUAGE LEARNERS

Beginning	Intermediate	Advanced
Write Sentences Provide model sentences based on the Journal Prompt: *Jennie had a problem. She wanted to ____, but ____. I helped Jennie ____. Now she can ____.* Help students write a concluding sentence.	**Explain** Ask students to write three sentences based on the Journal Prompt. Have them end with a concluding sentence. Provide a model if necessary. Read their sentences, correcting grammar and spelling as needed.	**Narrate** Ask students to respond to the Journal Prompt. They should give details and be sure to include a concluding sentence.

Write

Objectives
- Write a conclusion
- Create a bibliography entry
- Write strong paragraphs

Materials
- Writer's Notebooks
- Teacher's Resource Book, p. 207

ELL

Review Vocabulary Write these words and phrases on the board: *World War I, Veterans Day, veterans, honor, celebrate.* Say each and have students repeat it. Discuss the meaning. Then give a clue for each. Have students name the word or phrase that goes with each clue.

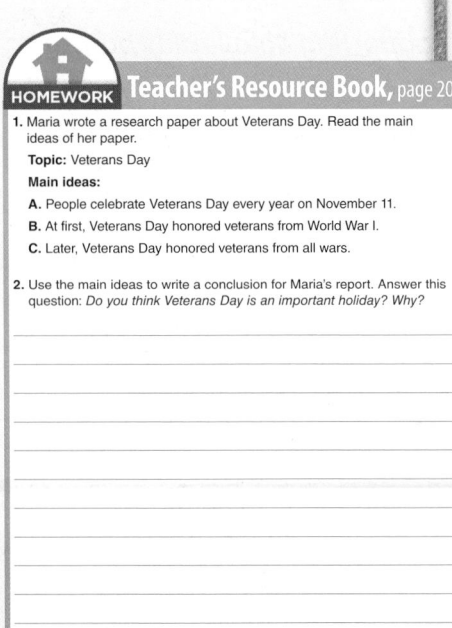

HOMEWORK Teacher's Resource Book, page 207

1. Maria wrote a research paper about Veterans Day. Read the main ideas of her paper.

Topic: Veterans Day

Main ideas:

A. People celebrate Veterans Day every year on November 11.

B. At first, Veterans Day honored veterans from World War I.

C. Later, Veterans Day honored veterans from all wars.

2. Use the main ideas to write a conclusion for Maria's report. Answer this question: *Do you think Veterans Day is an important holiday? Why?*

Minilessons

Minilesson 1 | Organization/Write a Conclusion

TEACH/MODEL

Remind students that they have been working on concluding sentences and paragraphs. Today they will practice that again. Have students use **Teacher's Resource Book** page 207. Ask students to read the directions, the topic, and the main ideas.

PRACTICE/APPLY

Have students work independently to use the main ideas to write a concluding paragraph. Remind students that a conclusion sums up the main ideas of a piece of writing. When they have finished, ask students to share their work during Sharing Circle.

Minilesson 2 | Conventions/Creating a Bibliography

TEACH/MODEL

Explain that good writers get their information from different sources, including reference books and reliable Web sites (for example, those ending in *.edu, .gov, .org*). Tell students that all reference sources must be listed in a bibliography, or works-cited page, at the end of a research report. Write the following bibliography entries.

> **Bibliography**
>
> Landau, Elaine. *Veterans Day: Remembering Our War Heroes.* Berkeley Heights, NJ: Enslow Elementary, 2002.
>
> *U.S. Army Center of Military History,* "The History of Veterans Day," http://www.history.army.mil/faq/vetsday/vetshist.htm

Explain that the first entry is an entry for a book, and the second is a Web site. Point out the features of each entry.

PRACTICE/APPLY

In their Writer's Notebooks, have students rewrite the following information in the correct form for a bibliography entry.

> The book is *Veterans Day* by Marlene Targ Brill. It was published by First Avenue Editions in 2005. First Avenue Editions is in Minneapolis, MN.

Conferencing Routine

Dynamic Feedback System

 Step 1 Read and appreciate the writing.

 Step 2 Notice how the student uses the targeted skill. (e.g., writing conclusions: Ask: *Does the writer include a concluding sentence or a concluding paragraph?*)

 Step 3 Write comments that show how the writing has an impact on you. Direct your comments to those places in the piece where the student has used the targeted skill.

 Step 4 Meet with and give the student a revision assignment.

Write Effective Comments

Organization At least one of your comments should highlight the way the student **writes a conclusion**. Here are some sample comments.

- This is a great conclusion! It helps me understand what you think about your topic.

- Something is missing here. Maybe you can add a conclusion that sums up all your ideas.

- I like your paragraphs. They all have main ideas, supporting details, and concluding sentences.

Revision Assignments

Organization Here are some examples of effective revision assignments for writing conclusions.

 - ***Reread your entry.*** *Find a paragraph in your entry where you think there should be a stronger concluding sentence. Write one.*

 - **[Underline a section.]** Mark a specific section of a student's writing and ask the student to revise it in a specific way.

 - **[Underline a section.]** *Read the part that I underlined. Does your conclusion summarize the main ideas? Do you use strong words? Rewrite your conclusion.*

Connect Language Arts

WHOLE GROUP

✔ **VOCABULARY**
- Tested Words

✔ **SPELLING**
- Prefixes and Suffixes

✔ **GRAMMAR**
- Sentences Using Prepositions

SMALL GROUP

- Differentiated Instruction, pp. 801I–801HH

Practice Book, page 269

Idioms are phrases that have a meaning different from the meaning of each word in them. For example: "pulling my leg". This group of words means "to trick or to tease." You can use a **dictionary** or context clues to help you understand the meaning of an idiom.

1. Read the sentence; then circle the meaning of "out of the blue."

The news came *out of the blue*, so Isaac was shocked.

a. suddenly   b. out of the sky

2. Use "out of the blue" in a sentence. **Possible response provided.**
The announcement came out of the blue.

3. Read the sentence; then circle the meaning of "to wind up."

The meeting was almost over when Janet said, "Let's *wind up* by six o'clock."

a. change time on the clock   b. finish

4. Use "wind up" in a sentence. **Possible response provided.**
Let's wind this up and go for a walk.

5. Read the sentence; then circle the meaning of "under the weather."

Zachary was rarely sick, so his teacher was surprised to hear that he was *under the weather.*

a. lying under a cloud   b. feeling sick

6. Use "under the weather" in a sentence. **Possible response provided.**
I have to go see the doctor because I've been under the weather for a week.

Approaching Reproducible, page 269
Beyond Reproducible, page 269

Build Robust Vocabulary

Day 1 Teach/Practice

CONNECT TO WORDS

- Practice this week's vocabulary words using the following prompts:

1. Would you laugh or cry if something were *hilarious*?

2. What kind of *mischief* is not allowed in your household?

3. How much *independence* do you have at school?

4. What kinds of activities make you feel *dizzy*?

5. In what ways is your life different *nowadays* than it was five years ago?

6. What kinds of materials *came in handy* when you did your math homework?

ACADEMIC VOCABULARY

- Review the important academic vocabulary words for the week. These words include *generate, perspective, rate, accuracy, conclusion, prefix, suffix, idiom.*

- Write each word on the board. Define each one using student-friendly language, and ask students to select the word you are defining. Then point to words in random order for students to define.

Day 2 Review

CONNECT TO WORDS

- Review the definitions of this week's vocabulary words using **Student Book** pages 776–777. Then discuss the words using the following prompts:

1. Describe a *hilarious* situation in which you have been involved.

2. What happens to students in your school who cause *mischief*?

3. How do you think America's *independence* has changed the country?

4. Why might you feel *dizzy* when you are sick?

5. What inventions *nowadays* make use of electricity, which was discovered by Ben Franklin?

6. What supplies might *come in handy* during a lightning storm?

IDIOMS

- Remind students that an idiom is an expression that is not intended to be taken literally. The words in the phrase take on a different meaning.

- Display **Transparency 59**. Read the first sentence and model how to figure out the meaning of the idiom.

- Have students find the clues in the remaining sentences that help clarify the idiom's intended meaning.

- Have students write a brief story in their Writer's Notebooks. Direct them to use at least two of the idioms from the transparency in their story.

Day 3 Reinforce

CONNECT TO WORDS

- Ask students to create Word Squares for each word in their Writer's Notebooks.

- In the first square, students write the word. (Example: *nowadays*)

- In the second square, students write their own definition of the word and any related words, such as synonyms. (Example: *today, currently, these days*)

- In the third square, students draw a simple illustration that will help them remember the word. (Example: drawing of a time line with an arrow labeled "nowadays" pointing to the present year)

- In the fourth square, students write nonexamples, including antonyms for the word. (Example: *previously, in the future, another time*)

RELATED WORDS

- Help students generate words related to *hilarious*. The classification of synonyms can help improve students' vocabularies.

- Draw a word web on the board. Write *hilarious* in the middle.

- Have students write words that have similar meanings to *hilarious*. Ask students to use a thesaurus to find words. Responses might include *funny, amusing, entertaining, comical, hysterical*.

Day 4 Extend

CONNECT TO WORDS

- Review this week's vocabulary using the following sentence stems. Have students orally complete each one.

1. It was hilarious when ____.
2. I got into mischief after ____.
3. My independence allowed me to ____.
4. After ____, I felt dizzy.
5. Nowadays, I do not ____ like I did several years ago.
6. A ____ and some ____ came in handy when we were building a treehouse.

MORPHOLOGY

- Learning about Greek roots and affixes can help raise students' word consciousness. Use the additional selection vocabulary word *odometer* as a springboard for students to learn other words.

- Write the word *odometer* on the board. Underline *-meter*. Explain that *-meter* is Greek for "measure." The word part *odo-* comes from the Greek word *hodor*, meaning "distance." Thus, an *odometer* measures distance.

- Write *speedometer* and *thermometer* on the board. Have students underline *-meter* in each word.

- Use the word parts to define each word. Explain that a *speedometer* is a measure of speed, while a *thermometer* is a measure of heat, or temperature.

Day 5 Assess and Reteach

POSTTEST

- Display **Transparency 60**. Have students complete the cloze sentences using one of this week's vocabulary words.

- Note how quickly and accurately students can complete this task. Work with students who make errors or require too much time to complete this task during Small Group time.

CONNECT TO WRITING

- Have students write sentences in their Writer's Notebooks using this week's vocabulary. Tell them to write sentences that provide information they learned from this week's readings.

- **ELL** Provide the Day 4 sentence stems for students needing extra support.

PERIODIC REVIEW

- Check students' mastery of all the words from Unit 6. Use the Day 1 prompts from each week. Continue to use these words during classroom discussions to reinforce their meanings and usage.

Go to pages T14–T15 for **Differentiated Spelling Lists**.

 # Prefixes and Suffixes

Spelling Words

unchanged	displease	deflate
unnamed	action	semiweekly
restate	establishment	happily
reverse	oversized	kindness
infrequent	prejudge	finally
invisible	interstate	fearful
prepaid	intersect	

Review really, handful, goodness
Challenge transplant, superhuman

Dictation Sentences

1. My grade remained <u>unchanged</u>.
2. An <u>unnamed</u> man saved the baby.
3. I will <u>restate</u> the facts of the case.
4. Mom put the car in <u>reverse</u> and backed out of the driveway.
5. Mr. Jones is an <u>infrequent</u> visitor.
6. Jan bought <u>invisible</u> ink.
7. I used a <u>prepaid</u> phone card.
8. Don't <u>displease</u> your teacher.
9. We took <u>action</u> to fix the problem.
10. It was a popular <u>establishment</u>.
11. I sat in an <u>oversized</u> chair.
12. It is unwise to <u>prejudge</u> others.
13. Dad uses the <u>interstate</u> daily.
14. Those two streets <u>intersect</u>.
15. I <u>deflated</u> the soccer ball.
16. The council meets <u>semiweekly</u>.
17. Brad <u>happily</u> helped at the party.
18. The boy's <u>kindness</u> was obvious.
19. I **finally** cleaned my room.
20. Jed was <u>fearful</u> about the test.

Review/Challenge Words

1. It is <u>really</u> hot outside today.
2. I grabbed a <u>handful</u> of jelly beans.
3. We admire his <u>goodness</u>.
4. Tina has to <u>transplant</u> a tree today.
5. The masked man had <u>superhuman</u> strength.

The word in **bold** is from this week's selections.

Day 1 Pretest

ASSESS PRIOR KNOWLEDGE

- Model for students how to spell the word *review*. Segment the word syllable-by-syllable, then attach a spelling to each sound. Point out that the prefix *re-* and the base word *view* can be used to sound out the word.

- Use the Dictation Sentences. Say the underlined word, read the sentence, and repeat the word. Have students write the words.

- Have students self-correct their tests. Point out that identifying the prefix or suffix before spelling the word can help them sound it out and spell it correctly.

- Have students cut apart the **Spelling Word Cards BLM** on **Teacher's Resource Book** page 103 and figure out a way to sort them. Have them save the cards for use throughout the week.

Day 2 Word Sorts and Review

SPIRAL REVIEW

Review common suffixes. Write *really, handful, tasteless,* and *goodness* on the board. Have students identify the suffixes and name other words with the same suffixes.

WORD SORTS

- Have students take turns sorting the spelling words and explaining how they sorted them. When students have finished the sort, discuss any words that have unexpected pronunciations (*unnamed, happily*).

- Review the spelling words, pointing out the prefixes and suffixes. Use the cards on the Spelling Word Cards BLM. Write a key word for each prefix and suffix on the board. Model how to sort the words by prefix or suffix. Place one or two cards beneath the correct key words.

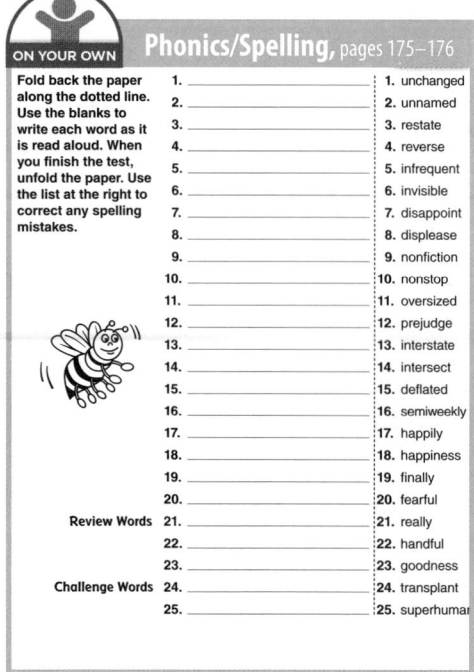

ON YOUR OWN — **Phonics/Spelling,** pages 175–176

Fold back the paper along the dotted line. Use the blanks to write each word as it is read aloud. When you finish the test, unfold the paper. Use the list at the right to correct any spelling mistakes.

1.	1. unchanged
2.	2. unnamed
3.	3. restate
4.	4. reverse
5.	5. infrequent
6.	6. invisible
7.	7. disappoint
8.	8. displease
9.	9. nonfiction
10.	10. nonstop
11.	11. oversized
12.	12. prejudge
13.	13. interstate
14.	14. intersect
15.	15. deflated
16.	16. semiweekly
17.	17. happily
18.	18. happiness
19.	19. finally
20.	20. fearful
Review Words 21.	21. really
22.	22. handful
23.	23. goodness
Challenge Words 24.	24. transplant
25.	25. superhuman

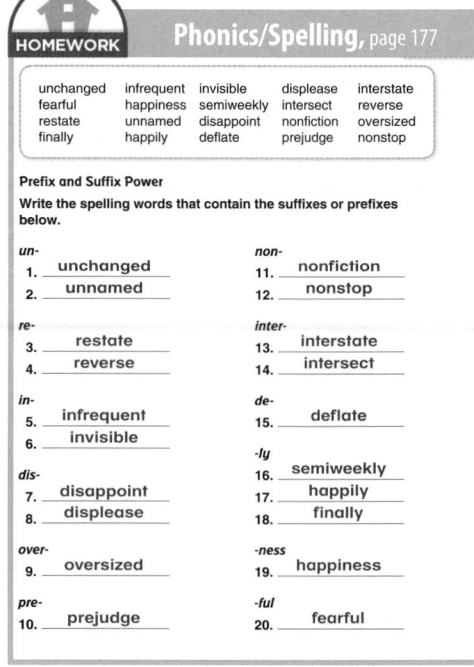

HOMEWORK — **Phonics/Spelling,** page 177

unchanged	infrequent	invisible	displease	interstate
fearful	happiness	semiweekly	intersect	reverse
restate	unnamed	disappoint	nonfiction	oversized
finally	happily	deflate	prejudge	nonstop

Prefix and Suffix Power

Write the spelling words that contain the suffixes or prefixes below.

un-
1. unchanged
2. unnamed

re-
3. restate
4. reverse

in-
5. infrequent
6. invisible

dis-
7. disappoint
8. displease

over-
9. oversized

pre-
10. prejudge

non-
11. nonfiction
12. nonstop

inter-
13. interstate
14. intersect

de-
15. deflate

-ly
16. semiweekly
17. happily
18. finally

-ness
19. happiness

-ful
20. fearful

Day 3 — Word Meanings

CATEGORIES

Read each definition below. Have students copy the definitions into their Writer's Notebooks, matching each definition to the spelling word it describes.

1. cannot be seen (invisible)
2. make unhappy (displease)
3. at last (finally)
4. afraid (fearful)
5. say again (restate)

Challenge students to come up with brief definitions for other words, and have other students guess the spelling word, challenge word, or review word that each definition describes.

Have partners write a sentence for each spelling word, leaving a blank space where the word should go. Direct them to exchange papers and fill in the blanks.

Day 4 — Proofread

PROOFREAD AND WRITE

Write these sentences on the board. Have students circle and correct each misspelled word.

1. We finaly finished our semmiweekly meeting. (*finally, semiweekly*)
2. Paul got an ovarsized poodle that is still unamed. (*oversized, unnamed*)
3. The club president had to reestate the rules at the semiweeklee meeting. (*restate, semiweekly*)
4. The store sold envisable cloaks enfrequantly. (*invisible, infrequently*)

Error Correction Remind students that they should first identify the prefix or suffix and the base word before spelling the word.

Day 5 — Assess and Reteach

POSTTEST

Use the Dictation Sentences on page 801E for the Posttest.

If students have difficulty with any words in the lesson, have them place the words in a list entitled *Spelling Words I Want to Remember* in their Writer's Notebooks. Look for students' use of these words in their writings.

Challenge students to find words with each prefix or suffix reviewed and write them in their Writer's Notebooks. Have partners use print resources such as a dictionary and electronic resources such as a spelling check tool on the computer to check each other's words. Partners should discuss what the words mean and write sentences using the words.

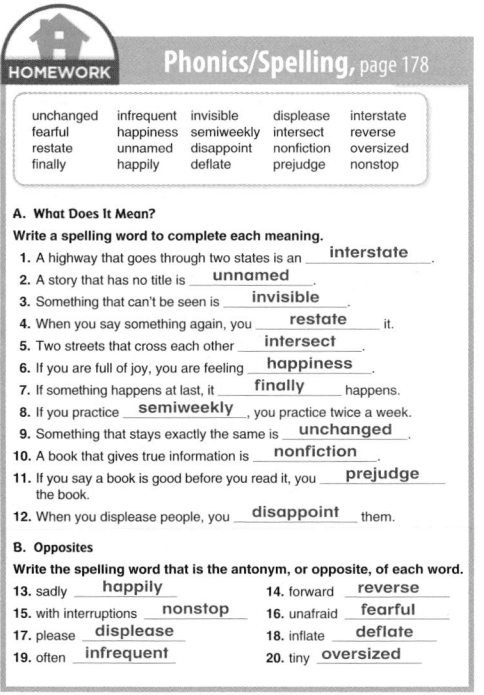

HOMEWORK — Phonics/Spelling, page 178

unchanged	infrequent	invisible	displease	interstate
fearful	happiness	semiweekly	intersect	reverse
restate	unnamed	disappoint	nonfiction	oversized
finally	happily	deflate	prejudge	nonstop

A. What Does It Mean?
Write a spelling word to complete each meaning.

1. A highway that goes through two states is an __interstate__
2. A story that has no title is __unnamed__
3. Something that can't be seen is __invisible__
4. When you say something again, you __restate__ it.
5. Two streets that cross each other __intersect__
6. If you are full of joy, you are feeling __happiness__
7. If something happens at last, it __finally__ happens.
8. If you practice __semiweekly__, you practice twice a week.
9. Something that stays exactly the same is __unchanged__
10. A book that gives true information is __nonfiction__
11. If you say a book is good before you read it, you __prejudge__ the book.
12. When you displease people, you __disappoint__ them.

B. Opposites
Write the spelling word that is the antonym, or opposite, of each word.

13. sadly __happily__
14. forward __reverse__
15. with interruptions __nonstop__
16. unafraid __fearful__
17. please __displease__
18. inflate __deflate__
19. often __infrequent__
20. tiny __oversized__

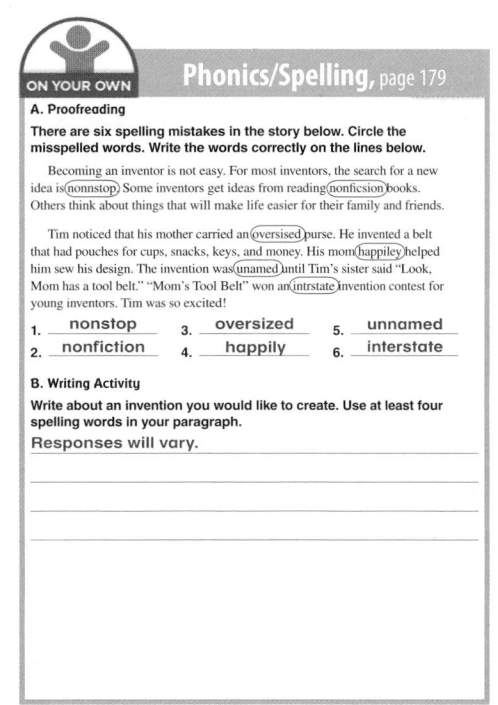

ON YOUR OWN — Phonics/Spelling, page 179

A. Proofreading
There are six spelling mistakes in the story below. Circle the misspelled words. Write the words correctly on the lines below.

Becoming an inventor is not easy. For most inventors, the search for a new idea is (nonstop) Some inventors get ideas from reading (nonficsion) books. Others think about things that will make life easier for their family and friends.

Tim noticed that his mother carried an (oversised) purse. He invented a belt that had pouches for cups, snacks, keys, and money. His mom (happiey) helped him sew his design. The invention was (unamed) until Tim's sister said "Look, Mom has a tool belt." "Mom's Tool Belt" won an (intrstate) invention contest for young inventors. Tim was so excited!

1. __nonstop__
2. __nonfiction__
3. __oversized__
4. __happily__
5. __unnamed__
6. __interstate__

B. Writing Activity
Write about an invention you would like to create. Use at least four spelling words in your paragraph.

Responses will vary.

HOMEWORK — Phonics/Spelling, page 180

Look at the words in each set below. One word in each set is spelled correctly. Use a pencil to fill in the circle next to the correct word. Before you begin, look at the sample set of words. Sample A has been done for you. Do Sample B by yourself. When you are sure you know what to do, you may go on with the rest of the page.

Sample A:
- Ⓐ hopefil
- Ⓑ hopefull
- Ⓒ hopefil
- Ⓓ hopeful ●

Sample B:
- Ⓔ unty
- Ⓕ uhnty
- Ⓖ untie ●
- Ⓗ uhntie

1.
- Ⓐ ovirsized
- Ⓑ oaversized
- Ⓒ oversized
- Ⓓ ovursized

2.
- Ⓔ fearfull
- Ⓕ fearful
- Ⓖ feerfull
- Ⓗ feerful

3.
- Ⓐ reverse
- Ⓑ riverse
- Ⓒ raverse
- Ⓓ ruhverse

4.
- Ⓔ unnchanged
- Ⓕ unchainged
- Ⓖ unchanged
- Ⓗ unchainged

5.
- Ⓐ daflait
- Ⓑ deflait
- Ⓒ diflate
- Ⓓ deflate

6.
- Ⓔ invisable
- Ⓕ invisible
- Ⓖ invisuble
- Ⓗ invisabel

7.
- Ⓐ dissplease
- Ⓑ displeeze
- Ⓒ displease
- Ⓓ displeese

8.
- Ⓔ interstate
- Ⓕ inturstate
- Ⓖ intarstate
- Ⓗ interstait

9.
- Ⓐ happyness
- Ⓑ happiness
- Ⓒ happyniss
- Ⓓ happyniss

10.
- Ⓔ resstait
- Ⓕ resstate
- Ⓖ restait
- Ⓗ restate

11.
- Ⓐ happily
- Ⓑ happyly
- Ⓒ happiley
- Ⓓ happyley

12.
- Ⓔ nonficshun
- Ⓕ nonnfiction
- Ⓖ nofiction
- Ⓗ nonfiction

13.
- Ⓐ priejudge
- Ⓑ prejudge
- Ⓒ preejudge
- Ⓓ preejuge

14.
- Ⓔ semyweekly
- Ⓕ semiweekly
- Ⓖ semeweekly
- Ⓗ simiweekly

15.
- Ⓐ innamed
- Ⓑ uneamed
- Ⓒ unnamed
- Ⓓ unamed

16.
- Ⓔ innfrequer
- Ⓕ imfrequint
- Ⓖ infrequent
- Ⓗ infrequint

17.
- Ⓐ disappoint
- Ⓑ disappoir
- Ⓒ disapoint
- Ⓓ dissapoint

18.
- Ⓔ noanstop
- Ⓕ nonnstop
- Ⓖ nonstop
- Ⓗ nostop

19.
- Ⓐ intirsect
- Ⓑ intursect
- Ⓒ intesect
- Ⓓ intersect

20.
- Ⓔ finaly
- Ⓕ finally
- Ⓖ fighnly
- Ⓗ finley

Daily Language Activities

Write the sentences on the board.

DAY 1

My friends and me work together good. We built a treehouse on a tree. (1: My friends and I; 2: well; 3: in a tree.)

DAY 2

I sang in the school play. The play was last week. My dad came and watch me. (1: I sang in the school play last week.; 2: and watched me.)

DAY 3

In the morning I ate cereal. For lunch I had a sandwhich. What will I have for dinner. (1: morning,; 2: lunch,; 3: sandwich; 4: dinner?)

DAY 4

If there weren't no school I would play outside. Its important to exercise. (1: were no; 2: school,; 3: It's)

DAY 5

Grapes grow good in california. They grow on much farms. don't pick them until their ripe. (1: Grapes grow well on many farms in California.; 2: Don't; 3: they're)

Practice Activity Write on the board: *After school, Jenny went to the library. She went with Cindy.* Model how to combine the sentences using prepositions. Then create simple sentences with students and write them on the board. Have groups practice combining the sentences using prepositions. Read each group's sentence aloud, correcting for grammar and pronunciation as needed.

Sentences Using Prepositions

Day 1 — Introduce the Concept

INTRODUCE SENTENCES USING PREPOSITIONS

- A **preposition** is a word that links a subject or action with a descriptive phrase (**prepositional phrase**). A prepositional phrase modifies a noun, a verb, or an adjective: I sat *in the sun.*

- Two or more ideas in simple sentences may be combined into one sentence: The dog was barking. The dog was *on the porch*; The dog *on the porch* was barking.

- Prepositional phrases can convey location (*in the corner*), time (*at noon*), and direction (*to the right*) or can provide more details. Adding prepositional phrases to simple sentences makes the writing more fluent.

See Grammar Transparency 146 for modeling and guided practice.

HOMEWORK — **Grammar,** page 146

- Two sentences can be combined by adding a **prepositional phrase** to one sentence.

Combine the pairs of sentences below by adding a prepositional phrase. Then underline the words you added to join the two sentences.

1. Today our class went bird-watching. We were at the park.
   Today our class went bird-watching at the park.

2. There were many birds to see. They were in the trees.
   There were many birds to see in the trees.

3. I could see a baby bird. It was inside a small nest.
   I could see a baby bird inside a small nest.

4. The baby bird was crying. It was crying with its mouth open.
   The baby bird was crying with its mouth open.

5. There was a mother bird. She was above the baby.
   There was a mother bird above the baby.

6. The mother fed the baby. She fed the baby by giving her a worm.
   The mother fed the baby by giving her a worm.

7. The baby bird hid. She hid inside the nest.
   The baby bird hid inside the nest.

8. The mother bird flew across. She flew to another tree.
   The mother bird flew across to another tree.

Day 2 — Teach the Concept

REVIEW SENTENCES USING PREPOSITIONS

Review with students how to identify a preposition and how to determine what the prepositional phrase modifies.

INTRODUCE RULES FOR USING PREPOSITIONAL PHRASES

- A prepositional phrase may be placed at the beginning, in the middle, or at the end of a sentence: We studied math *after lunch.*

- A comma is often inserted after a prepositional phrase if the phrase begins a sentence. A comma is also frequently added after a prepositional phrase to make a sentence clearer: *To the gardener, ants are pests.*

See Grammar Transparency 147 for modeling and guided practice.

ON YOUR OWN — **Grammar,** page 147

Two sentences can be combined by adding a **prepositional phrase** to one sentence. If the prepositional phrase begins the sentence, a comma is often inserted at the end of the phrase.

A. Rewrite the pairs of sentences below, using the prepositional phrase to combine them into one sentence.

1. Ants make their anthills by digging. They dig through dirt.
   Ants make their anthills by digging through dirt.

2. Ants scoop dirt. They scoop dirt with their jaws.
   Ants scoop dirt with their jaws.

3. Ants live like people. They live in social communities.
   Ants live in social communities like people.

4. Most ants live and work together. They live under the ground.
   Most ants live and work together under the ground.

5. The queen ant lays eggs. She does this inside the hive.
   The queen ant lays eggs inside the hive.

B. Combine each pair sentences below. Begin the new sentence with a preposition. Add a comma at the end of the prepositional phrase.

6. Male ants die. They die after mating with the queen.
   After mating with the queen, male ants die.

7. Ant eggs develop into adult ants. They develop after three months.
   After three months, ant eggs develop into adult ants.

Day 3 Review and Practice	**Day 4** Review and Proofread	**Day 5** Assess and Reteach

REVIEW USING PREPOSITIONS

Review what prepositional phrases are and the rules for using them.

MECHANICS AND USAGE: COMBINING SENTENCES

- When different adverbs modify the same verb in more than one sentence (She ran *there*. She ran *swiftly*.), the sentences can be combined: She ran *there swiftly*.

- When different prepositional phrases modify the same verb in more than one sentence (I am *at home*. I am *on the sofa*.), the sentences can likewise be combined: I am *at home on the sofa*.

- Remember that sentences can also be combined using appositives and adjectives and using conjunctions in compound sentences. Be sure to use proper subject-verb agreement.

See Grammar Transparency 148 for modeling and guided practice.

REVIEW SENTENCES USING PREPOSITIONS

Review how to write sentences with prepositions, including combining short, related sentences with prepositional phrases, and where to put commas when needed.

PROOFREAD

Have students correct errors in the following sentences.

1. The groundhog was, under the ground. (was under)

2. In the evening people cook dinner. (In the evening,)

3. I put together my bicycle, by myself. (bicycle by)

4. I stood, on my toes, to see over the counter. (stood on my toes to)

See Grammar Transparency 149 for modeling and guided practice.

ASSESS

Use the Daily Language Activity or **Grammar Practice Book** page 150 for assessment.

RETEACH

Use Grammar Practice Book page 150 and selected pages from the **Grammar and Writing Handbook** for additional reteaching. Tell students it is important to use prepositional phrases correctly when speaking and writing.

Check students' writing for use of the skill, and listen for it in their speaking. Assign Grammar Revision assignments in their Writer's Notebooks, as needed.

If necessary, review how to use commas and conjunctions when combining sentences. Model combining sentences using correlative conjunctions such as *either/or*.

See Grammar Transparency 150 for modeling and guided practice.

HOMEWORK — Grammar, page 148

- **Adverbs** can be used to combine two sentences into one longer sentence.
- **Prepositional phrases** can be used to combine two sentences into one longer sentence.

Possible responses provided.
Combine each pair of sentences. Write the new sentence.

1. Eric got a new computer game. The game was about the California Gold Rush.
Eric got a new computer game about the California Gold Rush.

2. Eric pressed a button, and the boys were standing in the mountains. They got there suddenly.
Eric pressed a button, and the boys were suddenly standing in the mountains.

3. They had traveled to the Gold Rush. They had traveled back in time.
They had traveled back in time to the Gold Rush.

4. Many people came to California during the Gold Rush. They came from all around the world.
Many people came to California from all around the world during the Gold Rush.

5. Many Forty-niners panned gold. They panned tirelessly.
Many Forty-niners panned gold tirelessly.

6. Gold dust traveled in the river. It traveled downstream.
Gold dust traveled downstream in the river.

ON YOUR OWN — Grammar, page 149

Read the passage below. Combine each pair of underlined sentences into one sentence by adding a prepositional phrase. Write the combination sentences on the lines below.

I read an interesting book. It was about ants. The book says that ants are one of the greatest insects around. Ants protect plants. They protect them from other insects. Also, they feed the dirt with good things so that we can grow pretty flowers, like Mr. Chang's pink roses! There are three kinds of ants that help each other. They help to get things done.

Worker ants look after the other ants. They do this by gathering food, watching the queen and her eggs, and building the anthill. Male ants don't live long, but they help the queen produce lots of eggs. Finally, there's the queen ant. She is the mother of all the ants. Without her, none of the ants would have anything to do! I recommend this book to all kids who want to learn more about ants and the way they live.

1. **I read an interesting book about ants.**

2. **Ants protect plants from other insects.**

3. **There are three kinds of ants that help each other to get things done.**

4. **Worker ants look after the other ants by gathering food, watching the queen and her eggs, and building the anthill.**

HOMEWORK — Grammar, page 150

Study the sentences below. Then circle the choice in which the sentences are combined correctly.

1. They saw the ant crawling. It was crawling up an old tree.
   a. They saw a crawling ant up the tree.
   b. They saw a tree ant crawling.
   c. They saw the ant crawling up an old tree.

2. It was carrying a big breadcrumb. The breadcrumb was in its jaws.
   a. It was carrying a big breadcrumb in its jaws.
   b. It was carrying its big jaws.
   c. A big breadcrumb was carrying its jaws.

3. Then the breadcrumb dropped. It dropped to the ground.
   a. Then the ground dropped.
   b. Then the breadcrumb dropped.
   c. Then the breadcrumb dropped to the ground.

4. The ant ran down the tree. It ran into the nest.
   a. The ant ran down the nest.
   b. The ant ran down the tree into the nest.
   c. The nest ran into the ant.

5. Another ant came out. It came from inside the nest.
   a. Another ant was inside the nest.
   b. Another ant came out from another nest.
   c. Another ant came out from inside the nest.

6. Together, they pushed the breadcrumb. They pushed it up the tree.
   a. Together, they pushed the breadcrumb into the tree.
   b. Together, they pushed the breadcrumb up the tree.
   c. They pushed the breadcrumb and the tree together.

Approaching Level

Prepare to Read

	Daily Planner	
DAY 1	• Prepare to Read • Academic Language • Vocabulary (Preteach)	
DAY 2	• Comprehension • Leveled Reader Lesson 1	
DAY 3	• Phonics/Decoding • Leveled Reader Lesson 2	
DAY 4	• Phonics/Decoding • Vocabulary (Review) • Leveled Reader Lesson 3	
DAY 5	• High-Frequency Words • Fluency • Self-Selected Reading	

Interactive Student Book

If you wish to preteach the main selection, use StudentWorks Plus for:

• Vocabulary Preteaching

• Word-by-Word Highlighting

• Think Aloud Prompts

Academic Language

Academic words include those harder Tier 2 words that appear in much of students' reading materials as well as the language of instruction. The words chosen for instruction were selected from the **Living Word Vocabulary** list and Avril Coxhead's list of **High-Incidence Academic Words**.

Objective Preview *How Ben Franklin Stole the Lightning*
Materials • **StudentWorks Plus** • self-stick notes

PREVIEW THE MAIN SELECTION

- Have students preview *How Ben Franklin Stole the Lightning* using **StudentWorks Plus**. This version of the Student Book contains oral summaries in multiple languages, story recording, word-by-word highlighting, Think Aloud prompts, and comprehension monitoring questions.

- Remind students that listening carefully to and following along with the word-by-word reading will help them prepare for the reading of the selection with the class. Ask students to place self-stick notes on any challenging words or places that confuse them. Discuss these with students prior to the reading of the selection with the rest of the class.

- Ask students to write three or four sentences in their Writer's Notebooks telling what they learned about Franklin's experiments.

Academic Language

Objective Teach academic language
Materials • none

PRETEACH LANGUAGE OF INSTRUCTION

Tell students that there are many important lesson words you will be using this week. You want them to become familiar with these words *before* the lessons. These words also appear in the directions of the tests they will be taking this year.

Preteach the following academic words: *biography, generate, perspective, conclusions, idiom, figurative language, alliteration.*

- Define each word using student-friendly language. Tell students that a *biography* is a person's life story written by someone else. Explain that *bio-* means "life" and *-graph* means "write," so *biography* means "a story written about someone's life."

- In addition, relate each word to known words. For example, connect *figurative language* to *similes and metaphors; alliteration* to *repeating the same beginning consonant sound; idiom* to *a group of words with a meaning different from that of the individual words;* and *concrete poem* to *a poem with a definite, or concrete, shape.*

- Highlight these words when used throughout the week and reinforce their meanings.

Approaching Level

Phonics/Decoding

Objectives   Decode words with prefixes and suffixes
Materials   • **Approaching Reproducible**, p. 262
                 • **Word-Building Cards**

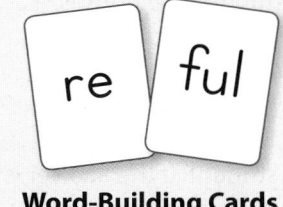

Word-Building Cards

PHONICS MAINTENANCE

Tier 2

- Distribute **Word-Building Cards** to each student. Review the spellings for skills previously taught, including prefixes, suffixes, and syllable types. Have students find the Word-Building Cards for prefixes and suffixes.

- Review the spelling of each prefix, suffix, or syllable by providing a sample word containing that word part. Guide students to write the word. Model how to segment the word and write the spelling for each syllable, as needed. In addition, point out spelling hints, such as that prefixes always form their own syllable and usually do not change the spelling of the base word.

- Dictate the following words for students to spell: *inventor, button, replay, garden, safely, tightness, nonsense, unhappy, helpful, careless.* Write each word on the board and have students self-correct their work.

RETEACH SKILL

Prefixes and Suffixes   Write the prefixes *dis-, non-, un-,* and *mis-* and the suffixes *-ly, -y, -ful, -less,* and *-ness* on the board, and review the spelling for each.

- Write the words below. Provide a sample word and discuss the meaning of the prefix or suffix and the word's meaning. Then have students read through the words, observing the prefix or suffix in each one.

- When completed, point to the words in random order for students to chorally read. Repeat several times.

nonslip	nonstop	nondrip	nonstick	nonsmoker	nonfiction
disagree	disappear	dislike	distrust	disable	discolor
unable	unafraid	unlike	unload	unlined	unlock
misread	mistreat	misstep	misspell	mistype	mislead
hardy	hardly	harmful	harmless	happiness	hardiness
weakly	weakness	weighty	weightless	wiggly	watchful

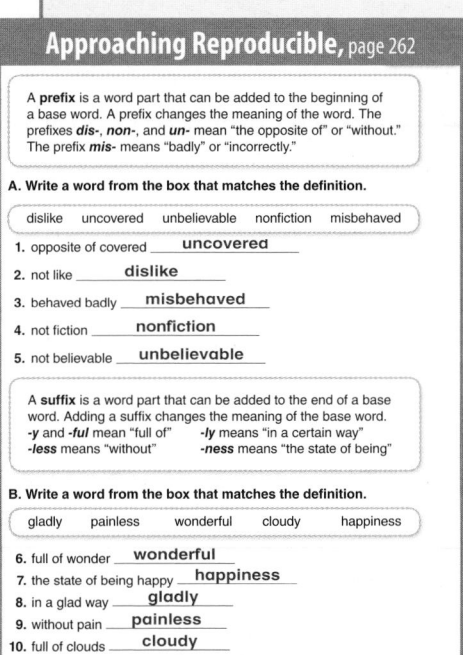

Approaching Reproducible, page 262

A **prefix** is a word part that can be added to the beginning of a base word. A prefix changes the meaning of the word. The prefixes *dis-, non-,* and *un-* mean "the opposite of" or "without." The prefix *mis-* means "badly" or "incorrectly."

A. Write a word from the box that matches the definition.

dislike	uncovered	unbelievable	nonfiction	misbehaved

1. opposite of covered ____ **uncovered**
2. not like ____ **dislike**
3. behaved badly ____ **misbehaved**
4. not fiction ____ **nonfiction**
5. not believable ____ **unbelievable**

A **suffix** is a word part that can be added to the end of a base word. Adding a suffix changes the meaning of the base word.
-y and **-ful** mean "full of"   **-ly** means "in a certain way"
-less means "without"   **-ness** means "the state of being"

B. Write a word from the box that matches the definition.

gladly	painless	wonderful	cloudy	happiness

6. full of wonder ____ **wonderful**
7. the state of being happy ____ **happiness**
8. in a glad way ____ **gladly**
9. without pain ____ **painless**
10. full of clouds ____ **cloudy**

Corrective Feedback

Throughout the lessons, provide feedback based on students' responses. If the answer is correct, ask another question. If the answer is tentative, restate key information to assist the student. If the answer is wrong, provide corrective feedback such as hints or clues, refer to a visual such as a Sound-Spelling Card or story illustration, or probe with questions to help the student clarify any misunderstanding.

Approaching Level
Vocabulary

Objective   Preteach selection vocabulary

Materials
- **Visual Vocabulary Resources**
- **Vocabulary Cards**
- **Approaching Reproducible**, p. 263

PRETEACH KEY VOCABULARY

Tier 2

Introduce the Words   Use the **Visual Vocabulary Resources** to preteach the key selection words *hilarious, mischief, independence, dizzy, nowadays,* and *came in handy*. Use the following routine, which appears in detail on the cards.

- Define the word in English, and provide the example given.
- Define the word in Spanish, if appropriate, and indicate if the word is a cognate.
- Display the picture, and explain how it illustrates or demonstrates the word. Engage students in structured partner-talk about the image, using the key word.
- Ask students to chorally say the word three times.
- Point out any known sound-spellings, or focus on a key aspect of phonemic awareness related to the word.
- You may wish to also distribute copies of the Vocabulary Glossary in the **ELL Resource Book**.

REVIEW PREVIOUSLY TAUGHT VOCABULARY

Display the **Vocabulary Cards** from the previous four weeks. Say the meanings of the words, one by one, and have students identify them. Then point to words in random order for students to provide definitions and related words they know.

Context Clues   Remind students that context clues are clues within the text that help a reader figure out what a word means and can include definitions, examples, synonyms, antonyms, descriptions, or grammatical clues related to how the word is used in the sentence. Have students write a context sentence for each vocabulary word. For example, *The insect was so small, I had to* magnify *it to see it clearly.*

Approaching Reproducible, page 263

| hilarious | dizzy | nowadays |
| came in handy | mischief | independence |

A. Write each vocabulary word next to its meaning.

1. having a spinning feeling   dizzy
2. useful   came in handy
3. freedom   independence
4. being naughty   mischief
5. in the present   nowadays
6. very funny   hilarious

B. Write two sentences using words from the box.
Possible responses provided.

7. The 20-dollar bill came in handy during my school trip.

8. "What mischief could I get into in the museum gift shop with this?" I thought.

Approaching Level

Vocabulary

Objective   Review vocabulary and high-frequency words
Materials   • **Vocabulary Cards**   • **High-Frequency Word Cards**

REVIEW VOCABULARY

Review the Words Display the **Vocabulary Cards** *hilarious, mischief, independence, dizzy, nowadays,* and *came in handy*. Point to each word, read it aloud, and have students chorally repeat.

Then provide the following word sets. Ask students to identify the word or phrase in each set that is not related to the other words.

- independence, free, leaning on others, self-ruling
- hilarious, comical, funny, hilltop
- dizzy, wobbly, sturdy, shaky
- nowadays, in the present, currently, ancient
- came in handy, proved helpful, was useful, handed off
- mischief, obedient, naughty, trouble

HIGH-FREQUENCY WORDS

Tier 2

Top 250 Words The ability to read accurately and effortlessly the most frequently used words in written English will help students develop reading fluency. Display **High-Frequency Word Cards 241–247**. Then do the following:

- Display one card at a time, and ask students to chorally state each word.
- Have students spell each word aloud.
- Ask students to write each word in their Writer's Notebooks as they state aloud each letter. Then have them read the word again.
- When completed, quickly flip through the word card set as students chorally read the words.
- Provide opportunities for students to use the words in speaking and writing. For example, provide sentence starters, such as *Tom said he will* <u>write</u> _____ , for oral and written practice. Or point to a word card and ask a question, such as *What word is an adjective?* (when pointing to the *yellow* word card).
- Continue the routine throughout the week.

ELL

Practice Vocabulary Pair students of different proficiency. Orally model the vocabulary in sentences. For example: *I felt dizzy after the roller coaster ride.* On the board, provide sentence frames for pairs to copy and complete using the vocabulary. For example: The comedian told _____ jokes during his routine. (hilarious)

Word Webs

Have students create Word Webs in their Writer's Notebooks for each vocabulary word. Write the related words provided, and ask students to add other words, phrases, and illustrations.

Student Book

Approaching Level

Comprehension

Objective Reteach generate questions and author's perspective

Materials • **Student Book:** "He Made the World Brighter"

RETEACH THE STRATEGY: GENERATE QUESTIONS

Tier 2

- **Define** Review with students that asking questions as they read will help them check their understanding of the story and focus on important ideas. Asking and answering questions about the text can help them determine why the author organized facts about the subject in a particular way.

- **Relate to Real Life** Ask students to imagine that they are reading a biography and want to know how the main character will solve a particular problem. One way to find out would be to ask themselves questions about this topic and then read the section of the book that deals with the topic to find the answer.

- **Set Purposes** Remind students that good readers generate questions to help themselves understand the information being presented. If the reader can state the most important ideas or events, he or she reads on. If not, the reader generates questions and rereads to find the answers.

RETEACH THE SKILL: AUTHOR'S PERSPECTIVE

- **Define** Tell students that the author's perspective is the author's attitude toward the subject about which he or she is writing. Different writers can have different perspectives on the same subject.

- **Relate to Real Life** Ask students to think of a story they have read recently. What are their opinions and attitudes toward the story? How might their friends' perspective on the story differ from their own?

- **Set Purposes** Remind students that determining the author's perspective, or attitude, toward what he or she is writing about can help them understand the author's word choice and the sequence in which the story is presented.

- **Apply** Work with students to generate questions about Thomas Edison. Help them use the questions to find clues that reveal the author's perspective on Edison and his accomplishments. Students will apply this strategy and skill to a simpler text as they read *Who Invented It?*

Corrective Feedback

Read each paragraph with students. Ask: *What questions do you have about Edison?* Model how to generate questions and reread or read on to clarify your understanding or learn important facts about the subject. Explain that generating questions helps you find out about the problems the subject of a biography faces and the steps the person takes to solve, or find a solution to, the problems.

Approaching Level

Leveled Reader Lesson 1

Objective   Read to apply skills and strategies
Materials   • **Leveled Reader**: *Who Invented It?*

Leveled Reader

BEFORE READING

Preview and Predict   Have students read the title and preview the first chapter. Ask students to generate questions about the subject before they read. They should note any questions they have before reading.

Review the Vocabulary Words   Have students read the vocabulary words on the inside front cover. Briefly define each one, and ask students to state related words they have learned.

Set a Purpose for Reading   *Let's read to find out about many different inventions, and who invented them.*

DURING READING

STRATEGY
GENERATE QUESTIONS

Remind students that asking questions helps readers check their understanding of the story and focus on important ideas.

SKILL
AUTHOR'S PERSPECTIVE

Remind students to look for clues that show the author's perspective, or point of view, as they read. Read chapter 1 with students. Help complete the Author's Perspective Map.

As you read, help students decode unknown words. In addition, ask open-ended questions to facilitate rich discussion, such as *What is the author telling us about the different inventions? What does the author want us to know about how they solve problems?* Build on students' responses to help them develop a deeper understanding of the text.

Stop after every two pages and ask students to generate questions to check their understanding before reading on. If they struggle, help them reread the difficult pages or passages. Model how asking questions can help you identify clues to the author's perspective.

AFTER READING

Ask: *Which invention that you read about do you think was most important? Explain your answer.*

Digital Learning

Use the **Leveled Reader Audio CD** for fluency building *after* students read the book with your support during Small Group time.

Leveled Reader

Approaching Level

Leveled Reader Lesson 2

Objective	Reread to apply skills and strategies and develop fluency
Materials	• **Leveled Reader**: *Who Invented It?*
	• **Approaching Reproducible**, p. 266

BEFORE READING

 **Review the Strategy and Skill** Review students' completed Author's Perspective Maps from the first read. Remind them that the the author's perspective is the author's attitude and feelings toward the subjects described in the book.

Review Vocabulary Words Have students search the book for each vocabulary word. Ask students to read aloud the sentence containing the word and state the word's definition or provide related words. Point out any idioms and discuss their meanings.

Set a Purpose for Reading *Let's reread to check our understanding of the information in the book and to work on our reading fluency.*

DURING READING

Reread *Who Invented It?* with students. Have them read silently, two pages at a time, or read aloud to a partner. Stop and have students generate questions before reading the next two pages. Model generating questions, as needed.

AFTER READING

Check Comprehension Have partners complete the Comprehension Check on page 20. Review students' answers. Help them find evidence for their answers in the text.

MODEL FLUENCY

Model reading the fluency passage on **Approaching Reproducible** page 266. Tell students to pay close attention to your rate and accuracy as you read. Then read one sentence at a time, and have students echo-read the sentences, copying your rate and accuracy.

During independent reading time, have students use the fluency passage with a partner. One student reads aloud, and the other repeats each sentence. If students need additional support, have them listen to the "practice speed" version of the passage on the **Fluency Solutions Audio CD**.

Approaching Reproducible, page 266

As I read, I will pay attention to my reading rate and accuracy.

	A wounded soldier lies on the battlefield. He calls out
10	for help. The sound of gunfire is closer than before. He
21	looks up to see a woman. She gives him water. Then she
33	begins to clean his wounds. The year is 1862 and the Civil
44	War has begun. The woman is Clara Barton.
52	Clara Barton was a woman with an idea. She thought
62	that all wounded soldiers should get medical treatment.
70	She believed that a group of volunteers could be set up to
82	make sure that this happened. She wanted this group
91	to provide help for everyone, not only in times of war, but
103	whenever help was needed. She found others to help her.
113	Her work left us with a life-saving idea — the American
124	Red Cross. 126

Comprehension Check

1. What is the main idea of the first paragraph? **Main Idea and Details Clara Barton helps the wounded soldier on the battlefield.**
2. What problem did Clara Barton see, and what did she do about it? **Problem and Solution Clara Barton believed that injured soldiers needed better medical treatment. She organized a group of volunteers, which eventually became the American Red Cross.**

	Words Read	−	Number of Errors	=	Words Correct Score
First Read		−		=	
Second Read		−		=	

Approaching Level

Leveled Reader Lesson 3

Objectives Build fluency

Materials
- **Leveled Reader**: *Who Invented It?*
- **Approaching Reproducible**, p. 266

FOCUS ON FLUENCY

Timed Reading Tell students that they will be doing a final timed reading of the fluency passage on **Approaching Reproducible** page 266 that they have been practicing. With each student, follow these directions:

- Place the passage facedown.
- When you say "Go," the student begins reading the passage aloud.
- When you say "Stop," the student stops reading the passage.

As they read, note words students mispronounce and their overall expression. Stop after one minute. Help students record and graph the number of words they read correctly.

REREAD PREVIOUSLY READ BOOKS

- Distribute copies of the past six **Leveled Readers**. Have students select two to reread. Tell students that rereading the books will help them develop their skills. The more times they read the same words, the quicker they will learn those words. This will make the reading of other books easier.

- Circulate and listen in as students read. Stop them periodically and ask how they are figuring out difficult words and how they are monitoring their comprehension. Note students who need additional work with specific decoding or comprehension skills.

- Have students read other previously read Leveled Readers during independent reading time or for homework.

Meet Grade-Level Expectations

As an alternative to this day's lesson, guide students through a reading of the On Level Leveled Reader. See page 801U. Since both books contain the same vocabulary, phonics, and comprehension skills, the scaffolding you provided will help most students gain access to this more challenging text.

Book Talk

Bringing Groups Together Students will work with peers of various language and reading abilities to discuss this week's Leveled Readers. Refer to page 162 in the **Teacher's Resource Book** for more about how to conduct a Book Talk.

Student Book

Student Book

Approaching Level

Fluency

Objectives Reread selections to develop fluency; develop speaking skills

Materials • **Student Book**: *How Ben Franklin Stole the Lightning*, "He Made the World Brighter"

REREAD FOR FLUENCY

- Have students reread a portion of *How Ben Franklin Stole the Lightning*. Remind them to focus on two to four of their favorite pages from the selection. Work with students to read the pages with the appropriate rate and accuracy.

- Provide time for students to read their sections of text to you. Comment on their rate and accuracy, and provide corrective feedback by modeling proper fluency.

DEVELOP SPEAKING/LISTENING SKILLS

- Have students practice reading the selection "He Made the World Brighter."

- Work with students to read at an appropriate rate, and with accuracy. Model reading a few lines at a time. Emphasize how you read the words accurately, pay attention to punctuation, and vary your speed appropriately for the kind of information you are presenting.

- Provide time for partners to read aloud the passage. Ask students to identify places where their partner varied his or her reading speed, paid attention to punctuation, or read difficult words accurately.

- Have students use the selection to create a brief oral presentation about Edison, using details from the selection, and deliver it to their partner. Suggest that students begin with a question, such as *Why is Thomas Edison an inspiration to many people?*

Decodable Text

Use the decodable stories in the **Teacher's Resource Book** to help students build fluency with basic decoding patterns.

Approaching Level

Self-Selected Reading

Objective Read independently to determine the author's perspective

Materials • **Classroom Library** • other informational books

APPLY SKILLS AND STRATEGIES TO INDEPENDENT READING

- **Read Independently** Have students choose an informational book or a **Leveled Classroom Library** book for sustained silent reading. (See the **Theme Bibliography** on pages T8–T9 for book suggestions.) Remind them that the author's perspective is the author's attitude toward the subject of the book. Have students read their books and record their clues on an Author's Perspective Map.

- **Show Evidence of Reading** While reading, students may generate a reading log or journal. After reading, have students use their Author's Perspective Maps and logs to paraphrase the content of the book, maintaining meaning and logical order. They may write or orally state a summary of the book. Ask students to share their summaries and reactions to the book while participating in Book Talks. Ask: *Would you recommend this book to a classmate who was interested in the subject? Why or why not?*

Approaching

Leveled Classroom Library
See Leveled Classroom
Library lessons on pages T2–T7.

Daily Planner

DAY 1	• Vocabulary • Phonics
DAY 2	• Leveled Reader Lesson 1
DAY 3	• Leveled Reader Lesson 2
DAY 4	• Fluency
DAY 5	• Self-Selected Reading

ELL

Practice Vocabulary Pair ELL students with native speakers. On the board, provide sentence frames for pairs to copy and complete using the vocabulary and additional words when necessary. For example: The _____ comedian told many _____. (hilarious; jokes)

Sound-Spelling WorkBoard

On Level

Vocabulary

Objectives Review vocabulary
Materials • **Vocabulary Cards**

REVIEW PREVIOUSLY TAUGHT WORDS

Review the Words Display the **Vocabulary Cards** *hilarious, mischief, independence, dizzy, nowadays,* and *came in handy*. Point to each word, read it aloud, and have students chorally repeat.

Have students respond to the following suggestions. Use their responses to determine each student's depth of word knowledge.

- Describe something you read or saw that was hilarious.
- Tell about a time when you got into mischief.
- Describe a time when you asserted your independence.
- Name an activity that would make someone feel dizzy.
- Give an example of a technology that is different nowadays than it was in the past
- Name something that would come in handy for a school project.

Phonics/Word Study

Objective Decode multisyllabic words with prefixes and suffixes
Materials • **Word-Building Cards** • **Sound-Spelling Workboards**

RETEACH SKILL

- **Prefixes and Suffixes** Point to the prefixes *dis-, non-, un-* and *mis-,* and the suffixes *-ly, -y, -ful, -less,* and *-ness* on the **Word-Building Cards**, and review the spellings for each. Give a sample word and discuss the meaning of the word and its prefix or suffix.

- Write the words below on the board. Divide the words into syllables using the syllable-scoop technique to help students read one syllable at a time. When completed, point to the words in random order for students to chorally read.

misplace	misfile	disconnect	disobey	disapprove
healthy	unhealthy	healthful	gratefully	gracefully
nonbreakable	nonliving	brightness	lightness	lifeless

- **Spelling** Dictate the following words for students to spell on their **WorkBoards**: *shoeless, uncomfortably, uneventful, nonsense, displeasing, misunderstood*. Have students use the Sound-Spelling Cards to segment words syllable by syllable.

On Level

Fluency

Objectives Reread selections to develop fluency; develop speaking skills

Materials • **Student Book**: *How Ben Franklin Stole the Lightning,* "He Made the World Brighter"

REREAD FOR FLUENCY

- Have students reread parts of *How Ben Franklin Stole the Lightning.* Work with students to read at an appropriate rate, with accuracy.

- Allow time for students to read a section of text to you. Comment on their rate and accuracy and provide corrective feedback.

DEVELOP SPEAKING/LISTENING SKILLS

- Have students practice reading "He Made the World Brighter."

- Work with students to read at an appropriate rate and with accuracy. Model reading a few lines at a time. Emphasize how you read the words accurately, pay attention to punctuation, and vary your speed appropriately, based on the information you read.

- Have students read aloud the second page to partners. Ask them to comment on their partners' rate and accuracy.

- Have students use the selection to create a brief oral presentation about Edison, using details from the selection, and deliver it to their partner. Suggest that students begin with a question, such as *Why is Thomas Edison an inspiration to many people?*

Student Book

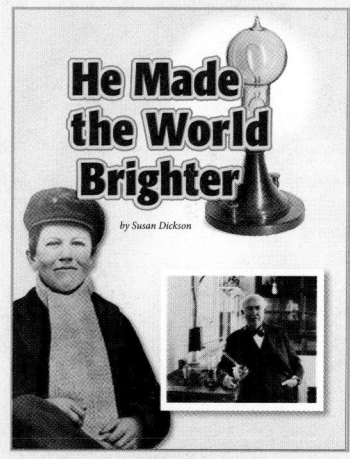

Student Book

Self-Selected Reading

Objective Read independently to generate questions and determine the author's perspective

Materials • **Leveled Classroom Library** • other informational books

APPLY SKILLS AND STRATEGIES TO INDEPENDENT READING

- **Read Independently** Have students choose an informational book for sustained silent reading. (See the **Theme Bibliography** on pages T8–T9 for book suggestions.) Ask students to read their books, recording the author's perspective and the clues that helped them identify it, on an Author's Perspective Map.

- **Show Evidence of Reading** While reading, students may generate a reading log or journal. After reading, have students use their Author's Perspective Maps and logs to paraphrase the content of the book, maintaining meaning and logical order. They may write or orally state a summary of the book. Ask students to share their summaries and reactions to the book while participating in Book Talks. Ask: *Would you recommend this book to a classmate? Explain.*

On Level

Leveled Classroom Library
See Leveled Classroom
Library lessons on pages T2–T7.

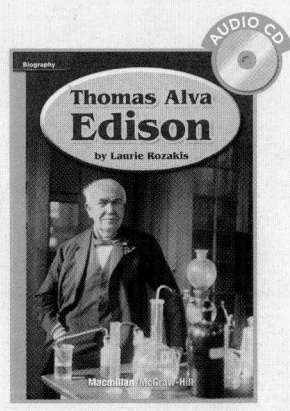

Leveled Reader

On Level

Leveled Reader Lesson 1

Objectives   Read to apply strategies and skills

Materials   • **Leveled Reader**: *Thomas Alva Edison*

BEFORE READING

Preview and Predict   Have students read the title and preview the book by reading the chapter titles and looking at the illustrations. Ask students to predict what they might learn about Thomas Edison.

Review the Vocabulary Words   Have students read the vocabulary words on the inside front cover. Ask them to identify any idioms in the text and discuss their meanings.

Set a Purpose for Reading   *Let's read to find out about the problems Thomas Edison faced and how he solved them.*

DURING READING

STRATEGY
GENERATE QUESTIONS

Remind students that asking questions helps readers check their understanding of the story and focus on important ideas. Generating literal, interpretive, and evaluative questions during reading helps direct readers to look for specific information. If they cannot answer the questions, they reread to find the information needed to answer them.

SKILL
AUTHOR'S PERSPECTIVE

Tell students to think about the author's perspective on Thomas Edison and his accomplishments.

Read Chapter 1 with students. Ask open-ended questions to facilitate rich discussion, such as *What is the author telling us about the problems Edison faced? What does she want us to know about the kind of person Edison was?* Build on students' responses to help them develop a deeper understanding of the text. Have students fill in the first section of the Author's Perspective Map, then continue reading.

Idioms   As they read, have students point out this week's new vocabulary words and any idioms the author includes. Have them share and discuss the meanings of any idioms they find.

AFTER READING

Ask students to discuss Edison's solutions to the problems he faced. Have them comment on the most interesting facts they learned about Thomas Edison and his inventions.

On Level

Leveled Reader Lesson 2

Objective Reread to apply skills and strategies and develop fluency
Materials
• **Leveled Reader**: *Thomas Alva Edison*
• **Practice Book**, p. 266

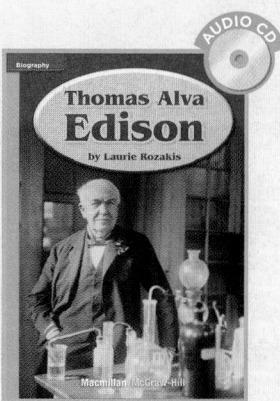

Leveled Reader

BEFORE READING

Review the Strategy and Skill Review students' completed Author's Perspective Maps from the first read. Remind them that the author's perspective is the author's point of view. Generating questions can help clarify information for readers and help them identify the author's perspective.

If students' Author's Perspective Maps are incomplete, provide a model chart or use a student chart and revise it as a group. Have students copy the revised chart in their Writer's Notebooks.

Set a Purpose for Reading *Let's reread to check our understanding of the information in the book and to work on our reading fluency.*

DURING READING

Reread *Thomas Alva Edison* with students. Have them read silently, two pages at a time, or read aloud to a partner. Stop and have students generate questions before they read the next two pages. Model generating questions, as needed.

AFTER READING

Check Comprehension Have partners complete the Comprehension Check on page 20. Review students' answers. Help them find evidence for their answers in the text.

MODEL FLUENCY

Model reading the fluency passage on **Practice Book** page 266. Tell students to pay close attention to your rate, or pacing, and your accuracy as you read. Then read one sentence at a time and have students echo-read the sentences, copying your rate and accuracy.

During independent reading time, have students use the fluency passage with a partner. One student reads aloud, and the other repeats each sentence. If students need additional support, have them listen to the "practice speed" version of the passage on the **Fluency Solutions Audio CD**.

Book Talk

Bringing Groups Together
Students will work with peers of various language and reading abilities to discuss this week's **Leveled Readers**. Refer to page 160 in the **Teacher's Resource Book** for more about how to conduct a Book Talk.

Practice Book, page 266

As I read, I will pay attention to my reading rate and accuracy.

	What would the world be like without light bulbs?
9	We have Thomas Edison to thank for that bright idea!
19	He also invented the phonograph and motion pictures.
27	Thomas Edison is the most famous American inventor.
35	He came up with more than 1,000 new devices. He worked
45	with electricity and technology to make our daily lives
54	better.
55	Find out how this one man changed history through his
65	inventions.
66	The 1800s have been called "The Age of Invention."
74	That is because many things were invented at that time.
84	It seemed like a whirlwind of inventions!
91	The first steamboat, steam-engine train, and airplane
98	were invented during this time. The telephone was invented
107	too. These inventions changed the way people lived and
116	worked. 117

Comprehension Check

1. How did Thomas Edison's inventions solve problems? **Problem and Solution** Thomas Edison worked with electricity and technology to make our daily lives better.
2. When the author says that Thomas Edison is the most famous American inventor, is this statement a fact or opinion? **Main Idea and Details** This is an opinion.

	Words Read	−	Number of Errors	=	Words Correct Score
First Read		−		=	
Second Read		−		=	

Daily Planner

DAY 1	• Leveled Reader Lesson 1
DAY 2	• Leveled Reader Lesson 2
DAY 3	• Phonics
DAY 4	• Vocabulary • Fluency
DAY 5	• Self-Selected Reading

ELL

Self-Monitor Vocabulary
Have student pairs of different proficiency identify and define unfamiliar words from the main selection using a dictionary. Challenge students to use the new words in sentences. Monitor students as they complete the activity.

Beyond Level

Phonics/Word Study

Objective Decode multisyllabic words with prefixes and suffixes
Materials • none

EXTEND/ACCELERATE

■ **Read Multisyllabic Words with Prefixes and Suffixes** Write the words below on the board. Challenge students to read the words, using known word parts. When completed, point to the words in random order for students to chorally read.

nondrinkable	nonactive	unsatisfactory	unqualified
mispronounce	misdiagnose	disadvantage	disable
regardless	colorless	unhappiness	inventiveness
wonderfully	beautifully	unsuccessfully	incredible

■ **Define the Words** Ask students to use their knowledge of word parts to figure out the meanings of the above words. Then have partners find the words in a dictionary and confirm or revise the meanings. Challenge students to use these words in this week's writing assignments.

■ **Spell Words with Prefixes and Suffixes** Dictate the following words for students to spell on their **WorkBoards**: *tastefully, disregard, unhappily, undesirably, nonabrasive, mispronounce, thoughtlessly*. Write the words for students to self-correct.

Vocabulary

Objective Review alliteration; compare poems
Materials • poetry anthologies

ENRICH VOCABULARY

■ **Review Alliteration** Remind students that the author of the poem "Light Bulb" used alliteration to make the poem more interesting. Review that alliteration is the repetition of beginning consonant sounds. Select a consonant, such as *b*, and brainstorm a list of words that begin with that letter; for example, *bulb, brightest, baffle, behavior, boasted, bolt, bifocals, believed,* and *burn*.

■ **Compare Poems** Have students search for other poems related to Ben Franklin, Thomas Edison, or another famous person. Have them present and compare the poems they find. Have students draw conclusions about which poem is their favorite and why. They should identify any strong examples of figurative language and memorable vocabulary.

Gifted & Talented

Beyond Level

Fluency

Objectives Reread selections to develop fluency; develop speaking skills

Materials • **Student Book**: *How Ben Franklin Stole the Lightning*, "He Made the World Brighter"

REREAD FOR FLUENCY

- Have students reread parts of *How Ben Franklin Stole the Lightning*. Work with them to read at an appropriate rate, with accuracy.

- Allow time for students to read a section of text to you. Comment on their rate and accuracy, and provide corrective feedback.

DEVELOP SPEAKING/LISTENING SKILLS

- Have students practice reading "He Made the World Brighter."

- Work with students to read at an appropriate rate and with accuracy. Model reading a few lines at a time. Emphasize reading the words accurately, paying attention to punctuation, and varying reading rate, based on the information you read.

- Have students read aloud the second page to partners. Ask them to critique their partners' reading rate and accuracy.

- Have students create and deliver an oral presentation about Edison, using details from the selection.

Self-Selected Reading

Objective Read independently to determine the author's perspective

Materials • **Leveled Classroom Library** • other informational books

APPLY SKILLS AND STRATEGIES TO INDEPENDENT READING

- **Read Independently** Ask students to choose an informational book for sustained silent reading. (See the **Theme Bibliography** on pages T8–T9 for book suggestions.) Have students read their books and fill out an Author's Perspective Map.

- **Show Evidence of Reading** While reading, students may generate a reading log or journal. After reading, have them use their Author's Perspective Maps and logs to paraphrase the content of the book, maintaining meaning and logical order. They may write or state a summary of the book. Ask students to share their summaries and reactions to the book during Book Talks. Ask: *Would you recommend this book to a classmate? Why or why not?*

- **Evaluate** Challenge students to discuss how the self selected books they have chosen relate to the unit theme, Problem Solving. Ask: *What problem did you read about in your book? How was it solved?*

Student Book

Student Book

Beyond

Leveled Classroom Library
See Leveled Classroom
Library lessons on pages T2–T7.

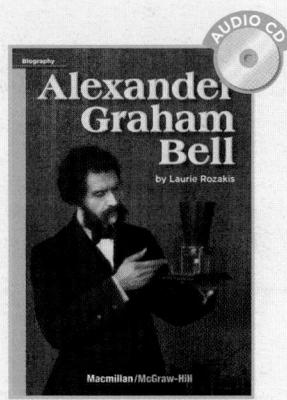

Leveled Reader

Beyond Level

Leveled Reader Lesson 1

Objective	Read to apply strategies and skills
Materials	• **Leveled Reader**: *Alexander Graham Bell*

BEFORE READING

Preview and Predict Have students read the title and preview the book by reading the chapter titles and looking at the illustrations. Ask students to predict what they might learn about Alexander Graham Bell.

Review the Vocabulary Words Have students read the vocabulary words on the inside front cover. Ask students to state each definition and any related words they have learned.

Set a Purpose for Reading *Let's read to find out about the problems Alexander Graham Bell faced and how he solved them.*

DURING READING

STRATEGY
GENERATE QUESTIONS

Ask students to define the term *generate questions.* Remind them that asking questions helps readers direct their reading. If the reader cannot answer the questions, he or she rereads to look for the information.

SKILL
AUTHOR'S PERSPECTIVE

Ask students to define the term *author's perspective.* Discuss different attitudes authors might have toward the invention of the telephone.

Read the book with students. Ask open-ended questions to facilitate rich discussion, such as *What is the author telling us about Bell's life? How does the author present major events in Bell's life?* Build on students' responses to help them develop a deeper understanding of the text. Have students fill in the Author's Perspective Map independently as they read.

AFTER READING

Formulate Questions Ask students to discuss the steps Alexander Graham Bell took to resolve one of his problems. Prompt them to develop questions about Bell that they would like to research.

Analyze Ask students to discuss what kind of person Alexander Graham Bell was, based on details from the story. Instruct them to research the lives of other inventors and compare and contrast their qualities. Have them share their findings with the other students.

Gifted Talented

Beyond Level

Leveled Reader Lesson 2

Objective Reread to apply skills and strategies and develop fluency

Materials • **Leveled Reader**: *Alexander Graham Bell*
• **Beyond Reproducible**, p. 266

BEFORE READING

✔ **Review the Strategy and Skill** Review students' completed Author's Perspective Maps from the first read. Remind them that the author's perspective may not be stated outright. They may have to ask and answer questions to determine the author's perspective.

If students' Author's Perspective Maps are incomplete, provide a model map or use a student's map and revise it as a group. Have students copy the revised Author's Perspective Map in their Writer's Notebooks.

Set a Purpose for Reading *Let's reread to check our understanding of the information in the book and work on our reading fluency.*

DURING READING

Have students reread *Alexander Graham Bell* silently or with a partner. If reading in pairs, prompt students to stop every two pages and generate questions or ask their partner probing questions.

AFTER READING

Check Comprehension Have students independently complete the Comprehension Check on page 24. Review students' answers. Help students find evidence for their answers in the text.

Synthesize Thomas Edison said that the telephone "brought the human family closer in touch." Ask students to write a paragraph explaining what he meant by this. Then have them write a poem expressing these ideas. Encourage them to use sensory details.

MODEL FLUENCY

Model reading the fluency passage on **Beyond Reproducible** page 266. Tell students to pay close attention to your reading rate, or speed, and your accuracy as you read. Then read one sentence at a time and have students echo-read the sentences, copying your rate and accuracy.

During independent reading time, have students work with a partner using the fluency passage. One student reads aloud, while the other repeats each sentence. Students can check their fluency by reading along with the "expert speed" version of the passage on the **Fluency Solutions Audio CD**.

Leveled Reader

Book Talk

Bringing Groups Together Students will work with peers of various language and reading abilities to discuss this week's **Leveled Readers**. Refer to page 160 in the **Teacher's Resource Book** for more about how to conduct a Book Talk.

Beyond Reproducible, page 266

As I read, I will pay attention to my reading rate and accuracy.

	Scotland in the 1800s was an exciting place. Scientists
8	were making many discoveries. There was a whirlwind
16	of inventing going on. New gas lamps lit the streets.
26	Railroads carried people and supplies across the country.
34	The telegraph could send messages with great speed.
42	Alexander Bell was born in Edinburgh, Scotland, on
50	March 3, 1847. Sound shaped his whole life. His mother
58	Eliza was hearing impaired. His father and his grandfather
67	studied speech. They taught people how to speak clearly in
77	public. They helped people overcome speech problems.
84	Bell's mother taught Alexander and his two brothers at
93	home. When Bell was 11 years old, his parents sent him to
104	Royal Edinburgh High School. He did not like school and
114	left after four years without graduating.
120	Bell had not worked hard at his schoolwork. Instead,
129	he asked lots of questions and explored the countryside.
138	He did not get into mischief or make trouble, however. In
149	fact, Bell's childhood was perfect for an inventor! 157

Comprehension Check

1. What kind of person was Alexander Bell? **Draw Conclusions** He liked to learn and explore. He did not like school.

2. What opinion does the author express about Scotland in the 1800s? **Main Idea and Details** The author says that Scotland was an exciting place in the 1800s.

	Words Read	–	Number of Errors	=	Words Correct Score
First Read		–		=	
Second Read		–		=	

Daily Planner

DAY 1	• Build Background Knowledge • Vocabulary
DAY 2	• Vocabulary • Access to Core Content *How Ben Franklin Stole the Lightning*
DAY 3	• Vocabulary • Grammar • Access to Core Content *How Ben Franklin Stole the Lightning*
DAY 4	• Vocabulary • Writing/Spelling • Access to Core Content "Light Bulb" and "Lightning Bolt" • Leveled Reader *A Great Inventor*
DAY 5	• Vocabulary • Leveled Reader *A Great Inventor* • Self-Selected Reading

StudentWorks Plus
Interactive Student Book

Use StudentWorks Plus for:
- Vocabulary preteaching
- Word-by-word highlighting
- Think Aloud prompts

Cognates

Help students identify similarities and differences in pronunciation and spelling between English and Spanish cognates.

invent	*inventar*
independence	*independencia*
author	*autor*
perspective	*perspectiva*
prepositions	*preposiciones*

ELL ENGLISH LANGUAGE LEARNERS

Prepare to Read

Content Objective Describe how Ben Franklin solved the problem of electricity

Language Objective Use key words to describe how inventions can improve our lives

Materials • StudentWorks Plus

BUILD BACKGROUND KNOWLEDGE

All Language Levels

- Have students preview *How Ben Franklin Stole the Lightning* using **StudentWorks Plus**, which contains oral summaries in multiple languages, online multilingual glossaries, word-by-word highlighting, and questions that assess and build comprehension.

- Students can build their word-reading fluency by reading along as the text is read or by listening during the first reading and, at the end of each paragraph, returning to the beginning of the paragraph and reading along.

- Students can build their comprehension by reviewing the definitions of key words in the online glossary and by answering the comprehension questions. When appropriate, the text required to answer the question is highlighted to provide students with additional support and scaffolding.

- After reading, ask students to respond to these questions: *What invention has helped to improve your life? How? What ideas do you have for new inventions that could improve the way we live?*

Academic Language

Language Objective Use academic language in classroom conversations

All Language Levels

- This week's academic words are **boldfaced** throughout the lesson. Define the word in context, and provide a clear example from the selection. Then ask students to generate an example or a word with a similar meaning.

Academic Language Used in Whole Group Instruction

Theme Words	Key Selection Words	Strategy and Skill Words
invent **discovery** **innovative**	**hilarious** **mischief** **independence** **dizzy** **nowadays** **came in handy**	**generate questions** **author's perspective** **prepositions** **idioms**

ELL ENGLISH LANGUAGE LEARNERS

Vocabulary

Language Objective Demonstrate understanding and use of key words by describing how inventions can improve our lives

Materials • **Visual Vocabulary Resources**
• **ELL Resource Book**

Visual Vocabulary Resources

PRETEACH KEY VOCABULARY

Use the **Visual Vocabulary Resources** to preteach the key selection words *hilarious, mischief, independence, dizzy, nowadays,* and *came in handy.* Focus on two words per day. Use the following routine, which appears in detail on the cards.

Beginning/Intermediate

- Point out any known sound-spellings, or focus on a key aspect of phonemic awareness related to the word.

All Language Levels

- Define the word in English, and provide the example given.

- Define the word in Spanish, if appropriate, and indicate if the word is a cognate.

- Display the picture, and explain how it illustrates the word. Engage students in a structured activity, using the key word.

- Ask students to chorally say the word three times.

- Distribute copies of the Vocabulary Glossary in the **ELL Resource Book**, page 346.

PRETEACH FUNCTION WORDS AND PHRASES

All Language Levels

Use the Visual Vocabulary Resources to preteach the function words and phrases *goes to figure, lickety-split, newfangled,* and *storm brewing.* Focus on one word or phrase per day. Use the detailed routine on the cards.

- Define the word in English and, if appropriate, in Spanish. Point out if the word is a cognate.

- Refer to the picture and engage students in talk about the word. For example, students will partner-talk using sentence frames.

- Ask students to chorally repeat the word three times.

TEACH BASIC WORDS

Beginning/Intermediate

Use the Visual Vocabulary Resources to teach the basic words *eclipse, thunderstorm, lightning, forecast, odometer,* and *bifocal.* Teach these "science" words using the routine provided on the card.

ELL Resource Book, page 346

Use the word chart to study this week's vocabulary words.
Write a sentence using each word in your writer's notebook.

Word	Context Sentence	Illustration
hilarious	My brother thinks I am hilarious. He laughs at everything I say.	
dizzy	He spun around in circles until he was dizzy.	
mischief	My cat loves to get into mischief.	
independence	Getting around on my own has given me more independence.	
came in handy	The umbrella came in handy when it started to rain.	
nowadays	Once, people walked many places. Nowadays they drive.	What do kids play with nowadays that they didn't have 20 years ago?

ELL Resource Book

ELL ENGLISH LANGUAGE LEARNERS

Access to Core Content

Content Objective Read grade-level text

Language Objective Discuss text, using key words and sentence frames

Materials • **ELL Resource Book,** pp. 334–345

PRETEACH MAIN SELECTION (PAGES 778–795)

> **All Language Levels**

Use the Interactive Question-Response Guide on **ELL Resource Book** pages 334–343 to introduce students to *How Ben Franklin Stole the Lightning.* Preteach half of the selection on **Day 2** and half on **Day 3**.

- Use the prompts provided in the guide to develop meaning and vocabulary. Use the partner-talk and whole-class responses to engage students and increase student-talk.

- When completed, have partners reread the story.

PRETEACH PAIRED SELECTIONS (PAGES 798–799)

> **All Language Levels**

Use the Interactive Question-Response Guide on ELL Resource Book pages 344–345 to preview the paired selections "Light Bulb" and "Lightning Bolt." Preteach the selections on **Day 4**.

Beginning	Intermediate	Advanced
Use Visuals During the Interactive Reading, select several illustrations. Describe them and have students summarize what you said. Then help them generate questions about what they want to learn, based on the description.	**Describe** During the Interactive Reading, select a few lines of text. After you have read and explained it, have students generate questions about what they learned or what they want to learn, based on the text.	**Discuss** During the Interactive Reading, select a passage of text. After you have read and explained it, have students generate questions about what they learned or what they want to learn, based on the passage.

ELL ENGLISH LANGUAGE LEARNERS

Fluency

Content Objectives Reread selections to develop fluency; develop speaking skills

Language Objective Tell a partner what a selection is about

Materials • **Student Book**: *How Ben Franklin Stole the Lightning,* "Light Bulb," and "Lightning Bolt"
• **Teacher's Resource Book**

REREAD FOR FLUENCY

Beginning

■ Have students read the decodable passages in the **Teacher's Resource Book,** pages 38–39.

Intermediate/Advanced

■ Have students reread a portion of *How Ben Franklin Stole the Lightning.* Work with students to read the pages with the appropriate rate and accuracy. For example, read each sentence of the first paragraph and have students echo. Then have students chorally read additional paragraphs.

■ Provide time for students to read their sections of text to you. Comment on their rate and accuracy, and provide corrective feedback by modeling proper fluency.

DEVELOP SPEAKING/LISTENING SKILLS

All Language Levels

■ Have students practice reading "Light Bulb" and "Lightning Bolt." Work with them to read with the appropriate rate and accuracy.

■ Provide time for students to recite one of the poems to a partner. Ask students to tell their partner about the poem. Provide the sentence frame *This poem is about ___.*

Student Book

Self-Selected Reading

Content Objective Read independently

Language Objective Orally retell information learned

Materials • **Leveled Classroom Library** • other informational books

APPLY SKILLS AND STRATEGIES TO INDEPENDENT READING

All Language Levels

■ Have students choose an informational book or **Leveled Classroom Library** book for independent reading. (See the Theme Bibliography on pages T8–T9 for book suggestions.)

■ After reading, ask students to orally summarize and share their reactions to the book with classmates. Ask: *Would you recommend this book to a classmate? Why or why not?*

Leveled Classroom Library
See Leveled Classroom
Library Lessons on pages T2–T7.

Transfer Skills

Sentence Structure In Cantonese, there are no exact equivalents of English prepositions, although there are words to mark location and movement. Therefore, these students may omit prepositions when combining sentences. For example, *Lightning rods rooftops helped prevent many fires.* Model correct usage and have students repeat. See language transfers on pages T16–T31.

Corrective Feedback

During whole group grammar lessons, follow the routine on the **Grammar Transparencies** to provide students with extra support. This routine includes completing the items with English Language Learners while other students work independently, having students reread the sentences with partners to build fluency, and providing a generative task such as writing a new sentence using the skill.

ELL ENGLISH LANGUAGE LEARNERS

Grammar

Content Objective Combine sentences with prepositions
Language Objective Speak in complete sentences, using sentence frames

SENTENCES USING PREPOSITIONS

Beginning/Intermediate

- Review prepositions with students. Remind them that two ideas in simple sentences can be combined into one sentence by using a prepositional phrase. Write the following on the board: *Franklin chased a whirlwind. He chased the whirlwind over the hills and forests.* Tell students that the ideas in both sentences can be combined into one sentence. Write: *Franklin chased a whirlwind over the hills and forests.* Underline the prepositional phrase. Point out that using prepositional phrases can make writing more fluent.

All Language Levels

- Review how to combine sentences using prepositional phrases. Write sentence pairs on the board, such as those below. Have students combine each pair by using a prepositional phrase.

    Ben flew a special kite. He flew the kite toward a big rain cloud.

    Franklin captured lightning. The lightning traveled along the kite string.

PEER DISCUSSION STARTERS

All Language Levels

- Write the following sentence on the board.

    I learned that Ben Franklin ___.

- Pair students and have them complete the sentence frame. Ask them to expand on their sentences by providing as many details as they can from this week's readings. Circulate, listen in, and take note of each student's language use and proficiency.

Beginning	Intermediate	Advanced
Use Visuals Describe the illustrations in *How Ben Franklin Stole the Lightning* to students. Ask: *What do you see?* Help them point and describe what they see using prepositions and prepositional phrases.	**Describe** Ask students to describe the illustrations in *How Ben Franklin Stole the Lightning* using sentences with prepositions. Model sentences as needed.	**Discuss** Ask students to describe the illustrations in *How Ben Franklin Stole the Lightning* using sentences with prepositions.

ELL ENGLISH LANGUAGE LEARNERS

Writing/Spelling

Content Objective Spell words correctly

Language Objective Write in complete sentences, using sentence frames

All Language Levels

- Write the key vocabulary words on the board: *hilarious, convinced, mischief, independence, nowadays, came in handy*. Have students copy each word on their **WorkBoards**. Then help them say each word and write a sentence for it. Provide sentence starters such as:

    The show was so hilarious that ____.

    The last time I got into mischief ____.

    I want independence from ____.

    My brother felt dizzy when ____.

    Nowadays, it's easy to ____.

    My umbrella came in handy when ____.

Beginning/Intermediate

- Help students spell words using their growing knowledge of English sound-spelling relationships. Model how to segment the word students are trying to spell, and attach a spelling to each sound (or spellings to each syllable if a multisyllabic word). Use the Sound-Spelling Cards to reinforce the spellings for each English sound.

Advanced

- Dictate the following words for students to spell: *unchanged, deplane, happiness, fearful, unhappy, deflate, roughness,* and *careful*. Use the Sound-Spelling Cards to guide students as they spell each word.

- When completed, review the meanings of words that can be easily demonstrated or explained. Use actions, gestures, and available pictures.

Sound-Spelling WorkBoard

Phonics/Word Study

For English Language Learners who need more practice with this week's phonics/spelling skill, see the Approaching Level lesson on page 801J. Focus on minimal contrasts, articulation, and those sounds that do not transfer from the student's first language to English. See language transfers on pages T16–T31.

Leveled Reader

Vocabulary

Preteach Vocabulary Use the routine in the **Visual Vocabulary Resources**, pages 521–526, to preteach the ELL Vocabulary listed in the inside front cover of the Leveled Reader.

ELL ENGLISH LANGUAGE LEARNERS

Leveled Reader

Content Objective Read to apply skills and strategies

Language Objective Retell information, using complete sentences

Materials • **Leveled Reader**: *A Great Inventor*
• **ELL Resource Book,** p. 347
• **Visual Vocabulary Resources,** pp. 521–526

BEFORE READING

> **All Language Levels**

- **Preview** Read the title *A Great Inventor*. Ask: *What's the title? Say it again.* Repeat with the author's name. Then page through the photographs. Use simple language to tell about each page. Immediately follow up with questions, such as *What makes an inventor great? What did Thomas Edison invent?*

- **Review Skills** Use the inside front cover to review the comprehension skill and vocabulary words.

- **Set a Purpose** Say: *Let's read to find out about Thomas Edison and his inventions.*

DURING READING

> **All Language Levels**

- Have students whisper-read each page, or use the differentiated suggestions below. Circulate, listen in, and provide corrective feedback, such as modeling how to blend a decodable word or clarifying meaning by using techniques from the Interactive Question-Response Guides.

- **Retell** After every two pages, ask students to state the main ideas they have learned so far. Help them to complete the Author's Perspective Map. Restate students' comments when they have difficulty using story-specific words. Provide differentiated sentence frames to support students' responses and engage students in partner-talk where appropriate.

Beginning	Intermediate	Advanced
Echo-Read Have students echo-read after you.	**Choral-Read** Have students read chorally with you.	**Choral-Read** Have students read chorally.
Check Comprehension Point to pictures and ask questions, such as *Do you see the photo of Edison as a boy? Point to it.*	**Check Comprehension** Ask questions/prompts, such as *Describe what you see in this photo. What did the author tell us about Edison and telegraph machines?*	**Check Comprehension** Ask: *What did you learn about Thomas Edison on this page? Read sentences that tell about his inventions.*

AFTER READING

Use the chart below and **Think and Compare** questions in the Leveled Reader to determine students' progress.

Think and Compare	Beginning	Intermediate	Advanced
1 Look back at pages 2–3. What does the text tell you about the author's perspective? **(Author's Perspective)**	Possible responses: Nonverbal response. Invention is good. Inventions help people.	Possible responses: The author believes inventions help people live better.	Possible responses: The author believes that inventions help people live better and can change the world.
2 Edison believed he could accomplish anything he set out to do. Do you agree? Why or why not? **(Evaluate)**	Possible responses: Nonverbal response. Yes. Can do anything. Need to work hard.	Possible responses: Yes, I agree. Anything is possible. I need to work hard.	Possible responses: Yes, I agree with Edison because anything is possible if I work hard at it.
3 The phonograph is used to play music. What other things do you know have been invented to play music? **(Apply)**	Possible responses: Nonverbal response. CD player. Computer.	Possible responses: CD players and computers play music.	Possible responses: We can use CD players and computers to play music.

BOOK TALK

Develop Listening and Speaking Skills Distribute copies of **ELL Resource Book**, page 347, and form small groups. Help students determine the leader to discuss the Book Talk questions. Tell students to remember the following while engaged in the activity:

■ Distinguish between formal and informal English and know when to use each one. Remind students to note whether the selection is written in formal or informal English. Ask: *Why do you think it is written in this way?* Remind students that they may use informal English when speaking with their classmates, but they should use formal language when they talk to teachers or write essays.

ELL Resource Book

Book Talk

Bringing Groups Together Students will work with peers of varying language abilities to discuss the questions for the Book Talk activity. Form groups so that students who read Beyond Level, On Level, Approaching Level, and English Language Learner Leveled Readers are in the same group for the activity.

Progress Monitoring
Weekly Assessment

ASSESSED SKILLS

- Vocabulary: Vocabulary Words, Dictionary: Idioms
- Comprehension: Author's Perspective
- Grammar: Sentences Using Prepositions
- Phonics/Spelling: Prefixes and Suffixes

Selection Test for **How Ben Franklin Stole the Lightning** *Also Available*

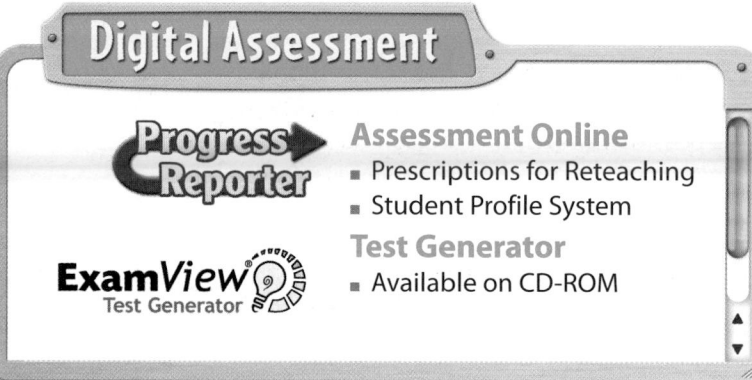

Digital Assessment

Progress Reporter

Assessment Online
- Prescriptions for Reteaching
- Student Profile System

ExamView Test Generator

Test Generator
- Available on CD-ROM

**Weekly Assessment
Unit 6 Week 5**

Fluency Assessment

Assess fluency for one group of students per week.
Use the Oral Fluency Record Sheet to track the number of words read correctly. Fluency goal for all students:
113–133 words correct per minute (WCPM).

Approaching Level	Weeks 1, 3, 5
On Level	Weeks 2, 4
Beyond Level	Week 6

Fluency Assessment

Diagnose		Prescribe
Review the assessment answers with students. Have them correct their errors. Then provide additional instruction as needed.		
	IF...	**THEN...**
VOCABULARY WORDS VOCABULARY STRATEGY Dictionary: Idioms	0–2 items correct . . .	See **Vocabulary Intervention Teacher's Edition.** **LOG ON** Online Practice: Go to www.macmillanmh.com. **CD-ROM** Vocabulary PuzzleMaker
COMPREHENSION Skill: Author's Perspective	0–3 items correct . . .	See **Comprehension Intervention Teacher's Edition.** **SPIRAL REVIEW** See Author's Perspective lesson in Unit 5 Week 1, page 563B.
GRAMMAR Sentences Using Prepositions	0–1 items correct . . .	See **Writing and Grammar Intervention Teacher's Edition.**
PHONICS AND SPELLING Prefixes and Suffixes	0–1 items correct . . .	**LOG ON** Online Practice: Go to www.macmillanmh.com. See **Phonics Intervention Teacher's Edition.**
FLUENCY	109–112 WCPM	**AUDIO CD** Fluency Solutions Audio CD
	0–108 WCPM	See **Fluency Intervention Teacher's Edition.**

Response to Intervention

To place students in Tier 2 or Tier 3 Intervention use the *Diagnostic Assessment*.

• Phonics
• Vocabulary
• Comprehension
• Fluency
• Writing and Grammar

Week 6 ★ At a Glance

Review and Assess

 ### Writing Project
- **Research Report**
- **Writer's Resources:** Note Taking

 ### Show What You Know
- **Test Practice**
- **Literacy Activities:** Comprehension, Word Study, Drama, Genre Study, Research

 ### Theme Project
- **Problem Solving**
- **Research Strategy:** Use Text Features
- **Listening/Speaking**

 ### Computer Literacy
- **Adding to a Presentation**

 ### Media Literacy
- **Online vs. In Print**

 ### Assessment
- **Unit Assessment**

Key

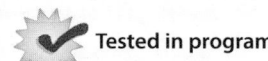 Tested in program

Digital Learning

Digital solutions to help plan and implement instructions

☑ Teacher Resources

LOG ON ▶

ONLINE www.macmillanmh.com

▶ **Teacher's Edition**
- Lesson Planner and Resources also on CD-ROM

 TeacherWorks *Plus*

▶ **Formative Assessment**
- ExamView® on CD-ROM also available

Progress Reporter

▶ **Instructional Resources**
- Unit Videos
- Classroom Presentation Toolkit

 VIDEO

▶ **Professional Development**
- Video Library

Professional Development

☑ Student Resources

LOG ON ▶

ONLINE www.macmillanmh.com

▶ **Interactive Student Book**

 StudentWorks *Plus*

▶ **Leveled Reader Database**

▶ **Activities**
- Research Toolkit
- Oral Language Activities
- Vocabulary/Spelling Activities

 Listening Library
- Recordings of Student Books and Leveled Readers

 Fluency Solutions
- Fluency Modeling and Practice

Show What You Know

Spiral Review

Show What You Know provides a spiral review of reading comprehension and vocabulary skills and strategies previously taught. After reading fiction and nonfiction selections, students will answer questions that assess reading comprehension and vocabulary.

Have students turn to **Student Book** page 802 and read "Pitch for Fish" independently. Distribute pages 21–22 from **Show What You Know**. Have students complete the questions.

Share Your Thinking

After students have completed the questions, model your own thinking on how to arrive at correct answers.

Question **1** **Cause and Effect** *Why are Alison, Rosa, and Javier having a meeting?*

Explain that students must **combine** the details in the story to find the **stated** answer. Alison calls the meeting to order and tells the group they need to decide what they will do for the school fair. (B) THINK AND SEARCH

Question **2** **Problem and Solution** *What is Rosa's problem in the story?*

Tell students they must **connect** the clues in the story to the **unstated** answer. Rosa is afraid to speak up, but doesn't agree with Alison's plan to give away fish for prizes. (J) AUTHOR AND ME

Show What You Know

Review

Problem and Solution
Cause and Effect
Fact and Opinion
Idioms
Primary Source

"Order! This meeting will now come to order!" barked Alison as she slammed her fist down on the desk. Rosa and Javier rolled their eyes at one another as Alison kept talking. "We have to decide what to do for the school fair. I think we should do a game of some sort. Like the game where people throw a ball in a jar from three feet away. And if they get it in, they win a prize."

"They'll win a prize? What?" asked Javier.

"A goldfish!" said Alison excitedly. "Don't you just love the idea of seeing all those little goldfish bowls lined up together? We can call our booth *Pitch for Fish*!"

Javier bit his lip. He nodded, knowing his opinion was insignificant. It didn't matter what he thought. Alison wanted a goldfish game and Alison always got what she wanted.

"Great," Alison said. "Rosa? What about you? Don't you think this is the best idea ever?"

802

Genre

Fiction

Fiction is a story that comes from imagination and not from fact.

Setting: The time and place where the story takes place.

Characters: The people, animals, or things that appear in the story.

Plot: The structure of the story; how the events are arranged in a story.

Theme: The central lesson or message of the story.

Rosa looked down, her face burning. She didn't want to [sa]y anything to upset Alison, but she didn't like the idea.

Alison frowned. "Okay, you agree then. Now, I hate [pa]inting so you two have to lend a hand. You should construct [th]e booth and paint it pink. The letters should be—"

"Alison," Rosa interrupted.

Alison paused at the timid interruption. She looked [an]gry. "Did you just interrupt me, Rosa?"

When she heard the anger in Alison's voice, Rosa felt [m]ore intimidated than ever. But she thought of those poor [fis]h, trapped in tiny bowls, and gained enough courage to [sa]y, "I think goldfish make terrible prizes."

"Well, I think it's a great idea. And Javier agrees."

"He didn't hear my side yet." Rosa took a deep breath. [I]t's not fair to the fish. Getting a pet is an important [de]cision. You have to really want one and be willing [to] take care of it. You should never give someone a [pe]t as a prize or present. Most people who win a [fis]h won't take care of it. Most of those fish will be [de]ad in a few weeks and it will be our fault. I don't [w]ant to be responsible for that."

Alison looked stunned. She was not used to people [di]sagreeing with her.

"Actually, I agree with Rosa," Javier said in a firm voice. ["W]e can still have the pitching game, but let's think of [an]other prize. We shouldn't give away something live."

Alison looked really upset. Rosa knew they were right, [bu]t she didn't want to rub it in.

"Let's give away stuffed fish instead," Rosa [su]ggested. "Then we can still use your name, [Al]ison. Pitch for Fish is a great name."

Alison smiled again. "It is, isn't it?"

803

GRADE 4

Treasures

Show What You Know

Spiral Review

Macmillan/McGraw-Hill

pages 21–22

Question 3 **Idioms** *In the sixth paragraph, the phrase "lend a hand" means —*

Remind students to **connect** the context clues in the paragraph with the **unstated** answer. Alison says they must lend a hand by painting and building a booth. To lend a hand must mean to help out. (C) AUTHOR AND ME

Question 4 **Cause and Effect**
When Rosa interrupts Alison, she —

Students should **connect** the clues in the story with the **unstated** answer. When Rosa interrupts, she can hear anger in Alison's voice, so she knows that she is angry. (F) AUTHOR AND ME

Question 5 **Problem and Solution**
How do the students solve their problem? Explain your answer and support it with evidence from the story. AUTHOR AND ME

Possible response: They decide to have a "Pitch for Fish" game, as Alison suggested. Rosa suggests that they give away stuffed fish instead of live goldfish as prizes, and everyone agrees.

Use the Short-Answer Reading Rubric on page 170 in the Teacher's Resource Book to score students' written responses.

Have students turn to page 804 in the **Student Book** and read "Caves" independently. Distribute **Show What You Know** pages 23–24. Have students complete the questions.

Share Your Thinking

After students have completed the questions, model your own thinking on how to arrive at correct answers.

Question 1 Fact and Opinion *Use the diagram to answer the question below. Which idea from the article belongs in the empty box?*

Tell students that this is a fact and opinion chart with the fact side filled in. The students need to **combine** the clues and evidence to find an opinion. The sentence, "Caves can be exciting places to explore" cannot be supported by text evidence- it tells how a person might feel about exploring caves. That is an opinion. (C)

THINK AND SEARCH

Question 2 Fact and Opinion *Which sentence from the article shows how solution caves are formed?*

Students should **locate** the **stated** answer by finding the facts in the text. The second paragraph says solution caves are formed from the flow of water dissolving away the rocks. (G)

RIGHT THERE

CAVES
MYSTERIOUS UNDERGROUND WORLDS

ARE YOU LOOKING for something new to explore? Check out a cave! Caves are natural spaces, like rooms, that have openings you can reach from the inside. They are often so deep below the ground that natural light does not reach inside. There are about 40,000 caves in the United States. This means there is a very good chance you can find one somewhere near you. There are caves in every state except Louisiana and Rhode Island.

There are four basic types of caves: **solution caves**, **sea caves**, **lava caves**, and **glacier caves**. Solution and sea caves are both formed by water. The constant flow of water dissolves and wears away the rock. Over time, the path deepens and creates a cave. Lava caves are formed from volcanic eruptions. The outer layer of lava cools and hardens while the center stays hot and keeps flowing. When the lava in the center drains, it creates a cave. Glacier caves form when melting water runs through a glacier.

Many caves are protected by state law. This ensures cavers respect the caves while exploring them!

804

Genre

Nonfiction

A nonfiction article may tell about an event, a person, or a place.

Introduction: Tells the topic of the selection.

Body: The main text of the selection; gives more detail about the topic.

Conclusion: Gives a summary of the most important ideas from the article.

Text Features: Give information in a variety of formats, such as charts, graphs, or maps, to supplement the text.

Caves can be exciting places explore, but they can also be angerous. The number one rule to member is never to go in a cave one. It is best to go with an expert ho knows the cave well. You also ed to be prepared. Remember, ere is no natural light in a cave, you need to bring your own ght with you. Most cave explorers ear a helmet that has a light on e front. The light allows you to e and to inspect the wonders of e cave. It also helps you in tricky eas that might need more of your tention because you do not have hold a light in your hands. This

is important because then your hands are free to help you keep your balance.

Choose your clothing carefully before you go caving. Wear comfortable shoes that help you keep your balance on steep or slippery paths. Temperatures are often colder in caves, so wear layers of clothing that you can add or remove as necessary. Wearing cotton as the inside layer and wool as the outside layer will help you keep dry and trap in heat.

Finally, you also need to be sure not to cause any damage. Do not go off alone or remove any objects. Be sure to leave the cave exactly the way you found it. That way, other people can enjoy the same mysterious underground world!

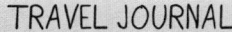

TRAVEL JOURNAL

June 20-21
This weekend, my family and I visited Mammoth Cave National Park. Did you know Mammoth is the longest cave in the United States? It is about 169 miles long and right here in our home state of Kentucky. My brother and I took a tour and got to crawl and slide through really narrow parts of the cave. After that, we decided to call it a day and go back to the campsite for a dinner of hotdogs and hot chocolate!

June 27-29
My family and I traveled to Cumberland Caverns in Kentucky. All I can say is WOW! Even though Cumberland is shorter than Mammoth, I think I liked it better. The cave is 23 miles long but very tricky. We brought sleeping bags and did an overnight tour. It was scary but a lot of fun!

805

GRADE 4

Treasures

Show What You Know

Spiral Review

Macmillan/McGraw-Hill

pages 23–24

Question 3 Primary Source
Look at the "Travel Journal" on page 805. The reader can tell that this journal is an example of a primary source because it —

Students should **connect** the clues in the journal to the **unstated** answer. The journal is a first person account of events in which he or she participated. This makes it a primary source. (D)
AUTHOR AND ME

Question 4 Idioms *In the "Travel Journal," the phrase "call it a day" means —*

Students must **connect** the details in the journal to the **unstated** answer. The kids explored the cave, then stopped and "called it a day." To *call it a day* means to stop what you are doing. (F) AUTHOR AND ME

Question 5 Primary Source
According to the "Travel Journal," what did the writer's family do on June 20–21 and June 27–29? Explain your answer and support it with details from the story.
AUTHOR AND ME

Possible response: They visited Mammoth Cave National Park on June 20–21 and took a tour through the cave. On June 27–29, they visited Cumberland Caverns and did an overnight tour.

Use the Short-Answer Reading Rubric on page 170 in the Teacher's Resource Book to score students' written responses.

Show What You Know

 ## Spiral Review

Show What You Know Unit Review provides a spiral review of the core skill taught in this unit. Students will review by answering questions and completing short, targeted activities.

Have students turn to pages 806 and 807 of the Student Book. Have students note their responses on a separate sheet of paper.

Share Your Thinking

Read the questions for each activity in the **Student Book** with students. If additional review is needed, go back to the lessons in the Teacher's Edition if necessary.

Comprehension: Using Text Features
Review with students what text features are and what they do. Have students offer different examples of text features. Read the activity on page 806 of the Student Book. Complete the activity as a class, making predictions about the article using its text features.

Comprehension

Using Text Features

- Text features in expository text, such as a magazine article, give an overview of the article. As you look at an article think about what information you can learn from the title, the headings, and the photographs.

- Graphic aids such as maps, graphs, and diagrams will also give an overview of the information that is being presented.

- Look at the article "Taking the Lead" on pages 734–737. On a separate sheet of paper, answer the following questions: *What can you tell about the topic of the article by reading the title, the question under the title, and the other headings? What kind of information do the photographs and captions provide?*

A B C Word Study

Suffixes

- A suffix is a word part added to the end of a base word or root that changes the meaning of the word. Many suffixes used in English come from Greek, Latin, and other languages. Some suffixes change a word from a noun to an adjective. For example: *joy* + *-ful* = "joyful."

- Some suffixes change a verb into a noun. For example: *teach* + *-er* = the noun "teacher."

- Create at least eight words using the following suffixes: *-or, -er, -less, -ful.* Then sort the words by putting the nouns in one column and the adjectives in another column.

806

Genre

Expository Text

- Expository text, such as a magazine article, presents facts and information about an event, person, place, or thing.

- The introduction tells what the article is about and usually includes a topic sentence. The main text of the article gives information, facts, and details about the topic. Text features provide details and facts in easy-to-read formats.

- The conclusion gives the author's ideas about what is the most important information in the article.

- With a partner read a magazine article. Together write a summary of the article.

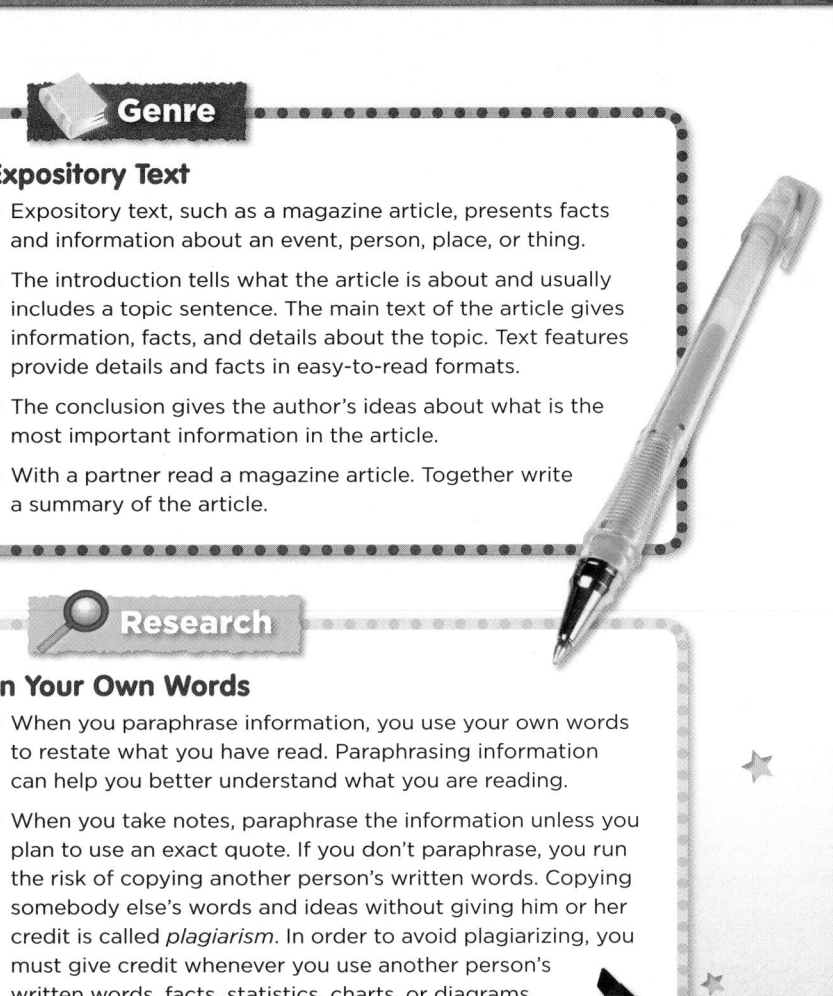

Research

In Your Own Words

- When you paraphrase information, you use your own words to restate what you have read. Paraphrasing information can help you better understand what you are reading.

- When you take notes, paraphrase the information unless you plan to use an exact quote. If you don't paraphrase, you run the risk of copying another person's written words. Copying somebody else's words and ideas without giving him or her credit is called *plagiarism*. In order to avoid plagiarizing, you must give credit whenever you use another person's written words, facts, statistics, charts, or diagrams.

- Choose a reference book. Paraphrase part of a chapter and write the source of your information. When you write the source include the author, title, place published, publisher, and year of publication.

LOG ON **StudentWorks** *Plus* Interactive Student Book
Media Literacy Activities www.macmillanmh.com

807

Word Study: Suffixes Have a student explain what a suffix is. Remind students that sometimes when suffixes are added to a base word it turns the word into a different part of speech. Read the activity on page 806 of the Student Book. Have students complete the activity. Make sure they create real words, using a dictionary to check their work. **To review, see lesson on page 706 of the Teacher's Edition.**

Genre: Expository Text Discuss with students the elements of expository text. Read the activity on page 807 of the Student Book. Have students complete the activity with a partner. When they have finished, allow students to read their summaries to the class.

Research: In Your Own Words Review with students the difference between paraphrasing and plagiarism. Have students discuss why plagiarism is wrong. Guide students to see that by directly quoting somebody without citing them, they are stealing that author's ideas. Read the activity on page 807 of the Student Book. Have students complete the activity individually.

StudentWorks *Plus*
Interactive Student Book

Media Literacy Activities
See Teacher's Edition p. 807J.

Objectives

- Identify features of a research report
- Plan and organize ideas by using a graphic organizer to prewrite
- Draft and revise a research report
- Proofread, publish, and present a research report

Materials

- Writing Transparencies 99–104
- proofreading marks, Teacher's Resource Book, p. 171

Features of a Research Report

- It has a clear **topic** and gives information and answers questions about the topic.
- It starts with an **introduction** and ends with a **conclusion**.
- Paragraphs have **main ideas** stated in **topic sentences.**
- It includes **supporting details** that give facts, examples, or explanations.
- It uses **transition words and phrases** to connect ideas or indicate a conclusion.
- It presents information from **reliable sources** and lists the sources in a **bibliography**.

ELL

Model the Process Choose a topic of interest. Help students brainstorm questions they would ask about the topic. With their help, create a KWL chart. Provide many examples of questions for students to use as models.

Research Report

Read Like a Writer

Tell students that you will read an excerpt from a research report. Ask students to listen for

- the **topic** of the report;
- **supporting details** that give facts, examples, or explanations about the **main ideas** of the paragraphs;
- **transition words** that connect ideas;
- evidence that information came from **reliable sources**.

The Inspiring Falls

One of the most famous attractions in North America, Niagara Falls, can be seen in Canada or the United States. The mighty cataract lies on the border between Ontario and New York. According to the official Canadian and U.S. tourism Web sites, the Falls bring millions of visitors each year.

The section nearest the Canadian bank, known as Horseshoe Falls, is about 185 feet tall and 2,200 feet across. The American Falls comes crashing down at a similar height of about 190 feet. Although both sections are awe-inspiring, the American Falls is smaller at 1,060 feet across.

According to a United States Geological Survey, nearly one third of Horseshoe Falls lies within U.S. territory. Nevertheless, the best views of this section are from the Canadian bank at Queen Victoria Park.

Discuss the Features

After reading, discuss the following questions with students.

- **What is the topic of this report?** (Niagara Falls)
- **What is one main idea?** (Possible responses: Niagara Falls is famous attraction; Horseshoe Falls is awe-inspiring.)
- **What are supporting details for that main idea?** (Possible responses: location, visitors, size)
- **What transition words are used?** (*although, nevertheless*)
- **What sources does the author refer to?** (official tourism Web sites and a United States geological survey)

 # Prewrite

Set a Purpose Remind students that the purpose of a research report is to inform the reader about an interesting topic.

Know the Audience Ask students to think about who will read their reports, such as classmates. *How much do your readers already know about the topic? What do you want them to learn?*

Choose a Topic Tell students they should choose an animal that interests them. Suggest that they use KWL charts to focus and plan their reports.

What I Know	What I Want to Know	What I Learned
Bats are not birds.	What class of animal are bats?	They are mammals.

Minilesson **Organization**

Display **Writing Transparency 99**. Explain that this is an example of an outline that a girl named Emmy used to develop ideas for her research report. Point out the following about the outline:

- Emmy states her topic in the first section, or **introduction**.

- She writes a topic sentence for each **main idea** after each Roman numeral.

- She organizes **supporting details** under each topic sentence.

- She includes a **conclusion** based on what she has learned.

Organize Ideas Tell students they will create their own outlines to plan their research reports. Use Writing Transparency 99 to guide students in using an outline to organize their ideas.

Writer's Resources

Note-Taking Brainstorm a list of reliable resources students can use to gather information about their topics (encyclopedias, books, newspapers, magazines, Web sites, interviews with experts). Demonstrate how to take notes by reading aloud an excerpt and paraphrasing the information. Point out that you include key words and phrases but that you use your own words to avoid plagiarism, or copying someone's work without citing the source. Review how to cite sources.

Writing Prompt

Write a research report about an animal that you would like to learn more about.

Transparency 99

Bats

I. Bats are amazing animals.
   A. They live on all continents except Antarctica.
   B. They are misunderstood.

II. Bats are mammals, not birds.
   A. They are the only flying mammal.
   B. They have hair like other mammals.
   C. They are born alive and feed on milk.

III. Bats are not blind.
   A. They depend on their ears more than their eyes.
   B. They make noises and listen for echoes.

IV. Bats are helpful.
   A. They don't get rabies any more than other animals.
   B. They eat insects that cause disease or harm farm crops.
   C. Their waste is used as fertilizer.

V. If people knew more about bats, they might appreciate them better.

Writing Transparency

Draft

Categorize Information Help students determine a main idea for their research reports. Call on volunteers to share their topics. Ask open-ended questions to help them formulate ideas. Write down their ideas and work together to create a single topic sentence that expresses the main idea.

Minilesson | **Main Idea and Details**

Display **Writing Transparency 100**. Explain that this is a first draft that Emmy will revise and proofread later. Then point out the following features:

- Emmy introduces the **topic** in the **introduction**.

- Each paragraph has a **main idea** that tells about the topic. Emmy uses **supporting details** to tell about the main ideas.

- Emmy uses **transition words and phrases**, such as *but, like,* and *though,* to connect ideas.

- Emmy ends with a **conclusion**.

Review Your Outline Have students review their outlines before they write. Remind them to refer to their outlines frequently as they draft their research reports.

Write the Draft Remind students that the purpose of a first draft is to get their ideas on paper. They will have time to revise and correct their work later. Share the following tips:

- Write a strong introduction to capture the reader's interest.

- Use the material in each Roman numeral from your outline as a topic sentence that states the main idea of a paragraph. The capital letters can provide information for supporting details.

- Use transition words and phrases to connect ideas.

- Write a conclusion that sums up what you learned.

- Include a bibliography, or works-cited page.

 Transparency 100

Bats
by Emmy K.

The bat, which lives on all continents except antarctica, is one of the world's most amazing animals. It is also among the most misunderstood.

Bats are mammals. Bats are the only mammals that really fly. Like other mammals, bats have hair, are born alive, and feed on milk from their mothers.

Despite the phrase blind as a bat, bats aren't blind. Most see very good, though they depend on their ears more than their eyes. Bats make high-pitched noises that humans can't never hear. When these sounds hit something, an echo bounces back. Bats use echoes to help them find food and avoid flying into objects.

Many people worry that bats are harmfull because they carry rabies. But bats are no more likely to get rabies than any other mammal. Bats are quite helpful. They eat insects that can cause disease or harm crops. A final contribution comes from bat waste. People in many parts of the world use it as fertilizer.

As a matter of fact learning about bats will help humans appreciate these interesting animals.

Writing Transparency

Writer's Resources

Write a Bibliography Demonstrate how to write bibliographical entries. Ask students to name sources they used when they took notes. List the sources on the board. Explain that different types of sources include different kinds of information. Point out and discuss the following: source title, author name, article title, publisher, date or year of publication, Web-site address. Show examples:

Bibliography

Gibbons, Gail. <u>Bats</u>. New York: Holiday House, 1999.

Macmillan/McGraw-Hill Education Web site. "Bats." http://www.macmillanmh.com

Revise

Display **Writing Transparency 101** and point out ways Emmy revises her good research report to make it excellent.

- Emmy adds the transition words *in fact* and *actually* to better connect ideas. (Sentence Fluency/Organization)

- She crosses out the words *as a matter of fact* because they disrupt rather than connect ideas. (Sentence Fluency)

- She elaborates by adding a fact about the number of mosquitoes bats can eat. (Development of Ideas)

Remind students that Emmy focused on her ideas while revising. In the next step, she will fix errors in spelling, punctuation, and capitalization. Guide students to think about the following writing elements as they evaluate and revise the draft of their research reports:

Focus and Coherence Is your report focused on one **topic**? Are your paragraphs in a logical order? Did you gather information from reliable sources?

Organization Do you begin with a strong **introduction**? Do you end with a **conclusion** that sums up your ideas? Does each paragraph include a **topic sentence** and **supporting details**?

Word Choice Do you choose vivid and precise words?

Voice Can readers sense your enthusiasm and knowledge about the topic?

Conventions/Sentence Fluency Do you vary your sentences? Do you connect ideas with **transition words and phrases**? Did you use a dictionary and thesaurus to check spelling and word choices?

Peer Review

Think, Pair, Share Have partners listen to each other's drafts for places where there are unnecessary words that make sentences sound choppy. Ask students to share how they improved their reports.

Flexible Pairing Option Consider pairing students who have strong writing skills with those who need support and encouragement.

ELL

Use Resource Materials If students need to add facts and details as they revise, help them identify appropriate key words to use as search terms for their topics. Guide students in using key words to search the Internet or an electronic encyclopedia.

Transparency 101

Bats
by Emmy K.

The bat, which lives on all continents except antarctica, is one of the world's most amazing animals. It is also among the most misunderstood.

In fact,
Bats are mammals. Bats are the only mammals that really fly. Like other mammals, bats have hair, are born alive, and feed on milk from their mothers.

Despite the phrase blind as a bat, bats aren't blind. Most see very good, though they depend on their ears more than their eyes. Bats make high-pitched noises that humans can't never hear. When these sounds hit something, an echo bounces back. Bats use echoes to help them find food and avoid flying into objects.

Many people worry that bats are harmfull because they carry rabies. But bats are no more likely to get rabies than any other mammal. Actually, Bats are quite helpful. They eat insects that can Some bats eat half their weight in mosquitoes in a single night. cause disease or harm crops. A final contribution comes from bat waste. People in many parts of the world use it as fertilizer.

As a matter of fact learning about bats will help humans appreciate these interesting animals.

Writing Transparency

Speaking and Listening

Have students read their research reports aloud. Invite them to share visuals. Share these strategies.

SPEAKING STRATEGIES

- Speak clearly and pace your presentation.

- Include facts and details that help listeners focus.

- Make eye contact with your listeners.

LISTENING STRATEGIES

- Listen attentively and ask relevant questions.

- Listen for and restate main ideas or supporting details.

- Make constructive comments after the presentation.

Minilesson Conventions

Display **Writing Transparency 102** to point out Emmy's corrections.

- She indents the first paragraph, capitalizes the proper noun *Antarctica*, adds quotation marks, and corrects the spelling of *harmful*.

- She uses the adverb *well* to describe the verb *see*.

- She deletes *never* to correct a double negative.

- She combines a sentence and a fragment to make a compound sentence.

Have students reread their research reports to find and correct grammar, spelling, and punctuation mistakes. Review the proofreading marks with students on page 171 of the **Teacher Resource Book**. Remind students to use prepositional phrases to add details, such as time, location, or direction, to their report.

Peer Review

Check Conventions Have partners proofread one another's edited drafts. Ask them to check for grammar, punctuation, and spelling. Have students discuss any corrections.

TEACHER CONFERENCE

Use the rubric on page 807G to evaluate student writing and help you formulate questions to foster self-assessment.

- *What are two reliable sources that you used?*

- *How did transition words improve your report?*

- *What conclusion did you include at the end of your report?*

Publish and Share

Ask students to write or type final copies of their research reports. Remind them to check the spacing between words, sentences, and paragraphs.

PRESENTATION Hold a "knowledge fair" during which students can share their published work with classmates and guests. Students should share visuals that will help their audience understand the topic.

Transparency 102

Bats
by Emmy K.

¶ The bat, which lives on all continents except antarctica, is one of the world's most amazing animals. It is also among the most misunderstood.

In fact,
Bats are mammals. Bats are the only mammals that really fly. Like other mammals, bats have hair, are born alive, and feed on milk from their mothers.

Despite the phrase "blind as a bat," bats aren't blind. Most see very good, though they depend
well
on their ears more than their eyes. Bats make high-pitched noises that humans can't never hear. When these sounds hit something, an echo bounces back. Bats use echoes to help them find food and avoid flying into objects.

harmful
Many people worry that bats are harmfull because they carry rabies. But bats are no more likely to get rabies than any other mammal.
Actually,
Bats are quite helpful. They eat insects that can
Some bats eat half their weight in mosquitoes in a single night
cause disease or harm crops. A final contribution comes from bat waste. People in many parts of the world use it as fertilizer.

As a matter of fact learning about bats will help humans appreciate these interesting animals.

Writing Transparency

Using Rubrics

READ AND SCORE

Display **Writing Transparency 103**. Tell students to follow along as a volunteer reads the research report aloud. Then have students use the student rubric on page 214 of the **Teacher's Resource Book** to assess the writing sample. Guide students to understand that this report is only a fair writing sample that would score a 2, and that they will work together in groups to improve it.

RAISE THE SCORE

Point out the following shortfalls in the writing sample:

Focus and Coherence Tracy tells about hummingbirds but does not write a catchy introduction to catch a reader's interest.

Organization Two different main ideas are included in the third paragraph: how hummingbirds fly and what they eat. Tracy should separate the ideas into two paragraphs.

Development of Ideas/Word Choice Tracy does not use transition words, so the ideas are not always connected.

Have students work in small groups to revise the research report. Remind them to refer to the student rubric.

SHARE AND COMPARE

Ask groups to share their revised versions, explaining how they improved the writing. Then display **Writing Transparency 104** to show the same report written at an excellent level. Have each group compare its revised version with the transparency. Remind students that although two papers vary, they may both be considered excellent. Then have students review the research reports they wrote and try to raise their own scores.

Objective

- Revise a research report to raise the writing score from a 2 to a 4

CREATE A RUBRIC

Teacher-Developed Rubric
You may want to copy, enlarge, and then distribute the blank rubric form on page 216 in the Teacher's Resource Book. Remind students that the rubric should assess whether or not the research report focuses on the topic, is logically organized, includes main ideas, supporting details, and transition words, and demonstrates a strong command of language and conventions.

 Transparency 104

Hummingbirds
by Tracy W.

Can you imagine a bird that weighs less than a penny? That's the size of the bee hummingbird, the smallest bird in the world. Not all hummingbirds are as small as the bee hummingbird, but they are all interesting!

Hummingbirds have long, pointed wings. They can move their wings faster than the eye can see. The wings make a humming noise as they move. That's how the hummingbird got its name.

The rapid beat of the wings allows the bird to hover in midair. The hummingbird can also fly straight up, straight down, and even backwards! No other bird can do that.

Flying takes lots of energy, so hummingbirds eat often. They dip their long bills and tongues inside flowers to get the nectar. For some reason, they seem to like red flowers best. Hummingbirds also drink sugar water from hummingbird feeders. The bird hovers in midair as it sips the sweet liquid.

The hummingbird's size, ways of flying, and feeding style make it a special bird. Maybe someday you'll see one!

Writing Transparency

4-Point Writing Rubric

Use this four-point rubric to assess students' writing.

4-POINT SCORING RUBRIC

4 Excellent	**3** Good	**2** Fair	**1** Unsatisfactor
Focus and Coherence Sustained focus shows how ideas are related. Introduction and conclusion add depth and sense of completeness.	**Focus and Coherence** Focus generally shows clear relationship between ideas. Introduction and conclusion add some depth and sense of completeness.	**Focus and Coherence** Somewhat focused paragraphs may shift quickly among related ideas. Introduction and conclusion may be superficial, but composition has some sense of completeness.	**Focus and Coherence** Weak connection to prompt and abrupt sh among ideas show lac of focus. Composition lacks completeness, with minimal, if any, introduction and conclusion.
Organization Logical and controlled progression of thought, with meaningful transitions. Organizational strategy enhances presentation of ideas.	**Organization** Generally logical and controlled progression of thought, with mostly meaningful transitions. Generally effective organizational strategy is not affected by minor wordiness or repetition.	**Organization** Progression of thought may not be logical and needs more meaningful transitions. Organizational strategy is not effective, with some wordiness or repetition.	**Organization** Progression of though is not logical, and transitions are minima lacking. No evidence organizational strateg with random, wordy, repetitive ideas.
Development of Ideas/ Word Choice Thorough, insightful development of ideas creates depth of thought. Shows interesting connections between ideas and willingness to take compositional risks. Precise word choice enhances quality of content.	**Development of Ideas/ Word Choice** Development of ideas reflects some depth of thought. Presentation of some ideas may be thoughtful but shows little evidence of willingness to take compositional risks. Word choice suits purpose.	**Development of Ideas/ Word Choice** Superficial development of ideas, using lists or brief explanations, is general, inconsistent, or contrived and shows little evidence of depth of thinking. Word choice does not suit purpose.	**Development of Idea Word Choice** General or vague development of ideas. Omits words or uses chosen words incorre
Voice Authentic and original writing expresses unique perspective and sustains connection with reader.	**Voice** Mostly authentic and original writing generally expresses unique perspective and generally sustains connection with reader.	**Voice** Somewhat authentic or original but shows little unique perspective and fails to sustain connection with reader.	**Voice** Shows little or sense of individual vo and no connection wi reader.
Conventions/Sentence Fluency Demonstrates consistent command of spelling, capitalization, punctuation, grammar, usage, and sentence structure. Words, phrases, and sentence structure enhance overall effectiveness of communication.	**Conventions/Sentence Fluency** Demonstrates good command of spelling, capitalization, punctuation, grammar, usage, and sentence structure. Generally appropriate words, phrases, and sentence structure contribute to overall effectiveness of communication.	**Conventions/Sentence Fluency** Demonstrates limited command of spelling, capitalization, punctuation, grammar, usage, and sentence structure. Simple or inaccurate words or phrases and some awkward sentences limit overall effectiveness of communication.	**Conventions/Senten Fluency** Demonstrate little or no command spelling, capitalization punctuation, gramma usage, and sentence structure. May be difficult to read. Misu omitted, or awkward words, phrases, or sentences interfere wi communication.
Presentation Handwriting or typing is neat, consistent, and error free.	**Presentation** Margins are mostly even. Font is appropriate or handwriting is neat and mostly consistent.	**Presentation** Margins are inconsistent. Font is inappropriate or handwriting is difficult to read.	**Presentation** Spacing is uneven. Format is confusing or absent o handwriting is illegible in parts.

Anchor Papers

Use these Anchor Papers in the **Teacher's Resource Book** to evaluate students' writing.

Teacher's Resource Book, page 239

Teacher's Resource Book, page 240

Teacher's Resource Book, page 241

Teacher's Resource Book, page 242

Anchor Papers

Research Report Score: 4 Points

Bats
by Emmy K.

The bat, which lives on all continents except Antarctica, is one of the world's most amazing animals. It is also among the most misunderstood.

Bats are mammals. In fact, bats are the only mammals that really fly. Like other mammals, bats have hair, are born alive, and feed on milk from their mothers.

Despite the phrase "blind as a bat," bats aren't blind at all. Most see very well, though they depend on their ears more than their eyes. Bats make high-pitched noises that humans can't hear. When these sounds hit something, an echo bounces back. Bats use echoes to help them find food and avoid flying into objects.

Many people worry that bats are harmful because they carry rabies, but bats are no more likely to get rabies than any other mammal. Actually, bats are quite helpful. They eat insects that can cause disease or that harm crops. Some bats eat half their weight in mosquitoes in a single night! A final contribution comes from bat waste. People in many parts of the world use it as fertilizer.

Learning more about these flying mammals will help humans appreciate these interesting and important animals.

Focus and Coherence The report is well focused on the topic, and all information is relevant. The report has a sense of completeness, with an engaging introduction and a thoughtful conclusion.

Organization The progression of ideas from sentence to sentence and paragraph to paragraph is smooth and controlled. Each well-crafted paragraph has a distinct main idea supported by relevant details. Meaningful transitions link ideas.

Development of Ideas/Word Choice All ideas are well developed. Supporting explanations and details are thorough yet succinct, and the language is precise.

Voice The writer shows originality throughout. The personal tone also adds to the interest of the report.

Conventions/Sentence Fluency The writer uses a variety of sentence structures to convey ideas and shows skill in most writing conventions.

Short-Answer Reading Rubric

Use the Short-Answer Reading Rubric to score students' short-answer responses to the weekly Comprehension Check questions and the short-answer questions on weekly and unit assessments.

SHORT-ANSWER READING RUBRIC

3 Excellent	**2** Good	**1** Fair	**0** Unsatisfactory
An **exemplary** response must • be thoughtful and insightful; • be strongly supported with accurate/relevant textual evidence; • show depth of understanding and ability to effectively connect textual evidence to the idea, analysis, or evaluation.	A **sufficient** response must • be reasonable; • be supported with accurate/relevant textual evidence; • be clear and specific.	A **partially sufficient** response may • be reasonable; • be supported by general, incomplete, partially accurate/relevant textual evidence, if any; • weakly connect textual evidence to the idea, analysis, or evaluation; • be somewhat unclear or vague.	An **insufficient** response may • not be reasonable or be too general or vague to determine whether it is reasonable; • not address the question or answer a different question than the one asked; • not be based on the selection; • incorrectly analyze or evaluate the text; • offer only incomplete or irrelevant textual evidence, if any; • lack clarity.

Evidence may consist of a direct quotation, a paraphrase, or a specific synopsis.

Objectives

- Improve a media presentation
- Insert clip art and text into a slide show presentation

Materials

- www.macmillanmh.com
- presentation application such as Microsoft PowerPoint

Vocabulary

presentation a show given for an audience

slide show a series of pictures presented in a certain order to display information

multimedia the use of more than one text, sound, video, and graphic source

Computer Literacy
Focus on Keyboard and Internet Skills and Media Literacy
www.macmillanmh.com

Remind students to get permission before downloading any type of file. Failing to doing so can result in accidentally downloading a virus, which could be harmful to the computer.

Computer Literacy
Adding to a Presentation

ACCESS PRIOR KNOWLEDGE

Discuss with students:

- When you present information to other people, what are some different ways to capture their attention?

- What are some effects that you could add to your presentation?

EXPLAIN

Introduce the lesson vocabulary by writing each word on the board and asking for a definition.

- Have students think about how they can make a **presentation** more interesting.

- Tell them that inserting **clip art** is just one of many ways to improve a presentation such as a **slide show**.

MODEL

- Show students how to open a slide show presentation.

- Show students how to use a search engine to find clip art that can be used in a presentation. Remind them that they cannot use any images that are copyrighted.

- Show how to save clip art and insert it into a slide show.

Technology Makes a Difference

Multimedia Presentations

▶ A **multimedia** presentation uses a combination of text, audio, video, and graphic files. Multimedia presentations can be used for a variety of purposes.

▶ Creating a multimedia presentation is an effective way to communicate large amounts of information and ideas to an audience in an interesting way.

Media Literacy

Online vs. In Print

ACCESS PRIOR KNOWLEDGE

Discuss with students:

- Have you ever read an online issue of a magazine or newspaper? In what ways was it different from the print edition?

- What are some advantages and disadvantages to having the same magazine or newspaper appear both in print and online?

- Why do you think so many publications have online editions?

EXPLAIN

Introduce the lesson vocabulary by writing each word on the board and asking for its definition.

- **Online magazines** and **online newspapers** are delivered over the Internet.

- Some online **publications** only exist online, while others are the **digital edition** of the **print edition** of a magazine or newspaper.

- Many new opportunities were created for newspapers and magazines by adding a digital edition. These publications can now interact with their readers, publish news more quickly, and attract more **advertisers**.

- Digital editions are considered more **environmentally friendly** because they use less paper and energy than print editions.

MODEL

- Show students both the print and digital editions of an age-appropriate magazine or newspaper. Explain that while much of the content is the same, the digital edition offers unique features such as forums where readers can comment on stories, blogs, polls, slide shows, video, and other interactive elements.

- Provide students with a newspaper or magazine article from the print edition of the publication. In small groups, have students brainstorm ideas for what the digital edition of the same publication would look like. Have students write a detailed description of what types of information and features their digital edition would include. Have students share their ideas and writing with their classmates.

Objective

- Compare written conventions used for digital media
- Distinguish between print and digital editions of newspapers and magazines

Materials

- examples of print and digital editions of publications

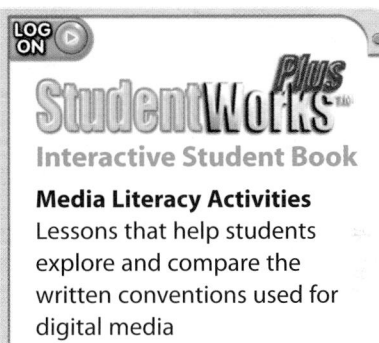

LOG ON

StudentWorks Plus

Interactive Student Book

Media Literacy Activities
Lessons that help students explore and compare the written conventions used for digital media

Theme Project Wrap-Up
Research/Organizing and Presenting Ideas

After students complete Step 1, Step 2, Step 3, and Step 4 of their project, have them work on the following:

 Step 5 Create the Presentation Have students present the information they gathered about their problem and solution in a booklet. In the booklet they should include graphic aids for clarification. Have students share their booklets with the class in an oral presentation.

 Step 6 Review and Evaluate Use these questions to help you and students evaluate their research and presentation.

Teacher's Checklist

Assess the Research Process

Planning the Project
- ✔ Generated a research topic and formulated open-ended questions.
- ✔ Created a research plan for gathering information.

Doing the Project
- ✔ Located relevant information in multiple credible sources.
- ✔ Recorded simple notes and sorted evidence.
- ✔ Organized information.

Assess the Presentation

Speaking
- ✔ Spoke clearly.
- ✔ Expressed an opinion supported by information.
- ✔ Presented an effective introduction and conclusion.

Representing
- ✔ Presented organized data and elaborated on main ideas.
- ✔ Clearly explained the problem and solution.
- ✔ Chose helpful graphic aids.

Assess the Listener

- ✔ Listened actively.
- ✔ Asked focused questions.
- ✔ Took notes.
- ✔ Made inferences.
- ✔ Connected ideas to those of the speaker.

Student's Checklist

Research Process
- ✔ Did you sort information into a graphic organizer?
- ✔ Did you research using both print and electronic sources?
- ✔ Did you evaluate the information you collected?

Presenting

Speaking
- ✔ Did you answer the audience's questions?
- ✔ Did you use speak clearly at an appropriate pace?

Representing
- ✔ Did your presentation clearly explain the problem and solution?
- ✔ Did your graphic aids clarify important facts and ideas?

SCORING RUBRIC FOR THEME PROJECT

④ Excellent	**③ Good**	**② Fair**	**① Unsatisfactory**
The student • presents the information in a clear and interesting way; • uses visuals that effectively present important information; • includes an effective introduction and conclusion.	The student • presents the information in a fairly clear way; • uses visuals that present relevant information; • includes an introduction and conclusion.	The student • struggles to present information clearly; • may use a few adequate visuals; • includes either an introduction or a conclusion.	The student • may not grasp the task; • may present sketchy information in a disorganized way; • does not have an introduction or conclusion.

Home-School Connection

■ Invite family members, other students, and members of the community to the presentation of the projects. Introduce each guest by name and relationship to the school community.

■ Videotape the presentations for family members to borrow or to show at the parent/teacher conferences.

■ Have students present their project to the whole grade or school or to a community organization. Include a question-and-answer period to clarify and interpret the presentation.

■ Make sure students adjust their language content to their audience and purpose.

■ Remind students to emphasize points in ways that help the listener or viewer to follow important ideas and concepts.

■ Have the class write a collaborative thank-you letter to those who attended.

Big Question Wrap-Up

Review the Big Question. Have students use their layered book organizers and what they learned to help them respond to the following questions: *What is a good way for people to go about solving a problem? Is there always one right way to solve a problem? Why or why not?* Students can sum up their major ideas by giving simple directions for problem-solvers.

Monitoring Progress

Administer the Test

UNIT 6 TEST

TESTED SKILLS AND STRATEGIES

COMPREHENSION STRATEGIES AND SKILLS

- Strategies: analyze story structure, generate questions
- Skills: problem and solution; cause and effect; fact and opinion; draw conclusions; author's perspective

VOCABULARY STRATEGIES

- Word parts: prefixes, suffixes, Latin, Greek, and other linguistic roots
- Multiple-meaning words
- Dictionary: unfamiliar words, idioms

TEXT FEATURES AND STUDY SKILLS

- Maps
- Functional documents
- Time lines

LITERARY ELEMENTS

- Imagery
- Figurative language
- Metaphor
- Alliteration

GRAMMAR, MECHANICS, USAGE

- Adverbs, comparing with adverbs
- Negatives, correcting double negatives
- Prepositions and prepositional phrases
- Punctuation and capitalization
- Using quotations
- Sentence combining

WRITING

- Expository: research report

Use Multiple Assessments for Instructional Planning

To create instructional profiles for your students, look for patterns in the results from any of the following assessments.

Fluency Assessment

Plan appropriate fluency-building activities and practice to help all students achieve the following goal: **113–133 WCPM**.

Running Records

Use the instructional reading level determined by the Running Record calculations for regrouping decisions.

Benchmark Assessment

Administer tests four times a year as an additional measure of both student progress and the effectiveness of the instructional program.

Digital Assessment

Assessment Online
- Prescriptions for Reteaching
- Student Profile System

Test Generator
- Available on CD-ROM

Analyze the Data

Use information from a variety of informal and formal assessments, as well as your own judgment, to assist in your instructional planning. Students who consistently score at the lowest end of each range should be evaluated for Intervention. Use the **Diagnostic Assessment** for guidelines for decision making.

Diagnose		Prescribe
ASSESSMENTS	**IF...**	**THEN...**
UNIT TEST	0–21 questions correct	Reteach tested skills using the **Intervention Teacher's Editions**.
FLUENCY ASSESSMENT		
Oral Reading Fluency	109–112 WCPM 0–108 WCPM	Fluency Solutions Reteach using the **Fluency Intervention Teacher's Edition**.
RUNNING RECORDS	Level 28 or below	Reteach Comprehension skills using the **Comprehension Intervention Teacher's Edition**. Provide additional Fluency activities.

Response to Intervention

To place students in Tier 2 or Tier 3 Intervention use the *Diagnostic Assessment*.

- Phonics
- Vocabulary
- Comprehension
- Fluency
- Writing and Grammar

Glossary

Introduce students to the Glossary by reading through the introduction and looking over the pages with them. Ask the class to talk about what they see.

Words in a glossary, like words in a dictionary, are listed in **alphabetical order**. Point out the **guide words** at the top of each page that tell the first and last words appearing on that page.

ENTRIES

Point out examples of **main entries**, or entry words, and entries. Read through a sample entry with the class, identifying each part. Have students note the order in which information is given: entry word(s), syllable division, pronunciation respelling, part of speech, definition(s), example sentence(s).

Note if more than one definition is given for a word, the definitions are numbered. Note the format used for a word that is more than one part of speech.

Review the **parts of speech** by identifying each in a sentence:

Inter.	*article*	*n.*	*conj.*	*adj.*	*n.*
Wow!	A	dictionary	and	useful	glossary

v.	*adv.*	*pron.*	*prep.*	*n.*
tell	almost	everything	about	words!

HOMOGRAPHS/HOMOPHONES/HOMONYMS

Point out that some entries are for multiple-meaning words called **homographs**. Homographs have the same spellings but have different origins and meanings, and, in some cases, different pronunciations.

Explain that students should not confuse homographs with **homophones** or **homonyms**. Homophones are words that have the same pronunciation but have different spellings and meanings. Homonyms are words that have the same pronunciation and spelling but have different meanings. Provide students with examples.

PRONUNCIATION KEY

Explain the use of the pronunciation key (either the short key, at the bottom of every other page, or the long key, at the beginning of the Glossary). Demonstrate the difference between primary stress and secondary stress by pronouncing a word with both. Pronounce the words both correctly and incorrectly to give students a clearer understanding of the proper pronunciations.

WORD HISTORY

The Word History feature explains the **etymology** of select words. Explain that etymology is the history of a word from its origin to its present form. A word's etymology explains which language it comes from and what changes have occurred in its spelling and/or meaning. Many English words are derivatives of words from other languages, such as Latin or Greek. Derivatives are formed from base or root words.

Glossary

What Is a Glossary?

A glossary can help you find the **meanings** of words in this book that you may not know. The words in the glossary are listed in **alphabetical order**. **Guide words** at the top of each page tell you the first and last words on the page.

Each word is divided into syllables. The way to pronounce the word is given next. You can understand the pronunciation respelling by using the **pronunciation key**. A shorter key appears at the bottom of every other page. When a word has more than one syllable, a dark accent mark (′) shows which syllable is stressed. In some words, a light accent mark (′) shows which syllable has a less heavy stress. Sometimes an entry includes a second meaning for the word.

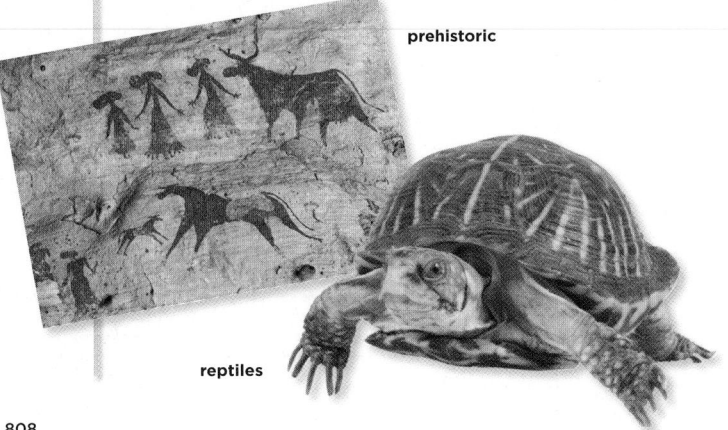

prehistoric

reptiles

808

Guide Words

script/splendid

First word on the page   Last word on the page

Sample Entry

Main entry & Syllable division — **sketch•es** (skech′əz) *plural noun.* Simple drawings that are done quickly. *I made several sketches before finally painting the tree.*

Pronunciation   Part of speech

Definition

Example sentence

Pronunciation Key

Phonetic Spelling	Examples	Phonetic Spelling	Examples
a	at, bad, plaid, laugh	d	dear, soda, bad
ā	ape, pain, day, break	f	five, defend, leaf, off, cough, elephant
ä	father, calm	g	game, ago, fog, egg
âr	care, pair, bear, their, where	h	hat, ahead
e	end, pet, said, heaven, friend	hw	white, whether, which
ē	equal, me, feet, team, piece, key	j	joke, enjoy, gem, page, edge
i	it, big, give, hymn	k	kite, bakery, seek, tack, cat
ī	ice, fine, lie, my	l	lid, sailor, feel, ball, allow
îr	ear, deer, here, pierce	m	man, family, dream
o	odd, hot, watch	n	not, final, pan, knife, gnaw
ō	old, oat, toe, low	ng	long, singer
ô	coffee, all, taught, law, fought	p	pail, repair, soap, happy
ôr	order, fork, horse, story, pour	r	ride, parent, wear, more, marry
oi	oil, toy	s	sit, aside, pets, cent, pass
ou	out, now, bough	sh	shoe, washer, fish, mission, nation
u	up, mud, love, double	t	tag, pretend, fat, dressed
ū	use, mule, cue, feud, few	th	thin, panther, both
ü	rule, true, food, fruit	th	these, mother, smooth
ù	put, wood, should, look	v	very, favor, wave
ûr	burn, hurry, term, bird, word, courage	w	wet, weather, reward
ə	about, taken, pencil, lemon, circus	y	yes, onion
b	bat, above, job	z	zoo, lazy, jazz, rose, dogs, houses
ch	chin, such, match	zh	vision, treasure, seizure

809

Aa

ab•sorbed (ab zôrbd′) *verb.* Soaked up something such as a liquid or the sun's rays. *It was a hot day, so the plant absorbed the water immediately.*

a•chieved (ə chēvd′) *verb.* To have done or carried out successfully. *She studied hard and achieved the grade she wanted.*

ac•quaint•ance (ə kwān′təns) *noun.* A person one knows, but who is not a close friend. *Carole is an acquaintance from camp.*

ac•tive (ak′tiv) *adjective.* Lively, busy. *Carlos is always active; he hardly ever sits still.*

ad•vanced (ad vanst′) *adjective.* Beyond the beginning level; not elementary. *As a singer, Sheila was really advanced for her age.*

ag•ile (aj′əl) *adjective.* Able to move and react quickly and easily. *Bonita is an agile softball player.*

al•loy (al′oi) *noun.* A metal formed by fusing two or more metals. *Brass is an alloy of copper and zinc.*

a•maze•ment (ə māz′mənt) *noun.* Great surprise or wonder. *To the amazement of the audience, the children played some difficult music perfectly.*

am•bu•lance (am′byə ləns) *noun.* A special vehicle that is used to carry sick or injured people to a hospital. *My neighbor once had to call an ambulance to take him to the hospital.*

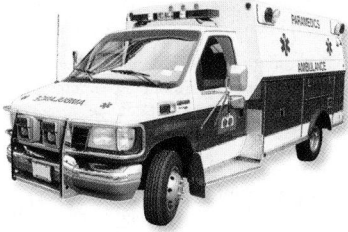

an•ces•tors (an′ses tərz) *plural noun.* People in the past from whom one comes. *Your great-grandparents are some of your ancestors.*

an•noyed (ə noid′) *adjective.* Bothered or disturbed. *Kevin looked annoyed when his little sister came out to join the game.*

an•nu•al (an′yü əl) *adjective.* Measured by the year. *The annual rainfall in our hometown is close to 20 inches.*

an•tic•i•pa•tion (an tis′ə pā′shən) *noun.* A feeling of excited expectation. *Tim was full of eager anticipation as he got on the roller coaster.*

a•pol•o•gize (ə pol′ə jīz′) *verb.* To say one is sorry or embarrassed; make an apology. *Aaron said, "I'd like to apologize for being late."*

ap•plaud•ed (ə plôd′əd) *verb.* Showed approval for or enjoyment of something by the clapping of hands. *The crowd applauded the soldiers as they came off the ship.*

ap•pre•ci•at•ed (ə prē′shē āt′əd) *verb.* Understood the value of; was grateful for something. *The boss appreciated how much his workers did for the company.*

as•sem•bled (ə sem′bəld) *verb.* To have put or fit together. *Anita and Grace assembled their wagon in just three hours.*

as•sured (ə shùrd′) *verb.* Made certain or sure. *Our hard work assured the success of the festival.*

a•void•ed (ə void′əd) *verb.* Stayed away from. *Butch avoided doing hard work.*

a•ware (ə wâr′) *adjective.* Knowing or realizing. *I don't wear headphones when I run, so I am aware of what is around me.*

awk•ward (ôk′wərd) *adjective.* Lacking grace in movement or behavior; clumsy or uncomfortable. *Until Julio learned the steps, his dancing was awkward.*

Bb

bar•be•cue (bär′bi kū′) *noun.* A meal, usually meat, cooked outdoors over an open fire. *We had a great barbecue in the park.*

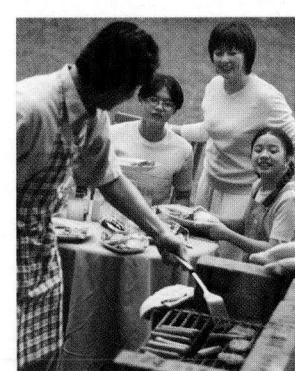

at; āpe; fär; câre; end; mē; it; īce; pîerce; hot; ōld; sông; fôrk; oil; out; up; ūse; rūle; pùll; tûrn; chin; sing; shop; thin; <u>th</u>is; hw in white; zh in treasure.

The symbol ə stands for the unstressed vowel sound in about, taken, pencil, lemon, and circus.

810

811

bar•gained (bär′gind) *verb.* To have talked over the terms of an agreement or sale. *My dad* **bargained** *with the salesperson to get a deal on our new car.*

bid•ding (bid′ing) *noun.* A period in which bids, offers of payments, are made or received. *The auction house started the* **bidding** *for the antiques.*

bor•der (bôr′dər) *noun.* A line between one country, state, county, or town and another. *A river runs along the* **border** *between the two states.*

boy•cotts (boi′kots) *plural noun.* Protests in which people refuse to buy from or work for a person, nation, or business. *The* **boycotts** *against the unfair company were very successful.*

Word History

Boycotts comes from Charles Boycott, who was shunned by Irish farmers for his harsh actions against them.

brit•tle (brit′əl) *adjective.* Likely to break or snap. *Susan's fingernails became* **brittle** *and started to break.*

Cc

cam•ou•flage (kam′ə fläzh′) *verb.* To hide or conceal by using shapes or colors that blend with the surroundings. *The chameleon is able to* **camouflage** *itself by changing the color of its skin.*

car•at (kar′ət) *noun.* A unit of weight equal to 1/5 of a gram, usually used to measure gems. *The ring had a three* **carat** *diamond in the center.*

chal•leng•es (chal′ənj ez) *plural noun.* Those things that call for work, effort, and the use of one's talents. *Ted's greatest* **challenges** *are in Art and Spanish.*

char•i•ty (char′i tē) *noun.* The giving of help to the poor or needy. *After the flood, some of the families refused to accept any* **charity***.*

cir•cu•lar (sûr′kyə lər) *adjective.* Having or making the shape of a circle. *The referee's arm made a* **circular** *motion as he blew the whistle.*

cit•i•zen (sit′ə zən) *noun.* A person who was born in a country or who chooses to live in and become a member of that country. *Carmine is an Italian* **citizen** *but often visits the United States.*

civ•i•li•za•tions (siv′əl ə zā′shəns) *plural noun.* Human societies in which agriculture, trade, government, art, and science are highly developed. *Charles studies the ancient* **civilizations** *of Asia.*

cli•mate (klī′mit) *noun.* The average weather conditions of a place or region through the year. *Most deserts have a hot, dry* **climate***.*

clus•tered (klus′tərd) *verb.* To have grown, or grouped together, things of the same kind. *The grapes were* **clustered** *in a bunch.*

col•lage (kə läzh′) *noun.* A picture made by pasting paper, cloth, metal, and other things in an arrangement on a surface. *Once I made a* **collage** *of my day's activities by using clippings from magazines.*

Word History

Collage comes from the French word *collage*, from *colle*, meaning "glue" or "paste."

col•o•ny (kol′ə nē) *noun.* A group of animals or plants of the same kind that live together. *I found a* **colony** *of ants in my yard.*

com•mo•tion (kə mō′shən) *noun.* A noisy disturbance; confusion. *We ran into the hall to see what was causing the* **commotion***.*

com•mu•ni•ca•tion (kə mū′ni kā′shən) *noun.* An exchange or sharing of feelings, thoughts, or information. *Music is one form of* **communication** *that does not require speech.*

com•ple•ted (kəm plēt′əd) *verb.* Finished; did. *I had to wait until I* **completed** *my homework before I could go to the movies.*

con•ceived (kən sēvd′) *verb.* To have formed an idea; thought up. *The plan was* **conceived** *after everyone had gone to bed.*

con•densed (kən densd′) *verb.* To have made thicker or more compact; to have reduced the volume of. *The chef* **condensed** *the sauce by boiling it for 20 minutes.*

con•di•tions (kən dish′əns) *plural noun.* The state something is in. *Because of the* **conditions** *at the playground, we weren't allowed to play there.*

at; āpe; fär; câre; end; mē; it; īce; pîerce; hot; ōld; sông; fôrk; oil; out; up; ūse; rūle; pûll; tûrn; chin; sing; shop; thin; this; hw in white; zh in treasure.

The symbol ə stands for the unstressed vowel sound in about, taken, pencil, lemon, and circus.

con•duc•ted (kən dukt′tid) *verb.* To have directed, led, guided, or transmitted. *When Susie lost her sneaker, she* **conducted** *a search of the entire locker room.*

con•sis•ted (kən sis′təd) *verb.* Contained; was made up. *The batter* **consisted** *of a cup of flour, one egg, and a cup of milk.*

con•vinced (kən vinst′) *verb.* To have caused a person to do or believe something. *Raj finally* **convinced** *his father he was old enough to go on the trip.*

crank•y (krang′kē) *adjective.* To be cross or in a bad temper; grouchy. *Roni is always* **cranky** *before she's had breakfast.*

cur•i•ous (kyúr′ē əs) *adjective.* Eager to learn new, strange, or interesting things. *We were all* **curious** *to know who our new teacher might be.*

cur•rent (kûr′ənt) *noun.* A portion of a body of water or of air flowing continuously in a definite direction. *The* **current** *took the raft far out to sea.*

Dd

dec•ades (dek′ādz) *plural noun.* Periods of ten years. *Our family has lived in the same city for nearly six* **decades***.*

Word History

Decades comes from the Greek *deka*, meaning "ten."

de•cayed (dē kād′) *adjective.* Having undergone the process of decomposition; rotted. *We walked in the woods past* **decayed** *stumps of trees.*

de•fend (di fend′) *verb.* Guard against attack or harm. *The rabbit could not* **defend** *itself against the snake, so it ran away.*

def•i•ni•tion (def′ə nish′ən) *noun.* An explanation of what a word or phrase means. *Our teacher Mr. Mitchell asked us what the* **definition** *of "like" is.*

de•mon•stra•ted (de′mən strā′təd) *verb.* Showed by actions or experiment. *The performer* **demonstrated** *great skill with both the piano and the drums.*

de•scen•dants (di send′ənts) *plural noun.* People who come from a particular ancestor. *My neighbors are* **descendants** *of a French explorer.*

de•signed (di zīnd′) *verb.* To have made a plan, drawing, or outline of something. *Penelope's sister* **designed** *the perfect sundress for her.*

des•per•ate (des′pər it) *adjective.* Very bad or hopeless. *I needed money, but the situation was not* **desperate***.*

di•ges•ted (di jes′tid) *verb.* To have broken down food in the mouth, stomach, and intestines. *After my dog had* **digested** *his dinner he was hungry again.*

dis•ap•point•ment (dis′ə point′mənt) *noun.* A feeling of being disappointed or let down. *Losing the match was a* **disappointment***, but I still like tennis.*

dis•miss (dis mis′) *verb.* To discard or reject. *John was able to* **dismiss** *the story he heard as a rumor.*

dis•play (di splā′) *noun.* A show or exhibit. *The children's artwork is the main* **display** *on the family refrigerator.*

dis•rupt (dis rupt′) *verb.* To throw into disorder or confusion. *An argument might* **disrupt** *the meeting.*

diz•zy (diz′ē) *adjective.* Having the feeling of spinning and being about to fall. *I was* **dizzy** *when I got off the Ferris wheel.*

dove (dōv) *verb.* Plunged head first into water. *We watched as the woman* **dove** *perfectly off the board and into the deep pool.*

dove (duv) *noun.* A medium-size bird of the pigeon family. *The* **dove** *cooed quietly on the window ledge.*

draw•backs (drô′bäks) *plural noun.* Things that make something more difficult or unpleasant. *One of the* **drawbacks** *of his job is the long hours.*

drought (drout) *noun.* A period of time in which there is little or no rainfall. *The terrible August* **drought** *affected the wheat crop.*

at; āpe; fär; câre; end; mē; it; īce; pîerce; hot; ōld; sông; fôrk; oil; out; up; ūse; rūle; pûll; tûrn; chin; sing; shop; thin; this; hw in white; zh in treasure.

The symbol ə stands for the unstressed vowel sound in about, taken, pencil, lemon, and circus.

Dust Bowl (dust bōl) *noun.* The region in the central United States that suffered from the great dust storms of the 1930s. *Oklahoma was part of the **Dust Bowl**.*

Ee

eaves•drop•ping (ēvz'drop'ing) *noun.* Listening to other people talking without letting them know you are listening. *He was **eavesdropping** on her neighbors.*

ech•o•lo•ca•tion (ek'ō lō kā'shən) *noun.* A way to find out where objects are by making sounds and interpreting the echo that returns. *Bats rely on **echolocation** when they hunt for insects.*

ee•rie (ir'ē) *adjective.* Strange in a scary way. *We heard an owl's **eerie** hooting as we walked home in the dark.*

e•lec•tri•cal (i lek'tri kəl) *adjective.* Relating to the form of energy carried in wires for use to drive motors or as light or heat. *Dad carefully connected the **electrical** cables to the new DVD player in the den.*

e•merge (i mûrj') *verb.* To come into view or become known. *After months in hibernation, the bears **emerge**.*

en•coun•ter (en koun'tər) *verb.* To meet or face, usually unexpectedly. *Katie listens to the traffic report so she does not **encounter** any delays.*

en•cour•aged (en kûr'ijd) *verb.* To have inspired with courage, hope, or confidence. *The bright sunlight **encouraged** us to continue our hike.*

end•less (end'lis) *adjective.* Having no limit or end. *The line of people for the show seemed **endless**.*

en•dured (en dûrd' or en dyûrd') *verb.* Survived or put up with. *The workers **endured** the hot sun all day.*

e•nor•mous (i nôr'məs) *adjective.* Much greater than the usual size, amount, or degree; extremely large. *The **enormous** pumpkin weighed over 300 pounds.*

en•ter•pris•ing (en'tər prī'zing) *adjective.* Showing energy and initiative; willing or inclined to take risks. *Brian, an **enterprising** young man, ran for class president and won.*

e•sta•blished (i stab'lishd) *verb.* To have begun, created, or set up. *We **established** a scholarship in memory of my mother.*

e•va•po•rate (i vap'ə rāt') *verb.* To change from a liquid or solid into a gas. *Heat makes water **evaporate**.*

Word History
Evaporate comes from the Latin *evaporatus*, "dispersed in vapor," from *ex*, "out," and *vapor*, "exhalation."

e•ven•tu•al•ly (i ven'chü ə lē) *adverb.* In the end; finally. *We **eventually** got a DVD player because the good movies were not being shown on television.*

ex•as•per•at•ed (eg zas'pər āt'əd) *verb.* Annoyed greatly; made angry. *Helping me with my math so **exasperated** my dad that my mom took over.*

ex•po•sure (ek spō'zhər) *noun.* The condition of being presented to view. *After each **exposure** to the new toy, the dog began to recognize it and would pick it up without being asked.*

Ff

fam•ished (fam'isht) *adjective.* Very hungry; starving. *After a long day of running and swimming, the children were **famished** and wanted to eat as soon as possible.*

flinched (flincht) *verb.* Drew back or away, as from something painful or unpleasant; winced. *When the door suddenly slammed, Myra **flinched**.*

fool•ish•ness (fü'lish nəs) *noun.* The act of not showing good sense. *I wanted to race across the street, but my mom will not allow that **foolishness**.*

frag•ile (fraj'əl) *adjective.* Easily broken; delicate. *My toothpick ship is too **fragile** to take to show-and-tell.*

freeze-dried (frēz'drī'd) *verb.* To dry while frozen under high vacuum for preservation. *On the camping trip, John mixed a cup of boiling water with a teaspoon of **freeze-dried** coffee.*

fre•quent•ly (frē'kwənt lē) *adverb.* Happening often. *I **frequently** eat cereal for breakfast.*

fron•tier (frun tîr') *noun.* The far edge of a country, where people are just beginning to settle. *Many Americans moved to the **frontier** in covered wagons.*

fu•els (fü'əlz) *plural noun.* Substances burned as a source of heat and power, such as coal, wood, or oil. *When the world runs out of fossil **fuels**, we will be forced to use alternate energy sources.*

at; āpe; fär; câre; end; mē; it; īce; pîerce; hot; ōld; sông; fôrk; oil; out; up; ūse; rüle; púll; tûrn; chin; sing; shop; thin; this; hw in white; zh in treasure. | The symbol ə stands for the unstressed vowel sound in about, taken, pencil, lemon, and circus.

Gg

gaped (gāpt) *verb.* Stared with the mouth open, as in wonder or surprise. *The audience **gaped** at the acrobats.*

gen•u•ine (jen'ū in) *adjective.* Sincere; honest. *My friends and I made a **genuine** effort to help all the kids that were new to the school.*

glanced (glansd) *verb.* To take a brief or hurried look. *He **glanced** at the magazines on the table.*

glist•ened (glis'ənd) *verb.* To shine with reflected light. *The snow on the fir trees **glistened** in the sun.*

globe (glōb) *noun.* Earth (as a shape). *Our **globe** is the home of billions of people.*

glo•ri•ous (glor'ē əs) *adjective.* Having or deserving praise or honor; magnificent. *The colors of the maple leaves in autumn are **glorious**.*

Great De•pres•sion (grāt'dē presh'ən) *noun.* A worldwide economic downturn that began in 1928. *My grandparents tell stories about how difficult it was to find a job during the **Great Depression**.*

guard•i•an (gär'dē ən) *noun.* A person or thing that guards or watches over. *My older brother sometimes acts like he is my **guardian**.*

Hh

hab•i•tat (hab'i tat') *noun.* The place where an animal or plant naturally lives and grows. *A swamp is a common **habitat** for many creatures.*

han•dy (han'dē) *adjective.* Within reach, nearby; easy to use. To **come in handy** is to be useful. *It's amazing how many times a dictionary can **come in handy**.*

harm•less (härm'les) *adjective.* Not able to do damage or hurt. *My dog looks mean, but really she is **harmless**.*

head•lines (hed'līnz) *plural noun.* Words printed at the top of a newspaper or magazine article. *The most important news has the biggest **headlines**.*

hi•ber•nate (hī'bər nāt') *verb.* To sleep or stay inactive during the winter. *Bears eat a lot to get ready to **hibernate**.*

hi•lar•i•ous (hi lâr'ē əs) *adjective.* Very funny. *Keisha tells **hilarious** jokes that make everyone laugh.*

hoist•ing (hoist'ing) *verb.* Lifting or pulling up. ***Hoisting** logs out of the water, the men soon grew tired.*

Ii

i•den•ti•fied (ī den'tə fīd) *verb.* Proved that someone or something is a particular person or thing. *The fingerprints on the gold watch **identified** the butler as the thief.*

im•pres•sive (im pres'iv) *adjective.* Deserving admiration; making a strong impression. *The track team won five races, which was its most **impressive** result all year.*

in•ci•dent (in'si dənt) *noun.* An event or act. *After the pep rally, there was a funny **incident** involving bales of hay and the school mascot.*

in•de•pen•dence (in'di pen'dəns) *noun.* Freedom from the control of another or others. *America gained its **independence** from Great Britain.*

in•jus•tice (in jus'tis) *noun.* Lack of justice; unfairness. *The workers felt it was an **injustice** that they could not vote on the issue.*

in•sec•ti•cides (in sek'ti sīdz') *plural noun.* Chemicals for killing insects. *Our family room was sprayed with **insecticides**.*

at; āpe; fär; câre; end; mē; it; īce; pîerce; hot; ōld; sông; fôrk; oil; out; up; ūse; rüle; púll; tûrn; chin; sing; shop; thin; this; hw in white; zh in treasure. | The symbol ə stands for the unstressed vowel sound in about, taken, pencil, lemon, and circus.

Glossary

in•spire (in spīr′) *verb.* To stir the mind, feelings, or imagination. *Nature can **inspire** some people to write poetry.*

in•sult (in′sult) *noun.* A remark or action that hurts someone's feelings or pride. *It would be an **insult** not to invite Marta to the party.*

in•tel•li•gent (in tel′i jənt) *adjective.* Able to understand and to think especially well. *An **intelligent** person was needed to solve the difficult puzzle.*

in•ter•act (in′tər akt′) *verb.* To act together, toward, or with others. *My teacher and our class **interact** on a daily basis.*

in•ter•fere (in′tər fîr′) *verb.* To take part in the affairs of others when not asked; to meddle. *My mom hates to **interfere** with my business, but she often gives me good advice.*

in•ter•vals (in′tər vəlz) *plural noun.* The spaces or time between two things. *There are **intervals** of 50 miles between each rest stop on the highway.*

in•ves•ti•gates (in ves′ti gāts′) *verb.* Looks at something carefully in order to gather information. *Every morning, our dog Lulu **investigates** our yard for cats.*

Word History

Investigates comes from the Latin *investigare*, meaning "to track."

is•sues (ish′üz) *plural noun.* 1. Subject matters under discussion. *2.* Individual copies of a magazine. *1. My brother and I disagree on certain **issues**. 2. All the **issues** of my favorite comic book were stacked on the shelf.*

i•tems (ī′təmz) *noun.* Things in a group or list. *Christine always makes a list of the **items** she needs from the grocery store.*

Jj

jour•ney (jûr′nē) *noun.* A trip, especially one over a considerable distance or taking considerable time. *Ping made a **journey** to China to meet his grandparents and uncles.*

jum•ble (jum′bəl) *noun.* A confused mixture or condition; mess. *My messy room is a **jumble** of toys and books.*

Ll

la•bor (lā′bər) *noun.* 1. Hard work. 2. People who work at jobs that require physical strength. *1. We all needed naps after a day of **labor** in the yard. 2. The **labor** unions asked for better pay.*

leg•a•cy (leg′ə sē) *noun.* Something handed down from the past; heritage. *The medical research foundation she founded will be her **legacy**.*

leg•en•dary (lej′ən der′ē) *adjective.* Relating to a legend, or a story that has been handed down for many years and has some basis in fact. *Johnny Appleseed's efforts to spread the apple tree have become **legendary**.*

log•i•cal (loj′i kəl) *adjective.* Sensible; being the action or result one expects. *When it rains, I do the **logical** thing and put my bicycle in the garage.*

loos•ened (lü′sənd) *verb.* Made looser; set free or released. *Brad **loosened** his necktie when the ceremony was over.*

lum•ber•ing (lum′bər ing) *adjective.* Moving in a slow, clumsy way. *Put a **lumbering** hippo in the water, and it becomes a graceful swimmer.*

lurk (lûrk) *verb.* To lie hidden. *Many animals **lurk** in their dens so they can surprise their prey when it walks by.*

Mm

mag•ni•fy (mag′nə fī′) *verb.* To make something look bigger than it really is. *Devices such as microscopes help to **magnify** small things.*

mas•sive (mas′iv) *adjective.* Of great size or extent; large and solid. *The sumo wrestler had a **massive** chest.*

at; āpe; fär; câre; end; mē; it; īce; pîerce; hot; ōld; sông; fôrk; oil; out; up; ūse; rūle; pùll; tûrn; chin; sing; shop; thin; this; hw in white; zh in treasure.

The symbol ə stands for the unstressed vowel sound in about, taken, pencil, lemon, and circus.

midst (midst) *noun.* A position in the middle of a group of people or things. *"There is a poet in our **midst**," said the principal, "and we need to clap for her."*

mi•grant work•ers (mī′grənt wûr′kərz) *plural noun.* Persons who move from place to place for work. *The **migrant workers** traveled from farm to farm.*

mis•chief (mis′chif) *noun.* Conduct that may seem playful but causes harm or trouble. *The kittens were always getting into **mischief** when we weren't home.*

mis•un•der•stood (mis′un dər stùd′) *verb.* Understood someone incorrectly; got the wrong idea. *I **misunderstood** the directions my teacher gave and did the wrong page for homework.*

mo•ti•vate (mō′tə vāt′) *verb.* To provide with a move to action. *The thought of a college scholarship will always **motivate** me to study hard.*

mut•tered (mut′ərd) *verb.* Spoke in a low, unclear way with the mouth closed. *I could tell he was mad by the way he **muttered** to himself.*

mys•te•ri•ous (mi stîr′ē əs) *adjective.* Very hard or impossible to understand; full of mystery. *The fact that the cookies were missing was **mysterious**.*

Nn

nat•u•ral (nach′ər əl) *adjective.* 1. Unchanged by people. 2. Expected or normal. *1. We hiked through **natural** surroundings of woods, streams, and meadows. 2. The **natural** home of the dolphin is the open ocean.*

ne•glec•ted (ni glekt′əd) *verb.* Failed to give proper attention or care to; failed to do. *I **neglected** to finish my science project and could not present it at the fair.*

now•a•days (nou′ə dāz′) *adverb.* In the present time. *People hardly ever write with typewriters **nowadays**.*

nu•mer•ous (nü′mər əs *or* nü′mər əs) *adjective.* Forming a large number; many. *The mountain climbers faced **numerous** problems, but they still had fun.*

nu•tri•ents (nü′trē ənts *or* nü′trē ənts) *plural noun.* Substances needed by the bodies of people, animals, or plants to live and grow. *Sometimes we get ill because we are not getting the proper **nutrients**.*

Oo

o•be•di•ence (ō bē′dē əns) *noun.* The willingness to obey, or to carry out orders, wishes, or instructions. *It is important to show **obedience** to safety rules.*

Word History

Obedience comes from the Latin word *obedire*, meaning "to hearken, yield, or serve."

o•pin•ions (ə pin′yənz) *plural noun.* Beliefs or conclusions based on a person's judgment rather than on what is proven or known to be true. *I want to find out what my classmates' **opinions** are about recycling.*

op•por•tu•ni•ties (op′ər tü′ni tēz) *plural noun.* Good chances or favorable times. *School offers students many **opportunities** to join clubs and organizations.*

or•a•to•ry (ôr′ə tôr′ē) *noun.* Eloquence and skill in public speaking. *The President was a master of campaign **oratory**.*

out•stretched (out′strechtd′) *adjective.* Stretched out; extended. *His **outstretched** palm held the quarter I had dropped.*

o•ver•flow•ing (ō′vər flō′ing) *verb.* To be so full that the contents flow over. *The trunk was **overflowing** with old toys.*

at; āpe; fär; câre; end; mē; it; īce; pîerce; hot; ōld; sông; fôrk; oil; out; up; ūse; rūle; pùll; tûrn; chin; sing; shop; thin; this; hw in white; zh in treasure.

The symbol ə stands for the unstressed vowel sound in about, taken, pencil, lemon, and circus.

Pp

par•a•lyzed (par′ə lizd′) *adjective.* 1. Having lost movement or sensation in a part of the body. 2. Powerless or helpless. *Sue was **paralyzed** by stage fright.*

part•ner•ship (pärt′nər ship′) *noun.* A kind of business in which two or more people share the work and profits. *Janell, Pat, and Erik formed a gardening **partnership**.*

pe•cul•iar (pi kūl′yər) *adjective.* Strange; not usual. *I had the **peculiar** feeling that I was being watched.*

per•sis•tence (pər sis′təns) *noun.* The ability to keep trying in spite of difficulties or obstacles. *In order to run a business, a person must have a lot of **persistence**.*

phras•es (frāz′iz) *plural noun.* Groups of words expressing a single thought but not containing both a subject and predicate. *When I proofread my report, I made **phrases** into complete sentences.*

pol•i•cy (pol′i sē) *noun.* A guiding plan that people use to help make decisions. *The school has a strict "no t-shirt" **policy**.*

pos•i•tive (poz′i tiv) *adjective.* Certain; sure. *I am **positive** I left my backpack right here on the counter.*

pre•his•tor•ic (prē′his tôr′ik) *adjective.* Belonging to a time before people started recording history. *Explorers found **prehistoric** drawings along the cave walls.*

pro•claimed (prə klāmd′ *or* prō klāmd′) *verb.* Announced publicly. *The principal **proclaimed** May 20 as the day for our class trips.*

prop•er•ties (prop′ər tēz) *plural noun.* Characteristics of matter that can be observed. *Scientists measured the **properties** of gold in their lab.*

pro•tes•ted (prō test′əd) *verb.* Complained against something. *When the workers lost their jobs in the factory, they **protested**.*

pur•chased (pûr′chəsd) *verb.* Got by paying money; got by sacrifice or hardship. *Sally **purchased** the chess board using what she saved from her monthly allowance.*

Rr

ranged (rānjd) *verb.* To go between certain limits. *The prices for a music player **ranged** from fifty to two hundred dollars.*

re•al•is•tic (rē′əlis′tik) *adjective.* Seeing things as they are; practical. *I dream of being a famous rock star, but I should also be **realistic** and stay in school.*

reef (rēf) *noun.* A ridge of sand, rock, or coral at or near the surface of the ocean. *Boaters have to be careful not to scrape against the **reef** below.*

ref•er•ence (ref′ər əns *or* ref′rens) *noun.* A statement that calls or directs attention to something. *The speech makes a **reference** to a play written by William Shakespeare.*

re•form (ri fôrm′) *noun.* A change for the better. *She worked for a **reform** of the political system.*

reg•i•ster (rej′i stər) *noun.* 1. A formal record or list. 2. The range of a voice or instrument. *verb.* To enroll. *Every college student must **register** before attending class.*

re•lays (rē′lāz) *plural noun.* Fresh sets, teams, or supplies that replace or relieve another. *Post office workers work in **relays** in order to get your letters from one place to another quickly.*

at; āpe; fär; câre; end; mē; it; īce; pîerce; hot; ōld; sông; fôrk; oil; out; up; ūse; rūle; pùll; tûrn; chin; sing; shop; thin; this; hw in white; zh in treasure.

The symbol ə stands for the unstressed vowel sound in about, taken, pencil, lemon, and circus.

re•leased (ri lēsd′) *verb.* To have set free or loose. *The girl opened the gate to the pen and **released** the pigs.*

re•lo•cat•ed (rē lō′kā tid) *verb.* To have moved to a different location. *The store **relocated** down the block from the park.*

rep•tiles (rep′tilz) *plural noun.* Cold-blooded vertebrates of the group Reptilia, which includes lizards, snakes, alligators, crocodiles, and turtles. *Most **reptiles** lay eggs, although some give birth to live young.*

res•i•dent (rez′i dənt) *noun.* A person who lives in a particular place. *The new **resident** shocked neighbors by planting the entire front yard with sunflowers.*

re•spon•si•bil•i•ty (ri spon′sə bil′i tē) *noun.* The quality or condition of having a job, duty, or concern. *Taking care of the dog was my **responsibility**.*

roamed (rōmd) *verb.* Moved around in a large area. *The grizzly bear **roamed** over the valley and the nearby mountains.*

route (rūt *or* rout) *noun.* A road or course used for traveling. *Trucks must follow a special **route**.*

rum•bling (rum′bling) *noun.* A heavy, deep, rolling sound. *The **rumbling** of thunder woke me up.*

Ss

sanc•tu•ar•y (sangk′chü er′ē) *noun.* A protected place for wildlife where predators are controlled and hunting is not allowed. *My friend runs a **sanctuary** for injured hawks and owls.*

scorn•ful•ly (skôrn′fəl ē) *adverb.* In a way that shows that something or someone is looked down upon and considered bad or worthless. *The critic was unhappy with the new artist's paintings so he spoke **scornfully** about them.*

seg•re•ga•tion (seg′ri gā′shən) *noun.* The practice of setting one racial group apart from another. *The Civil Rights movement fought against **segregation**.*

se•lec•ting (si lek′ting) *verb.* Picking out among many; choosing. *I spent a long time **selecting** the right gift.*

self•ish (sel′fish) *adjective.* Thinking only of oneself; putting one's own interests and desires before those of others. *A second piece of cake sounded good, but I didn't want to be **selfish**.*

sen•si•ble (sen′sə bəl) *adjective.* Having or showing sound judgment; wise. *If you make a mistake, the **sensible** thing to do is apologize.*

sev•e•ral (sev′ə rəl *or* sev′rəl) *adjective.* More than two, but not many. *Louisa slept for **several** hours.*

shim•mer (shim′ər) *verb.* To shine with a faint, wavering light; glimmer. *The lake began to **shimmer** in the rays of the setting sun.*

silk•en (sil′kən) *adjective.* 1. Made of silk. 2. Like silk in appearance. *1. The queen's **silken** robe was exquisite. 2. Antonio wrote a poem about the girl's long **silken** hair.*

Silk Road (silk rōd) *noun.* A trade route that connected China with the Roman Empire. *The **Silk Road** was about 4,000 miles long.*

sim•il•ar (sim′əl ər) *adjective.* Having many but not all qualities alike. *Zack and Nick have **similar** haircuts.*

sky•scrap•ers (skī′skrā′pərz) *plural noun.* Very tall buildings. *The city has many **skyscrapers**, and some of them are 50 stories tall!*

slen•der (slen′dər) *adjective.* Thin, especially in an attractive or graceful way. *The swan stretched its long **slender** neck and flapped its wings.*

slith•ered (slith′ərd) *verb.* Slid or glided like a snake. *When the snakes **slithered** across the ground, they moved quickly and hardly made a sound.*

snick•er•ing (snik′ər ing) *verb.* Laughing in a mean or disrespectful manner. *The children stopped **snickering** when their mother told them to be kinder.*

at; āpe; fär; câre; end; mē; it; īce; pîerce; hot; ōld; sông; fôrk; oil; out; up; ūse; rūle; pùll; tûrn; chin; sing; shop; thin; this; hw in white; zh in treasure.

The symbol ə stands for the unstressed vowel sound in about, taken, pencil, lemon, and circus.

Glossary

Glossary

soft•ware (sôft′wâr′) *noun.* Written or printed programs of information that are used on a computer. *The artist used a new design **software** to help plan her latest sculpture.*

sol•i•tar•y (sol′i ter′ē) *adjective.* Living, being, or going alone. *After everyone else quit, Jim was the **solitary** player left in the game.*

Word History

Solitary comes from the Latin *solitarius*, meaning "alone, lonely."

sores (sôrz) *plural noun.* Places where the skin has been broken and hurts. *My hands had **sores** after raking leaves all morning with no gloves on.*

spe•cial•ized (spesh′ə līzd′) *verb.* To have concentrated on a particular product, activity, branch of a profession, or field of study. *When she went to cooking school, she **specialized** in bread baking.*

spe•cial•ty (spesh′əl tē) *noun.* A special thing that a person knows a great deal about or can make very well. *Making quilts is my aunt Lisa's **specialty**.*

spin•off (spin′ôf′) *noun.* A product derived from another field. *This new plastic used in eyeglass frames is a **spinoff** from the aerospace industry.*

strikes (strīks) *plural noun.* 1. The stopping of work to protest something. 2. Pitched balls in the strike zone or that a batter swings at and misses. *1. The workers threatened **strikes** if conditions did not improve. 2. One rule of baseball is three **strikes** and you're out.*

strut•ting (strut′ing) *verb.* Walking in a self-important way. *When Marilyn returned from her trip to Europe, she came **strutting** in showing off her new Italian boots.*

stur•dy (stûr′dē) *adjective.* Having strength; hardy. *The bookshelf we built was **sturdy** enough to hold our entire collection of books.*

sub•urbs (sub′ûrbz) *plural noun.* The areas around a city where people live. *Many people commute from the **suburbs** to the city using public transportation.*

Word History

Suburbs comes from the Latin *suburbium*—from *sub-* "under" and *urbs*, meaning "city."

sul•tan (sul′tən) *noun.* The king or ruler in certain Muslim countries. *Modern-day Turkey was ruled by a **sultan** at one time.*

swarms (swôrmz) *plural noun.* Large groups of insects flying or moving together. *When the hive fell, **swarms** of angry bees flew out.*

Tt

tan•gles (tang′gəlz) *plural noun.* Knotted, twisted, confused masses. *The garden hose had not been rolled back up and was full of **tangles**.*

tech•nique (tek nēk′) *noun.* A method or way of bringing about a desired result in a science, an art, a sport, or a profession. *Part of Orli's **technique**, when she is running, is to breathe in and out through her mouth.*

Word History

Technique comes from the Greek word *teknikos*, meaning "relating to an art or a craft."

tech•nol•o•gy (tek nol′ə jē) *noun.* Electronic products and systems that have various uses. ***Technology** has changed the ways that artists create their work.*

tel•e•graph (tel′i graf′) *noun.* A system or equipment used to send messages by wire over a long distance. *Before the telephone, a **telegraph** may have been used to relay a message.*

tem•po•rar•y (tem′pə rer′ē) *adjective.* Lasting or used for a short time only. *We recorded a **temporary** message for the answering machine.*

at; āpe; fär; câre; end; mē; it; īce; pîerce; hot; ōld; sông; fôrk; oil; out; up; ūse; rūle; pu̇ll; tûrn; chin; sing; shop; thin; this; hw in white; zh in treasure.

The symbol ə stands for the unstressed vowel sound in about, taken, pencil, lemon, and circus.

---

ter•ri•to•ry (ter′i tôr′ē) *noun.* Any large area of land; region. *My brother's **territory** for selling medical office supplies is North Carolina.*

threat•ened (thret′ənd) *adjective.* Having a sense of harm or danger. ***Threatened** by the hawk circling above, the mouse escaped under a log.*

trans•form (trans fôrm′) *verb.* To change in form, appearance, or structure. *To **transform** a barn into a modern home, you need to invest a lot of time and expense.*

Word History

Transform comes from the Latin *transformare*, meaning "to change in shape."

trans•la•tion (trans lā′shən) *noun.* A changing of a speech or piece of writing into another language. *Maria's grandmother spoke only Spanish, so Maria needed a **translation** of the letter from her.*

Uu

un•fair (un fâr′) *adjective.* Not fair or just. *Punishing all of us for the actions of my little sister seemed **unfair**.*

un•ions (ūn′yənz) *plural noun.* Groups of workers joined together to protect their jobs and improve working conditions. *Some labor **unions** stage strikes to get workers the safety equipment they need.*

u•nique (ū nēk′) *adjective.* Having no equal; the only one of its kind. *The Everglades is **unique** in that there is no other place on Earth like it.*

un•sta•ble (un stā′bəl) *adjective.* Not settled or steady; easily moved or put off balance. *Although the raft looked **unstable**, it floated very well.*

Vv

var•ied (vâr′ēd) *adjective.* Consisting of many different kinds. *The organisms in this coral reef are **varied**.*

ven•ture (ven′chər) *noun.* A business or some other undertaking that involves risk. *Rea's new **venture** was a carpet-cleaning service.*

vi•o•lat•ed (vī′ə lā′tid) *verb.* To have failed to obey; to have broken. *Mel was yelled at because she **violated** the "no talking during a test" rule.*

vis•i•bly (viz′ə blē) *adverb.* Plainly seen. *The firemen were **visibly** fatigued.*

vol•un•teer (vol′ən tîr′) *noun.* A person who offers to help or does something by choice and usually without pay. *I am a **volunteer** at the nursing home.*

W

week•days (wēk′dāz′) *plural noun.* The days of the week except Saturday and Sunday. *We go to school only on **weekdays**.*

at; āpe; fär; câre; end; mē; it; īce; pîerce; hot; ōld; sông; fôrk; oil; out; up; ūse; rūle; pu̇ll; tûrn; chin; sing; shop; thin; this; hw in white; zh in treasure.

The symbol ə stands for the unstressed vowel sound in about, taken, pencil, lemon, and circus.

Instructional Routines

Professional Development

- Read the routine prior to using *Treasures*. Use the Routine QuickNotes as a reminder of key routine steps throughout Unit 6, or as needed.

- View the online classroom video clip through **TeacherWorks Plus**. Watch master teachers use these routines.

1. **Phonological Awareness/ Phonemic Awareness**
   Rhyme
   Oddity Tasks
   Sound Categorization
   Oral Blending
   Oral Segmentation
   Manipulation

2. **Phonics**
   Blending
   Introducing Sound-Spelling Cards
   Letter Recognition
   Building Words
   Building Fluency
   Reading Decodables
   Multisyllabic Words Routine

3. **Fluency**
   Strategies

4. **Vocabulary**
   Define/Example/Ask Routine
   Strategies

5. **High-Frequency Words**
   Read/Spell/Write Routine
   Reading Pre-decodables

6. **Spelling**
   Dictation

7. **Comprehension**
   Strategies
   Skills
   Reading Big Books
   Reading Student Book

8. **Writing**
   Conferences
   Revision Assignments
   Writing Process
   Using Rubrics
   Using Anchor Papers
   Writers' Express Sequence

9. **Research Process**
   Big Question Board

10. **Classroom Management**
    Workstation Flip Charts
    Contracts
    Centers
    Small Groups

11. **Listening/Speaking/Viewing**

12. **Assessment**

Objectives

- Generate questions
- Identify cause and effect
- Find problems and solutions
- Draw conclusions

Genre Informational Text/Expository

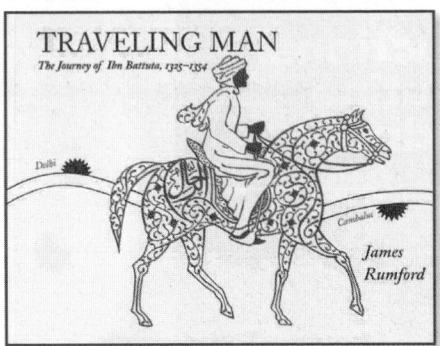

TRAVELING MAN
The Journey of Ibn Battuta, 1325–1354

Delhi

Córdoba

James Rumford

Approaching Level

Summary

As a child, Ibn Battuta dreamed of traveling east. He looked at maps and longed to sail on ships. As a young man, he became a scholar and set off for travels in Africa and Asia. This book recounts his adventures.

FYI for your information

Ibn Battuta lived from 1304 to about 1369, and was born and died in Morocco. He spent 30 years traveling around Africa and Asia and logged nearly 75,000 miles during that time. The original records of his travels were written in Arabic. This book is an adaptation of those records.

Traveling Man

by James Rumford

Before Reading

BUILD BACKGROUND

Tell students to brainstorm a list of faraway places they would like to visit. Ask students:

- *Why do you want to visit these places? What would you hope to see and do?*

- *Why have people always been curious about other places?*

PREVIEW AND SET PURPOSES

Have students look at the map and the glossary. Tell students that they can use these pages to help them understand what they read. Then have them set a purpose for reading, such as to discover to which places Battuta traveled.

During Reading

APPLY COMPREHENSION SKILLS AND STRATEGIES

Students may want to read the book in one sitting. Use the following Think Alouds and discussion questions to review comprehension strategies and skills taught in this unit.

Pages 1–7

STRATEGY
GENERATE QUESTIONS

Teacher Think Aloud I know that good readers ask themselves questions before, during, and after they read. Pausing to ask questions helps them to make sure they understand key ideas, events, and details. As I look through these pages, I have the following questions: *What places will Ibn Battuta visit during his journey? What are the places shown on the map, such as the Ocean of Darkness, called today?* Reading to find the answers to these questions will help me understand the journey of Battuta.

Cause and Effect Why does Ibn Battuta get rid of his extra baggage on the first part of his journey to Mecca? (His traveling companions are traveling very fast, in order to keep one step ahead of bandits, and Ibn is trying to keep up with them. He gets rid of his extra baggage to make the load lighter for the camel to carry.)

Pages 8–19

STRATEGY
GENERATE QUESTIONS

Teacher Think Aloud I will pause after reading this section and ask myself questions about what I have read. *Where did Battuta travel after leaving Alexandria?* Before I read the next section, I wonder, *Will Battuta's journey to China bring him good fortune?* As I read, I will think about and look for the answer to this question.

Problem and Solution What was Ibn Battuta's solution to escape the threat of the Sultan's assassins? (He prayed until the assassins finally left. The assassins would not kill him while he was praying.)

Pages 20–end

STRATEGY
GENERATE QUESTIONS

Teacher Think Aloud Asking questions before, during, and after reading will help me clarify the main ideas of this book. As I read I ask myself, *Will Battuta return home as he promised his parents? Will he have riches at the end of his journey?* After I finish reading the book, I will think about the questions I asked and review the answers I found.

Draw Conclusions How do you think Ibn Butatta feels about being a traveler? Use details from the text to explain your answer. (Ibn Butatta feels lonely as a traveler. When he sees the family in the Maldives he wants so much to have a home. Then when he returns home, he finds his parents have died and he is alone. He says traveling "leaves you a stranger in your own land.")

After Reading

LITERATURE CIRCLES

Use page 253 in the **Teacher's Resource Book** to review Listening and Speaking guidelines for a discussion. Use these questions to guide a discussion of the book in small groups:

- *Was this book hard to read? Explain your answers.*

- *What do you consider to be the most interesting place Ibn Battuta visited? Why do you think so?*

- *Do you think he thought traveling was worth the sacrifice? Explain.*

Write About It

Have students pretend to be newspaper reporters covering Ibn Battuta's return after 30 years of travel. Have them think of *who, what, where, when,* and *why* questions. Students can look for answers to their questions in the book and then write a short article about Ibn Battuta's adventures. Have students reread their writing to see that they have correctly used *more* and *most* and *-er* and *-est* with adverbs.

Social Studies Connect to Content

MAPS AND LOCATIONS

Have students choose one of Ibn Battuta's destinations and use print or online sources to find out where it is located. Distribute world maps, atlases, or globes. Have students locate the destination and record the coordinates of the place. Then have students find the coordinates of their town.

Tell students to compare the coordinates of the destination with the coordinates of their town by relating them to the equator, tropics, hemispheres, or North and South Poles. For example, Delhi is north of the equator and in the Eastern Hemisphere. My town is also north of the equator, but in the Western Hemisphere.

Objectives

- **Find problem and solution**
- **Generate questions**
- **Analyze story structure**
- **Identify cause and effect**

Genre Literary Text/Folktale

On Level

Summary

This book tells how a quick-thinking tortoise uses his smarts to make two bullies—an elephant and a hippopotamus—behave, restoring harmony to the banks of Lake Nyasa. The author includes some Kiswahili words to give the African folktale authenticity.

FYI for your information

The animals in *Clever Tortoise* think and behave just as humans do. This personification is common in folktales. Animals that assume human characteristics are called anthropomorphic.

Clever Tortoise

by Francesca Martin

 **Before Reading**

BUILD BACKGROUND

Help students brainstorm a list of animals that might live in East Africa. Write all the responses on the board. Spend a few minutes talking about the animals. Ask students:

- *How would you describe these animals?*
- *Do you think all animals get along? Explain.*
- *What animals might not get along? Explain.*
- *How might animals communicate with one another?*

PREVIEW AND SET PURPOSES

Tell students to look at the cover of the book. Ask them what questions they have. Suggest that students set a purpose for reading based on one of their questions about the cover illustration. For example, they may choose to read to find out what the tortoise said or did that was so clever.

 **During Reading**

APPLY COMPREHENSION SKILLS AND STRATEGIES

Students may want to read the book in one sitting. Use the following Think Alouds and discussion questions to review comprehension strategies and skills taught in this unit.

Pages 1–10

STRATEGY
GENERATE QUESTIONS

Teacher Think Aloud When I read a text, I can generate questions to help with my comprehension. As I begin this story, I wonder: *Will the tortoise be an important character in this story? Why do the Elephant and the Hippopotamus behave like they do? How will the tortoise help his friends?*

Problem and Solution What problem do the Rabbit, Snake, Lizard, and Warthog face? What solution does Clever Tortoise have? (The Elephant and the Hippopotamus are bullies. Clever Tortoise decides that they are going to play a trick on them to teach them a lesson.)

STRATEGY
GENERATE QUESTIONS

Teacher Think Aloud Asking questions about what I have read will ensure that I understand what is happening in the story. Why did Clever Tortoise tell the Elephant and the Hippopotamus that they were both the strongest? I know that folktales often have a lesson or moral. I think this will have something to do with the moral of the story. I will read on to find out.

Problem and Solution What trick does Clever Tortoise come up with to solve the problem? (Clever Tortoise is setting up a tug-of-war between the Hippopotamus and the Elephant. They each think they are matched with Clever Tortoise and are surprised by his strength.)

STRATEGY
ANALYZE STORY STRUCTURE

Teacher Think Aloud I know in the beginning of the story Clever Tortoise and the other animals had a problem. The Elephant and the Hippopotamus were bullies. As the story continued, Tortoise came up with a trick to have the bullies matched in a tug-of-war that they think is against him. At the end of the story, the Elephant and the Hippopotamus are no longer bullies. Tortoise's trick solved the problem.

Cause and Effect What effect does Clever Tortoise's trick have on the Elephant and the Hippopotamus? (The Elephant and the Hippopotamus are so ashamed that they lost to Clever Tortoise in a tug-of-war that they both stop acting like bullies.)

 **After Reading**

LITERATURE CIRCLES

Use page 253 in the **Teacher's Resource Book** to review Listening and Speaking guidelines for a discussion. Use these questions to guide a discussion of the book in small groups:

- *What did you find to be the most amusing part of the book?*
- *What are some examples of animals acting like humans?*
- *Was Tortoise's plan a good solution to the problem? Explain.*

Write About It

Point out the illustration in which the animals are complaining to Clever Tortoise. Have each student choose two of the animals shown in the drawing, name them, and write a dialogue between them. Remind students that the animals are upset before discussing possible solutions to the problem. Have students reread their writing to see that they have used quotation marks and dialogue punctuation correctly and that they have avoided using double negatives.

Connect to Content

GETTING ALONG

In this story, the Elephant and the Hippopotamus are bullies to the smaller animals. Discuss how smaller animals have adapted to survive such conditions. What characteristics do they have that help them survive in the world and around much larger animals?

Classroom Library

Objectives

- Analyze story structure
- Identify cause and effect
- Generate questions
- Find problem and solution

Genre Literary Text/Folktale

Beyond Level

Summary

This folktale tells about a widow who weaves beautiful brocades and uses her skill to copy a painting of a beautiful palace. A wind carries the brocade away, and one by one, each of the widow's three sons goes in search of it. Only the youngest completes the quest and succeeds in retrieving the brocade from the fairies who stole it.

FYI for your information

With over 1,500 years of history, Nanjing cloud-pattern brocades have been used exclusively by Chinese imperial families in dynasties like the Yuan, Ming, and Qing. Elaborate golden brocades with patterns of peacocks or clouds, dragons, and flowers were made in the Ming Dynasty (1368–1644) and the Qing Dynasty (1644–1911).

The Weaving of a Dream

by Marilee Heyer

 **Before Reading**

BUILD BACKGROUND

Create a word web with students about the term "favorite possession." Ask students:

- *What is your favorite possession? Why?*
- *How would you feel if you lost it?*
- *What would you do to recover it?*

PREVIEW AND SET PURPOSES

Tell students to look through the book at the colorful illustrations. Ask what this book might be about. Have students set a purpose for reading, such as to find out what dream is woven, as the title suggests.

 **During Reading**

APPLY COMPREHENSION SKILLS AND STRATEGIES

Students may want to read the book in one sitting. Use the following Think Alouds and discussion questions to review comprehension strategies and skills taught in this unit.

Pages 1–10

STRATEGY

ANALYZE STORY STRUCTURE

Teacher Think Aloud I know that character, setting, plot, and theme fit together to make a story's structure. I see the characters in this folktale are an old widow who weaves beautiful brocades to support herself and her three sons. The plot centers on a painting of everything the widow has ever desired. I think this painting will be important as the story goes on.

Cause and Effect How does the mother's decision to weave the painting affect the family? (The two brothers are upset that their mother is no longer selling her brocades to make money. They have to do extra work. The youngest brother decides to take on the extra work so that his mother can keep on weaving.)

STRATEGY

ANALYZE STORY STRUCTURE

Teacher Think Aloud I see the oldest and middle sons value gold more than their youngest brother does. They take the gold offered by the fortune-teller and do not return home. In contrast, the youngest son loves his mother deeply and, refusing the gold, finds the brocade and returns it to his dying mother.

Problem and Solution According to the fortune teller, what is the only solution for getting the brocade back from the fairies? (The son must knock out his own teeth to get the horse and endure the pain of riding through Flame Mountain and the Sea of Ice to get to the place where the fairies live.)

STRATEGY

ANALYZE STORY STRUCTURE

Teacher Think Aloud As I read the last part of the story, I see the folktale ends happily. When the brocade comes alive, the widow and her youngest son live there happily. The faithful son is rewarded for his goodness. I think the theme or message of this story is that goodness is rewarded and greed is punished. By discovering the theme, I understand what the author thinks is important and meaningful.

Problem and Solution How does Leje, the youngest son, solve the problem of the missing brocade? (Leje endures the pain of the fortune teller's directions and reaches Sun Mountain to retrieve the brocade. He must wait until the fairies are asleep to get the brocade back.)

After Reading

LITERATURE CIRCLES

Use page 253 in the **Teacher's Resource Book** to review Listening and Speaking guidelines for a discussion. Use these questions to guide a discussion of the book in small groups:

- *How did the illustrations help you understand the story events?*
- *Why do you think the brocade was so important?*
- *Why do you think Letuie walked away?*

Write About It

Have students select a favorite scene from the book and write a one-page play. Students can use dialogue from the story and use their imagination to extend the conversation between the characters. Encourage them to include stage directions as well. Have students reread their writing to see that they have incorporated prepositional phrases accurately.

Science
Connect to Content

SILK

The widow uses silk threads in her brocade. Explain that the Chinese were the first people to raise silkworms to produce silk thread. Tell students to find out about how the silkworm produces silk. Prompt them to show what they learn by creating a diagram that illustrates this characteristic.

Classroom Library

Additional Readings

UNIT 6

30 MINUTES DAILY

By the Authors and Illustrators

For additional information on authors, illustrators, and selection content, go to www.macmillanmh.com.

Garland, Michael. *Hooray José!* Marshall Cavendish, 2007. This vibrant book tells the lesson of José, the short mouse who never got picked to play basketball. See how his determination to play well (and a lot of practice) gives him the opportunity to play when one of the team members becomes injured.
APPROACHING

Leitich Smith, Cynthia. *Jingle Dancer.* Illustrated by Cornelius van Wright and Ying-Hwa Hu. Morrow, 2000. Jenna can hardly wait to perform the traditional Native American dance at the next powwow, but unfortunately she runs into some trouble. These warm illustrations will take you on the journey of how her dream does come true.
APPROACHING

Related to the Theme (spans 3+ grade levels)

Use these and other classroom or library resources to ensure students are reading at least 30 minutes a day outside of class. Enlist the help of your school librarian to teach students how to use library resources, such as card catalogs and electronic search engines, to find other books related to the unit theme.

Krull, Kathleen. *Harvesting Hope: The Story of Cesar Chavez.* Harcourt, 2003. An illustrated biography of César Chávez, a labor activist who fought to improve the working conditions of migrant farm workers.
APPROACHING

Martin, Francesca. *Clever Tortoise: A Traditional African Tale.* Candlewick, 2000. Tortoise leads the other jungle animals in teaching Elephant and Hippo a lesson by having them engage in a tug of war.
ON LEVEL

Bickerstaff, Linda. *Oil Power of the Future: New Ways of Turning Petroleum into Energy.* Rosen Publishing, 2002. This book presents the benefits and problems of using oil as fuel.
BEYOND

Brown, Don. *Odd Boy Out: Young Albert Einstein.* Houghton, 2004. This book is an engaging look into the life of the world's most famous scientist.
APPROACHING

Miller, Kimberly. *What If We Run Out of Fossil Fuels?* Children's Press, 2002. Examines our dependence on fossil fuels and describes alternative energy sources.
ON LEVEL

Goodall, Jane. *My Life with the Chimpanzees.* Houghton Mifflin, 1999. This is Jane Goodall's own story of the research she has conducted at the Gombe Research Center in Tanzania.
BEYOND

Library Resources

Encyclopedias

Tell students that they can use an encyclopedia to find more information on a topic they have read about. Point out that encyclopedias are located in the reference section of the library. Review how to find information in these reference books and how to use them effectively as an aid to expository writing.

Have students pick a topic covered in the unit and look it up in the encyclopedia. Then have students summarize something new they learned about the topic from the information they found in the encyclopedia. Discuss any similar information in unit selections.

Schanzer, Rosalyn. *Gold Fever!: Tales from the California Gold Rush.* **National Geographic Society, 1999.** Using eyewitness accounts from the real men, women, and children of the Gold Rush, this absorbing picture book combines the words of the gold seekers and vibrant folk-art-style paintings.
ON LEVEL

Briggs Martin, Jacqueline. *The Lamp, the Ice, and the Boat Called Fish.* **Houghton Mifflin, 2001.** This book tells the dramatic story of the Canadian Arctic Expedition that set off in 1913 to explore the high north.
BEYOND

Schanzer, Rosalyn. *Davy Crockett Saves the World.* HarperCollins, 2001. Davy Crockett stops the evil Halley's Comet from destroying the world and wins the heart of Sally Sugartree in the process.
ON LEVEL

Gibson, Diane. *Wind Power.* **Smart Apple Media, 2004.** This book describes wind energy and how it is generated.
APPROACHING

Matthews, Tom. *Always Inventing: A Photobiography of Alexander Graham Bell.* **National Geographic Society, 1999.** A biography of the life of Alexander Graham Bell, detailing his efforts to find ways to improve people's lives.
APPROACHING

Ray, Deborah Kogan. *The Flower Hunter: William Bartram, America's First Naturalist.* **Farrar, Straus and Giroux, 2004.** As Billy travels the colonial United States, he keeps a journal of all of the plant specimens he encounters.
APPROACHING

Osborne, Mary Pope. *Buffalo Before Breakfast.* **Random House, 1999.** Jack and his sister Annie are taken to the Great Plains, where they learn about the Lakota Indians.
ON LEVEL

Park, Linda Sue. *The Firekeeper's Son.* **Clarion, 2004.** After his father is hurt, it is up to Sang-hee to light the evening fire that signals all is well in the nineteenth-century Korean place where he lives.
ON LEVEL

VanCleave, Janice. *Janice VanCleave's Scientists Through the Ages.* **Wiley, 2004.** This book introduces numerous scientists, their contributions, and important discoveries.
ON LEVEL

Hill, Christine. *Robert Ballard: Oceanographer Who Discovered the Titanic.* **Enslow, 1999.** A biography of the man whose numerous explorations resulted in locating the wreck of the *Titanic*.
BEYOND

Kennedy, Mike. *Baseball.* **Franklin Watts, 2003.** This book offers historical background, rules, fundamentals, and a chapter on the people who have had an influence on the sport.
BEYOND

Waldman, Neil. *Wounded Knee.* **Atheneum, 2001.** An account of the events leading to the massacre at Wounded Knee, including a description of the battle itself.
BEYOND

Selection Honors, Prizes, and Awards

Leah's Pony

Unit 6, p. 678
by *Elizabeth Friedrich*
Illustrated by *Michael Garland*
Young Hoosier Award Nominee (1998–1999), Golden Kite Honor Book, *Parents* Magazine Best Book of the Year, National Council of Trade Books Award, IRA Teacher's Choice Award (1997), Texas Bluebonnet Award (1997–1998)

Illustrator: *Michael Garland,* winner of *Booklist* Editor's Choice and National Council on Social Studies/Children's Book Council Notable Children's Trade Book for *My Cousin Katie.*

Snowflake Bentley

Unit 6, p. 746
by *Jacqueline Briggs Martin*
Illustrated by *Mary Azarian*
Caldecott Medal (1999), The Lupine Award (1998), ALA Notable Book (1999)

Author: *Jacqueline Briggs Martin,* winner of the Lupine Award (1996) for *Grandmother Bryant's Pocket* and (2003) for *The Water Gift and the Pig of the Pig;* Smithsonian Magazine Notable Books for Children (2001) for *The Lamp, The Ice, and the Boat Called Fish.*

How Ben Franklin Stole the Lightning

Unit 6, p. 778
by *Rosalyn Schanzer*
Parent's Guide Children's Media Award for Outstanding Achievement in Children's Books (2003), IRA/CBC Children's Choice and Teacher's Choice (2004)

Author/Illustrator: *Rosalyn Schanzer,* winner of ALA Booklist "Book for Youth" Editor's Choice (2001), IRA/CBC Children's Choice Award (2002) for *Davy Crockett Saves the World;* National Council of Social Studies Notable Children's Trade Book (1997) for *How We Crossed the West: The Adventures of Lewis & Clark.*

Resources

Audio Bookshelf
44 Ocean View Drive
Middletown, RI 02842
800-234-1713
www.audiobookshelf.com

Discovery Education
One Discovery Place
Silver Spring, MD 20910
800-323-9084
http://discoveryeducation.com

Dorling Kindersley
375 Hudson Street
New York, NY 10014
Tel: 800-631-8571
Fax: 201-256-0000
http://us.dk.com

GPN Educational Media
1407 Fleet Street
Baltimore, MD 21231
800-228-4630
http://shopgpn.com

Innovative Educators
P.O. Box 520
Montezuma, GA 31063
888-252-KIDS (5437)
Fax: 888-536-8553
www.innovative-educators.com

Library Video Co.
P.O. Box 580
Wynnewood, PA 19096
800-843-3620
www.libraryvideo.com

Listening Library
400 Hahn Road
Westminster, MD 21157
800-733-3000
http://randomhouse.biz/educators/

Live Oak Media
P.O. Box 652
Pine Plains, NY 12567
800-788-1121
www.liveoakmedia.com

Macmillan/McGraw-Hill
220 East Danieldale Road
DeSoto, TX 75115-9960
Tel: 800-442-9685
Fax: 972-228-1982
www.macmillanmh.com

Microsoft Corp.
One Microsoft Way
Redmond, WA 98052
800-642-7676
www.microsoft.com

National Geographic Society
1145 17th Street N.W.
Washington, DC 20036
800-647-5463
www.nationalgeographic.com

Recorded Books
270 Skipjack Road
Prince Frederick, MD 20678
800-638-1304
www.recordedbooks.com

Sunburst Communications
Sunburst Technology
1550 Executive Drive
Elgin, IL 60123
888-321-7511 ext.3337
www.sunburst.com

Tom Snyder Productions
100 Talcott Avenue
Watertown, MA 02472
800-342-0236
www.tomsnyder.com

Weston Woods
143 Main Street
Norwalk, CT 06851
800-243-5020
www.teacher.scholastic.com/products/
westonwoods/

Web Sites

Go to www.macmillanmh.com.
Use the zip code finder to locate other resources in your area.

The Academy of Natural Sciences
http://www.ansp.org/

Acadia National Park
http://www.nps.gov/acad

Agriculture in the Classroom
http://www.agclassroom.org/

Arches National Park
http://www.nps.gov/arch

Asian American History Resources Online - CET
http://www.cetel.org/res.html

Association of Zoos and Aquariums
http://www.aza.org/

Bronx Zoo
http://www.bronxzoo.com/

Cincinnati Zoo
http://www.cincinnatizoo.org/

Colonial Williamsburg
http://www.history.org/

Denali National Park and Preserve
http://www.nps.gov/dena

Ellis Island
http://www.ellisisland.org/

Glacier National Park
http://www.nps.gov/glac

Grand Canyon National Park
http://www.nps.gov/grca

Grand Teton National Park
http://www.nps.gov/grte

High Museum of Art, Atlanta
http://www.high.org/

International Civil Rights Center and Museum
http://www.sitinmovement.org/

Japanese American National Museum
http://www.janm.org/

K12Station – Library of K–12 Education Links
http://www.k12station.com/k12link_library.html

Kids.gov
http://www.kids.gov/

KidsHealth in the Classroom
http://classroom.kidshealth.org/

Meteorology
http://www.wxdude.com/

The Metropolitan Museum of Art, New York
http://www.metmuseum.org/

Minneapolis Institute of Arts
http://www.artsmia.org/

Minnesota Zoo
http://www.mnzoo.com/

MoMA | The Museum of Modern Art
http://www.moma.org/

Monterey Bay Aquarium
www.montereybayaquarium.org

Mount Rushmore National Memorial
http://www.nps.gov/moru

Museum of Fine Arts, Boston
http://www.mfa.org/

Museum of Science, Boston
http://www.mos.org/

Museum of Science and Industry, Chicago
http://www.msichicago.org/

NASA
http://www.nasa.gov/

NASA Kids' Club
http://www.nasa.gov/audience/forkids/kidsclub/flash/index.html

National Air and Space Museum
http://www.nasm.si.edu/

National Civil Rights Museum
http://www.civilrightsmuseum.org/home.htm

National Museum of African American History and Culture
http://nmaahc.si.edu/

National Museum of American History
http://americanhistory.si.edu/

National Museum of the American Indian
http://www.nmai.si.edu/

National Museum of Women in the Arts
http://www.nmwa.org/

National Music Museum
http://www.usd.edu/smm/

National Park Service
http://www.nps.gov/

National Weather Service Education Resources
http://www.nws.noaa.gov/om/edures.shtml

National Women's History Museum
http://www.nwhm.org/

National Zoo
http://nationalzoo.si.edu/

Native American Facts for Kids: Resources on American Indians for Children and Teachers
http://www.native-languages.org/kids.htm

New England Aquarium
http://www.neaq.org/index.php

New York Aquarium
http://www.nyaquarium.com/

Newseum
http://www.newseum.org/

Omaha's Henry Doorly Zoo
http://www.omahazoo.com/

Philadelphia Museum of Art
http://www.philamuseum.org/

Philadelphia Zoo
http://www2.philadelphiazoo.org/

Plimoth Plantation
http://www.plimoth.org/

Redwood National and State Parks
http://www.nps.gov/redw

Rocky Mountain National Park
http://www.nps.gov/romo

Saint Louis Art Museum
http://www.slam.org/

San Diego Zoo
http://www.sandiegozoo.com/

San Francisco Museum of Modern Art
http://www.sfmoma.org/

Shedd Aquarium
http://www.sheddaquarium.org/

Smithsonian Education
http://www.smithsonianeducation.org/

Smithsonian: Science and Technology
http://www.si.edu/Encyclopedia_SI/science_and_technology/

Space Center Houston
http://www.spacecenter.org/

Tennessee Aquarium
http://www.tennis.org/

United States Holocaust Memorial Museum
http://www.ushmm.org/

University of California Museum of Paleontology
http://www.ucmp.berkeley.edu/

The White House Historical Association
http://www.whitehousehistory.org/

Yellowstone National Park
http://www.nps.gov/yell

Yosemite National Park
http://www.nps.gov/yose

Zion National Park
http://www.nps.gov/zion

Unit 6

Week		Vocabulary	Differentiated Spelling
1	**Leah's Pony**	items clustered overflowing sturdy glistened bidding	**APPROACHING** robin, button, bacon, reason, cotton, garden, eleven, cousin, ripen, woman, kitten, muffin, widen, wooden, person, common season, open, wagon, lemon **ON LEVEL** robin, button, bacon, reason, cotton, sunken, eleven, cousin, woven, raisin, **wagon**, muffin, widen, wooden, ridden, common, proven, often, penguin, skeleton **BEYOND** listen, salmon, pardon, certain, mountain, sunken, eleven, cousin, woven, raisin, straighten, muffin, kitchen, oxygen, mistaken, common, proven, often, penguin, skeleton
2	**The Gold Rush Game**	reference disappointment annoyed circular outstretched conducted	**APPROACHING** root, tale, peak, tail, prince, dough, oar, prints, herd, heard, whose, who's, route, blue, blew, peek, need, knead, doe, ore **ON LEVEL** **root**, tale, wade, tail, prince, dough, moose, prints, we've, weave, whose, **who's**, route, boulder, bolder, weighed, patience, patients, **doe**, mousse **BEYOND** taught, principle, straight, principal, presence, dough, moose, presents, weather, whether, whose, who's, taut, boulder, bolder, kernel, patience, patients, doe, mousse
3	**Taking the Lead**	decades active transform volunteer violated	**APPROACHING** disorder, displease, distaste, distrust, disloyal, misplace, mislabel, mislead, misstep, misnumber, nonfat, nonfiction, nonsense, nonstop, unable, unplug, unkind, unfair, uncover, unclean **ON LEVEL** discourage, disappoint, disbelief, distrust, disloyal, misplace, mislabel, mislead, misstep, misnumber, nonfat, nonfiction, nonsense, nonstop, unable, unplug, uncertain, uncomfortable, uncover, unclean **BEYOND** discourage, disappointment, disbelief, disappear, disloyal, mismanage, misheard, misfortune, misstep, misnumber, nonessential, nonfiction, nonsense, nonspecific, unable, unofficial, uncertain, uncomfortable, unpredictable, unnecessary

Key Spelling words in bold appear in the selection.

LOG ON For additional spelling activities, go to **www.macmillanmh.com**.

Unit 6 (continued)

Week		Vocabulary	Differentiated Spelling
4	**Snowflake Bentley**	technique foolishness inspire evaporate magnify annual	**APPROACHING** spotless, sunny, furry, really, hairy, barely, tasteless, handful, lifeless, illness, hopeful, shortness, goodness, foggy, purely, sickness, joyful, hopeless, cordless, hardly
			ON LEVEL spotless, sunny, furry, really, hairy, barely, tasteless, handful, lifeless, illness, hopefully, happiness, goodness, sorrowful, **gently**, sickness, joyfully, aimless, breathless, certainly
			BEYOND spotless, casually, furry, constantly, hurriedly, barely, tasteless, wonderful, lifeless, illness, hopefully, happiness, truthfulness, sorrowful, assuredly, foolishness, annually, aimless, breathlessly, certainly
5	**How Ben Franklin Stole the Lightning**	hilarious mischief independence dizzy nowadays came in handy	**APPROACHING** unchanged, unnamed, restate, reverse, underdog, invisible, prepaid, displease, action, establishment, oversized, prepack, interstate, intersect, deplane, semiweekly, happily, kindness, **finally**, fearful
			ON LEVEL unchanged, unnamed, restate, reverse, infrequent, invisible, prepaid, displease, action, establishment, oversized, prejudge, interstate, intersect, deflate, semiweekly, happily, kindness, **finally,** fearful
			BEYOND unchanged, unnamed, restated, reversible, infrequently, invisible, prepaid, displeased, inaction, establishment, oversized, prejudged, interstate, intersection, deflate, semiweekly, happily, kindness, **finally,** fearful

Key Spelling words in bold appear in the selection.

LOG ON For additional spelling activities, go to www.macmillanmh.com.

Language Transfers:

The Interaction Between English and Students' Primary Languages

Dr. Jana Echevarria
California State University, Long Beach

Dr. Donald Bear
University of Nevada, Reno

It is important for teachers to understand why English Language Learners (ELLs) use alternative pronunciations for some English words. Many English sounds do not exist or transfer to other languages, so English Learners may lack the auditory acuity to "hear" these English sounds and have difficulty pronouncing them. These students are not accustomed to positioning their mouth in a way the sound requires. The charts that appear on the following pages show that there is variation among languages, with some languages having more sounds in common and thus greater transfer to English than others.

For example, an English speaker may be able to pronounce the /r/ in the Spanish word *pero* ("but"), but not the /rr/ trill in *perro* ("dog"). The English speaker may also lack the auditory acuity to detect and the ability to replicate the tonal sounds of some Chinese words. Similarly, a Vietnamese speaker may have difficulty pronouncing /th/ in words such as *thin* or *thanks*.

Further, English Language Learners make grammatical errors due to interference from their native languages. In Spanish, the adjective follows the noun, so often English Language Learners say "the girl pretty" instead of "the pretty girl." While English changes the verb form with a change of subject (*I walk. She walks.*), some Asian languages keep the verb form constant across subjects. Adding /s/ to the third person may be difficult for some English Language Learners. Students may know the grammatical rule, but applying it consistently may be difficult, especially in spoken English.

When working with English Language Learners, you should also be aware of sociocultural factors that affect pronunciation. Students may retain an accent because it marks their social identity. Speakers of other languages may feel at a social distance from members of the dominant English-speaking culture.

English Language Learners improve their pronunciation in a nonthreatening atmosphere in which participation is encouraged. Opportunities to interact with native English speakers provide easy access to language models and give English Language Learners practice using English. However, students should not be forced to participate. Pressure to perform—or to perform in a certain way—can inhibit participation. In any classroom, teacher sensitivity to pronunciation differences contributes to a more productive learning environment.

Phonics, word recognition, and spelling are influenced by what students know about the sounds, word structure, and spelling in their primary languages. For example, beginning readers who speak Spanish and are familiar with its spelling will often spell short *o* with an *a*, a letter that in Spanish makes the short *o* sound. Similarly, English Language Learners who are unaccustomed to English consonant digraphs and blends (e.g., /ch/ and *s*-blends) spell /ch/ as *sh* because /sh/ is the sound they know that is closest to /ch/. Students learn about the way pronunciation influences their reading and spelling, beginning with large contrasts among sounds, then they study the finer discriminations. As vocabulary advances, the meaning of words leads students to the sound contrasts. For example, *shoe* and *chew* may sound alike initially, but meaning indicates otherwise. Students' reading and discussions of what they read advances their word knowledge as well as their knowledge in all language and literacy systems, including phonics, pronunciation, grammar, and vocabulary.

Phonics Transfers:
Sound Transfers

This chart indicates areas where a positive transfer of sounds and symbols occurs for English Language Learners from their native languages into English. This symbol (✔) identifies a positive transfer. "Approximate" indicates that the sound is similar.

Sound Transfers	Spanish	Cantonese	Vietnamese	Hmong	Korean	Khmer
Consonants						
/b/ as in bat	✔	approximate	approximate	approximate	approximate	✔
/k/ as in cake, kitten, peck	✔	✔	✔	✔	✔	✔
/d/ as in dog	✔	approximate	approximate	✔	approximate	✔
/f/ as in farm	✔	✔	✔	✔		
/g/ as in girl	✔	approximate	✔	approximate	approximate	
/h/ as in ham	✔	✔	✔	✔	✔	approximate
/j/ as in jet, page, ledge		approximate	approximate		approximate	
/l/ as in lion	✔	✔	✔	✔	✔	
/m/ as in mat	✔	✔	✔	✔	✔	✔
/n/ as in night	✔	✔	✔	✔	✔	✔
/p/ as in pen	✔	✔	✔	approximate	✔	✔
/kw/ as in queen	✔	approximate	✔		✔	✔
/r/ as in rope	approximate					✔
/s/ as in sink, city	✔	✔	✔	✔	✔	approximate
/t/ as in ton	✔	✔	approximate	approximate	✔	✔
/v/ as in vine	✔		✔	✔		
/w/ as in wind	✔	✔			✔	✔
/ks/ as in six	✔				✔	✔
/y/ as in yak	✔	✔		✔	✔	✔
/z/ as in zebra			✔			
Digraphs						
/ch/ as in cheek, patch	✔	approximate		✔	✔	✔
/sh/ as in shadow			✔	✔	✔	
/hw/ as in whistle					✔	✔
/th/ as in path	approximate		approximate			
/TH/ as in that	approximate					
/ng/ as in sting	✔	✔	✔	✔	✔	approximate

Sound Transfers	Spanish	Cantonese	Vietnamese	Hmong	Korean	Khmer
Short Vowels						
/a/ as in cat	approximate		approximate	✔	✔	
/e/ as in net	✔	approximate	approximate		✔	
/i/ as in kid	approximate	approximate			✔	
/o/ as in spot	approximate	approximate	approximate	approximate	approximate	✔
/u/ as in cup	approximate	approximate	✔		✔	✔
Long Vowels						
/ā/ as in lake, nail, bay	✔	approximate	approximate	approximate	✔	✔
/ē/ as in bee, meat, cranky	✔	approximate	✔	✔	✔	✔
/ī/ as in kite, tie, light, dry	✔	approximate	✔	✔	✔	✔
/ō/ as in home, road, row	✔	approximate	approximate		✔	
/ū/ as in dune, fruit, blue	✔	approximate	✔	✔	✔	✔
/yü/ as in mule, cue	✔	approximate			✔	
***r*-Controlled Vowels**						
/är/ as in far	approximate	approximate				
/ôr/ as in corn	approximate	approximate				
/ûr/ as in stern, bird, suburb	approximate	approximate				
/âr/ as in air, bear						
/îr/ as in deer, ear						
Variant Vowels						
/oi/ as in boil, toy	✔	approximate	approximate		✔	✔
/ou/ as in loud, down	✔	approximate	✔	approximate	✔	✔
/ô/ as in law	approximate	✔	✔	approximate	approximate	✔
/ô/ as in laundry	approximate	approximate	✔	approximate	approximate	✔
/ôl/ as in salt, call	approximate	approximate			approximate	✔
/ü/ as in moon, drew	✔	approximate	approximate	✔	✔	✔
/u̇/ as in look		approximate	approximate		approximate	✔
/ə/ as in askew			approximate		✔	

Phonics Transfers:
Sound-Symbol Match

Sound-Symbol Match	Spanish	Cantonese	Vietnamese	Hmong	Korean	Khmer
Consonants						
/b/ as in bat	✔		✔			
/k/ as in cake	✔		✔			
/k/ as in kitten	✔		✔	✔		
/k/ as in peck						
/d/ as in dog	✔		✔	✔		
/f/ as in farm	✔			✔		
/g/ as in girl	✔		✔			
/h/ as in ham			✔	✔		
/j/ as in jet, page, ledge						
/l/ as in lion	✔		✔	✔		
/m/ as in mat	✔		✔	✔		
/n/ as in night	✔		✔	✔		
/p/ as in pen	✔		✔	✔		
/kw/ as in queen			✔			
/r/ as in rope	approximate					
/s/ as in sink, city	✔		✔			
/t/ as in ton	✔		✔	✔		
/v/ as in vine	✔		✔	✔		
/w/ as in wind	✔					
/ks/ as in six	✔					
/y/ as in yak	✔			✔		
/z/ as in zebra						
Digraphs						
/ch/ as in cheek, patch	✔					
/sh/ as in shadow						
/hw/ as in whistle						
/th/ as in path			✔			
/TH/ as in that						
/ng/ as in sting	✔		✔			
Short Vowels						
/a/ as in cat			✔	✔		
/e/ as in net	✔		✔			
/i/ as in kid						
/o/ as in spot			✔	✔		
/u/ as in cup						

Sound-Symbol Match	Spanish	Cantonese	Vietnamese	Hmong	Korean	Khmer
Long Vowels						
/ā/ as in lake						
/ā/ as in nail						
/ā/ as in bay						
/ē/ as in bee						
/ē/ as in meat						
/ē/ as in cranky						
/ī/ as in kite, tie, light, dry						
/ō/ as in home, road, row						
/ū/ as in dune			✔	✔		
/ū/ as in fruit, blue						
/yü/ as in mule, cue						
r-Controlled Vowels						
/är/ as in far	✔					
/ôr/ as in corn	✔					
/ûr/ as in stern	✔					
/ûr/ as in bird, suburb						
/âr/ as in air, bear						
/îr/ as in deer, ear						
Variant Vowels						
/oi/ as in boil	✔		✔			
/oi/ as in toy	✔					
/ou/ as in loud						
/ou/ as in down						
/ô/ as in law						
/ô/ as in laundry						
/ôl/ as in salt	✔					
/ôl/ as in call						
/ü/ as in moon, drew						
/ù/ as in look						
/ə/ as in askew						

Phonics Transfers

How to Use the Phonics Transfer Charts

To read and speak fluently in English, English Language Learners need to master a wide range of phonemic awareness, phonics, and word study skills. The Phonics Transfer Charts are designed to help you anticipate and understand possible student errors in pronouncing or perceiving English sounds.

1. **Highlight Transferrable Skills** If the phonics skill transfers from the student's primary language to English, state that during the lesson. In most lessons an English Language Learner feature will indicate which sounds do and do not transfer in specific languages.

2. **Preteach Non-Transferrable Skills** Prior to teaching a phonics lesson, check the chart to determine if the sound and/or spelling transfers from the student's primary language into English. If it does not, preteach the sound and spelling during Small Group time. Focus on articulation, using the backs of the small **Sound-Spelling Cards**, and the minimal contrast activities provided.

3. **Provide Additional Practice and Time** If the skill does NOT transfer from the student's primary language into English, the student will require more time and practice mastering the sound and spellings. Continue to review the phonics skill during Small Group time in upcoming weeks until the student has mastered it. Use the additional resources, such as the extra decodable stories in the **Teacher's Resource Book**, to provide oral and silent reading practice.

Teaching Supports for Students Transitioning from Spanish to English

The **Sound-Spelling Cards** have been created to assist you in working with English Language Learners. For example:

1. The dotted border on many of the cards indicates that the sound transfers from Spanish to English. On these cards, the same image is used in both English and Spanish (e.g., *camel/camello*). Therefore, students learning the sound in Spanish can easily transfer that knowledge to English.

2. Students whose primary language is not English will need additional articulation support to pronounce and perceive non-transferrable English sounds. Use the articulation photos on the backs of the Sound-Spelling Cards and the student-friendly descriptions of how to form these sounds during phonics lessons.

Sound-Spelling Cards

Transfer Skill Support

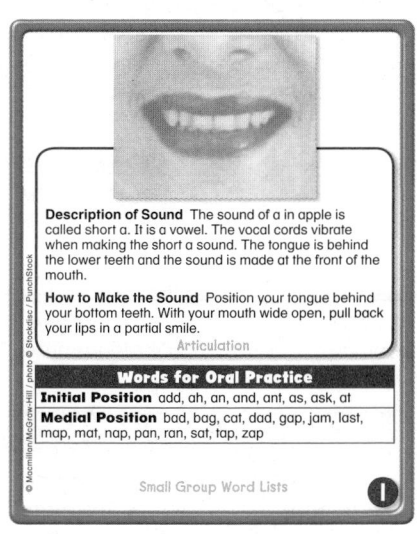

Articulation Support

Grammar Transfers:
Grammatical Form

This chart can be used to address common mistakes that some English Language Learners make when they transfer grammatical forms from their native languages into English.

Grammatical Form	Transfer Mistakes in English	Native Language	Cause of Difficulty
Nouns			
Plural Marker -s	**Forgets plural marker -s** *I have 3 sister.*	Cantonese, Haitian Creole, Hmong, Korean, Vietnamese, Khmer	Native language does not use a plural marker.
Countable and Uncountable Nouns	**Confuses countable and uncountable nouns** *the homeworks* or *the informations*	Haitian Creole, Spanish	Countable and uncountable nouns are different in English and native language.
Possessives	**Uses prepositions to describe possessives** *the book of my brother* as opposed to *my brother's book*	Haitian Creole, Hmong, Spanish, Vietnamese	Possession is often described using a prepositional phrase.
	Avoids using 's *dog my father* as opposed to *my father's dog*	Haitian Creole, Vietnamese, Khmer	A noun follows the object in the native language.
Articles			
	Consistently omits articles *He has book. They want dog not cat.*	Cantonese, Haitian Creole, Hmong, Korean, Vietnamese, Khmer	There is no article in the native language or no difference between *the* and *a*.
	Overuses articles *The English is difficult. The soccer is popular in the Europe.*	Haitian Creole, Hmong, Spanish	Some languages use articles that are omitted in English.
a/an	**Mistakes *one* for *a/an*** *She is one nurse.*	Haitian Creole, Hmong, Vietnamese	The native language either does not use articles or uses articles differently.
Pronouns			
Gender-Specific Pronouns	**Uses pronouns with the inappropriate gender** *He is my sister.*	Cantonese, Haitian Creole, Hmong, Korean, Spanish, Khmer	The third person pronoun in the native language is gender free, or the personal pronoun is omitted.
	Uses inappropriate gender, particularly with neutral nouns *The day is sunny. She is beautiful.*	Spanish	Nouns have feminine or masculine gender in the native language, and the gender may be carried over into English.

Grammatical Form	Transfer Mistakes in English	Native Language	Cause of Difficulty
Pronouns			
Object Pronouns	**Confuses subject and object pronouns** *Her talks to me.*	Cantonese, Hmong, Khmer	The same pronoun form is used for subject and object in the native language.
	Omits object pronouns *That girl is very rude, so nobody likes.*	Korean, Vietnamese	The native language does not use direct objects.
Pronoun and Number Agreement	**Uses the wrong number for pronouns** *I saw many red birds. It was pretty.*	Cantonese, Korean	The native language does not require number agreement.
Subject Pronouns	**Omits subject pronouns** *Mom isn't home. Is at work.*	Korean, Spanish	Subject pronouns may be dropped because in the native language the verb ending gives information about the number and/or gender.
Pronouns in Clauses	**Omits pronouns in clauses** *If don't do homework, they will not learn.*	Cantonese, Vietnamese	The native language does not need a subject in the subordinate clause.
Pronouns and Nouns	**Overuses pronouns with nouns** *This school, it very good.*	Hmong, Vietnamese	This is popular in speech in some languages. The speaker mentions a topic, then makes a comment about it.
	Avoids pronouns and repeats nouns *Carla visits her sister every Sunday, and Carla makes a meal.*	Korean, Vietnamese	In the native language, the speaker repeats nouns and does not use pronouns.
Pronoun *one*	**Omits the pronoun *one*** *I saw two dogs, and I like the small.*	Spanish	Adjectives can stand alone in the native language, but English requires a noun or *one*.
Possessive Forms	**Confuses possessive forms** *The book is my.*	Cantonese, Hmong, Vietnamese	Cantonese and Hmong speakers tend to omit the final *n* sound, which may create confusion between *my* and *mine*.

Grammar Transfers:
Grammatical Form

Grammatical Form	Transfer Mistakes in English	Native Language	Cause of Difficulty
Verbs			
Present Tense	**Omits -s in present tense, third person agreement** *He like pizza.*	Cantonese, Haitian Creole, Hmong, Korean, Vietnamese, Khmer	Subject-verb agreement is not used in the native language.
Irregular Verbs	**Has problems with irregular subject-verb agreement** *Tom and Sue has a new car.*	Cantonese, Hmong, Korean, Khmer	Verbs' forms do not change to show the number of the subject in the native language.
Inflectional Endings	**Omits tense markers** *I study English yesterday.*	Cantonese, Haitian Creole, Hmong, Korean, Vietnamese, Khmer	The native language does not use inflectional endings to change verb tense.
Present and Future Tenses	**Incorrectly uses the present tense for the future tense** *I go next week.*	Cantonese, Korean	The native language may use the present tense to imply the future tense.
Negative Statements	**Omits helping verbs in negative statements** *Sue no coming to school.*	Cantonese, Korean, Spanish	The native language does not use helping verbs in negative statements.
Present-Perfect Tense	**Avoids the present-perfect tense** *Marcos live here for three months.*	Haitian Creole, Vietnamese	The native language does not use the present-perfect verb form.
Past-Continuous Tense	**Uses the past-continuous tense for recurring action in the past** *When I was young, I was talking a lot.*	Korean, Spanish	In the native language, the past-continuous tense is used but in English the expression *used to* or the simple past tense is used.
Main Verb	**Omits the main verb** *Talk in class not good.*	Cantonese	Cantonese does not require an infinitive marker when using a verb as a noun. Speakers may confuse the infinitive for the main verb.
Main Verbs in Clauses	**Uses two or more main verbs in one clause without any connectors** *I took a book went studied at the library.*	Hmong	In Hmong, verbs can be used consecutively without conjunctions or punctuation.
Linking Verbs	**Omits the linking verb** *He hungry.*	Cantonese, Haitian Creole, Hmong, Vietnamese, Khmer	In some languages, *be* is implied in the adjective form. In other languages, the concept is expressed with a verb.
Helping Verb in Passive Voice	**Omits the helping verb in the passive voice** *The homework done.*	Cantonese, Vietnamese	In Cantonese and Vietnamese, the passive voice does not require a helping verb.

Grammatical Form	Transfer Mistakes in English	Native Language	Cause of Difficulty
Verbs			
Passive Voice	**Avoids the passive voice** *They speak English here.* *One speaks English here.* *English is spoken here.*	Haitian Creole	The passive voice does not exist in the native language.
Transitive Verbs	**Confuses transitive and intransitive verbs** *The child broke.* *The child broke the plate.*	Cantonese, Korean, Spanish	Verbs that require a direct object differ between English and the native language.
Phrasal Verbs	**Confuses related phrasal verbs** *I ate at the apple.* *I ate up the apple.*	Korean, Spanish	Phrasal verbs are not used in the native language, and there is often confusion over their meaning.
Have **and** *be*	**Uses** *have* **instead of** *be* *I have thirst.* *He has right.*	Spanish	Spanish and English have different uses for *have* and *be*.
Adjectives			
Word Order	**Places adjectives after nouns** *I saw a car red.*	Haitian Creole, Hmong, Spanish, Vietnamese, Khmer	Nouns often precede adjectives in the native language.
	Consistently places adjectives after nouns *This is a lesson new.*	Cantonese, Korean	Adjectives always follow nouns in the native language.
-er **and** *-est* **Endings**	**Avoids** *-er* **and** *-est* **endings** *I am more old than you.*	Hmong, Korean, Spanish, Khmer	The native language shows comparative and superlative forms with separate words.
-ing **and** *-ed* **Endings**	**Confuses** *-ing* **and** *-ed* **forms** *Math is bored.*	Cantonese, Korean, Spanish, Khmer	Adjectives in the native language do not have active and passive meanings.
Adverbs			
Adjectives and Adverbs	**Uses an adjective where an adverb is needed** *Talk quiet.*	Haitian Creole, Hmong, Khmer	Adjectives and adverb forms are interchangeable in the native language.
Word Order	**Places adverbs before verbs** *He quickly ran.* *He ran quickly.*	Cantonese, Korean	Adverbs usually come before verbs in the native language, and this tendency is carried over into English.
Prepositions			
	Omits prepositions *I like come school.*	Cantonese	Cantonese does not use prepositions the way that English does.

How to Use the Grammar Transfer Charts

The grammar of many languages differs widely from English. For example, a student's primary language may use a different word order than English, may not use parts of speech in the same way, or may use different verb tenses. The Grammar Transfer Charts are designed to help you anticipate and understand possible student errors in speaking and writing standard English. With all grammar exercises, the emphasis is on oral communication, both as a speaker and listener.

1. **Highlight Transferrable Skills** If the grammar skill transfers from the student's primary language to English, state that during the lesson. In many lessons an English Language Learner feature will indicate which skills do and do not transfer.

2. **Preteach Non-Transferrable Skills** Prior to teaching a grammar lesson, check the chart to determine if the skill transfers from the student's primary language into English. If it does not, preteach the skill during Small Group time. Provide sentence frames and ample structured opportunities to use the skill in spoken English. Students need to talk, talk, and talk some more to master these skills.

3. **Provide Additional Practice and Time** If the skill does NOT transfer from the student's primary language into English, the student will require more time and practice mastering it. Continue to review the skill during Small Group time. Use the additional resources, such as the grammar lessons in the **Intervention Kit** (K–3) or review lessons, in upcoming weeks.

4. **Use Contrastive Analysis** Tell students when a skill does not transfer and include contrastive analysis work to make the student aware of how to correct their speaking and writing for standard English. For example, when a student uses an incorrect grammatical form, write the student sentence on a **WorkBoard**. Then write the correct English form underneath. Explain the difference between the student's primary language and English. Have the student correct several other sentences using this skill, such as sentences in their Writer's Notebooks.

5. **Increase Writing and Speaking Opportunities** Increase the amount of structured writing and speaking opportunities for students needing work on specific grammatical forms. Sentence starters and paragraph frames, such as those found in the lessons, are ideal for both written and oral exercises.

6. **Focus on Meaning** Always focus on the meanings of sentences in all exercises. As they improve and fine-tune their English speaking and writing skills, work with students on basic comprehension of spoken and written English.

To help students move to the next level of language acquisition and master English grammatical forms, recast their responses during classroom discussions or provide additional language for them to use as they respond further. Provide leveled-language sentence frames orally or in writing for students to use as they respond to questions and prompts. Below are samples.

English Language Learner Response Chart

Beginning (will respond by pointing or saying one word answers)	**Sample Frames** (simple, short sentences) *I see a _____.* *This is a _____.* *I like the _____.*
Early Intermediate (will respond with phrases or simple sentences)	**Sample Frames** (simple sentences with adjectives and adverbs added, and compound subjects or predicates) *I see a _____ _____.* *The _____ animal is _____.* *There are _____ and _____.*
Intermediate (will respond with simple sentences and limited academic language)	**Sample Frames** (harder sentences with simple phrases in consistent patterns; some academic language included) *The animal's prey is _____ because _____.* *The main idea is _____ because _____.* *He roamed the park so that _____.*
Early Advanced (will begin to use more sophisticated sentences and some academic language)	**Sample Frames** (complex sentences with increased academic language, beginning phrases and clauses, and multiple-meaning words) *When the violent storm hit, _____.* *As a result of the revolution, the army_____.* *Since most endangered animals are _____, they _____.*
Advanced (will have mastered some more complex sentence structures and is increasing the amount of academic language used)	Use the questions and prompts provided in the lessons for the whole group. Provide additional support learning and using academic language. These words are boldfaced throughout the lessons and sentence starters are often provided.

Cognates

Cognates are words in two languages that look alike and have the same or similar meaning (e.g., *school/escuela, telephone/teléfono*) and can be helpful resources for English Language Learners. This list identifies some Spanish cognates for the academic language used during the lessons.

Students must also be aware of false cognates—words that look similar in two languages, but have different meanings, such as *soap* in English and *sopa* (meaning *soup*) in Spanish.

accent	*acento*	**context**	*contexto*
action	*acción*	**contrast**	*contrastar*
action verb	*verbo de acción*	**definition**	*definición*
adjective	*adjetivo*	**demonstrative**	*demostrativo*
adverb	*adverbio*	**denotation**	*denotación*
alphabetical order	*orden alfabético*	**description**	*descripción*
analogy	*analogía*	**dialogue**	*diálogo*
analyze	*analizar*	**dictionary**	*diccionario*
antecedent	*antecedente*	**direct**	*directo*
antonym	*antónimo*	**effect**	*efecto*
apostrophe	*apóstrofe*	**evaluate**	*evaluar*
article	*artículo*	**event**	*evento*
author	*autor*	**example**	*ejemplo*
cause	*causa*	**exclamation**	*exclamación*
classify	*clasificar*	**family**	*familia*
combine	*combinar*	**fantasy**	*fantasía*
compare	*comparar*	**figurative**	*figurativo*
complex	*complejo*	**fragment**	*fragmento*
comprehension	*comprensión*	**future**	*futuro*
conclusion	*conclusión*	**generalization**	*generalización*
confirm	*confirmar*	**generalize**	*generalizar*
conjunction	*conjunción*	**glossary**	*glosario*
connotation	*connotación*	**Greek**	*Griego*
consonant	*consonante*	**homophone**	*homófono*

idea	*idea*	**prefix**	*prefijo*
identify	*identificar*	**preposition**	*preposición*
illustration	*ilustración*	**prepositional**	*preposicional*
indirect	*indirecto*	**present**	*presente*
introduction	*introducción*	**problem**	*problema*
irregular	*irregular*	**pronunciation**	*pronunciación*
language	*lenguaje*	**punctuation**	*puntuación*
Latin	*Latín*	**reality**	*realidad*
myth	*mito*	**relationship**	*relación*
negative	*negativo*	**sequence**	*secuencia*
object	*objeto*	**singular**	*singular*
opinion	*opinión*	**solution**	*solución*
order	*orden*	**structure**	*estructura*
origin	*orígen*	**subject**	*sujeto*
paragraph	*párrafo*	**suffix**	*sufijo*
part	*parte*	**syllable**	*sílaba*
perspective	*perspectiva*	**synonym**	*sinónimo*
persuasion	*persuación*	**technique**	*técnica*
phrase	*frase*	**text**	*texto*
plural	*plural*	**theme**	*tema*
possessive adjective	*adjetivo posesivo*	**verb**	*verbo*
predicate	*predicado*	**visualize**	*visualizar*
prediction	*predicción*	**vowel**	*vocal*

English Language Learners

The **English Language Learners** in your classroom have a variety of backgrounds. An increasing proportion of English Language Learners are born in the United States. Some of these students are just starting school in the primary grades; others are long-term English Language Learners, with underdeveloped academic skills. Some students come from their native countries with a strong educational foundation. The academic skills of these newly arrived students are well developed and parallel the skills of their native English-speaking peers. Other English Learners immigrate to the United States with little academic experience.

These English Learners are not "blank slates." Their oral language proficiency and literacy in their first languages can be used to facilitate literacy development in English. Systematic, explicit, and appropriately scaffolded instruction and sufficient time help English Learners attain English proficiency and meet high standards in core academic subjects.

Beginning

This level of language proficiency is often referred to as the "silent" stage, in which students' receptive skills are engaged. It is important that teachers and peers respect a language learner's initial silence or allow the student to respond in his or her native language. It is often difficult for teachers to identify the level of cognitive development at this stage, due to the limited proficiency in the second language. It is important to realize that these beginning students have a wide range of abilities in their first language. They are able to transfer knowledge and skills from their first language as they develop English and learn grade-level content. Beginning students include those with limited formal schooling: young students just starting school, as well as older students. Other beginning students have had schooling in their native language and are academically parallel to nativeEnglish-speaking peers.

The Beginning Student...

- recognizes English phonemes that correspond to phonemes produced in primary language;
- is able to apply transferable grammar concepts and skills from the primary language;
- initially demonstrates more receptive than productive English skills;
- produces English vocabulary to communicate basic needs in social and academic settings;
- responds by pointing to, nodding, gesturing, acting out, and manipulating objects/pictures;
- speaks in one-or two-word responses as language develops;
- draws pictures and writes letters and sounds being learned.

Early Intermediate

this level, students are considered more dvanced beginning English Learners. They developing early production skills, but eir receptive skills are much more advanced an their speaking ability. At this stage it is itical that the students continue to listen to odel speakers.

The Early Intermediate Student...

- recognizes English phonemes that correspond to phonemes produced in primary language;
- is able to apply transferable grammar concepts and skills from the primary language;
- understands more spoken English than the beginning student;
- speaks in one- or two-word utterances;
- may respond with phrases or sentences;
- produces English vocabulary words and phrases to communicate basic needs in social and academic settings;
- begins to ask questions, role-play, and retell;
- begins to use routine expressions;
- demonstrates an internalization of English grammar and usage by recognizing and correcting some errors when speaking and reading aloud;
- increases correct usage of written and oral language conventions.

Intermediate

udents at this level begin to tailor eir English language skills to meet mmunication and learning demands with creasing accuracy. They possess vocabulary d knowledge of grammatical structures at allow them to more fully participate in assroom activities and discussions. They are enerally more comfortable producing both oken and written language.

The Intermediate Student...

- pronounces most English phonemes correctly while reading aloud;
- can identify more details of information that has been presented orally or in writing;
- uses more complex vocabulary and sentences to communicate needs and express ideas;
- uses specific vocabulary learned, including academic language;
- participates more fully in discussions with peers and adults;
- reads and comprehends a wider range of reading materials;
- writes brief narratives and expository texts;
- demonstrates an internalization of English grammar and usage by recognizing and correcting errors when speaking and reading aloud.

Early Advanced

Students at this language proficiency level possess vocabulary and grammar structures that approach those of an English-proficient speaker. These students demonstrate consistent general comprehension of grade-level content that is presented.

The Early Advanced Student...

- applies knowledge of common English morphemes in oral and silent reading;
- understands increasingly more nonliteral social and academic language;
- responds using extensive vocabulary;
- participates in and initiates more extended social conversations with peers and adults;
- communicates orally and in writing with fewer grammatical errors;
- reads with good comprehension a wide range of narrative and expository texts;
- writes using more standard forms of English on various content-area topics;
- becomes more creative and analytical when writing.

Advanced

The student at this language proficiency level communicates effectively with peers and adults in both social and academic situations. Students can understand grade-level text but still need some English language development support, such as preteaching concepts and skills. While the English language proficiency of these students is advanced, some linguistic support for accessing content is still necessary.

The Advanced Student...

- understands increasingly more nonliteral social and academic language;
- responds using extensive vocabulary;
- communicates orally and in writing with infrequent errors;
- creates more complex narratives and expository writing in all content areas.

English Language Learner Profiles
Facilitating Language Growth

Beginning

Student's Behaviors	Teacher's Behaviors	Questioning Techniques
■ Points to or provides other nonverbal responses ■ Actively listens ■ Responds to commands ■ Understands more than he or she can produce	■ Gestures ■ Focuses on conveying meanings and vocabulary development ■ Does not force students to speak ■ Shows visuals and real objects ■ Writes words for students to see ■ Pairs students with more proficient learners ■ Provides speaking and writing frames and models	■ Point to the _____. ■ Find the _____. ■ Put the _____ next to the _____. ■ Do you have the _____? ■ Is this the _____? ■ Who wants the _____?

Early Intermediate

Student's Behaviors	Teacher's Behaviors	Questioning Techniques
■ Speaks in one- or two-word utterances ■ Uses short phrases and simple sentences ■ Listens with greater understanding	■ Asks questions that can be answered by yes/no ■ Asks either/or questions ■ Asks higher-order questions with one-word answers ■ Models correct responses ■ Ensures supportive, low-anxiety environment ■ Does not overtly call attention to grammar errors ■ Asks short "wh" questions	■ Yes/no (Did you like the story?) ■ Either/or (Is this a pencil or a crayon?) ■ One-word responses (Why did the dog hide?) ■ General questions that encourage lists of words (What did you see in the book bag?) ■ Two-word responses (Where did I put the pen?)

Intermediate

Student's Behaviors	Teacher's Behaviors	Questioning Techniques
■ Demonstrates comprehension in a variety of ways ■ Speaks in short phrases or sentences ■ Begins to use language more freely	■ Provides frequent comprehension checks ■ Asks open-ended questions that stimulate language production	■ Why? ■ How? ■ How is this like that? ■ Tell me about _____. ■ Talk about _____. ■ Describe _____. ■ What is in your book bag?

Early Advanced

Student's Behaviors	Teacher's Behaviors	Questioning Techniques
■ Participates in reading and writing activities to acquire information ■ Demonstrates increased levels of accuracy and correctness and is able to express thoughts and feelings ■ Produces language with varied grammatical structures and academic language ■ May experience difficulties in abstract, cognitively demanding subjects	■ Fosters conceptual development and expanded literacy through content ■ Continues to make lessons comprehensible and interactive ■ Teaches thinking and study skills ■ Continues to be alert to individual differences in language and culture	■ What would you recommend/why? ■ How do you think this story will end? ■ What is this story about? ■ What is your favorite part of the story? ■ Describe/compare _____. How are these similar/different? ■ What would happen if _____? ■ Why do you think that? Yes, tell me more about _____.

Fostering Classroom Discussions

Strategies for English Language Learners

One of the most effective ways in which to increase the oral language proficiency of your English Language Learners is to give students many opportunities to do a lot of talking in the classroom. Providing the opportunities and welcoming all levels of participation will motivate students to take part in the class discussions. You can employ a few basic teaching strategies that will encourage the participation of all language proficiency levels of English Language Learners in whole class and small group discussions.

☑ WAIT/DIFFERENT RESPONSES

- Be sure to give students enough time to answer the question.

- Let students know that they can respond in different ways depending on their levels of proficiency. Students can

  - answer in their native language;

  - ask a more proficient ELL speaker to repeat the answer in English;

  - answer with nonverbal cues (pointing to related objects, drawing, or acting out).

> **Teacher:** Where is Charlotte?
>
> **ELL Response:** (Student points to the web in the corner of the barn.)
>
> **Teacher:** Yes. Charlotte is sitting in her web. Let's all point to Charlotte.

☑ REPEAT

- Give positive confirmation to the answers that each English Language Learner offers. If the response is correct, repeat what the student has said in a clear, loud voice and at a slower pace. This validation will motivate other ELLs to participate.

> **Teacher:** How would you describe the faces of the bobcats?
>
> **ELL Response:** They look scared.
>
> **Teacher:** That's right, Silvia. They are scared. Everyone show me your scared face.

☑ REVISE FOR FORM

- Repeating an answer allows you to model the proper form for a response. You can model how to answer in full sentences and use academic language.

- When you repeat the answer, correct any grammar or pronunciation errors.

> **Teacher:** Who are the main characters in the story *Zathura*?
>
> **ELL Response:** Danny and Walter is.
>
> **Teacher:** Yes. Danny and Walter <u>are</u> the main characters. Remember to use the verb <u>are</u> when you are telling about more than one person. Let's repeat the sentence.
>
> **All:** Danny and Walter <u>are</u> the main characters.

☑ REVISE FOR MEANING

- Repeating an answer offers an opportunity to clarify the meaning of a response.

> **Teacher:** Where did the golden feather come from?
>
> **ELL Response:** The bird.
>
> **Teacher:** That's right. The golden feather came from the Firebird.

☑ ELABORATE

- If students give a one-word answer or a nonverbal cue, elaborate on the answer to model fluent speaking and grammatical patterns.

- Provide more examples or repeat the answer using proper academic language.

> **Teacher:** Why is the girls' mother standing with her hands on her hips?
>
> **ELL Response:** She is mad.
>
> **Teacher:** Can you tell me more? Why is she mad?
>
> **ELL Response:** Because the girls are late.
>
> **Teacher:** Ok. What do you think the girls will do?
>
> **ELL Response:** They will promise not to be late again.
>
> **Teacher:** Anyone else have an idea?

☑ ELICIT

- Prompt students to give a more comprehensive response by asking additional questions or guiding them to get to an answer.

> **Teacher:** Listen as I read the caption under the photograph. What information does the caption tell us?
>
> **ELL Response:** It tells about the butterfly.
>
> **Teacher:** What did you find out about the butterfly?
>
> **ELL Response:** It drinks nectar.
>
> **Teacher:** Yes. The butterfly drinks nectar from the flower.

Making the Most of Classroom Conversations

Use all the speaking and listening opportunities in your classroom to observe students' oral language proficiency.

- Response to oral presentations
- Responding to text aloud
- Following directions
- Group projects
- Small Group work
- Informal, social peer discussions
- One-on-one conferences

The **English Language Learner Resource Book** provides Speaking and Listening Checklists to help you monitor students' oral language proficiency growth.

Treasures

Support for Students with Dyslexia

Characteristics of Dyslexia

A student with dyslexia is a student who continually struggles with reading and spelling but displays an ability to learn when there are no print materials involved. Even though the student receives the same classroom instruction as most other students, he continues to have difficulties with reading and spelling.

Students identified with dyslexia often have difficulties in the following areas

- reading words in isolation
- decoding nonsense words accurately
- oral reading (slow and inaccurate)
- learning to spell

The difficulties in these areas are usually the result of student's struggles with:

- phonological awareness: segmenting, blending, and manipulating words
- naming letters and pronouncing their sounds.
- phonological memory
- rapid naming of the letters of the alphabet or familiar objects

Effective Instruction

To address the needs of a student with dyslexia, instruction should be delivered in small groups. The instruction should be explicit, intensive, employ multisensory methods, as needed, and be individualized. It should include instruction on:

- phonemic awareness that has students detect, segment, blend and manipulate sounds
- phonics, emphasizing the sound/symbol relationships for decoding and encoding words
- morphology, semantics and syntax
- fluency with patterns of language
- strategies for decoding, encoding, word recognition, fluency and comprehension

Resources:
The International Dyslexia Association Website: www.interdys.org
The Dyslexia Handbook: Procedures Concerning Dyslexia and Related Disorders (Revised 2007) Texas Education Agency, Austin, TX, Publication Number: GE8721001

Treasures Reading and Language Arts Program

Treasures is a scientifically-based core program that offers sequential, explicit, and effective instruction in phonological awareness, phonics, morphology, fluency, vocabulary, and reading comprehension. Students are given many opportunities to practice and review these skills to help prevent reading difficulties before they begin.

 INTERVENTION

Weekly Small Group Lessons
Intervention Teacher's Editions

Tier 2 Instruction is provided in weekly small group lessons in the *Treasures* **Teacher's Editions**. These lessons provide targeted instruction in priority skills taught in the week. *Tier 2 Intervention* **Teacher's Editions** provide additional instruction for struggling students in the areas of phonemic awareness, phonics, vocabulary, fluency, and comprehension, grammar and writing.

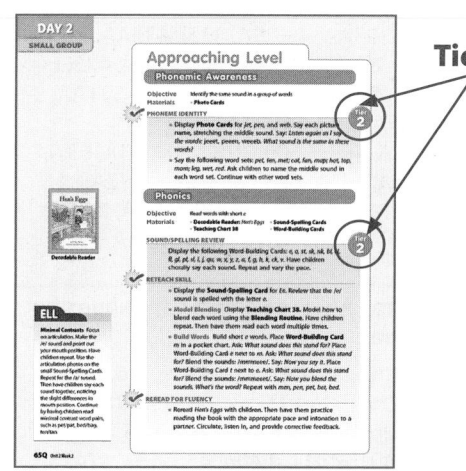

 INTERVENTION

Reading Triumphs
Intervention Program

Reading Triumphs provides intensive instruction. Explicit, sequential lessons delivered through clear instructional routines for all the key components of reading are embedded in the program. The "no assumption instruction" allows for both teacher and student success.

B

C

Key 6 = Unit 6

Key 6 = Unit 6

D

Daily Language Activities, **1**:37G, 65G, 77K, 103G, 125G, **2**:161G, 187G, 199K, 225G, 257G, **3**:291G, 325G, 337K, 367G, 395G, **4**:435G, 461G, 473K, 503G, 531G, **5**:569G, 597G, 609K, 637G, 663G, **6**:703G, 729G, 741K, 773G, 801G

Decodable Passages, **1**:37Q, 65Q, 77U, 103Q, 125Q, **2**:161Q, 187Q, 199U, 225Q, 257Q, **3**:291Q, 325Q, 337U, 367Q, 395Q, **4**:435Q, 461Q, 473U, 503Q, 531Q, **5**:569Q, 597Q, 609U, 637Q, 663Q, **6**:703Q, 729Q, 741U, 773Q, 801Q

Decoding. *See* Decodable Passages; Phonics/Word Study.

Denotation. *See* Vocabulary: denotation.

Details. *See* Comprehension skills: main ideas and details; Writer's Craft.

Diagrams. *See* Graphic Organizers: diagrams; Text features.

Dialogue, **1**:52, 58, 96, **4**:433A–433B, 434, **6**:722, 756, 768

    effective, **4**:435A

    identifying speaker in, **4**:461A

    mixing narration with, **4**:459A–459B, 460

    punctuation, **3**:291H, **4**:461A, **5**:570L

    telling statements replaced with, **4**:435A

Dictionary, use, **1**:S13, S30, 8, 37C, 80, 93, 103C, 103U, 106, 118, 131C, **2**:228, 236, **5**:554, 605C, 640, 650, 654, **6**:676, 685, 692, 703C, 703K, 703U, 714, 744, 751, 763, 776, 783, 784, 786, 790, 791, 792

    See also Study skills; Vocabulary: dictionary, using.

Differentiated instruction. *See* Approaching Level Options; Beyond Level Options; English Language Learners; On Level Options.

Digital Learning, **1**:4/5, S2–S3, 6B–6C, 6I–6J, 38B–38C, 38I–38J, 66B–66C, 66I–66J, 78B–78C, 78I–78J, 104B–104C, 104I–104J, 126B, **2**:134/135, 136B–136C, 136I–136J, 162B–162C, 162I–162J, 188B–188C, 188I–188J, 200B, 200I–200J, 226B–226C, 226I–226J, 258B, **3**:266/267, 267B–267C, 267I–267J, 292B–292C, 292I–292J, 326B–326C, 326I–326J, 338B–338C,

338I–338J, 368B–368C, 368I–368J, 396B, **4**:404/405, 406B–406C, 406I–406J, 436B–436C, 436I–436J, 462B–462C, 462I–462J, 474B–474C, 474I–474J, 504B–504C, 504I–504J, 532B, **5**:540/541, 542B–542C, 542I–542J, 570B–570C, 570I–570J, 598B–598C, 598I–598J, 610B–610C, 610I–610J, 638B–638C, 638I–638J, **6**:672/673, 674B–674C, 674I–674J, 704B–704C, 704I–704J, 730B–730C, 730I–730J, 742B–742C, 742I–742J, 774B–774C, 774I–774J, 802B

    See also **Technology.**

Drama. *See under* **Genre.**

Drawing conclusions. *See* **Comprehension skills: draw conclusions.**

Dyslexia, **1**:T38, **2**:T38, **3**:T38, **4**:T38, **5**:T38, **6**:T38

E

Editorial, **4**:430, 435W

Encyclopedia, **4**:498, 499, 501, 503W

End punctuation. *See* Grammar: punctuation.

Engagement Prompt. *See under* Writing prompts.

English Language Learners

    academic language, **1**:37AA, 65AA, 69A, 77EE, 81A, 103AA, 125AA, **2**:161AA, 165A, 187AA, 199EE, 225AA, 257AA, **3**:291AA, 325AA, 337EE, 367AA, 395AA, **4**:435AA, 461AA, 473EE, 503AA, 531AA, **5**:569AA, 597AA, 609EE, 637AA, 663AA, **6**:703AA, 729AA, 741EE, 773AA, 801AA

    access to core content, **1**:13, 37CC, 45, 65CC, 77GG, 85, 103CC, 111, 125CC, **2**:161CC, 169, 187CC, 199GG, 207, 225CC, 233, 257CC, **3**:275, 291CC, 299, 325CC, 337GG, 345, 367CC, 375, 395CC, **4**:413, 435CC, 443, 461CC, 473GG, 481, 503CC, 511, 531CC, **5**:549, 569CC, 577, 597CC, 609GG, 617, 637CC, 645, 663CC, **6**:681, 703CC, 711, 729CC, 741GG, 749, 773CC, 781, 801CC

    beginning/intermediate/advanced/ advanced high, **1**:7, 13, 37, 37BB, 37CC, 37DD, 37EE, 37FF, 37GG, 37HH, 39, 45, 65, 65BB, 65CC, 65DD,

65EE, 65FF, 65GG, 65HH, 67, 77FF, 77GG, 77HH, 77II, 77JJ, 77KK, 77LL, 79, 85, 103, 103BB, 103CC, 103DD, 103EE, 103FF, 103GG, 103HH, 105, 111, 125, 125BB, 125CC, 125DD, 125EE, 125FF, 125GG, 125HH, **2**:137, 143, 161, 161BB, 161CC, 161DD, 161EE, 161FF, 161GG, 161HH, 163, 169, 187, 187BB, 187CC, 187DD, 187EE, 187FF, 187GG, 187HH, 189, 199FF, 199GG, 199HH, 199II, 199JJ, 199KK, 199LL, 201, 207, 225, 225BB, 225CC, 225DD, 225EE, 225FF, 225GG, 225HH, 227, 233, 257, 257BB, 257CC, 257DD, 257EE, 257FF, 257GG, 257HH, **3**:269, 275, 291, 291BB, 291CC, 291DD, 291EE, 291FF, 291GG, 291HH, 293, 299, 325, 325BB, 325CC, 325DD, 325EE, 325FF, 325GG, 325HH, 327, 337FF, 337GG, 337HH, 337II, 337JJ, 337KK, 337LL, 339, 345, 367, 367BB, 367CC, 367DD, 367EE, 367FF, 367GG, 367HH, 369, 375, 395, 395BB, 395CC, 395DD, 395EE, 395FF, 395GG, 395HH, **4**:407, 413, 435, 435BB, 435CC, 435DD, 435EE, 435FF, 435GG, 435HH, 437, 443, 461, 461BB, 461CC, 461DD, 461EE, 461FF, 461GG, 461HH, 463, 473FF, 473GG, 473HH, 473II, 473JJ, 473KK, 473LL, 475, 481, 503, 503BB, 503CC, 503DD, 503EE, 503FF, 503GG, 503HH, 505, 511, 531, 531BB, 531CC, 531DD, 531EE, 531FF, 531GG, 531HH, **5**:543, 549, 569, 569BB, 569CC, 569DD, 569EE, 569FF, 569GG, 569HH, 571, 577, 597, 597BB, 597CC, 597DD, 597EE, 597FF, 597GG, 597HH, 599, 609FF, 609GG, 609HH, 609II, 609JJ, 609KK, 609LL, 611, 617, 637, 637BB, 637CC, 637DD, 637EE, 637FF, 637GG, 637HH, 639, 645, 663, 663BB, 663CC, 663DD, 663EE, 663FF, 663GG, 663HH, **6**:675, 681, 703, 703BB, 703CC, 703DD, 703EE, 703FF, 703GG, 703HH, 705, 711, 729, 729BB, 729CC, 729DD, 729EE, 729FF, 729GG, 729HH, 731, 741FF, 741GG, 741HH, 741II, 741JJ, 741KK, 741LL, 743, 749, 773, 773BB, 773CC, 773DD, 773EE, 773FF, 773GG, 773HH, 775, 781, 801, 801BB, 801CC, 801DD, 801EE, 801FF, 801GG, 801HH

    choral-read, **1**:37GG, 65GG, 77KK, 103GG, 125GG, **2**:161GG, 187GG, 199KK, 225GG, 257GG, **3**:291GG, 325GG, 337KK, 367GG, 395GG, **4**:435GG, 461GG, 473KK, 503GG, 531GG, **5**:569GG, 597GG, 609KK, 637GG, 663GG, **6**:703GG, 729GG, 741KK, 773GG, 801GG

Key 6 = Unit 6

M

Magazine article. *See* Genre: reading nonfiction; Writing applications: informational.

Main ideas. *See* Comprehension skills: main ideas and details.

proofreading, **1:**37F, 65F, 77J, 103F, 125F, **2:**161F, 187F, 187H, 199J, 225F, 257F, **3:**291F, 325F, 337J, 367F, 395F, **4:**435F, 461F, 473J, 503F, 531F, **5:**569F, 597F, 609J, 637F, 663F, **6:**703F, 729F, 741J, 773F, 801F

Spelling Inventory, **1:**S8, S27

Spiral Review, **1:**37E, 65E, 77I, 103E, 125E, **2:**161E, 187E, 199I, 225E, 257E, **3:**291E, 325E, 337I, 367E, 395E, **4:**435E, 461E, 473I, 503E, 531E, **5:**569E, 597E, 609I, 637E, 663E, **6:**703E, 729E, 741I, 773E, 801E

synonyms, **2:**187F, **4:**503F, **5:**597F

word lists, **1:**37E, 65E, 77I, 103E, 125E, **2:**161E, 187E, 199I, 225E, 257E, **3:**291E, 325E, 337I, 367E, 395E, **4:**435E, 461E, 473I, 503E, 531E, T14–T15, **5:**569E, 597E, 609I, 637E, 663E, T14–T15, **6:**703E, 729E, 741I, 773E, 801E, T14–T15

word meanings, **1:**37F, 65F, 77J, 103F, 125F, **2:**161F, 187F, 199J, 225F, 257F, **3:**291F, 325F, 337J, 367F, 395F, **4:**435F, 461F, 473J, 503F, 531F, **5:**569F, 597F, 609J, 637F, 663F, **6:**703F, 729F, 741J, 773F, 801F

words changing *y* to *i*, **4:**461E–461F, 461J

word sorts, **1:**37E, 65E, 77I, 103E, 125E, **2:**161E, 187E, 199I, 225E, 257E, **3:**291E, 325E, 337I, 367E, 395E, **4:**435E, 461E, 473I, 503E, 531E, **5:**569E, 597E, 609I, 637E, 663E, **6:**703E, 729E, 741I, 773E, 801E

words with /är/ and /ôr/, **2:**225E–225F, 225S

words with closed syllables, **5:**569E–569F, 569J, 569S

words with consonant + *le* syllables, **5:**663E–663F, 663S

words with digraphs, *th, sh, wh, ph, ch, tch,* **2:**187E–187F, 187J, 187S

words with *er, ir, ur,* **3:**291E–291F, 291J, 291S

words with final /ən/, **6:**703E–703F, 703J, 703S

words with homophones, **6:**729E–729F, 729J, 729S, 729W

words with inflectional endings, **4:**435E–435F, 435S, 461S

words with long vowels, **1:**65E–65F, 65S, 77I–77J, 77N, 77W, 103E–103F, 103J, 103S, 125E–125F, 125S

words with /ô/, **4:**531E–531F, 531J, 531S

words with /oi/ and /ou/, **4:**503E–503F, 503J, 503S

words with open syllables, **5:**597E–597F, 597S

words with plurals *s* and *es, y* to *i,* **3:**367E–367F, 367S, **4:**461E–461F, 461J, 461S

words with prefixes, **2:**161E–161F, 161J, 161S, **6:**741I–741J, 741N, 741W, 801E–801F, 801S

words with *r*-controlled vowel, **5:**637E–637F, 637J, 637S

words with *r*-controlled vowel syllables, **2:**225E–225F, 225S, **3:**291S

words with short vowels, **1:**37E–37F

words with silent letters, **3:**325E–325F, 325S

words with soft *c* and soft *g,* **3:**337I–337J, 337W

words with suffixes, **6:**773E–773F, 773J, 773S, 773W, 801E–801F, 801S, **2:**257E–257F, 257S

words with three-letter blends, **2:**199I–199J, 199W

words with /ü/, /û/, /u̇/, **4:**473I–473J, 473W, 473AA

words with vowel teams, **5:**609I–609J, 609W

Story structure. *See* Comprehension strategies: story structure.

Structural Analysis. *See* Phonics/Word Study; Vocabulary.

Structural elements. *See* Comprehension strategies: structural elements.

Study skills

See also **Text features.**

computers using. *See* Computer Literacy.

dictionary. *See* Dictionary, using.

explain/model/practice, **1:**73C–73D, **2:**195C–195D, **3:**333C–333D, **4:**469C–469D, **5:**605C–605D, **6:**737C–737D

functional documents, **6:**737C–737D

library and media center, using, **1:**73C–73D

author and title, subject searches, **1:**73C

call numbers, **1:**73C

electronic and print card catalog, using, **1:**73C–73D

organization in, **1:**73C

parts of a book, **2:**195C–195D

appendix, **2:**195C

copyright page, **2:**195C

glossary, **2:**195C

headings, **2:**195C

index, **2:**195C

preface, **2:**195C

subheadings, **2:**195C

table of contents, **2:**195C

title page, **2:**195C

skimming and scanning, **1:**xvii, **4:**469C–469D

Suffixes. *See* Phonics/Word Study: words with suffixes; Vocabulary: suffixes.

Summarizing. *See* Comprehension skills: summarize; Comprehension strategies: summarize.

Symbolism, **2:**227A, **5:**592, 594, 597W

Synonyms, **1:**40, 65C, 65K, 127, 129, **2:**187F, **3:**367U, 367W, 401, **4:**476, 503F, 503K, 503U, **5:**570K, 572, 597F, 597K, 597U

T

Talk About It. *See* Oral language.

Tall tale, **2:**225W

Teacher's Checklist, **1:**131K, **2:**263K, **3:**401K, **4:**537K, **5:**669K, **6:**807K

Teacher-to-Teacher, **1:**37B, 65B, 77C, 103B, 125B, **2:**161B, 187B, 199C, 225B, 257B, **3:**291B, 325B, 337C, 367B, 395B, **4:**435B, 461B, 473C, 503B, 531B, **5:**569B, 597B, 609C, 637B, 663B, **6:**703B, 729B, 741C, 773B, 801B

Teamwork, rules of, **1:**xvii, **2:**xvii, **3:**xvii, **4:**xvii, **5:**xvii, **6:**xvii

Technology

See also **Computer Literacy.**

audio CDs **1:**S27, 6B, 6D, 6J, 6K, 31A, 37N, 37O, 37U, 37V, 37Y, 37Z, 37GG, 37II, 37JJ, 38B, 38D, 38J, 59A, 65N, 65O, 65U, 65V, 65Y, 65Z, 65GG, 65II, 65JJ, 66B, 66D, 66J, 73A, 77R, 77S, 77Y, 77Z, 77CC, 77DD, 77KK, 77MM, 77NN, 78B, 78D, 78J, 78K, 97A, 103N, 103O, 103U, 103V, 103Y,

V

W

Key 6 = Unit 6

Acknowledgments

Photography

All photos by Ken Karp or Ken Cavanagh for MacMillan/McGraw-Hill except the following:

iv: (tl, tcl, tcr, ccl, bl, br) Macmillan/McGraw-Hill; (tr) Deborah Attoinese Photography; (ccr, cr) Anthony Colella/Richter-Colella Studios; (cl) Photography by Monet. v: (br) Macmillan/McGraw-Hill; (tl) Doug Martin; (tr) Ferguson & Katzman Photography. xii: (br) Thomas Kitchin & Victoria Hurst/Getty Images. xiii: (br) Macmillan/McGraw-Hill. 674A–B: Photodisc/Fotosearch. 674C: (inset) Dorothea Lange/Stringer/2005 GettyImage; (r) Corbis. 674I: Macmillan/McGraw-Hill. 703B: (b) Gabe Palmer/Corbis. 704A–B: Radius Images/Alamy. 704C: (r-bkgd, cr) Joe Ginsberg/Getty Images; (r) ImageDJ/Jupiter Images. 704I: Macmillan/McGraw-Hill. 730A–B: Digital Vision/Fotosearch. 730I: Macmillan/McGraw-Hill. 742A–B: Digital Vision/PunchStock. 742C: (cl) Richard Hutchings/Corbis; (l) Gary Buss/Getty Images. 742I: Macmillan/McGraw-Hill. 773B: (b) Jim Cummings/Corbis. 774A–B: John Anderson/Alamy. 774C: (cl) W. Dickson/Corbis; (c) Bettmann/Corbis; (tl) Schenectady Museum; Hall of Electrical History Foundation/Corbis. 774I: Macmillan/McGraw-Hill. 802A–B: Brad Perks Lightscapes/Alamy. 807B–F: Macmillan/McGraw-Hill. 807H: (br) Royalty Free/Corbis. 807L: (br) Comstock/SuperStock. Teacher's Notes: (marker) Royalty Free/Corbis; (sharpeners) Pixtal/PunchStock.

The publisher gratefully acknowledges permission to reprint the following copyrighted material:

"Adelina's Whales" text and photographs by Richard Sobol. Text and photographs copyright © 2003 by Richard Sobol. Reprinted by permission of Dutton Children's Books, a division of Penguin Books USA Inc.

"The Adventures of Ali Baba Bernstein" by Johanna Hurwitz. Copyright © 1985 by Johanna Hurwitz. Reprinted by permission of William Morrow and Company.

"The Ant and the Grasshopper" retold and illustrated by Amy Lowry Poole. Copyright © 2000 by Amy Lowry Poole. Reprinted by permission of Holiday House.

"The Astronaut and the Onion" by Ann Cameron from GLORIA RISING. Text copyright © 2002 by Ann Cameron. Reprinted by permission of Frances Foster Books, an imprint of Farrar, Straus and Giroux.

"At Home in the Coral Reef" by Katy Muzik, illustrated by Katherine Brown-Wing. Text and illustrations copyright © 1992 by Charlesbridge Publishing. Reprinted by permission.

"Because of Winn-Dixie" by Kate DiCamillo from BECAUSE OF WINN-DIXIE. Copyright © 2000 by Kate DiCamillo. Reprinted by permission of Candlewick Press.

"Brave New Heights" by Monica Kulling from MORE SPICE THAN SUGAR: POEMS ABOUT FEISTY FEMALES compiled by Lillian Morrison. Compilation copyright © 2001 by Lillian Morrison. Reprinted by permission of Marian Reiner from the author.

"The Cricket in Times Square" by George Selden, illustrated by Garth Williams from THE CRICKET IN TIMES SQUARE. Copyright © 1960 by George Selden Thompson and Garth Williams. Reprinted by permission of Farrar, Straus and Giroux. [McGraw-Hill acknowledges the use of a trademark due to illustrator restrictions.]

"Dear Mrs. LaRue" written and illustrated by Mark Teague. Copyright © 2002 by Mark Teague. Reprinted by permission of Scholastic Press, a division of Scholastic, Inc.

"How Ben Franklin Stole the Lightning" by Rosalyn Schanzer. Copyright © 2003 by Rosalyn Schanzer. Reprinted by permission of HarperCollins Publishers.

"I Love the Look of Words" by Maya Angelou from SOUL LOOKS BACK IN WONDER. Copyright © 1993 by Tom Feelings. Reprinted by permission of Dial Books, a division of Penguin Books USA Inc.

"Ima and The Great Texas Ostrich Race" by Margaret Olivia McManis, illustrated by Bruce Dupree. Text copyright © 2002 by Margaret McManis. Illustrations copyright © 2002 by Bruce Dupree. Reprinted by permission of Eakin Press/A Division of Sunbelt Media, Inc.

"Leah's Pony" by Elizabeth Friedrich, illustrated by Michael Garland. Text copyright © 1996 by Elizabeth Friedrich. Illustrations © 1996 by Michael Garland. Reprinted by permission of Boyds Mills Press.

"The Life and Times of the Ant" by Charles Micucci from THE LIFE AND TIMES OF THE ANT. Copyright © 2003 by Charles Micucci. Reprinted by permission of Houghton Mifflin Company.

"Light Bulb" and "Lightning Bolt" by Joan Bransfield Graham from FLICKER FLASH. Text copyright © 1999 by Joan Bransfield Graham. Reprinted by permission of Houghton Mifflin Company.

"Me and Uncle Romie" by Claire Hartfield, paintings by Jerome Lagarrigue. Text copyright © 2002 by Claire Hartfield, paintings copyright © 2002 by Jerome Lagarrigue. Reprinted by permission of Dial Books, a division of Penguin Books USA Inc.

"Mighty Jackie: The Strike-Out Queen" by Marissa Moss, illustrated by C. F. Payne. Text copyright © 2004 by Marissa Moss, illustrations copyright © 2004 by C. F. Payne. Reprinted by permission of Simon & Schuster Books for Young Readers.

"Mountains and plains" and "No sky at all" from AN INTRODUCTION TO HAIKU: AN ANTHOLOGY OF POEMS AND POETS FROM BASHŌ TO SHIKI. Copyright © 1958 by Harold G. Henderson. Reprinted by permission of Doubleday Anchor Books, a Division of Doubleday & Company, Inc.

"My Brother Martin: A Sister Remembers, Growing Up with the Rev. Dr. Martin Luther King, Jr." by Christine King Farris, illustrated by Chris Soentpiet. Text copyright © 2003 by Christine King Farris, illustrations copyright © 2003 by Chris Soentpiet. Reprinted by permission of Simon & Schuster Books for Young Readers.

"My Brothers' Flying Machine" by Jane Yolen, paintings by Jim Burke. Text copyright © 2003 by Jane Yolen, illustrations copyright © 2003 by Jim Burke. Reprinted by permission of Little, Brown and Company.

"My Diary from Here to There" story by Amada Irma Pérez, illustrations by Maya Christina Gonzalez from MY DIARY FROM HERE TO THERE. Story copyright © 2002 by Amada Irma Pérez, illustrations copyright © 2002 by Maya Christina Gonzalez. Reprinted by permission of Children's Book Press.

"Mystic Horse" by Paul Goble. Copyright © 2003 by Paul Goble. Reprinted by permission of HarperCollins Publishers.

"The New Kid" from AT THE CRACK OF THE BAT: Baseball Poems compiled by Lillian Morrison, illustrated by Steve Cieslawski. Text copyright © 1992 by Lillian Morrison. Illustrations copyright © 1992 by Steve Cieslawski. Reprinted by permission of Hyperion Books for Children.

"Roadrunner's Dance" by Rudolfo Anaya, pictures by David Diaz. Text copyright © 2000 by Rudolfo Anaya, illustrations copyright © 2000 by David Diaz. Reprinted by permission of Hyperion Books for Children.

"Snowflake Bentley" by Jacqueline Briggs Martin, illustrated by Mary Azarian. Text copyright © 1998 by Jacqueline Briggs Martin, illustrations copyright © 1998 by Mary Azarian. Reprinted by permission of Houghton Mifflin Company.

"The snow is melting" and " Winter solitude" from THE ESSENTIAL HAIKU: VERSIONS OF BASHŌ, BUSON, AND ISSA. Introduction and selection copyright © 1994 by Robert Hass. Unless otherwise noted, all translations copyright © 1994 by Robert Hass. Reprinted by permission of The Ecco Press.

Excerpt from "So Long, It's Been Good to Know Yuh." Words and music by Woody Guthrie. www.woodyguthrie.org Copyright © 1940 (Renewed), 1950 (Renewed), 1951 (Renewed) by TRO-Folk. Reprinted by permission of The Richmond Organization (TRO).

"A Walk in the Desert" by Rebecca L. Johnson with illustrations by Phyllis V. Saroff from A WALK IN THE DESERT. Text copyright © 2001 by Rebecca L. Johnson, illustrations copyright © 2001 by Phyllis V. Saroff. Reprinted by permission of Carolrhoda Books, Inc.

"When I Went to the Library" by Ken Roberts from WHEN I WENT TO THE LIBRARY edited by Debora Pearson. Copyright © 2001 by Ken Roberts. Reprinted by permission of Groundwood Books/Douglas & McIntyre.

"Wild Horses: Black Hills Sanctuary" by Cris Peterson, photographs by Alvis Upitis. Text copyright © 2003 by Cris Peterson, photographs copyright © 2003 by Alvis Upitis. Reprinted by permission of Boyds Mills Press, Inc.

ILLUSTRATIONS

Cover Illustration: Gloria Domingo Manuel.

10–31: Maya Christina Gonzalez. 40–41: Ginger Nielson. 42–59: Brian Biggs. 60–63: Olwyn Whelan. 65: Ken Bowser. 80: Kim Johnson. 82–97: Anna Rich. 120–121: Robert Casilla. 125: Viviana Diaz. 140–155: Chris Soentpiet. 166–183: C.F. Payne. 184–185: Steve Cieslawski. 220–223: Ande Cook. 230–251: Paul Goble. 258–259: Darryl Ligasan. 270: Ann Boyajian. 272–285: Nicole Wong. 296–319: Mark Teague. 330: Dean Macadam. 340–341: David LaFleur. 342–361: Renato Alarcão. 362: Wendy Born Hollander. 363: (tr)(ml) Renato Alarcão; (bl)(cr) Wendy Born Hollander. 364: (t) Renato Alarcão; (tr)(bl) Wendy Born Hollander. 365: (bkgd) Renato Alarcão; (insets) Wendy Born Hollander. 372–391: Jerome Lagarrigue. 396–397: Susan Swan. 408–409: Loretta Krupinski. 410–429: Garth Williams. 433: Argosy. 440–455: Charles Micucci. 456–459: Amy Lowry Poole. 465: Bridget Starr Taylor. 476–477: James Bentley. 478–497: Bruce Dupree. 508–525: Jim Burke. 527: Jim Burke. 528–529: Bandelin-Dacey Studios. 532–533: Bill Cigliano. 534–535: Argosy. 548: Laura Westlund. 550–559: Phyllis V. Saroff. 574–595: David Diaz. 614–631: Katherine Brown-Wing. 632–635: David Groff. 658: Richard Sobol. 660–661: Jesse Reisch. 664–665: Fabricio Vandenbroeck. 666–667: Marion Eldrige. 676–677: Stacey Schuett. 678–697: Michael Garland. 706–707: Greg Shed. 708–723: Ying-Hwa Hu & Cornelius Van

832

Acknowledgments

Wright. 746–769: Mary Azarian. 770–771: Tina Fong. 778–797: Rosalyn Schanzer. 802–803: Stacey Schuett. 804: Paul Mirocha.

PHOTOGRAPHY

iv: Purestock/SuperStock. v: (t) Jeff Greenberg/PhotoEdit; (b) © 2005 Twentieth Century Fox. All rights reserved. vi: Kayte M. Deioma/PhotoEdit. vii: (t) Brian Bahr/Getty Images. viii: Masterfile. ix: Masterfile. x: Bob Daemmrich/PhotoEdit. xi: Bill Heinsohn/Alamy. xii: (tl) Lon Lauber/OSF/Animal Animals/Earth Scenes; (cl) Martin J. Miller/Visuals Unlimited; (cl-bkgd) Tom Bean. xiii: William Smithey Jr/Getty Images. xiv: Comstock/SuperStock. xv: AP Images/Neil Eliot. 2–3: Purestock/SuperStock. 4: Veronique Krieger/Getty Images. 4–5: Ryan McVay/Getty Images. 5: Bettmann/Corbis. 6–7: Jose Luis Pelaez/Corbis. 8: Rusty Hill/FoodPix/Jupiter Images. 9: David Hiser/Getty Images. 30: (tl, c) Children's Book Press. 32: (bl) Ted Streshinsky/Corbis. 33: (c) Morton Beebe/Corbis; (br) Najlah Feanny/Corbis. 34: (bl) Arthur Schatz/Time Life Pictures/Getty Images; (tr) PunchStock. 35: Walter P. Reuther Library/Wayne State University. 37: Myrleen Ferguson Cate/PhotoEdit. 38–39: Tom & Dee Ann McCarthy/Corbis. 58: (bl) Brian Biggs; (tr) Ben Hurwitz. 65: Photodisc/Getty Images. 66–67: Jeff Greenberg/PhotoEdit. 68: (t) Getty Images; (cr) Russel Illig/Photodisc/PunchStock; (br) C Squared Studios/Getty. 70–71: (all) Mi Won Kim /Time For Kids. 72: (t) Esta Shapiro/Time For Kids; (bl) Courtesy David Hsu. 73: Courtesy David Hsu. 74: Lewis Wickes Hines/Corbis. 77: (tcr) Brand X Pictures/PunchStock; (cr) PhotoLink/Getty Images. 78–79: Mitch Tobias/Masterfile. 81: Stock Trek/Getty. 96: (tl) Das Anuda/Courtesy Farrar, Straus and Giroux; (cr) Courtesy Anna Rich. 98: NASA Johnson Space Center Collection. 98–99: (bkgd) NASA/CORBIS. 99: (br) PatitucciPhoto/Aurora Photos; (t) NASA Johnson Space Center Collection. 100: (tr) GustoImages/Artemi Kyriacou/Jupiter Images. 100–101: (bkgd) BigStockPhoto. 101: (tr) NASA/Roger Ressmeyer/Corbis; (br) NASA/Corbis. 103: Dan Bigelow/Getty Images. 104–105: Don Mason/Blend Images/Jupiter Images. 106:Steven Weinrebe/Index Stock Imagery. 107: Don Smetzer/Stone/Getty Images. 108–114: © 2005 Twentieth Century Fox. All rights reserved. 116–117: (bkgd) Wetzel & Company. 117: © 2005 Twentieth Century Fox. All rights reserved. 120: (tr) Courtesy Candlewick Press, (bl) © 2005 Twentieth Century Fox. All rights reserved. 121: © 2005 Twentieth Century Fox. All rights reserved. 124: © 2005 Twentieth Century Fox. All rights reserved. 125: Ryan McVay/Getty Images. 126: Brand X Pictures/PunchStock. 128: Michael Okoniewski/AP-Wide World Photos. 129: (br) Michael Okoniewski/AP-Wide World Photos; (bl) Hemera Technologies/Alamy. 131: (cr) Nic Hamilton/Alamy; (tr) Ryan McVay/Getty Images; (br) Pixtal/PunchStock. 132–133: Kayte M. Deioma/PhotoEdit. 134: Digital Vision Photography/Veer. 134–135: Ingram Publishing/AGEfotostock. 135: Owen Franken/Corbis. 136–137: Bettmann/Corbis. 138: Bettmann/Corbis. 139: (cl,cr) Bettmann/Corbis. 154: (c) Courtesy Chris Soentpiet/www.soentpiet.com. 156: Bettmann/Corbis. 156–159: Macmillan/McGraw-Hill. 157: AP Photo. 158: Jack Balletti/Bettmann/Corbis. 161: Michael Newman/PhotoEdit. 162–163: Lori Adamski Peek/Getty Images. 164: Bettmann/Corbis. 165: Bernard Hoffman/Getty. 182: (cr) Courtesy C.F. Payne. 187: Royalty-Free/Corbis. 188–189: Brian Bahr/Getty Images. 190: (t) Brian Nicholson/AP. (b) Bryn Lennon/Getty Images. 191: (tr) Al Grillo/AP Photo; (bl) Phil Cole/Getty Images. 192: Brian Bahr/Getty Images. 193: (tr) Todd Warshaw/Pool/Getty Images; (bl) Petros Giannakouris/AP Photos. 194: Nadia Borowski Scott/Zuma Press/Newscom. 195: (tr) STR/AFP/Getty Images; (bl) Petros Giannakouris/AP Photo. 196:Tamara Reynolds. 199: (bl) Photodisc/PunchStock; (bc) Ana de Sousa/Shutterstock; (r) Stockdisc/PunchStock. 200-201: Steve Bloom Images/Alamy. 202: Scott Neville/AP Photos. 204–217: (all) Alvis Upitis. 218: (tl) Boydsmills Press; (cr) Alvis Upitis. 218–219: Alvis Upitis. 225: Kevin Peterson/Getty Images. 226–227: Carson Ganci/Design Pics Inc./Alamy. 228: TiConUno s.r.l./Alamy. 228–229: (bkgd) Photographers Choice RF/SuperStock. 229: Macmillan/McGraw-Hill. 250: Courtesy Paul Goble. 252: (bl) Getty Images; (bkgd) Wetzel & Company. 253: Getty Images. 253–255: (bkgd) Wetzel & Company. 257: Robert Llewellyn/Alamy. 260: (br) Michael St. Maur Sheil/Corbis; (t) Jerry Driendl/Getty Images. 260–261: Jerry Driendl/Getty Images. 263: (tr) Stockbyte/PunchStock; (cr) Royalty-Free/Corbis; (bl) McVay/Getty Images. 264–265: Masterfile. 266: Dennis MacDonald/AGEfotostock America. 266–267: Gary He/Macmillan/McGraw-Hill. 267: Charles Krupa/AP Images. 268–269: Whit Preston/Stone/Getty Images. 271: (tl) Daryl Balfour/Getty Images; (cr) Stephen Cooper/Getty Images. 284: (tl) Courtesy Groundwood Books; (cr) Courtesy Nicole Wong. 286: John Cancalosi/DRK. 287: Michael & Patricia Fogden/Minden. 288: (tl) Michael Fogden/Animal Animals; (bl) Bruce Coleman, Inc/Alamy. 291: Tipp Howell/Getty Images. 292–293: Masterfile Royalty-Free. 294: (bl) Ulrike Schanz/Animal Animals; (b) Royalty-Free/Corbis. 295: Mary Grace Long/Asia Images/Getty Images. 318: Courtesy Scholastic. 320: Okapia/Hund/Kramer/Photo Researchers.

321–323: Manuela Hartling/Reuters/Corbis. 325: Royalty-Free/Corbis. 326–327: Masterfile. 328: Time & Life Pictures/Getty Images. 329: (tl) Time & Life Pictures/Getty Images; (tr) Corbis. 331: Marc Longwood. 332: Eric L. Stewart/Lyon College. 333: Warner Brothers/Everett Collection. 337: (tcr, br) Brand X Pictures/PunchStock; (cr) Siede Preis/Getty Images; (bl) PhotoLink/Getty Images; (bc) Ana de Sousa/Shutterstock; (b) Michael Scott/Macmillan/McGraw-Hill. 338: Group 4/Image Source Black/Alamy. 360: (tl) Courtesy Peachtree Publishers; (br) Courtesy Renato Alarcão. 367: Amos Morgan/Getty Images. 368–369: Jeff Greenberg/Alamy. 370: (bl) Chris Steele-Perkins/Magnum; (bc) Getty Images; (br) Comstock Images/Getty Images. 371: Photodisc/Getty Images. 390: (cl) Courtesy of Penguin Group; (tr) Photo by Jessica Tampas. Courtesy Claire Hartfield. 392: Frank Chmura/Alamy. 395: Alan Levenson/AGEfotostock America. 398: Time & Life Pictures/Getty Images. 399: Danita Delimonte/Alamy. 401: (bl) Pixtal/PunchStock; (cr) Stockdisc/PunchStock. 402–403: Bob Daemmrich/Photo Edit. 404: Marta Lavandier/AP Images. 404–405: (bkgd wooden blocks) Dynamic Graphics/Jupiter Images; (bkgd wood texture) Dynamic Graphics/PunchStock; (bkgd close-up of wood grain) Ryan McVay/Getty Images. 405: The Granger Collection, New York. 406–407: Gabe Palmer/Corbis. 428: (tl) Marcia Johnston. Courtesy Farrar, Straus & Giroux; (cr) Courtesy Estate of Garth Williams c/o Frost National Bank. 430: (tr) B. G. Thomson/Photo Researchers; (cr) Karen Marks/Bat Conservation International/Photo Researchers. 430–431: Steve Kaufman/Corbis. 431: Pat Little/AP Images. 432: Jeff Lepore/Photo Researchers. 432–433: Tim Flach/Stone/Getty Images. 435: Dan Bigelow/Getty Images. 436–437: Michael & Patricia Fogden/Corbis. 438: Masterfile. 439: Steve Hopkin/Ardea. 454: Anita Lambrinos/Courtesy Charles Micucci. 461: Amos Morgan/Getty Images. 462–463: Bill Heinsohn/Alamy. 464: Bob Stefko/Getty Images. 465: (tr) Bettmann/Corbis; (tl) Christopher and Sally Gable/Getty Images. 466: Stephen Pingry/AP Photo. 467: AGEfotostock/SuperStock. 468: Doug Mazell/Jupiter Images. 469: Mary Altaffer/AP Photo. 470: OJPhotos/Alamy. 473: (cr) Ryan McVay/Getty Images; (bl) PhotoLink/Getty Images; (bc) Ana de Sousa/Shutterstock; (br) Photodisc/PunchStock. 474–475: Troy Wayrynen. 496: (tl) Justin A. Woods; (br) Donna Freeman courtesy of Pelican Publishing Company. 498: Richard Hutchings. 499: North Wind Picture Archives/Alamy. 500: (tl) The Ima Hogg Papers/The Center for American History/The University of Texas at Austin; (b) Travelwide/Alamy. 501: Thais Llorca/epa/Corbis. 503: Rubberball Productions/Getty Images. 504–505: Library of Congress/Getty Images. 506–507: Bettmann/Corbis. 507: Science Museum, London/Topham-HIP/Image Works. 526: (tr) Jason Stemple/Curtis Brown Limited; (bcl) Courtesy Jim Burke. 531: Frank Siteman/AGEfotostock America, Inc. 537: (l) Brand X Pictures/PunchStock; (cr) Ken Cavanagh/Macmillan/McGraw-Hill; (br) Stockbyte/PunchStock. 538–539: Lon Lauber/OSF/Animal Animals/Earth Scenes. 540: George H. H. Huey/Corbis. 540–541: Brand X Pictures/PunchStock. 541: Jeff Foott/Getty Images. 542–543: Stephen Krasemann/NHPA. 544: Jack Barrie/Bruce Coleman. 545: Dave Tipling/Alamy. 546–547: Bruce Clendenning/Visuals Unlimited. 547: Martin J Miller/Visuals Unlimited. 549: (tr) Steve Warble; (b) Brian Vikander. 550: Barbara Gerlach/Visuals Unlimited. 551: (t) Richard Day/Daybreak Imagery; (b) Tom Bean. 552: (tr) Bayard A. Brattstrom/Visuals Unlimited; (br) Rob Simpson/Visuals Unlimited. 553: John Cunningham/Visuals Unlimited. 554: (t) LINK/Visuals Unlimited; (b) John and Barbara Gerlach/Visuals Unlimited. 555: Hal Beral/Visuals Unlimited. 556: Malowski/Visuals Unlimited. 557: John Gerlach/Visuals Unlimited. 558: (tr) Barbara Gerlach/Visuals Unlimited; (b) Joe McDonald/Visuals Unlimited. 559: Tom J. Ulrich/Visuals Unlimited. 560-561: Bruce Clendenning/Visuals Unlimited. 562: (tr) Courtesy Lerner Publishing Group; (b) Martin J Miller/Visuals Unlimited. 562–563: Bruce Clendenning/Visuals Unlimited. 563: (bl) Barbara Gerlach/Visuals Unlimited; (bc) Rob Simpson/Visuals Unlimited; (br) Steve Warble. 564: Mitsuaki Iwago/Minden Pictures. 565: (tl) Steve Kazlowski/Danita Delimont.com; (br) Robert W. Ginn/Alamy. 566: (tl) Inside OutPix/PunchStock; (cl) Renee Morris/Alamy; (bc) blickwinkel/Alamy; (br) Andrew Harrington/Alamy. 567: Royalty-Free/Corbis. 569: Jim Jordan/Getty Images. 570–571: Joel Sartore/National Geographic Image Collection. 572–573: John Cancalosi/Ardea. 573: ZSSD/SuperStock. 590: (tl) Photo by Mimi. Courtesy Rudolfo Anaya; (cr) Courtesy of David Diaz. 597: BananaStock/Alamy. 598–599: William Smithey Jr/Getty Images. 600: Frank Staub/Index Stock Imagery. 601: Corey Rich/Aurora Photos. 602–603: Ken Wilson/Wildfaces. 605: William Campbell/Corbis Sygma. 606: Galen Rowell/Corbis. 609: (cr) PhotoLink/Getty Images; (bc) Ana de Sousa/Shutterstock; (br) Stockbyte/PunchStock. 610–611: Jupiter Images/Comstock/Alamy. 612: (t) Boden/Ledingham/Masterfile; (bl) Brandon Cole Marine Photography/Alamy. 612–613: Boden/Ledingham/Masterfile. 613: Brandon Cole/Visuals Unlimited. 616–629: (bkgd) Wetzel & Company/Janice McDonald. 630: Yuusuke Itagaki, Courtesy Charlesbridge Publishers. 630–631: (bkgd) Wetzel & Company/

833

Acknowledgments

Janice McDonald. 637: BananaStock/AGEfotostock. 638-639: (bkgd) James Watt/Animal Animals/Earth Scenes. 640: (tr) Amos Nachoum/Corbis; (br) Roger Tidman/Corbis. 640-641: (bkgd) Stephen Frink Collection/Alamy. 642-657: Richard Sobol. 658: (author) Courtesy Robert Sobol. 658-659: Richard Sobol. 663: (cr) Rubberball Productions/Getty Images. 669: (cr) Stockdisc/PunchStock; (br) Tracy Montana/PhotoLink/Getty Images. 670-671: Comstock/SuperStock. 672: Comstock/SuperStock. 673: Underwood & Underwood/Corbis. 672-673: Digital Vision/Getty Images. 674-675: Corbis. 696: Alice Garland. 698-699: Corbis. 699: Dorothea Lange/Stringer/2005 Getty Images. 700: (t) John Springer Collection/Corbis; (c) Bettmann/Corbis. 703: Comstock Images/Alamy. 704-705: The Granger Collection, New York. 722: (tr) Rob Layman; (cl) Courtesy Cornelius Van Wright and Ying-Hwa Hu. 724: James L. Amos/Corbis. 724-725: Joe Ginsberg/Getty Images. 725: (t) Pat Roque/Associated Press; (b) Joe Ginsberg/Getty Images. 726: (t) Victoria & Albert Museum, London/Art Resource, NY. 726-727: Joe Ginsberg/Getty Images. 727: ImageDJ/Jupiter Images. 729: Tipp Howell/Getty Images. 730-731: Damian Dovarganes/AP Photo. 732: Brian Harkin/Getty Images. 733: (all) Taro Yamasaki. 734: Ric Francis/AP Photo. 735 (all) Arthur Schatz/Time Life Pictures/Getty Images. 736-

737: Aurelia Ventura/La Opinion Photos/Newscom. 738: Staples, Inc. 741: (br) Royalty-Free/Corbis; (bc) Ana de Sousa/Shutterstock. 742-743: Randy Olson/National Geographic/Getty Images. 744: Gary Buss/Getty Images. 745: Richard Hutchings/Corbis. 768: (tl) Sharron L. McElmeel/McBookwords LLC; (cr) Courtesy Mary Azarian. 773: ImageState/Alamy. 774-775: Justin Sullivan/Getty Images. 776: (tr) Schenectady Museum; Hall of Electrical History Foundation/Corbis; (bl) W. Dickson/Corbis. 777: Bettmann/Corbis. 796: Courtesy Roz Schanzer. 801: Michael Newman/PhotoEdit. 804-805: Chris Howes/Wild Places Photography/Alamy. 807: (tr) Stockdisc/PunchStock; (br) Photodisc/PunchStock. 808: (l) Digital Vision Ltd./Getty Images; (r) Ingram Publishing/Alamy. 810: Comstock/Alamy. 811: Photodisc Collection/Getty Images. 814: Creatas/SuperStock. 815: Adam Jones/Visuals Unlimited. 818: Jeremy Woodhouse/Getty Images. 819: Charles George/Visuals Unlimited. 821: Mel Curtis/Getty Images. 822: Jeff Foott/Discovery Images/Getty Images. 825: Digital Vision Ltd./Getty Images. 826: (r) S. Solum/PhotoLink/Getty Images; (l) Ingram Publishing/Alamy. 829: Digital Vision Ltd. 830: Peter Yates/Corbis. 831: Robert Harding World Imagery/Getty Images.

834